Practical Perspectives on Inclusive and Immersive Learning Environments

Hector Cardona-Reyes
https://orcid.org/0000-0002-9626-6254
Center for Research in Mathematics, Mexico

Klinge Orlando Villalba-Condori
https://orcid.org/0000-0002-8621-7942
The Catholic University of Santa María, Peru

Alexis Edmundo Gallegos-Acosta
Center for Research in Mathematics. Mexico

Miguel Angel Ortiz-Esparza
Center for Research in Mathematics, Mexico

IGI Global
Scientific Publishing
Publishing Tomorrow's Research Today

Vice President of Editorial | Melissa Wagner
Director of Acquisitions | Mikaela Felty
Director of Book Development | Jocelynn Hessler
Production Manager | Mike Brehm
Cover Design | Jose Rosado

Published in the United States of America by
IGI Global Scientific Publishing
701 East Chocolate Avenue
Hershey, PA, 17033, USA
Tel: 717-533-8845 | Fax: 717-533-7115
Website: https://www.igi-global.com E-mail: cust@igi-global.com

Library of Congress Cataloging-in-Publication Data

Names: Cardona Reyes, Héctor editor | Villalba-Condori, Klinge Orlando, 1974- editor | Gallegos Acosta, Alexis Edmundo editor | Ortiz Esparza, Miguel Angel editor
Title: Practical perspectives on inclusive and immersive learning environments / Edited by Hector Cardona-Reyes, Klinge Orlando Villalba-Condori, Alexis Edmundo Gallegos-Acosta, Miguel Angel Ortiz-Esparza.
Description: Hershey, PA : IGI Global Scientific Publishing, [2026] | Includes bibliographical references and index. | Summary: "This book explores how emerging technologies like AR, VR, and AI can foster inclusive, equitable learning. Combining research, real-world examples, and critical insights, it examines strategies to break barriers, enhance engagement, and create transformative educational experiences that respect and reflect learner diversity"-- Provided by publisher.
Identifiers: LCCN 2025038336 (print) | LCCN 2025038337 (ebook) | ISBN 9798337351889 hardcover | ISBN 9798337351896 paperback | ISBN 9798337351902 ebook
Subjects: LCSH: Inclusive education | Virtual reality in education | Shared virtual environments | Artificial intelligence--Educational applications
Classification: LCC LC1200 .P73 2026 (print) | LCC LC1200 (ebook)
LC record available at https://lccn.loc.gov/2025038336
LC ebook record available at https://lccn.loc.gov/2025038337

British Cataloguing in Publication Data
A Cataloguing in Publication record for this book is available from the British Library.

Table of Contents

Preface xii

Chapter 1
Artificial Intelligence and Adaptive Learning for Equity 1
P. Selvakumar, Department of Science and Humanities, Nehru Institute of Technology, Coimbatore, India

Chapter 2
Bridging the Gap: The Role of Immersive Technologies for Learners With Disabilities 27
Özgür Örün, Izmir Institute of Technology, Turkey
Mesut Türk, Amasya University, Turkey

Chapter 3
Designing Immersive Learning Experiences for Neurodiverse Learners: A Practical Framework for Inclusive Educational Technology 59
Muhammad Usman Tariq, Abu Dhabi University, UAE & University College Cork, Ireland

Chapter 4
Designing Inclusive Education With AI-Driven Pedagogies and Learning Analytics: Bridging Instructional Design, Equity, and Impact 87
Ashraf Alam, Alliance University, Bengaluru, India

Chapter 5
Ethical and Social Considerations in the Deployment of AI in Education 121
P. Selvakumar, Department of Science and Humanities, Nehru Institute of Technology, Coimbatore, India

Chapter 6
Inclusive Instructional Design Through Digital Pedagogies and Active Learning Approaches 147
Rampelli Manojkumar, BVRIT HYDERABAD College of Engineering for Women, India
T. Aditya Sai Srinivas, Ravindra College of Engineering for Women, India
Venkanna Mekala, BVRIT HYDERABAD College of Engineering for Women, India

Chapter 7
Minds and Machines: The Interdisciplinary Challenge of AI's Influence in Education 181
Pankaj Bhambri, Guru Nanak Dev Engineering College, Ludhiana, India
Suresh Kumar, Maharishi Markandeshwar University, Mullana, India

Chapter 8
Practical Inclusive Education Approaches in Immersive Learning Environments 201
Marubini Christinah Sadiki, University of South Africa, South Africa

Chapter 9
STEAM Camp Impact on Mexican Female Teachers' Technological, Pedagogical, and Disciplinary Knowledge 233
Ricardo Murillo Alfaro, Centro Regional de Formación Docente e Investigación Educativa, Mexico
Alhelí Segovia Sánchez, Escuela Normal federal de Educadoras Maestra Estefanía Castañeda, Mexico
Ezra Federico Parra-González, Center for Research in Mathematics (CIMAT), Zacatecas, Mexico

Chapter 10
The Short Story as a Teaching Tool for Educating Readers in Primary School 275
Oscar Ernesto Cabral Mier, Escuela Normal Rural "Gral. Matías Ramos Santos", Mexico
Selso Loera-Serrano, Benemérita Escuela Normal "Manuel Ávila Camacho", Mexico
Sergio Rodríguez-Ayala, Escuela Normal Benemérita "Manuel Ávila Camacho", Mexico

Chapter 11
Virtual Reality-Based Intensive Care Unit (VRIcuLAB) Design 299
Cem Deniz Kumral, Isparta University of Apllied Sciences, Turkey
Mevlüt Ersoy, Süleyman Demirel University, Turkey
Sıddıka Ersoy, Süleyman Demirel University, Turkey
Hamit Armağan, Süleyman Demirel University, Turkey
Tuncay Yiğit, Süleyman Demirel University, Turkey

Compilation of References 337

About the Contributors 405

Index 415

Detailed Table of Contents

Preface.. xii

Chapter 1
Artificial Intelligence and Adaptive Learning for Equity 1
P. Selvakumar, Department of Science and Humanities, Nehru Institute of Technology, Coimbatore, India

Artificial Intelligence fundamentally by unprecedented opportunities, fosters inclusivity, and bridges long-standing gaps in access to quality education worldwide. As a suite of advanced technologies designed to simulate human and intelligent tutoring, all of which collectively provide personalized, adaptive, and scalable educational experiences. At its core, AI's integration into education aims the of teaching processes but also to promote equity by making educational resources more accessible, affordable, learners. Traditionally, has been limited by geographic, economic, and social barriers. Students in remote or under-resourced regions need qualified teachers, curricula, and supportive learning environments. Furthermore, learners with disabilities or those requiring special accommodations frequently face systemic obstacles that hinder their academic progress. AI, however, has the potential to mitigate many of these challenges by democratizing knowledge and creating more inclusive educational ecosystems.

Chapter 2
Bridging the Gap: The Role of Immersive Technologies for Learners With Disabilities 27
Özgür Örün, Izmir Institute of Technology, Turkey
Mesut Türk, Amasya University, Turkey

Accessibility gaps in learning environments can cause various problems, especially in achieving the learning goals of individuals with special needs. At this point, immersive technologies such as augmented and virtual reality are technologies that have the potential to create accessible and equal environments for students with special needs and to compensate for accessibility problems. These technologies can provide special learning environments that meet the unique needs of individuals with sensory, cognitive and motor problems. Some of the advantages provided by immersive technologies include visual, auditory and tactile support, adaptive controllers, eye-tracking interfaces, voice command systems, real-time subtitles, and interactive learning environments enhanced with acceleration. Additionally, immersive environments can increase engagement, motivation, and skill acquisition for students with learning disabilities. In this context, this chapter examines the use of immersive technologies to address accessibility gaps in educational settings for individuals with disabilities.

Chapter 3
Designing Immersive Learning Experiences for Neurodiverse Learners: A Practical Framework for Inclusive Educational Technology 59
Muhammad Usman Tariq, Abu Dhabi University, UAE & University College Cork, Ireland

Creating engaging learning experiences for students who think and learn differently requires a thoughtful and inclusive approach that combines new ideas with ensuring everyone can access them. This guide provides practical strategies for making educational technology effective for a diverse range of learning styles, sensory preferences, and communication needs, particularly for individuals with autism, ADHD, and dyslexia. By incorporating ideas from Universal Design for Learning, ethical data handling practices, and standards such as WCAG and ISO/IEC 24751, this guide enables teachers and technology designers to create learning environments that are engaging, adaptable, and equitable. Essential aspects of this design include managing the amount of sensory input provided, utilizing various methods to present information, allowing users to customize settings, and collaborating directly with students to tailor the experience to their individual needs.

Chapter 4
Designing Inclusive Education With AI-Driven Pedagogies and Learning Analytics: Bridging Instructional Design, Equity, and Impact............................ 87
Ashraf Alam, Alliance University, Bengaluru, India

This chapter specifies an equity-optimizing sociotechnical stack for inclusive education that fuses UDL-as-compiled accessibility, capability-expanding pedagogy, equity-constrained adaptive mastery, and interpretability-first learning analytics into a single accountable operating model. It translates justice constructs such as targeted universalism, intersectional parity, epistemic justice, and care ethics into backlog-ready design grammars, contestable AI affordances, and privacy-by-design governance with portability, deletion verification, and recourse pathways. The chapter formalizes low-resource resilience through offline-first architectures, edge inference, and progressive enhancement, while constraining personalization via calibration parity, anti-proxy feature governance, and latency-disciplined time-to-support protocols. Five matrices operationalize theory-to-requirements, use-case safeguards, orchestration heuristics, signal-to-action logic, and implementation roadmaps, enabling auditable inclusion dividends across languages, disabilities, and bandwidth ecologies.

Chapter 5
Ethical and Social Considerations in the Deployment of AI in Education 121
P. Selvakumar, Department of Science and Humanities, Nehru Institute of Technology, Coimbatore, India

Processes while simultaneously raising profound ethical questions that demand careful examination, promises through data analytics, thereby potentially increasing educational equity and efficiency. Adaptive learning platforms, powered by sophisticated algorithms, tailor instructional content to learning speeds, preferences, and an engaging environment. Virtual teaching assistants, software can reduce on enable more immediate and personalized feedback for learners, which can significantly improve outcomes. Additionally, AI learners' customized assistance, including text-to-speech functionalities, makes education more accessible. The promise of AI in education also extends to facilitating which crucial. However, alongside these exciting prospects, brings it significant perils ethical dilemmas that stakeholders must address. One major concern is the issue of heavily storage, vast amounts student ranging from to behavioral patterns even biometric information. This extensive data collection raises critical especially when sensitive information is involved.

Chapter 6
Inclusive Instructional Design Through Digital Pedagogies and Active Learning Approaches 147
Rampelli Manojkumar, BVRIT HYDERABAD College of Engineering for Women, India
T. Aditya Sai Srinivas, Ravindra College of Engineering for Women, India
Venkanna Mekala, BVRIT HYDERABAD College of Engineering for Women, India

This chapter examines how inclusive instructional design, supported by digital pedagogies and active learning, transforms higher education. It argues that integrating frameworks like Universal Design for Learning (UDL) with flipped classrooms, simulations, and problem-based learning creates equitable, adaptive, and engaging environments. By prioritizing flexibility, personalization, and real-world relevance, these strategies empower diverse learners and reduce barriers to success, making inclusion a foundational principle rather than an afterthought.

Chapter 7
Minds and Machines: The Interdisciplinary Challenge of AI's Influence in Education 181
Pankaj Bhambri, Guru Nanak Dev Engineering College, Ludhiana, India
Suresh Kumar, Maharishi Markandeshwar University, Mullana, India

The integration of Artificial Intelligence (AI) into education transcends its role as a mere efficiency tool, becoming an active, "unseen classroom partner" that shapes cognitive, social, and ethical dimensions of learning. This chapter employs an interdisciplinary conceptual analysis to argue that understanding AI's profound influence requires synthesizing perspectives from computer science, psychology, sociology, and philosophy. Moving beyond a technocentric view, we critically examine AI's dual potential to enhance metacognition and personalization while simultaneously risking algorithmic dependency, eroded autonomy, and the amplification of societal biases. The analysis extends to AI's role in shaping trust, motivation, and classroom dynamics, with particular attention to its integration within immersive and inclusive learning environments. We confront key ethical dilemmas surrounding data privacy, surveillance, and algorithmic fairness.

Chapter 8
Practical Inclusive Education Approaches in Immersive Learning Environments 201
Marubini Christinah Sadiki, University of South Africa, South Africa

Immersive learning environments, driven by cutting-edge technologies such as virtual reality (VR), augmented reality (AR), and interactive simulations, present substantial opportunities to enhance inclusive education. These technologies empower educators to create engaging and personalized learning experiences that cater to a diverse array of learning styles, abilities, and preferences. Central to this inclusive strategy is the Universal Design for Learning (UDL) framework, which advocates for adaptable methods of content delivery, learning assessment, and student engagement. When combined with immersive technologies, UDL facilitates the development of accessible educational resources that are advantageous for learners with disabilities, as well as those from varied linguistic and cultural backgrounds. An essential aspect of this methodology is the incorporation of multi-sensory learning tools, which are particularly beneficial for students facing cognitive or sensory challenges.

Chapter 9
STEAM Camp Impact on Mexican Female Teachers' Technological, Pedagogical, and Disciplinary Knowledge 233
Ricardo Murillo Alfaro, Centro Regional de Formación Docente e Investigación Educativa, Mexico
Alhelí Segovia Sánchez, Escuela Normal federal de Educadoras Maestra Estefanía Castañeda, Mexico
Ezra Federico Parra-González, Center for Research in Mathematics (CIMAT), Zacatecas, Mexico

This chapter per the authors examines the impact of a STEAM camp on the technological, pedagogical, and disciplinary knowledge of female upper secondary school teachers in priority groups within the COBAT system in Tamaulipas, Mexico, utilizing the TPACK model as a theoretical framework. Methodologically, it employs a quantitative, explanatory, longitudinal, non-experimental design with a sample of 20 female teachers, using the validated TPACK-21 questionnaire administered after three STEAM camps. Results reveal solid baseline strengths in CK, PK, and PCK, with significant improvements in TCK ($p = .042$), TPK ($p = .030$), and TPACK ($p = .037$) dimensions, indicating enhanced integration of technology with pedagogy and content through hands-on activities. The discussion interprets these findings in light of gender equity and regional inequalities, while conclusions underscore the camp's role in empowering teachers, promoting equitable STEAM education, and informing policies for sustainable professional development in vulnerable contexts.

Chapter 10
The Short Story as a Teaching Tool for Educating Readers in Primary School 275
Oscar Ernesto Cabral Mier, Escuela Normal Rural "Gral. Matías Ramos Santos", Mexico
Selso Loera-Serrano, Benemérita Escuela Normal "Manuel Ávila Camacho", Mexico
Sergio Rodríguez-Ayala, Escuela Normal Benemérita "Manuel Ávila Camacho", Mexico

This research examines the effectiveness of short stories as a teaching tool for strengthening the development of literary readers and reading comprehension in primary school. A project conducted with fourth-grade elementary school students, based on the strategies of Isabel Solé (1992) and a constructivist approach, was carried out in twelve public schools in the municipality of Loreto, Zacatecas, during the 2023–2024 school year. Using a mixed methodology and an action research process, 286 students and 24 teachers participated, applying teaching sequences centered on short stories. The results showed a 32% increase in reading comprehension and an improvement in motivation for recreational reading. From a qualitative perspective, three categories emerged: reading motivation, teacher mediation, and reading as a social practice. Therefore, it is concluded that short stories, when approached pedagogically, constitute an effective means to promote critical reading, the pleasure of reading, and reading autonomy in rural school settings.

Chapter 11
Virtual Reality-Based Intensive Care Unit (VRIcuLAB) Design 299
Cem Deniz Kumral, Isparta University of Apllied Sciences, Turkey
Mevlüt Ersoy, Süleyman Demirel University, Turkey
Sıddıka Ersoy, Süleyman Demirel University, Turkey
Hamit Armağan, Süleyman Demirel University, Turkey
Tuncay Yiğit, Süleyman Demirel University, Turkey

The integration of immersive technologies has transformed nursing education, yet existing solutions often lack holistic ICU workflow experiences. This chapter presents VRicuLAB, a Virtual Reality-Based Intensive Care Unit designed to provide nursing students with a realistic, risk-free, and process-oriented learning environment. VRicuLAB enables users to perform procedures, operate virtual devices, and monitor patients through high-fidelity simulations. Beyond technical architecture, the system integrates data-driven tracking and educator dashboards for objective assessment and personalized feedback. By combining engineering precision with instructional design, VRicuLAB aims to enhance accessibility, inclusivity, and engagement. The chapter discusses theoretical foundations, educational rationales for design decisions, and sustainable immersive learning approaches, bridging the gap between engineering and healthcare disciplines.

Compilation of References 337

About the Contributors 405

Index 415

Preface

INTRODUCTION

Inclusive and immersive learning environments have moved from aspirational ideals to urgent educational imperatives. Across global contexts, educators and institutions are called upon to address persistent inequities related to access, ability, geography, and socio-economic conditions. This edited volume, Practical Perspectives on Inclusive and Immersive Learning Environments, emerges from the convergence of these equity-driven goals and the transformative possibilities of modern technology.

As editors, we recognize that inclusion is not a static concept, nor is immersion merely a matter of hardware sophistication. True inclusion requires intentional design, ethical awareness, and sustained engagement with learners' diverse cognitive, physical, and emotional needs. Consequently, learning environments—regardless of the specific medium employed—must be evaluated not only for their technical innovation but for their capacity to reduce barriers and expand meaningful participation.

However, the transition to these advanced pedagogies is not without significant friction. The integration of immersive tools and automated systems introduces complex challenges regarding infrastructure, sustainability, and the digital divide. Beyond the technical requirements, there are profound human and ethical hurdles: the need for rigorous data privacy, the risk of algorithmic bias, and the urgent necessity for teacher training and digital literacy. It is not enough to simply introduce tools; we must also cultivate the pedagogical ecosystems that sustain them. This volume explicitly acknowledges that technology can inadvertently exacerbate the very inequalities it aims to solve if not deployed with a critical, sociotechnical perspective.

The chapters collected in this book reflect interdisciplinary, international, and practice-oriented perspectives, offering insights from education, engineering, computer science, psychology, healthcare, and the social sciences. Contributors examine these dynamics across formal and informal settings, from primary education to teacher professional development and specialized training. Together, these works provide educators, researchers, instructional designers, and policymakers with actionable frameworks to navigate these challenges and build truly equitable learning ecosystems.

CHAPTER OVERVIEW

Chapter 1 explores the role of adaptive systems in fostering equity. It examines how data-driven personalization can address long-standing barriers related to geography, resources, and learner diversity, particularly for marginalized and underserved populations.

Chapter 2 focuses on the use of immersive technologies such as virtual and augmented reality to bridge accessibility gaps for learners with disabilities. The authors highlight practical design features and assistive affordances that enhance engagement, motivation, and skill development.

Chapter 3 presents a practical framework for designing immersive learning experiences for neurodiverse learners. Grounded in Universal Design for Learning (UDL) and international accessibility standards, this chapter offers concrete strategies for managing sensory load, customization, and ethical technology design.

Chapter 4 introduces a pedagogical and learning analytics framework that integrates equity, instructional design, and accountability. It operationalizes justice-oriented educational principles into actionable design grammars and implementation models suitable for diverse and low-resource contexts.

Chapter 5 addresses the ethical and social considerations surrounding the deployment of intelligent systems in education. It critically examines issues of data privacy, surveillance, bias, and governance, emphasizing the need for responsible and transparent integration.

Chapter 6 explores inclusive instructional design through digital pedagogies and active learning approaches in higher education. By integrating frameworks such as UDL with flipped classrooms and problem-based learning, the chapter demonstrates how inclusion can become a foundational design principle.

Chapter 7 adopts an interdisciplinary lens to examine the broader cognitive, social, and ethical influence of advanced technology in education. It positions these tools as active participants in learning environments, raising important questions about autonomy, trust, and human–machine collaboration.

Chapter 8 focuses on practical inclusive education approaches within immersive environments. Anchored in the UDL framework, the chapter demonstrates how multisensory tools can support diverse learners across cultural and linguistic contexts.

Chapter 9 examines the impact of STEAM camps on the technological, pedagogical, and disciplinary knowledge of female teachers in Mexico. Using the TPACK framework, the chapter highlights professional development as a pathway toward gender equity and inclusive STEM education.

Chapter 10 shifts attention to literacy and foundational education, exploring the short story as a pedagogical tool in primary schools. The chapter demonstrates how culturally responsive and constructivist approaches can enhance reading comprehension, motivation, and autonomy in rural contexts.

Chapter 11 presents the design and implementation of a virtual reality–based intensive care unit laboratory for nursing education. By integrating immersive simulation with instructional design and assessment tools, the chapter illustrates inclusive and accessible training in healthcare education.

CONCLUSION

Collectively, the chapters in this volume underscore that inclusive learning environments are not defined by technology alone, but by the values, pedagogies, and ethical commitments that guide their design. Whether addressing neurodiversity, disability, displacement, gender equity, or professional development, the contributors demonstrate that meaningful inclusion requires intentional alignment between technological affordances and human-centered educational goals.

This book also highlights the importance of contextual sensitivity. The diversity of geographic regions, educational levels, and learner populations represented in this volume reinforces the idea that solutions must be adaptable to local needs rather than universally prescribed. At the same time, shared frameworks such as Universal Design for Learning and participatory design provide a common foundation for scalable innovation.

As editors, we hope this volume serves not only as a reference but as a catalyst for reflective practice. By bringing together practical perspectives and empirical insights, Practical Perspectives on Inclusive and Immersive Learning Environments aims to support the ongoing transformation of education toward systems that are equitable, resilient, and deeply inclusive for all learners.

Chapter 1
Artificial Intelligence and Adaptive Learning for Equity

P. Selvakumar
https://orcid.org/0000-0002-3650-4548
Department of Science and Humanities, Nehru Institute of Technology, Coimbatore, India

ABSTRACT

Artificial Intelligence fundamentally by unprecedented opportunities, fosters inclusivity, and bridges long-standing gaps in access to quality education worldwide. As a suite of advanced technologies designed to simulate human and intelligent tutoring, all of which collectively provide personalized, adaptive, and scalable educational experiences. At its core, AI's integration into education aims the of teaching processes but also to promote equity by making educational resources more accessible, affordable, learners. Traditionally, has been limited by geographic, economic, and social barriers. Students in remote or under-resourced regions need qualified teachers, curricula, and supportive learning environments. Furthermore, learners with disabilities or those requiring special accommodations frequently face systemic obstacles that hinder their academic progress. AI, however, has the potential to mitigate many of these challenges by democratizing knowledge and creating more inclusive educational ecosystems.

DOI: 10.4018/979-8-3373-5188-9.ch001

THE ROLE OF AI IN EDUCATION: PROMOTING EQUITY AND ACCESS

Artificial Intelligence fundamentally by unprecedented opportunities, fosters inclusivity, and bridges long-standing gaps in access to quality education worldwide. As a suite of advanced technologies designed to simulate human and intelligent tutoring, all of which collectively provide personalized, adaptive, and scalable educational experiences. At its core, AI's integration into education aims the of teaching processes but also to promote equity by making educational resources more accessible, affordable, learners. Traditionally, has been limited by geographic, economic, and social barriers. Students in remote or under-resourced regions need qualified teachers, curricula, and supportive learning environments. Furthermore, learners with disabilities or those requiring special accommodations frequently face systemic obstacles that hinder their academic progress. AI, however, has the potential to mitigate many of these challenges by democratizing knowledge and creating more inclusive educational ecosystems. Through AI-powered platforms and tools, learners can receive customized instruction suited to their pace, learning style, and prior knowledge, thus fostering engagement and reducing dropout rates. In terms of access, AI also plays a vital role by breaking down linguistic and cultural barriers. Natural language processing technologies facilitate real-time translation and transcription services, enabling learners to engage with educational content in their native languages.

This linguistic inclusivity enhances comprehension and participation, fostering a more equitable learning environment across multicultural classrooms and global online platforms. Furthermore, AI-powered educational tools and virtual learning environments (VLEs) significantly extend educational opportunities beyond traditional classroom platforms. Powered by AI can reach millions of learners worldwide, including those in low-income and rural areas who might otherwise lack access to quality education. These platforms often provide flexible schedules and personalized convenience without geographic or socioeconomic constraints. With disabilities is also transformative, and computer vision-based tools are educational and accessible, all require policymakers, communities to establish standards frameworks that prioritize the rights and needs of underserved populations. Holds remarkable promoting equity and access through personalized learning, data-driven support, linguistic inclusivity, and assistive technologies. Its ability to transcend traditional barriers opens pathways for millions of learners worldwide to receive quality education tailored to their unique contexts and abilities. However, realizing this vision demands vigilant attention to ethical implementation and sustained commitment to inclusivity, empowerment exclusion. As educational institutions increasingly embrace AI, the focus must remain on more equitable, accessible, for all.

ADAPTIVE LEARNING: PERSONALIZED EDUCATION FOR DIVERSE LEARNERS

Unlike educational models, which often rely on standardized curricula and uniform teaching methods, adaptive learning systems' instructional strategies are efficient, process, especially for diverse learners who bring different backgrounds, skills to the classroom. These technologies continuously analyze students' responses, behavior patterns, and progress to identify strengths and weaknesses (Taylor D L., et al, 2021). Based on these insights, the system modifies the difficulty level, presents targeted feedback, and recommends resources tailored to each learner's specific needs. For example, math might provide alternative explanations, or interactive simulations, while another who masters the topic quickly could be challenged with advanced material or enrichment activities. Adaptive learning systems are especially valuable in addressing the educational needs of diverse learners, including those with varying cognitive abilities, learning disabilities, language proficiencies, and cultural backgrounds. By personalizing instruction, these systems help to mitigate the one-size-fits-all limitations of traditional classrooms, where teachers may struggle to meet the needs of every student simultaneously. For learners with disabilities, adaptive technologies can integrate assistive features such as text-to-speech, speech recognition, or alternative input methods, enhancing accessibility and participation (Mirari K., 2022). Similarly, English language learners benefit from adaptive platforms that can modify vocabulary complexity, provide multilingual support, and offer scaffolded language development resources. The benefits of adaptive learning extend beyond individualized instruction to include improvements in learner motivation and engagement. Instructors also benefit from adaptive systems as they receive granular, actionable data on student performance, enabling targeted interventions and more efficient use of instructional time.

Educational institutions this broader allocate resources effectively, and improve curriculum design to better serve their student populations (Soler Costa R., et al, 2021). Moreover, adaptive learning fosters equity in education by leveling the playing field for learners who may have been marginalized or underserved by conventional educational methods, linguistic, personalized learning experiences that respect their contexts and support their academic growth. This inclusivity contributes to reducing achievement gaps and promoting social mobility, aligning with all. In practice, many educational platforms and tools today incorporate adaptive learning features ranging Examples include intelligent tutoring systems, adaptive testing, and learning management systems that adjust course materials in real time. Adaptive technologies as schools and universities, sought solutions to deliver personalized education remotely (Jiang Z., 2024). This shift highlighted both the opportunities and the digital divides that remain, underscoring the need for continued investment in infrastructure, training, and equitable access. Looking to the future, adaptive learning and advanced natural language processing promise even richer, more immersive personalized learning experiences. These advancements could transform contextual, responsive ways people learn.

EQUITY IN EDUCATION: THE POTENTIAL OF AI-DRIVEN SOLUTIONS

Equity is a fundamental principle that ethnicity, language, gender, or abilities have learning that meet needs enable them to succeed academically and socially. Unlike equality, which implies providing the same resources to everyone, equity acknowledges the diverse barriers and circumstances learners face and calls for tailored supports to bridge these gaps. Despite widespread recognition of its importance, achieving true equity in education remains a global challenge, as persistent disparities continue to limit opportunities for marginalized and underserved populations (Sato E., et al, 2024). In this context, and promising advance in equity by personalizing learning, expanding access, and enabling data-driven interventions that address educational inequities at scale. The potential of AI-driven solutions to promote equity in education lies in their capacity to adapt to the varied backgrounds, learning styles, and proficiency levels of individual students. Traditional education systems often struggle, especially in overcrowded classrooms or under-resourced schools where one-size-fits-all curricula prevail. AI-powered dynamically assesses students' knowledge and skills accordingly. This personalization ensures that students who may need additional support receive it promptly, while advanced learners are challenged appropriately, thereby minimizing achievement gaps and fostering inclusive learning environments (Li H., 2023). Moreover, AI can enhance equity by breaking down physical, linguistic, and cultural barriers that historically restrict learners' access and provide AI-driven, affordable alternatives to traditional schooling. Natural language processing tools facilitate translation and language support, allowing students to native tongues or languages. These technologies also provide accessibility features, customized user interfaces, enabling them to participate fully in learning activities. By democratizing access and tailoring experiences to diverse learner profiles, AI helps level the educational playing field.

In addition to personalizing instruction and expanding access, AI equips educators and administrators with powerful data analytics capabilities that enhance decision-making and resource allocation aimed at promoting equity. By analyzing large volumes of student data—from attendance and participation to assessment results and engagement metrics—AI can identify patterns indicative of learning difficulties or social challenges, supporting vulnerable populations and preventing disparities from widening over time. Furthermore, insights generated by AI inform policy development and institutional strategies focused on equity, helping to ensure that investments and reforms prioritize the needs of underserved communities. One critical concern is the risk of reinforcing existing biases through AI algorithms trained on non-representative or biased data sets (Sundari M S., et al, 2024). Ensuring algorithmic transparency, fairness, and accountability build against discrimination. Possess substantial devices or skills that benefit from AI-driven educational technologies. Without addressing infrastructure and accessibility issues, AI risks exacerbating rather than alleviating educational inequalities. Looking ahead, the future of equity in education will likely depend on a collaborative and multi-faceted approach that integrates AI innovations with systemic reforms, inclusive policies, and community engagement. Advances in AI continue to expand the possibilities for personalized, accessible, and data-informed education, but realizing this potential requires intentional design and equitable deployment. By doing so, AI-driven solutions can contribute significantly to transforming education into a truly inclusive and empowering experience for learners around the world (Sakthivel M., et al, 2025). In summary, AI holds transformative promise for promoting equity in education by personalizing learning, expanding access, supporting educators with actionable insights, and enabling targeted interventions for underserved populations. Its capacity to adapt educational experiences to diverse learner needs and contexts makes it a powerful catalyst for closing opportunity gaps and fostering inclusive educational ecosystems. Nonetheless, careful attention to ethical considerations, algorithmic digital equity critical AI technologies fulfill their potential as instruments of justice and empowerment. When thoughtfully implemented, AI-driven solutions can be instrumental in creating educational environments, thereby advancing a global vision of equitable, high-quality education for all.

PERSONALIZED LEARNING PATHS: AI-GENERATED CONTENT AND RECOMMENDATIONS

Personalized learning paths represent a transformative approach in education, driven increasingly by Artificial Intelligence (AI), that tailors instructional assessments to individual needs, preferences, and goals. Unlike traditional educational models that often deliver a standardized curriculum to all students regardless of their unique backgrounds, abilities, or interests, personalized learning paths leverage AI-generated content and recommendations to create adaptive, flexible, and learner-centered experiences. AI-powered learners' interactions, performance, preferences, and even emotional states, using sophisticated algorithms to map out tailored educational pathways. These systems dynamically generate and recommend relevant content.

Appropriately challenging, skill level demonstrates proficiency in AI might suggest advancing to more complex topics or exploring interdisciplinary applications, whereas if a learner struggles, it can recommend targeted practice exercises, multimedia explanations, or alternative instructional methods such as gamified learning modules or interactive simulations (Maheswaran K., et al, 2025). This continuous feedback loop between learner input and AI adaptation enables real-time customization, allowing education to move away from rigid, linear curricula toward more organic and personalized learning experiences. Machine learning models identify patterns in student behavior and outcomes, enabling predictive insights about the most effective instructional strategies for each individual. Natural language processing enhances the system's ability to interpret and generate educational content in various formats, including text, audio, and video, while also supporting personalized communication and tutoring through conversational agents or chatbots. These AI-driven capabilities collectively empower educational platforms to curate content from vast digital repositories or even create novel learning materials, such as customized quizzes or scenario-based problems, tailored specifically to the learner's needs. Personalized learning paths are especially beneficial in diverse educational settings, supporting learners across different ages, cultural backgrounds, language proficiencies, and cognitive abilities (Binhammad M H Y., et al, 2024). By addressing each learner's unique profile, AI-generated recommendations help bridge gaps caused by socio-economic disparities, language barriers, and limited prior knowledge. A subject can receive foundational resources and scaffolded instruction, while advanced learners can explore enrichment opportunities that challenge their critical thinking and creativity. Furthermore, these personalized paths enhance learner autonomy and agency, allowing students to take ownership of their education by setting goals, choosing learning modalities, and pacing their progress with AI-guided support.

Educators also stand to benefit significantly from AI-driven personalized learning systems. These technologies provide teachers with progress, potential challenges, enabling more informed instructional decisions and targeted interventions. Instead of spending excessive time on routine content delivery or grading, educators can address social-emotional needs. AI-generated recommendations thus complement, rather than replace, human teaching by augmenting educators' capacity to meet diverse learner needs in a scalable manner (Yekollu R K., et al, 2024). Numerous real-world applications and platform paths enabled Coursera, Duolingo to adaptively recommend courses, modules, and practice activities tailored to individual progress and goals. In K-12 education, systems such as DreamBox Learning and Smart Sparrow offer personalized math and science curricula, improving engagement and learning outcomes. Higher education institutions also employ AI to design personalized degree pathways and professional development plans, reflecting learners' aspirations and workforce demands. These implementations illustrate how AI-generated personalized learning can transform educational delivery across contexts, making learning more relevant, effective, and inclusive. Looking ahead, the future of personalized learning paths AI includes deeper learning analytics dashboards that provide real-time, immersive feedback. These innovations promise even richer, more interactive, and context-aware learning experiences tailored to individual cognitive, emotional, and social dimensions. Furthermore, collaborative AI systems that engage not only learners and educators but also families and communities could foster more holistic support networks, enhancing educational outcomes and equity (Ni A., et al, 2023). In conclusion, AI-generated personalized learning paths represent a paradigm shift toward learner-centered education that acknowledges and embraces diversity in learning needs and goals. By dynamically customizing content and recommendations, these systems promote deeper engagement, improved achievement, and greater learner autonomy. While challenges related to ethics, access, and implementation persist, thoughtful design and inclusive policies can ensure that AI-powered personalization fulfills its potential to make education more equitable, effective, and empowering for learners worldwide. As education continues to evolve in the digital age, personalized learning paths driven by AI stand at the forefront of innovation, redefining how knowledge is acquired, applied, and valued in a rapidly changing world.

INTELLIGENT TUTORING SYSTEMS: AI-POWERED SUPPORT FOR LEARNERS

Intelligent Tutoring Systems represent cutting-edge (AI) interactive, learning experiences that closely mimic the one-on-one guidance of a human tutor. By combining principles from cognitive science, user modeling, ITS, tailored instruction feedback based on individual learner needs, pacing, and knowledge gaps. These systems aim to optimize learning by continuously assessing student performance and adapting content in real time to maximize understanding, retention, and skill acquisition. As a result, ITSs are emerging as powerful tools that support learners across diverse educational contexts, helping to overcome traditional challenges such as limited teacher availability, large class sizes, and variable learner abilities. Heart capacity creates a dynamic interaction between the learner and the system, and adjusts to evolving (Basri W S., 2024). Unlike static educational software, ITS actively analyzes student input—whether through typed answers, spoken responses, or problem-solving steps—to diagnose misconceptions, predict errors, and tailor subsequent instruction. This adaptive process involves several core skills learned, current understanding progress, tutoring decides how to teach based on the other models, and a user interface that facilitates interaction. Together, these elements enable ITS to offer hints, explanations, remedial exercises, and challenges precisely when and where the learner needs them, fostering efficient pathways. ITS can provide immediate, targeted feedback, which research has shown to be critical for learning and motivation. Unlike traditional classroom settings where teachers may be unable to attend individually to every student, ITS ensures timely guidance for difficulties and learning pace. This responsiveness helps to maintain learner engagement, reduce frustration, and encourage persistence. Furthermore, ITSs are capable of accommodating needs, including through multimodal interactions, customizable interfaces, and assistive technologies. By offering a learner-centered experience, ITS helps bridge gaps caused by varying prior knowledge, language proficiency, or cognitive abilities, thus contributing to greater educational equity (Mounkoro I., et al, 2024). In addition to supporting learners directly, Intelligent Tutoring Systems serve as valuable tools for educators by providing detailed analytics and insights into student performance. These systems generate rich data on how learners interact with content, the errors they make, and the strategies they employ to solve problems. Such information enables teachers to monitor progress more effectively, identify students who require additional support, and tailor classroom instruction to address common challenges. ITS thereby augments the teacher's role rather than replaces it, allowing educators pedagogical foster critical thinking, attending to social-emotional aspects of learning.

Several ITS implementations across different disciplines and educational levels illustrate their versatility and impact. For example, systems like Carnegie Learning's Cognitive Tutor have been widely adopted in mathematics education, demonstrating significant improvements in student achievement through personalized problem-solving guidance. In language learning, ITS platforms provide conversational practice and corrective feedback, enhancing speaking and writing skills. Medical education benefits from ITS, whose diverse applications highlight the broad potential of ITS to transform education by providing scalable, personalized tutoring across subject areas (Okeke N I., et al, 2024). Developing accurate student models and domain representations requires extensive expertise and resources, making ITS costly and complex to design and maintain. Additionally, ensuring that AI-driven feedback is pedagogically sound, culturally sensitive, and free from bias is critical to avoid unintended negative impacts on learners. Technical challenges such as natural language understanding and the interpretation of open-ended student responses remain areas of active research. Ethical considerations also come to the forefront with ITS deployment. Protecting student-given sensitive nature records and detailed behavioral data that ITS collects. Transparency in how these systems make decisions and recommendations is necessary to build trust among learners, educators, and parents. Moreover, integrating ITS into existing educational frameworks requires thoughtful planning to complement rather than disrupt teacher-student relationships and curricular goals (Hubballi R B., et al, 2025). Looking forward, advances in AI, including deep learning, affective computing, and multimodal interaction, promise to enhance the sophistication and human-likeness of Intelligent Tutoring Systems. Future ITS may be capable of recognizing and responding to learners' emotional states, providing more empathetic and motivating offers in immersive learning environments where ITS guides students through complex, hands-on experiences. Additionally, collaborative ITS that support group learning and peer interactions hold potential for developing social and communication skills alongside academic competencies.

REAL-TIME FEEDBACK: AI-DRIVEN ASSESSMENT AND EVALUATION

Real-time feedback, assessment evaluation in education by offering immediate, personalized responses that help learners recognize and correct mistakes, reinforce understanding, and accelerate skill development. Unlike traditional assessments that often rely on periodic testing and delayed grading, AI-driven systems enable continuous monitoring and instantaneous feedback during the learning process itself. This timely intervention is not only crucial for reinforcing knowledge retention and preventing the accumulation of misconceptions but also fosters greater learner autonomy, motivation, and engagement. As educational environments become increasingly digital and personalized, real-time feedback stands at the forefront of a shift toward dynamic, formative assessment practices that support individualized learning paths (Thirunagalingam A., et al, 2025). Significant advantages of real-time feedback its facilitates formative assessment—assessment for learning—rather than relying solely on summative assessments that measure learning outcomes after instruction has concluded. Formative feedback is vital for promoting a growth mindset and allowing students to iterate, practice, and improve continuously. By receiving feedback as they work, students gain a clearer sense of their progress, which empowers them to take ownership about proceed. Moreover, because the feedback is personalized, students at different skill levels receive support that is appropriate to their needs, helping to close achievement gaps and foster equity. AI-based real-time feedback is increasingly being integrated into a variety of educational tools and platforms. In language learning applications such as Duolingo or Grammarly, learners receive instant corrections and suggestions that help refine grammar, vocabulary, and sentence structure in real time. Intelligent tutoring systems and adaptive learning platforms further extend these capabilities by dynamically adjusting content based on the learner's response history, delivering feedback that evolves as the learner progresses. These systems do not merely point out errors but often guide students through metacognitive strategies, encouraging reflection on how they learn and helping build self-regulation skills (Wongvorachan T., et al, 2022). AI models trained in natural language understanding are capable of evaluating narrative structure, coherence, argument strength, and even tone. For example, tools like Turnitin's Revision Assistant or Google's WriteLab offer formative feedback on students' drafts, suggesting improvements in clarity, grammar, and logic. These tools help learners become better writers by engaging in an iterative process of revision and improvement, guided by immediate, data-informed recommendations. In doing so, they simulate a more continuous and interactive teacher-student dialogue, even in environments where teacher time is limited.

Figure 1. The Promise of AI-Based Adaptive Learning

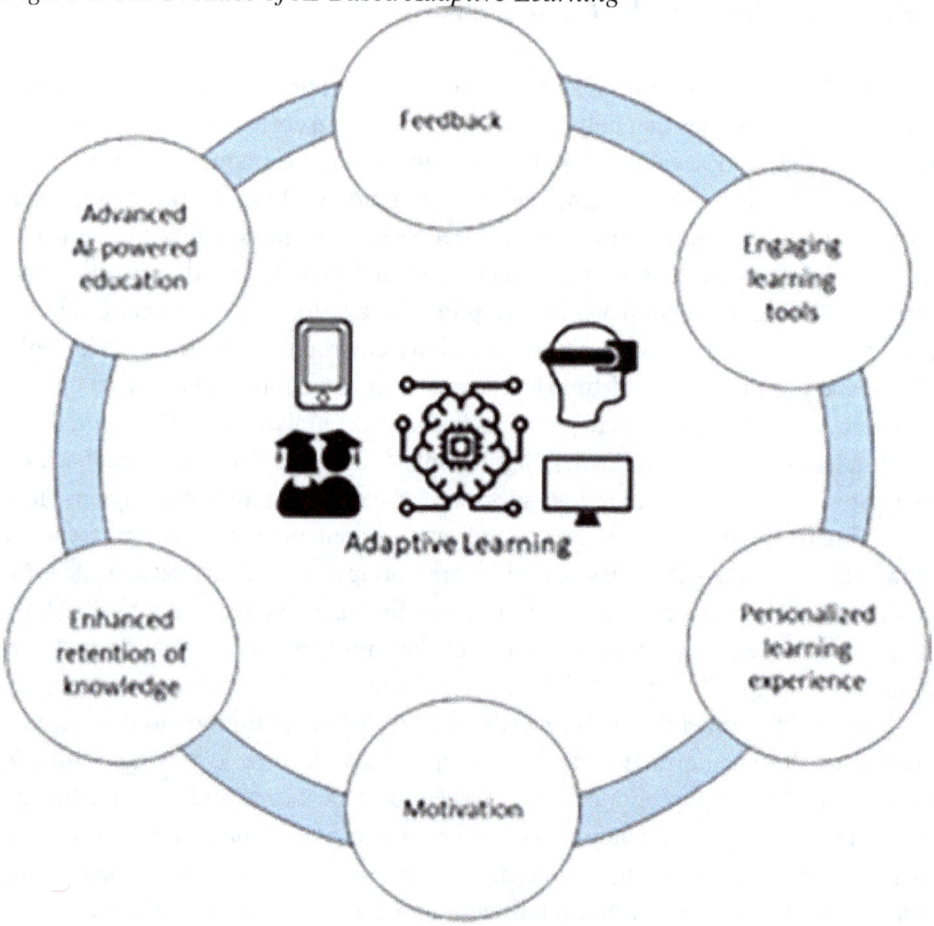

Teachers and educators also benefit significantly from AI-driven feedback systems. These tools provide instructors with real-time dashboards that visualize student progress, common errors, and levels of engagement across a class or cohort. Such analytics allow teachers to intervene promptly, differentiate instruction, and address specific learning needs more efficiently. For example, if a large portion of a class is struggling with a concept, the teacher's lesson plan reinforces learning. Moreover, AI systems can automate time-consuming grading tasks, particularly in large classes or MOOCs, freeing up qualitative tasks such as mentoring, discussion facilitation, and emotional support (Singh T M., et al, 2025). Not well designed, AI systems may provide vague, incorrect, or unhelpful feedback that confuses rather than supports learners. Ensuring that AI feedback aligns with curriculum goals and reflects best teaching practices requires interdisciplinary collaboration among educators, technologists, and learning scientists. Additionally, while AI can recognize patterns and surface insights, it lacks the contextual sensitivity and empathy of a human teacher, which can be critical in nuanced or emotionally charged learning situations. As such, AI should be viewed as a complement to, not a replacement for, human interaction in education. To ensure inclusive impact, education systems must invest in infrastructure, training, and support mechanisms that allow all students to take advantage of these tools. Furthermore, safeguarding learner privacy is paramount, as real-time feedback systems often collect detailed data on individual learning behaviors. Transparent data governance policies and ethical AI design are necessary to protect student rights and build trust among users. Looking ahead, the future of AI-driven real-time feedback is promising and full of potential. Emerging technologies such as affective computing, which enables systems to detect emotional states through voice tone, facial expression, or keystroke patterns, may enhance the emotional intelligence of AI tutors and provide more compassionate, responsive feedback. In coding education, AI systems like GitHub Copilot are already assisting learners by providing real-time code suggestions and error diagnostics, a trend likely to expand into more disciplines (Sajja R., et al, 2023). These advancements could create even more responsive, personalized, and human-centered learning environments. In conclusion, AI-driven real-time feedback represents a pivotal advancement in educational assessment and evaluation. By delivering immediate, individualized guidance, these systems support deeper learning, encourage student agency, and enhance teaching effectiveness. From language learning and mathematics to writing and coding, real-time feedback helps bridge gaps between instruction and understanding, enabling learners to thrive in increasingly complex and digital learning environments. While challenges remain in ensuring quality, equity, and ethical use, the ongoing evolution of AI technologies promises to refine and expand the capabilities of real-time feedback systems. As educators, technologists, and policymakers collaborate to integrate these tools thoughtfully and inclusively, AI-driven feedback is poised to become an essential pillar of modern, learner-centric education.

ADDRESSING LEARNING GAPS: AI-DRIVEN INTERVENTIONS

Learning gaps—disparities between what a student knows and what they are expected to know at a given point in their educational journey—are a long-standing challenge in both traditional and modern educational systems. These gaps can emerge due to a range of factors, including socioeconomic status, inconsistent access to quality instruction, language barriers, cognitive differences, disabilities, or interruptions in schooling. The COVID-19 pandemic, for instance, significantly widened existing learning gaps, especially among students from marginalized or under-resourced backgrounds. Traditional methods of addressing these gaps, such as after-school tutoring or remedial classes, have limited scalability and often fail to identify and address the root causes of individual learning deficiencies (Strielkowski W., et al, 2025). In contrast, Artificial Intelligence (AI) offers powerful, scalable, and data-driven solutions that can detect, analyze, and respond to learning gaps with precision and personalization, transforming how educators intervene and support student progress. AI-driven interventions begin with advanced diagnostic capabilities. These algorithms construct detailed learner profiles and can detect subtle indicators of misunderstanding or disengagement far earlier than traditional assessments. Consistently multi-digit multiplication performs well on single-digit operations, AI systems can pinpoint this specific skill gap, rather than broadly labeling the student as "weak in math." This granular level of analysis helps educators avoid generalizations and craft interventions that target the exact skill or concept where learning has broken down. Once a learning gap is identified, AI-powered systems can provide targeted interventions in real-time. These may take the form of adaptive practice exercises, scaffolded instructional content, gamified activities, or intelligent tutoring systems that deliver step-by-step guidance. The content and difficulty adjust automatically to receive just-in-time support that's neither too easy nor too hard (Owoade S J., et al, 2024). Importantly, these interventions are designed to be nonjudgmental and supportive, encouraging a growth mindset by reinforcing the idea that struggle is a normal part of learning. AI also facilitates early-warning systems that help educators and administrators proactively intervene before learning gaps widen into persistent academic failures. These systems monitor behavioral and academic quiz performance, engagement with content be at at-risk. For instance, a drop in participation in a learning management system (LMS) combined with declining test scores can trigger alerts to teachers or counselors. With this information, educators can initiate personalized outreach, provide additional resources, or refer students to support services. These predictive analytics make it possible to move from reactive to proactive educational support, which is critical in closing achievement gaps before they become entrenched.

Beyond academic achievement, AI-driven interventions also support students' social-emotional learning and well-being, which are often intertwined with academic gaps. Some systems integrate affective computing capabilities—technologies that recognize emotions through facial expressions, voice patterns, or written language. This emotional data, when used ethically, can be shared with educators to help them understand when a student's learning struggles may be tied to stress, anxiety, or external life circumstances. Tailoring interventions to include emotional support or adjusting instructional strategies based on students' affective states can significantly enhance the effectiveness of learning gap remediation. Despite their promise, AI-driven interventions face several critical issues, including inequities, underrepresentation of demographics, or biased grading practices—they may perpetuate or even exacerbate learning disparities (Cao Y., et al, 2022). For instance, an AI system might interpret slower typing speed as a lack of comprehension without recognizing that a student is using assistive technology. To mitigate this risk, developers must be inclusive, regularly audited. Include explainability features that make their decisions transparent to educators and students, enabling meaningful human oversight and adjustment. Another challenge is the digital divide. Bridging this divide requires coordinated policy action and investment in equitable access to digital resources, as well as training for both educators and students on how responsibly. Looking forward, the future of AI in addressing learning gaps lies in more sophisticated, empathetic, and integrative technologies. Advances in multimodal learning analytics—combining textual, visual, and behavioral data—promise more accurate and holistic learner profiling. AI systems may also become more collaborative, engaging students in dialogue about their progress and encouraging metacognition. Further integration with virtual and augmented reality could create immersive, interactive interventions tailored to specific learning needs (Upadhyaya A N., et al, 2025). In the long term, policy frameworks must evolve to ensure that AI-driven educational interventions are designed and implemented with equity, inclusivity, and sustainability in mind. In conclusion, AI-driven interventions offer a powerful solution for identifying and addressing learning gaps with speed, precision, and personalization that traditional methods struggle to achieve. By detecting gaps early, customizing instructional responses, and supporting educators with actionable insights, AI transforms remediation into a proactive and student-centered process. While significant challenges around equity, ethics, and infrastructure remain, the responsible and inclusive deployment of AI holds the potential to reduce educational disparities, promote learning continuity, and ensure that no learner is left behind. As education systems worldwide seek to recover from disruptions and reimagine the future of learning, AI-powered interventions will be an indispensable tool in building a more just, responsive, and effective educational landscape.

INCREASING ACCESS: AI-DRIVEN EDUCATION FOR UNDERSERVED COMMUNITIES

One education today is persistent inequality in access to high-quality learning opportunities. Millions of learners in underserved communities—including rural populations, low-income urban areas, conflict-affected regions, and economically disadvantaged countries—face systemic barriers to education. By automating instruction, translating content, adapting to diverse learners' needs, and scaling personalized education, AI-driven solutions are redefining what is possible in global education delivery, making it more accessible, inclusive, and flexible for underserved populations. A core advantage of AI is its scalability. Traditional education relies heavily on human labor, which is costly and unevenly distributed. Many underserved regions face acute shortages of qualified teachers, especially in subjects such as science, mathematics, and languages (Soundariya A., et al, 2025). AI-powered learning platforms can supplement or partially fill this gap by delivering consistent, high-quality content to students regardless of their location. These platforms include intelligent tutoring systems, mobile learning apps, and adaptive assessment tools that guide students through subject matter at their own pace, providing real-time feedback and personalized learning pathways. Mobile technologies have become a vital vehicle for AI-driven education access. In many underserved communities, while broadband infrastructure may be lacking, mobile phone penetration is relatively high. AI-powered mobile learning applications leverage this accessibility by turning basic devices into portable classrooms. Beyond content delivery, AI can support underserved learners by offering remote mentoring, career counseling, and life skills training. Chatbots and virtual counselors, powered by AI, provide guidance on educational pathways, scholarships, vocational training, and job readiness. These digital mentors are especially valuable in areas where access to school counselors or career advisors is limited or nonexistent. AI can also help identify at-risk students through behavioral data analytics, flagging disengagement, declining performance, or irregular attendance, and enabling timely interventions (Rane N., 2023). In contexts where human intervention may be constrained by geography or personnel shortages, AI offers a way to monitor learner progress and needs, ensuring that no student falls through the cracks. Educational equity also depends on the accessibility of content to learners with disabilities, a group often doubly marginalized in underserved communities. AI technologies support inclusive education through adaptive user interfaces, voice control, text-to-speech conversion, and intelligent captioning systems. These accommodations make it possible for education on an equal footing. In areas where special education resources are rare or nonexistent, AI-enhanced devices and apps can provide a foundational level of access that would otherwise be unavailable. Organizations like Benetech and Bookshare use AI to convert books into accessible formats, offering visually impaired students in low-resource settings the opportunity to read and learn independently.

AI is also revolutionizing teacher support and professional development in underserved communities. Many educators in these regions lack access to updated pedagogical training or subject-matter expertise. AI-driven coaching platforms can provide teachers with real-time feedback on instructional delivery, suggest adaptive lesson plans, and offer resources tailored to local curricula and language. Additionally, virtual training modules—available offline or on mobile devices—use AI to personalize content for individual teacher learning needs. These innovations not only improve classroom instruction but also empower teachers with the tools to become more confident and effective facilitators of learning. Another major challenge is ensuring digital literacy among learners and educators (Zuhair V., et al, 2024). For AI-driven solutions to be truly impactful, users must be able to navigate interfaces, interpret feedback, and interact with technology confidently. Investment in foundational digital skills training is crucial, particularly in communities where exposure to technology is limited. Moreover, equitable access requires that gender disparities in education and technology use be addressed. In many regions, girls and women face cultural, economic, or logistical barriers to digital learning. AI interventions must be deliberately inclusive, with content and delivery methods that support gender equity. Ethical considerations are also paramount in deploying AI in underserved settings. Data privacy, consent, and algorithmic fairness must be ensured, particularly when working with vulnerable populations. Many AI systems collect extensive data on learners' behaviors, responses, and personal characteristics. Without strong data governance frameworks, there is a risk of surveillance, misuse, or exploitation. Transparent design, open-source development, and community engagement are key strategies for building ethical, accountable, and trustworthy AI tools in these contexts. Looking forward, the future of AI-driven education for underserved communities will likely involve greater integration with other technologies such as blockchain for credentialing, satellite-based internet for remote delivery, and open educational resources (OER) enhanced by AI for localization and customization (Rekha K., et al, 2024). There is also increasing potential for community-led innovation, where local educators, technologists, and students co-create AI tools tailored to their unique needs and cultural contexts. International partnerships and collaborations will scale successful models and ensure sustainable impact. In conclusion, AI offers transformative possibilities for increasing educational access in underserved communities worldwide. By addressing barriers related to geography, language, disability, teacher shortages, and socio-economic exclusion, AI-driven education can democratize learning and support the global mission of education for all. The effectiveness of these interventions, however, depends on thoughtful design, ethical implementation, and sustained investment in local capacity building. When combined with human-centered pedagogy, inclusive policies, and robust infrastructure, AI has the power to close long-standing gaps in educational opportunity, ensuring that every learner, regardless of their circumstances, can realize their full potential.

ENHANCED STUDENT ENGAGEMENT: AI-POWERED INTERACTIVE LEARNING

Student engagement is a crucial factor in successful learning, performance, and long-term outcomes. Yet keeping students actively engaged—especially in digital or large-scale classrooms—has always posed a challenge for educators. Traditional teaching methods often struggle to accommodate varied attention spans, learning preferences, and motivational drivers, resulting in passive participation and reduced retention. However, the rise of interactive learning allows students to connect with educational content. AI technologies can personalize instruction, adapt in real time to students' needs and behaviors, and create interactive, immersive experiences that maintain interest and stimulate deeper learning. By blending data-driven insights with engaging digital interfaces, AI-powered systems are making learning more dynamic, responsive, and emotionally resonant, ultimately driving higher levels of student engagement across diverse learning environments (Alam A., et al, 2022). AI enhances gamified learning by dynamically adjusting game mechanics based on learner input. For example, AI can increase the difficulty of a task if a student is performing well or provide additional scaffolding if they are struggling. Badges, leaderboards, narrative storylines, and levels are personalized to match learners' progress and preferences, making them more meaningful and motivating. Platforms such as Classcraft, Duolingo, and Prodigy integrate AI-driven gamification to create highly engaging learning environments. These systems foster achievement autonomy that motivates students to return to learning tasks repeatedly. AI is also central to the development of conversational agents and virtual tutors, which enhance engagement by simulating human-like interaction. These AI-powered chatbots or avatars can answer questions, explain concepts, provide hints, or guide students through learning activities. Their natural language processing (NLP) capabilities allow for fluid dialogue, enabling students to interact with content conversationally rather than passively consuming it (Banik B G., et al, 2025). For example, Carnegie Learning's Mika and Google's Socratic app offer on-demand tutoring that mimics peer or instructor support, keeping students mentally and emotionally involved in the learning process. This "always-on" support system ensures that learners remain engaged, even in self-paced or asynchronous environments. Importantly, AI-driven engagement strategies are proving especially impactful in online and hybrid learning environments, where maintaining attention and connection can be more difficult. Remote learners often face distractions, isolation, and reduced motivation. AI helps combat these issues by personalizing content, offering interactive elements, and creating a sense of presence through conversational agents or virtual classrooms. Platforms such as Coursera, Edmodo, and Khan Academy have incorporated AI features to improve engagement metrics like course completion rates, daily logins, and time-on-task, especially among students who previously struggled in self-directed settings.

Overuse or poor implementation of AI tools can lead to excessive screen time, reliance on extrinsic motivation (e.g., badges over intrinsic interest), or reduction in critical human interaction. Systems must be designed to balance digital engagement with authentic learning goals and opportunities for reflection and dialogue. Moreover, if engagement metrics are used solely for behavioral tracking without a pedagogical purpose, they risk becoming surveillance tools rather than supports for student growth. Transparency about how AI monitors and uses engagement data is essential to maintaining trust and ethical standards (Almusaed A., et al, 2023). Another issue is equitable access to engaging AI technologies. Students in under-resourced schools or regions may lack access to the devices, bandwidth, or software needed to benefit from advanced AI systems. Additionally, language barriers, disabilities, or lack of digital literacy may inhibit full participation in AI-enhanced activities. To address this, developers and educators must prioritize inclusive design, mobile compatibility, multilingual interfaces, and adaptive accommodations that ensure all students can engage meaningfully with AI-powered content. Looking forward, the future of AI-powered engagement lies in deeper personalization, greater interactivity, and more human-like responsiveness. As generative AI, multimodal interfaces, and social robotics evolve, we will see the emergence of virtual learning companions that not only teach but also relate, support, and inspire learners. These companions could act as peer collaborators, role-playing characters, or even mentors, responding not just to what students know, but how they feel and why they learn. Furthermore, ethical AI design will ensure that these systems empower rather than replace human relationships in learning environments, keeping the emotional and social core of education intact. In conclusion, AI-powered interactive learning is fundamentally transforming how students engage with education (Samal A., et al, 2025). By tailoring content, recognizing emotions, simulating real-world experiences, and facilitating meaningful interaction, AI technologies foster deeper cognitive, emotional, and social involvement in learning. They make education more enjoyable, relevant, and accessible, especially in digital or diverse settings. While challenges remain around equity, ethics, and implementation, the thoughtful integration of AI into teaching and learning holds enormous potential to keep students actively involved, curious, and excited about their educational journey. As schools and institutions embrace these innovations, student engagement, long a challenge, can become a strength and a catalyst for lifelong learning.

DATA-DRIVEN INSIGHTS: AI-GENERATED ANALYTICS FOR EDUCATORS

Modern data vital asset—offering instructional quality, and improving student outcomes educational often exceeds human capacity to interpret and act on it in real time. This is where plays through amounts of educational uncover patterns, predict outcomes, and generate actionable insights for educators. These data-driven insights are reshaping teaching practices by empowering educators with precise, timely, and contextually relevant information, thereby making education more responsive, equitable, and effective (Chib S., et al, 2025). Analytics collect and process a wide array of data points from student interactions, ranging from grades, test scores, attendance, and time-on-task to behavioral cues such as mouse clicks, keystrokes, discussion forum participation, and even sentiment in written responses. Unlike traditional assessment tools that provide static snapshots of student performance, AI continuously monitors learning activities, enabling real-time diagnostics and longitudinal analysis. This dynamic data processing allows educators to move beyond intuition or anecdotal evidence and make evidence-based decisions tailored to individual and group learning. AI also facilitates formative assessment and continuous feedback, providing teachers with a fine-grained understanding of what each student knows and where they are struggling. Instead of relying solely on end-of-unit exams or standardized tests, educators can use AI-powered dashboards to access real-time updates on student comprehension and progress. These systems analyze micro-interactions—such as how long a student pauses before answering a question, whether they revisit learning materials, or how they approach problem-solving tasks—to infer mastery levels (Dwivedi A., et al, 2024). Teachers can then use this insight to adjust lesson pacing, revisit misunderstood concepts, or provide personalized scaffolding. In addition to individual student tracking, AI-driven analytics enable classroom-level and school-wide insights that inform instructional planning and curriculum development. For example, analytics can highlight which topics consistently cause difficulty for students across multiple classes or identify instructional strategies that correlate with higher engagement or performance. These macro-level insights support professional learning communities, enabling educators to collaborate around shared challenges and best practices. Curriculum designers can use aggregated data to refine learning materials and align them more closely with learner needs strategically, intervening in the areas where they are most needed.

Another valuable feature of AI-generated analytics is learning style and preference analysis. By observing how students interact with different types of content (e.g., video lectures, text articles, interactive simulations), AI systems can infer individual preferences and recommend resources accordingly. For instance, a student who consistently performs better with visual aids might receive infographics or video explanations, while another who excels with text-based information might be directed to reading materials. These personalized content recommendations help students stay engaged and achieve a deeper understanding, while also giving teachers a better sense of how to differentiate instruction. Also key supporting competency-based education, where progression is based on demonstrated mastery rather than time spent in class. AI analytics can provide clear visualizations of which competencies each student has mastered and which remain areas for development (Mishra S., et al, 2025). Teachers can use these insights to group students by skill level, design personalized learning pathways, and ensure that no student moves ahead with unresolved knowledge gaps. This granular, competency-level visibility is especially useful in STEM fields, language learning, and vocational training, where cumulative understanding is critical for long-term success. For educators involved in assessment and grading, AI can offer efficiency and objectivity. Automated scoring systems powered by natural language processing can evaluate essays, short answers, and even creative writing for content accuracy, coherence, grammar, and sentiment. While human oversight remains essential, these tools can dramatically reduce grading time and highlight common misconceptions across a class, design mini-lessons, or provide more meaningful individual feedback. Moreover, grading analytics can reveal bias patterns, such as unintentional disparities in how different demographic groups are evaluated, helping educators reflect on and refine their assessment practices. AI-generated analytics are also transforming teacher professional development (Faresta R A., 2024). By tracking patterns in student performance and classroom dynamics, AI can suggest areas where a teacher might benefit from training or new strategies. For instance, if students in a certain class consistently struggle with higher-order thinking questions, the system might recommend professional learning modules on inquiry-based instruction. These recommendations can be aligned with teacher growth goals, observation feedback, and school improvement plans, creating a coherent and data-informed professional development experience. Additionally, educator readiness training is critical to the successful adoption of AI analytics, not only technical skills to use dashboards to interpret data, but also with the pedagogical knowledge to act on insights effectively. Data without interpretation is useless—or worse, misleading. Schools and districts must invest in professional development, coaching, and support structures that help teachers become confident, reflective, and data-literate practitioners.

CONCLUSION

(AI) Promises profoundly reshape the landscape of education, unlocking unprecedented opportunities for equity and inclusion. AI lies in experiences, democratizes access to quality education, supports diverse learners, and provides educators with powerful tools to address systemic inequalities. However, realizing this future requires intentional design, ethical stewardship, and a commitment to bridging existing gaps to ensure AI benefits all learners. Compelling opportunities offer the advancement of personalized learning at scale, which can fundamentally alter how students engage with education. Traditional education models often apply teaching and progress measured uniformly, leaving behind those who learn differently or need additional support. Learner real-time—including performance metrics, engagement levels, and learning preferences—to craft tailored learning paths that adapt dynamically. This personalization matched pace, style, and needs, addressing gaps in understanding before they widen. For learners with disabilities or language barriers, AI can provide customized accommodations such as text-to-speech, sign language avatars, or real-time translation, thereby fostering inclusion and reducing barriers to participation. Beyond personalization, AI can serve as a gateway to educational resources for underserved and marginalized populations worldwide. By leveraging cloud computing and mobile technology, AI-driven platforms can reach remote areas where qualified teachers and physical infrastructure are scarce. Initiatives employing AI tutors or chatbots are already providing learners in rural communities with 24/7 access to instructional support, homework help, and exam preparation services previously unavailable or inconsistent. As internet connectivity improves globally, these AI tools can help bridge the gap between privileged urban centers and resource-poor rural regions, democratizing access to quality education. Importantly, AI can curate culturally relevant content in local languages, respecting diversity and promoting engagement, which is crucial for fostering equitable learning environments. The future also promises AI-enhanced support for educators, empowering teachers to focus more on student interaction and less on administrative overhead. AI-driven analytics and dashboards can offer actionable insights on student progress, highlight emerging learning gaps, suggest differentiating instruction effectively, and allocate their time strategically to maximize impact. In under-resourced schools, AI can supplement teacher shortages by providing intelligent tutoring systems that guide learners through complex subjects, thereby reducing educational disparities. Ethical considerations also demand attention. The number of personal learner AI systems rises. Robust policies and safeguards are essential to protect vulnerable populations, especially children, and to build trust in AI-driven educational tools. Equally important is maintaining the human-centered nature of education. AI should augment—not replace—the relational, empathetic, and social aspects of teaching that are critical for holistic development. The future of AI in education must emphasize partnership between technology and educators, respecting teachers' professional judgment and fostering human connection. Looking forward, interdisciplinary collaboration among policymakers, technologists, educators, and civil society will be crucial to harness AI's potential for equity. National and international frameworks can set standards and guidelines to promote the use, innovations in educational equity objectives. Investments in research and development can further refine AI tools to serve diverse learning contexts and support marginalized groups. Additionally, empowering learners to understand and critically engage with AI technologies fosters digital citizenship, preparing them for an increasingly AI-infused world. In summary, immense to transform learning landscapes by promoting access, personalization, and inclusivity on a global scale. Through thoughtful implementation, ethical governance, and equitable access, AI can become a catalyst for dismantling longstanding educational barriers and fostering a more just and inclusive society. Embracing AI's potential with vigilance and purpose will be essential to ensuring that learners in the digital age, unlocking human potential, and creating opportunities for generations to come.

REFERENCES

Alam, A., & Mohanty, A. (2022). Facial analytics or virtual avatars: Competencies and design considerations for student-teacher interaction in AI-powered online education for effective classroom engagement. In International conference on communication, networks and computing (pp. 252–265). Springer. https://doi.org/DOI: 10.1007/978-3-031-43145-6_21

Almusaed, A., Almssad, A., Yitmen, I., & Homod, R. Z. (2023). Enhancing student engagement: Harnessing 'AIED''s power in hybrid education—A review analysis. *Education Sciences*, *13*(7), 632. Advance online publication. DOI: 10.3390/educsci13070632

Banik, B. G., & Gullapelly, A. (2025). AI-powered gamification and interactive learning tools for enhancing student engagement. In *Driving quality education through AI and data science* (p. 28). IGI Global., DOI: 10.4018/979-8-3693-8292-9.ch013

Basri, W. S. (2024). Effectiveness of AI-powered tutoring systems in enhancing learning outcomes. *Eurasian Journal of Educational Research*, *110*, 1–15. DOI: 10.14689/ejer.2024.110.003

Binhammad, M. H. Y., Othman, A., Abuljadayel, L., Al Mheiri, H., Alkaabi, M., & Almarri, M. (2024). Investigating how generative AI can create personalized learning materials tailored to individual student needs. *Creative Education*, *15*, 1499–1523. DOI: 10.4236/ce.2024.157091

Cao, Y., & Zhai, J. (2022). A survey of AI in finance. *Journal of Chinese Economic and Business Studies*, *20*(2), 125–137. DOI: 10.1080/14765284.2022.2077632

Chib, S., Mehta, A. K., Selvakumar, P., Saravanan, A., Mishra, B. R., & Manjunath, T. C. (2025). Mental health challenges and solutions in high-pressure work environments. In Harriott, S. (Ed.), *Innovative approaches to managing conflict and change in diverse work environments* (pp. 247–272). IGI Global Scientific Publishing., DOI: 10.4018/979-8-3693-9556-1.ch011

Dwivedi, A., Dsouza, M., & Aggarwal, A. (2024). AI-driven school management system: A React-based web application enhancing educational administration and student performance analytics. *International Journal of Innovative Science and Research Technology*, *8*(5), 811–816. DOI: 10.38124/ijisrt/ijisrt24apr2465

Faresta, R. A. (2024). AI-powered education: Exploring the potential of personalised learning for students' needs in Indonesia education. *Traektoriâ Nauki*, *10*(5), 3012–3022. DOI: 10.22178/pos.104-19

Hubballi, R. B., Selvakumar, P., Seenivasan, R., Basava Aradhya, S. G., Dinesh, N., & Seelam, P. K. (2025). Overview of current AI technologies in education. In Kyei-Blankson, L., & Ntuli, E. (Eds.), *Transformative AI practices for personalized learning strategies* (pp. 1–26). IGI Global Scientific Publishing., DOI: 10.4018/979-8-3693-8744-3.ch001

Jiang, Z. (2024). Research on the advancement of equity in higher education driven by artificial intelligence. *Journal of Higher Education Research*, *5*(2), 88–102. DOI: 10.32629/jher.v5i2.2427

Li, H. (2023). AI in education: Bridging the divide or widening the gap? Exploring equity, opportunities, and challenges in the digital age. Advances in Education. *Humanities and Social Sciences*, *8*(1), 355–370. DOI: 10.56028/aehssr.8.1.355.2023

Maheswaran, K., Selvakumar, P., Shaikh, M., Shashank, G., Gupta, S., & Manjunath, T. C. (2025). The evolution of smart urban mobility with emerging technologies. In Ponnusamy, S., Assaf, M., Youssef, B., Jeon, G., & Kalyanaraman, S. (Eds.), *Leveraging VANETs and blockchain technology for urban mobility* (pp. 1–28). IGI Global Scientific Publishing., DOI: 10.4018/979-8-3373-0265-2.ch001

Mirari, K. (2022). The effectiveness of adaptive learning systems in personalized education. *Journal of Education Review Provision*, *2*(3), 70–76. DOI: 10.55885/jerp.v2i3.194

Mishra, S., Afaq, A., Mishra, T. K., & Mathur, N. (2025). Integrating generative AI-driven learning programs to enhance marketing skills. In *Generative artificial intelligence and ethics: Standards, guidelines, and best practices* (p. 38). IGI Global., DOI: 10.4018/979-8-3693-3691-5.ch009

Mounkoro, I., & Rafique, T.. (2024). AI-powered tutoring systems: Revolutionizing individualized support for learners. *Library Progress International*, *44*(2), 1–20. DOI: 10.48165/bapas.2024.44.2.1

Ni, A., & Cheung, A. (2023). Understanding secondary students' continuance intention to adopt AI-powered intelligent tutoring system for English learning. *Education and Information Technologies*, *28*, 3191–3216. DOI: 10.1007/s10639-022-11305-z PMID: 36119127

Okeke, N. I., Alabi, O. A., Igwe, A. N., & Ofodile, O. C. (2024). AI in customer feedback integration: A data-driven framework for enhancing business strategy. *World Journal of Advanced Research and Reviews*, *24*(1), 2036–2052. DOI: 10.30574/wjarr.2024.24.1.3207

Owoade, S. J., Uzoka, A., Akerele, J. I., & Ojukwu, P. U. (2024). Innovative cross-platform health applications to improve accessibility in underserved communities. *International Journal of Applied Research in Social Sciences*, *6*(11), 2727–2743. DOI: 10.51594/ijarss.v6i11.1723

Rane, N. (2023). Roles and challenges of ChatGPT and similar generative artificial intelligence for achieving the sustainable development goals (SDGs) [Preprint]. *SSRN*. https://doi.org/DOI: 10.2139/ssrn.4603244

Rekha, K., Gopal, K., Satheeskumar, D., Anand, U., Doss, D., & Elayaperumal, S. (2024). AI-powered personalized learning system design: Student engagement and performance tracking system. In *Proceedings of the 4th international conference on advanced computing and intelligent technologies* (Vol. 28, pp. 1125–1130). IEEE. https://doi.org/DOI: 10.1109/icacite60783.2024.10617155

Sajja, R., Sermet, Y., Cwiertny, D., & Demir, I. (2023). Integrating AI and learning analytics for data-driven pedagogical decisions and personalized interventions in education [Preprint]. arXiv. https://doi.org//arXiv.2312.09548DOI: 10.48550

Sakthivel, M., Jaganathan, A., & Mohanraj, M. Mohit, & Manjunath, T. (2025). Brand loyalty through AI and personalisation: AI-generated content for financial marketing. In A. J. Nair, S. Manohar, Y. B. Limbu, & B. A. Huhmann (Eds.), Intersecting natural language processing and FinTech innovations in service marketing (pp. 77–96). IGI Global Scientific Publishing. https://doi.org/DOI: 10.4018/979-8-3693-9944-6.ch006

Samal, A., & Misra, L. I. Mohit, Pougajendy, S., Chandel, P. S., & Manjunath, T. C. (2025). Musealization and tourism practices. In S. Oflazoğlu & M. Dora (Eds.), Preserving cultural heritage in post-disaster urban renewal (pp. 115–142). IGI Global Scientific Publishing. https://doi.org/DOI: 10.4018/979-8-3693-9097-9.ch006

Sato, E., Shyyan, V., Chauhan, S., & Christensen, L. (2024). Putting AI in fair: A framework for equity in AI-driven learner models and inclusive assessments. *Journal of Measurement and Evaluation in Education and Psychology*, *15*(Special Issue), 263–281. DOI: 10.21031/epod.1526527

Singh, T. M., Reddy, C. K. K., Murthy, B. V. R., & Nag, A. (2025). AI and education: Bridging the gap to personalized, efficient, and accessible learning. In *Internet of behavior-based computational intelligence for smart education systems* (p. 30). IGI Global., DOI: 10.4018/979-8-3693-8151-9.ch005

Soler Costa, R., Tan, Q., Pivot, F., Zhang, X., & Wang, H. (2021). Personalized and adaptive learning: Educational practice and technological impact. *Texto Livre*, *14*(3), 33445. Advance online publication. DOI: 10.35699/1983-3652.2021.33445

Soundariya, A., Behera, N. K., Chandel, P. S., Gupta, S., & Manjunath, T. C. (2025). AI and environmental ethics: The role of AI in addressing climate change—Ethical considerations in AI-driven environmental solutions. In Chakraborty, S. (Ed.), *Human values, ethics, and dignity in the age of artificial intelligence* (pp. 321–346). IGI Global Scientific Publishing., DOI: 10.4018/979-8-3693-9035-1.ch013

Strielkowski, W., & Grebennikova, V.. (2025). AI-driven adaptive learning for sustainable educational transformation. *Sustainable Development, 33*(2), 1921–1947. DOI: 10.1002/sd.3221

Sundari, M. S., Penthala, H. R., & Nayyar, A. (2024). Transforming education through AI-enhanced content creation and personalized learning experiences. In *Impact of artificial intelligence on society* (p. 21). Chapman and Hall/CRC., DOI: 10.1201/9781032644509-7

Taylor, D. L., Yeung, M., & Bashet, A. Z. (2021). Personalized and adaptive learning. In *Innovative learning environments in STEM higher education* (pp. 17–34). Springer., DOI: 10.1007/978-3-030-58948-6_2

Thirunagalingam, A., & Selvakumar, P. (2025). Application of automation and robotics in the oil and gas industry. In Abdullayev, V., & Khang, A. (Eds.), *Revolutionizing AI and robotics in the oil and gas industry* (pp. 229–244). IGI Global Scientific Publishing., DOI: 10.4018/979-8-3693-8156-4.ch011

Upadhyaya, A. N., Debnath, P., Rani, P., Manjunath, T. C., & Bhattacharya, S. (2025). AI-based disaster prediction and early warning systems. In Mobo, F. (Ed.), *AI and emerging technologies for emergency response and smart cities* (pp. 55–74). IGI Global Scientific Publishing., DOI: 10.4018/979-8-3693-9770-1.ch003

Wongvorachan, T., Lai, K. W., Bulut, O., & Tsai, Y. S. (2022). Artificial intelligence: Transforming the future of feedback in education. Journal of Applied Testing Technology, 23(Special Issue 1), 95–116. https://doi.org/DOI: 10.1386/jpm_00003_1

Yekollu, R. K., Bhimraj Ghuge, T., Sunil Biradar, S., Haldikar, S. V., & Mohideen Abdul Kader, O. F. (2024). AI-driven personalized learning paths: Enhancing education through adaptive systems. In International conference on smart data intelligence (pp. 507–517). Springer. https://doi.org/DOI: 10.1007/978-981-97-3191-6_38

Zuhair, V., Babar, A., Ali, R., & Oduoye, M. O.. (2024). Exploring the impact of artificial intelligence on global health and enhancing healthcare in developing nations. *Journal of Primary Care & Community Health, 15*, 1–10. DOI: 10.1177/21501319241245847 PMID: 38605668

Chapter 2
Bridging the Gap:
The Role of Immersive Technologies for Learners With Disabilities

Özgür Örün
https://orcid.org/0000-0001-7131-7265
Izmir Institute of Technology, Turkey

Mesut Türk
https://orcid.org/0000-0001-5988-5075
Amasya University, Turkey

ABSTRACT

Accessibility gaps in learning environments can cause various problems, especially in achieving the learning goals of individuals with special needs. At this point, immersive technologies such as augmented and virtual reality are technologies that have the potential to create accessible and equal environments for students with special needs and to compensate for accessibility problems. These technologies can provide special learning environments that meet the unique needs of individuals with sensory, cognitive and motor problems. Some of the advantages provided by immersive technologies include visual, auditory and tactile support, adaptive controllers, eye-tracking interfaces, voice command systems, real-time subtitles, and interactive learning environments enhanced with acceleration. Additionally, immersive environments can increase engagement, motivation, and skill acquisition for students with learning disabilities. In this context, this chapter examines the use of immersive technologies to address accessibility gaps in educational settings for individuals with disabilities.

DOI: 10.4018/979-8-3373-5188-9.ch002

1. INTRODUCTION

Immersive technologies such as augmented reality (AR), virtual reality (VR), and mixed reality (MR) have the potential to change the way we teach and learn (Trivedi, 2024). The potential for the application of these technologies in the education of students with special needs has been investigated for a long time, and research is expanding thanks to various applications. These technologies offer dynamic and interactive platforms that blend digital content with the physical world, and offer learning environments adapted to the various needs of students with learning disabilities (Intarapreecha and Sangsawang, 2023). Immersive technologies offer various possibilities to create a variety of learning experiences. For example, AR adds digital elements to our physical environment, allowing students to interact with both real and virtual components simultaneously (Carmigniani et al., 2011). Such a directional interaction can transform lessons into engaging applications that help students with special needs grasp complex ideas in a more relatable way. On the other hand, VR users are completely exposed (immersed) in virtual environments and can explore or practice in a safe area. This can be useful for students with special needs because they are allowed to experience life skills and social interactions without the pressure of the real world. Meanwhile, MR offers a blend of both AR and VR, allowing students to manipulate virtual objects in their real environment. Such an environment can facilitate a deeper understanding of difficult-to-understand or learn topics (Carmigniani et al., 2011) and encourage students to collaborate with their classmates and teachers. Moreover, the potential of immersive technologies extends beyond traditional teaching methods. These technologies can create personalized and adaptable learning experiences that address individual needs and are especially beneficial for students with sensory, cognitive, and motor needs (Mokmin & Rassy, 2024; Trivedi, 2024; Voultsiou & Moussiades, 2025). Moreover, immersive technologies can help develop social skills and emotional intelligence through simulated interactions in safe environments. Most students with special needs can succeed in such interactive environments because these technologies can provide scaffolding and personalized learning paths that traditional methods cannot provide (Intarapreecha & Sangsawang, 2023).

Immersive technologies have the potential to significantly reduce the digital divide experienced by students with disabilities and overcome all these barriers (Chalkiadakis et al., 2024; Creed et al., 2023; Creed et al., 2024; Macdonald & Clayton, 2012; Trivedi, 2024; Voultsiou and Moussiades, 2025). In addition, these technologies hold promise in contributing to educational technology due to their immersive nature, their ability to share information in new and engaging ways, and their potential to offer virtual experiences that can reduce barriers caused by cost or distance (Dick, 2021). In summary, the integration of immersive technologies into learning and teaching environments with various pedagogies can help eliminate accessibility and participation issues, especially for students with special needs (Intarapreecha & Sangsawang, 2023). It provides various opportunities in developing context-sensitive digital content, providing more accessible environments that suit the needs of students (Mokmin & Rassy, 2024), creating customized educational content thanks to the flexibility it offers, allowing students to learn at their own pace and receive the support they need (Intarapreecha & Sangsawang, 2023). This is especially advantageous for those with learning disabilities who may need extra time and guidance when learning certain concepts and developing skills. In brief, these immersive technologies have an undeniable potential to contribute to quality education for students with special needs.

Despite the rapid growth of immersive technologies, such as virtual, augmented and mixed reality, in educational contexts, learners with disabilities still face barriers relating to accessibility, instructional design and achieving meaningful learning outcomes. While existing research has demonstrated promising results in terms of engagement and motivation, the literature is fragmented, covering different technologies, disability categories and pedagogical approaches. Consequently, there is limited conceptual integration that systematically links immersive technologies with inclusive pedagogical principles, long-term learning outcomes, and institutional implementation considerations.

This chapter aims to address this gap by providing a critical and integrative synthesis of current research on immersive technologies in education for learners with disabilities. Rather than providing a descriptive overview, the chapter brings together technological capabilities, accessibility considerations, and instructional design principles to identify emerging patterns, limitations, and research gaps. In doing so, it supports researchers, educators and policymakers in making informed decisions about designing, adopting and evaluating immersive learning environments that promote inclusion and educational equity.

2. UNDERSTANDING ACCESSIBILITY CHALLENGES IN EDUCATION FOR LEARNERS WITH DISABILITIES

Educational equity is a fundamental requirement in contemporary society, particularly for students, learners with disabilities. United Nations (2015) sustainable development agenda targeted this goal as "Ensure inclusive and equitable quality education and promote lifelong learning opportunities for all" by 2030. With the context of this goal efforts are being made to achieve "eliminate gender inequalities in education and ensure equal access to education and vocational training at all levels for vulnerable people, including persons with disabilities, indigenous peoples and vulnerable children (United Nations, 2015)". However, there are still different type of barriers to accessibility in education in both physical and cognitive dimensions. The core problem addressed in this chapter lies not in the availability of immersive technologies, but in the lack of integrated frameworks that connect accessibility needs, pedagogical design, and measurable educational outcomes for learners with disabilities.

According to Newman et al. (2011) accessibility barriers in educational settings could cause to lower graduation rates, reduced post-graduation enrolment for upper degree, and limited career opportunities for individuals with disabilities. CAST (2024) offers a framework called Universal Design for Learning (UDL) principles, which aims to reduce barriers and create meaningful learning opportunities for learners with and without disabilities. This framework is quite fruitful for educators, learners and both. Getzel and Thoma (2008) found that many educational institutions focus on minimum compliance rather than comprehensive accessibility. This discrepancy between targeted policy and practice perpetuates barriers that restrict educational opportunities for students with disabilities.

Accessibility challenges in education for learners with disabilities could classified as physical accessibility barriers, technology and equipment barriers, cognitive accessibility barriers, and communication and language barriers.

Many traditional learning environments (school buildings), constructed before accessibility legislation came into force, feature designs that present significant challenges for students with mobility impairments, visual impairments and other physical disabilities (Imrie, 2011). Inadequate ramp systems, narrow doorways, inaccessible restroom facilities, poorly designed circulation routes, stairways without adequate alternatives, elevated platforms in classrooms and laboratories, and insufficient accessible parking spaces are several mobility-based physical accessibility barriers (Agbabiaka et al., 2024; Kapsalis et al., 2022; Pivik, 2010).

The availability and quality of assistive technology plays crucial role in educational accessibility. Despite technological advances, many educational institutions lack adequate assistive technology resources or provide outdated equipment that fails to meet student needs (Bouck, 2016). Common technology barriers include incompatible software systems, lack of alternative document format, absence of screen readers or magnification(zooming) software, and insufficient technical support for assistive technology devices (Babu & Vinutha, 2024; Fichten et al., 2009; Jacob, et al., 2022; Roberts et al., 2011).

Traditional teaching methods and materials are based on standardized educational approaches and curricula regarding cognitive processing styles and learning preferences. This can be challenging for students with learning disabilities, attention deficit disorder, and autism spectrum disorder (Chalkiadakis et al., 2024; Ralabate, 2011). Time constraints, format limitations, speed differences, auditory processing difficulties, and traditional assessment methods can negatively affect the learning outcomes of students with cognitive disabilities (Hrastinski et al., 2023; Kettler et al., 2012; Zentall, 2007).

Another barrier that needs to be overcome for those with learning disabilities can be expressed as communication and language barriers. Students with communication difficulties may avoid expressing themselves in class, answering questions, and making presentations (Light et al., 2019). According to Bellini et al. (2007), social communication and language barriers not only affect interpersonal relationships but also affect students' academic performance by reducing their opportunities for collaboration and increasing their anxiety levels.

3. THE ROLE OF IMMERSIVE TECHNOLOGIES IN ENHANCING ACCESSIBILITY

Traditional learning and teaching environments may have various limitations in meeting the varying sensory, cognitive and motor needs of students with special needs (Rose and Strangman, 2007). In this context, immersive technologies offer practical solutions by providing customizable, multimodal experiences that can be adapted to individual learning preferences and accessibility needs (Creed et al., 2024; Macdonald and Clayton, 2012; Obaid, 2013; Trivedi, 2024). As previously reiterated, these technologies have an undeniable potential to facilitate communication, collaboration and interaction. This section focuses on immersive technologies and how they can be used in multisensory learning approaches, personalized learning experiences, special solutions for sensory impairments and increasing student participation to improve accessibility.

Multi-sensory Learning Approaches: Senses are critical in learning, and with immersive technologies, it is possible to create multi-sensory learning environments that use visual and auditory senses as well as tactile channels simultaneously. Thanks to this opportunity, the user's sense of touch is activated with tactile interfaces, interactions are enriched and learning experiences can be improved (Wang et al., 2024). This multi-sensory approach in immersive technologies can be used for students with special needs who cannot use certain sensory channels. For example, with VR, realistic simulations can be created that help such students practice social interactions and daily skills in a controlled environment, thus increasing their self-confidence and readiness for real-life situations (Voultsiou & Moussiades, 2025). Tan et al. (2024) stated that these technologies attract students' attention significantly more than traditional methods. By integrating these immersive experiences into their activities, educators can work to bridge the gap between students with special needs and their peers, creating inclusive classrooms that encourage collaboration and understanding. The virtual learning environment allows students to explore and interact freely, while keeping them away from real-world dangers or embarrassment (Ip & Li, 2021).

Specific Solutions for Sensory Impairments: Immersive technologies can offer innovative solutions for visually impaired students through enhanced spatial audio, haptic feedback, and tactile interfaces. Asatryan et al. (2023) designed an AR system to provide a multi-sensory learning experience that will help visually impaired children understand and interact with their physical environment. It was concluded that students in the AR-based experimental group had higher levels of engagement and motivation during spatial awareness training, and this result showed that the AR system is effective for students who have difficulty understanding spatial concepts using traditional education methods (Asatryan et al., 2023). Immersive technologies can also provide enhanced visual feedback, spatial vibration tactile cues, and sign language integration within a multi-sensory infrastructure for hearing impaired students. Seol et al. (2021) reported that enriching speech with visual information has a significant impact on hearing impaired students with the help of the integration of audio and visual cues. In instructional materials created with these technologies, real-time subtitles, audiovisual cues, and contextual information about the learning environment can be projected directly into the student's field of vision. These features provide a richer learning environment with auditory and tactile support without distracting from the actual educational content. In addition to these features, adaptive controllers, eye-tracking interfaces, and voice command systems can be used in immersive learning experiences for students with motor disabilities. In this context, immersive technologies appear to be a highly effective solution for students with motor disabilities and the rehabilitation of motor skills (Cheng, 2024; Dascal et al., 2017; Ferreira and Menezes, 2020; Vibhuti et al., 2025).

Personalized Learning Experiences: The traditional "one size fits all" approach ignores the vast individual differences in learning disabilities, challenges, and interests (Rose & Strangman, 2007). This traditional approach creates a divide between the accessibility, participation, and academic success of students with and without disabilities. When traditional environments and curricula are not sufficient, new learning environments or activities are needed to meet the unique needs of students who are on the "margins" of the everyday classroom, such as students with disabilities and/or exceptional abilities (Meyer & Rose, 2005). With immersive technologies, students can adjust visual contrast, audio frequency ranges, interaction styles, and navigation methods to suit their specific needs and preferences (Microsoft, 2024). VR enables students to engage with information at their own pace by providing personalized learning activities through interactive games, 3D simulations, and virtual storytelling (Babu & Vinutha, 2024). AI-powered adaptive learning systems can track student progress and performance in real time and adjust the difficulty, pace, and presentation format of content in immersive environments accordingly. Moreover, these adaptive systems learn from user interaction data and can continuously improve feedback mechanisms to support learning outcomes. Thanks to these features, students can be provided with immersive learning experiences, which can increase engagement, academic success, motivation, and reduce cognitive load (Liu et al., 2022)

Student Engagement: The level of interaction is important for students to engage. With immersive technologies, students with disabilities are given control over the elements they interact with at a level that is not possible in the real world (Serafin et al., 2023). Moreover, in addition to providing a manageable, reflective learning experience that includes audio, video, and graphics, these technologies provide student engagement, interaction, and fun (Osypova et al., 2021). In particular, the gamification element plays a role in making learning more effective while providing instant feedback and better achievement and retention scores. Kaur et al. (2022) suggested that interactive technologies have significant potential in terms of improving student learning outcomes, facilitating cognitive processes, and achieving high user experience, student engagement, technological acceptance, and usability of developed systems. A significant number of studies have emphasized the effectiveness of immersive technologies in making abstract concepts more concrete in educational environments, and have stated that a deeper understanding is developed through experiential learning (Alhazzaa & Yan, 2025; Kaur et al., 2022; Tene et al., 2024; Sviridova et al., 2023; Suh & Prophet, 2018; Zhang & Miao, 2025).

Taken together, the studies discussed across these thematic areas suggest that, when aligned with inclusive instructional design principles, immersive technologies can meaningfully support learners with disabilities by enhancing engagement, accessibility, and experiential learning. The effectiveness of immersive environments appears to depend more on how pedagogical goals, accessibility features and learner needs are integrated into the design process than on the technology itself. However, despite the breadth of existing research, the evidence base remains fragmented, with limited comparative analysis across disability groups and a predominant focus on short-term outcomes. These patterns highlight the need for more systematic, longitudinal and theory-informed research to better understand how immersive technologies can support sustainable, equitable learning experiences.

4. IMMERSIVE TECHNOLOGIES IN LEARNING DISABILITY

Learning disabilities (LD) are complex neurological conditions that significantly affect an individual's ability to process information, leading to difficulties in acquiring and using skills related to listening, speaking, reading, writing, reasoning, or mathematics, despite average or above-average intelligence (Grigorenko et al., 2020; Lyon, 1996; Nugraha et al., 2025). These difficulties are intrinsic to the individual, presumed to be due to central nervous dysfunction, and may occur across a lifespan (Vinumol et al., 2013). According to the UK Department of Health and Social Care (DHSC), a learning disability is defined as a "significant reduced ability to understand new or complex information, to learn new skills (impaired intelligence), with a reduced ability to cope independently impaired social functioning), which started before adulthood, with a lasting effect on development" (DHSC, 2001). According to the Individuals with Disabilities Education Act (IDEA), LDs are defined as disorders in one or more basic psychological processes involved in understanding or using language, which may manifest in difficulties with listening, speaking, reading, writing, spelling, or mathematical calculations (Lyon, 1996). These disorders are intrinsic to the individual, presumed to be due to central nervous system dysfunction, and can persist across the lifespan (Grigorenko et al., 2020). Significantly, LDs are not attributed to visual, hearing, or motor disabilities, intellectual disabilities, emotional disturbances, or environmental, cultural, or economic disadvantages (Perelmutter et al., 2017). The prevalence of LDs among school-aged children ranges from 5% to 15%, with reading disabilities being the most common (Grigorenko et al., 2020; Lyon, 1996). Furthermore, learning disabilities often co-occur with social skill deficits and emotional or behavioural disorders, complicating the educational and social experiences of affected individuals (Tan et al., 2024). Students with learning difficulties often perform below average concerning their age, level of education, and intelligence, facing challenges in fundamental skills like reading, writing, or basic mathematics (Ahuja et al., 2025). Beyond academic struggles, students with LD frequently experience socio-emotional difficulties, such as anxiety and social rejection, which can hinder academic progress and self-esteem (Nugraha et al., 2025). The broader term of "disability" encompasses physical, cognitive, sensory, or mental impairments that lead to substantial limitations in one or more major life activities (Chalkiadakis et al., 2024). Specific learning difficulties (SpLD) include conditions such as dyslexia, dysgraphia, dyscalculia, dyspraxia, perceptual disabilities, brain injury, minimal brain dysfunction, and developmental aphasia (Ahuja et al., 2025). Neurodevelopmental disorders (NDDs), encompassing intellectual and developmental disabilities (IDDs) like autism spectrum disorder (ASD) and Down syndrome, are characterized by severe deficits in cognitive, emotional, and motor areas, leading to significant impairments in social functioning (Almuaqel, 2023; Chalkiadakis et al., 2024; Garzotto et al., 2017; Wu & Tsai, 2024).

In the literature, it is emphasized that students with IDD often struggle with functional life skills such as social skills, vocational skills, behavioral control, and disciplinary knowledge acquisition (Wu and Tsai, 2024). Given the complex nature of these challenges, individualized education and specialized teaching techniques are important for students with disabilities to build self-confidence and achieve their full potential (Babu & Vinutha, 2024; Yenioglu et al., 2023). AR, VR, and MR, along with recent developments in instructional technologies, have shown promising results in supporting students with learning disabilities (LD). Through these technologies, interactive and multisensory experiences that help address the challenges faced by these students can be provided, increasing engagement and improving learning outcomes (Ahuja et al., 2025; Bryant and Hemsley, 2024; Tan et al., 2024; Voultsiou & Moussiades, 2025). This section focuses on how AR, VR, and MR can help students with various special needs. Several reviews (e.g., Grigorenko et al., 2020; Perelmutter et al., 2017; Vasquez et al., 2015), while emphasizing that the combined evidence is still evolving, indicate that immersive environments frequently improve engagement, motivation, and skill acquisition for students with dyslexia, autism spectrum disorder (ASD), intellectual disability, attention-deficit/hyperactivity disorder (ADHD), and sensory impairments. In the following sections, we categorize studies by type of learning disability, summarizing key findings in each paragraph and indicating the technology used.

4.1. General Learning Disabilities / Specific Learning Difficulties (SpLDs)

Immersive technologies can have positive effects on the learning processes and overall development of students with general learning disabilities. AR applications attract attention by increasing student engagement, providing more accessible educational environments, and facilitating personalized learning (Chalkiadakis et al., 2024; Kapetanaki et al., 2022; Rahman et al., 2020). AR technology can help students develop their social skills and relationships and increase their motivation (Kapetanaki et al., 2022; Jdaitawi et al., 2022). AR has been found to be especially effective in improving academic skills (Jdaitawi et al., 2022; Perelmutter et al., 2017), vocabulary (McMahon et al., 2015), and decision-making abilities (Baragash et al., 2020). AR can make learning more fun, engaging, and similar to real-life experiences by providing contextual prompts directly in the real world (Cakir & Korkmaz, 2019; McMahon et al., 2015). The integration of various multimedia elements such as sound, graphics, animation, and video can significantly increase student motivation and active participation (Rahman et al., 2020). Studies have reported that AR is effective in improving spatial orientation skills in physical education (Intarapreecha & Sangsawang, 2023) and in improving reading comprehension skills in early childhood students (Shaaban & Mohamed, 2024). AR can also function as an assistive technology or instructional technology. By providing text labels, reading difficult terms aloud, and presenting video instructions and tips for independent living, AR can serve as a teaching tool and help students build self-confidence and develop social, physical, and cognitive skills (Mokmin & Rassy, 2024).

VR offers an immersive experience that removes the physical world from view, creating a simulated environment (Babu & Vinutha, 2024; Rueda and Lara, 2020). VR applications are advantageous because they provide safe and repeatable activities that can be generalized to everyday life situations (Franze et al., 2024; Malaquias et al., 2016; Mitsea et al., 2023). They can be successfully employed to support the teaching of logical-mathematical concepts, facilitate leisure activities, and provide instruction against unintentional injuries (Malaquias et al., 2016). VR contributes to motor skill learning (Perez-Muñoz et al., 2024).

Students interact with the environments created by repeatedly watching actions, slowing them down, examining them from different angles, and even directly participating in the simulated action. In this context, VR allows individuals with physical disabilities to experience activities that would otherwise be inaccessible, such as mountain climbing or extreme sports (Mokmin & Ridzuan, 2022). It also enables customized and individualized training, addressing educational gaps that may arise where traditional methods are inadequate (Chalkiadakis et al., 2024).

4.2. Specific Learning Disabilities

Attention-Deficit/Hyperactivity Disorder (ADHD): Research findings have illustrated the potential of VR in the treatment of ADHD, a condition characterized by deficits in planning, patience, and self-regulation, all of which negatively affect academic outcomes (Almuaqel, 2023). The integration of AR/VR technologies in literacy and language acquisition for students with ADHD facilitates the creation of immersive, gamified educational experiences that effectively maintain attention and foster motivation (Voultsiou & Moussiades, 2025). A gaming environment utilizing AR has been developed to enhance the behavioral outcomes for individuals diagnosed with ADHD (Alqithami et al., 2019). The application of AR technology has been scrutinized in relation to enhancing literacy and mathematical competencies among students suffering from ADHD (Kapetanaki et al., 2022). In particular, a specialized AR literacy initiative has been investigated to address reading and orthographic challenges in children identified with ADHD (Creed et al., 2023; Tosto et al., 2021).

Dyslexia: For those with dyslexia, AR and VR technologies can extend customized help. AR can yield positive effects on learning outcomes, bolster confidence, enhance commitment, and stimulate interest, while simultaneously providing avenues for autonomous learning. An AR-based Intelligent Tutoring System (ITS) enriched the educational experiences of learners with dyslexia (Ahuja et al., 2025). Tools supported by AR enhanced academic performance in engineering disciplines for students with learning disabilities (Fitzpatrick et al., 2013). An interactive textbook utilizing AR improved comprehension by transforming key terms into three-dimensional visuals, audio components, and video content (Vinumol et al., 2013).

VR environments may be advantageous for multisensory pedagogical approaches by providing safe and controlled environments characterized by high interactivity, where student efforts are encouraged without criticism through avatar functions (Maskati et al., 2021). Research shows that VR training programs can increase visual attention and motor skills, potentially resulting in significant improvements in reading abilities. Interaction with action video games and VR applications has been associated with improvements in short-term memory, reading speed, visuospatial attention, and multisensory integration in children with dyslexia (Flores-Gallegos et al., 2022). Furthermore, sustained effectiveness of virtual reality rehabilitation in improving reading proficiency has been demonstrated (Maresca et al., 2024). Cano et al. (2022) focused their efforts on the development of user-friendly VR and AR tools specifically aimed at the inclusion, treatment, and rehabilitation of individuals with dyslexia. Software applications such as "DiDoc" have helped alleviate reading difficulties by scanning and vocalizing the text (Cano et al., 2022).

Dysgraphia: Supportive AR and VR tools have been developed to address dysgraphia (Creed et al., 2023). This includes Kinect-based therapy games designed with dynamic difficulty adjustment to assist individuals with dysgraphia (Hutama et al., 2021).

Dyscalculia: AR and VR have also yielded supportive tools for dyscalculia. An AR serious game has been specifically designed for children with dyscalculia (Avila-Pesantez et al., 2018), and AR learning environments have been explored for mathematics learning (Kapetanaki et al., 2022).

4.3. Autism Spectrum Disorder (ASD)

For individuals with ASD, immersive technologies are particularly valuable for addressing social and behavioral challenges. VR applications are utilized to impart social skills in controlled environments, offering realistic interactions and enabling the automatic assessment of cognitive and emotional states during training (Almuaqel, 2023). These tools can be effective in addressing low representational flexibility in ASD. VR environments, such as EVA Park (see https://evapark.city.ac.uk), have been used for social interaction and tele-therapy for individuals with communication disabilities, showing high compliance and positive therapy experiences (Amaya et al., 2018; Galliers et al., 2017). VR headsets can enhance affective expression and social reciprocity (Ip et al., 2024), and VR gaming (e.g., virtual pink dolphins) can be beneficial for children with ASD (Lu et al., 2018). VR helps in the development and practice of social and problem-solving skills through real-world scenario simulations (Chalkiadakis et al., 2024; Zhang et al., 2021). Virtual vocational training programs also connect real-world instructors with trainees in virtual environments for individuals with intellectual disabilities, including those with ASD (Cano et al., 2022).

AR applications for ASD include smart glasses systems for social communication and behavioral coaching (Liu et al., 2017). These AR learning environments can facilitate the acquisition of social and behavioral skills, science vocabulary, and general skills (Kapetanaki et al., 2022). AR has been used to teach phoneme and word reading to first-grade students with autism and developmental delays (Saunders et al., 2024), and specific mobile applications like “AReal-Vocab” help with English vocabulary for children with mild autism (Hashim et al., 2022). AR is also applied in teaching bakery skills and developing assistive learning tools using speaking albums and visual auditory schedulers (Vullamparthi et al., 2013). Review highlights that AR research for ASD largely focuses on language use, vocabulary acquisition, speech sounds, and phonics skills (Bryant et al., 2024). AR can also support the teaching of mathematics (Kellems et al., 2020; Morris et al., 2022), functional living skills, and vocational/employment skills (Saunders et al., 2024).

4.4. Intellectual and Developmental Disabilities (IDDs) / Cognitive Disabilities

Immersive technologies can provide support to individuals with IDD and cognitive disabilities in areas such as daily living skills, education, and personal autonomy. VR environments help teach logical-mathematical concepts and prevent injuries (Malaquias et al., 2016). VR creates recreational opportunities for young adults with physical and mental disabilities (Malaquias et al., 2016; Weiss et al., 2003). Immersive VR has been shown to be superior to non-immersive devices in improving real-world skills among individuals with intellectual disabilities (Franze et al., 2024). The “Joker” Wearable Immersive Virtual Reality (WIVR) application aimed to improve traditional educational strategies for children with NDD, particularly in attention skills (Garzotto et al., 2017). VR technologies are vital for engaging students with intellectual and sensory disabilities, given their multisensory and interactive environments that benefit those who have difficulty in traditional environments (Chalkiadakis et al., 2024). They also support the acquisition of basic academic skills and the promotion of independent living (Malaquias et al., 2016).

AR applications involving individuals with intellectual disabilities have targeted various areas, including education, personal autonomy, and health promotion. Portable AR devices are preferred due to their comprehensive intervention options and potential to promote personal autonomy (Gómez-Puerta et al., 2019). Their advantages include improved learning outcomes, motivation, task enjoyment, better understanding of information, better orientation, and increased participation

(Gómez-Puerta et al., 2019). An AR-based prompt system has been developed for vocational tasks for individuals with cognitive disabilities (Chang et al., 2013). AR has been shown to be effective in teaching daily living skills to adults with intellectual disabilities, and it has been concluded that this increases independence (Bridges et al., 2020).

AR supported educational materials are considered suitable for learners with cognitive disabilities and provide visual aids for activity support and decision-making (Jdaitawi et al., 2022). AR has been applied to introduce animals to students with intellectual disabilities (Pangestu et al., 2024) and to teach mathematics and science (Kapetanaki et al., 2022; Saunders et al., 2024). AR-based video prompted teaching models can increase student motivation and independent learning abilities by showing immediate, maintenance and generalization effects on functional life skills (Wu & Tsai, 2024). AR also facilitates independent learning and task performance for students with intellectual disabilities through cognitive enhancement (Voultsiou & Moussiades, 2025).

The body of literature strongly supports the transformative potential of AR and VR technologies for individuals with a broad spectrum of disabilities. These immersive technologies demonstrably enhance learning outcomes, boost motivation, and improve critical life skills across diverse populations, including those with specific learning disabilities like dyslexia, dysgraphia, and dyscalculia, as well as broader categories such as autism spectrum disorder, intellectual and developmental disabilities, and sensory impairments. AR's ability to overlay digital information onto the real world provides context-relevant, hands-free support, proving effective in teaching academic subjects, daily living skills, and vocational tasks, while also fostering social interaction and independence (Jdaitawi et al., 2022; Mokmin & Rassy, 2024; Gómez-Puerta et al., 2019; Saunders et al., 2024; Wu & Tsai, 2024). VR provides immersive environments for skill development and training, advantageous for individuals with cognitive and physical challenges (Chalkiadakis et al., 2024; Franze et al., 2024; Malaquias et al., 2016).

In conclusion, despite these significant advantages, there are a number of challenges to the widespread adoption and optimal implementation of AR and VR in special education. These include high development and implementation costs, technical barriers, and lack of teacher readiness and specialized training (Ahuja et al., 2025; Chalkiadakis et al., 2024; Kapetanaki et al., 2022). Existing studies are often based on small sample sizes and short-term interventions, which limits the generalizability of findings and long-term understanding of effects (Bryant et al., 2024; Kapetanaki et al., 2022). Moreover, concerns about privacy, potential for overstimulation, and the need for personalized content remain valid (Babu and Vinutha, 2024; Tan et al., 2024; Voultsiou and Moussiades, 2025). In addition, the application of instructional design elements in immersive technologies is another important issue.

To provide a structured overview of how immersive technologies have been applied across different types of learning disabilities, Table 1 summarizes key study foci and reported outcomes.

Table 1. Use of Immersive Technologies for Different Types of Learning Disabilities

Learning Disability Type	Immersive Technology Used	Focus of Studies / Applications	Key Outcomes Reported
General Learning Disabilities / SpLDs	AR, VR	Academic skills, vocabulary development, decision-making, spatial orientation, motor skills, social skills, independent living	Increased engagement and motivation; improvement in academic performance, vocabulary acquisition, spatial orientation, motor learning, and self-confidence; enhanced personalization and contextual learning
ADHD	AR, VR	Attention regulation, literacy and language acquisition, mathematics learning, behavioral outcomes	Improved attention span and motivation; enhanced literacy and mathematical competencies; positive behavioral regulation through gamified and immersive environments
Dyslexia	AR, VR	Reading skills, comprehension, visual attention, multisensory learning, rehabilitation	Improved reading speed, comprehension, short-term memory, visuospatial attention, and multisensory integration; increased learner confidence and sustained reading improvements over time
Dysgraphia	AR, VR	Writing skills, motor coordination, therapy-based interventions	Improved fine motor control and writing-related skills through adaptive and game-based therapeutic environments
Dyscalculia	AR, VR	Mathematics learning, number sense, problem-solving	Enhanced mathematical understanding and engagement through serious games and interactive learning environments
Autism Spectrum Disorder (ASD)	AR, VR	Social communication, behavioral coaching, language and vocabulary, vocational skills, daily living skills	Improved social interaction, affective expression, communication skills, and vocational competencies; safe practice of real-world scenarios; increased engagement and compliance
Intellectual and Developmental Disabilities (IDDs) / Cognitive Disabilities	AR, VR	Daily living skills, logical-mathematical concepts, vocational training, autonomy, injury prevention	Enhanced independence, motivation, and participation; improved real-world skill transfer; better understanding of academic and functional content; increased personal autonomy

5. INSTRUCTIONAL DESIGN CONSIDERATIONS IN LEARNING OF LEARNERS WITH DISABILITIES

When designing instructional materials, learning experiences, or teaching environments for students with disabilities through immersive technologies, it is necessary to identify and address some important issues. In this section, we aimed to categorize and systematically synthesize these issues related to instructional design and technology by reviewing the relevant academic literature.

5.1. Instructional Design Considerations

Personalization and adaptability are two relevant elements to meet the diverse needs of students with disabilities. This includes being able to change visual and auditory components such as typography, color schemes, contrast, and text sizes to reduce distractions and cognitive overload specifically for dyslexia (Almuaqel, 2023). For example, in AR applications for dyslexia, words can be highlighted during reading and visual images can be presented to improve word recognition (Babu & Vinutha, 2024). On the other hand, adaptive systems powered by AI can customize learning experiences and enhance educational experiences by providing real-time feedback at the pace of each student (Chalkiadakis et al., 2024). Virtual reality environments provide an adaptable environment where teaching methodologies can be employed to adjust teaching content to address the individual cognitive, sensory, and motor abilities of students with special needs (Voultsiou & Moussiades, 2025). This adaptability encompasses a variety of methods of presenting educational materials, including interactive games, 3D simulations, and virtual narratives (Babu & Vinutha, 2024; Intarapreecha & Sangsawang, 2023; Mokmin & Ridzuan, 2022). In addition, interfaces and content for students with cognitive disabilities should be organized with clear instructions that AI can modify to increase understanding and recall of the complexity of the content (Chalkiadakis et al., 2024; Voultsiou & Moussiades, 2025).

Enhancing engagement and motivation is key advantage of immersive technologies. AR and VR are inherently engaging technologies that can significantly increase student engagement, interest, and enthusiasm (Babu and Vinutha, 2024; Gulboy & Denizli-Gulboy, 2025; Jdaitawi and Kanan, 2022; Rahman et al., 2020; Shaaban & Mohamed, 2024). These technologies can provide positive educational experiences by promoting immersive and interactive environments, making lessons more fun, stimulating, and engaging (Ahuja et al., 2025; Babu and Vinutha, 2024; Chalkiadakis et al., 2024; Franze et al., 2024; Maskati et al., 2021; Shaaban and Mohamed, 2024; Tan et al., 2024). For students with intellectual disabilities, augmented reality can facilitate virtual experiments that allow interaction with scientific concepts in a safe and orderly context, thereby increasing motivation and self-esteem (Gulboy & Denizli-Gulboy, 2025).

Multi-sensory interaction and experience are another critical element in the instructional design of immersive technologies for effective learning. AR integrates digital content with physical environments and enhances real-world experiences (Bryant & Hemsley, 2024). This method increases user engagement and situational awareness (Bryant & Hemsley, 2024; Creed et al., 2023). VR creates immersive environments that connect theoretical concepts to practical applications (Chalkiadakis et al., 2024). Utilizing visual cues, interactive elements, and multisensory feedback significantly benefits students with dyslexia (Babu & Vinutha, 2024; Khasawneh, 2024; Voultsiou & Moussiades, 2025). For individuals with visual impairments, key features include enhanced contrast, audio descriptions, and tactile feedback (Voultsiou & Moussiades, 2025).

Focusing on skill development and generalization is a significant application area for immersive technologies. They provide safe, controlled, and repeatable environments for hands-on learning, making it easier to acquire life skills, social skills, and vocational abilities (Almuaqel, 2023; Franze et al., 2024; Jdaitawi & Kanan, 2022; Malaquias & Malaquias, 2016; Tan et al., 2024). Examples include teaching waste management, grocery shopping, street crossing, job interview skills, and functional living skills like cooking (Franze et al., 2024; Jdaitawi & Kanan, 2022; Nabors et al., 2020; Wu & Tsai, 2024). AR can also improve navigation skills, support daily and independence skills, and enhance academic skills in math and science (Gulboy & Denizli-Gulboy, 2025; Jdaitawi & Kanan, 2022; Kapetanaki et al., 2022; Saunders et al., 2024; Wu & Tsai, 2024). For certain skills, structured and repetitive tasks within the immersive environment can be highly effective in improving skill acquisition and executive functions (Carreon et al., 2022). The immersive qualities foster engagement and contextualize learning, which are key for skill acquisition and transfer to real-world situations (Carreon et al., 2022; Franze et al., 2024; Malaquias & Malaquias, 2016; Nabors et al., 2020).

Careful user interface and experience (UI/UX) Design is paramount to ensure the applications are intuitive, user-friendly, and accessible (Almuaqel, 2023; Babu & Vinutha, 2024; Bryant et al., 2024; Bryant & Hemsley, 2024; Carreon et al., 2022; Chalkiadakis et al., 2024; Creed et al., 2024; Garzotto et al., 2017; Jdaitawi & Kanan, 2022; Kapetanaki et al., 2022; Kellems et al., 2020; Mokmin & Ridzuan, 2022; Nabors et al., 2020; Rahman et al., 2020; Voultsiou & Moussiades, 2025). Design decisions should consider optimal font styles, colors, contrast levels, and text size to enhance readability and reduce cognitive load for learners with dyslexia (Babu & Vinutha, 2024). Providing multiple input options (e.g., voice control, gaze mapping) and allowing personalization of stimuli (e.g., slower speeds, lower sound) can mitigate physical and mental fatigue and accommodate diverse interaction requirements (Creed et al., 2023). The ability to freely control learning progress, rewind, and pause content is also beneficial (Mokmin & Ridzuan, 2022).

Providing adequate teacher and caregiver support and training is essential for successful implementation (Babu & Vinutha, 2024; Bryant et al., 2024; Bryant & Hemsley, 2024; Cano et al., 2022; Perez-Munoz et al., 2024; Chalkiadakis et al., 2024; Creed et al., 2023; Kapetanaki et al., 2022; Nabors et al., 2020; Shaaban & Mohamed, 2024; Voultsiou & Moussiades, 2025). Educators need to be familiar with the technology, understand intervention goals, and be proficient in facilitating AR/VR experiences (Babu & Vinutha, 2024). Ongoing support and professional development opportunities are necessary to ensure effective implementation (Babu & Vinutha, 2024; Chalkiadakis et al., 2024). It is also important to involve end-users, including children with disabilities, their parents, and education/health professionals, in the design phase to ensure applications are fit for purpose and address unique needs (Bryant & Hemsley, 2024; Bryant, Hemsley, & Brunner, 2024; Creed et al., 2023; Kapetanaki et al., 2022; Voultsiou & Moussiades, 2025). Beyond technological considerations, the effective use of immersive technologies in inclusive education hinges on teacher preparedness. Teachers need to be familiar with technology and understand how to align it with learning objectives, accessibility requirements and the needs of different learners. Without targeted professional development and instructional support, the pedagogical potential of immersive environments may go unfulfilled or be implemented inconsistently.

6. CHALLENGES AND LIMITATIONS

Despite their potential, immersive technologies face significant challenges in accessibility for learners with disabilities. The high costs of necessary equipment and training hinder scalability, particularly in under-resourced educational environments (Babu & Vinutha, 2024; Chalkiadakis et al., 2024; Voultsiou & Moussiades, 2025). If not universally accessible, these technologies may exacerbate the digital divide (Creed et al., 2024). Access to hardware, funding, and technical support are essential factors to consider (Babu & Vinutha, 2024). At the institutional level, adopting immersive technologies requires adequate infrastructure, technical support and organizational commitment. Issues such as resource allocation, staff training and compliance with accessibility standards play a critical role in determining whether immersive solutions can be integrated into curricula sustainably, rather than remaining isolated pilot initiatives.

Technical barriers and usability issues can hinder effective implementation of immersive technologies into learning environments. Issues like cybersickness (i.e., simulation sickness, nausea or discomfort from VR use), display performance problems (e.g., slow frame rate, distortion), and the general complexity of certain assistive technologies can make them inaccessible for students with disabilities (Creed et al., 2024; Franze et al., 2024; Jdaitawi & Kanan, 2022; Maskati et al., 2021; Mokmin & Ridzuan, 2022; Voultsiou & Moussiades, 2025). Environmental constraints such as lighting, reflective surfaces, and occlusions can affect object detection and tracking in AR experiences (Babu & Vinutha, 2024). There is also a lack of standardized frameworks for applying these tools effectively (Voultsiou & Moussiades, 2025).

Research gaps and methodological limitations are highlighted as important research gaps and methodological limitations (Almuaqel, 2023; Kapetanaki et al., 2022; Nabors et al., 2020; Tan et al., 2024; Wu and Tsai, 2024). A significant number of studies indicate limitations due to limited sample sizes, short experimental time frames, and lack of assessments for skill generalization and maintenance, thus questioning the external validity and longitudinal validity of the results (Gomez-Puerta et al., 2019; Jdaitawi and Kanan, 2022; Kapetanaki et al., 2022; Nabors et al., 2020; Tan, Shendyapina, and Tay, 2024; Wu and Tsai, 2024). Additionally, the lack of studies focusing on different disabilities is also highlighted. Therefore, it can be stated that there is a need for rigorous generalization of results across different disability groups (Jdaitawi & Kanan, 2022; Shaaban & Mohamed, 2024). Moreover, it can be said that there is a critical need for more detailed empirical analyses designed to evaluate the effectiveness of AR/VR interventions that go beyond basic skill acquisition and compare them with different pedagogical strategies (Almuaqel, 2023; Ahuja et al., 2025; Jdaitawi & Kanan, 2022; Perelmutter et al., 2017).

Resistance to adoption can arise from a variety of stakeholders, including special education professionals and parents (Perez-Munoz et al., 2024; Chalkiadakis et al., 2024; Nabors et al., 2020; Voultsiou & Moussiades, 2025). Such resistance may arise from inadequate training, uncertainty and concerns about the impact of assistive technologies on professional roles, or a lack of understanding of their advantages (Chalkiadakis et al., 2024; Voultsiou & Moussiades, 2025). In order to overcome this challenge, in-service professional development initiatives and the development of positive adoption intentions are a necessity (Perez-Munoz et al., 2024; Voultsiou & Moussiades, 2025).

Ethical concerns must be considered when integrating these technologies into learning environments for students with disabilities. These include privacy risks, the potential for malicious digital attacks, and algorithmic biases that may portray people with disabilities in a limited light (Ahuja et al., 2025; Chalkiadakis et al., 2024; Voultsiou & Moussiades, 2025). There are also concerns about the potential for over-reliance on these tools to inhibit the development of critical thinking skills or reduce human agency and creativity in the learning process (Chalkiadakis et al., 2024). It has been stated that measures should be taken to protect against misuse and bias in order to reduce inequalities and promote equitable learning environments (Chalkiadakis et al., 2024).

Beyond technical hurdles, deploying immersive technologies for vulnerable learners requires a robust data governance framework. Immersive devices can capture detailed biometric data, such as gaze patterns and physiological responses, raising significant privacy concerns. Furthermore, as AI becomes integrated into these environments, there is a risk of algorithmic bias, whereby standardized models may misinterpret the atypical behavior of students with neurodevelopmental disorders, potentially leading to exclusionary educational pathways.

7. CONCLUSION

Inclusion and equity within the educational sphere, particularly for learners with disabilities, represent core objectives of modern societies. As elucidated in this section, immersive technologies such as AR and VR possess capabilities to bridge accessibility disparities within educational settings for individuals with special requirements. These technological innovations surpass conventional methodologies by providing tailored interventions for students with sensory, cognitive, and motor challenges through multisensory pedagogical frameworks, individualized experiences, and interactive platforms. For instance, VR facilitates students diagnosed with Autism Spectrum Disorder (ASD) in honing their social competencies within a secure environment, whereas AR can render abstract concepts more concrete for learners experiencing difficulties such as dyslexia. Such advancements underscore the capacity to foster a more inclusive educational milieu by enhancing student engagement, motivation, and skill development.

Nonetheless, significant challenges are identified that impede the widespread adoption of immersive technologies. Elevated costs, intricate technical requirements, and the necessity for specialized training for educators constitute formidable obstacles, particularly in educational contexts that are constrained by limited resources. Furthermore, for these technologies to yield effective outcomes, it is imperative that instructional design incorporates diverse pedagogical frameworks; user-friendly, intuitive, and adaptable tools catering to varying needs must be developed, and media should be meticulously crafted. Conversely, the gaps in existing research literature are conspicuous. Given that current studies predominantly focus on small cohorts, it is articulated that further investigations are warranted to explore long-term implications. Additionally, ethical dilemmas, including privacy vulnerabilities and an overreliance on technology, represent critical considerations.

In summary, the prospects presented by immersive technologies are too significant to overlook concerning their capacity to engender more accessible and equitable educational environments for students with special needs. However, it must also be indicated that collaboration among researchers, educators, policymakers, and technology developers is important for realization of this potential. In this regard, augmenting research and development investments, establishing comprehensive training programs for educators to proficiently utilize these technologies, and adhering to universal design principles will underpin this initiative. From a sustainability perspective, long-term success depends on evaluating not only immediate engagement or usability but also learning retention, skill transfer, and the capacity of institutions to maintain and update immersive systems over time. Sustainable implementation therefore requires alignment between pedagogical goals, institutional strategies, and ongoing evaluation mechanisms. The pursuit of immersive technologies to dismantle educational barriers and ensure that every student receives a learning experience commensurate with their capabilities can be regarded not merely as an option but as an ethical obligation.

REFERENCES

Agbabiaka, H. I., Olatunji, S. A., Saleh, M., Sodangi, A. B., & Muhammad, H. (2024). Students with disabilities (SWDs) and facilities accessibility in a northern Nigerian public university: Dismantling exclusion in achieving SDG4. *Facilities*, *42*(11/12), 928–946.

Ahuja, N. J., Dutt, S., Choudhary, S. L., & Kumar, M. (2025). Intelligent tutoring system in education for disabled learners using human–computer interaction and augmented reality. *International Journal of Human-Computer Interaction*, *41*(3), 1804–1816.

Alhazzaa, K., & Yan, W. (2025). Immersive technologies in education: Exploring user experience and engagement in building energy simulations through AR and VR. *Computers & Education: X Reality*, 6, 100097. https://doi.org/DOI: 10.1016/j.cexr.2025.100097

Almuaqel, I. A. (2023). Virtual reality and inclusive learning of individuals with intellectual and developmental disabilities: A review of findings and the path ahead. *IEEE Transactions on Learning Technologies*, *16*(3), 365–377.

Alqithami, S., Alzahrani, M., Alzahrani, A., & Mostafa, A. (2019). Modeling an augmented reality game environment to enhance behavior of ADHD patients. In *Brain Informatics: 12th International Conference, BI 2019, Haikou, China, December 13–15, 2019* [Springer International Publishing.]. *Proceedings*, *12*, 179–188.

Amaya, A., Woolf, C., Devane, N., Galliers, J., Talbot, R., Wilson, S., & Marshall, J. (2018). Receiving aphasia intervention in a virtual environment: The participants' perspective. *Aphasiology*, *32*(5), 538–558.

Asatryan, S., Svajyan, A., & Antonyan, S. (2023). Augmented reality in education for children with special needs. *Armenian Journal of Special Education*, *7*(1), 56–62. DOI: 10.24234/se.v6i1.304

Avila-Pesantez, D. F., Vaca-Cardenas, L. A., Delgadillo Avila, R., Padilla Padilla, N., & Rivera, L. A. (2018, August). Design of an augmented reality serious game for children with dyscalculia: a case study. In *International Conference on Technology Trends* (pp. 165-175). Cham: Springer International Publishing.

Babu, C. V. S., & Vinutha, S. (2024). Impact of AR/VR in the Learning Process of Children with Dyslexia. In V. A. Devi, W. Singh, & Y. Kumar (Eds.), *Augmented reality and virtual reality in special education* (pp. 161–188). Scrivener Publishing LLC.

Baragash, R., Al-samarrie, H., Azahrai, A., & Alfarraj, O. (2020). Augmented reality in special education: A meta-analysis of single-subject design studies. *European Journal of Special Needs Education, 35*(3), 382–397. DOI: 10.1080/08856257.2019.1703548

Bellini, S., Peters, J. K., Benner, L., & Hopf, A. (2007). A meta-analysis of school-based social skills interventions for children with autism spectrum disorders. *Remedial and Special Education, 28*(3), 153–162.

Bouck, E. C. (2016). A national snapshot of assistive technology for students with disabilities. *Journal of Special Education Technology, 31*(1), 4–13. DOI: 10.1177/0162643416633330

Bridges, S. A., Robinson, O. P., Stewart, E. W., Kwon, D., & Mutua, K. (2020). Augmented reality: Teaching daily living skills to adults with intellectual disabilities. *Journal of Special Education Technology, 35*(1), 3–14. DOI: 10.1177/0162643419836411 PMID: 38911489

Bryant, L., Bailey, B., & Hemsley, B. (2024). Developing and evaluating an immersive augmented reality application for children with developmental communication disability: InterPlay for language learning. *International Journal of Speech-Language Pathology*, •••, 1–14. DOI: 10.1080/17549507.2024.2361734 PMID: 39135408

Bryant, L., Decates, J., Bailey, B., & Hemsley, B. (2024). Views on augmented reality and neurodevelopmental communication disability: Survey of parents, educators, and health professionals. *Journal of Autism and Developmental Disorders*, •••, 1–9. DOI: 10.1007/s10803-024-06686-8 PMID: 39708077

Bryant, L., & Hemsley, B. (2024). Augmented reality: A view to future visual supports for people with disability. *Disability and Rehabilitation. Assistive Technology, 19*(3), 800–813. PMID: 36149835

Cakir, R., & Korkmaz, O. (2019). The effectiveness of augmented reality environments on individuals with special education needs. *Education and Information Technologies, 24*(2), 1631–1659.

Cano, S. R., Delgado-Benito, V., & Gonçalves, V. (2022). Educational technology based on virtual and augmented reality for students with learning disabilities: Specific projects and applications. In *Emerging advancements for virtual and augmented reality in Healthcare* (pp. 26–44). IGI Global Scientific Publishing.

Carmigniani, J., Furht, B., Anisetti, M., Ceravolo, P., Damiani, E., & Ivkovic, M. (2011). Augmented reality technologies, systems and applications. *Multimedia Tools and Applications, 51*(1), 341–377. DOI: 10.1007/s11042-010-0660-6

Carreon, A., Smith, S. J., Mosher, M., Rao, K., & Rowland, A. (2022). A review of virtual reality intervention research for students with disabilities in K–12 settings. *Journal of Special Education Technology, 37*(1), 82–99. DOI: 10.1177/0162643420962011

CAST. (2024). Universal Design for Learning Guidelines version 3.0. Retrieved June 3, 2025, from https://udlguidelines.cast.org

Chalkiadakis, A., Seremetaki, A., Kanellou, A., Kallishi, M., Morfopoulou, A., Moraitaki, M., & Mastrokoukou, S. (2024). Impact of artificial intelligence and virtual reality on educational inclusion: A systematic review of technologies supporting students with disabilities. *Education Sciences, 14*(11), 1223. DOI: 10.3390/educsci14111223

Chang, Y. J., Kang, Y. S., & Huang, P. C. (2013). An augmented reality (AR)-based vocational task prompting system for people with cognitive impairments. *Research in Developmental Disabilities, 34*(10), 3049–3056. DOI: 10.1016/j.ridd.2013.06.026 PMID: 23880030

Cheng, M. (2024). *Immersive Virtual Reality for Motor Rehabilitation in Individuals With Neurodevelopmental Disorders* [Doctoral dissertation, Northeastern University]. ProQuest Dissertations & Theses Global. https://www.proquest.com/dissertations-theses/immersive-virtual-reality-motor-rehabilitation/docview/3130515297/se-2?accountid=25074

Creed, C., Al-Kalbani, M., Theil, A., Sarcar, S., & Williams, I. (2023). Inclusive augmented and virtual reality: A research agenda. *International Journal of Human-Computer Interaction, 40*(20), 6200–6219. DOI: 10.1080/10447318.2023.2247614

Creed, C., Al-Kalbani, M., Theil, A., Sarcar, S., & Williams, I. (2024). Inclusive AR/VR: Accessibility barriers for immersive technologies. *Universal Access in the Information Society, 23*(1), 59–73. DOI: 10.1007/s10209-023-00969-0

Dascal, J., Reid, M., IsHak, W. W., Spiegel, B., Recacho, J., Rosen, B., & Danovitch, I. (2017). Virtual reality and medical inpatients: A systematic review of randomized, controlled trials. *Innovations in Clinical Neuroscience, 14*(1-2), 14. PMID: 28386517

DHSC [Department for Health and Social Care] (2001). *Valuing people: A new strategy for learning disability for the 21st century.* Retrieved June 3, 2025, from https://www.gov.uk/government/publications/valuing-people-a-new-strategy-for-learning-disability-for-the-21st-century

Dick, E. (2021). The promise of immersive learning: Augmented and virtual reality's potential in education. *Information Technology and Innovation Foundation, 1*, 1–10.

Ferreira, B., & Menezes, P. (2020). Gamifying motor rehabilitation therapies: Challenges and opportunities of immersive technologies. *Information (Basel), 11*(2), 88. DOI: 10.3390/info11020088

Fitzpatrick, V., Reed, T., Gilger, J., Brophy, S., & Imbrie, P. K. (2013, October). First-year engineering students with dyslexia: Comparison of spatial visualization performance and attitudes. In *2013 IEEE Frontiers in Education Conference (FIE)* (pp. 1254–1256). IEEE.

Flores-Gallegos, R., Rodríguez-Leis, P., & Fernández, T. (2022). Effects of a virtual reality training program on visual attention and motor performance in children with reading learning disability. *International Journal of Child-Computer Interaction, 32*, 100394.

Franze, A., Loetscher, T., Gallomarino, N. C., Szpak, A., Lee, G., & Michalski, S. C. (2024). Immersive virtual reality is more effective than non-immersive devices for developing real-world skills in people with intellectual disability. *Journal of Intellectual Disability Research, 68*(12), 1358–1373. DOI: 10.1111/jir.13177 PMID: 39169557

Galliers, J., Wilson, S., Marshall, J., Talbot, R., Devane, N., Booth, T., & Greenwood, H. (2017). Experiencing EVA park, a multi-user virtual world for people with aphasia. [TACCESS]. *ACM Transactions on Accessible Computing, 10*(4), 1–24.

Garzotto, F., Gelsomini, M., Occhiuto, D., Matarazzo, V., & Messina, N. (2017, June). Wearable immersive virtual reality for children with disability: a case study. In *Proceedings of the 2017 conference on interaction design and children* (pp. 478-483).

Getzel, E. E., & Thoma, C. A. (2008). Experiences of college students with disabilities and the importance of self-determination in higher education settings. *Career Development for Exceptional Individuals, 31*(2), 77–84.

Gómez-Puerta, M., Chiner, E., Melero-Pérez, P., & Lorenzo Lledó, G. (2019). Research review on augmented reality as an educational resource for people with intellectual disabilities. *International Journal of Developmental and Educational Psychology, 1*(2), 473–485. DOI: 10.1177/00224669241258225

Grigorenko, E. L., Compton, D. L., Fuchs, L. S., Wagner, R. K., Willcutt, E. G., & Fletcher, J. M. (2020). Understanding, educating, and supporting children with specific learning disabilities: 50 years of science and practice. *The American Psychologist, 75*(1), 37–51. DOI: 10.1037/amp0000452 PMID: 31081650

Gulboy, E., & Denizli-Gulboy, H. (2025). Evaluating augmented reality to teach science for secondary students with intellectual disability. *The Journal of Special Education, 59*(1), 3–15. DOI: 10.1177/00224669241258225

Hashim, H. U., Yunus, M. M., & Norman, H. (2022). 'AReal-Vocab': An augmented reality English vocabulary mobile application to cater to mild autism children in response towards sustainable education for children with disabilities. *Sustainability, 14*(8), 4831.

Hrastinski, I., Bonetti, A., & Hedjever, M. (2023). Relationship between auditory processing skills and academic achievement of elementary school children. *Specijalna Edukacija i Rehabilitacija, 22*(2), 95–116. DOI: 10.5937/specedreh22-37415

Hutama, B. A. A., Sihwi, S. W., & Salamah, U. (2021, November). Kinect based therapy games to overcome misperception in people with dysgraphia using dynamic difficulty adjustment. In *2021 IEEE International Conference on Computing (ICOCO)* (pp. 230-235). IEEE.

Imrie, R. (2011). Universalism, universal design and equitable access to the built environment. *Disability and Rehabilitation, 34*(10), 873–882. DOI: 10.3109/09638288.2011.624250 PMID: 22054109

Intarapreecha, N., & Sangsawang, T. (2023). Incorporating augmented reality to enhance learning for students with learning disabilities: A focus on spatial orientation in physical. *Journal of Applied Data Sciences, 4*(3), 245-253. dhttps://DOI: <ALIGNMENT.qj></ALIGNMENT>10.47738/jads.v4i3.126

Ip, H. H., Wong, S. W., Chan, D. F., Li, C., Kon, L. L., Ma, P. K., Lau, K. S. Y., & Byrne, J. (2024). Enhance affective expression and social reciprocity for children with autism spectrum disorder: Using virtual reality headsets at schools. *Interactive Learning Environments, 32*(3), 1012–1035. DOI: 10.1080/10494820.2022.2107681

Ip, H. H. S., & Li, C. (2021). Introducing immersive learning into special education settings: A comparative review of two studies. In Hui, A., & Wagner, C. (Eds.), *Creative and Collaborative Learning Through Immersion: Interdisciplinary and International Perspectives* (pp. 135–150). Springer., DOI: 10.1007/978-3-030-72216-6

Jacob, U. S., Pillay, J., Misitura Oyundoyin, B., & Oyundoyin, J. O. (2022). Barriers to and benefits of online learning among special education undergraduates. *Multicultural Education, 8*(4), 9–21. DOI: 10.5281/zenodo.6416145

Jdaitawi, M. T., & Kanan, A. F. (2022). A decade of research on the effectiveness of augmented reality on students with special disability in higher education. *Contemporary Educational Technology, 14*(1), ep332. DOI: 10.30935/cedtech/11369

Kapetanaki, A., Krouska, A., Troussas, C., & Sgouropoulou, C. (2022). Exploiting augmented reality technology in special education: A systematic review. *Computers, 11*(10), 143. DOI: 10.3390/computers11100143

Kapsalis, E., Jaeger, N., & Hale, J. (2022). Disabled-by-design: Effects of inaccessible urban public spaces on users of mobility assistive devices – A systematic review. *Disability and Rehabilitation. Assistive Technology, 19*(3), 604–622. DOI: 10.1080/17483107.2022.2111723 PMID: 35984675

Kaur, D. P., Kumar, A., Dutta, R., & Malhotra, S. (2022). The role of interactive and immersive technologies in higher education: A survey. *Journal of Engineering Education Transformations, 36*(2), 79–86. DOI: 10.16920/jeet/2022/v36i2/22156

Kellems, R. O., Eichelberger, C., Cacciatore, G., Jensen, M., Frazier, B., Simons, K., & Zaru, M. (2020). Using video-based instruction via augmented reality to teach mathematics to middle school students with learning disabilities. *Journal of Learning Disabilities, 53*(4), 277–291. DOI: 10.1177/0022219420906452 PMID: 32065040

Kettler, R. J., Elliott, S. N., Davies, M., & Griffin, P. (2012). Testing a multi-stage screening system: Predicting performance on Australia's national achievement test using teachers' ratings of academic and social behaviors. *School Psychology International, 33*(1), 93–111. DOI: 10.1177/01430343114030

Khasawneh, M. A. S. (2024). The potential for utilizing virtual reality technology in educating students with learning disabilities. *Journal of Infrastructure. Policy and Development, 8*(13), 6802. DOI: 10.24294/jipd6802

Light, J., McNaughton, D., Beukelman, D., Fager, S. K., Fried-Oken, M., Jakobs, T., & Jakobs, E. (2019). Challenges and opportunities in augmentative and alternative communication: Research and technology development to enhance communication and participation for individuals with complex communication needs. *Augmentative and Alternative Communication, 35*(1), 1–12. DOI: 10.1080/07434618.2018.1556732 PMID: 30648903

Liu, R., Salisbury, J. P., Vahabzadeh, A., & Sahin, N. T. (2017). Feasibility of an autism-focused augmented reality smartglasses system for social communication and behavioral coaching. *Frontiers in Pediatrics, 5*, 145. PMID: 28695116

Liu, R., Wang, L., Koszalka, T. A., & Wan, K. (2022). Effects of immersive virtual reality classrooms on students' academic achievement, motivation and cognitive load in science lessons. *Journal of Computer Assisted Learning, 38*(5), 1422–1433. DOI: 10.1111/jcal.12688

Lu, A., Chan, S., Cai, Y., Huang, L., Nay, Z. T., & Goei, S. L. (2018). Learning through VR gaming with virtual pink dolphins for children with ASD. *Interactive Learning Environments*, *26*(6), 718–729.

Lyon, G. R. (1996). Learning disabilities. *The Future of Children*, *6*(2), 54–75. PMID: 8689262

Macdonald, S. J., & Clayton, J. (2012). Back to the future, disability and the digital divide. *Disability & Society*, *28*(5), 702–718. DOI: 10.1080/09687599.2012.732538

Malaquias, O., & Malaquias, R. F. (2016). The role of virtual reality in the learning process of individuals with intellectual disabilities. *Technology and Disability*, *28*(4), 133–138. 10.3233_TAD-160454

Maresca, G., Corallo, F., De Cola, M. C., Formica, C., Giliberto, S., Rao, G., Crupi, M. F., Quartarone, A., & Pidalà, A. (2024). Effectiveness of the use of virtual reality rehabilitation in children with dyslexia: Follow-up after one year. *Brain Sciences*, *14*(7), 655. DOI: 10.3390/brainsci14070655 PMID: 39061396

Maskati, E., Alkeraiem, F., Khalil, N., Baik, R., Aljuhani, R., & Alsobhi, A. (2021). Using virtual reality (VR) in teaching students with dyslexia. [IJET]. *International Journal of Emerging Technologies in Learning*, *16*(9), 291–305. DOI: 10.3991/ijet.v16i09.19653

McMahon, D., Cihak, D., & Wright, R. (2015). Augmented reality as a navigation tool to employment opportunities for postsecondary education students with intellectual disabilities and autism. *Journal of Research on Technology in Education*, *47*(3), 157–172. DOI: 10.1080/15391523.2015.1047698

Meyer, A., & Rose, D. H. (2005). The future is in the margins: the role of technology and disability in educational reform. In Rose, D. H., Meyer, A., & Hitchcock, C. (Eds.), *The Universally Designed Classroom: Accessible Curriculum and Digital Technologies* (pp. 18–51). Harvard Education Press.

Microsoft. (2024, March 7). Ability Summit 2024: Advancing accessibility with AI technology and innovation. The Official Microsoft Blog. Retrieved May, 29, 2025 from https://blogs.microsoft.com/blog/2024/03/07/ability-summit-2024-advancing-accessibility-with-ai-technology-and-innovation/

Mitsea, E., Drigas, A., & Skianis, C. (2023). VR gaming for meta-skills training in special education: The role of metacognition, motivations, and emotional intelligence. *Education Sciences*, *13*(7), 639.

Mokmin, N. A. M., & Rassy, R. P. (2024). Review of the trends in the use of augmented reality technology for students with disabilities when learning physical education. *Education and Information Technologies*, *29*(2), 1251–1277. DOI: 10.1007/s10639-022-11550-2

Mokmin, N. A. M., & Ridzuan, N. N. I. B. (2022). Immersive technologies in physical education in malaysia for students with learning disabilities. *IAFOR Journal of Education*, *10*(2), 91–110.

Morris, J. R., Hughes, E. M., Stocker, J. D., & Davis, E. S. (2022). Using video modeling, explicit instruction, and augmented reality to teach mathematics to students with disabilities. *Learning Disability Quarterly*, *45*(4), 306–319.

Nabors, L., Monnin, J., & Jimenez, S. (2020). A scoping review of studies on virtual reality for individuals with intellectual disabilities. *Advances in Neurodevelopmental Disorders*, *4*(4), 344–356. DOI: 10.1007/s41252-020-00177-4

Newman, L., Wagner, M., Knokey, A. M., Marder, C., Nagle, K., Shaver, D., Wei, X., Cameto, R., Contreras, E., Ferguson, K., Greene, S., & Schwarting, M. (2011). The post-high school outcomes of young adults with disabilities up to 8 years after high school: A report from the National Longitudinal Transition Study-2 (NLTS2). National Center for Special Education Research. Retrieved May, 28, 2025 from https://files.eric.ed.gov/fulltext/ED524044.pdf

Nugraha, R. A., Sunardi, S., Asrowi, A., Murwaningsih, T., Yusuf, M., & Supratiwi, M. (2025). Development and validation of augmented reality media for social and emotional learning in children with learning disabilities (SEAKAR). *AL-ISHLAH: Jurnal Pendidikan*, *17*(1), 1355–1366.

Obaid, M. A. S. (2013). The impact of using multi-sensory approach for teaching students with learning disabilities. *Journal of International Education Research*, *9*(1), 75.

Osypova, N., Kokhanovska, O., Yuzbasheva, G., & Kravtsov, H. (2021). Implementation of Immersive Technologies in Professional Training of Teachers. In Bollin, A. (Eds.), *Information and Communication Technologies in Education, Research, and Industrial Applications. ICTERI 2020. Communications in Computer and Information Science, 1308*. Springer., DOI: 10.1007/978-3-030-77592-6_4

Pangestu, Y., Wulandari, S., & Handayani, I. (2024). Implementation of augmented reality in animal introduction learning for students with intellectual disabilities. [IJSECS]. *International Journal Software Engineering and Computer Science*, *4*(1), 263–272. DOI: 10.35870/ijsecs.v4i1.2214

Perelmutter, B., McGregor, K. K., & Gordon, K. R. (2017). Assistive technology interventions for adolescents and adults with learning disabilities: An evidence-based systematic review and meta-analysis. *Computers & Education, 114*, 139–163. DOI: 10.1016/j.compedu.2017.06.005 PMID: 29276334

Pérez-Muñoz, S., Castaño Calle, R., Morales Campo, P. T., & Rodríguez-Cayetano, A. (2024). A systematic review of the use and effect of virtual reality, augmented reality and mixed reality in physical education. *Information (Basel), 15*(9), 582. DOI: 10.3390/info15090582

Pivik, J. R. (2010). The perspective of children and youth: How different stakeholders identify architectural barriers for inclusion in schools. *Journal of Environmental Psychology, 30*(4), 510–517. DOI: 10.1016/j.jenvp.2010.02.005

Rahman, N. A., Mailok, R., & Husain, N. M. (2020). Mobile augmented reality learning application for students with learning disabilities. *International Journal of Academic Research in Business & Social Sciences, 10*(2), 133–141. DOI: 10.6007/IJARBSS/v10-i2/6896 PMID: 40715120

Ralabate, P. K. (2011). Universal design for learning: Meeting the needs of all students. *ASHA Leader, 16*(10), 14–17. DOI: 10.1044/leader.FTR2.16102011.14

Roberts, K. D., Park, H. J., Brown, S., & Cook, B. (2011). Universal design for instruction in postsecondary education: A systematic review of empirically based articles. *Journal of Postsecondary Education and Disability, 24*(1), 5–15.

Rose, D. H., & Strangman, N. (2007). Universal design for learning: Meeting the challenge of individual learning differences through a neurocognitive perspective. *Universal Access in the Information Society, 5*, 381–391. DOI: 10.1007/s10209-006-0062-8

Rueda, J., & Lara, F. (2020). Virtual reality and empathy enhancement: Ethical aspects. *Frontiers in Robotics and AI, 7*, 506984. DOI: 10.3389/frobt.2020.506984 PMID: 33501297

Saunders, T. L., Coleman, M. B., Smith, C. C., Carter, A., & Alshehri, A. (2024). The effects of using augmented reality on phoneme and word reading for first grade students with autism and developmental delays. *Journal of Special Education Technology, 0*(0), 1–13. 10.1177_01626434251314007

Seol, H. Y., Kang, S., Lim, J., Hong, S. H., & Moon, I. J. (2021). Feasibility of virtual reality audiological testing: Prospective study. *JMIR Serious Games, 9*(3), e26976. DOI: 10.2196/26976 PMID: 34463624

Serafin, S., Adjorlu, A., & Percy-Smith, L. M. (2023). A review of virtual reality for individuals with hearing impairments. *Multimodal Technologies and Interaction, 7*(4), 36. DOI: 10.3390/mti7040036

Shaaban, T. S., & Mohamed, A. M. (2024). Exploring the effectiveness of augmented reality technology on reading comprehension skills among early childhood pupils with learning disabilities. *Journal of Computers in Education, 11*(2), 423–444. DOI: 10.1007/s40692-023-00269-9

Suh, A., & Prophet, J. (2018). The state of immersive technology research: A literature analysis. *Computers in Human Behavior, 86*, 77–90. DOI: 10.1016/j.chb.2018.04.019

Sviridova, E., Yastrebova, E., Bakirova, G., & Rebrina, F. (2023). Immersive technologies as an innovative tool to increase academic success and motivation in higher education. *Frontiers in Education, 8*, 1192760. DOI: 10.3389/feduc.2023.1192760

Tan, S. Z. K., Shendyapina, M., & Tay, L. N. S. (2024). Evaluating the use of immersive interactive mixed reality (i2MR) technology in special needs education in Singapore. *Technology. Knowledge and Learning, 29*(2), 781–802. DOI: 10.1007/s10758-023-09648-8

Tene, T., Marcatoma Tixi, J. A., Palacios Robalino, M. D. L., Mendoza Salazar, M. J., Vacacela Gomez, C., & Bellucci, S. (2024). Integrating immersive technologies with STEM education: A systematic review. *Frontiers in Education, 9*, 1410163. DOI: 10.3389/feduc.2024.1410163

Tosto, C., Hasegawa, T., Mangina, E., Chifari, A., Treacy, R., Merlo, G., & Chiazzese, G. (2021). Exploring the effect of an augmented reality literacy programme for reading and spelling difficulties for children diagnosed with ADHD. *Virtual Reality (Waltham Cross), 25*, 879–894.

Trivedi, P. (2024). Immersive Learning's Promise: The educational potential of augmented and virtual reality. *Augmented Reality and Virtual Reality in Special Education*, 91–102.

United Nations. (2015). Transforming our world: The 2030 agenda for sustainable development Retrieved May, 28, 2025 from https://sdgs.un.org/2030agenda

Vasquez, E., Nagendran, A., Welch, G. F., Marino, M. T., Hughes, D. E., Koch, A., & Delisio, L. (2015). Virtual learning environments for students with disabilities: A review and analysis of the empirical literature and two case studies. *Rural Special Education Quarterly*. Advance online publication. DOI: 10.1177/875687051503400306

Vibhuti, Kumar, N., Kataria, C., & Aroura, S. (2025). Assessing the efficacity of immersive computing and electroencephalogram in the rehabilitation of upper extremity neuro-motor dysfunctions: A systematic review. *International Journal of Human-Computer Interaction*, •••, 1–27. DOI: 10.1080/10447318.2025.2470284

Vinumol, K. P., Chowdhury, A., Kambam, R., & Muralidharan, V. (2013, May). Augmented reality based interactive text book: An assistive technology for students with learning disability. In *2013 XV symposium on virtual and augmented reality* (pp. 232–235). IEEE. https://doi.org/DOI: 10.1109/SVR.2013.26

Voultsiou, E., & Moussiades, L. (2025). A systematic review of AI, VR, and LLM applications in special education: Opportunities, challenges, and future directions. *Education and Information Technologies*, •••, 1–41. DOI: 10.1007/s10639-025-13550-4

Vullamparthi, A. J., Nelaturu, S. C. B., Mallaya, D. D., & Chandrasekhar, S. (2013). Assistive learning for children with autism using augmented reality. Speaking albums and visual auditory schedulers. In *2013 IEEE Fifth International Conference on Technology for Education* (pp. 43-46). doi: DOI: 10.1109/T4E.2013.18

Wang, Y., Liang, J., Yu, J., Shan, Y., Huang, X., Lin, W., Pan, Q., Zhang, T., Zhang, Z., Gao, Y., Yu, X., Wei, L., & Yang, Z. (2024). Multiscale haptic interfaces for metaverse. *Device*, *2*(6), 100326. Advance online publication. DOI: 10.1016/j.device.2024.100326

Weiss, P. L., Bialik, P., & Kizony, R. (2003). Virtual reality provides leisure time opportunities for young adults with physical and intellectual disabilities. *Cyberpsychology & Behavior*, *6*(3), 335–342. PMID: 12855092

Wu, C.-L., & Tsai, Y.-H. (2023). Effects of video prompting with augmented reality on functional living skills of students with intellectual and developmental disabilities. *Journal of Special Education Technology*, *39*(1), 3–14. DOI: 10.1177/01626434231170594

Yenioglu, B. Y., Yenioglu, S., Sayar, K., & Ergulec, F. (2023). Using augmented reality based intervention to teach science to students with learning disabilities. *Journal of Special Education Technology*, *39*(1), 108–119. DOI: 10.1177/01626434231184829

Zentall, S. S. (2007). Math performance of students with ADHD: Cognitive and behavioral contributors and interventions. In Berch, D. B., & Mazzocco, M. M. M. (Eds.), *Why is math so hard for some children? The nature and origins of mathematical learning difficulties and disabilities* (pp. 219–243). Paul H. Brookes Publishing Co.

Zhang, M., Ding, H., Naumceska, M., & Zhang, Y. (2022). Virtual reality technology as an educational and intervention tool for children with autism spectrum disorder: Current perspectives and future directions. *Behavioral Sciences (Basel, Switzerland)*, *12*(5), 138. PMID: 35621435

Zhang, Y., & Miao, Z. (2025). Enhancing EFL learners' engagement and motivation through immersive technologies: The role of artificial intelligence, augmented reality, virtual Reality, and mobile applications. *European Journal of Education*, *60*(2), e70128. DOI: 10.1111/ejed.70128

Chapter 3
Designing Immersive Learning Experiences for Neurodiverse Learners:
A Practical Framework for Inclusive Educational Technology

Muhammad Usman Tariq
https://orcid.org/0000-0002-7605-3040
Abu Dhabi University, UAE & University College Cork, Ireland

ABSTRACT

Creating engaging learning experiences for students who think and learn differently requires a thoughtful and inclusive approach that combines new ideas with ensuring everyone can access them. This guide provides practical strategies for making educational technology effective for a diverse range of learning styles, sensory preferences, and communication needs, particularly for individuals with autism, ADHD, and dyslexia. By incorporating ideas from Universal Design for Learning, ethical data handling practices, and standards such as WCAG and ISO/IEC 24751, this guide enables teachers and technology designers to create learning environments that are engaging, adaptable, and equitable. Essential aspects of this design include managing the amount of sensory input provided, utilizing various methods to present information, allowing users to customize settings, and collaborating directly with students to tailor the experience to their individual needs.

DOI: 10.4018/979-8-3373-5188-9.ch003

INTRODUCTION

In today's rapidly evolving digital world, the concept of inclusion is changing significantly. In the past, inclusion in schools and workplaces meant ensuring that people with diverse abilities, backgrounds, and identities were part of the same group. However, as technology transforms how we communicate, learn, and connect, inclusion must also change accordingly. In the digital age, being in a place is not enough; being able to engage with and derive value from it is essential. These technologies can help reshape our understanding of inclusivity. For teachers, content creators, and professionals, these tools provide an opportunity to design learning spaces from the outset, with inclusion in mind. Unlike traditional classrooms or offices, which often require changes to be more inclusive, an immersive experience can be gained to serve a wide variety of users (Schmidt et al., 2024). This is especially helpful for neurodiverse individuals who may find regular learning methods challenging. VR can create calm and safe spaces for learners with sensory issues. AR can offer additional support to help people understand better. MR can provide highly interactive and personalized experiences that cater to the unique ways in which different people think and learn. However, there are also risks associated with this approach. Although these technologies can help some people, they can also make others feel left out if not designed carefully. For instance, VR can be too intense for individuals with specific sensory issues. AR can be challenging for individuals with visual impairments or those who struggle with spatial thinking (Cook-Chennault, 2025). Additionally, suppose an immersive experience is overly complicated or overwhelming. In that case, it may be too much for some people, especially those who are neurodiverse, making it difficult for them to focus or learn (Tariq, 2025).

Another problem is that many of these experiences are created by teams that lack diverse backgrounds and experiences. This can lead to hidden biases in the design. The usual user might be assumed to be neurotypical and non-disabled, which excludes others. In such cases, these tools may exacerbate the digital divide instead of helping to close it (Schmidt et al., 2024). Additionally, without designing for inclusion, the content may not present diverse viewpoints. This leads to a narrow, one-sided story that misses the complete picture of what it means to be human. Features such as voice commands, customizable settings, or other alternative ways to use technology are often ignored or not considered at all. When these tools are created and used with fairness in mind, they can help make inclusion possible for people with disabilities. The key is to design with intention and place people at the center. For neurodiverse learners, these tools can offer different methods of learning that respect and support their unique thinking and learning styles. Instead of a single approach that suits everyone, immersive platforms can offer adjustable sensory settings, flexible pacing, and various ways of receiving information. For example, a VR science lab could allow one student to learn through pictures while another uses sounds or physical feedback (Schmidt et al., 2024). This type of personalization enables learners to connect with content in a way that suits them best, leading to deeper understanding and increased engagement.

To maximize this potential, teachers, instructional designers, and developers require a clear and adaptable framework for creating immersive learning experiences that prioritize inclusivity. This framework should begin with the understanding that inclusion is not just about adjusting; it is about how we design from the outset. This means recognizing that everyone has different abilities, needs, and expectations, and ensuring that these differences inform every aspect of the design. Instead of adding fixes after problems are found, the goal is to prevent these problems from occurring in the first place. Figure 1 illustrates a triadic and interdependent framework in which Universal Design for Learning (UDL), neurodiversity-responsive strategies, and co-design practices operate in continuous dialogue rather than as isolated components. Co-design acts as the entry point of the framework, ensuring that the lived experiences of neurodiverse learners inform design decisions from the outset.

Figure 1. Framework for Inclusive Immersive Learning Design

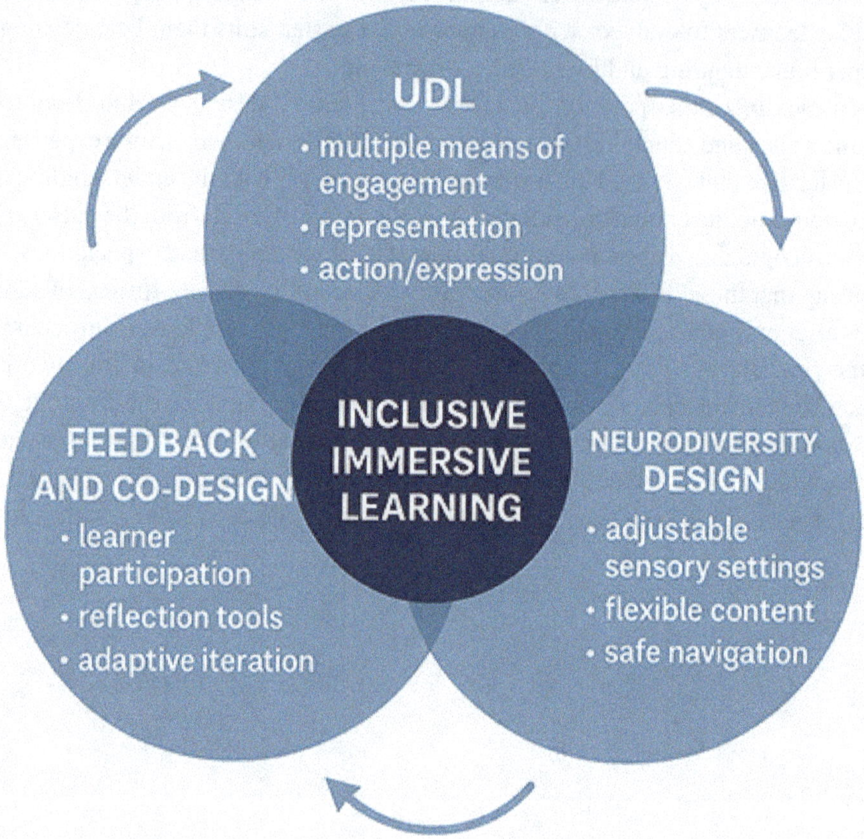

Including neurodiverse learners in the creation and testing process helps to ensure that their perspectives are incorporated into the design of the experience. This not only makes the experience more accessible and practical but also gives learners a sense of control and respect for their opinions (Schmidt et al., 2024). Practitioners should also utilize Universal Design for Learning (UDL) principles, which support various ways of engaging with learning. UDL aligns well with immersive tools because they enable various media and interaction methods that cater to different types of learners. Equity-focused immersive design also means being prepared to continually improve and receive feedback. Immersive experiences should not remain the same; they should change based on what users need and what they say. Practitioners need to collect both quantitative data and personal insights, such as users' comfort levels, their level of involvement, the accessibility of the experience, and the extent of their learning. Tools like in-app surveys or reflections after the experience can show unexpected problems and help find better ways to improve. Additionally, evaluating the accessibility of the experience should be part of the development plan, with clear standards to measure its inclusivity. Another essential part of this approach is training educators and practitioners. Many people may not be familiar with immersive technology or how to utilize it in inclusive ways (Schmidt et al., 2024). Building skills through training is key so that tools are not only available but also used effectively and adequately. Training should encompass both technical skills and ethical considerations, such as protecting privacy, obtaining consent, and considering the emotional impact of immersive experiences. It is also essential to recognize the broader issues that prevent people from accessing and feeling included in the world of immersive tech (Cook-Chennault, 2025). Cost is a significant concern, as high-end VR gear and matching software are often too expensive for many schools, communities, and learners. To address this, the approach should support solutions that are easier to use and less costly, such as AR or MR tools that work on mobile devices or through web browsers, which do not require expensive hardware. Collaborating among tech companies, schools, and groups advocating for inclusion can help address resource gaps and ensure everyone has fair access.

Content variety is another crucial aspect of creating inclusive, immersive experiences. These experiences should show a wide range of cultures, languages, identities, and life stories. Seeing themselves represented is especially important for people with different neurotypes, who often do not see themselves in familiar stories. Content creators should avoid simple, clichéd portrayals and instead show the full, rich diversity of people's lives. This may involve collaborating with individuals who have diverse neurotypes, researchers, and educators to create content that feels authentic and meaningful to various groups. Ultimately, this chapter aims to provide a practical guide for designing and implementing immersive learning experiences that prioritize fairness and inclusion. This guide is intended to help, not dictate specific actions to individuals. It offers ideas, methods, and valuable tools that can be adapted to each situation, encouraging deep thinking, gradual change over time, and collaborative efforts to create experiences that are thoughtful and respectful of all individuals (Cook-Chennault, 2025). As immersive technologies shape our digital future, the choices we make today will determine whether they help connect people or create divides. By making equity a central part of every decision, practitioners can envision a new approach to inclusion, not as something added later, but as an integral part of everything they do.

UNDERSTANDING NEURODIVERSITY IN EDUCATIONAL CONTEXTS

Understanding neurodiversity in schools means truly grasping how people perceive, think, and interact with the world in different ways. Neurodiversity is a term that encompasses the various ways the brain functions, including autism spectrum disorder, ADHD, dyslexia, dyspraxia, and other cognitive differences. These are not just problems or weaknesses; they are natural variations in how brains are built. In schools, it is crucial to recognize and accept this diversity, ensuring that everyone has a fair chance to learn and succeed. Each neurodiverse person has their special strengths and some challenges. For example, individuals with autism may excel at noticing details, remembering things, and focusing intensely on their areas of interest. However, they may have a harder time interacting with others, understanding social norms, or adapting to changes. Those with ADHD may be creative and full of energy, able to come up with new ideas, but they often struggle to stay focused, control their impulses, or organize their time and tasks. People with dyslexia often struggle with reading smoothly, spelling, and recognizing words, but they can excel at seeing patterns, solving problems, and telling stories. These students bring something unique to the classroom, and when teachers understand their needs, they can help them reach their full potential (Tariq, 2025). Dyspraxia, or Developmental Coordination Disorder (DCD) is a disorder associated with difficulties in motor coordination, spatial awareness and planning physical actions. In schools, dyspraxic students can be unable to accomplish activities requiring fine motor control, sequencing, or physical maneuvering. Immersive technologies provide specific opportunities to assist such learners in case they are developed properly. In the case of Augmented Reality (AR), especially, it will be possible to display real-time visual overlays and stepwise motor guidance pegged to physical space to aid activities such as lab work or demonstrations. VR may also be useful in a well-considered manner where the learners get to practice the movements and the spatial activities in low-risk, repeatable settings with no time pressure. The reduction of cognitive load with the assistance of such features as slowed interactions, guided paths, simplified spatial layouts can help to support the development of coordination and confidence.

Although more people are becoming aware of neurodiversity, many schools still adhere to rules and methods that make it challenging for neurodivergent students to succeed. These schools often employ traditional, text-focused teaching methods and standardized tests that fail to accommodate diverse learning styles and needs. Classrooms might have strict routines and expectations that do not work well for neurodivergent learners (Schmidt et al., 2024). For example, a student with dyslexia may struggle to keep up with extensive reading, while a student with ADHD may have difficulty staying still and paying attention during extended discussions. Also, classroom environments like bright lights, loud noises, and crowded spaces can be overwhelming for students who are sensitive to their senses, like those on the autism spectrum. These issues do not just affect learning; they can lower confidence and harm mental health, too. The challenges do not stop at school classrooms. Online learning, while flexible and beneficial for some, can also pose challenges for neurodivergent students. Many websites and tools are not made with neurodiversity in mind. Messy websites, difficult-to-use designs, and confusing menus can be challenging to navigate. For students with ADHD, the lack of structure and the ability to learn at their own pace can make it hard to manage time and stay focused (Cook-Chennault, 2025). Videos without captions, text that's not easy to read, or materials that mix audio and visual info can be tough for students with dyslexia or hearing processing issues. Additionally, online spaces often lack clear signals or feedback that help people learn and stay motivated, making it more challenging for some neurodivergent individuals to remain engaged. To make these spaces more inclusive, educators and designers should focus on providing multiple ways for individuals to interact, learn, and express their ideas. This means avoiding a one-size-fits-all approach and instead giving learners choices (Schmidt et al., 2024). Options like visual displays, audio guides, physical activities, and written text can help each learner access information in a way that suits them. For example, a history lesson in VR could be experienced as a visual tour, an interactive story, or an audio guide, based on the learner's preference. Letting students choose how they learn not only respects their individual needs but also helps them feel more in control of their learning (Tariq, 2025).

Another critical aspect is ensuring the environment is aware of and responsive to the sensory needs of individuals. This involves understanding how different senses can affect a person and adjusting the setting to prevent overstimulation or discomfort in immersive environments. This might involve letting users control elements such as background noise, lighting, or visual effects (Cook-Chennault, 2025). Providing tools that help manage sensory input, such as the ability to pause or slow down an experience, can help learners stay comfortable and focused. For example, a VR science lab might allow students to adjust the brightness or volume of virtual instruments or select between high- and low-stimulation modes based on their individual needs.

Responsive design takes this step further by creating systems that adapt to how a learner interacts. This is especially helpful for neurodivergent learners, who may require additional support during their learning process. For example, a language-learning app could use AI to track a learner's progress and adjust the activity based on their responses. If a student with dyslexia is struggling with spelling, the system may offer different ways to view the words, such as visual support or extra time (Schmidt et al., 2024). For a learner with ADHD who is losing focus, the app can gently remind them or offer interactive cues to help refocus them on the activity. Responsive design helps create a learning space that adapts to changes in attention, mood, and performance, which are common for individuals with neurodivergent conditions. To successfully implement these kinds of designs, teachers, instructional designers, and tech developers need to work closely with individuals who are neurodivergent. Their personal experiences and feedback are crucial in finding and testing solutions. Involving neurodivergent users in the development of educational tools can lead to more flexible, user-friendly, and inclusive products. When teachers possess these skills, they can create environments where neurodivergent students are not only tolerated but also fully included and valued (Cook-Chennault, 2025). Ultimately, incorporating neurodiversity into education is about more than just addressing problems; it is about acknowledging the unique strengths and perspectives that diverse minds bring to the learning process. Neurodivergent individuals often have fresh, non-linear ways of thinking that can lead to creative and innovative solutions. When education is designed to welcome and celebrate these differences, everyone benefits. Differentiated teaching encourages teachers to rethink traditional standards and adopt more flexible approaches that support a range of learners (Schmidt et al., 2024). Thoughtful environments improve well-being and engagement for all students, not just those who are more sensitive. Adaptive technologies make learning more personalized and interactive, helping improve outcomes for everyone. As society becomes more diverse and technology becomes more immersive, the need to create fair and accessible educational experiences becomes more pressing. Understanding neurodiversity is not just a minor issue; it is a crucial aspect of effective teaching and design. Whether in physical classrooms, digital spaces, or virtual worlds, education must honor the full range of human minds and experiences. By doing so, we not only remove obstacles but also unlock the potential of every learner, creating a future where different ways of thinking are viewed not as problems to fix but as valuable strengths to be embraced.

INCLUSIVE DESIGN PRINCIPLES FOR IMMERSIVE LEARNING

Inclusive design in these immersive environments means creating experiences that are naturally adaptable, flexible, and welcoming for all learners. At the heart of this approach is Universal Design for Learning (UDL). This framework supports multiple ways of engaging with content, receiving information, and expressing understanding, which helps meet the diverse needs, strengths, and preferences of all learners (Schmidt et al., 2024). Using UDL in immersive settings ensures that these tools benefit everyone, not just those who are most comfortable with new formats and tools.

In AR, VR, and MR environments, applying UDL involves creating content and experiences that are flexible from the start. Instead of creating a single fixed path through a lesson or activity, UDL encourages offering multiple options. For example, a virtual biology lab could allow learners to explore content visually through 3D models, audibly through explanations, and engage in hands-on interactions. These choices are not just extra features for some learners; they are essential parts of the design (Cook-Chennault, 2025). By providing various ways to access information and demonstrate understanding, immersive learning spaces can better support learners with diverse cognitive, sensory, and physical needs, as well as those from different cultural and linguistic backgrounds. UDL also helps give learners more control, allowing them to choose how they engage with the material, how quickly they progress through it, and how they reflect on what they have learned (Tariq, 2025). A key part of designing inclusive immersive environments is managing sensory input. These technologies often provide a wealth of sensory stimulation, combining visual, auditory, and sometimes tactile experiences to create rich and engaging learning spaces. To help, immersive environments should offer ways to adjust or limit certain sensory elements. Options like reducing background sounds, lowering visual effects like flashing lights or fast movement, and controlling the speed of information delivery can help. Thoughtful spatial design is also essential, ensuring that spaces are neither too crowded nor overly complex, and that important information stands out without being lost in clutter. Offering a simpler, calmer version of the environment can be very useful for learners who need a more controlled and less intense experience. Although VR, AR, and MR are commonly used in the same context, they have different affordances and risks to neurodiverse learners. Virtual Reality can be fully immersive and can help improve concentration and experiential learning but can also expose learners to excessive sensory effects, dizziness, or disorientation especially when those students are susceptible to extreme visual or vestibular stimuli. Augmented Reality has continuous association with the real world and it would be a better choice compared to situations where the learners feel anxious when not in touch with the real world or where physical contact is needed. Mixed Reality lies between virtual and physical, allowing a connection with both, yet it can be taxing on the cognitive load without appropriate scaffolding. The knowledge of these trade-offs enables teachers and designers to make wise choices concerning the type of technology that is more suitable to address particular learner needs and learning goals.

Another important aspect of inclusive design in immersive environments is using content in different ways. Not all learners process information in the same way, and designers can present content through multiple modes of delivery. A single lesson might include spoken narration, on-screen text, sign language, interactive visuals, and even tactile feedback, helping learners choose the methods that work best for them. Multimodal delivery enhances accessibility and facilitates better understanding and retention of content by engaging multiple senses simultaneously (Schmidt et al., 2024). For instance, in a virtual chemistry lab, a learner could hear a description of a chemical reaction, see an animation of how molecules interact, read a summary, and even take control of the virtual elements to perform the reaction themselves. This layered approach ensures that all learners, regardless of their preferred learning style, can fully grasp the material (Tariq, 2025).

Predictability and easy navigation are also essential in inclusive design. For many learners, especially those with anxiety, autism, or difficulties with planning and organization, unpredictability can be a big challenge. Immersive spaces should be designed with clear, consistent paths that help users know where to go, what to do next, and what to expect. Visual guides, clear directions, and simple user interfaces help learners feel in control and confident. For example, a virtual trip to an ancient city might include a map, arrows showing the way, and prompts explaining each site. Providing a virtual guide or companion can make the experience more predictable and supportive. The ability to pause, rewind, or replay parts of the experience is also helpful for learners who need more time or want to review content at their own pace. Inclusive immersive environments often use built-in features that help meet a wide range of learner needs. This might include adjusting the lighting, changing the color contrast, muting the background music, or switching to a less visually intense version of the scene. These options let learners create a space that feels safe and manageable, which helps them focus more on learning. For example, a student exploring a virtual art museum could switch between a detailed, richly textured version and a simpler, high-contrast version depending on their visual needs.

Guided tutorials play a crucial role in creating an inclusive and immersive learning experience. Providing clear step-by-step instructions that explain how to use the interface, navigate through it, and understand the learning goals helps everyone get started more easily (Cook-Chennault, 2025). These tutorials should be available in various forms, such as videos, text, audio, or interactive guides, to accommodate the diverse learning styles of different individuals. A good tutorial might teach you how to navigate space, interact with objects, communicate with others in a group activity, and seek additional help. By providing this support early on, designers help prevent frustration and keep learners from becoming discouraged, especially those who may feel nervous about new technology or require more time to adjust to it. By following these principles, immersive learning can achieve more than just being a modern tool; it can become a transformative experience. It can become a way to create a fairer education system. Inclusive design ensures that this change benefits all learners, not just those who are already tech-savvy or fit into traditional learning styles. It opens new opportunities for those who have been left behind, giving them fresh ways to access knowledge, connect with others, and express themselves (Forde et al., 2025). In that way, it helps shape the future of learning into something as varied, lively, and creative as the people it aims to serve.

CASE STUDY: BUILDING A VIRTUAL SCIENCE LAB FOR SECONDARY STUDENTS WITH ASD

A school district collaborated with an edtech company to develop a virtual science lab tailored for secondary students with an autism spectrum disorder. The lab was designed in collaboration with teachers, therapists, and the students themselves to ensure it met their sensory and learning needs (Schmidt et al., 2024). Special features, such as speech-to-text tools, adjustable background sounds to help mitigate sensory sensitivity, and avatars that display emotions, were added to enhance the learning experience. These thoughtful features allow students to explore science experiments at their own pace in a calm, stress-free environment. Teachers noticed that students were more engaged, stayed focused for more extended periods, and retained more information, demonstrating the importance of having inclusive and flexible tools in education.

CO-DESIGN WITH LEARNERS: METHODS AND LESSONS LEARNED

Designing learning spaces that genuinely meet the needs of neurodiverse students cannot happen without involving them directly. Co-design, also known as participatory design, is a method where students are treated as partners in the process, rather than just users of the final product. Especially when working with neurodiverse learners, this approach is vital. Neurodivergent students often experience the world in unique ways that can be misunderstood or ignored by those who have not shared similar experiences. By including neurodiverse students in testing and creating educational tools, such as AR and VR, we can learn what works best for them, what causes obstacles, and what can help them thrive. This is not only about making things accessible, but also about fairness, respect, and innovation.

One of the most effective ways to engage neurodiverse students in the design process is through participatory design workshops. These are structured sessions where students can share their thoughts, generate ideas, try out early versions of tools, and provide feedback. It is essential to plan these workshops carefully to ensure they are inclusive and accessible (Moon, 2024). This often means offering different ways for students to participate, such as talking, drawing, writing, using technology, or presenting ideas with objects. Facilitators should avoid assuming how students will communicate or interact with each other. Some individuals may prefer to express themselves visually rather than verbally, while others may require more time to think things through or benefit from having questions prepared in advance.

When facilitating participatory design with neurodiverse students, it is key to focus on flexibility and respect. Sessions should have a structure but also allow for different ways of interacting that feel safe and comfortable. Clear rules, predictable routines, and visual timetables can help reduce anxiety and encourage participation (Schmidt et al., 2024). It is essential to value all input equally, regardless of how it is presented. Facilitators should be trained not only in design methods but also in understanding neurodiversity. This includes awareness of sensory issues, communication styles, and how people process information. Including neurodivergent individuals as co-facilitators or advisors can help make the process more genuine and inclusive. When working with neurodiverse students, ethical considerations are critical. The consent must be explicit and easy to understand, and students should be aware of how their input will be used. Privacy and data protection are also key, as is ensures that the environment does not cause anyone discomfort or emotional distress (Moon, 2024). Designers and researchers must avoid treating a single neurodiverse individual as representative of an entire group. Instead, they should aim for ongoing, meaningful collaboration. This means involving a diverse range of neurodiverse students and allowing their voices to shape every aspect of the design process.

Feedback is a crucial component of co-design. It is not enough to listen to learners' ideas and then disappear to build something based on assumptions. Instead, feedback should be part of a continuous cycle of testing, thinking, and improving. Once a design or prototype is created, it should be shared back with the students for review. Their experiences, what worked and what did not, should guide the following changes (Hutson & Hutson, 2024). This process fosters trust and leads to more effective outcomes. For example, a neurodiverse student might test a VR learning game and say the interface is too busy or moving too fast. These insights can lead to changes in layout, navigation, or speed. The new version is then tested again, maybe by the same student or a different group, and the process continues. One advantage of iterative refinement is that it enables gradual improvements based on real-world use. It acknowledges that no design will be perfect from the start and that learners' needs are complex and change over time (Savickaite et al., 2024). Over time, these improvements create a product that is shaped by those who will use it. Iteration also helps designers discover unexpected challenges and insights. For instance, an activity that appears simple may turn out to be confusing or difficult to use, highlighting the need for more precise instructions, distinct controls, or varied feedback. Involving neurodiverse learners in this cycle ensures these changes are based on real experience rather than guesswork.

Despite the benefits, co-designing with neurodiverse learners also brings real challenges. Communication styles can vary a lot among participants, and not all ways of expressing ideas are easy to understand. Some students may use different methods to communicate, such as pictures or special tools, which can require more time and necessitate extra support (Hutson & Hutson, 2024). Others might reveal their preferences through actions, such as gestures or facial expressions, which require careful observation and understanding in the proper context. This means facilitators must be attentive and open-minded and be ready to ask questions without pushing participants to respond in a certain way. Another challenge is interpreting the feedback collected during the co-design process. Unlike regular surveys or group discussions, these sessions may produce non-linear, visual, or mixed-form feedback. Students might draw, create storyboards, or rearrange objects to show their ideas. Transforming this into helpful design ideas requires a thorough understanding of both the message and the situation. It often involves collaborating with designers and researchers, and sometimes even participants, to accurately interpret the data. Engaging neurodiverse learners deeply can be time-consuming and requires more resources than usual. It may require additional staff, specialized materials, and repeated sessions. Schools and organizations might not always have the money or capacity to support this level of involvement. However, when co-design is a priority, the long-term benefits, such as improved tools, increased engagement, and greater inclusion, often make the investment worthwhile (Glaser et al., 2025). Also, involving learners early can help identify problems before they become costly to fix. Working with neurodiverse students in co-design has taught us the importance of fostering trust and building strong relationships. Students are more likely to share honest feedback and creative ideas when they feel safe, respected, and valued. Taking the time to understand their interests and strengths, and involving them as equals, makes a big difference. Trust also facilitates open conversations about what is not working, which is crucial for making improvements. When students know that their feedback will lead to fundamental changes, they are more likely to participate fully.

Designers need to be ready for unexpected things. Not every session will go as planned. A workshop might be disrupted by sensory overload, or a participant may need to leave early due to fatigue. Flexibility is important. Having different formats and backup plans, along with a calm and understanding attitude, helps keep the process inclusive even when things do not go smoothly (Hutson & Hutson, 2024). It can also be helpful to involve families, caregivers, or support staff when needed, as they can provide essential insights into how a student communicates and engages most effectively. Through this process, many valuable insights come up, not just about the technology being developed, but also about how learning can be more inclusive overall. Co-design sessions often highlight broader themes, such as the need for independence, more explicit instructions, or the value of visual support. These lessons can influence not only the specific project but also broader educational practices. For example, one team working with autistic students found that consistent visual cues significantly improved engagement and lessened anxiety for all participants (Moon, 2024). This led to broader changes in how visual information was used in other areas of the curriculum.

Ultimately, co-designing with neurodiverse learners is both a challenge and a chance. It needs patience, creativity, and humility. It means stepping back from traditional design methods and accepting the messiness of genuine collaboration (Bali & Zsido, 2024). However, it also leads to deeper, more meaningful solutions that are not only technically accessible but also truly inclusive. By including the voices of often-overlooked groups, we create technology that's more human, more adaptable, and better suited for today's diverse learners. In a world where technology is increasingly shaping education, co-design offers a way to ensure that innovation does not leave anyone behind. It reminds us that the best solutions come from genuine partnerships, not top-down decisions. Moreover, when neurodiverse students are given the chance to help shape the tools they will use, the result is not just better technology, but also a more fair and caring approach to learning.

TEACHER READINESS AND PEDAGOGICAL INTEGRATION

Just because a classroom has headsets or an AR app does not automatically mean students will learn better. For these technologies to be effective, teachers need to be well-prepared, not just in terms of knowing how to use the technology, but also in how to teach with it, manage the classroom, and feel confident about it (Nuguri et al., 2025). Supporting teachers through training, ensuring that immersive activities align with what students are meant to learn, managing classrooms where digital and physical learning coexist, and helping teachers feel comfortable with new technology are all essential components of the process. Without these, even the best tools might not make a big difference in how students learn.

Professional development is crucial in helping teachers feel prepared to utilize these new tools. Many teachers are excited about technology but unsure of where to begin. Unlike older digital tools like slides or learning websites, immersive tech can be confusing because it utilizes new hardware, different interaction methods, and complex software to create content. Training should go deeper than just showing off a few features. It should enable teachers to explore, create, and consider how they can utilize the tools. Training should happen over time, not just once (Sgambelluri & Placanica, 2024). It should provide teachers with an opportunity to try out the tools, practice using them, seek assistance when needed, and discuss with other teachers how they utilize these tools in their classes. Having a group of teachers who can share what they are learning and what is working can be helpful. However, the training should not just focus on the tools themselves. How teachers utilize technology in their lessons is just as important. They need help connecting immersive experiences to what students are supposed to learn. If it is not tied to goals, the tech might be a distraction. For instance, a VR experience of a historical event can be powerful, but only if it is used to help students analyze history, think critically, and meet educational standards. Teachers should learn how to fit these experiences into their lesson plans, link them with assessments, and plan follow-up activities. It is about going beyond the cool factor of the tech to its actual purpose. Teachers must understand not only how the tools work, but also when and why they should be used to support learning (Shadmehr, 2024). Using immersive tools also means understanding how they can help different kinds of learners. Some students struggle with traditional methods, like those with learning differences, attention issues, or language challenges. Immersive tech offers new ways for these students to learn by visualizing abstract ideas, learning through experience, and exploring at their own pace. Teachers need to be prepared to identify these opportunities and adjust their teaching methods accordingly. Training should include real classroom examples, lesson ideas, and group planning sessions to help teachers see how these tools integrate into their subjects and meet the diverse needs of their students.

Another significant challenge arises from managing the classroom, particularly when combining immersive tools with traditional methods. Teachers face new challenges, such as how to keep students on task while they are wearing headsets, how to manage time when some students are using immersive tools and others are working on other activities, and how to ensure all students stay engaged. When some are in a virtual world and others are reading or writing, keeping everyone on the same page can be tough. Clear rules and routines are essential (Glaser et al., 2025). Teachers may need to establish rules regarding headset use, switching between different types of learning, and communication methods during immersive activities. In mixed environments, flexible grouping can be beneficial, as it enables pairing or rotating students to allow everyone to participate, and utilizes reflection sessions to bring the class back together after an immersive task. Creating a classroom where teachers and students feel safe to try new things is also essential. For many teachers, using immersive tech can feel overwhelming. Worrying about technical problems, feeling pressured to do everything right, or lacking confidence in their tech skills can prevent them from using these tools. Therefore, building confidence is a crucial component of any plan to introduce these technologies (Nuguri et al., 2025). This starts by understanding that learning takes time and that it is okay to make mistakes. Teachers need time to figure things out, chances to ask questions without fear, and support when things go wrong. Knowing they do not have to be perfectly willing to try can make a big difference in helping them feel more comfortable and ready to use the tech.

School leaders and tech coaches play a crucial role in helping teachers adopt a curious and open mindset. When school leaders, such as principals, department heads, or instructional leaders, show enthusiasm for immersive learning, it makes teachers feel more comfortable trying new things as well. Recognizing teachers' efforts, even when outcomes are not perfect, can boost morale and keep things moving forward. Highlighting projects led by teachers, celebrating small wins, and offering opportunities to collaborate can make teachers feel like they own the learning process and get excited about it (Mercier, 2025). Confidence grows when teachers see how immersive tools help their students become more engaged, curious, and expressive. When students show these positive changes, it reinforces the value of the work and encourages teachers to keep exploring.

At the same time, we must consider the genuine challenges of utilizing technology. Teachers need reliable devices, good internet, and support to use them effectively. If they spend too much time fixing broken technology instead of teaching, their confidence and motivation can drop quickly. Schools should not only purchase devices but also invest in maintenance, IT support, and classroom setups that facilitate effective immersive learning (Yeganeh et al., 2025). This means having space for movement, charging stations for devices, and quiet areas for focused work. It is also essential that all students have equal access to these tools, not just those in better-funded classrooms. One way to make it easier for teachers to use immersive tech is by providing ready-to-use content. Not all teachers have the time or skills to create their own VR or AR experiences. Providing them with high-quality, ready-to-use resources that align with lesson plans can help them get started (Levterova-Gadjalova et al., 2024). These could include simulations, virtual field trips, 3D models, or games that align with the material being taught. Professional development can then focus on how to utilize and adapt these resources for different learners, rather than on creating new content. As teachers become more comfortable with the tools, they may choose to try more complex designs, but this should be optional, not something they are forced to do immediately.

Reflection is another essential tool for building teacher readiness. Encouraging teachers to reflect on their experiences with immersive technology helps them identify what worked, what did not, and what they can improve upon next time. This can happen in teacher groups, mentoring sessions, or digital records where they track their learning. When teachers share these reflections with others, it builds a culture of innovation and shared knowledge. Reflection also shows that using technology in teaching is a process that involves trial and error, adjustment, and improvement over time. Teacher readiness for immersive instruction is a journey, not a finish line

(Qian et al., 2025). It evolves, shaped by professional growth, classroom experience, support from the school, and collaboration with other teachers. By focusing on all these areas, schools can help make immersive learning a regular part of teaching. Teachers are essential to this change. When they are confident, well-prepared, and supported, immersive tech can become a tool that enhances learning instead of distracting from it. This journey also requires a shift in how we approach educational technology. We should not focus only on new tools for their own sake. Instead, we should think about what learners need and what teachers know best. Immersive tools should support the curriculum, not replace it. They should enhance good teaching methods rather than replace them. This mindset empowers teachers to view themselves not just as users of technology but as designers of learning experiences, creating meaningful paths that utilize immersion to deepen understanding, spark curiosity, and connect students to the world in new and innovative ways. When educators possess the knowledge, skills, and support to utilize immersive technologies thoughtfully and meaningfully, they become leaders in driving change. Their confidence helps students stay engaged, their teaching ideas drive innovations, and their openness to new possibilities ensures that immersive learning reaches its full potential. In this way, the future of education is not just about the technology we use, but also about how we help teachers utilize it with purpose, care, and vision.

EVALUATION AND FEEDBACK IN IMMERSIVE INCLUSIVE SETTINGS

In classrooms where virtual reality (VR), augmented reality (AR), and mixed reality (MR) are used as part of the teaching process, especially for students who may have different learning needs, it is essential to measure how engaged students are, how well they understand the material, and how they are growing. The way we assess learning in these environments should match the hands-on and interactive nature of the tools used. Evaluation is not just about knowing the content, but also about observing how students respond to the environment, how they feel during the experience, and how that translates into real learning. Creating feedback systems that are flexible, fast to respond, and inclusive helps teachers support each student in a way that respects their unique needs and abilities.

These engagement signals are beneficial when working with students who may not express themselves in usual ways. For instance, a student who does not speak or talk much might seem quiet in a group discussion. Still, their eye movements and interaction data in a VR environment could show they are intensely focused and understand the material (Zaugg, 2024). Understanding these small clues helps teachers avoid wrong assumptions about how much a student is participating or how much they can learn. However, it is essential to track this data in a manner that's fair and transparent. Students and their families should be aware of precisely what information is being collected, why it is being collected, and how it will be used. Ensuring privacy and respecting students' rights should always be a top priority. In addition to tracking engagement, using assessments that change and adapt to the learner's needs is also essential in immersive environments. Traditional tests, such as multiple-choice questions or written essays, often fail to accurately assess what students have learned when they are using an experience-based or spatial learning environment. In immersive setups, assessment can be built into the learning activity itself. For example, in a VR science lab, students demonstrate their understanding of the material by correctly using virtual equipment, following steps, and interpreting results. The system can provide instant feedback, prompt students to reflect on what they have learned, or present new challenges based on their performance. Figure 2 represents an iterative evaluation loop that integrates learner feedback, behavioral interaction data, and adaptive design responses. Rather than positioning assessment as a final stage, the model emphasizes continuous feedback throughout the learning experience.

Figure 2. Immersive Inclusive Learning Evaluation Loop

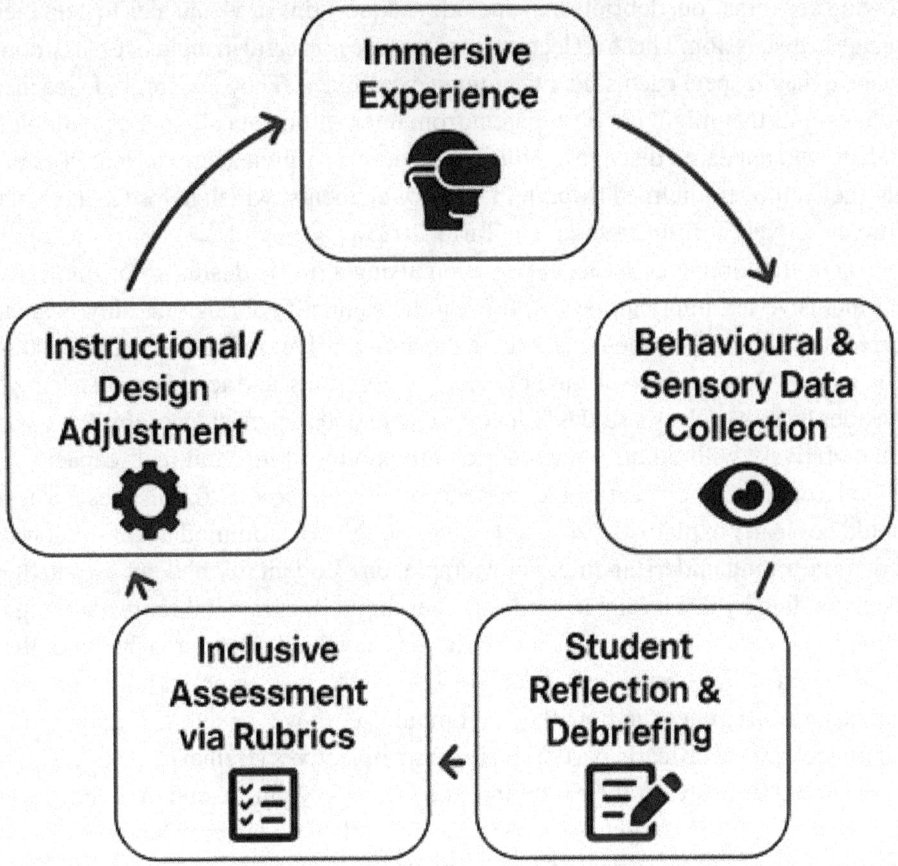

In addition to these built-in assessment methods, reflective journaling and debriefing are essential for giving ongoing feedback. Immersive experiences can be intensely emotionally powerful and complex. Offering students the chance to reflect on what they did, how they felt, and what they learned helps them solidify their understanding and learn how to think critically about their learning process (Sbeiti, 2024). Reflective journaling can take many different forms, and it is essential to offer neurodiverse learners diverse options. Some might prefer to write, others might draw, record audio, or use symbols or images to express their thoughts. The key is to create a space that allows for both organized reflection and flexibility. Debriefing, whether conducted one-on-one or in a small group, helps students make sense of their experiences and connect them to broader learning objectives. After a VR trip through a rainforest, for example, a teacher might lead a discussion about what surprised students, how the environment made them feel, or what questions they have left (Harrison et al., 2024). For students who are less comfortable with free-flowing conversation, debriefs may include set questions or visual aids to help them engage in discussion. These reflection practices are powerful in inclusive classrooms because they respect each student's unique experience. They also provide teachers with insights that might not be apparent from interaction data alone. For example, a student who appeared disengaged during the activity might share during reflection that they felt overwhelmed by certain sensory elements, which helps teachers plan more effectively for future sessions (Tariq, 2025).

To ensure fair and consistent evaluation, using a rubric designed for immersive and inclusive learning can be helpful. Unlike standard rubrics that only evaluate correct answers or completed assignments, an inclusive, immersive rubric takes a broader view. It considers various behaviors, expressions, and achievements. It might consider factors such as a student's level of engagement, persistence, ability to work collaboratively with others, creative problem-solving skills, and their capacity for self-reflection on their learning experience (Yeganeh et al., 2025). These criteria should be clearly explained, yet also flexible enough to accommodate different ways of demonstrating understanding. For example, one student might demonstrate their understanding by discussing it, while another might illustrate it through drawing or acting it out in a virtual world. The rubric should value both approaches equally.

When creating rubrics for neurodiverse learners, it is essential not to penalize students for differences in how they communicate, move, or interact, unless those differences are specifically part of the learning objectives (Belhaj et al., 2025). The focus should be more on their thinking, the effort they put in, and how they grow. For instance, a rubric might ask students to show they understand how ecosystems work, and they could do this by describing a food chain, arranging animals in a VR environment, or drawing a diagram in a virtual notebook. Similarly, a category like "works respectfully with others on shared tasks" should acknowledge different ways people communicate, including the use of gestures or assistive devices. This type of rubric helps teachers recognize and value learning in various forms. Evaluating in immersive and inclusive settings needs to be an ongoing process. As new immersive tools emerge and more students utilize them, our understanding of what constitutes good assessment also evolves (Efthymiou, 2024). Teachers should continually reflect on how they assess, solicit student feedback, and remain open to adapting their methods. Sometimes, involving students in helping create the assessment criteria can be empowering and lead to more student engagement. Neurodiverse learners often have deep insights into what helps them show what they have learned. Their input can help create more real and fair assessment practices.

There are still some challenges. Not all immersive platforms have built-in mechanisms for assessing learning and collecting and analyzing interaction data can be a complex process. Teachers may need assistance in understanding data from eye tracking or movement, and there is a learning curve when designing assessments that can be adjusted based on students' performance. There is also the risk of being too focused on data, which can make students feel like they are being watched instead of being supported. Finding the right balance between providing helpful feedback and respecting students' privacy and autonomy needs careful planning and ongoing discussion between teachers, tech experts, and learners. Another key point is making sure the assessment process is meaningful for students. If learners feel that their actions in an immersive environment are being judged without their understanding or consent, they may stop engaging. Transparency is essential (Forde et al., 2025). Teachers should clearly explain what is being observed or tracked, why it is essential, and how students can use feedback to improve. Assessment should feel like a team effort, not like a way to monitor students. When students understand the purpose and see the benefits, such as personalized feedback, growth opportunities, and recognition of their strengths, they are more likely to welcome it.

In short, assessment and feedback in immersive and inclusive environments need to be as flexible and varied as the learning experiences themselves. Using tools like eye tracking, gesture analysis, adaptive pathways, reflective journaling, and inclusive rubrics can help educators build systems that truly reflect the depth of student learning (Naruka & Upadhyay, 2024). These systems should be created with care, based on teaching principles, and responsive to the many ways students think, feel, and express themselves. In doing this, we not only support better learning outcomes but also build classrooms where all students feel seen, understood, and empowered to succeed in their way.

ETHICAL, SAFETY, AND ACCESSIBILITY CONSIDERATIONS

One of the first concerns in immersive learning is how these experiences can overstimulate the senses or lead to digital fatigue. Immersive tech is designed to fully involve users with strong visuals, spatial audio, and interactive features. While this can make learning more vivid for some, it can be overwhelming for others, especially those with sensory sensitivities, like many autistic learners. Bright lights, loud or unexpected sounds, busy visuals, or complicated navigation can cause stress, confusion, or even trigger anxiety and physical problems like dizziness or nausea (Manekar et al., 2024). Digital fatigue, which already arises from excessive screen use, can worsen in immersive setups that require intense focus and physical movement. These issues can affect not just health but also how well people learn and stay engaged. The use of biometric or behavioral data such as eye-tracking, gesture or movement analysis when using immersive systems makes informed consent especially important, particularly with children involved. Consent procedures must be presented in straightforward and comprehensible wording and clearly signify what information is gathered, how it will be utilized, who will have access to it and how it will be kept. Authentic options should be provided to learners and their caregivers such as being able to switch off certain data collection features without being locked out of the learning process. Continued consent must also be considered, as it can be understood that the levels of comfort may fluctuate.

On the sustainability front, the long-term technical management issue is a viable issue to schools implementing immersive technologies. To maintain the safety and durability of the gadgets the regular maintenance activities like the hygiene of the visor as well as regular software updates, storage of the device and the charging arrangements are necessary. Technical support planning, replacement cycles, and employee training can be used to avoid unnecessary immersive tools and their obsolescence. These logistical issues, as well as ethical considerations, will help to institute responsible and sustainable implementation at an institutional level.

To help reduce overstimulation, immersive settings should allow users to customize their sensory experiences. Giving people control over aspects such as sound levels, visual complexity, lighting, and animation speed helps them adjust their experience to what feels comfortable for them. Having modes with less stimulation, such as simpler visuals and quieter sounds, makes learning easier without causing discomfort. Sessions in immersive environments should also be limited in time and broken into smaller parts, with clear breaks and opportunities to rest (Videla et al., 2025). Designing for comfort means not just avoiding intense stimuli but also helping users know when they need a pause. Visual or audio reminders to take breaks, messages to blink or stretch, and guided ways to cool down can all support well-being. Teachers also need training to spot signs of sensory overload and respond with understanding and flexibility. Equal access is another significant issue in utilizing immersive technology for learning. While these tools can help some learners, they can also widen the gap if not used carefully. VR headsets, powerful computers, and fast internet are often expensive and not equally available everywhere. Students in schools with limited resources, in rural areas, or from low-income families may miss out on these experiences simply because they cannot afford the necessary tools and equipment (Tariq, 2025).

To address this digital divide, schools and governments must collaborate to make immersive tools more accessible. Schools could utilize shared devices, mobile AR apps compatible with smartphones, and explore ways to fund programs that include more students (Yeganeh et al., 2025). Teamwork between the public and private sectors may help reduce the cost of these technologies, and open-source platforms can lower the cost of software. Content creators should also ensure that experiences are compatible with a variety of devices, from high-end headsets to web-based versions, so that more people can access them. Schools need to consider the additional costs of immersive learning, including technical support, training, device maintenance, and plans for long-term access. Along with expanding access, immersive learning must meet accessibility standards to make sure everyone can use it (Kirk, 2025). For example, in a VR setting, all important sounds should have visual or textual options, and interactive features should be usable without requiring precise movements.

ISO/IEC 24751 is designed to make digital systems adaptable to individual needs. It emphasizes that learning tools should be flexible enough to accommodate the unique preferences and needs of each learner. Features like voiceovers for text, captions for audio, and navigation options that work with switches, eye tracking, or other alternative controls should be standard, not optional. These features should be incorporated into the design from the outset, not added as afterthoughts later.

Developers and educators should collaborate with individuals with disabilities and neurodivergent individuals to ensure that accessibility claims are practical and effective in real-life applications. User feedback can uncover issues that are not obvious in theory or simulations (Velazquez-Solis et al., 2025). This hands-on approach enhances accessibility and fosters a more inclusive and respectful culture. Ethically, it is essential to be thoughtful about the content and how it is represented. Immersive experiences can have a profound emotional impact, especially when they recreate real-life situations or tackle complex topics. Designers must be mindful of the psychological effects of their work and refrain from including content that could cause trauma or distress to others. For neurodivergent learners, representations of disabilities or social situations must be accurate, respectful, and meaningful. Using stereotypes or trying to include disability in a tokenistic way can be harmful and may reduce the educational value of the experience. It is essential to consult with neurodivergent communities and utilize their real-life experiences to inform design choices in a manner that's authentic and avoids harm. Ethical immersive education also means continuously evaluating and responding to user needs. This includes not only evaluating the system's performance but also gathering feedback on how users feel, the challenges they encounter, and the support they require. Feedback should be collected in a manner that is easily accessible and taken seriously. Systems should be updated regularly based on user needs, and educators should be encouraged to voice their suggestions for improvements. Ethics in technology is not something set in stone; it is an ongoing process that involves reflection, accountability, and continuous improvement. In short, utilizing immersive technology in education offers significant potential but also carries substantial responsibilities (Yeganeh et al., 2025). Ensuring these experiences are safe, respectful, and inclusive requires careful planning and collaboration among developers, educators, institutions, and learners. Taking steps to manage sensory overload and digital fatigue helps protect students' well-being. Protecting data privacy and ensuring informed consent respects their right to make choices. Promoting equal access helps close opportunity gaps, and following accessibility standards makes sure nobody is excluded. The ethical use of immersive technology in education must be built on empathy, inclusion, and commitment to fairness, because the future of learning should open doors, not close them.

CONCLUSION

Inclusive innovation in immersive education starts with understanding people and continues through teamwork. When teachers, creators, and students come together, technology can help connect rather than separate. By focusing on making things accessible, adhering to ethical guidelines, and being flexible, we create learning spaces that respect diverse needs and learning styles. The way forward is through careful planning, listening to what works, and always thinking about how we can improve. Real innovation is not just about what technology can achieve; it is about who benefits and how they do so. With purposeful effort, immersive tools can support every learner, helping to create a fairer and more exciting future for education that includes everyone.

REFERENCES

Bali, C., & Zsido, A. N. (2024). Optimizing Learning Outcomes of Educational Applications Enhanced with Multimedia and Interactive Features: A Review. *Education, Development and Intervention: Toward Participatory and Integrated Solutions*, 167-184.

Belhaj, R., Ait Ali, N., & Browlahrouf, I. (2025). Gamified Hybrid Learning for Neurodiverse Students: Designing Universally Accessible Instructional Models. *Journal Neosantara Hybrid Learning*, *3*(1), 38–46.

Cook-Chennault, K. (2025). *Examining Access and Inclusion in STEM Fields in Higher Education: Digital Learning Environments*. Personalized Learning, and Institutional Change to Advance Educational Opportunity.

Efthymiou, E. (Ed.). (2024). *Revolutionizing Inclusive Education: Mindfulness, Neurodiversity, and Executive Functioning Skills: Mindfulness, Neurodiversity, and Executive Functioning Skills*. IGI Global.

Forde, D., Carstens, C., Haihambo, C. K., Sivunen, U., O'Neill, C., & Galletti, A. (2025). Creating a Framework for an Inclusive Learning Environment.

Glaser, N., Li, S., Nuguri, S. S., Calyam, P., & Joshi, A. C. (2025). Piloting a Virtual Reality Cybersecurity Game for Neurodivergent Adults: Findings from a User-Centered Formative Evaluation. *Immersive Learning Research-Academic*, 67-77.

Glaser, N., Parishani, Z., Joshi, A. C., & Calyam, P. (2025). Leveraging Virtual Reality for Neurodivergent Representation in Cybersecurity Education: An Emerging Technology Report. *Technology, Knowledge and Learning*, 1-14.

Harrison, M., Rowlings, J., White, E. H., Vallence, M., & Potemkin, N. (2024). Neurodiversity and digital inclusion: creating the conditions for inclusive education through universal learning design.

Hutson, J., & Hutson, P. (2024). Conclusion: Future Directions for Neuro-inclusivity in Museums and Heritage Sites. In *Inclusive Smart Museums: Engaging Neurodiverse Audiences and Enhancing Cultural Heritage* (pp. 229–240). Springer Nature Switzerland.

Hutson, J., & Hutson, P. (2024). Immersive technologies. In *Inclusive brilliant museums: Engaging neurodiverse audiences and enhancing cultural heritage* (pp. 153–228). Springer Nature Switzerland.

Hutson, J., & Hutson, P. (2024). *Inclusive smart museums: Engaging neurodiverse audiences and enhancing cultural heritage*. Springer Nature.

Kirk, V. (2025). A sensory-friendly learning environment through design: user experience and implementation.

Levterova-Gadjalova, D., Terlemezyan, H., Tagareva, K., & Tsokov, G. (2024). Metaverse of Learning Disabilities in Higher Educational Institutions. In *Applied Assistive Technologies and Informatics for Students with Disabilities* (pp. 209–234). Springer Nature Singapore.

Manekar, A., Gade, V., Unhale, R., Manker, H., & Dhole, R. (2024). Exploring an Immersive AR/VR Pedagogical Approach: Experiential Learning for Autism Spectrum Disorder (ASD). *Education.*

Mercier, S. (Ed.). (2025). *Design for All Learners: Create Accessible and Inclusive Learning Experiences.* American Society for Training and Development.

Moon, J. (2024). Learning experience design of verbal prompts in virtual reality-based training for autistic children. *Research in Learning Technology*, •••, 32.

Naruka, V. S., & Upadhyay, S. (2024). Virtual Reality (VR) and Neurodiversity: Therapeutic and Educational Applications. *As the editors of Transforming Learning. Power and Education*, •••, 151.

Nuguri, S. S., Kambhampati, A., Glaser, N., Calyam, P., Li, S., Bates, C., . . . Nuguri, S. (2025, January). Adaptive Virtual Reality Learning Environment with a Reinforcement Learning-Driven Pedagogical Agent. In *2025 IEEE 22nd Consumer Communications & Networking Conference (CCNC)* (pp. 1-4). IEEE.

Qian, C., Videla, R., Videla, R., Parada, F. J., Aros, M. B., Ramírez, P., ... & Molina, B. (2025). Breaking barriers in education: leveraging 3E approach and technology to foster inclusion for SEN students.

Savickaite, S., Oyebisi, J., Stockman, T., & Bourguet, M. L. (2024). Instructional Design and Authoring of Accessible and Inclusive Extended Reality Learning Experiences. *The Journal of Applied Instructional Design, 13*(4).

Sbeiti, S. A. (2024). Technology Integration in Support of Wellness for Neurodiverse Students. *Journal of Educational Informatics, 5*(1), 58–73.

Schmidt, M., Lu, J., Huang, R., Francois, M. S., Lee, M., Wang, X., & Feijóo-García, P. G. (2024). Participatory, human-centered, equitable, neurodiverse, and inclusive XR. *Journal of Educational Technology & Society, 27*(4), 283–301.

Schmidt, M., Newbutt, N., Lee, M., Lu, J., Francois, M. S., Antonenko, P. D., & Glaser, N. (2024). Toward a strengths-based model for designing virtual reality learning experiences for autistic users. *Autism, 28*(7), 1809–1827. PMID: 37937531

Sgambelluri, R., & Placanica, F. (2024). Designing educational-inclusive contexts through artificial intelligence from the perspective of Life Designing.

Shadmehr, R. (2024). Designing an Individualized Virtual Reality Environment for Training: A Design Case Study with Autistic Learners.

Tariq, M. U. (2025). AI in the Classroom: Revolutionizing Instruction and Student Engagement. In M. Kessinger, G. Nelson, L. Lennex, & K. Nettleton (Eds.), *Enhancing Classroom Instruction and Student Skills With AI* (pp. 35-62). IGI Global Scientific Publishing. https://doi.org/DOI: 10.4018/979-8-3373-4576-5.ch002

Tariq, M. U. (2025). Integrating Advanced Technologies for Multi-Stakeholder Collaboration: Driving Sustainability in Supply Chains Through Industry 4.0. In Frichi, Y., & Jawab, F. (Eds.), *Multi-Stakeholder Collaboration for Sustainable Supply Chain* (pp. 313–334). IGI Global Scientific Publishing., DOI: 10.4018/979-8-3693-8925-6.ch014

Tariq, M. U. (2025). Harnessing Collective Power-Multi-Stakeholder Synergies for Sustainable Supply Chain Transformation. In Frichi, Y., & Jawab, F. (Eds.), *Multi-Stakeholder Collaboration for Sustainable Supply Chain* (pp. 245–264). IGI Global Scientific Publishing., DOI: 10.4018/979-8-3693-8925-6.ch011

Velazquez-Solis, P. E., Correa, M. E. G., Martinez, M. A., Arroyo, J. G., & Marquez, M. Y. (2025). Designing Teaching Strategies Using Artificial Intelligence for Neurodivergent Students in Higher Education. In *Exploring Psychology, Social Innovation and Advanced Applications of Machine Learning* (pp. 191-208). IGI Global Scientific Publishing.

Videla, R., Aros, M. B., Parada, F., Kausel, L., Sandoval-Obando, E., Jorquera, D., & Ramírez, P. (2025). Neurodiversity: Post-cognitivist foundations of the 3E approach for educational inclusion of autistic students with technology. *Frontiers in Human Neuroscience, 18*, 1493863. PMID: 39963287

Videla, R., Parada, F. J., Aros, M. B., Ramírez, P., Sarzosa, A., Jorquera, D., & Kausel, L. (2025, June). Breaking barriers in education: Leveraging 3E approach and technology to foster inclusion for SEN students. [). Frontiers Media SA.]. *Frontiers in Education, 10*, 1554314.

Yeganeh, L. N., Fenty, N. S., Chen, Y., Simpson, A., & Hatami, M. (2025). The future of education: A multi-layered metaverse classroom model for immersive and inclusive learning. *Future Internet*, *17*(2), 63.

Zaugg, T. (2024). Future innovations for assistive technology and universal design for learning. *Assistive technology and universal design for learning: Toolkits for inclusive instruction*, 275-318.

KEY TERMS AND DEFINITIONS

Immersive Educational Technology: Collaborative digital tools simulating real-world learning environments.

Sensory Load Management: Lessening overwhelming stimuli for better learner focus.

Universal Design for Learning: Flexible learning environments accepting diverse learning needs.

Chapter 4
Designing Inclusive Education With AI-Driven Pedagogies and Learning Analytics:
Bridging Instructional Design, Equity, and Impact

Ashraf Alam
https://orcid.org/0000-0001-6178-1187
Alliance University, Bengaluru, India

ABSTRACT

This chapter specifies an equity-optimizing sociotechnical stack for inclusive education that fuses UDL-as-compiled accessibility, capability-expanding pedagogy, equity-constrained adaptive mastery, and interpretability-first learning analytics into a single accountable operating model. It translates justice constructs such as targeted universalism, intersectional parity, epistemic justice, and care ethics into backlog-ready design grammars, contestable AI affordances, and privacy-by-design governance with portability, deletion verification, and recourse pathways. The chapter formalizes low-resource resilience through offline-first architectures, edge inference, and progressive enhancement, while constraining personalization via calibration parity, anti-proxy feature governance, and latency-disciplined time-to-support protocols. Five matrices operationalize theory-to-requirements, use-case safeguards, orchestration heuristics, signal-to-action logic, and implementation roadmaps, enabling auditable inclusion dividends across languages, disabilities, and bandwidth ecologies.

DOI: 10.4018/979-8-3373-5188-9.ch004

1. INTRODUCTION

1.1 Inclusive Education as a Rights-and-Capabilities Project in the Digital Age

Inclusive education in digitally mediated systems must be treated as a non-negotiable entitlement to *capability expansion*, not a discretionary service contingent on geography, income, or institutional prestige. The operative unit is the learner's real freedom to participate, progress, and thrive across formal learning, wellbeing, and future opportunity, under explicit constraints of *conversion factors* such as disability profile, language repertoire, time poverty, device ecology, and bandwidth volatility (Acharya & Mohbey, 2024; Stalmach et al., 2024). A credible inclusion agenda therefore requires a *sociotechnical operating model* where pedagogy specifies the learning aims and evidence pathways, technology implements accessible affordances and adaptive supports, and governance guarantees dignity, remedy, and portability through verifiable rules for consent, minimization, and role-scoped access. This chapter frames education as critical infrastructure that must deliver *auditability*, *reversibility*, and *agency-preserving personalization*, preparing the ground for a design grammar that is scalable, culturally sustaining, and procurement-enforceable.

1.2 Persistent Exclusion Patterns as Emergent Properties of Systems

Digital exclusion is rarely a single-point failure, it is an emergent property of tightly coupled choices across curriculum, interface defaults, assessment regimes, and institutional incentive structures. When platforms privilege synchronous video, high-bandwidth assets, and monolingual textuality, they silently impose a participation tax on learners facing intermittent connectivity, shared devices, migration-linked discontinuity, or dialectal variation (Rane, 2023; Pitychoutis & Al Rawahi, 2024; Sowell, 2023). When interfaces violate *accessibility conformance* expectations such as keyboard path integrity, contrast adequacy, caption availability, and assistive interoperability, the system performs exclusion through routine interaction friction rather than overt denial. When assessment is anchored to a narrow modality such as timed writing, it converts linguistic diversity, neurodivergent pacing, and sensory variance into artificial performance deficits (Wu, Zhang, & Lee, 2023; Berezi, 2025). Intersectional compounding makes these effects nonlinear, producing distinctive risk signatures where, for example, low bandwidth and language mismatch jointly depress completion, while disability and punitive analytics jointly elevate attrition. The chapter treats these patterns as system dynamics that demand multi-node re-design, not remedial patches.

1.3 Technology as Equity Infrastructure and as Risk Multiplier

Technology can function as equity infrastructure when it operationalizes *multimodal equivalence*, *mastery-oriented pacing*, and *assistive interoperability* while preserving teacher authority and learner autonomy through transparent controls. Adaptive sequencing can accelerate learning when it respects prerequisite topology, uncertainty bounds, and subgroup-calibrated mastery thresholds, and when it remains contestable through human override semantics (Eltahir & Babiker, 2024; Urbaite, 2024; Anwar et al., 2025). Multilingual mediation can widen epistemic access when it supports translanguaging, dialect tolerance, readability calibration, and script-aware rendering without degrading latency or imposing surveillance. The same stack becomes a risk multiplier when opaque optimization targets reward throughput over understanding, when proxy features encode protected attributes, or when risk scores are treated as deterministic labels that trigger punitive gatekeeping (Mintz et al., 2024; AlArabi et al., 2023; Ader et al., 2023). The chapter therefore treats *fairness constraints*, *calibration parity*, *counterfactual explainability*, and *privacy-by-design* as engineering requirements, not ethical aspirations, positioning analytics as care-oriented decision support rather than compliance theater or behavioral control.

1.4 Chapter Contributions, Scope, and Structure

This chapter delivers a conceptual-theoretical blueprint that fuses *UDL-grounded pedagogy*, *accessible AI affordances*, and *interpretable learning analytics* into a single equity-optimizing apparatus that can survive low-resource realities and global heterogeneity. The scope is explicitly non-empirical, focused on design logics, governance instruments, and implementation architectures that enable institutions to translate inclusion into verifiable properties across product releases, classroom routines, and procurement contracts. Section 2 formalizes learning-science and justice foundations, and introduces Table 1 as a theory-to-requirements matrix for release gates and institutional accountability. Section 3 specifies AI-driven instructional design patterns and presents Table 2 as a use-case-to-safeguards schema for multilingual, disability-inclusive, and offline-resilient functionality. Section 4 operationalizes classroom ecosystems with Table 3 as an orchestration playbook, Section 5 builds equity analytics with Table 4 as a signals-to-interventions logic, and Section 6 provides execution architectures with Table 5 as a time-bound roadmap and risk register, culminating in a compact set of non-negotiables in Section 7.

2. THEORETICAL AND ETHICAL FOUNDATIONS FOR INCLUSIVE AI PEDAGOGIES

2.1 Learning-Science Convergences for Inclusive Digital Instructional Ecologies

Inclusive AI pedagogy must be grounded in a convergent learning-science account that treats learning as socially mediated meaning-making, cognitively constrained information processing, and motivationally regulated persistence. *Sociocultural learning* frames competence as participation, making *guided participation*, *scaffold fading*, and *shared regulation* central to platform orchestration and classroom routines (AlAli & Wardat, 2024; Khalid, Abdullah, & Fadzil, 2024; Zhan et al., 2025). *Cognitive apprenticeship* requires explicit modeling, coached rehearsal, and progressive transfer of control, which implies transparent task decomposition, worked-example overlays, and teacher-configurable hint policies. *Cognitive load theory* and *multimedia learning* demand coherence, signaling, segmenting, and dual-channel alignment so that extraneous burden is suppressed and germane processing is amplified, especially for learners navigating disability-related access friction or second-language processing (Jadán-Guerrero et al., 2024; Shanthi et al., 2025). *Self-regulated learning* and *metacognitive calibration* require goal-setting, progress visualization, and recourse pathways, while *self-determination* and *expectancy-value* constructs require autonomy-supportive choice architectures and mastery-oriented feedback, operationalized through the design commitments consolidated in Table 1.

2.2 Equity-and-Justice Design Grammars for Capability-Expanding Sociotechnical Stacks

Equity becomes operational only when justice lenses are compressed into non-negotiable design grammars that bind curriculum intent, interface behavior, model objectives, and governance duties into a single auditable unit. In practice, inclusion fails when universal goals are pursued through uniform pathways that ignore conversion factors, or when the system treats linguistic, sensory, and executive-function variability as deviation rather than expected heterogeneity (Borah, Nischith, & Gupta, 2024; Yeh, 2025; Feng & Ng, 2024). Table 1 is therefore positioned as a translation matrix that encodes *capability* and *targeted universalism* into pathway heterogeneity, *critical disability* into configurability as a first-order outcome, and *responsible AI* into contestability and data sovereignty, while retaining learning-science constraints that prevent pseudo-personalization and cognitive overload. The matrix is intentionally framed as release-gate logic and procurement-ready acceptance criteria, so design teams, educators, and administrators can enforce parity-sensitive outcomes without reducing inclusion to performative compliance.

Table 1. Justice-to-Design Translation for Inclusive AI Pedagogies in Practice

Theory-Infused Foundation	Exclusion Mechanism Neutralized	Pedagogy and UX Implementation Commitments	Model and Data Governance Constraints	Equity Assurance Verification Signals
Sociocultural Constructivism	Isolation through solitary tasking, fixed pacing, and brittle progression	Adaptive scaffolds with fade logic, peer co-regulation affordances, teacher override for regrouping and re-sequencing	Human-in-the-loop escalation, audit trails for overrides, prohibition of automated high-stakes gating	Time-to-independence trends, scaffold fade stability, participation balance across groups
Cognitive Load and Multimedia Learning	Cognitive overload from clutter, redundant media, and incoherent signaling	Progressive disclosure, segmenting into micro-tasks, synchronized captions-transcripts, low-distraction modes	Feature governance to prevent attention-harvesting dark patterns, latency budgets for assistive pathways	Task efficiency without drop-off, error distribution compression, perceived effort consistency
Universal Design for Learning	Single-modality gates, rigid inputs, and narrow demonstrations of competence	Parallel representations, alternative input channels, flexible evidence submission across modalities	Accessibility conformance as release gate, assistive interoperability regression testing, defect remediation SLAs	Access-incident reduction, modality diversity indices, assistive compatibility pass rates
Capability and Targeted Universalism	Aggregate gains masking subgroup loss through unequal conversion factors	Branching routes for language, bandwidth, and time poverty, resumable sessions and catch-up scaffolds	Subgroup-calibrated objectives, small-n protections for disaggregation, anti-proxy feature constraints	Parity deltas on progression, continuity under outages, uptake equity across contexts
Critical Disability and Crip Technoscience	Normative UX penalizing sensory variance and neurodivergent pacing	Configurability-first controls, motion reduction, contrast tuning, executive-function scaffolds and pacing elasticity	No inferred disability labeling, consent-bounded accommodations, dignity-preserving data minimization	Accommodation uptake without stigma, abandonment risk decline, latency tolerance consistency
Responsible AI and Data Sovereignty	Opaque scoring, extractive data flows, and non-contestable decisions	Scope transparency, recourse pathways, local explanations framed as actionable next steps	Purpose limitation, RBAC, retention discipline, portability and deletion verification guarantees	Flag reversal rates, explanation uptake, consent completeness, calibration parity checks

Table 1 functions as a shared control surface for institutional alignment, because each row binds a normative commitment to implementable behaviors and verifiable signals, reducing interpretive drift across stakeholders. The pedagogy and UX commitments translate justice into interaction-level affordances, while the governance constraints prevent algorithmic determinism, surveillance drift, and proxy discrimination from entering through convenience features. Verification signals are framed as distribution-sensitive indicators, so equity is evaluated as parity in participation, progression, and recourse, not as averaged activity counts (Rana et al., 2024; Kusmawan, 2023; Lampropoulos, 2023). By treating accessibility conformance, contestability, and portability as release gates, the matrix turns inclusion into an engineered property of the stack rather than a remedial service. Subsequent sections operationalize this matrix by linking adaptive engines and multilingual mediation to the same constraints, ensuring that instructional design in Section 3 and classroom orchestration in Section 4 remain coherent with the accountability primitives encoded here.

2.3 Responsible AI, Privacy-by-Design, and Contestable Algorithmic Accountability Regimes

Ethical assurance in inclusive education requires that *fairness*, *accountability*, *transparency*, *explainability*, and *privacy* be treated as measurable constraints on system behavior, not as aspirational values. Fairness must be specified as calibration parity and error-balance across intersectional slices, with explicit recognition that optimizing one parity condition can perturb another, requiring documented trade-off governance and bounded-risk thresholds (Sethi & Jain, 2024; Shireesha & Jeevan, 2024; Pradeep et al., 2024). Explainability must be implemented as *actionable recourse* and *counterfactual guidance* that describes what a learner can do next within feasible constraints, rather than abstract feature attribution that invites stereotyping. Accountability must be procedural as well as technical, embedding *due process* through teacher override semantics, auditable decision logs, and low-friction appeal channels that are stigma-resistant (Marques, Santos, & Dias, 2024; Rajora et al., 2024; Sabri et al., 2024). Privacy-by-design must operationalize minimization, purpose limitation, role-based access control, retention discipline, and deletion verification, while data sovereignty requires portability and community-legible consent language. These commitments are concretized in Table 1 through governance constraints and verification signals, and they provide the compliance spine for all downstream adaptivity and analytics.

2.4 Translational Synthesis into Non-Negotiable Design, Evaluation, and Deployment Principles

Translational fidelity is achieved when abstract commitments are compressed into backlog-ready requirements, testable acceptance criteria, and monitoring signals that survive procurement cycles, platform updates, and institutional turnover. The non-negotiable baseline begins with *UDL-as-compiled property*, meaning accessibility is continuously verified through regression testing and structured audits, rather than promised through policy statements, a logic operationalized through Table 1 release gates. The second invariant is *contestability*, where every automated flag is treated as a hypothesis and is paired with recourse options, teacher annotations, and reversible workflows, preserving agency and preventing automation bias (Haj-Bolouri, Katende, & Rossi, 2023; Adetunla et al., 2024; Wang & Yu, 2024). The third invariant is *resilience engineering* for low-resource realities, requiring offline-first architectures, progressive enhancement, and device-heterogeneous interoperability so that inclusion does not collapse under bandwidth volatility. The fourth invariant is equity evaluation as distributional improvement, using parity-sensitive indicators rather than aggregate means. This synthesis prepares the transition to Section 3, where adaptive and generative mechanisms are constrained by the same justice-to-design grammar introduced in Table 1.

3. AI-DRIVEN INSTRUCTIONAL DESIGN AND CONTENT GENERATION FOR DIVERSE LEARNERS

3.1 Mastery-Gradient Personalization, Probabilistic Sequencing, and Equity-Constrained Optimization

AI-driven instructional design becomes inclusion-relevant when personalization is re-specified as *mastery learning* with uncertainty-aware progression, rather than convenience-driven content recommendation (Xu, 2024; Bu u, 2024; Liu et al., 2024). A rigorously engineered pathway begins with *learning progressions* and prerequisite graphs that encode conceptual dependency, then overlays *cognitive diagnostic modeling*, *item response theory* logics, and *Bayesian knowledge tracing* to estimate latent competence with confidence bounds that prevent premature gatekeeping (Di Natale et al., 2024; Ai, Hu, & Zhao, 2025; Kumar et al., 2024). Sequencing can be formalized through *multi-armed bandit* allocation or *Markov decision process* policies, but the objective function must be equity-constrained, optimizing expected learning gain subject to subgroup parity, cold-start protections, and discontinuous attendance tolerance. Teacher authority remains a constitutional layer through override semantics, group-level reconfiguration, and justification notes that feed institutional learning memory, consistent with the contestability and governance requirements already encoded in Table 1. Table 2 then translates these abstractions into implementable inclusion archetypes, making the personalization stack legible to curriculum, platform, and policy actors.

3.2 Multilingual Mediation, Generative Authoring Pipelines, and Accessibility-First Content Semantics

Multilingual mediation is not a cosmetic translation layer, it is epistemic infrastructure that must support translanguaging, dialectal variation, and script heterogeneity without collapsing latency budgets or interpretability (Munthe et al., 2024; Sombilon et al., 2024; Dalle, Aydin, & Wang, 2024). *Automatic speech recognition* and *neural machine translation* must be coupled with constrained decoding, domain glossaries, and teacher-verified post-edit loops to stabilize terminology and reduce semantic drift, while readability control and plain-language transforms protect comprehension without impoverishing conceptual depth (Akintayo et al., 2024; Alam & Mohanty, 2024; Cano & Troya, 2023). Inclusive generative authoring must be blueprint-governed, using coverage constraints, difficulty calibration, and representation diversity rules so that generated items and exemplars remain aligned to learning maps and valid evidence models. Accessibility is operationalized as content semantics, where every asset carries structured captions, transcripts, alt-text scaffolds, and interaction hints that preserve multimodal equivalence and assistive interoperability (Ayeni et al., 2024; Mhlongo et al., 2023; Marín, Sampedro, & Morales-Diaz, 2025). The compact tuples in Table 2 specify how these pipelines should be assembled for distinct inclusion challenges, while remaining compatible with the release-gate logic introduced in Table 1.

Table 2. Inclusion Use Cases, AI Modalities, and Safeguard Signals

Inclusion Challenge Archetype	AI Modality Stack	Instructional Design Move	Accessibility and Linguistic Affordance	Safeguards and Evidence Signals
Translanguaging and Script Variability	Multilingual ASR, NMT with constrained decoding, glossary-aware generation	Bidirectional mediation that preserves reasoning while adapting register and reading level	Script toggles, RTL-safe rendering, synchronized captions and transcripts	Terminology fidelity checks, dialect parity diagnostics, classroom latency stability
Connectivity Volatility and Edge Constraints	On-device inference, adaptive caching, bandwidth-aware media selection	Asynchronous mastery cycles with resumable sessions and recovery-friendly pacing	Offline packs, progressive enhancement, lightweight interaction surfaces	Uptime-under-outage targets, sync-integrity audits, completion parity across modes
Executive Function Variability and Time Poverty	Knowledge tracing, spacing schedules, micro-prompt orchestration	Chunked task design with explicit goals, staged hints, and self-regulation cues	Distraction-reduced views, checklist scaffolds, visible progress and pause-resume	Re-engagement stability, overload incident monitoring, equitable time-to-support signals
Sensory Accessibility for Vision and Hearing	Multimodal alignment, TTS-STT pipelines, caption-timestamp fusion	Parallel representations with equivalence mapping across audio, text, and visual anchors	Keyboard-path integrity, contrast controls, captions, alt-text semantics	Assistive compatibility validation, access-incident reduction, comprehension equivalence probes
Cold Start and Sparse Observability	Bayesian priors, hybrid defaults, human-in-the-loop calibration	Low-stakes diagnostics followed by rapid personalization with transparent starting points	Retry logic, scaffolded hints, non-punitive baselines with learner agency	Calibration-to-accuracy tracking, early misclassification suppression, override uptake review
Cultural Locality and Epistemic Plurality	Content selection with fairness constraints, locality-aware retrieval, provenance tracking	Community-anchored exemplars and culturally situated problems linked to core standards	Local-language UI, culturally legible imagery, flexible prompt templates	Representation balance auditing, relevance ratings, subgroup outcome parity monitoring

Table 2 functions as a procurement-ready specification, because each row binds an inclusion challenge to a concrete modality stack, an instructional move, a user-facing affordance, and a measurable assurance regime that prevents ambiguity from turning into inequitable defaults. The modality column guides engineering decomposition into components, while the instructional move column constrains pedagogy so the system remains mastery-oriented rather than novelty-oriented. The affordance column enforces accessibility and linguistic usability as compiled properties, not optional settings, and the safeguards column defines verification signals that can be embedded into release gates, coaching routines, and governance dashboards. This table also creates continuity with Table 1 by ensuring that multilingual mediation, offline resilience, and configurability are implemented within contestable, privacy-preserving, parity-aware constraints.

3.3 Dialogic Tutoring, Metacognitive Scaffolding, and Assistive Interoperability as Learning Infrastructure

Intelligent tutoring becomes inclusion-supportive when it is designed as *dialogic pedagogy* with state-aware scaffolding, not as automated adjudication. A robust tutoring loop couples fine-grained task models with error-class inference and *worked example* fading, enabling graduated hints, self-explanation prompts, and strategy feedback that builds transfer and not mere compliance (McDermott et al., 2023; Sá & Serpa, 2023; Miles & Boltin, 2025). Metacognition is operationalized through *self-regulated learning* routines such as goal-setting, monitoring prompts, calibration checks, and implementation-intention cues, while executive-function supports reduce cognitive friction through chunking, timers, and pause-resume continuity aligned to time-poverty realities. Assistive interoperability must be treated as a systems contract, ensuring keyboard navigation integrity, screen-reader semantics, caption fidelity, stable STT-TTS latency, and AAC compatibility so the same competence can be demonstrated through modality-diverse pathways (Alam & Mohanty, 2023; Nurfadila, Hajar, & Arsyad, 2024). The executive-function and sensory-accessibility archetypes in Table 2 constrain tutoring behavior and affordance design, while Table 1 ensures that every tutoring suggestion remains contestable, auditable, and bounded by dignity-preserving governance.

3.4 Bias-Robustness, Privacy-Preserving Computation, and Safety Engineering for High-Stakes Learning Contexts

Inclusive AI requires a reliability regime that anticipates distribution shift across languages, devices, curricula, and socio-economic ecologies, treating *dataset shift* and *concept drift* as routine operational risks rather than edge cases. Bias-robustness depends on stratified evaluation, calibration parity, and intersectional error auditing, combined with anti-proxy feature governance so protected attributes are not reconstructed through correlated behavioral traces (Aloizou et al., 2025; Solmaz, Kester, & Van Gerven, 2024). Privacy-preserving computation should prioritize minimization, on-device processing where feasible, and constrained data retention with deletion verification, while allowing federated or enclave-based patterns when institutional risk models demand stronger isolation. Safety engineering must include harmful-output controls, academically honest assistance policies, and escalation workflows that route ambiguous cases to human judgment, preventing automated sanctions that violate due process (Singh et al., 2025; Adera, 2025). Table 2 provides the concrete safeguards and evidence signals that can be instrumented into monitoring pipelines, and Table 1 supplies the governance constraints that keep personalization and generation aligned with contestability, transparency, and sovereignty under real-world operational pressure.

4. DIGITAL PEDAGOGIES AND THE INCLUSIVE CLASSROOM ECOSYSTEM

4.1 Instructional Architectures for Equitable Participation and Legitimate Epistemic Access

An inclusive classroom ecosystem is stabilized when pedagogy is engineered as the primary actuator of equity, and technology functions as orchestration substrate that renders participation, progression, and belonging predictable under real constraints. Instructional architectures must embed multiple entry points, elastic pacing, and modality-diverse demonstrations of competence so discontinuous attendance does not translate into reputational penalty or epistemic exclusion (Mouboua, Atobatele, & Akintayo, 2024; Al-Kfairy et al., 2024). *Mastery learning* provides the pacing backbone, while *evidence-centered design* protects construct validity by permitting equivalent evidentiary pathways across oral explanation, performance tasks, project artifacts, and reflective narratives. *Sociocultural learning* and *communities of practice* require structured collaboration, legitimate peripheral participation, and role rotation so talk time, feedback authority, and intellectual risk-taking are equitably distributed (Alam & Mohanty, 2022; Papaioannou et al., 2023). *Trauma-informed pedagogy* and *care ethics* reposition relational safety, non-punitive recovery windows, and respectful critique as infrastructure rather than soft add-ons. This section operationalizes these paradigms through the orchestration grammars specified in Table 3, aligned to the justice-to-design constraints already encoded in Table 1 and the inclusion archetypes in Table 2.

4.2 Teacher Orchestration, Professional Praxis, and Improvement-Science Decision Routines

Teacher orchestration is the governance layer where analytics, adaptive supports, and classroom realities are reconciled through situated judgment, preventing automation bias and protecting learner dignity. Effective praxis requires dashboard literacies that interpret concept heatmaps, prerequisite bottlenecks, and uncertainty-bounded mastery estimates as hypotheses, not verdicts, while respecting small-number protections and avoiding rank-order display cultures that catalyze stigma (Bourguet & Omfalos, 2024; Minghelli, D'anna, & Vastola, 2023). Professional integration can be framed through *TPACK* as competence in aligning content, pedagogy, and technology, and through *improvement science* routines that conduct micro-tests of change, such as adjusting hint timing, regrouping logic, or multimodal evidence pathways, then observing distribution-sensitive deltas. Table 3 functions as a portable playbook that binds pedagogical paradigm, required enablers, orchestration heuristics, and evidence signals into a single unit, enabling consistent enactment across teachers, schools, and modalities (Adeleye, Eden, & Adeniyi, 2024; Rana et al., 2023). This table also provides the practical bridge to Section 5, because the evidence signals in Table 3 are designed to be legible within equity analytics frameworks without collapsing into surveillance.

Table 3. Pedagogy-to-Inclusion Orchestration for Classroom Ecosystems

Pedagogical Paradigm Anchor	Inclusion Dividend Profile	Digital and Assistive Enablers	Teacher Orchestration Heuristics	Evidence Signals and Equity Checks
Flipped Mastery and Retrieval-Rich Sequencing	Anxiety reduction through self-pacing, error-tolerant repetition, competence consolidation	Offline micro-lectures, transcripted segments, mastery maps, low-bandwidth practice sets	Pre-class diagnostics, in-class micro-clinics, targeted re-teach with scaffold fading	Time-to-mastery parity, retake yield distribution, low-bandwidth completion equivalence
HyFlex Equivalence and Mode-Parity Design	Attendance elasticity, caregiver-friendly continuity, reduced exclusion from schedule shocks	Device-agnostic rooms, asynchronous forums, auto-captioning, resumable submissions	Equivalence mapping across modes, cohort twinning, parity checks on workload and assessment	Cross-mode outcome parity, access-minutes distribution, submission modality fairness
Project Inquiry Studio and Portfolio Validity	Agency growth, authentic transfer, identity-safe knowledge production	Shared workspaces, versioned artifacts, rubric coders, multimodal portfolio vaults	Role rotation, critique protocols, checkpoint retrospectives, evidence triangulation	Artifact quality trajectory, rubric reliability parity, reflection depth consistency
Simulation, Game-Based Learning, and Safe Failure Loops	Rapid feedback, strategic exploration, misconception surfacing without stigma	Lightweight simulations, telemetry instrumentation, adaptive difficulty, accessible control schemes	Debrief cycles, misconception cataloging, optional challenge paths with autonomy support	Misconception resolution rates, engagement stability, adaptive gains parity

continued on following page

Table 3. Continued

Pedagogical Paradigm Anchor	Inclusion Dividend Profile	Digital and Assistive Enablers	Teacher Orchestration Heuristics	Evidence Signals and Equity Checks
Peer Tutoring and Cooperative Sensemaking	Belonging, reciprocal explanation, language practice, distributed cognition	Pairing algorithms, shared scratchpads, talk-time meters, collaborative annotation layers	Heterogeneous grouping, scaffolded roles, equitable turn-taking norms, tutor rotation	Talk-time balance, hint quality calibration, mutual learning deltas parity
Community-Anchored Service Learning and Civic Epistemics	Relevance, civic efficacy, epistemic justice through local problem framing	Mobile data capture, geo-tagged tasks, consentable media uploads, badgeable portfolios	Community co-design, risk review routines, ethical clearance checks, reciprocity agreements	Community satisfaction indices, relevance ratings, longitudinal impact markers

Table 3 makes equity operational by specifying how pedagogical structures distribute voice, time, and evidentiary legitimacy, and by binding those distributions to enablers and checks that can be monitored without becoming punitive. The enablers column prevents procurement drift by clarifying which platform capabilities are non-optional for each pedagogy, including offline resilience, caption integrity, and multimodal portfolio storage. The orchestration heuristics column preserves teacher sovereignty by formalizing decision routines that translate signals into humane action, including role rotation, regrouping, and equivalence mapping across HyFlex modalities. The evidence signals column is intentionally distribution-sensitive, emphasizing parity, reliability, and stability rather than crude activity counts, thereby aligning classroom practice with the contestability and fairness constraints introduced in Table 1 and the safeguard signals formalized in Table 2.

4.3 Decolonial, Culturally Sustaining, and Community-Governed Learning Ecologies

A globally relevant inclusion ecosystem must treat culture and language as epistemic infrastructure, not decorative contextualization, operationalizing *epistemic justice* through curricular locality, representation balance, and community-legible governance. *Culturally sustaining pedagogy* and *funds of knowledge* logics require that learners encounter local exemplars, regionally salient problems, and community datasets as legitimate objects of inquiry, while *translanguaging* normalizes bilingual prompts, code-switch tolerant rubrics, and dual-language artifacts that evaluate reasoning quality independent of accent or orthographic variance (Mystakidis & Lympouridis, 2023; Kokkinos, 2024). Decolonial commitments must be rendered as procedural safeguards, including community review boards for sensitive content, provenance tracking for revisions, and reciprocity norms for data extraction so local communities retain interpretive authority over their narratives. Table 3 embeds these commitments through community-anchored service learning routines and portfolio legitimacy, and it complements Table 2 by specifying how cultural locality constrains content selection, prompt templates, and relevance metrics. These ecologies also create structural protection against stigma, because belonging is cultivated through recognition, reciprocity, and voice, rather than manufactured through superficial engagement features.

4.4 Resilience Engineering, Wellbeing Safeguards, and Care-Oriented Classroom Systems

Resilience must be engineered as a default operating condition, assuming intermittent power, shared devices, constrained bandwidth, and crisis shocks as routine realities in many regions, including humanitarian, rural, and peri-urban contexts (Belda-Medina, 2024; Lin et al., 2024). Mobile-first and offline-first design becomes pedagogically meaningful only when it is coupled to asynchronous mastery cycles, resumable submissions, and recovery-friendly pacing so learners are not penalized for volatility they cannot control. Wellbeing safeguarding must be treated as a governance-in-practice layer, where *psychological safety* is maintained through anti-harassment protocols, respectful critique norms, privacy-preserving defaults, and non-stigmatizing intervention logistics that prioritize support over classification (Chukwuemeka & Garba, 2024; Alam, 2023a). *Care ethics* translates into time-to-support commitments, configurable notification cadence, and restorative pathways after setbacks, while *risk governance* requires escalation routes that keep human judgment in the loop for sensitive cases. The parity-oriented evidence checks in Table 3, including cross-mode equivalence, talk-time balance, and low-bandwidth completion equivalence, function as early-warning signals for inclusion drift, and they set the stage for Section 5 where analytics-to-action pipelines formalize these signals into disciplined, interpretable interventions.

5. LEARNING ANALYTICS FOR INCLUSION

5.1 Purposes, Limits, and Ethical Guardrails for Equity Analytics

Learning analytics for inclusion is best understood as *decision intelligence* for care-oriented action, not as surveillance instrumentation or performative accountability. Its legitimate purposes are tightly delimited, early identification of reversible learning friction, precision scaffolding for concept mastery, workload leveling for teachers through triage that preserves dignity, and governance-grade visibility into distributional equity across participation, progression, and recourse (Monica et al., 2025; Zhu & Xie, 2023). The primary limit is that analytics must never collapse into deterministic labeling, because *algorithmic subjectification* and rank-order cultures can convert probabilistic signals into stigma, self-fulfilling withdrawal, and punitive sorting. Guardrails therefore require *interpretability-first modeling*, role-scoped visibility, minimization, purpose limitation, and contestability through override and appeals, consistent with Table 1 constraints and the implementation tuples in Table 2 and Table 3. Table 4 operationalizes these guardrails by binding each signal family to misreading hazards, inclusive heuristics, intervention protocols, and latency-disciplined verification indicators.

5.2 Interoperable Data Foundations and Signal Semantics for Equitable Sensemaking

Equity analytics depends on semantic discipline, because heterogeneous tools generate noisy traces whose meaning drifts unless event vocabularies are standardized and pedagogically plausible. A robust substrate uses interoperable schemas and consistent verbs for attempts, hints, revisions, peer feedback, and portfolio submissions, while encoding missingness and uncertainty so intermittent connectivity does not masquerade as disengagement (Alam, 2023b; Hossain, 2024). Identity handling must support pseudonymous analytic keys with revocable linkage, enabling teacher attribution where duty-of-care requires it, while preventing unnecessary exposure through least-privilege access and auditable retrieval. Data minimization and retention discipline reduce chilling effects, and privacy-preserving aggregation protects small cohorts from re-identification while still enabling intersectional diagnostics (Binytska et al., 2023; Hajahmadi et al., 2024). Table 4 provides the operational grammar that converts these event streams into equitable sensemaking, neutralizing common misreads that turn activity into false mastery and silence into false apathy.

Table 4. Equity Analytics Signal-to-Action Map with Latency and Interpretability Discipline

Signal Family	Dominant Misreading Hazard	Inclusive Sensemaking Heuristic	Care-Oriented Intervention Protocol	Verification Indicator with Time-to-Support
Attendance and Access Continuity	Absence treated as apathy, intermittency treated as low commitment	Separate connectivity friction, caregiving constraints, and motivational withdrawal using contextual annotation	Offer asynchronous catch-up windows, low-bandwidth alternatives, and restorative re-entry conferences	Recovery within two learning sessions, stabilized access-minutes parity across groups
Interaction and Dwell Microdynamics	Long dwell treated as mastery, rapid clicks treated as disengagement	Distinguish productive struggle, confusion loops, and interface accessibility friction through pattern signatures	Trigger just-in-time exemplars, modality switches, and interface simplification with teacher confirmation	Error reduction within three tasks, reduced abandonment risk within one cycle
Assessment Evidence and Attempt Histories	Single score masks pathway diversity, language fluency conflated with concept mastery	Inspect concept-level evidence, attempt trajectories, and modality equivalence before interpreting proficiency	Provide targeted reattempts with spacing schedules, alternative demonstrations, and rubric-aligned feedback	Mastery progression within one week, improved retry-yield parity across cohorts
Discourse and Collaboration Traces	Talk volume treated as understanding, silence treated as non-participation	Weight contribution quality, role distribution, and epistemic access rather than raw frequency	Rotate roles, seed structured prompts, and deploy peer tutoring pairings with equitable turn-taking norms	Talk-time balance within a collaboration cycle, improved rubric-alignment within two cycles
Device and Network Telemetry	Low data use treated as laziness, low video time treated as low engagement	Recognize cost constraints, shared devices, and bandwidth volatility as structural conversion factors	Switch to offline packs, progressive enhancement modes, and resumable submissions without penalty	Completion-rate parity within one module, verified sync integrity within forty-eight hours
Risk Flags and Recourse Signals	Risk scores treated as fate, automated flags treated as authoritative judgments	Present flags as probabilistic hypotheses with confidence bounds and counterfactual levers	Convene brief learner-teacher conferences, adjust pacing plans, and document overrides with recourse	Flag reversal rate improvement within two weeks, reduced false positives across subgroups

Table 4 is deliberately engineered as a boundary object that can travel intact into coaching playbooks, administrative dashboards, and vendor acceptance criteria, without losing semantic fidelity. Each row names a misreading hazard that commonly emerges from cognitive heuristics and institutional incentive structures, then replaces it with an inclusive heuristic grounded in conversion-factor realism, interpretability discipline, and dignity-preserving practice. The intervention protocols are framed as actionable routines that teachers and systems can execute with minimal latency, aligning analytics with the orchestration logics already specified in Table 3, and the governance safeguards consolidated in Table 1. Verification indicators are explicitly time-bound, preventing slow, bureaucratic response cycles that allow inequities to compound, while keeping the analytic stance hypothesis-driven and contestable rather than deterministic.

5.3 Interpretable Modeling, Fairness Diagnostics, and Causal Pragmatics for Actionable Insights

Interpretability is a structural requirement for equitable analytics, because opaque models amplify power asymmetries and invite automation bias, especially under high workload and low analytic literacy. An interpretability-first ladder privileges calibrated, monotonic, and audit-friendly predictors, then layers *counterfactual explanations* that specify feasible levers such as additional practice sets, modality switches, scaffold intensity changes, or deadline elasticity, rather than abstract attributions that reproduce deficit narratives (Pattiasina, Lamaloang, & Santoso, 2025; Levesque & Duncan, 2024). Fairness diagnostics must be continuous, examining calibration parity, false-positive asymmetries, and error concentration across intersectional slices, while explicitly guarding against proxy features that reconstruct protected attributes through behavioral residues. Causal pragmatics strengthens actionability by distinguishing correlational risk markers from manipulable intervention levers, using design logic that treats analytics as *policy instruments* rather than prediction engines (Navas-Bonilla et al., 2025; Ghoulam & Bouikhalene, 2024). Table 4 anchors this by requiring every flag to map to a care protocol and a latency expectation, thereby aligning model outputs with executable support rather than classificatory labeling.

5.4 Governance, Rights, and Community Accountability for Inclusion-Centered Analytics

Analytics legitimacy is sustained through governance that operationalizes rights as procedures, not slogans, ensuring due process, transparency, and remedy at the point of decision. Consent must be intelligible, revisable, and scope-bounded, paired with purpose limitation and retention discipline, while role-scoped visibility prevents gratuitous exposure and minimizes chilling effects on learner voice (Alam, 2023c; Asitah et al., 2024). Contestability must be implemented as low-friction appeals, teacher override semantics, and auditable rationale trails, so automated inferences cannot silently harden into irreversible educational trajectories. Community accountability requires public reporting of distribution-sensitive indicators such as access incidents, parity deltas, and flag reversal dynamics, using aggregation safeguards that protect small cohorts from re-identification and stigmatization (Ahmad et al., 2024; Zhang et al., 2024). Procurement and platform governance should bind service levels to the verification indicators and time-to-support discipline specified in Table 4, thereby making vendor performance accountable to equity outcomes rather than engagement throughput. This governance frame also maintains coherence with Table 1 constraints and the pedagogical integrity encoded in Table 3, ensuring analytics remains care-oriented, interpretably actionable, and globally adaptable.

6. IMPLEMENTATION ARCHITECTURES FOR READINESS, GOVERNANCE, PROCUREMENT, CAPACITY, SUSTAINABILITY, AND MEL

6.1 Institutional Readiness, Maturity Stratification, and Change-Management Political Economy

Institutional readiness for inclusive AI-enabled education is a multi-pillar capacity state that must be formalized as a maturity stratification across strategy, pedagogy, accessibility, data governance, infrastructure resilience, workforce capability, and community compact, because partial readiness produces brittle implementations and predictable equity regressions. A viable rubric differentiates *Emergent*, *Established*, and *Optimizing* strata through observable entry criteria, budget-gated progression triggers, and accountability duties that bind leadership incentives to distribution-sensitive outcomes rather than procurement throughput (Barbu et al., 2025; Bekteshi, 2025). Readiness must include *implementation fidelity* and *adaptive fit* logics, ensuring core components such as *UDL-as-compiled property*, contestability, portability, and low-bandwidth continuity remain invariant even as local contextualization evolves. Change management must be treated as sociological and organizational engineering, aligning adoption cadence to academic calendars, cognitive load budgets, unionized labor realities, and bureaucratic procurement cycles, while building legitimacy through participatory governance (Dai, 2024; Lalotra & Kumar, 2024). Tables 1 through 4 already specify non-negotiable constraints and operational heuristics, and the implementation logic must treat them as enforceable program invariants.

6.2 Reference Architecture, Workstream Sequencing, and Execution Logic

A reference architecture for inclusive platforms must be layered, modular, and interoperability-first, because locked-in monoliths obstruct portability, weaken auditability, and reduce local innovation capacity. Identity and access should support shared-device ecologies through rapid role switching, revocable permissions, and pseudonymous analytics keys, while the data layer must implement open event semantics that preserve the interpretive grammar in Table 4 and the orchestration evidence in Table 3. Learning services should be composable, enabling tutoring, content, assessment, and assistive integrations to evolve without destabilizing the whole stack, while edge services must deliver offline caching, resumable sessions, and sync integrity to prevent bandwidth volatility from becoming educational penalty (Almuaqel, 2023; Eden, Chisom, & Adeniyi, 2024). The roadmap in Table 5 sequences these dependencies into an execution logic that is fiscally credible, governance-enforceable, and equity-triggered, translating the theory-to-design constraints of Table 1 and the use-case safeguards of Table 2 into a time-bound operating plan.

Table 5. Time-Bound Equity Implementation Roadmap with Risk Discipline

Implementation Phase	Priority Workstream Bundle	Accountable Governance Actors	Embedded Equity Safeguards	Success Metrics and Trigger Thresholds
Discovery and Baseline	Readiness audit, data mapping, accessibility gap closure, scope discipline for analytics	Ethics council, data stewards, accessibility lead, instructional core team	Consent templates, small-number protections, audit log activation, language access verification	Baseline parity index established, consent completeness stabilized, audit closure rate sustained
Pilot and Calibration	Offline-first modes, mastery-map publishing, tutor calibration, dashboard prototyping	Product owner, lead teachers, analytics steward, platform administrator	Subgroup error checks, override logging, appeal workflow rehearsals, assistive regression tests	Flag reversal stability, access incident decline, time-to-support within defined window
Adaptation and Scale	Content localization, translanguaging workflows, teacher coaching cycles, threshold tuning	Curriculum unit, coach cadre, community review panel, school leadership	Representation balance rules, role-scoped views, counterfactual recourse defaults, privacy minimization	Subgroup mastery parity improves, relevance ratings rise, dashboard adoption reaches target

continued on following page

Table 5. Continued

Implementation Phase	Priority Workstream Bundle	Accountable Governance Actors	Embedded Equity Safeguards	Success Metrics and Trigger Thresholds
Institutionalization and Procurement Reset	SLA renegotiation, portability proofing, policy codification, retention discipline	Procurement office, legal counsel, leadership council, records custodian	Model cards required, deletion verification, exportable portfolios, vendor lock-in constraints	Contract compliance rate verified, portability tests pass, retention reduction validated
Sustainment and Optimization	Green compute tuning, repair ecosystem buildout, continuous monitoring, public learning reports	Vendor liaison, facilities lead, community board, monitoring cell	Energy budgets, repairability standards, transparency cadence, incident response drills	Energy per session declines, device uptime stabilizes, public reporting punctuality maintained
Transition and Exit	Continuity drills, data handback, service substitution, staff re-onboarding routines	CIO function, governance secretariat, vendor liaison, training lead	Secure escrow, transfer proofs, learner portfolio continuity, decommission safeguards	Zero data loss verified, downtime minutes bounded, continuity certification achieved

Table 5 compresses sequencing, accountability, safeguards, and success triggers into a single operational artifact that can be budgeted, calendared, and audited without interpretive drift. The phases are dependency-aware, ensuring infrastructure primitives such as offline continuity, consent discipline, and assistive interoperability are hardened before scale-up, while governance primitives such as contestability, portability, and deletion verification become contractually binding at institutionalization. The safeguards column functions as the enforcement bridge from Table 1 constraints, while the metrics column mirrors the time-to-support and parity logic articulated in Table 4, preventing slow response cycles that allow inequities to compound. This roadmap also preserves pedagogical integrity by sequencing coaching and localization as core workstreams rather than optional enhancements, thereby maintaining coherence with the orchestration heuristics in Table 3 and the inclusion archetypes in Table 2.

6.3 Procurement, Vendor Accountability, and Workforce Capacity as Institutional Muscle

Procurement must be treated as a constitutional lever for inclusion, converting the technical and ethical constraints in Table 1 and the safeguard tuples in Table 2 into enforceable requirements, acceptance criteria, and remedies that activate when parity or time-to-support thresholds are breached. Vendor accountability should be structured through auditable deliverables such as model documentation, data provenance transparency, portability proofs, and deletion verification, combined with recurring red-teaming, calibration reviews, and drift governance that examine intersectional error distributions and recourse efficacy (Wang & Huang, 2025; Hutson & McGinley, 2023). Workforce capacity is not generic digital literacy, it is role-specific professionalization, where teachers develop *dashboard sensemaking*, scaffold orchestration, equitable grouping, and contestation routines, leaders develop readiness governance and public accountability discipline, and data stewards develop minimization enforcement, RBAC hygiene, retention control, and small-number suppression competence. Capacity must be institutionalized through coaching cycles, communities of practice, and versioned playbooks so operational knowledge compounds despite staff churn (Alam, 2022; Alvarado, Guerrero, & Serón, 2023). The execution logic in Table 5 assumes these capabilities as prerequisites, not downstream add-ons.

6.4 Sustainability, Costing Realism, and Monitoring-Evaluation-Learning as a Closed-Loop Control System

Sustainability must be engineered as financial, ecological, and institutional durability, because inclusion collapses when total cost of ownership is underestimated or when compute and hardware practices generate unsupportable externalities. Costing realism requires explicit line items for coaching time, accessibility audits, device refresh and repair ecosystems, connectivity subsidies, governance operations, and incident response, avoiding projectized funding that evaporates after initial deployment (Cao, Ng, & Ye, 2023; Singh, Sun, & Zheng, 2024). Green implementation requires *model compression*, on-device inference where feasible, caching strategies, and energy-per-session monitoring to reduce carbon intensity while preserving latency and privacy, alongside certified e-waste handling and secure destruction routines to protect data dignity. Monitoring-evaluation-learning must operate as a closed-loop control system, specifying a theory-of-change logic, time-bound indicators aligned to Table 4, and mixed-method sensemaking that integrates telemetry with structured learner voice and teacher annotation (Fernandes et al., 2023; Fitrianto & Saif, 2024). Continuous improvement must prioritize distributional equity, recourse effectiveness, and wellbeing safeguards, with continuity drills ensuring the transition discipline in Table 5 remains a routine governance capability rather than an emergency improvisation.

7. CONCLUSION

7.1 Integrative Synthesis of the Equity-Optimizing Sociotechnical Stack

This chapter consolidates inclusive education as an engineered property of learning systems, where equity outcomes emerge from the disciplined coupling of *UDL-as-compiled accessibility*, *capability-expanding pedagogy*, *contestable AI supports*, and *interpretability-first analytics* under enforceable governance. Inclusion is reframed from distributive inputs to realized *conversion-factor* performance, meaning that disability access, linguistic mediation, time poverty, and bandwidth volatility are treated as first-order design variables, not contextual noise. The theoretical architecture binds learning-science constructs such as *scaffold fading*, *cognitive load management*, *retrieval-rich mastery*, and *metacognitive calibration* to justice constructs such as *targeted universalism*, *epistemic justice*, and *care ethics*, producing a coherent design grammar that resists both techno-solutionism and compliance theater. The operational spine is procedural and measurable, accessibility and parity become release gates, recourse becomes a standard pathway, and portability and data sovereignty become institutional invariants. The resulting apparatus is globally adaptable because it is modular, offline-resilient, culturally sustaining, and governance-legible across policy, workforce, and technical domains.

7.2 Non-Negotiables, Immediate Commitments, and Future-Compatible Governance

Institutionalization requires non-negotiables that are testable, budgetable, and enforceable, beginning with accessibility verification as a continuous regression discipline, not a one-time audit, and extending to parity diagnostics that are intersectional, distribution-sensitive, and protected by small-number safeguards. Adaptive engines must publish *learning maps*, mastery thresholds, and uncertainty bounds, and must preserve teacher sovereignty through override semantics, auditable annotations, and stigma-resistant appeal pathways that operationalize due process. Analytics must remain care-oriented, using hypothesis-driven flags, counterfactual recourse, and latency-disciplined interventions, while avoiding rank-order display regimes that catalyze stigma and algorithmic subjectification. Procurement must encode these requirements into contracts through portability proofs, deletion verification, model documentation, and service levels tied to parity and time-to-support, preventing vendor lock-in from eroding institutional autonomy. Future-compatibility depends on modular reference architectures, green compute practices such as compression and edge inference, resilient repair ecosystems, and continuity drills for exit and

transition, ensuring that governance survives leadership turnover and technological drift while preserving learner dignity, agency, and epistemic access at scale.

REFERENCES

Acharya, M., & Mohbey, K. K. (2024). Virtual environment role in higher education students learning enhancement with intellectual disabilities. In *Applied assistive technologies and informatics for students with disabilities* (pp. 35–57). Springer Nature Singapore.

Adeleye, O. O., Eden, C. A., & Adeniyi, I. S. (2024). Innovative teaching methodologies in the era of artificial intelligence: A review of inclusive educational practices. *World Journal of Advanced Engineering Technology and Sciences, 11*(2), 069-079.

Ader, L. G. M., Crowley, K., Kuhn, S., Caraffini, F., Altındağ, T., & Colreavy-Donnelly, S. (2023, September). Extended Reality, Augmented Users, and Design Implications for Virtual Learning Environments. In *2023 IEEE International Symposium on Technology and Society (ISTAS)* (pp. 1-8). IEEE.

Adera, N. (2025). Innovative learning spaces and blended learning: Quest for 21st century competency teaching and learning approaches. *Creating Dynamic Space in Higher Education: Modern Shifts in Policy, Competencies, and Governance*, 139-174.

Adetunla, A., Akinlabi, E., Jen, T. C., Okokpujie, I. P., & Ajibade, S. S. (2024, April). A review on the Challenges and Prospects in Harnessing Virtual Reality in Education. In *2024 International Conference on Science, Engineering and Business for Driving Sustainable Development Goals (SEB4SDG)* (pp. 1-5). IEEE.

Ahmad, I., Sharma, S., Singh, R., Gehlot, A., Gupta, L. R., Thakur, A. K., & Twala, B. (2024). Inclusive learning using industry 4.0 technologies: Addressing student diversity in modern education. *Cogent Education, 11*(1), 2330235.

Ai, Y., Hu, Y., & Zhao, W. (2025). Interactive learning: Harnessing technology to alleviate foreign language anxiety in foreign literature education. *Interactive Learning Environments, 33*(3), 2440–2459.

Akintayo, O. T., Eden, C. A., Ayeni, O. O., & Onyebuchi, N. C. (2024). Inclusive curriculum design: Meeting the diverse needs of students for social improvement. *International Journal of Applied Research in Social Sciences, 6*(5), 770–784.

AlAli, R., & Wardat, Y. (2024). Opportunities and challenges of integrating generative artificial intelligence in education. *International Journal of Religion, 5*(7), 784–793.

Alam, A. (2022). Impact of university's human resources practices on professors' occupational performance: empirical evidence from India's higher education sector. In *Inclusive businesses in developing economies: Converging people, profit, and corporate citizenship* (pp. 107–131). Springer International Publishing.

Alam, A. (2023a). Media multitasking with M-learning technology in real-time classroom learning: Analysing the dynamics in formal educational settings for the future of E-learning in India. In *2023 2nd International Conference on Smart Technologies and Systems for Next Generation Computing (ICSTSN)* (pp. 1-6). IEEE.

Alam, A. (2023b). The secret sauce of student success: Cracking the code by navigating the path to personalized learning with educational data mining. In *2023 2nd International Conference on Smart Technologies and Systems for Next Generation Computing (ICSTSN)* (pp. 1-8). IEEE.

Alam, A. (2023c). Intelligence unleashed: An argument for AI-enabled learning ecologies with real world examples of today and a peek into the future. In *International Conference on Innovations in Computer Science, Electronics & Electrical Engineering*-2022 (Vol. 2717, No. 1, p. 030001). AIP Publishing LLC.

Alam, A., & Mohanty, A. (2022, December). Facial analytics or virtual avatars: competencies and design considerations for student-teacher interaction in AI-powered online education for effective classroom engagement. In *International Conference on Communication, Networks and Computing* (pp. 252-265). Cham: Springer Nature Switzerland.

Alam, A., & Mohanty, A. (2023, January). Learning on the move: a pedagogical framework for state-of-the-art mobile learning. In *International Conference on Data Management, Analytics & Innovation* (pp. 735-748). Singapore: Springer Nature Singapore.

Alam, A., & Mohanty, A. (2024). Integrated constructive robotics in education (ICRE) model: A paradigmatic framework for transformative learning in educational ecosystem. *Cogent Education, 11*(1), 2324487.

AlArabi, K., Alsalhi, N. R., Almarashdi, H. S., Zakarneh, B., & Annamalai, N. (2023). The Role of Computer Simulations (CSs) and artificial intelligence on student learning: Moderating the impact of the learning environment. [Social Space]. *Przestrzeń Społeczna, 23*(3), 103–122.

Al-Kfairy, M., Alzaabi, M., Snoh, B., Almarzooqi, H., & Alnaqbi, W. (2024, May). Metaverse-based classroom: the good and the bad. In *2024 IEEE Global Engineering Education Conference (EDUCON)* (pp. 1-7). IEEE.

Almuaqel, I. A. (2023). Virtual reality and inclusive learning of individuals with intellectual and developmental disabilities: A review of findings and the path ahead. *IEEE Transactions on Engineering Management, 71*, 13049–13065.

Aloizou, V., Linardatou, S., Boloudakis, M., & Retalis, S. (2025). Integrating a movement-based learning platform as core curriculum tool in kindergarten classrooms. *British Journal of Educational Technology, 56*(1), 339–365.

Alvarado, Y., Guerrero, R., & Serón, F. (2023). Inclusive learning through immersive virtual reality and semantic embodied conversational agent: A case study in children with autism. *Journal of Computer Science and Technology, 23*(2), e09–e09.

Anwar, M. S., Yang, J., Frnda, J., Choi, A., Baghaei, N., & Ali, M. (2025). Metaverse and XR for cultural heritage education: Applications, standards, architecture, and technological insights for enhanced immersive experience. *Virtual Reality (Waltham Cross), 29*(2), 51.

Asitah, N., Murni, A. W., Lestari, W. M., Aini, N., & Kartikasari, H. L. (2024, September). Virtual Reality in Inclusive Basic Education: A Systematic Review of Roles and Application for Future Education Directions. In *2024 International Conference on ICT for Smart Society (ICISS)* (pp. 1-6). IEEE.

Ayeni, O. O., Al Hamad, N. M., Chisom, O. N., Osawaru, B., & Adewusi, O. E. (2024). AI in education: A review of personalized learning and educational technology. *GSC Advanced Research and Reviews, 18*(2), 261–271.

Barbu, M., Iordache, D. D., Petre, I., Barbu, D. C., & Băjenaru, L. (2025). Framework Design for Reinforcing the Potential of XR Technologies in Transforming Inclusive Education. *Applied Sciences (Basel, Switzerland), 15*(3), 1484.

Bekteshi, L. (2025). Education in the Era of AI and Immersive Technologies: A Systematic Review. *Journal of Research in Engineering and Computer Sciences, 3*(1), 01-14.

Belda-Medina, J. (2024). Inclusive education through digital comic creation in higher learning environments. *Social Sciences, 13*(5), 272.

Berezi, I. U. (2025). Virtual Learning Environment: Redefining Higher Educational Delivery for Efficiency and Accessibility. *International Journal of Educational Management, Rivers State University., 1*(1), 451-467.

Binytska, K. M., Bilyakovska, O. O., Yankovych, O. I., Greskova, V. V., & Ocheretna, I. P. (2023). Exploring the potential of immersive technologies in university education worldwide.

Borah, A. R., Nischith, T. N., & Gupta, S. (2024, January). Improved learning based on GenAI. In *2024 2nd International Conference on Intelligent Data Communication Technologies and Internet of Things (IDCIoT)* (pp. 1527-1532). IEEE.

Bourguet, M. L., & Omfalos, E. (2024). Work-in-Progress—Student's Co-creation of Collaborative Learning Spaces on the Metaverse. Immersive Learning Research-Academic, 217-233.

Bu u, A. F. (2024). AI-Powered Classrooms: A Revolution in Learning Environments. *Analele Universităţii din Craiova, Seria Ştiinţe Filologice. Limbi Străine Aplicate*, (1), 96–103.

Cano, C. A. G., & Troya, A. L. C. (2023). Artificial Intelligence applied to teaching and learning processes. *LatIA*, (1), 2.

Cao, Y., Ng, G. W., & Ye, S. S. (2023). Design and evaluation for immersive virtual reality learning environment: A systematic literature review. *Sustainability*, *15*(3), 1964.

Chukwuemeka, E. J., & Garba, M. (2024). Technology as a catalyst for learning and unlearning: A tool for navigating education in a dynamic society. *European Journal of Interactive Multimedia and Education*, *5*(2), e02404.

Dai, C. P. (2024). Applying machine learning to augment the design and assessment of immersive learning experience. In *Machine learning in educational sciences: Approaches, applications and advances* (pp. 245–264). Springer Nature Singapore.

Dalle, J., Aydin, H., & Wang, C. X. (2024). Cultural dimensions of technology acceptance and adaptation in learning environments. *Journal of Formative Design in Learning*, •••, 1–14.

Di Natale, A. F., Bartolotta, S., Gaggioli, A., Riva, G., & Villani, D. (2024). Exploring students' acceptance and continuance intention in using immersive virtual reality and metaverse integrated learning environments: The case of an Italian university course. *Education and Information Technologies*, *29*(12), 14749–14768.

Eden, C. A., Chisom, O. N., & Adeniyi, I. S. (2024). Harnessing technology integration in education: Strategies for enhancing learning outcomes and equity. *World Journal of Advanced Engineering Technology and Sciences, 11*(2), 001-008.

Eltahir, M. E., & Babiker, F. M. E. (2024). The influence of artificial intelligence tools on student performance in e-learning environments: Case study. *Electronic Journal of e-Learning*, *22*(9), 91–110.

Feng, B., & Ng, L. L. (2024). The spatial influence on vocabulary acquisition in an immersive virtual reality-mediated learning environment. [IJCALLT]. *International Journal of Computer-Assisted Language Learning and Teaching*, *14*(1), 1–17.

Fernandes, F. A., Rodrigues, C. S. C., Teixeira, E. N., & Werner, C. M. (2023). Immersive learning frameworks: A systematic literature review. *IEEE Transactions on Learning Technologies*, *16*(5), 736–747.

Fitrianto, I., & Saif, A. (2024). The role of virtual reality in enhancing Experiential Learning: a comparative study of traditional and immersive learning environments. *International Journal of Post Axial: Futuristic Teaching and Learning*, 97-110.

Ghoulam, K., & Bouikhalene, B. (2024). From classrooms to cyberspace: Understanding pedagogical approaches and outcomes in Metaverse learning environments. *Advances in Mobile Learning Educational Research*, *4*(1), 983–993.

Hajahmadi, S., Clementi, L., López, M. D. J., & Marfia, G. (2024, March). Arele-bot: Inclusive learning of spanish as a foreign language through a mobile app integrating augmented reality and chatgpt. In *2024 IEEE Conference on Virtual Reality and 3D User Interfaces Abstracts and Workshops (VRW)* (pp. 335-340). IEEE.

Haj-Bolouri, A., Katende, J., & Rossi, M. (2023, May). A mid-range theory for designing sustainable safe spaces of immersive learning environments: a design-science based gamification approach. In *International Conference on Design Science Research in Information Systems and Technology* (pp. 449-469). Cham: Springer Nature Switzerland.

Hossain, K. I. (2024). Reviewing the role of culture in English language learning: Challenges and opportunities for educators. *Social Sciences & Humanities Open*, *9*, 100781.

Hutson, J., & McGinley, C. (2023). Neuroaffirmative approaches to extended reality: Empowering individuals with autism spectrum condition through immersive learning environments. *International Journal of Technology in Education and Science*, *7*(3).

Jadán-Guerrero, J., Tamayo-Narvaez, K., Méndez, E., & Valenzuela, M. (2024, June). Adaptive learning environments: Integrating artificial intelligence for special education advances. In *International Conference on Human-Computer Interaction* (pp. 86-94). Cham: Springer Nature Switzerland.

Khalid, I. L., Abdullah, M. N. S., & Fadzil, H. M. (2024). A systematic review: Digital learning in STEM education. *Journal of Advanced Research in Applied Sciences and Engineering Technology*, *51*(1), 98–115.

Kokkinos, L. (2024). Revolutionizing education: The dynamic intersection of technology and learning. [IJMCER]. *Educational Research*, *6*(1), 26–32.

Kumar, K. S., Selvan, T., Mahendraprabu, M., Ganesan, K., Ramnath, R., & Kumar, N. S. (2024). Examining the Role of Virtual Reality, Augmented Reality, and Artificial Intelligence in Adapting STEM Education for Next-Generation Inclusion. *International Journal of Emerging Knowledge Studies*, *2*(12), 876–883.

Kusmawan, U. (2023). Redefining teacher training: The promise of AI-supported teaching practices. *Journal of Advances in Education and Philosophy*, *7*(9), 332–335.

Lalotra, G. S., & Kumar, V. (2024). The impact of virtual reality and augmented reality in inclusive education. In *Applied Assistive Technologies and Informatics for Students with Disabilities* (pp. 71–94). Springer Nature Singapore.

Lampropoulos, G. (2023). Augmented reality and artificial intelligence in education: Toward immersive intelligent tutoring systems. In *Augmented reality and artificial intelligence: The fusion of advanced technologies* (pp. 137–146). Springer Nature Switzerland.

Levesque, E., & Duncan, J. (2024). Inclusive education for deaf students: Pass or fail. *Deafness & Education International*, *26*(2), 125–126.

Lin, X. F., Luo, G., Luo, S., Liu, J., Chan, K. K., Chen, H., & Li, Z. (2024). Promoting pre-service teachers' learning performance and perceptions of inclusive education: An augmented reality-based training through learning by design approach. *Teaching and Teacher Education*, *148*, 104661.

Liu, Y., Razman, M. R., Zakaria, S. Z. S., Ern, L. K., Hussain, A., & Chamola, V. (2024). Utilizing ubiquitous learning to foster sustainable development in rural areas: Insights from 6G technology. *Computers in Human Behavior*, *161*, 108418.

Marín, V., Sampedro, B. E., & Morales-Diaz, M. (2025). Secondary education teacher's views on mixed reality in inclusive environments. *Journal of New Approaches in Educational Research*, *14*(1), 4.

Marques, B., Santos, B. S., & Dias, P. (2024). Ten years of immersive education: Overview of a virtual and augmented reality course at postgraduate level. *Computers & Graphics*, *124*, 104088.

McDermott, G., Byrne, A., McLaughlin, R., O'Connor, N., & Griselain, S. (2023). *Exploring the use of immersive technologies to enhance the student experience.* Ubiquity Proceedings.

Mhlongo, S., Mbatha, K., Ramatsetse, B., & Dlamini, R. (2023). Challenges, opportunities, and prospects of adopting and using smart digital technologies in learning environments: An iterative review. *Heliyon*, *9*(6). PMID: 37274691

Miles, P., & Boltin, K. (2025). Creation and use of SBS's The Boat; principles for the co-creation of online interactive learning environments for innovative digital pedagogy. *Pedagogies*, *20*(3), 364–380.

Minghelli, V., D'anna, C., & Vastola, R. (2023). A biopsychosocial approach to plan inclusive learning environments in physical education. *Journal of Physical Education and Sport*, *23*(9), 2492–2502.

Mintz, J., Connolly, C., O'Brien, E., Daniela, L., & Ceallaigh, T. Ó. (2024). Inclusive digital education: Contexts, practices and perspectives. *Computers in the Schools*, *41*(2), 115–119.

Monica, J. A., Malar, J. H., Arun, C., Sharmila, L., & Arif, M. (2025). Leveraging technology and universal design for inclusive and engaging learning in Indian higher education. In *Educational Philosophy and Sociological Foundation of Education* (pp. 177–212). IGI Global.

Mouboua, P. D., Atobatele, F. A., & Akintayo, O. T. (2024). Multilingual education and social equity: A comparative study of integration policies in multicultural societies. *GSC Advanced Research and Reviews, 19*(2), 032-042.

Munthe, R. G., Abbas, M., Fernandez, R., & Ulita, N. (2024). The impact of educational information systems on learning accessibility in higher education. [ITEE]. *International Transactions on Education Technology*, *3*(1), 94–103.

Mystakidis, S., & Lympouridis, V. (2023). Immersive learning. *Encyclopedia*, *3*(2), 396–405.

Navas-Bonilla, C. D. R., Guerra-Arango, J. A., Oviedo-Guado, D. A., & Murillo-Noriega, D. E. (2025, February). Inclusive education through technology: A systematic review of types, tools and characteristics. []. Frontiers Media SA.]. *Frontiers in Education*, *10*, 1527851.

Nurfadila, M. Y., Hajar, S., & Arsyad, N. F. (2024). Utilizing quizizz for game-based learning in elementary science education. *Journal of Education and Computer Applications*, *1*(1), 12–19.

Papaioannou, G., Volakaki, M. G., Kokolakis, S., & Vouyioukas, D. (2023). Learning spaces in higher education: A state-of-the-art review. *Trends in Higher Education*, *2*(3), 526–545.

Pattiasina, P. J., Lamaloang, L. K., & Santoso, R. Y. (2025). The role of communication in creating inclusive and collaborative learning environments. *INJOSEDU: International Journal of Social and Education*, *2*(3), 577–591.

Pitychoutis, K. M., & Al Rawahi, A. (2024). Smart teaching: The synergy of multiple intelligences and artificial intelligence in English as a foreign language instruction. In *Forum for Linguistic Studies* (Vol. 6, No. 6, pp. 249-260).

Pradeep, K., Sulur Anbalagan, R., Thangavelu, A. P., Aswathy, S., Jisha, V. G., & Vaisakhi, V. S. (2024, December). Neuroeducation: Understanding neural dynamics in learning and teaching. [). Frontiers Media SA.]. *Frontiers in Education, 9*, 1437418.

Rajora, R., Rajora, A., Sharma, B., Aggarwal, P., & Thapliyal, S. (2024, February). The integration of IoT in learning environments: Assessing the impact of educational empowerment and addressing its challenges. In *2024 4th International Conference on Innovative Practices in Technology and Management (ICIPTM)* (pp. 1-5). IEEE.

Rana, M., Norbisrath, U., Vainikko, E., & Rossi, B. (2023, September). Transforming affordable virtual reality headsets into effective learning environments. In *2023 International Conference on Intelligent Metaverse Technologies & Applications (iMETA)* (pp. 1-8). IEEE.

Rana, S., Sheshadri, T., Malhotra, N., & Basha, S. M. (2024). Creating Digital Learning Environments: Tools and Technologies for Success. In *Transdisciplinary Teaching and Technological Integration for Improved Learning: Case Studies and Practical Approaches* (pp. 1-21). IGI Global.

Rane, N. (2023). Chatbot-enhanced teaching and learning: Implementation strategies, challenges, and the role of ChatGPT in education. *Challenges, and the Role of ChatGPT in Education (July 21, 2023).*

Sá, M. J., & Serpa, S. (2023). Metaverse as a learning environment: Some considerations. *Sustainability, 15*(3), 2186.

Sabri, S. M., Ismail, I., Annuar, N., Rahman, N. R. A., Abd Hamid, N. Z., & Abd Mutalib, H. (2024). A conceptual analysis of technology integration in classroom instruction towards enhancing student engagement and learning outcomes. *Integration (Amsterdam), 9*(55), 750–769.

Sethi, S. S., & Jain, K. (2024). AI technologies for social emotional learning: Recent research and future directions. *Journal of Research in Innovative Teaching & Learning, 17*(2), 213–225.

Shanthi, B., Ravichandran, C., Manimegalai, V., Parashar, A. K., & BS, H. (2025). Critical Thinking in Higher Education Through Innovative Strategies: Out-of-the-Box Thinking. In *Global Practices in Inclusive Education Curriculum and Policy* (pp. 365-398). IGI Global.

Shireesha, M., & Jeevan, J. (2024). The Role of Artificial Intelligence in Personalized Learning: A Pathway to Inclusive Education. *Library of Progress-Library Science, Information Technology & Computer, 44*(3).

Singh, B., Kaunert, C., Lal, S., & Arora, M. K. (2025). Enhancing AI-Augmented Classrooms: Teacher-Centric Integration of Intelligent Tutoring Systems and Adaptive Learning Environments. In *Fostering Inclusive Education With AI and Emerging Technologies* (pp. 99-130). IGI Global.

Singh, M., Sun, D., & Zheng, Z. (2024). Enhancing university students' learning performance in a metaverse-enabled immersive learning environment for STEM education: A community of inquiry approach. *Future in Educational Research, 2*(3), 288–309.

Solmaz, S., Kester, L., & Van Gerven, T. (2024). An immersive virtual reality learning environment with CFD simulations: Unveiling the Virtual Garage concept. *Education and Information Technologies, 29*(2), 1455–1488. PMID: 37361838

Sombilon, E. V., Rahmanov, S. S., Jachecki, K., Rahmanov, Z., & Peisachovich, E. (2024). Ethical considerations when designing and implementing immersive realities in nursing education. *Cureus, 16*(7). PMID: 39130836

Sowell, J. (2023). Making Learning Inclusive in Digital Learning Environments. In *English Teaching Forum* (Vol. 61, No. 1, pp. 2-13). US Department of State. Bureau of Educational and Cultural Affairs, Office of English Language Programs, SA-5, 2200 C Street NW 4th Floor, Washington, DC 20037.

Stalmach, A., D'Elia, P., Di Sano, S., & Casale, G. (2024). Digital methods to promote inclusive and effective learning in schools: A mixed methods research study. *Open Education Studies, 6*(1), 20240023.

Urbaite, G. (2024). The role of technology in modern language education. *Euro-Global Journal of Linguistics and Language Education, 1*(1), 3–10.

Wang, D., & Huang, X. (2025). Transforming education through artificial intelligence and immersive technologies: Enhancing learning experiences. *Interactive Learning Environments*, ●●●, 1–20.

Wang, Q., & Yu, Z. (2024). Deep Learning-Based Scene Processing and Optimization for Virtual Reality Classroom Environments: A Study. *TS. Traitement du Signal, 41*(1).

Wu, J. G., Zhang, D., & Lee, S. M. (2023). Into the brave new metaverse: Envisaging future language teaching and learning. *IEEE Transactions on Learning Technologies, 17*, 44–53.

Xu, Z. (2024). AI in education: Enhancing learning experiences and student outcomes. *Applied and Computational Engineering*, *51*(1), 104–111.

Yeh, H. C. (2025). The synergy of generative AI and inquiry-based learning: Transforming the landscape of English teaching and learning. *Interactive Learning Environments*, *33*(1), 88–102.

Zhan, Z., Zhou, X., Cai, S., & Lan, X. (2025). Exploring the effect of competing mechanism in an immersive learning game based on augmented reality. *Journal of Computers in Education*, *12*(2), 449–475.

Zhang, H., Wang, Z., Zong, S., Wu, H., Jiang, R., Cui, Y., & Luo, H. (2024). Impact of intelligent learning environments on perception and presence of hearing-impaired college students. *Journal of Educational Technology & Society*, *27*(4), 352–374.

Zhu, Q., & Xie, X. (2023). Users' needs and expectations of immersive learning spaces in an academic library: A survey. *Journal of Librarianship and Information Science*, *55*(2), 371–382.

Chapter 5
Ethical and Social Considerations in the Deployment of AI in Education

P. Selvakumar
https://orcid.org/0000-0002-3650-4548
Department of Science and Humanities, Nehru Institute of Technology, Coimbatore, India

ABSTRACT

Processes while simultaneously raising profound ethical questions that demand careful examination, promises through data analytics, thereby potentially increasing educational equity and efficiency. Adaptive learning platforms, powered by sophisticated algorithms, tailor instructional content to learning speeds, preferences, and an engaging environment. Virtual teaching assistants, software can reduce on enable more immediate and personalized feedback for learners, which can significantly improve outcomes. Additionally, AI learners' customized assistance, including text-to-speech functionalities, makes education more accessible. The promise of AI in education also extends to facilitating which crucial. However, alongside these exciting prospects, brings it significant perils ethical dilemmas that stakeholders must address. One major concern is the issue of heavily storage, vast amounts student ranging from to behavioral patterns even biometric information. This extensive data collection raises critical especially when sensitive information is involved.

DOI: 10.4018/979-8-3373-5188-9.ch005

OVERVIEW

Processes while simultaneously raising profound ethical questions that demand careful examination, promises through data analytics, thereby potentially increasing educational equity and efficiency. Adaptive learning platforms, powered by sophisticated algorithms, tailor instructional content to learning speeds, preferences, and an engaging environment. Virtual teaching assistants, software can reduce on enable more immediate and personalized feedback for learners, which can significantly improve outcomes. Additionally, AI learners' customized assistance, including text-to-speech functionalities, makes education more accessible. The promise of AI in education also extends to facilitating which crucial. However, alongside these exciting prospects, brings it significant perils ethical dilemmas that stakeholders must address. One major concern is the issue of heavily storage, vast amounts student ranging from to behavioral patterns even biometric information. This extensive data collection raises critical especially when sensitive information is involved. Furthermore, algorithmic within systems disproportionately affecting marginalized or underrepresented student groups. for tutor reflects societal prejudices or is skewed towards certain demographics, the system may deliver unfair or suboptimal educational recommendations, thereby entrenching disparities rather than mitigating them.

Another ethical challenge concerns the transparency and many AI models operate as "black boxes," understand how particular recommendations or evaluations are generated. This opacity undermines particularly influence high-stakes decisions such as grading, admissions, or identifying learning difficulties. The question of who holds responsibility for AI-driven decisions—whether it be educators, developers, or institutions—further complicates the ethical landscape. Additionally, the increased devaluation roles, risking a mechanized approach to teaching that overlooks the nuanced, empathetic, and socio-emotional dimensions of education that machines cannot replicate. AI education is an inclusive dialogue involving all stakeholders—students, teachers, administrators, policymakers, and technologists—that deployment broader goals and values. Develop robust and transparent protection of student rights. Data stewardship, the responsible design implementation of AI tools. Ensuring digital literacy and critical thinking skills among learners is also vital, equipping them to engage with AI responsibly and understand its capabilities and limitations. In sum, it embodies powerful duality: on one hand, it revolutionizes learning it accessible, effective; on the other hand, it poses significant ethical risks that, if left unaddressed, could undermine equity, privacy, and trust in educational systems. Ethical reflection, rigorous, and inclusive policymaking are crucial to harnessing its benefits while mitigating its dangers. Only through a balanced, conscientious approach can education systems ensure force good is fostered and educators alike exacerbate challenges or create new forms of injustice.

THE IMPORTANCE OF ETHICS IN AI-DRIVEN EDUCATION

Incorporating AI into classrooms learning environments supports the well-being, while fostering equitable and effective educational outcomes. The transformative is accompanied by complex moral and social responsibilities. Without a firm grounding in ethics, AI applications risk perpetuating inequalities, violating privacy, undermining trust, and compromising the integrity of education itself. Thus, the ethical stewardship of AI in education emerges as a critical imperative for educators, developers, policymakers, and society at large (Khine M S., 2024). One of the foremost reasons ethics is vital in AI-driven education is the sheer scale and sensitivity of data that AI systems collect and process. Educational AI tools often gather extensive personal and behavioral information about students, including academic performance, learning habits, emotional responses, and sometimes biometric data. This trove of data, if not handled ethically, can lead to breaches of privacy, unauthorized surveillance, or exploitation of vulnerable populations. Ethical frameworks mandate informed consent, transparency about data use, and robust safeguards to protect student information from misuse or cyber threats. These protections are essential to legal to trust that students, parents, and educators place in educational institutions and technologies. Moreover, ethical considerations address the critical issue of fairness and inclusivity in AI-driven education and algorithms. If training data reflects societal or disability, the AI may reinforce discriminatory practices and unfairly disadvantage certain groups of learners (Klimova B., et al, 2023). For example, an AI tutor might inadvertently favor students from particular backgrounds, or automated grading systems might misjudge the work of students with non-traditional writing styles or those for whom English is a second language. Ethics demands a proactive commitment to identifying, mitigating, and correcting biases, ensuring that AI tools promote equity and do not exacerbate existing educational disparities.

Transparency and accountability represent another pillar. Many models are "black boxes," logic complex, opaque, and readily users. Undermine confusion and resentment among students and educators, especially when AI influences critical decisions such as grading, student placement, or intervention strategies. Ethical principles call for explainability, where AI systems provide clear, understandable reasons for their outputs, enabling educators and learners to make informed decisions and appeal unfair results. Accountability mechanisms must be established to delineate responsibility among AI developers, educators, and institutions, ensuring that when AI-driven errors or harms occur, there is a pathway for redress and improvement (Eden C A., et al, 2024). Ethics in AI-driven education also emphasizes the importance of preserving the human dimension of automating many tasks offer support, which cannot replicate the empathy, mentorship, and social engagement that human educators provide. Ethical deployment of AI involves designing technologies that complement rather than replace human teachers, empowering them with tools to better understand and support their students. It also involves cultivating critical digital literacy among learners so they can navigate and question AI applications thoughtfully, recognizing both their capabilities and limitations. In addition, demands inclusive participation in decision-making processes. Students, educators, parents, and communities must have a voice in shaping how AI is integrated into educational settings. This inclusivity ensures that diverse perspectives on governance technologies, reflecting societal values and educational goals. It also continues ethical reflection, which is essential as AI evolves and new challenges emerge. Furthermore, calls for common guidelines for AI in education (Samal A., et al, 2025). Differing cultural values, legal frameworks, and educational priorities must be reconciled to respect rights universally while allowing flexibility to adapt to local contexts. Ethical leadership at the institutional, national, and international levels is crucial to promote transparency, protect vulnerable populations, and educational opportunities. Ultimately, ethics education is the role of a compass guiding the deployment of powerful forces that shape minds futures of learners. At innovation, education systems harness transformative potential while safeguarding human dignity, promoting fairness, and fostering trust. As education continues to evolve in the digital age, ethics provides the foundation upon which AI can truly enhance learning, empower educators.

SOCIAL IMPLICATIONS OF AI IN EDUCATION: A CRITICAL EXAMINATION

As AI technologies permeate classrooms, learning management systems, and educational policy frameworks, their social implications become increasingly complex and multifaceted, warranting critical examination. These implications extend far beyond the immediate benefits of enhanced personalization or efficiency, touching upon issues of social equity, cultural norms, workforce transformation, and the democratization of knowledge. The widespread adoption of AI in education reshapes social relationships, power dynamics, and access to opportunity, raising crucial questions about who benefits, who is marginalized, and how societies navigate this technological transition. Significant social implications, impact on social equity and inclusion. AI-driven educational tools promise to potentially bridge gaps for learners who have traditionally been underserved or marginalized (Soundariya A., et al, 2025). For instance, AI can offer support for students with disabilities, language learners, or those in remote or under-resourced areas, theoretically democratizing access to quality education. However, the reality is often more nuanced. The deployment of AI systems frequently depends on the availability of technological infrastructure, digital literacy, and socioeconomic resources. This can exacerbate existing disparities, creating a digital divide where only students in well-funded schools or affluent regions can fully benefit from AI-enhanced learning. Furthermore, algorithms they perpetuating or amplifying social inequalities, thus reinforcing systemic disadvantages rather than alleviating them. The social fabric of education, therefore, faces a paradox where technology meant to empower may inadvertently marginalize, highlighting the need for conscious, inclusive design and policy interventions. From a broader societal perspective, the infusion of AI into education intersects with labor market trends and workforce development, generating far-reaching social implications. As AI automates certain educational functions, it reshapes the roles and demands placed on educators, requiring new skills and continuous professional development (Al-Zahrani A M., et al, 2024). This evolution can create tensions around job security, professional identity, and equitable access to retraining opportunities. At the same time, AI-driven education aims to prepare students for a future workforce dominated by automation and digital technologies. This raises critical questions about how education systems can balance foundational knowledge with emergent thinking, creativity, qualities not easily replicated by AI. The social contract between education and society is thus being renegotiated in the context of AI, with implications for social mobility, economic opportunity, and the capacity of education to foster informed, engaged citizens.

Culturally, AI in education challenges existing norms, values, and pedagogical traditions. The global proliferation of AI technologies risks imposing dominant cultural paradigms embedded in algorithms designed primarily in Western contexts, potentially marginalizing indigenous knowledge systems, local languages, and alternative ways of knowing. This cultural homogenization threatens educational diversity and pluralism, which are vital for fostering intercultural understanding and respect (Berson I R., et al, 2024). Moreover, AI's influence on knowledge dissemination and curriculum design can centralize control in the hands of technology providers and policymakers, limiting community and educator agency. The social implications here involve a shift in who sets educational priorities, shapes narratives, and determines what counts as valid knowledge, with consequences for cultural identity and social cohesion. Ethical considerations intertwined with social implications are critically pervasive in the commodification of student data. The social expectation of confidentiality and trust between students and educators is challenged by AI systems that sometimes monetize information. Potential misuse of data can lead to stigmatization, discrimination, or manipulation, eroding the foundational social trust necessary for effective education. Additionally, issues emerge as complex and social; this skepticism or resistance toward AI technologies influences public perception and acceptance (Bearman M., et al, 2023). Social implications of education profoundly affect equity, social relationships, cultural diversity, workforce dynamics, and ethical norms. A critical examination reveals that while AI holds transformative potential to enhance educational access and quality, it simultaneously poses risks that could deepen social inequalities, alter human interactions, and reshape cultural landscapes. Addressing these implications demands a concerted effort to embed ethical principles, inclusive design, and participatory governance into AI development and deployment. By doing so, societies can harness AI's benefits while safeguarding social values and promoting an equitable, inclusive, and socially responsive educational future.

BIAS AND FAIRNESS: ENSURING AI SYSTEMS ARE EQUITABLE

Bias in AI arises when algorithms, datasets, or system designs systematically produce prejudiced outcomes that disadvantage certain disability or other characteristics. Socially, such bias can have profound consequences, perpetuating inequality and undermining the promise of AI as a tool for empowerment and inclusion. Therefore, the pursuit of fairness in AI is not merely a technical problem but an ethical and social imperative that demands rigorous attention and multifaceted strategies. Typically originates from machine learning. Since AI learns patterns from historical data, it is susceptible to inheriting the biases embedded in that data. Educational system data shows that it fails to accurately understand or serve students from underrepresented groups (Farukh Arslan., et al, 2024). Historical inequalities, stereotypes, and exclusionary practices are thus encoded into datasets, leading AI to replicate or amplify these injustices. Moreover, data can be incomplete, noisy, or unrepresentative, further skewing AI outcomes. This phenomenon is often referred to as "algorithmic bias," and it reflects not just technical shortcomings but also deeper societal biases. Beyond data, bias can also stem from the design choices of AI developers and the objectives set for AI systems. The framing of a problem, the selection of performance metrics, and the exclusion of diverse perspectives during development can inadvertently introduce unfairness. For example, an AI grading system efficiency and nuanced forms of expression used by students from different cultural backgrounds. Similarly, transparency or concealing biased processes, making it difficult for users and challenging the "black box" of many AI, exacerbates accountability trust. Multifaceted, that resists simple definitions or solutions. It encompasses various dimensions, including distributive fairness (equitable allocation of resources or benefits), procedural fairness (transparency and consistency of processes), and representational fairness (inclusive and respectful portrayal of all groups) (Pulivarthy P., et al, 2025). Different contexts and stakeholders may prioritize these aspects differently, leading to trade-offs and tensions. For instance, maximizing overall accuracy may conflict with achieving equal error rates across demographic groups. Thus, fairness must be approached as a contextual, value-laden concept requiring careful negotiation and deliberation. On the technical front, researchers and practitioners develop methods to detect, quantify, and mitigate bias at various stages of AI development. Techniques include balanced and diverse data collection, bias-aware model training, fairness constraints, and post-processing adjustments. Algorithmic is increasingly used before and after deployment. However, technical fixes alone are insufficient without organizational commitment to inclusive design and continuous monitoring.

Organizationally, fostering diversity in AI development teams and engaging stakeholders from affected communities are critical to identifying and addressing potential biases early. Inclusive design processes encourage the incorporation of multiple perspectives, ethical reflection, and participatory decision-making. These practices help surface implicit assumptions and power dynamics that might otherwise be overlooked. Educational institutions, companies, and policymakers bear responsibility for embedding fairness as a core value, providing training, resources, and governance mechanisms to support ethical AI development (Rashidi H H., et al, 2025). Policy setting standards, and protecting individuals from harm. International organizations recognizing risks of biased AI are proposing legislation, guidelines, and principles aimed at example, requirements, rights to explanation, and data protection laws help create an environment where AI systems are subject to scrutiny and correction. Collaboration across sectors and borders is essential to harmonize these efforts and address the global nature of AI deployment. Importantly, ensuring fairness in AI is an achievement. AI systems operate societal values, and user behaviors evolve. Continuous evaluation, feedback loops, and adaptability are necessary to detect emerging biases and respond effectively. Conclusion, bias, and fairness represent central challenges to realizing full, equitable progress. Recognizing and confronting bias requires acknowledging the interplay of technical, social, and ethical dimensions of AI systems (Upadhyaya A N., et al, 2025). By integrating rigorous bias detection and mitigation techniques, fostering inclusive design and governance, and establishing robust policy frameworks, societies can work toward AI systems that truly embody fairness. In education and beyond, equitable AI not only mitigates harm but actively contributes to dismantling systemic inequalities, promoting dignity, opportunity, and justice for all individuals. The journey toward fair AI is complex and ongoing, but it is indispensable for building a future where technology serves the collective good without reinforcing historical injustices.

DATA PRIVACY: PROTECTING STUDENT INFORMATION IN AI-DRIVEN EDUCATION

The rapid integration into educational settings data collection, analysis, and personalized learning. While innovations function, they simultaneously raise urgent and complex concerns about data education or regulatory issues, foundational ethical issues that affect trust, safety, equity, and the very integrity of educational institutions. The sensitive nature of records, analytics, biometric identifiers, and even emotional responses demands stringent safeguards to prevent misuse, which could cause lasting harm to families and communities. At the heart of data privacy concerns in AI-driven education lies the sheer volume and granularity of data collected. Unlike traditional educational records, AI systems often aggregate vast streams of real-time data, including keystrokes, eye tracking, facial expressions, and interaction patterns (Thirunagalingam A., et al, 2025). These datasets enable powerful insights but also increase the risk of invasive surveillance and profiling. The detailed nature of such data can reveal intimate aspects of a student's personality, mental health, learning disabilities, and socio-emotional state—information that, if mishandled, could lead to stigmatization or discrimination. For example, as "at-risk" behavior patterns, but if this data is improperly shared or leaked, it could negatively impact the student's academic opportunities or social standing. Thus, the ethical stewardship of student data requires a robust understanding of the risks inherent in its collection and use. The question of consent and agency is central to protecting data privacy in education. Students—especially minors—and their guardians must be adequately informed about how long it will be retained. Unfortunately, data processing makes transparency challenging, leaving many families unaware of the scope and implications of data collection. Ethical data practices demand clear, accessible communication and mechanisms for meaningful consent, allowing students and parents, where appropriate. Empowering students with digital literacy to understand their rights and the trade-offs of data use is equally important for fostering trust and autonomy in AI-enabled learning environments (Rosenstrauch D., et al, 2023). Data privacy also intersects with issues of equity and justice. Students from marginalized or vulnerable populations may face heightened risks if their data is exploited or exposed. For instance, students in low-income schools or those belonging to racial minorities might have less access to privacy protections or be disproportionately targeted by surveillance technologies purportedly aimed at improving safety or behavior. Such disparities can exacerbate educational inequities and contribute to a climate of mistrust and fear. Ensuring that data privacy protections are applied equitably requires proactive rights and dignity for all, particularly those historically underserved or vulnerable.

Acts establish standards for data collection, consent, access, and breach notification. However, the rapid pace of AI innovation often outstrips the development and enforcement of such regulations, creating gaps that can be exploited. Policymakers must therefore update and harmonize privacy laws flows, and data portability, while balancing innovation and protection. Collaboration between regulators, educators, technologists, and civil society is crucial for crafting comprehensive policies that reflect the complex realities of AI in education. Beyond compliance, ethical leadership in educational institutions is critical to cultivating a culture of privacy and respect (Oyeniran C O., et al, 2022). This includes training educators and administrators on data protection principles, establishing privacy officers or committees, and engaging students and families in ongoing conversations about data use and rights. Transparency reports and open communication channels can build community trust and demonstrate institutional commitment to safeguarding student information. Furthermore, ethical AI development involves designing systems that incorporate privacy by design and default, embedding data protection mechanisms from the earliest stages of technology creation rather than as afterthoughts. The implications of failing to protect student data privacy are profound. Breaches can lead to identity theft, psychological harm, loss of educational opportunities, and erosion of trust in educational institutions and technologies. Beyond individual harm, widespread privacy violations risk undermining public confidence in AI-driven education, hindering adoption and innovation. Therefore, protecting student data privacy is essential not only for individual rights but also for sustainable systems (Luca E., 2023). Protecting student information in AI-driven education is a multifaceted challenge that demands technical rigor, legal oversight, ethical commitment, and active stakeholder engagement. The sensitive nature of educational data, coupled with calls for vigilant, proactive measures to safeguard privacy and surveillance or exploitation. By prioritizing transparency, consent, equity, and security, educators and policymakers can build trust and foster an environment where AI enhances learning while respecting the fundamental rights of every student. As AI continues to evolve, maintaining a steadfast commitment to data privacy will be paramount in shaping an educational future that is innovative, inclusive, and just.

TRANSPARENCY AND ACCOUNTABILITY: UNDERSTANDING AI DECISION-MAKING

As artificial intelligence (AI) systems become increasingly embedded in critical societal domains—including education, healthcare, criminal justice, and public administration accountability decision-making becomes ever more urgent. Clarity with which systems reveal their inner workings, methodologies, and decision logic to users, stakeholders, and regulators. Accountability involves the mechanisms through which individuals and organizations can be held outcomes produced, harms addressed, and ethical standards upheld. Together, transparency and accountability form the ethical backbone of trustworthy AI, fostering confidence, fairness, and legitimacy in the deployment of automated decision-making tools. Understanding how AI decisions are made and who is responsible for them is fundamental to preventing abuses, mitigating biases, and enabling informed participation by affected individuals (Rousi R., et al, 2024). Operate "black boxes," processing vast amounts of data through intricate, multi-layered architectures that defy straightforward human interpretation. While the outputs—such as predictions, classifications, or recommendations—may be clear, the rationale behind these outputs is frequently opaque, even to the developers who create the systems. This opacity poses significant risks in contexts like education, where AI might influence student assessment, placement, or support services. Without understanding how and why decisions are made, educators, students, and parents may feel powerless to question or contest AI-generated outcomes, potentially perpetuating unfairness or error. Transparency is thus not merely about revealing technical details but about making AI systems comprehensible and accessible to diverse audiences, enabling meaningful scrutiny and dialogue. Achieving transparency requires both technical innovations and organizational commitments. Develop models or post-hoc tools that provide interpretable explanations of AI decisions, highlighting key features, decision pathways, or confidence levels. For example, an AI system assessing student essays might indicate which aspects of grammar, content, or structure influenced the final grade. These explanations empower understanding of challenge reasoning, facilitating collaborative decision-making and trust-building (Kolenbrander J., et al, 2025). However, explainability must balance detail with clarity, avoiding overwhelming users with technical jargon or excessive information. Additionally, transparency extends to data provenance and model development processes, including disclosures about training data sources, potential biases, and limitations, allowing systems. In education, accountability may rest with AI developers, school administrators, teachers, or policymakers, depending on the context and nature of AI use. Establishing accountability frameworks involves creating policies, standards, and regulatory mechanisms that define duties, rights, and remedies. For instance, regulatory bodies may require impact assessments before AI deployment, mandates for periodic audits, and mechanisms for redress or appeals when AI decisions adversely affect students. Accountability also entails documenting and reporting on AI performance and errors, fostering transparency in institutions.

Critical component accountability is the legal and ethical principle of human oversight. Despite AI's autonomy in processing and decision-making, ultimate responsibility should reside with human agents who can interpret, override, or halt AI actions when necessary. This "human-in-the-loop" approach safeguards against blind reliance on automated systems, ensuring that ethical judgment, empathy, and contextual understanding guide final decisions. In educational settings, teachers and administrators must retain authority to review AI recommendations, considering broader social and individual factors that AI may not capture. Human oversight also protects against algorithmic determinism, where AI outputs are perceived as infallible or final, which can undermine agency and critical thinking (Patty J., 2024). Transparency and accountability are intertwined with broader social values such as justice, fairness, and democratic participation. Transparent AI systems enable affected communities to engage in governance processes, voice concerns, and influence how AI is designed and deployed. This participatory dimension helps prevent technology providers from being institutional actors, democratizing AI governance. Accountability mechanisms reinforce social trust, as stakeholders see that there are meaningful consequences for negligence or abuse, and that AI is subject to ethical and legal standards akin to those governing human actors. Without transparency and accountability, AI risks becoming a source of alienation, discrimination, and social fragmentation rather than a tool for empowerment and inclusion. However, transparency and accountability face practical and philosophical challenges. Complete transparency may conflict with proprietary business interests, intellectual property rights, or security concerns, limiting the amount of information that developers can disclose. There is also the risk of "transparency overload," where excessive or poorly presented information hinders rather than helps understanding. Philosophically, the question arises whether fully interpreting complex AI models is feasible or even desirable, given the trade-offs between model performance and explainability (Hubballi R B., et al, 2025). Moreover, accountability frameworks must grapple with distributed responsibility in AI ecosystems involving multiple actors, from data suppliers to algorithm designers and end-users, complicating the attribution of blame or liability. To address these challenges, multidisciplinary collaboration among technologists, ethicists, legal experts, educators, and civil society is essential. Standards and best practices for transparency and accountability must be co-created and iteratively refined, reflecting technological advances and societal values. Educational programs can raise awareness and build capacity among stakeholders to engage critically with AI systems. Public policies should incentivize transparency and accountability through regulatory oversight, certification processes, and mechanisms for public participation. International cooperation is also necessary to harmonize approaches and ensure that AI governance respects human rights globally.

THE DIGITAL DIVIDE: ENSURING ACCESS TO AI-DRIVEN EDUCATION

As technologies become educational systems worldwide, the issue of the digital divide emerges as a critical barrier to equitable learning opportunities. Persistent individuals and communities, including adequate hardware, software, and reliable internet connectivity, and those who do not. In the context of AI-driven education, this divide transcends simple access to devices; it encompasses disparities in digital literacy, quality of AI tools available, and the ability to effectively engage with AI-powered learning platforms. Thus that education does not reinforce or deepen societal inequities but instead fosters inclusive and democratic learning environments. At the most fundamental level, it reflects the unequal necessity that is necessary for AI-driven education. High-speed internet, modern computers, tablets, and smartphones are prerequisites for interacting with AI platforms that offer personalized tutoring, adaptive assessments, and immersive educational experiences (Maheswaran K., et al, 2025). However, millions of students globally lack reliable internet connections or up-to-date devices, limiting their ability to benefit from AI-enhanced learning. For example, rural areas often suffer from poor broadband infrastructure, while economically disadvantaged families may struggle to afford multiple devices for children, especially in households with several students. The COVID-19 pandemic starkly highlighted these disparities as education shifted rapidly online, revealing that access issues are not only a technological problem but also a socio-economic challenge intertwined with broader patterns of poverty and marginalization. Beyond hardware and connectivity, the digital divide extends into disparities in knowledge required to evaluate, use AI-driven educational tools, often assuming a baseline of digital competence that not all students, teachers, or parents possess. Training students to engage meaningfully with AI platforms, while educators may find it difficult to integrate these tools into their pedagogical practices. This gap limits the effectiveness of AI-driven education and risks creating a two-tiered system where only digitally literate populations can harness the full advantages of technology-enhanced learning (Akinrinola O., et al, 2024). Moreover, digital literacy is closely linked to socio-cultural factors, including language proficiency, educational background, and cognitive abilities, underscoring the need for culturally responsive and accessible AI solutions. Another dimension of the digital divide involves the quality and relevance of AI educational content and tools available to different populations. AI systems are often developed and tested in technologically advanced, resource-rich environments, resulting in products that may not be culturally appropriate, linguistically inclusive, or sensitive to the specific educational contexts of underserved communities. Consequently, students without access to localized or contextually relevant AI tools may receive suboptimal educational experiences, reducing engagement and learning outcomes. This issue highlights the importance of inclusive AI design that incorporates diverse data sources, stakeholder input, and adaptive functionalities to serve varied learner needs and backgrounds.

The digital divide also raises critical equity concerns related to the perpetuation of systemic inequalities. Students lacking access to AI-driven education face not only immediate learning disadvantages but also long-term impacts on social mobility, economic opportunity, and civic participation. In an increasingly digital and automated world, AI literacy and proficiency become essential skills, and exclusion from these technologies risks reinforcing cycles of poverty and disenfranchisement. Additionally, the digital divide social stratification, including gender, requires intersectional approaches to policy and practice that address multiple axes of disadvantage simultaneously (Williams R., et al, 2022). Addressing the digital divide in AI-driven education demands coordinated efforts across multiple levels of society. Governments play a pivotal role in investing in digital infrastructure, subsidizing internet access, and providing devices to underserved populations. Public-private partnerships can mobilize resources and expertise to expand connectivity and develop affordable, high-quality AI educational tools tailored to diverse contexts. Educational institutions must prioritize digital literacy training for students, educators, and families, embedding these competencies within curricula and professional development programs. Furthermore, inclusive AI design principles should be institutionalized, ensuring that AI products are accessible, culturally sensitive, and adaptable to minority language groups. Policy frameworks and funding mechanisms must also evolve to support sustainable solutions that bridge the digital divide. This includes incentivizing innovation in low-cost AI technologies, mandating equity-focused impact assessments, and enforcing accountability standards for AI vendors to prevent exclusionary practices (Muthusubramanian M., et al, 2024). Community engagement and participatory governance are essential to identify local barriers and co-create strategies that reflect lived realities. For example, community-based digital hubs or learning centers can provide shared access points and technical support in areas where home connectivity is limited. In conclusion, the digital divide represents one of the most significant challenges to equitable Without deliberate, inclusive, sustained efforts to ensure access to technology, digital literacy, and culturally relevant AI tools, AI-driven education risks deepening existing disparities and excluding millions of learners from the benefits of technological innovation. By prioritizing equitable access, digital inclusion, and participatory design, society can harness AI's transformative power to create educational environments that are truly inclusive, empowering, and capable of preparing all students for a rapidly changing future.

STUDENT AGENCY: EMPOWERING LEARNERS IN AI-DRIVEN EDUCATION

Fostering student agency emerges as a fundamental principle for ensuring that learners are active participants in their educational journeys rather than passive recipients of automated instruction. Student agency refers to the capacity of learners to make choices, take initiative, and exercise control over their learning processes. It embodies empowerment, autonomy, and self-efficacy—qualities essential not only for academic success but for lifelong learning and adaptive problem-solving in a complex, technology-saturated world. As AI systems increasingly personalize learning, recommend resources, and guide instructional paths, the challenge and opportunity lie in designing these technologies and pedagogical approaches to support and enhance student agency, thereby nurturing motivated, confident, and critically engaged learners (Li H., 2023). At its core, student agency involves learners' ability to set goals, reflect on their progress, make decisions about their learning strategies, and seek feedback to improve. AI-driven education platforms hold immense potential to facilitate these dimensions by providing personalized, real-time insights tailored to individual strengths, weaknesses, and interests. Adaptive learning technologies, for example, can empower students to explore subjects at their own pace, select pathways that align with their curiosity, and receive scaffolded support that responds dynamically to their evolving needs. Moreover, AI can enhance metacognitive skills—learners' awareness and regulation of their cognition, which are central to student agency. Through interactive dashboards, progress trackers, and reflective prompts, AI platforms can help students monitor their understanding, identify areas for improvement, and plan subsequent learning activities. This data-driven self-awareness transforms students into reflective practitioners who actively participate in shaping their educational trajectories. Such empowerment aligns with contemporary educational theories that emphasize learner-centeredness, self-regulation, and critical thinking as pillars of effective education. However, realizing genuine student agency in AI-driven education is complex and fraught with challenges (Gašević D., et al, 2023). A primary concern is that AI systems, if designed and deployed without careful attention to learner autonomy, risk creating overly prescriptive or deterministic learning experiences. When AI algorithms tightly control content sequencing, pacing, or assessment criteria without room for student input, they can inadvertently undermine agency by constraining choice and fostering passivity. For instance, an AI tutor that rigidly directs learners to remediate specific skills without considering student interests or alternative strategies might diminish motivation and reduce engagement. Therefore, AI-driven platforms must be designed with flexibility and transparency, enabling learners to understand and influence how AI guides their learning.

Figure 1. Ethical AI Explained

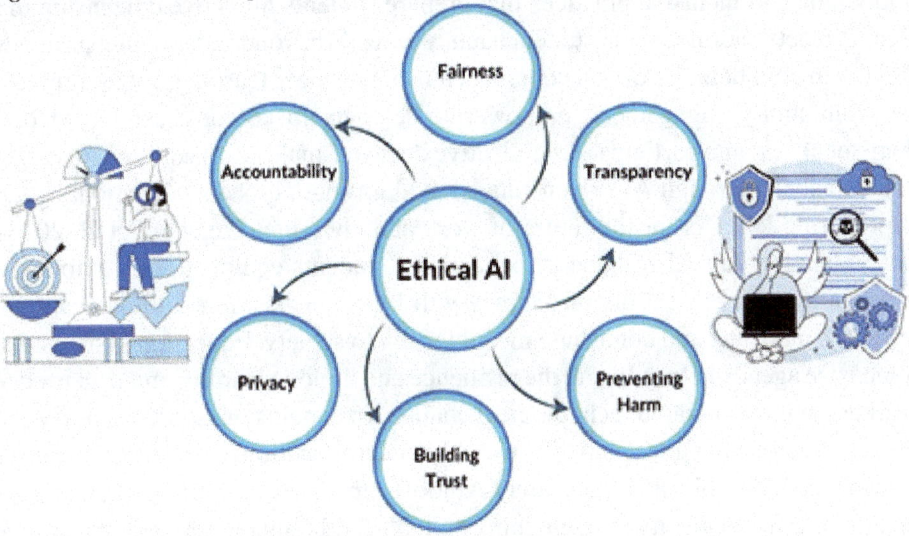

Another challenge involves equity and inclusivity. Students come from diverse cultural, linguistic, socio-economic, and cognitive backgrounds, and their experiences with agency vary widely. AI systems must be sensitive to these differences, avoiding biases that limit certain groups' opportunities for autonomous learning or that impose normative standards of engagement. For example, learners with disabilities may require alternative interaction modes or additional supports to exercise agency effectively. Similarly, culturally responsive AI design is necessary to respect and incorporate diverse values, languages, and ways of knowing. Without these considerations, AI-driven education risks perpetuating existing inequities by marginalizing voices and experiences that do not conform to dominant paradigms. Empowering student agency also requires educators to play an active role in mediating AI interactions and fostering environments conducive to autonomy and critical inquiry (Ellikkal A., et al, 2024). Teachers must be equipped not only to interpret AI-generated data but to coach learners in goal-setting, self-reflection, and decision-making skills. This pedagogical guidance helps students leverage AI as a tool for empowerment rather than feeling overwhelmed or controlled by technology. Professional development and curriculum redesign are vital to integrate

AI literacy and agency-supportive practices into classrooms, promoting a culture where students and teachers collaborate in shaping AI-mediated learning experiences. To cultivate student agency effectively, participatory design approaches are gaining prominence, involving learners directly in the development and evaluation of AI educational technologies. Designers' platforms reflect learners' preferences, needs, and aspirations. This collaborative process itself reinforces agency, modeling democratic and inclusive practices that prepare students for active citizenship in a digital society. Furthermore, student agency extends beyond individual learning to social and collaborative dimensions. AI can support peer learning, group projects, and community engagement, empowering learners to co-construct knowledge, share feedback, and participate in collective decision-making. In addition, fostering student agency through AI-driven education aligns with broader educational goals of preparing learners for the future of work and civic life (Eager B., et al, 2023). As automation and AI reshape labor markets, students equipped with autonomy, adaptability, and critical digital literacy will be better positioned to navigate uncertainty, innovate, and contribute meaningfully to society. Education systems that emphasize agency help cultivate the resilience and lifelong learning mindset needed in an era marked by rapid technological change. In conclusion, student agency is a vital cornerstone of ethical and effective AI-driven education experiences. Through personalized, flexible, and transparent AI tools supported by thoughtful pedagogy, education can become more engaging, equitable, and transformative. Overcoming challenges related to design, equity, and ethics requires collaborative efforts among technologists, educators, policymakers, and learners themselves. Ultimately, fostering student agency in AI-enhanced learning environments not only improves educational outcomes but also nurtures empowered individuals capable of thriving in and shaping a complex, AI-infused future.

THE IMPACT OF AI ON LEARNING OUTCOMES: OPPORTUNITIES AND CHALLENGES

Artificial intelligence (AI) has rapidly transformed the educational landscape, offering both unprecedented opportunities and significant challenges in shaping learning outcomes. At its best, AI holds the promise of revolutionizing how students acquire knowledge and skills, delivering highly personalized, adaptive, and engaging learning experiences that can optimize individual potential. Yet, despite its potential, it is complex, nuanced, and contingent upon factors such as implementation fidelity, contextual relevance, and equitable access. Understanding both the opportunities and challenges power to improve educational effectiveness while mitigating unintended consequences (Xiao Y., et al, 2023). Lauded advantages AI instruction meets the unique needs of each learner, thereby potentially enhancing mastery and retention in real time, adjusting difficulty, modality to fit individual learning styles and proficiencies. This is in traditional classrooms due to teacher-to-student ratios and time constraints. By providing differentiated instruction, AI can help close achievement gaps and support learners who might otherwise struggle in a one-size-fits-all environment. For example, language can receive customized scaffolding, which facilitates deeper understanding and reduces frustration, contributing to improved academic outcomes. Moreover, AI can enhance engagement through interactive and immersive intelligent tutoring systems, and gamified platforms leverage AI to create stimulating educational experiences that motivate learners and foster active participation. Research suggests that increased engagement correlates strongly with better learning outcomes, as motivated students are more likely to persist through challenges, retain information, and develop higher-order cognitive skills (Labadze L., et al, 2023). Instant, specific guidance that helps correct mistakes and refine skills continuously. This immediate feedback loop supports formative assessment practices, enabling learners to take ownership of their progress and educators to intervene more effectively. In addition to individual learning gains, AI facilitates data-driven insights that can inform instructional strategies and curriculum design, potentially improving outcomes at systemic levels. By aggregating and analyzing vast datasets, AI tools identify patterns of success and difficulty across populations, highlighting effective pedagogical approaches and content areas requiring enhancement. These insights empower educators to refine teaching methods and policymakers to allocate resources more strategically. AI can also automate administrative tasks related to assessment, reporting, educators higher-order that contribute to better student learning experiences.

Another challenge quality, transparency that drive learning outcomes, incomplete datasets, inequities, resulting in differential learning experiences and outcomes among diverse student groups. For instance, if an AI platform favors certain cultural norms, languages, or cognitive approaches, it may marginalize learners from underrepresented backgrounds, limiting their educational progress. The opacity of many AI algorithms also poses difficulties in understanding how decisions and recommendations are made, complicating efforts to evaluate their educational impact and fairness. Ensuring algorithmic accountability and incorporating inclusive design principles are therefore crucial to prevent harm and promote equitable learning. Additionally, the effectiveness of AI in improving learning outcomes is highly dependent on context, including teacher readiness, institutional support, and infrastructure quality (Owan V J., et al, 2023). Without adequate training and professional development, educators may struggle to integrate AI tools effectively, diminishing their potential benefits. Schools with limited technological resources or unstable internet connectivity may find it difficult to implement AI-driven solutions, perpetuating disparities in educational quality. Furthermore, curricular alignment is necessary to ensure that AI applications reinforce learning objectives and standards rather than distract or detract from coherent instruction. Empirical research on AI's impact on learning outcomes remains nascent and mixed, highlighting the need for rigorous, long-term studies that consider diverse educational contexts and learner populations. While many pilot studies and small-scale implementations report positive effects such as improved test scores, engagement, and motivation, these findings often vary and may not scale uniformly. Research must examine not only cognitive gains but also affective, social, and ethical dimensions to paint a holistic picture of AI's educational impact. Continuous evaluation, feedback, and iterative refinement of AI tools are necessary to optimize learning outcomes and minimize adverse effects (Sakthivel M., et al, 2025). Looking forward, the future impact of AI on learning outcomes will likely depend on a balanced, human-centered approach that integrates technological innovation with pedagogical expertise, equity considerations, and ethical stewardship. AI can serve as a powerful amplifier of educational quality by augmenting teacher capacity, providing personalized support, and enabling data-informed decision-making. However, its benefits will be realized only if deployed within inclusive, well-supported, and transparent educational ecosystems that prioritize student well-being and holistic development. In conclusion, AI presents both transformative opportunities and profound challenges for learning outcomes. Its capacity to personalize instruction, enhance engagement, and provide actionable insights holds promise for raising achievement and fostering equity. Yet, risks related to diminished human interaction, algorithmic bias, contextual limitations, and ethical concerns necessitate careful, thoughtful integration. Only through such a balanced and inclusive approach can AI contribute meaningfully and equitably to improved learning outcomes across diverse educational landscapes.

CHANGING ROLES OF TEACHERS: ADAPTING TO AI-DRIVEN EDUCATION

The advent of the traditional role of teachers compelled educators to adapt to new pedagogical paradigms, technological tools, and evolving expectations. Far from rendering teachers obsolete, AI is transforming the profession by shifting responsibilities, amplifying instructional capabilities, and demanding new skills, mindsets, and ethical considerations. As AI systems take on tasks such as content delivery, personalized tutoring, assessment, and administrative duties, teachers find their roles evolving from primary sources of knowledge to facilitators of learning, mentors, and critical interpreters of AI-generated insights (Kotte K R., et al, 2025). This transformation is multifaceted, encompassing pedagogical, relational, and professional dimensions that redefine what it means to be a teacher in an AI-enhanced educational environment. One of the most significant shifts in teachers' roles concerns their relationship with knowledge and instruction. Traditionally, teachers have been viewed as the primary conveyors of information, guiding students through curriculum content and providing explanations. However, AI-driven education platforms can now deliver personalized lessons, adaptive exercises, and instant feedback tailored to individual learner needs, enabling students to explore content independently and at their own pace. In this context, teachers transition from "sage on the stage" to "guide on the side," focusing less on direct instruction and more on facilitating inquiry, critical thinking, and problem-solving. They become designers of rich learning experiences, curators of resources, and coaches who support learners in navigating AI-mediated educational pathways. This pedagogical shift emphasizes higher-order cognitive skills and learner autonomy, requiring teachers to cultivate environments where students actively construct knowledge rather than passively receive it (Aghaziarati A., et al, 2023). The integration of AI also demands that teachers develop new competencies in data literacy and technology fluency. AI systems about which teachers must be informed to make informed instructional decisions. This requires skills in analyzing dashboards, understanding algorithmic outputs, and integrating data-driven insights with professional judgment and contextual knowledge. Teachers are increasingly tasked with mediating between AI recommendations and the complex, dynamic realities of the classroom, ensuring that technology augments rather than dictates pedagogy. Consequently, ongoing professional development in AI literacy, ethical use of data, and adaptive teaching strategies becomes essential. Educators recognize their limitations, advocate for equitable and transparent applications that serve diverse learners effectively.

Beyond instructional roles, AI reshapes the relational and emotional dimensions of teaching. As AI handles routine content delivery, teachers have more time for interpersonal relationships, fostering motivation, addressing social-emotional needs, and creating supportive learning communities. Emotional intelligence, empathy, and cultural responsiveness become even more critical competencies as teachers guide students through complex cognitive and affective landscapes. This human-centered focus reinforces the irreplaceable value of teachers in nurturing students' holistic development, resilience, and ethical reasoning, aspects that AI cannot replicate. AI's rise may underscore the importance of these uniquely human qualities, positioning teachers as advocates for student well-being and facilitators of meaningful human connection in increasingly technology-mediated classrooms (Hutson J., et al, 2023). Moreover, the changing educational ecosystem calls for teachers to embrace lifelong learning and adaptability as core professional attributes. Rapid technological advancements and shifting societal demands require educators to continuously update their knowledge, pedagogical approaches, and technical skills. This dynamic professional landscape fosters a culture of experimentation, innovation, and reflective practice, where teachers actively participate in co-designing AI-enhanced learning environments. By engaging in collaborative networks, professional learning communities, and interdisciplinary partnerships, teachers can share best practices, troubleshoot challenges, and contribute to the evolving knowledge base about AI in education. Such professional growth not only benefits individual teachers but also strengthens the capacity of education systems to integrate AI thoughtfully and sustainably. The transformation of teacher roles is not without challenges and tensions. Some educators may feel threatened or fear job displacement or loss of autonomy. Others may encounter resistance due to a lack of adequate training, infrastructural support, or clear guidance on integrating AI tools effectively. Addressing these concerns requires comprehensive strategies that prioritize teacher agency, voice, and well-being. Policymakers and educational leaders must invest in accessible professional development, equitable resource distribution, and supportive infrastructures that empower teachers to adapt confidently. Additionally, fostering a positive culture around AI adoption—characterized by transparency, collaboration, and trust—can alleviate anxieties and promote constructive engagement with technological innovation. In practical terms, AI-driven education is catalyzing a reconceptualization of teacher identity and professional purpose (Pillai R., et al, 2024). The teacher of the future is envisioned not simply as a content expert or classroom manager but as an orchestrator of complex learning ecosystems, a mediator between humans and intelligent machines, and a champion of ethical, equitable, and student-centered education. This expanded role calls for rethinking teacher education programs to incorporate interdisciplinary training in AI, ethics, data science, and collaborative problem-solving. Equipping future educators with these competencies will prepare them to thrive in hybrid learning environments and to lead innovation in educational practice. In conclusion, the roles of teachers are undergoing a profound transformation in response to AI-driven education. While AI automates and enhances various instructional and administrative functions, it simultaneously elevates the importance of human qualities such as empathy, critical judgment, and ethical stewardship. Teachers are called upon to adapt to new pedagogical models, develop data and technology literacy, advocate for equitable AI use, and foster holistic student development. Navigating this transition demands systemic support, ongoing professional growth, and active teacher involvement in AI integration processes. Ultimately, synergizing human and learning is dynamic, inclusive, and deeply human-centered, where teachers remain indispensable catalysts of curiosity, creativity, and critical thinking.

CONCLUSION

Its integration into education holds tremendous promise for transforming how knowledge is delivered, personalized, and assessed. Envisions intelligent systems capable of learning, facilitating personalized learning paths, automating administrative tasks, supporting educators with actionable insights, and fostering inclusive environments that accommodate diverse learners. Innovations AI-powered intelligent content creation, data-driven decision support, are poised to make education more accessible, engaging, and effective. However, this wave of technological innovation brings with it profound ethical, social, and practical challenges that require careful balancing of creativity and responsibility. The future of AI in education will depend not only on the sophistication of technology but also on how well stakeholders embed principles of fairness, transparency, privacy, and human-centeredness into its design, deployment, and governance. Looking forward, AI's role in personalizing education will likely become more nuanced and sophisticated. Leveraging advances in affective computing, AI could better understand learners' cognitive states, emotional engagement, and contextual backgrounds, tailoring instruction and feedback with unprecedented precision. This personalized approach holds the potential to close achievement gaps by addressing individual thus promoting equity analytics could empower customized curriculum design. Moreover, the capacity to automate routine administrative record-keeping would free mentorship, creativity, and social-emotional support, overall. In parallel, AI-powered content generation and immersive technologies like augmented and virtual reality promise to revolutionize educational resources. Intelligent systems could dynamically generate customized learning materials, simulate complex experiments, or facilitate virtual field trips, thereby enriching engagement and deepening understanding. Multilingual AI tools could break down language barriers, fostering global collaboration and inclusivity. Furthermore, AI's ability to facilitate lifelong learning and skill development by offering micro-credentials, adaptive assessments, and career guidance can help learners navigate the evolving demands of the digital economy. The convergence of AI for credential verification for classrooms could further enhance transparency, security, and interactivity in education. Despite these exciting prospects, significant challenges must be addressed to avoid unintended harms. One primary concern is the risk of exacerbating existing inequities due to could marginalize students from low-income or rural backgrounds, undermining the inclusive potential of AI-driven education. Addressing infrastructure gaps and ensuring affordable, equitable access to AI tools will be critical to realizing their benefits broadly. Another challenge lies in mitigating systems, which can lead to unfair treatment if left unchecked. As AI increasingly influences decisions around admissions, assessment, and student support, robust frameworks for fairness, accountability, and bias mitigation future.

Crucially, the dimension of must remain central in the AI-driven future. Teachers will continue to play indispensable roles as facilitators, mentors, and ethical stewards who interpret AI insights within pedagogical and social contexts. Rather than replacing educators, AI should augment their capabilities, providing tools that enhance creativity, empathy, and human connection. Preparing teachers with AI literacy and professional development will be essential to maximize the positive impacts of AI while mitigating risks. Similarly, empowering students to understand and critically engage with AI technologies cultivates digital citizenship and agency, enabling learners' world. Governance and policy frameworks will be pivotal in shaping the trajectory of AI in education. Multi-stakeholder collaboration among educators, technologists, policymakers, students, parents, and civil society will be necessary to co-create ethical guidelines, standards, and accountability mechanisms. Transparent AI systems with explainability features will build trust and enable contestability of automated decisions. Ethical review boards and impact assessments should be standard practice before widespread AI adoption. International cooperation can foster harmonized standards that promote equitable access and responsible innovation across contexts. also demands continuous research to understand long-term impacts, emergent ethical dilemmas, and effectiveness across different populations and settings. Interdisciplinary inquiry combining AI technology, pedagogy, psychology, and sociology can inform evidence-based practices and guide iterative improvements. Open dialogue and knowledge sharing about successes, failures, and lessons learned will accelerate responsible innovation and avoid repeating past mistakes. In conclusion, the future holds remarkable opportunities, personalized, accessible, and engaging. Yet, these innovations must be pursued with deliberate care to uphold ethical standards, protect privacy, ensure fairness, and preserve the essential human elements of teaching and learning. Balancing innovation with responsibility, excellence with foresight, robust governance, and inclusive stakeholder engagement. By embracing this balanced vision, the educational community can transform effective, human-centered learning environments that prepare learners 21st century beyond.

REFERENCES

Aghaziarati, A., Nejatifar, S., & Abedi, A. (2023). Artificial intelligence in education: Investigating teacher attitudes. *AI and Tech in Behavioral and Social Sciences, 1*(1), 35–42. DOI: 10.61838/kman.aitech.1.1.6

Akinrinola, O., Okoye, C. C., Ofodile, O. C., & Ugochukwu, C. E. (2024). Navigating and reviewing ethical dilemmas in AI development: Strategies for transparency, fairness, and accountability. *GSC Advanced Research and Reviews, 18*(3), 50–58. DOI: 10.30574/gscarr.2024.18.3.0088

Al-Zahrani, A. M., & Alasmari, T. M. (2024). Exploring the impact of artificial intelligence on higher education: The dynamics of ethical, social, and educational implications. *Humanities & Social Sciences Communications, 11*, 03432. Advance online publication. DOI: 10.1057/s41599-024-03432-4

Arslan, F., Haydar, B., & Ullah, F. (2024). *Bridging theory and practice: AI applications in learning and teaching in Pakistan's education system*. ResearchGate., DOI: 10.3847/rg.2024.383206313

Bearman, M., Ryan, J., & Ajjawi, R. (2023). Discourses of artificial intelligence in higher education: A critical literature review. *Higher Education, 86*, 369–385. DOI: 10.1007/s10734-022-00937-2

Berson, I. R., & Berson, M. J. (2024). AI in K-12 social studies education: A critical examination of ethical and practical challenges. In Artificial intelligence in education conference proceedings (pp. 101–112). Springer. https://doi.org/DOI: 10.1007/978-3-031-64315-6_8

Eager, B., & Brunton, R. (2023). Prompting higher education towards AI-augmented teaching and learning practice. *Journal of University Teaching & Learning Practice, 20*(5), 1–20. DOI: 10.53761/1.20.5.02

Eden, C. A., Chisom, O. N., & Adeniyi, I. S. (2024). Integrating AI in education: Opportunities, challenges, and ethical considerations. *Magna Scientia Advanced Research and Reviews, 10*(2), 6–13. DOI: 10.30574/msarr.2024.10.2.0039

Ellikkal, A., & Rajamohan, S. (2024). AI-enabled personalized learning: Empowering management students for improving engagement and academic performance. *Vilakshan-XIMB Journal of Management, 22*(1), 88–102. DOI: 10.1108/xjm-02-2024-0023

Gašević, D., Siemens, G., & Sadiq, S. (2023). Empowering learners for the age of artificial intelligence. *Computers and Education: Artificial Intelligence*, *4*, 100130. Advance online publication. DOI: 10.1016/j.caeai.2023.100130

Hubballi, R. B., Selvakumar, P., Seenivasan, R., Basava Aradhya, S. G., Dinesh, N., & Seelam, P. K. (2025). Overview of current AI technologies in education. In Kyei-Blankson, L., & Ntuli, E. (Eds.), *Transformative AI practices for personalized learning strategies* (pp. 1–26). IGI Global Scientific Publishing., DOI: 10.4018/979-8-3693-8744-3.ch001

Hutson, J., & Ceballos, J. (2023). Rethinking education in the age of AI: The importance of developing durable skills in the Industry 4.0. *Journal of Information Economics*, *1*(2), 9–26. DOI: 10.58567/jie01020002

Khine, M. S. (2024). Ethics, and the future of education in an AI-driven world. In *Artificial intelligence in education: A machine learning perspective* (pp. 629–735). Springer., DOI: 10.1007/978-981-97-9350-1_6

Klimova, B., Pikhart, M., & Kacetl, J. (2023). Ethical issues of the use of AI-driven mobile apps for education. *Frontiers in Public Health*, *10*, 1118116. Advance online publication. DOI: 10.3389/fpubh.2022.1118116 PMID: 36711343

Kolenbrander, J., & Michaels, A. J. (2025). Personality emulation utilizing large language models. *Applied Sciences (Basel, Switzerland)*, *15*(12), 6636. Advance online publication. DOI: 10.3390/app15126636

Kotte, K. R., & Attaluri, V. (2025). Revolutionising retail banking with AI and virtual technologies: AI-driven financial training. In Nair, A. J., Manohar, S., Limbu, Y. B., & Huhmann, B. A. (Eds.), *Intersecting natural language processing and FinTech innovations in service marketing* (pp. 421–440). IGI Global Scientific Publishing., DOI: 10.4018/979-8-3693-9944-6.ch020

Labadze, L., Grigolia, M., & Machaidze, L. (2023). Role of AI chatbots in education: Systematic literature review. *International Journal of Educational Technology in Higher Education*, *20*, 56. Advance online publication. DOI: 10.1186/s41239-023-00426-1

Li, H. (2023). AI in education: Bridging the divide or widening the gap? Exploring equity, opportunities, and challenges in the digital age. Advances in Education. *Humanities and Social Sciences*, *8*(1), 355–370. DOI: 10.56028/aehssr.8.1.355.2023

Luca, E. (2023). Transforming education with AI: Cloud-based personalized learning and data protection strategies. *International Journal of AI in Education*, *15*(6), 225–240.

Maheswaran, K., Selvakumar, P., Shaikh, M., Shashank, G., Gupta, S., & Manjunath, T. C. (2025). The evolution of smart urban mobility with emerging technologies. In Ponnusamy, S., Assaf, M., Youssef, B., Jeon, G., & Kalyanaraman, S. (Eds.), *Leveraging VANETs and blockchain technology for urban mobility* (pp. 1–28). IGI Global Scientific Publishing., DOI: 10.4018/979-8-3373-0265-2.ch001

Muthusubramanian, M., Jangoan, S., Sharma, K. K., & Krishnamoorthy, G. (2024). Demystifying explainable AI: Understanding, transparency and trust. *International Journal of AI Ethics and Governance*, *6*(2), 88–102. DOI: 10.36948/ijfmr.2024.v06i02.14597

Owan, V. J., Abang, K. B., Idika, D. O., & Etta, E. O. (2023). Exploring the potential of artificial intelligence tools in educational measurement and assessment. *Eurasia Journal of Mathematics, Science and Technology Education*, *19*(4), 13428. Advance online publication. DOI: 10.29333/ejmste/13428

Oyeniran, C. O., Adewusi, A. O., Adeleke, A. G., Akwawa, L. A., & Azubuko, C. F. (2022). Ethical AI: Addressing bias in machine learning models and software applications. *Computer Science & AI Ethics Journal*, *9*(3), 88–102.

Patty, J. (2024). The use of AI in language learning: What you need to know. Jurnal Review Pendidikan dan Pengajaran (JRPP), 7(1), 642–658.

Pillai, R., Sivathanu, B., Metri, B., & Kaushik, N. (2024). Students' adoption of AI-based teacher-bots (T-Bots) for learning in higher education. *Information Technology & People*, *37*(1), 328–355. DOI: 10.1108/ITP-02-2021-0152

Pulivarthy, P., & Whig, P. (2025). Bias and fairness addressing discrimination in AI systems. In *Ethical dimensions of AI development* (pp. 103–126). IGI Global., DOI: 10.4018/979-8-3693-4147-6.ch005

Rashidi, H. H., Pantanowitz, J., Hanna, M. G., Tafti, A. P., Sanghani, P., Buchinsky, A., Fennell, B., Deebajah, M., Wheeler, S., Pearce, T., Abukhiran, I., Robertson, S., Palmer, O., Gur, M., & Tran, N. K. (2025). Introduction to artificial intelligence and machine learning in pathology and medicine: Generative and nongenerative artificial intelligence basics. *Modern Pathology*, *38*(4), 100688. Advance online publication. DOI: 10.1016/j.modpat.2024.100688 PMID: 39755237

Rosenstrauch, D., Mangla, U., Gupta, A., & Masau, C. T. (2023). Artificial intelligence and ethics. In *Digital health entrepreneurship* (pp. 225–239). Springer., DOI: 10.1007/978-3-031-33902-8_16

Rousi, R., Alanen, H. K., & Wilson, A. S. (2024). Data privacy, ethics and education in the era of AI–A university student perspective. In Proceedings of the 7th conference on technology ethics (TETHICS 2024) (Vol. 3901, pp. 81–95). CEUR-WS.

Sakthivel, M., Jaganathan, A., & Mohanraj, M. Mohit, & Manjunath, T. (2025). Brand loyalty through AI and personalisation: AI-generated content for financial marketing. In A. J. Nair, S. Manohar, Y. B. Limbu, & B. A. Huhmann (Eds.), Intersecting natural language processing and FinTech innovations in service marketing (pp. 77–96). IGI Global Scientific Publishing. https://doi.org/DOI: 10.4018/979-8-3693-9944-6.ch006

Samal, A., & Misra, L. I. Mohit, Pougajendy, S., Chandel, P. S., & Manjunath, T. C. (2025). Musealization and tourism practices. In S. Oflazoğlu & M. Dora (Eds.), Preserving cultural heritage in post-disaster urban renewal (pp. 115–142). IGI Global Scientific Publishing. https://doi.org/DOI: 10.4018/979-8-3693-9097-9.ch006

Soundariya, A., Behera, N. K., Selvakumar, P., Chandel, P. S., Gupta, S., & Manjunath, T. C. (2025). AI and environmental ethics: The role of AI in addressing climate change—Ethical considerations in AI-driven environmental solutions. In Chakraborty, S. (Ed.), *Human values, ethics, and dignity in the age of artificial intelligence* (pp. 321–346). IGI Global Scientific Publishing., DOI: 10.4018/979-8-3693-9035-1.ch013

Thirunagalingam, A., & Selvakumar, P. (2025). Application of automation and robotics in the oil and gas industry. In Abdullayev, V., & Khang, A. (Eds.), *Revolutionizing AI and robotics in the oil and gas industry* (pp. 229–244). IGI Global Scientific Publishing., DOI: 10.4018/979-8-3693-8156-4.ch011

Upadhyaya, A. N., Debnath, P., Rani, P., Manjunath, T. C., & Bhattacharya, S. (2025). AI-based disaster prediction and early warning systems. In Mobo, F. (Ed.), *AI and emerging technologies for emergency response and smart cities* (pp. 55–74). IGI Global Scientific Publishing., DOI: 10.4018/979-8-3693-9770-1.ch003

Williams, R., Cloete, R., Cobbe, J., Cottrill, C., Edwards, P., Markovic, M., Naja, I., Ryan, F., Singh, J., & Pang, W. (2022). From transparency to accountability of intelligent systems: Moving beyond aspirations. *Data & Policy*, *4*, e7. Advance online publication. DOI: 10.1017/dap.2021.37

Xiao, Y., & Zhi, Y. (2023). An exploratory study of EFL learners' use of ChatGPT for language learning tasks: Experience and perceptions. *Languages (Basel, Switzerland)*, *8*(3), 212. Advance online publication. DOI: 10.3390/languages8030212

Chapter 6
Inclusive Instructional Design Through Digital Pedagogies and Active Learning Approaches

Rampelli Manojkumar
https://orcid.org/0000-0002-8141-0321
BVRIT HYDERABAD College of Engineering for Women, India

T. Aditya Sai Srinivas
Ravindra College of Engineering for Women, India

Venkanna Mekala
https://orcid.org/0000-0003-0418-3281
BVRIT HYDERABAD College of Engineering for Women, India

ABSTRACT

This chapter examines how inclusive instructional design, supported by digital pedagogies and active learning, transforms higher education. It argues that integrating frameworks like Universal Design for Learning (UDL) with flipped classrooms, simulations, and problem-based learning creates equitable, adaptive, and engaging environments. By prioritizing flexibility, personalization, and real-world relevance, these strategies empower diverse learners and reduce barriers to success, making inclusion a foundational principle rather than an afterthought.

DOI: 10.4018/979-8-3373-5188-9.ch006

INTRODUCTION

In the twenty-first century, education is undergoing a profound transformation shaped by rapid advances in digital technology, evolving social needs, and the persistent demand for inclusive and equitable learning opportunities. Traditional approaches to teaching and learning, often centered on standardized delivery and teacher-led instruction, are increasingly recognized as insufficient for addressing the diverse needs of today's learners. Instead, the current educational landscape emphasizes inclusivity, personalization, and adaptability—principles that align with the broader global push toward equity in education. Inclusive instructional design, supported by digital pedagogies and active learning strategies, has emerged as a central framework for achieving these objectives. This chapter begins by examining the role of inclusive instructional design in higher education, before analyzing the contributions of digital pedagogies such as flipped learning, simulation-based learning, and problem-based approaches in creating equitable, engaging, and meaningful educational experiences for all learners.

Inclusive instructional design refers to the systematic creation of educational environments that are accessible, equitable, and responsive to the diverse characteristics of learners. At its core, it emphasizes designing learning experiences that consider differences in culture, language, ability, socioeconomic background, and learning preferences. Hardwick et al. (2022) argue that designing for inclusion is also designing for care, as it involves anticipating barriers to learning and proactively creating pathways for every student to succeed. This approach requires educators to adopt a mindset that values diversity as a strength rather than a challenge. Such thinking is echoed in the Universal Design for Learning (UDL) framework, which has become an important reference point for inclusive pedagogy. By encouraging multiple means of engagement, representation, and expression, UDL provides a flexible blueprint that empowers students to interact with content in ways that align with their abilities and preferences. Wojdak et al. (2024) demonstrate that integrating UDL with active learning strategies in biology open educational resources not only improves access but also enhances student motivation and engagement. These insights underscore the fact that inclusivity must be embedded in the design stage of pedagogy rather than retrofitted as an afterthought.

Digital technologies serve as both catalysts and enablers of inclusive instructional design. They allow educators to design learning pathways that are adaptive to different learning speeds, provide immediate and meaningful feedback, and offer diverse modalities of content delivery. The Flexible Learning by Design (FLeD) project, for instance, highlights how the development of faculty digital competence is critical for achieving inclusive learning outcomes (Afonso et al., 2025). Through structured professional development initiatives, the FLeD project enhanced educators' ability to design and deliver digital learning experiences that promote flexibility and student engagement. Such projects illustrate that the success of digital pedagogies depends not only on the availability of technological tools but also on the pedagogical and emotional readiness of educators to deploy them inclusively. Indeed, without faculty who are confident in digital literacy and empathetic toward diverse learners, the promise of technology for inclusion may remain underutilized.

One of the most prominent digital pedagogies aligned with inclusivity is the flipped classroom model. The flipped classroom inverts the traditional order of instruction: instead of receiving lecture content in class and practicing afterward, students first engage with instructional materials—such as pre-recorded videos, readings, or interactive resources—on their own time. Classroom sessions are then dedicated to discussion, application, and collaborative learning. Research has shown that this model has several benefits for inclusion. First, it allows learners to engage with new content at their own pace, providing opportunities for repetition and review that are especially valuable for students with processing difficulties or language-related challenges (Yeleussizkyzy et al., 2023). Second, it creates a more interactive and social classroom dynamic where teachers can address individual needs and misconceptions in real time. Third, the model promotes autonomy and accountability, encouraging students to take ownership of their learning. These outcomes are evident in multiple contexts: Zafirova-Malcheva et al. (2019) found that incorporating flipped classroom approaches into teacher training improved inclusivity in instructional design courses, while Blasco-Serrano et al. (2022) demonstrated that preservice teachers who experienced flipped classroom models became more confident in designing ICT-based inclusive education practices themselves. Similarly, Andujar and Nadif (2022) showed that a flipped approach in blended English as a Foreign Language (EFL) classroom improved equity in learner participation and access to resources. More recently, Kamalı-Arslantaş and Baser (2025) confirmed that using interactive videos within flipped classrooms significantly improved pre-service special education teachers' engagement, showing that even within specialized contexts, the flipped model supports inclusivity. Collectively, these findings highlight how flipped learning operationalizes inclusivity by blending flexibility, personalization, and collaborative engagement.

Another important dimension of inclusive digital pedagogy lies in simulation-based and experiential learning. Simulation-based learning immerses students in realistic scenarios where they can apply theoretical knowledge to practical challenges, often in a safe and controlled environment. This is particularly valuable for inclusive education because it allows learners with different cognitive styles to engage with content in multimodal ways. For instance, visual and kinesthetic learners benefit from interactive interfaces that allow them to manipulate variables, visualize outcomes, and experience learning dynamically. Chernikova et al. (2020), in their meta-analysis, found that simulation-based learning has substantial positive effects on conceptual understanding, skill acquisition, and knowledge retention in higher education. Similarly, Duchatelet et al. (2022) emphasize that simulation-based activities enhance professional training by allowing learners to experiment with complex problems while receiving structured feedback. Vermunt (2023) further expands this perspective by highlighting the dual benefit of simulation-based learning: while students acquire applied competencies, instructors also develop deeper insights into learners' progress and misconceptions. In a more recent meta-analysis, Chernikova et al. (2025) examined the role of personalization in simulations, differentiating between adaptivity (system-driven personalization) and adaptability (learner-driven personalization). They concluded that both mechanisms, when appropriately designed, increase inclusivity by accommodating learner diversity. Together, these studies reveal that simulations are not only effective for content mastery but also equitable in their design, offering multiple points of access for learners with different needs.

Problem-based learning (PBL) is similarly recognized as an inclusive and equity-enhancing strategy. Unlike traditional instruction, which emphasizes the transmission of content, PBL situates learning within real-world and contextually relevant problems. This approach provides learners with opportunities to draw upon their varied skill sets, collaborate with peers, and engage in self-directed inquiry. Youngerman and Culver (2024) argue that PBL enhances equity in graduate education by giving students access to authentic problems of practice that connect academic learning to professional and community contexts. This form of engagement is particularly valuable for learners from underrepresented backgrounds, as it validates their lived experiences and situates them as contributors to knowledge. Likewise, Horak et al. (2024) demonstrate that problem-based professional learning models can create access for gifted learners, many of whom experience barriers to enrichment within traditional instruction. Overall, the evidence suggests that problem-based learning not only improves cognitive outcomes but also cultivates a sense of belonging and recognition among diverse learners.

Taken together, the integration of flipped learning, simulation-based strategies, and problem-based approaches illustrates the powerful synergy between digital pedagogies and inclusive instructional design. Each of these pedagogies addresses different dimensions of learner diversity: flipped classrooms offer flexibility in pacing and engagement, simulations provide experiential and multimodal access, and problem-based approaches build real-world relevance while valuing diverse skill sets. Moreover, the emphasis on active learning across these methods shifts the role of the learner from passive recipient to active co-constructor of knowledge. This shift is critical for inclusion because it validates different ways of knowing, supports autonomy, and encourages collaboration among students with varied strengths and challenges. Importantly, however, the success of these pedagogies depends on the competence and commitment of educators. As the FLeD project (Afonso et al., 2025) demonstrates, developing faculty digital competence is essential for designing and sustaining inclusive learning environments. Without adequate preparation and ongoing support, educators may inadvertently reproduce exclusionary practices despite the availability of advanced technologies.

Another critical consideration is the role of formative assessment and feedback in inclusive digital pedagogy. Real-time feedback tools—ranging from automated graders to coding evaluation platforms—allow learners to test their understanding continuously and receive instant, personalized responses. These systems support mastery learning, where students are permitted multiple attempts until they achieve competence. For students who may hesitate to participate due to fear of failure, such as neurodiverse learners or first-generation students, real-time feedback reduces anxiety and builds confidence. Although not directly discussed in the references provided, this theme intersects with the broader findings on UDL and digital competence. It reinforces the idea that inclusivity is not merely about access to content but also about the quality and adaptability of the learning process.

In synthesizing the above perspectives, it becomes clear that inclusive instructional design through digital pedagogies and active learning approaches is not only an educational innovation but a social imperative. In an era where global education systems are increasingly diverse, designing for inclusion ensures that higher education remains relevant, equitable, and empowering. The references reviewed here collectively underscore that inclusivity must be embedded in every stage of instructional design, from content creation and technological integration to classroom practice and assessment. Whether through flipped classrooms that democratize access to content, simulations that create equitable and immersive learning experiences, or problem-based learning that validates diverse perspectives, digital pedagogies have the potential to transform higher education into a truly inclusive space. At the same time, the responsibility rests heavily on educators to embrace digital competence, empathy, and adaptability in their practice.

The Figure 1 shows how Inclusive Instructional Design integrates flipped, simulation-based, and problem-based learning approaches to foster active learning, ultimately resulting in equitable, adaptive, and empowering higher education outcomes

Figure 1. Inclusive instructional design

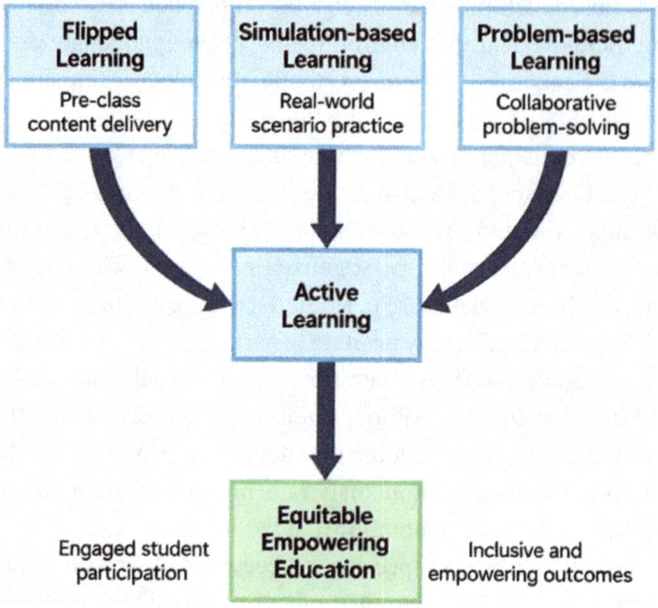

This chapter, therefore, sets out to examine inclusive instructional design through the lens of digital pedagogies and active learning. By weaving together research on UDL, flipped learning, simulations, and PBL, it offers a comprehensive framework for designing equitable and adaptive learning environments. The chapter argues that inclusivity is not achieved through a single strategy but through the thoughtful integration of multiple approaches that collectively support diversity in higher education. It will demonstrate how digital tools, when guided by inclusive design principles, can empower learners, reduce barriers, and foster deeper engagement. Ultimately, this work seeks to contribute to ongoing conversations about the role of education in promoting equity, not only by identifying challenges but also by highlighting practical pathways forward. In doing so, it underscores the transformative potential of inclusive instructional design in shaping the future of education.

DIGITAL PEDAGOGIES FOR FEEDBACK AND MASTERY LEARNING

In contemporary education, digital technologies have revolutionized the ways students learn, receive feedback, and achieve mastery. Feedback is widely recognized as a critical component of effective learning, serving not only to inform learners of their progress but also to guide them toward deeper conceptual understanding

(Barana, Marchisio, & Sacchet, 2021). Mastery learning, a pedagogical approach emphasizing progression upon demonstrating competence, has traditionally faced challenges in classroom scalability and individualized attention. However, the integration of digital tools—ranging from automated assessment systems to AI-driven learning platforms—has made it possible to provide immediate, personalized, and adaptive feedback, thereby aligning instructional practices with mastery learning principles (Jones & Bomash, 2018; Nurhaswinda, Pebriana, & Nurmalina, 2025).

The rise of digital pedagogies has brought a dual benefit: students gain access to real-time guidance tailored to their unique needs, and instructors acquire data-driven insights into learner performance, enabling more informed instructional decisions. Universal Design for Learning (UDL) principles complement these digital strategies by promoting inclusivity and adaptability, ensuring that learners with diverse abilities, cognitive styles, and socio-cultural backgrounds can benefit from structured, feedback-rich learning experiences (Kurtts, 2006; Navaitienė & Stasiūnaitienė, 2021; Espada-Chavarria et al., 2023).

Real-Time Feedback in Digital Learning Environments

Real-time feedback is a cornerstone of digital pedagogy for mastery learning. Such feedback mechanisms provide learners with immediate responses to their performance, allowing them to correct errors, consolidate understanding, and sustain motivation. Barana, Marchisio, and Sacchet (2021) demonstrated that interactive feedback in mathematics digital environments improves both engagement and conceptual comprehension. Similarly, Barley and Mikhailova (2020) showed that in online language classrooms, immediate formative assessment enables learners to self-regulate their performance, fostering a sense of autonomy and confidence in their learning trajectory.

Technologies such as Google Forms, quizzes embedded in Learning Management Systems (LMS), and adaptive assessment platforms allow educators to implement scalable real-time feedback. Haddad and Kalaani (2014) highlighted how Google Forms could function as a formative assessment tool, automatically processing responses and guiding students through adaptive learning pathways. This approach ensures that feedback is timely, precise, and relevant to each learner's performance level, aligning with mastery learning principles that prioritize competency over time-based progression.

The application of digital feedback is not limited to simple correctness checks. Platforms can provide hints, scaffolded support, and alternative problem-solving pathways, encouraging learners to explore concepts from multiple perspectives. Piccoli et al. (2020) emphasized the importance of designing digital assessment systems for accuracy and timeliness, particularly in practical skill acquisition, noting that immediate feedback not only enhances learning outcomes but also reduces learner frustration and disengagement.

Adaptive Learning Platforms for Personalized Mastery

Adaptive learning platforms represent a transformative approach to mastery learning by leveraging algorithms that tailor learning pathways based on individual student performance. These platforms continuously assess learners' knowledge and adapt content delivery, difficulty levels, and feedback mechanisms to optimize learning outcomes. Nurhaswinda, Pebriana, and Nurmalina (2025) found that technology-driven adaptive learning significantly improved conceptual mastery in mathematics for primary education students, demonstrating that personalization is key to fostering deep understanding.

Liu (2022) reported that adaptive learning in Taiwanese elementary schools allowed teachers to implement "precision education," whereby instructional interventions were tailored to the specific needs and progress of each learner. Similarly, Kochurina, Fedorova, and Zakharov (2022) highlighted that adaptive platforms increase learner motivation by providing challenges that are aligned with students' competence levels, offering continuous formative feedback, and reinforcing mastery through iterative practice.

Jones and Bomash (2018) examined Knewton Alta's adaptive learning framework, illustrating that mastery learning validated through adaptive systems improves both learning efficiency and retention. The adaptive nature of these platforms ensures that learners are neither over-challenged nor under-challenged, fostering optimal engagement and progression. By providing personalized scaffolding, adaptive platforms embody key UDL principles, ensuring multiple means of engagement, representation, and action/expression (Kurtts, 2006; Navaitienė & Stasiūnaitienė, 2021).

Flipped Classrooms and Formative Assessment

Flipped classroom models, where instructional content is delivered outside class and in-person sessions focus on application and interaction, provide a natural synergy with real-time feedback and mastery learning. Othman et al. (2023) found that integrating formative assessment within flipped classrooms enhances learner engagement and understanding, as students receive feedback on pre-class materials and enter class better prepared for collaborative problem-solving. Ziegenfuss and Furse (2021) illustrated that flipped classrooms in engineering education enabled formative assessment to function seamlessly within class activities, allowing instructors to monitor understanding and provide individualized guidance in real time.

Digital tools, including interactive quizzes, learning analytics dashboards, and collaborative platforms, enhance the efficacy of flipped classrooms. Loizou (2022) demonstrated that in primary education, digital tools combined with flipped pedagogy improved student participation, allowed repeated practice, and promoted mastery through iterative feedback cycles. By leveraging these tools, instructors can accommodate diverse learning paces and ensure that every student attains competence before progressing, a core tenet of mastery learning.

Moreover, flipped classrooms allow instructors to design learning experiences that align with inclusive practices. Students with different cognitive abilities, language proficiency levels, or learning preferences can engage with pre-class digital content at their own pace, while classroom interactions provide opportunities for peer learning, clarification, and feedback. This integration of flipped learning, real-time assessment, and digital pedagogy exemplifies how instructional design can operationalize both mastery and inclusion simultaneously (Kurtts, 2006; Espada-Chavarria et al., 2023).

AI-Powered Feedback and Assessment

Artificial Intelligence (AI) is increasingly transforming feedback and assessment processes in higher education. AI-powered platforms analyse learner data to provide adaptive, personalized feedback at scale, often surpassing the capacity of traditional classroom methods. Tariq (2026) highlighted that AI-driven assessment platforms enhance learning outcomes by offering precise, actionable feedback tailored to individual learner profiles. Similarly, de Amorim Silva et al. (2025) demonstrated that AI-powered personalized learning systems map learner progress, predict potential gaps, and automatically generate targeted exercises, facilitating mastery in complex subjects.

Vashishth et al. (2024) explored the role of AI-driven learning analytics in higher education, showing that platforms can provide predictive feedback, identify at-risk learners, and recommend remedial interventions in real time. Zhu (2025) further emphasized that AI feedback engines optimize vocational education assessment by continuously analysing student performance and adjusting evaluation criteria, thereby increasing the accuracy, efficiency, and inclusivity of assessment practices.

AI integration in mastery learning not only provides timely and personalized feedback but also supports scalable instructional design. Large classes, diverse learner profiles, and multiple learning objectives can be managed effectively through AI analytics, ensuring that all learners receive the attention and guidance necessary to achieve competence. The alignment of AI systems with UDL principles ensures accessibility, flexibility, and engagement for all learners, bridging gaps that traditional pedagogies may leave unaddressed (Navaitienė & Stasiūnaitienė, 2021; Espada-Chavarria et al., 2023).

Universal Design for Learning and Inclusive Feedback

Inclusive education requires that feedback and mastery learning strategies accommodate a broad range of learner needs. Universal Design for Learning (UDL) provides a foundational framework for implementing inclusive digital pedagogies, advocating multiple means of engagement, representation, and action/expression (Kurtts, 2006). Navaitienė and Stasiūnaitienė (2021) emphasized that UDL encourages designing learning experiences that allow all students—from novice to expert—to access content, receive feedback, and demonstrate mastery according to their strengths.

Espada-Chavarria et al. (2023) showed that UDL-informed digital strategies, including adaptive platforms, AI feedback systems, and interactive assessment tools, foster inclusive higher education environments. By integrating UDL principles into mastery-focused digital pedagogies, educators ensure that feedback is meaningful, personalized, and actionable for all learners, including those with cognitive, linguistic, or socio-cultural differences. In essence, UDL serves as a guiding philosophy that underpins the design and deployment of digital tools for feedback and mastery learning, ensuring equity and accessibility remain central to instructional innovation.

Digital pedagogies for feedback and mastery learning represent a paradigm shift in contemporary education, enabling personalized, timely, and inclusive learning experiences. Real-time feedback mechanisms, adaptive learning platforms, flipped classroom models, and AI-powered assessment systems collectively support mastery learning by ensuring learners progress upon demonstrating competence. These approaches are further strengthened by Universal Design for Learning, which ensures accessibility, engagement, and inclusivity across diverse learner populations.

Through the strategic integration of these tools, educators can design learning experiences that are not only effective in achieving mastery but also equitable and responsive to individual needs. The literature consistently demonstrates that digital feedback and adaptive instructional strategies enhance conceptual understanding, motivation, and engagement, while also allowing scalable and precise evaluation. This synthesis underscores that digital pedagogies, when combined with mastery learning and inclusive principles, provide a comprehensive framework for enhancing learning outcomes in diverse educational settings.

An example showing the activity of MATLAB grader that provides instant feedback on coding assignments, directly supporting mastery learning is shown in Figure 2.

Figure 2. MATLAB Grader activity

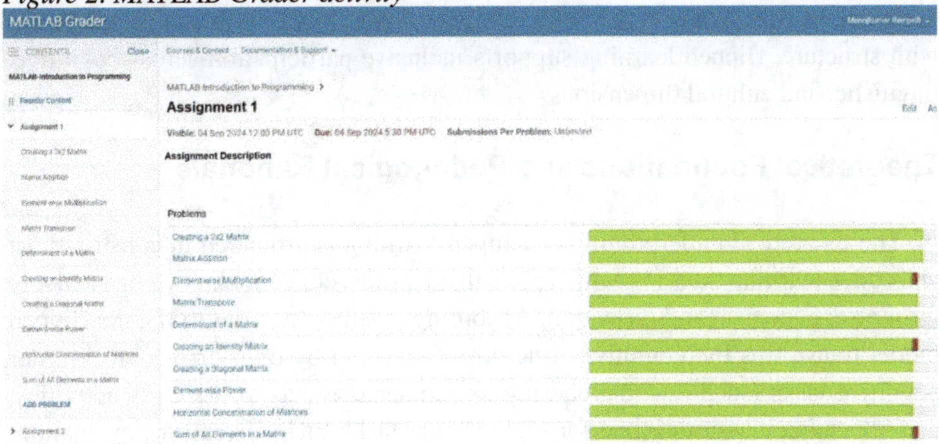

FLIPPED LEARNING AND ACTIVE ENGAGEMENT STRATEGIES

Flipped learning represents a transformative pedagogical shift that redefines the role of both teachers and learners in the educational process. Instead of delivering knowledge through direct in-class instruction, flipped learning inverts the traditional sequence of learning activities. Learners first engage with instructional materials—such as recorded lectures, digital resources, or readings—outside the classroom, while class time is reserved for active engagement, discussion, and problem-solving (Li, Lund, & Nordsteien, 2023). This inversion promotes self-paced learning, facilitates differentiated instruction, and transforms classroom spaces into environments of collaborative inquiry rather than passive knowledge reception.

The emergence of flipped learning coincides with a global emphasis on student-centred and active learning pedagogies, particularly in response to challenges posed by remote and hybrid learning contexts (Collado-Valero et al., 2021). The pedagogical shift aligns strongly with inclusive education principles by offering flexibility, autonomy, and multiple means of engagement for diverse learners. As such, flipped learning serves not only as an instructional innovation but also as a framework for designing equitable, technology-enhanced learning experiences that accommodate various learning preferences, abilities, and contexts.

The integration of digital technologies—such as learning management systems (LMS), artificial intelligence (AI)-driven analytics, speech recognition tools, and gamified learning environments—has significantly amplified the effectiveness of flipped classrooms. These tools enable personalized learning trajectories, continuous feedback, and adaptive content delivery, thereby enhancing learners' motivation and participation (Wang et al., 2023; Cueva & Inga, 2022). By blending flexibility with structure, flipped learning supports inclusive participation across cognitive, linguistic, and cultural dimensions.

Theoretical Foundations and Pedagogical Rationale

The theoretical underpinning of flipped learning is grounded in constructivist and active learning theories, which posit that learners construct knowledge actively through engagement and reflection. According to Bredow et al. (2021), the flipped model transforms the cognitive structure of learning by transferring lower-order cognitive tasks (such as remembering and understanding) to pre-class activities, and allocating classroom time for higher-order tasks such as analysis, evaluation, and creation—consistent with Bloom's revised taxonomy. This cognitive realignment allows educators to facilitate deeper conceptual understanding through peer collaboration, feedback, and real-world application.

The approach also aligns with self-determination theory, which emphasizes autonomy, competence, and relatedness as essential psychological needs for motivation (Fang, Vong, & Fang, 2022). In flipped classrooms, students exercise autonomy over their learning pace, engage in collaborative meaning-making, and develop a stronger sense of belonging through interactive class sessions. The flexibility of flipped instruction supports the differentiated pacing needed for inclusivity—allowing students with language barriers, cognitive diversity, or varied prior knowledge to engage meaningfully without the constraints of synchronous lecture delivery (Howell, 2021).

Moreover, the flipped approach complements Universal Design for Learning (UDL) principles by providing multiple means of representation (e.g., videos, readings, interactive modules), engagement (e.g., discussions, simulations, quizzes), and expression (e.g., collaborative projects, digital portfolios). By embedding these design principles, flipped learning promotes equitable participation and reduces systemic barriers in learning environments.

Flipped Learning in Higher Education: Evidence from Practice

The flipped classroom has gained significant traction in higher education due to its potential to enhance engagement, performance, and satisfaction. Fisher, Perényi, and Birdthistle (2021) demonstrated that flipped and blended learning approaches improve students' cognitive engagement and overall satisfaction by transforming classroom time into a space for interactive inquiry. Similarly, Cho et al. (2021) reported that engineering students participating in flipped learning activities perceived enhanced understanding and higher performance outcomes compared to traditional lecture formats.

Empirical research consistently highlights the benefits of flipped classrooms in promoting sustainable learning. Collado-Valero et al. (2021) found that during the COVID-19 pandemic, flipped classrooms supported continuity of learning and sustained motivation even under social distancing constraints. This was achieved through structured digital pre-class content and active online discussions. Li et al. (2023) further reinforced that flipped and active learning pedagogies are interconnected, as both rely on learner participation, instructor facilitation, and peer collaboration to achieve meaningful learning outcomes.

Flipped learning models have also demonstrated inclusivity benefits across disciplines. Cevikbas and Kaiser (2022) observed that students in a flipped secondary mathematics classroom displayed higher engagement and reduced anxiety, particularly among learners who typically struggle in traditional lecture environments. Similarly, Fang et al. (2022) emphasized that student engagement in fully flipped classrooms fosters ownership of learning and helps bridge participation gaps in culturally diverse settings. These outcomes highlight how flipped classrooms embody inclusive pedagogy in practice by creating equitable spaces for diverse learners to succeed.

Technology Integration in Flipped Classrooms

Technology acts as the enabler and catalyst for the success of flipped learning. Modern flipped classrooms leverage digital platforms to curate, deliver, and assess content efficiently while providing real-time analytics on learner progress. According to Jiang et al. (2021), the use of automatic speech recognition technology within flipped English as a Foreign Language (EFL) classroom improved learners' oral complexity and self-efficacy by offering instant corrective feedback. Similarly, Wang et al. (2023) illustrated how ChatGPT and AI-driven prompt engineering could optimize information retrieval, enhance inquiry-based learning, and personalize support for learners in flipped settings.

Cueva and Inga (2022) demonstrated that Information and Communication Technologies (ICTs) integrated within flipped classrooms expand opportunities for both synchronous and asynchronous engagement. Tools like interactive whiteboards, discussion forums, and polling systems promote participation and allow instructors to gauge understanding continuously. Furthermore, Klochko et al. (2021) highlighted that digital resources—such as simulation tools and online quizzes—support self-paced learning and cognitive reinforcement, especially beneficial for learners who require repetition or additional time for concept mastery.

Gamification, as another technological innovation, enhances motivation and engagement within flipped classrooms. Elzeky et al. (2022) reported that gamified flipped classroom designs in nursing education significantly improved skill competency and motivation. Integrating game elements such as leaderboards, challenges, and badges transforms routine practice into meaningful competition and cooperation, reinforcing both cognitive and affective learning outcomes.

Active Learning and Student Engagement in Flipped Environments

Active learning constitutes the core of the flipped classroom experience. By replacing passive lecture consumption with problem-solving, discussion, and collaborative projects, students actively construct understanding through engagement and dialogue. Howell (2021) emphasized that flipped classrooms promote reflective practices and engagement with sustainability topics by situating learning within real-world contexts. Similarly, Fisher et al. (2021) found that active learning in flipped environments improves academic achievement while nurturing critical thinking and teamwork skills.

Student engagement manifests cognitively (deep processing of content), behaviourally (participation and effort), and emotionally (interest and enjoyment). Fang et al. (2022) observed that flipped classrooms enhance these dimensions by fostering autonomy and accountability. The inclusion of pre-class materials encourages cognitive engagement, while interactive classroom tasks reinforce behavioural and emotional involvement. According to Samaila and Al-Samarraie (2024), the introduction of quiz-enhanced flipped classroom models further elevates engagement by providing immediate feedback loops, helping learners identify misconceptions early, and promoting self-regulation.

Flipped Classrooms in Discipline-Specific Contexts

The effectiveness of flipped classrooms has been documented across a wide range of academic disciplines. In engineering education, Cho et al. (2021) demonstrated that flipped approaches improved conceptual understanding of complex topics such as mechanical systems, while increasing students' perceptions of learning value. Similarly, in EFL instruction, Kawinkoonlasate (2024) showed that a digital-flipped classroom enhanced writing skills and fostered an active learning environment for Thai learners, emphasizing the cross-disciplinary adaptability of the model.

In teacher education, Candel, de-la-Peña, and Yuste (2024) found that pre-service teachers exposed to active methodologies like flipped learning and gamification developed positive perceptions toward student-centred instruction, reinforcing the potential for pedagogical transformation. Campillo-Ferrer and Miralles-Martínez (2021) further reported that flipped models improved motivation and resilience among higher education students during the COVID-19 pandemic. Their findings underline that flipped classrooms not only sustain engagement during crisis-driven transitions but also nurture independent, reflective learners capable of managing self-directed learning pathways.

Furthermore, Fang et al. (2022) identified that flipped pedagogies promote engagement across professional programs, such as business and management, by connecting theoretical content with real-world case discussions.

Student Readiness and the Role of Instructor Facilitation

Although flipped learning promotes autonomy and flexibility, its success depends largely on students' readiness and the instructor's facilitative role. Wut et al. (2022) emphasized that students' readiness—comprising self-regulation, digital literacy, and time management—directly influences their intention to participate and their learning outcomes. Instructors must therefore scaffold learner readiness through clear expectations, structured content, and support mechanisms.

Instructor presence and facilitation are equally crucial. The role of the teacher in flipped classrooms evolves from being a "content deliverer" to a "learning facilitator." Fang et al. (2022) argued that instructors in flipped environments must foster an inclusive culture of inquiry, provide timely feedback, and ensure equitable participation across diverse learner groups. Digital tools can aid this process by offering analytics that help instructors identify learners who may require additional guidance.

The social constructivist dimension of flipped classrooms underscores the importance of collaboration. Group discussions, peer feedback sessions, and cooperative projects strengthen interpersonal skills and promote empathy among learners (Li et al., 2023). In inclusive contexts, instructors can design group roles that cater to diverse strengths—such as analytical reasoning, creativity, or communication—ensuring all learners contribute meaningfully.

Challenges and Design Considerations in Implementing Flipped Learning

Despite its advantages, flipped learning presents several implementation challenges. The preparation of pre-class materials requires significant instructor time and digital competency. Students may also initially resist the shift in responsibility for pre-class learning. Cueva and Inga (2022) noted that technical infrastructure and access disparities can hinder equitable participation, particularly in low-resource contexts. Similarly, Fang et al. (2022) reported that maintaining engagement in fully flipped online environments requires intentional design strategies to sustain motivation and peer interaction.

Effective flipped learning design should therefore balance content delivery, interaction, and reflection. Bredow et al. (2021) recommended integrating structured feedback mechanisms—such as formative quizzes and peer review—to maintain engagement and accountability. Additionally, multimodal content formats (videos, simulations, readings) help accommodate different learning preferences and accessibility needs (Howell, 2021).

Another critical consideration involves aligning assessment strategies with active learning objectives. Summative assessments should be complemented by continuous formative evaluations to encourage reflection and improvement. As Samaila and Al-Samarraie (2024) demonstrated, integrating low-stakes quizzes and peer evaluation promotes continuous feedback and sustains learner motivation.

Emerging technologies such as artificial intelligence (AI) and learning analytics are redefining the future of flipped classrooms. Wang et al. (2023) illustrated how AI-driven systems like ChatGPT can personalize learning support through dynamic feedback, adaptive questioning, and information retrieval. Similarly, digital dashboards can provide instructors with real-time insights into student engagement patterns, enabling targeted interventions for struggling learners.

The integration of AI also supports inclusivity by offering adaptive pacing, multilingual translation tools, and automated accessibility features. Howell (2021) proposed that technology-mediated flipped learning can serve as a model for sustainability education, promoting reflective practice and systems thinking. Furthermore, as flipped learning expands into hybrid and blended formats, future designs should emphasize digital ethics, data privacy, and equitable access.

The future of flipped learning lies in its adaptability. As Cevikbas and Kaiser (2022) highlighted, continuous refinement of digital tools and pedagogical models is essential to ensure that flipped classrooms remain inclusive, engaging, and contextually relevant. This evolution will rely on ongoing collaboration between educators, technologists, and learners to co-create meaningful educational experiences.

Flipped learning embodies the intersection of pedagogy, technology, and inclusivity. By restructuring instructional time and leveraging digital tools, it transforms classrooms into dynamic, student-centred spaces where active engagement replaces passive reception. The model's success in enhancing motivation, participation, and performance has been evidenced across disciplines—from engineering to education and language learning (Cho et al., 2021; Fisher et al., 2021; Kawinkoonlasate, 2024). Moreover, its alignment with Universal Design for Learning principles ensures that learners of diverse abilities and backgrounds are supported through flexible, multimodal pathways.

The chapter section has demonstrated that the flipped learning model, when integrated with active engagement strategies, not only fosters cognitive growth but also nurtures collaboration, self-regulation, and inclusivity. As digital technologies continue to evolve, flipped classrooms will remain a cornerstone of innovative pedagogy, guiding the shift toward equitable, participatory, and sustainable learning environments.

An example showing the conduction of flipped class room activity is shown in Figure 3 where classroom time is used for interactive, applied learning.

Figure 3. Flipped class room activity

SIMULATION-BASED AND EXPERIENTIAL APPROACHES TO INCLUSION

The growing complexity of contemporary education systems and the diversity of student populations have intensified the need for pedagogical models that not only convey content knowledge but also cultivate inclusive mindsets, empathy, and reflective practice among future educators. Simulation-based and experiential learning approaches are increasingly recognized as effective mechanisms to address these needs, offering dynamic, immersive, and reflective spaces for teachers and students to engage with real-world complexities in safe, controlled, and authentic contexts (Langan et al., 2025; Frei-Landau et al., 2022).

Experiential learning theories, grounded in the work of Dewey, Kolb, and Vygotsky, posit that knowledge is best constructed through active engagement and reflection on direct experiences. Simulation-based learning extends this paradigm by creating interactive, situationally rich experiences where learners enact roles, make decisions, and receive immediate feedback (Kozyar et al., 2022). These methods promote cognitive, emotional, and social dimensions of learning that are essential for inclusive education—helping educators and students confront bias, empathize with diverse learners, and test strategies for equitable instruction (Kasperski & Crispel, 2022).

The convergence of experiential learning and digital simulation technologies marks a significant transformation in inclusive education. As Langan et al. (2025) emphasize in their scoping review, simulation-based learning in online environments enables personalized, flexible, and inclusive engagement, particularly in disciplines like nursing and teacher education.

Simulation-Based Pedagogies for Inclusive Teacher Education

Simulation-based learning (SBL) has become a cornerstone of innovative teacher education, fostering both professional competencies and inclusive dispositions. Through structured, scenario-driven experiences, pre-service teachers can explore complex classroom interactions, engage in reflective dialogue, and develop inclusive communication skills (Kasperski & Crispel, 2022).

In teacher education, SBL allows preservice educators to rehearse inclusive teaching before entering real classrooms. For instance, Adl-Amini, Meßner, and Hardy (2025) developed a simulation game focused on decision-making related to student placement and inclusion. The study found that participants showed increased reflection, empathy, and belief transformation regarding inclusion practices. Similarly, Yilmaz and Hebebci (2022) reported that virtual simulation environments enhanced trainee teachers' ability to handle diverse student needs and adapt pedagogical strategies, indicating the value of simulated practice in bridging theory and classroom realities.

Furthermore, simulation provides a risk-free environment for practicing challenging interactions—such as engaging with parents, managing behavioural issues, or accommodating special educational needs—without fear of negative consequences. Frei-Landau et al. (2022) introduced the notion of *mimetic learning*, wherein observation within simulation environments allows teachers to internalize both effective and ineffective teaching behaviours. Observers in these simulations experience what the authors term *vicarious inclusion learning*, recognizing how pedagogical decisions influence classroom equity.

Beyond skill development, simulation contributes to identity formation in teacher education. Learners reconstruct their understanding of what it means to be an inclusive educator through embodied participation. Kozyar et al. (2022) observed that future translators trained via simulation developed heightened intercultural and empathic communication abilities—an outcome highly relevant to inclusive pedagogy across disciplines. Thus, simulation-based learning not only builds competence but also nurtures the reflective, humanistic dimensions of inclusive teaching practice.

Experiential Learning Models and Inclusive Pedagogical Practice

Experiential learning extends beyond simulated experiences into real-world, community, and reflective engagements. In inclusive education, it serves as a bridge between theory and practice, offering learners opportunities to directly confront diversity, engage with marginalized groups, and design solutions that address educational inequities (Williams & Sembiante, 2022).

Yazici and Uzuner (2024) proposed an *Inclusive Experiential Model (IEM)* for teacher education, combining school-based mentoring with reflective inquiry. Their findings highlight that immersive, school-embedded learning fosters self-efficacy and empathy among pre-service teachers, equipping them to better accommodate learners with varied needs. Similarly, Resch and Schrittesser (2023) demonstrated the efficacy of *service-learning approaches* in connecting theoretical frameworks of inclusion to community-based action. This approach cultivates professional reflection and ethical responsibility while reinforcing that inclusion is a lived, relational practice rather than a mere policy objective.

In higher education, Valiente-Riedl, Anderson, and Banki (2022) argue that experiential approaches "cut both ways," meaning they challenge both educators and students to embody inclusive values. Their research underscores that experiential tasks, such as co-creating curricula or facilitating intercultural dialogues, foster mutual understanding and accountability in inclusive learning spaces.

Immersive and Virtual Environments for Inclusive Learning

The rapid advancement of digital technologies has expanded the scope of experiential and simulation-based learning through immersive environments such as virtual reality (VR), augmented reality (AR), and metaverse platforms. These tools facilitate embodied and multisensory learning, allowing learners to engage inclusively across geographic and physical barriers (Yeganeh et al., 2025).

Toto et al. (2024) conducted a systematic review on technologies for inclusive education and concluded that immersive tools enable differentiated instruction, empathy training, and accessibility through adaptable learning interfaces. Similarly, Baxter and Hainey (2024) demonstrated how immersive technologies can personalize learning pathways, giving students autonomy while maintaining inclusivity through universal design features.

Virtual environments are particularly impactful for developing empathy and cross-cultural competence. Sapkaroski, Mundy, and Dimmock (2022) compared virtual reality simulations with traditional role-play in medical education and found VR to be more effective in fostering empathic communication skills. Likewise, Dai et al. (2023) explored VR-supported simulation in teacher education, revealing that well-designed scenarios enhance reflection and sustain learning outcomes over extended periods.

The potential of immersive inclusion extends further with metaverse classrooms, which integrate virtual worlds, avatars, and interactive scenarios. Yeganeh et al. (2025) introduced a *multi-layered metaverse model* for inclusive education, combining spatial, social, and cognitive dimensions of immersion. This model encourages equitable participation by giving learners diverse modes of presence—verbal, visual, or embodied—thus accommodating neurodiverse and physically disabled learners. Such technologies also align with Universal Design for Learning (UDL) principles by offering multiple means of representation, engagement, and expression. Immersive inclusion ensures that learning is not only accessible but also deeply participatory and personalized, reinforcing the social model of disability that focuses on removing barriers rather than "fixing" learners.

Empathy, Role-Play, and Reflective Inclusion Practices

Empathy and emotional intelligence are central to inclusive pedagogy. Simulation and role-play have long been recognized as effective methods to cultivate these attributes by enabling learners to step into others' perspectives and experience complex emotional and social dynamics (Löfstrand & Zakrisson, 2025; Grech et al., 2024). Deniz et al. (2024) demonstrated that peer role-play simulations among pharmacy students significantly enhanced empathy and emotional intelligence, attributes vital for inclusive professional practice. Similarly, Löfstrand and Zakrisson (2025) explored the psychological impact of role-playing exercises, concluding that they activate both cognitive and affective processes, leading to sustained changes in attitudes toward others. In the design disciplines, Grech, Wodehouse, and Brisco (2024) employed empathic modelling to analyse user interactions and social dynamics in collaborative design tasks. This approach not only improved problem-solving but also nurtured an inclusive mindset that values diverse perspectives in group processes.

From a pedagogical standpoint, these practices support the affective dimension of inclusion, emphasizing that inclusive educators must be capable of emotional awareness as much as cognitive understanding. Sapkaroski et al. (2022) and Deniz et al. (2024) both confirmed that empathy-based simulations—whether digital or in-person—enhance interpersonal skills and awareness of bias, thereby contributing to equitable classroom dynamics. The reflective component of simulation is equally crucial. Observational and debriefing phases allow learners to articulate insights, question assumptions, and align their experiences with theoretical principles (Frei-Landau et al., 2022). This reflective loop transforms experience into learning and consolidates empathy into practice, anchoring inclusive pedagogy in both awareness and action.

Integrating Simulation and Experiential Approaches: Toward Inclusive Digital Pedagogies

Integrating simulation-based and experiential methodologies requires a deliberate pedagogical framework that aligns technological affordances with inclusive learning outcomes. The fusion of digital simulations, immersive technologies, and experiential reflection fosters a multidimensional approach to inclusion—one that engages cognitive, emotional, and social learning simultaneously.

Langan et al. (2025) emphasize that online simulation environments democratize access to experiential learning, particularly for students who face barriers to physical participation. Similarly, Toto et al. (2024) and Baxter & Hainey (2024) suggest that digital inclusion can be achieved through adaptive systems that respond to learner diversity in real time.

The integration of simulation and experiential learning is not merely technical but conceptual. As Valiente-Riedl et al. (2022) assert, experiential learning transforms educational spaces into communities of practice where inclusion is *experienced*, not just *taught*. Likewise, Adl-Amini et al. (2025) argue that simulation-based decision-making exercises instil reflective belief change, aligning learners' professional identities with inclusive principles.

To maximize impact, institutions must design inclusive simulation ecosystems that combine experiential mentorship (Yazici & Uzuner, 2024), service-learning (Resch & Schrittesser, 2023), and digital immersion (Yeganeh et al., 2025). Such ecosystems allow for sustained, iterative engagement where learners oscillate between virtual scenarios, real-world applications, and critical reflection.

This integrative model echoes the ethos of Universal Design for Learning, ensuring that all learners—regardless of ability, background, or learning preference—can engage meaningfully. It also addresses the call by Löfstrand and Zakrisson (2025) for pedagogies that not only teach inclusion but also *perform* it through authentic, empathic engagement.

The reviewed studies collectively demonstrate that such approaches foster empathy, communication, and reflective practice—core attributes for inclusive educators. From virtual reality simulations that nurture empathic communication (Sapkaroski et al., 2022) to metaverse classrooms that dissolve accessibility barriers (Yeganeh et al., 2025), these innovations embody inclusion in design and practice alike. Ultimately, inclusion cannot be achieved through didactic instruction alone. It must be experienced, enacted, and reflected upon—and simulation-based experiential learning offers precisely this transformative pathway. By merging technology with empathy and reflection, educators can move toward a more equitable, human-centred model of learning that truly prepares students for the diversity of the 21st-century classroom.

An example showing the activity problem of experiential learning and the solution through simulation in LTspice software is given in Figure 4 and Figure 5 respectively.

Figure 4. Example activity problem for experiential learning

NAS question 1 :

Design the underdamped, overdamped, and critically damped series RLC circuit byfixing L and C values as given follows for unit step input.

L= (last two digits of your roll number) *10-1 H i.e., if your roll number is 22WH1A0472,then L=72*10-1 H=7.2 H, C = (last two digits of your roll number after interchanging)

***10-2 F i.e., if your roll number is 22WH1A0405, then C=50*10-2 F=0.5 F**

Figure 5. Solution of the problem of activity for experiential learning through simulation in LTspice software

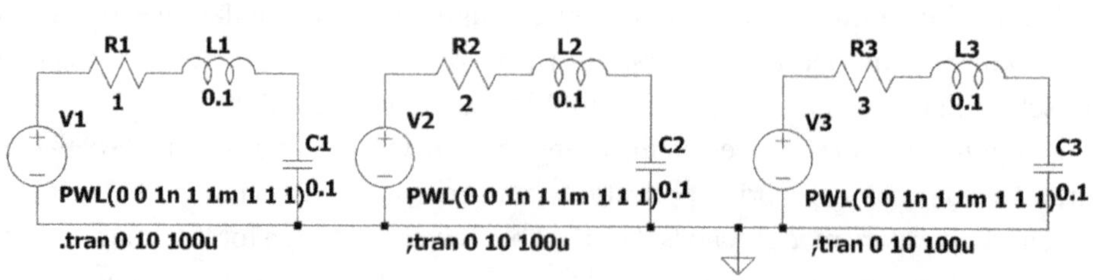

PROBLEM-BASED LEARNING AND REAL-WORLD RELEVANCE

Problem-Based Learning (PBL) has emerged as a transformative pedagogical strategy that bridges the gap between theoretical understanding and practical application. It shifts the focus from passive knowledge acquisition to active, inquiry-driven learning centred on real-world problems (Liu & Pásztor, 2022).

In the context of higher education, the growing complexity of societal and industrial challenges—driven by digital transformation, sustainability imperatives, and globalization—demands learning models that cultivate not just cognitive mastery but also problem-solving resilience and social awareness (Salvador et al., 2023). Real-world relevance in pedagogy connects academic content to contemporary challenges, thus fostering intrinsic motivation and ensuring that learning outcomes extend beyond classroom walls.

This section explores the role of problem-based learning and real-world integration in higher education, drawing insights from recent studies across disciplines. It examines the pedagogical principles, implementation models, and outcomes associated with PBL, emphasizing its effectiveness in developing critical thinking, entrepreneurial competencies, creativity, and employability skills.

PBL is grounded in constructivist learning theory, which posits that knowledge is actively constructed by learners through experience, reflection, and social interaction. Instead of following linear instructional sequences, students in PBL environments confront open-ended, ill-structured problems that require interdisciplinary thinking (Alfares, 2021). This approach was first popularized in medical education but has since evolved into a universal teaching model across disciplines such as business, engineering, and the social sciences. The PBL cycle typically involves problem identification, research, collaborative analysis, hypothesis formulation, and reflection. Learners assume responsibility for their learning trajectory, while instructors function as facilitators who guide, inquiry and provide feedback. According to Liu and Pásztor (2022), PBL not only enhances domain-specific knowledge but also promotes metacognitive skills that are essential for continuous learning. Their meta-analysis revealed significant improvements in students' critical thinking, creativity, and knowledge retention when compared to traditional lecture-based methods.

The fourth industrial revolution—characterized by automation, digitalization, and data-driven innovation—has redefined the competencies needed for employability. Salvador et al. (2023) argue that traditional higher education curricula often struggle to align with the dynamic needs of Industry 4.0 workplaces. Through their cross-program study, they found that PBL enables students to integrate technological, analytical, and collaborative skills, making them more adaptable to multidisciplinary industrial contexts.

In Industry 4.0-oriented PBL frameworks, students engage in real-world projects involving smart manufacturing, robotics, or data analytics. These projects mirror the challenges encountered in professional environments and require students to synthesize theoretical concepts into actionable solutions. The findings of Salvador et al. (2023) demonstrate that such industry-linked PBL not only enhances technical competence but also fosters systems thinking and ethical decision-making, vital for sustainable innovation.

PBL and Development of Critical and Creative Thinking

Developing higher-order thinking skills is one of the most cited advantages of PBL. Dolapcioglu and Doğanay (2022) demonstrated through action research in mathematics education that authentic learning environments—closely related to PBL principles—improve students' ability to reason critically, question assumptions, and construct new knowledge. Similarly, Liu and Pásztor's (2022) meta-analysis confirms that PBL interventions significantly elevate critical thinking outcomes across disciplines. Unlike rote learning, where knowledge recall dominates, PBL compels students to engage in reasoning, hypothesis testing, and argumentation. These cognitive processes contribute to a deeper conceptual understanding and foster creative approaches to problem-solving.

The element of creativity becomes even more pronounced in contexts where PBL integrates real-world maker education. Weng, Chiu, and Tsang (2022) demonstrated that engaging students in real-world, problem-based maker activities promote entrepreneurial thinking and creative design skills. Students learn to prototype, test, and iterate ideas in ways that mirror actual innovation processes in technology and design industries.

Entrepreneurship and Innovation Through PBL

In today's entrepreneurial ecosystem, where adaptability and innovation are key to success, PBL acts as an effective pedagogical framework for cultivating entrepreneurial competencies. Sousa and Costa (2022) emphasize that entrepreneurship education grounded in PBL allows students to discover competencies such as opportunity recognition, risk assessment, and decision-making. Their study of higher education students revealed that PBL fosters self-directed learning and encourages learners to translate theoretical business concepts into practical entrepreneurial ventures. By placing students in simulated or real entrepreneurial contexts, PBL bridges the gap between abstract management theory and the dynamic nature of startup ecosystems. It nurtures innovation not as a spontaneous act but as a process driven by curiosity, experimentation, and reflection. Additionally, Almazroui (2023) highlights the integration of project-based learning (PBL)—closely aligned with PBL—in developing 21st-century skills such as collaboration, communication, and moral reasoning. In the UAE's moral education context, Almazroui demonstrates that experiential projects grounded in real-life dilemmas improve students' ethical awareness and empathy, illustrating that PBL's impact extends beyond cognitive skills to affective and social dimensions of learning.

Problem-Based Learning as a Driver for Employability

The emphasis on employability skills has become central in higher education policy worldwide. According to Rohm, Stefl, and Ward (2021), live project-based learning that incorporates real business or community challenges develops students' leadership, communication, and problem-solving abilities—skills that are directly transferable to the workplace. Through real-world exposure, students not only acquire technical knowledge but also develop professional behaviours and interpersonal competencies. Grant (2025) reinforces this point, noting that experiential and community-engaged learning methods transform theoretical coursework into actionable experience, thereby enhancing career readiness.

Experiential Learning Integration

Experiential learning is closely intertwined with problem-based learning, forming a continuum that moves from guided inquiry to real-world practice. Grant (2025) and Upadhyay and Malik (2024) both highlight that experiential learning allows students to "learn by doing," reinforcing the application of knowledge through reflection and feedback. Upadhyay and Malik (2024) argue that in the globalized education era, experiential learning fosters cross-cultural awareness, digital adaptability, and skill diversification — all essential for employability. When PBL is embedded within experiential frameworks, it transforms students into active participants in constructing and testing solutions within authentic contexts.

The combination of problem-based and experiential methods also encourages emotional engagement. Students experience ownership of their learning process, thereby deepening motivation and persistence. This pedagogical alignment has been shown to increase long-term retention of knowledge and promote lifelong learning habits (Grant, 2025).

Real-World Relevance and Authentic Assessment

Real-world relevance is the essence of PBL's success. The problems students tackle are not hypothetical exercises but mirror contemporary challenges faced in industries, communities, or policy contexts. This authenticity enhances engagement and promotes the transfer of learning to practical settings. Authentic assessment—evaluating students through performance-based tasks such as case analyses, design projects, and reflective journals—complements PBL by emphasizing understanding over memorization. Salvador et al. (2023) note that such assessments more accurately capture students' ability to apply knowledge in dynamic contexts.

Pedagogical Challenges and Implementation Considerations

Despite its numerous advantages, PBL implementation presents several challenges. Faculty often face difficulties in designing open-ended problems that are both relevant and appropriately complex (Salvador et al., 2023). Time constraints, assessment standardization, and faculty training remain significant obstacles. Alfares (2021) also found that technology-mediated PBL, such as through Blackboard systems, requires careful instructional design to maintain engagement and support self-regulation. Instructors must balance structure with autonomy, ensuring that students have the necessary scaffolding to succeed in self-directed inquiry. As Dolapcioglu and Doğanay (2022) suggest, educators must embrace flexible, iterative instructional models that accommodate diverse learning paths and interdisciplinary collaboration.

Theoretical and Practical Synergy

PBL's success lies in its ability to merge theory with practice. It provides a platform where theoretical models are continuously tested against real-world situations, enabling students to appreciate the relevance of academic knowledge. This synergy transforms learning into a dynamic, reflective, and iterative process. Weng et al. (2022) demonstrate that when students are engaged in maker-based, problem-centred projects, their understanding of abstract theories deepens through tangible experimentation. Likewise, Rohm et al. (2021) confirm that such integrative experiences cultivate the self-efficacy and resilience necessary for lifelong learning and professional adaptability.

The problem-based learning provides a robust framework for developing not only cognitive and technical competencies but also the ethical, creative, and social dimensions of learning. By grounding education in authentic, real-world contexts, it empowers learners to become proactive problem-solvers capable of navigating the complexities of an ever-changing world.

CONCLUSIONS

In conclusion, this chapter has demonstrated that inclusive instructional design, underpinned by digital pedagogies and active learning strategies, is fundamental to creating equitable and empowering higher education experiences. The synergistic integration of frameworks like Universal Design for Learning with specific approaches—such as flipped classrooms, simulation-based learning, and problem-based learning—provides a comprehensive and adaptable model for addressing learner diversity. These methods collectively foster flexibility, personalization, real-world relevance, and collaborative engagement, ensuring all students have multiple pathways to succeed. Crucially, the effective implementation of these pedagogies hinges on developing faculty digital competence and a reflective, empathetic mindset. As the educational landscape continues to evolve, this holistic approach, which embeds inclusivity at the very core of curriculum and assessment design, is not merely an enhancement but a necessary imperative. It transforms higher education into a truly responsive and transformative space, preparing a diverse generation of learners to navigate and shape a complex world.

REFERENCES

Adl-Amini, K., Meßner, M. T., & Hardy, I. (2025). A simulation game for placement decision-making: Fostering reflection and belief change about inclusion in teacher education. *International Journal of Inclusive Education*, *29*(7), 1197–1213.

Afonso, A., Morgado, L., Noguera, I., Sepúlveda-Parrini, P., Hernandez-Leo, D., Alkhasawneh, S. N., & Carvalho, I. C. (2025). Flexible learning by design: Enhancing faculty digital competence and engagement through the FLeD Project. *Education Sciences*, *15*(7), 934.

Alfares, N. (2021). The effect of problem-based learning on students' problem-solving self-efficacy through Blackboard system in higher education. *International Journal of Education and Practice*, *9*(1), 185–200.

Almazroui, K. M. (2023). Project-based learning for 21st-century skills: An overview and case study of moral education in the UAE. *Social Studies*, *114*(3), 125–136.

Andujar, A., & Nadif, F. Z. (2022). Evaluating an inclusive blended learning environment in EFL: A flipped approach. *Computer Assisted Language Learning*, *35*(5–6), 1138–1167.

Barana, A., Marchisio, M., & Sacchet, M. (2021). Interactive feedback for learning mathematics in a digital learning environment. *Education Sciences*, *11*(6), 279.

Barley, N., & Mikhailova, I. (2020). Real-time formative assessment in online language classroom. In *ICERI2020 Proceedings* (pp. 4671–4678). IATED.

Baxter, G., & Hainey, T. (2024). Using immersive technologies to enhance the student learning experience. *Interactive Technology and Smart Education*, *21*(3), 403–425.

Blasco-Serrano, A. C., González, I. B., & Coma-Roselló, T. (2022). Incorporation of ICT into preservice teacher training using the flipped classroom to enhance inclusive education. *Edutec, 79. Article*, *10*, 21556.

Bredow, C. A., Roehling, P. V., Knorp, A. J., & Sweet, A. M. (2021). To flip or not to flip? A meta-analysis of the efficacy of flipped learning in higher education. *Review of Educational Research*, *91*(6), 878–918.

Campillo-Ferrer, J. M., & Miralles-Martínez, P. (2021). Effectiveness of the flipped classroom model on students' self-reported motivation and learning during the COVID-19 pandemic. *Humanities & Social Sciences Communications*, *8*(1), 1–9. PMID: 38617731

Candel, E. C., de-la-Peña, C., & Yuste, B. C. (2024). Pre-service teachers' perception of active learning methodologies in history: Flipped classroom and gamification in an e-learning environment. *Education and Information Technologies*, *29*(3), 3365–3387.

Cevikbas, M., & Kaiser, G. (2022). Student engagement in a flipped secondary mathematics classroom. *International Journal of Science and Mathematics Education*, *20*(7), 1455–1480.

Chernikova, O., Heitzmann, N., Stadler, M., Holzberger, D., Seidel, T., & Fischer, F. (2020). Simulation-based learning in higher education: A meta-analysis. *Review of Educational Research*, *90*(4), 499–541.

Chernikova, O., Sommerhoff, D., Stadler, M., Holzberger, D., Nickl, M., Seidel, T., & Heitzmann, N. (2025). Personalization through adaptivity or adaptability? A meta-analysis on simulation-based learning in higher education. *Educational Research Review*, *46*, 100662.

Cho, H. J., Zhao, K., Lee, C. R., Runshe, D., & Krousgrill, C. (2021). Active learning through flipped classroom in mechanical engineering: Improving students' perception of learning and performance. *International Journal of STEM Education*, *8*(1), 46. PMID: 34312588

Collado-Valero, J., Rodríguez-Infante, G., Romero-González, M., Gamboa-Ternero, S., Navarro-Soria, I., & Lavigne-Cerván, R. (2021). Flipped classroom: Active methodology for sustainable learning in higher education during social distancing due to COVID-19. *Sustainability*, *13*(10), 5336.

Cueva, A., & Inga, E. (2022). Information and communication technologies for education considering the flipped learning model. *Education Sciences*, *12*(3), 207.

Dai, C. P., Ke, F., Dai, Z., & Pachman, M. (2023). Improving teaching practices via virtual reality-supported simulation-based learning: Scenario design and the duration of implementation. *British Journal of Educational Technology*, *54*(4), 836–856.

Deniz, E. U., Ceylan, C., Eren, R., & Memiş, O. B. (2024). Advancing empathy and emotional intelligence among pharmacy students: A comparative mixed-methods study with peer role-play simulation intervention. *Currents in Pharmacy Teaching & Learning*, *16*(8), 102112. PMID: 38795610

Dolapcioglu, S., & Doğanay, A. (2022). Development of critical thinking in mathematics classes via authentic learning: An action research. *International Journal of Mathematical Education in Science and Technology*, *53*(6), 1363–1386.

Espada-Chavarria, R., González-Montesino, R. H., López-Bastías, J. L., & Díaz-Vega, M. (2023). Universal design for learning and instruction: Effective strategies for inclusive higher education. *Education Sciences*, *13*(6), 620.

Fang, J., Vong, J., & Fang, J. (2022). Exploring student engagement in fully flipped classroom pedagogy: Case of an Australian business undergraduate degree. *Journal of Education for Business*, *97*(2), 76–85.

Fisher, R., Perényi, A., & Birdthistle, N. (2021). The positive relationship between flipped and blended learning and student engagement, performance and satisfaction. *Active Learning in Higher Education*, *22*(2), 97–113.

Frei-Landau, R., Orland-Barak, L., & Muchnick-Rozonov, Y. (2022). What's in it for the observer? Mimetic aspects of learning through observation in simulation-based learning in teacher education. *Teaching and Teacher Education*, *113*, 103682.

Grant, K. A. (2025). Experiential learning. In *Practical Applications of Experiential and Community-Engaged Learning Methods in Business* (Vol. 1, pp. 91–109). High-Impact Teaching Practices in Business Education.

Grech, A., Wodehouse, A., & Brisco, R. (2024). Empathic empowerment: An exploration and analysis of a situated interaction through empathic modelling and role-play. *Proceedings of the Design Society*, *4*, 2373–2382.

Haddad, R. J., & Kalaani, Y. (2014). Gaming against plagiarism (GAP): A game-based approach to illustrate research misconduct to undergraduate engineering students.

Hardwick, J., Whittington-Walsh, F., Bezanson, K., Miller, A., & Sawatzky, E. (2022). Designing for inclusion. In *Designing for Care.*

Horak, A., Daly, K., & King, S. (2024). *Creating equity and access for gifted learners: Implementing a problem-based professional learning experience using the ExCEL model.* Routledge.

Howell, R. A. (2021). Engaging students in education for sustainable development: The benefits of active learning, reflective practices and flipped classroom pedagogies. *Journal of Cleaner Production*, *325*, 129318.

Jiang, M. Y. C., Jong, M. S. Y., Lau, W. W. F., Chai, C. S., & Wu, N. (2021). Using automatic speech recognition technology to enhance EFL learners' oral language complexity in a flipped classroom. *Australasian Journal of Educational Technology*, *37*(2), 110–131.

Jones, A., & Bomash, I. (2018, June). Validating mastery learning: assessing the impact of adaptive learning objective mastery in Knewton Alta. In *International Conference on Artificial Intelligence in Education* (pp. 433-437). Cham: Springer International Publishing.

Kamalı-Arslantaş, T., & Baser, D. (2025). Effects of implementing interactive videos in an online flipped classroom on preservice special education teachers. *European Journal of Education*, *60*(4), e70234.

Kasperski, R., & Crispel, O. (2022). Preservice teachers' perspectives on the contribution of simulation-based learning to the development of communication skills. *Journal of Education for Teaching*, *48*(5), 521–534.

Kawinkoonlasate, P. (2024). Utilizing a digital-flipped classroom approach to enhance writing skills and foster an active learning environment among Thai EFL learners.

Klochko, O., Fedorets, V., Tkachenko, S., & Maliar, O. (2021). The use of digital technologies for flipped learning implementation. *IEEE EAEEIE Annual Conference Proceedings,* 1–6.

Kochurina, S. A., Fedorova, O. O., & Zakharov, K. P. (2022, April). Learning Motivation of Students of Adaptive Learning Platforms. In Proceedings of the Conference "Integrating Engineering Education and Humanities for Global Intercultural Perspectives" (pp. 303-310). Cham: Springer International Publishing.

Kozyar, M. M., Pasichnyk, S. M., Kopchak, M. M., Burmakina, N. S., & Suran, T. (2022). Simulation-based learning as an effective method of practical training of future translators. *Journal of Curriculum and Teaching*, *11*(1), 298–308.

Kurtts, S. A. (2006). Universal design for learning in inclusive classrooms. *Electronic Journal for Inclusive Education*, *1*(10), 7.

Langan, L., Frazer, K., Darley, A., Goodman, L., Browne, F., Fulfilled, P., & Redmond, C. (2025). Inclusive pedagogy in online simulation-based learning in undergraduate nursing education: A scoping review. *Journal of Advanced Nursing*, *81*(2), 591–606. PMID: 38940383

Li, R., Lund, A., & Nordsteien, A. (2023). The link between flipped and active learning: A scoping review. *Teaching in Higher Education*, *28*(8), 1993–2027.

Liu, Y., & Pásztor, A. (2022). Effects of problem-based learning instructional intervention on critical thinking in higher education: A meta-analysis. *Thinking Skills and Creativity*, *45*, 101069.

Löfstrand, P., & Zakrisson, I. (2025). Exploring the impact of role-playing exercises on cognitive and emotional processes: A social-and educational psychological perspective. *Frontiers in Psychology*, *16*, 1645213. PMID: 41030334

Nurhaswinda, N., Pebriana, P. H., & Nurmalina, N. (2025). The Impact of Technology-Driven Adaptive Learning on Mathematical Conceptual Mastery in Primary Education. G-Couns: Jurnal Bimbingan dan Konseling, 9(3), 2383-2397.

Rohm, A. J., Stefl, M., & Ward, N. (2021). Future proof and real-world ready: The role of live project-based learning in students' skill development. *Journal of Marketing Education*, *43*(2), 204–215.

Salvador, R., Barros, M. V., Barreto, B., Pontes, J., Yoshino, R. T., Piekarski, C. M., & de Francisco, A. C. (2023). Challenges and opportunities for problem-based learning in higher education: Lessons from a cross-program Industry 4.0 case. *Industry and Higher Education*, *37*(1), 3–21.

Sapkaroski, D., Mundy, M., & Dimmock, M. R. (2022). Immersive virtual reality simulated learning environment versus role-play for empathic clinical communication training. *Journal of Medical Radiation Sciences*, *69*(1), 56–65. PMID: 34706398

Sousa, M. J., & Costa, J. M. (2022). Discovering entrepreneurship competencies through problem-based learning in higher education students. *Education Sciences*, *12*(3), 185.

Tariq, M. U. (2026). AI-Powered Assessment Platforms: Transforming Higher Education Evaluation. In *Innovating Assessment and Evaluation in Higher Education: Inclusive Practices and Technological Advancements* (pp. 117-146). IGI Global Scientific Publishing.

Toto, G. A., Marinelli, C. V., Cavioni, V., di Furia, M., Traetta, L., Iuso, S., & Petito, A. (2024). What is the role of technologies for inclusive education? A systematic review. In *International Conference on Higher Education Learning Methodologies and Technologies Online* (pp. 533–565). Springer, Cham.

Upadhyay, M., & Malik, F. A. (2024). Societal and economic impact of Atmanirbhar Bharat: A long-term vision through education. Empowering India's Future: NEP. Skill Development and Cultural Expression, 17.

Valiente-Riedl, E., Anderson, L., & Banki, S. (2022). Practicing what we teach: Experiential learning in higher education that cuts both ways. *Review of Education, Pedagogy & Cultural Studies*, *44*(3), 231–252.

Vermunt, J. D. (2023). Understanding, measuring and improving simulation-based learning in higher education: Student and teacher learning perspectives. *Learning and Instruction*, *86*, 101773.

Weng, X., Chiu, T. K., & Tsang, C. C. (2022). Promoting student creativity and entrepreneurship through real-world problem-based maker education. *Thinking Skills and Creativity*, *45*, 101046.

Williams, L., & Sembiante, S. F. (2022). Experiential learning in US undergraduate teacher preparation programs: A review of the literature. *Teaching and Teacher Education*, *112*, 103630.

Yazici, M. S., & Uzuner, F. G. (2024). School-based inclusive mentoring within the scope of an experiential learning model (IEM) for teacher education. *Teaching and Teacher Education*, *152*, 104799.

Yeganeh, L. N., Fenty, N. S., Chen, Y., Simpson, A., & Hatami, M. (2025). The future of education: A multi-layered metaverse classroom model for immersive and inclusive learning. *Future Internet*, *17*(2), 63.

Yilmaz, O., & Hebebci, M. T. (2022). The use of virtual environments and simulation in teacher training. *International Journal on Social and Education Sciences*, *4*, 446–457.

Youngerman, E., & Culver, K. C. (2024). Increasing equity through project-based learning in graduate and professional schools: Problems of practice, cases, and clinics. In *Promoting Meaningful Student-Faculty Experiences in Graduate Education* (pp. 62–84). Routledge.

Chapter 7
Minds and Machines: The Interdisciplinary Challenge of AI's Influence in Education

Pankaj Bhambri
https://orcid.org/0000-0003-4437-4103
Guru Nanak Dev Engineering College, Ludhiana, India

Suresh Kumar
https://orcid.org/0009-0009-1272-5053
Maharishi Markandeshwar University, Mullana, India

ABSTRACT

The integration of Artificial Intelligence (AI) into education transcends its role as a mere efficiency tool, becoming an active, "unseen classroom partner" that shapes cognitive, social, and ethical dimensions of learning. This chapter employs an interdisciplinary conceptual analysis to argue that understanding AI's profound influence requires synthesizing perspectives from computer science, psychology, sociology, and philosophy. Moving beyond a technocentric view, we critically examine AI's dual potential to enhance metacognition and personalization while simultaneously risking algorithmic dependency, eroded autonomy, and the amplification of societal biases. The analysis extends to AI's role in shaping trust, motivation, and classroom dynamics, with particular attention to its integration within immersive and inclusive learning environments. We confront key ethical dilemmas surrounding data privacy, surveillance, and algorithmic fairness.

DOI: 10.4018/979-8-3373-5188-9.ch007

1 INTRODUCTION: THE UNSEEN CLASSROOM PARTNER

The integration of Artificial Intelligence (AI) into educational settings is often celebrated for its efficiency and personalization, promising a revolution in how we teach and learn. However, this narrative frequently overlooks a more profound and subtle transformation. Beyond the interactive tutors and automated grading systems, AI has become an "unseen classroom partner"—a pervasive force that actively, if imperceptibly, shapes the educational environment, influencing not just what students learn, but how they think, feel, and perceive knowledge itself. This chapter moves beyond a technocentric view to investigate this multifaceted influence, arguing that to understand modern education, we must account for the silent, formative role of these intelligent systems. AI is not a neutral tool but an active participant in the educational dynamic (Lobanova et al., 2024). Its algorithms curate information, its feedback mechanisms guide behavior, and its very presence alters traditional classroom interactions and power structures. By framing AI in this way, we set the stage for a critical exploration of its cognitive, social, and ethical ramifications. The goal is to shift the conversation from what AI does for education to what AI is doing to education, prompting a necessary and interdisciplinary examination of our new learning reality.

This chapter intentionally bridges the interdisciplinary study of AI in education with the specific challenges and opportunities of immersive and inclusive learning environments, such as VR-based simulations, AI-driven digital twins, and adaptive gamified platforms. By doing so, it aligns directly with this book's focus on practical, inclusive, and immersive educational futures.

1.1 Methodological Approach

This chapter adopts an interdisciplinary conceptual analysis and synthesis to deconstruct the layered influence of AI in education. It does not present new empirical data but constructs a robust theoretical framework by critically integrating findings and theories from diverse fields. The methodology involves: (1) a critical review of contemporary literature (2024-2025) from computer science, educational psychology, sociology, ethics, and learning design; (2) the identification and interconnection of key themes across these disciplines (e.g., linking algorithmic design to cognitive offloading and social bias); and (3) the application of this synthesized understanding to propose a principled framework for human-centric AIED. This approach is chosen to bridge disciplinary silos and provide a holistic, critical lens on a complex socio-technical phenomenon, moving from diagnosis of challenges to normative design principles.

This chapter adopts an interdisciplinary conceptual analysis and synthesis to deconstruct the layered influence of AI in education, with a focused lens on immersive and inclusive learning contexts. It does not present new empirical data but constructs a robust theoretical framework by critically integrating findings and theories from diverse fields. The methodology involves: (1) a critical review of contemporary literature (2024–2025) from computer science, educational psychology, sociology, ethics, and learning design, with particular attention to studies on VR, AR, gamification, and inclusive AIED tools; (2) the identification and interconnection of key themes across these disciplines (e.g., linking algorithmic design to cognitive offloading and social bias in simulated learning environments); and (3) the application of this synthesized understanding to propose a principled framework for human-centric AIED that is actionable in immersive and inclusive settings.

1.2 From Tool to Agent: Redefining AI's Role

Traditionally, educational technology has been understood as a tool—an instrument wielded by human intention, like a calculator or a pencil. Its function was to augment human capability without independent influence. Contemporary AI, particularly with the advent of generative models and adaptive learning platforms, shatters this paradigm (Vatankhah et al., 2024). These systems are not passive instruments; they are active agents that make decisions, generate content, and provide personalized feedback based on complex, often opaque, internal logic. This shift from a static tool to a dynamic agent represents a fundamental change in the human-machine relationship within the learning process.

This redefinition is critical because an agent exerts a different kind of influence than a tool. An agent can initiate interaction, adapt strategies in real-time, and assert a form of "expertise." When a student interacts with an AI writing tutor that suggests structural changes to an essay, or an adaptive learning platform that alters the difficulty of problems based on performance, the AI is acting as a pedagogical agent (Yıldız, 2025). This agency directly impacts the learner's journey, delegating certain aspects of guidance and judgment to the machine. Consequently, we can no longer evaluate AI solely on its technical performance but must also assess its pedagogical actions and their consequences on student autonomy, trust, and intellectual development.

1.3 The Central Thesis: Why an Interdisciplinary Lens is Essential

The central thesis of this chapter is that the profound challenges and opportunities posed by AI in education are inherently interconnected and cannot be adequately understood or addressed through a single disciplinary silo (Creely & Blannin, 2025). A computer scientist can optimize an algorithm for efficiency, but cannot alone grasp its potential to erode metacognitive skills. A psychologist might study learning outcomes, but may lack the framework to analyze how algorithmic bias perpetuates social inequities. Similarly, an ethicist can outline principles for fairness, but requires insights from sociology and education to implement them in practice. The complexity of AI's influence demands a synthesis of these perspectives. Therefore, an interdisciplinary lens is not merely beneficial but essential (Rani et al., 2024). It allows us to see the full picture: how a cognitive effect (e.g., algorithmic dependency) is linked to a technical design (e.g., high-powered recommendations), which in turn raises an ethical concern (e.g., diminished student agency) and a social consequence (e.g., changed classroom dynamics). This chapter argues that only by integrating insights from computer science, psychology, sociology, philosophy, and educational theory can we develop a holistic understanding of AI as an "unseen classroom partner" and craft effective, human-centric responses that harness its power while mitigating its risks.

1.4 Chapter Roadmap

This chapter is structured to systematically unpack the layered influence of AI, guiding the reader from the internal cognitive processes of the learner to the broader ethical and societal implications. We begin by exploring the Cognitive Layer, investigating how AI impacts thinking patterns, metacognition, and tangible learning outcomes. From there, we expand to the Affective and Social Layer, analyzing the formation of student attitudes, perceptions of AI reliability, and the reshaping of classroom relationships and social biases, with specific attention to immersive learning contexts (Rana & Bhambri, 2024a). The third section delves into the Ethical and Philosophical Dimension, confronting the fundamental questions of autonomy, data privacy, and equity that AI introduces. The final section synthesizes these explorations to propose a way forward. In Toward an Interdisciplinary Response, we will integrate the threads from the preceding layers to construct a collaborative framework for researchers, designers, educators, and policymakers (Lamberti et al., 2025). This roadmap is designed to build a cumulative argument, demonstrating that each domain of influence is inextricably linked and that a siloed approach is insufficient for navigating the future of education—particularly in evolving immersive and inclusive environments—in an age of intelligent machines. The conclusion will offer a forward-looking perspective on steering the symbiotic relationship between human minds and artificial agents.

2 THE COGNITIVE LAYER: AI'S IMPACT ON THINKING AND LEARNING OUTCOMES

2.1 Enhancing or Eroding Metacognition?

AI systems, particularly those offering real-time feedback and learning analytics, hold significant promise for enhancing metacognition—the awareness and understanding of one's own thought processes (Ng et al., 2024). By providing students with detailed dashboards on their performance, struggle points, and time management, these tools act as external mirrors, reflecting their learning journey back to them. This can help learners develop a more accurate sense of their knowledge gaps, strengthen their ability to self-assess, and make more informed decisions about what to study next, thereby fostering self-regulated learning (Parker et al., 2025). In this capacity, AI serves as a powerful scaffold, helping students "learn how to learn" by making the learning process visible and actionable.

Conversely, an over-reliance on AI-driven guidance risks eroding the very metacognitive skills it aims to build (Nishat, 2025). If an AI system consistently curates content, predicts difficulties before they are deeply felt, and provides immediate corrective feedback, the student may become a passive recipient of information rather than an active manager of their own cognition. The internal struggle to monitor one's comprehension and the crucial experience of working through confusion—key drivers of deep learning—can be short-circuited (Peters et al., 2024). The danger is that the AI becomes a cognitive crutch, leading to "metacognitive offloading," where students no longer develop the intrinsic ability to plan, monitor, and evaluate their learning independently, leaving them ill-equipped for complex tasks in non-scaffolded, real-world environments. For example, in a VR-based engineering simulation, an AI tutor providing real-time feedback on design choices can help students reflect on their problem-solving process. However, if the AI prematurely corrects errors, it may prevent the learner from experiencing and learning from failure—a key component of deep learning in immersive contexts.

2.2 Personalized Learning Pathways and Knowledge Acquisition

The core promise of AI in education is the delivery of truly personalized learning pathways. By analyzing vast datasets of student interactions, AI can adapt the sequence, pace, and difficulty of content to match individual needs and aptitudes. This moves beyond the one-size-fits-all model, theoretically optimizing knowledge acquisition by ensuring students are consistently working within their "zone of proximal development." Such systems can identify and remediate specific misconceptions instantly, reinforce concepts as needed, and present information in modalities that align with a learner's preferences, potentially leading to more efficient and durable learning outcomes compared to traditional methods (Simões & Caldeira, 2024). However, this personalization raises critical questions about the nature of the knowledge being acquired. Highly algorithmically-curated pathways may lead to a fragmented or "siloed" understanding of a subject, where students miss the broader, interdisciplinary connections that a standardized curriculum often provides (Allison et al., 2025). Furthermore, the criteria for "optimal" pathways are defined by the algorithm's model of learning, which may prioritize measurable, short-term performance metrics (e.g., quiz scores) over deeper, more conceptual understanding or creative thinking. There is a risk of creating a generation of learners who are proficient in navigating narrow, pre-defined skill trees but lack the cohesive, integrated knowledge framework necessary for innovation and critical synthesis.

2.3 The Problem of "Algorithmic Dependency" and Critical Thinking

A primary cognitive risk associated with pervasive AI integration is the development of "algorithmic dependency"—a learned reliance on AI systems to the point where cognitive effort and intellectual autonomy diminish (Chen, 2025). When students habitually turn to an AI for answers, step-by-step solutions, or even ideation, they bypass the productive struggle that is essential for developing robust problem-solving skills and conceptual mastery. This dependency mirrors the "Google effect," where individuals forget information they believe can be easily retrieved, but extends it to the very process of thinking itself, potentially atrophying the cognitive muscles required for sustained intellectual effort.

This dependency poses a direct threat to critical thinking, the cornerstone of advanced learning. Critical thinking requires questioning assumptions, evaluating evidence, and constructing logical arguments—processes that are inherently internal and effortful (Khogali & Mekid, 2024). If an AI consistently provides pre-digested information, validated answers, and persuasive arguments, students may lose the motivation and capacity to engage in these foundational practices (Vatankhah et al., 2024). The challenge, therefore, is not just to prevent plagiarism, but to foster an environment where AI tools are used to stimulate and challenge thinking rather than replace it. Educators must design tasks that require students to critique, build upon, and apply AI-generated outputs, ensuring the technology serves as a catalyst for critical inquiry rather than a substitute for it (Kayyali, 2024). A tangible example of algorithmic dependency is seen when students use AI tools like ChatGPT to complete homework without engaging with the material. As one reviewer noted, when asked to explain their AI-generated submissions, students often cannot articulate the underlying concepts—illustrating how AI can bypass the cognitive struggle essential for genuine understanding.

3 THE AFFECTIVE AND SOCIAL LAYER: SHAPING ATTITUDES AND PERCEPTIONS

The chart of Figure 1 visualizes how an AI System directly influences three key affective and social domains (Trust & Relationships, Perception of Fairness & Bias, and Motivation & Engagement). These influences lead to specific alterations in classroom dynamics and student psychology, which collectively result in changed Student Attitudes and Learning Behaviours. Crucially, this outcome creates a feedback loop (indicated by the dotted line), as these new behaviours generate the data that is used to train and refine future AI systems, potentially creating a self-reinforcing cycle that can be either virtuous or vicious. In immersive learning environments—such as VR business simulations or AI-facilitated digital twins for engineering education (Rana & Bhambri, 2024a)—this cycle is intensified, as AI shapes behavior within a highly responsive and personalized digital space.

Figure 1. Cyclical relationship between AI systems and the affective/social dimensions of the learner

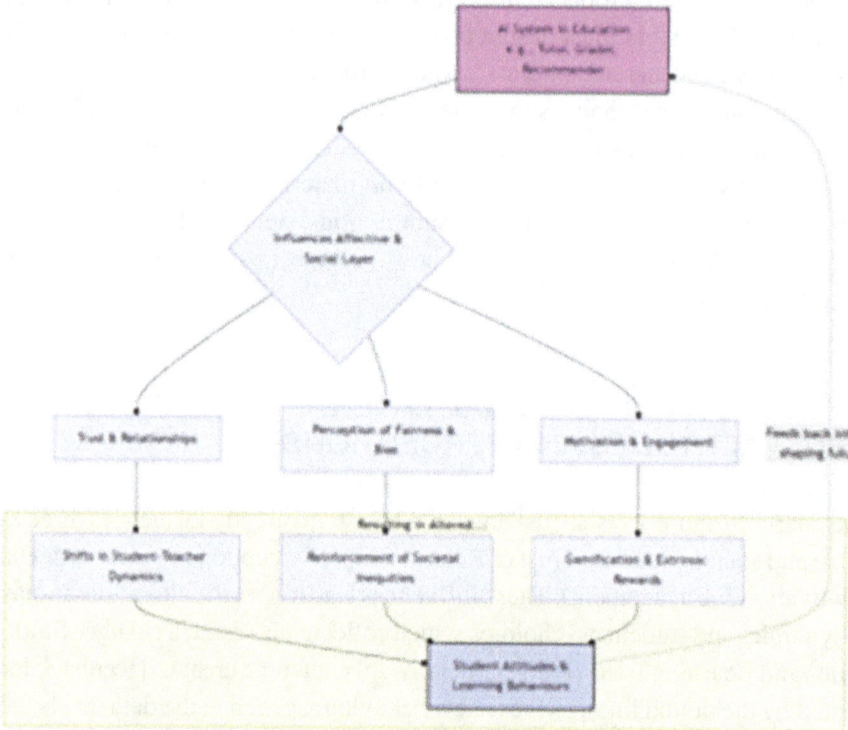

In immersive AI-driven simulations, such as a virtual business strategy lab, the AI not only adapts scenarios but also influences team dynamics and individual confidence. These environments intensify the feedback loop between AI guidance and student behavior, making the design of trust and fairness even more critical.

3.1 Trust, Reliability, and Student-Teacher Relationships

The integration of AI tutors and feedback systems fundamentally recalibrates the dynamics of trust in the classroom. Students may develop a transactional reliance on AI for immediate, unambiguous answers, which can erode their tolerance for the productive struggle essential for deep learning and diminish their perception of the teacher's role as the primary guide (Rong et al., 2024). Conversely, when AI systems provide erroneous or biased information, they can undermine student trust not only in the technology but also in the institution that deploys it. This shifting trust dynamic challenges educators to reassert their value as empathetic mentors and facilitators of critical thinking, moving beyond their traditional role as knowledge dispensaries to become interpreters and contextualizers of AI-generated information. In immersive settings, where an AI might control a virtual character or adapt a simulation scenario, establishing clear boundaries between machine operation and human mentorship becomes even more critical.

3.2 AI as a Mirror: Uncovering and Amplifying Societal Biases

AI systems in education do not operate in a vacuum; they are trained on data produced by a society laden with historical and social inequities. Consequently, these systems can act as a mirror, reflecting and often amplifying existing biases related to race, gender, socioeconomic status, and culture (Elamin, 2024). This can manifest in automated grading systems that penalize non-native language patterns, recommendation engines that steer students toward traditionally gendered career paths, or content that presents a predominantly Western canon. The peril lies in the perceived objectivity of the algorithm, which can cloak these biased outputs in a veil of neutrality, thereby legitimizing and institutionalizing discrimination under the guise of personalized, data-driven education. For inclusive immersive environments, this is a paramount concern; an AI-driven virtual learning world that fails to represent diverse perspectives or that allocates resources based on biased models directly contradicts the goal of equitable access and experience.

3.3 Motivation, Engagement, and the Gamification of Learning

AI-driven platforms frequently employ gamification—using elements like points, badges, and leaderboards—to boost student motivation and engagement. While this can make learning more immediately appealing and increase time-on-task, it risks promoting extrinsic over intrinsic motivation, where students engage for the reward rather than a genuine love of learning. This can shallowify the educational experience, focusing on measurable metrics of completion rather than deep conceptual understanding (Bhambri & Kant, 2025a). The interdisciplinary challenge is to design AI systems that use these engaging mechanisms not as an end, but as a scaffold to foster a more profound, self-sustaining curiosity and a growth mindset, ensuring that the "game" of learning serves the deeper goal of mastery. In immersive gamified environments, this design challenge is amplified, requiring careful balance to ensure the immersive experience enhances, rather than distracts from, core learning objectives.

4 THE ETHICAL AND PHILOSOPHICAL DIMENSION: NAVIGATING THE NEW TERRAIN

4.1 Autonomy, Agency, and the Hidden Curriculum of AI

AI systems, through their recommendations and adaptive pathways, inherently shape student choice. While intended to personalize learning, this can inadvertently curtail intellectual autonomy by creating "filter bubbles" of knowledge and pre-empting the productive struggle essential for deep understanding (Stolpe & Hallström, 2024). The hidden curriculum here is one of deference to algorithmic authority; students may learn to trust the machine's judgment over their own intellectual curiosity, potentially stifling the development of critical thinking and self-directed learning skills that are the hallmarks of genuine education (Huang & Qiao, 2024).

Furthermore, the very design of AI can compromise student agency. When a platform constantly dictates the "next best step," it reduces the learner's opportunity to make false starts, explore tangents, and exercise metacognitive control over their learning journey. Philosophically, this raises a critical question: are we educating students to be independent thinkers or efficient system-optimizers? Preserving human agency requires a deliberate design ethos that positions AI as a consultative tool that expands, rather than contracts, the space for authentic student choice and intellectual risk-taking (Bhambri & Rani, 2025). This is especially pertinent in simulated professional environments (e.g., a virtual business strategy lab), where over-guidance could undermine the development of real-world decision-making resilience.

4.2 Data Privacy, Surveillance, and the Digital Student

The data-driven nature of AI in education creates an unprecedented regime of surveillance, transforming the traditional classroom into a high-resolution panopticon. Every click, hesitation, and interaction can be captured, analyzed, and used to build a pervasive digital profile of the "digital student." This raises profound privacy concerns that extend beyond simple data security to the very right to learn in a space of intellectual safety, free from the constant pressure of performance monitoring and the potential for data to be repurposed in ways that harm a student's future opportunities (Storozhyk, 2024). In immersive VR classrooms, where eye-tracking, biometric responses, and interaction logs are continuously collected, the surveillance potential is magnified. This raises urgent ethical questions about student consent, data ownership, and the right to learn without being perpetually profiled.

The ethical dilemma lies in the tension between personalized learning, which requires data, and the protection of a child's developmental right to anonymity and error. Constant monitoring can instill anxiety, discourage creative experimentation, and normalize a culture of surveillance that students may carry into adulthood. An interdisciplinary response must, therefore, integrate pedagogical goals with legal and ethical frameworks from data protection (e.g., GDPR, FERPA) to establish clear boundaries, ensure meaningful consent, and protect students from being reduced to their data points (Jain & Raghuram, 2024). In immersive environments that track biometric data (e.g., eye movement, physiological responses), these concerns are exponentially greater.

4.3 Defining Equity and Fairness in Algorithmic Systems

The promise of AI to democratize education is shadowed by the significant risk of exacerbating existing inequalities. Algorithmic systems are trained on historical data, which often contains societal and historical biases (Patel & Indurkhya, 2025). An AI trained on data from privileged school districts, for example, may develop a model of "success" that systematically disadvantages students from underrepresented or non-traditional backgrounds, mistaking correlation for causation and cementing inequity under a veneer of technological objectivity.

Achieving fairness, therefore, requires moving beyond a purely technical definition. It is not enough for an algorithm to be mathematically "blind"; it must be actively designed for equity and justice. This demands an interdisciplinary approach where computer scientists collaborate with sociologists, ethicists, and educators to critically audit datasets and models for bias (Bhambri & Kant, 2025b). The goal must be to create systems that are not only fair in procedure but also just in their outcomes, actively working to identify and remedy opportunity gaps rather than perpetuating the status quo. For inclusive immersive learning, this means ensuring virtual environments and AI tutors are accessible, culturally responsive, and designed to support, not stereotype, diverse learners.

4.4 Practical Implementation in Immersive and Inclusive Environments: Bridging Theory and Classroom Reality

While the theoretical risks and promises of AI in education are well-documented, implementing AI in immersive and inclusive settings presents unique practical challenges. For instance, in VR-based collaborative simulations, AI must balance adaptive guidance with preserving student agency. Over-guidance can undermine decision-making resilience, while under-support can leave learners frustrated. Additionally, in inclusive classrooms, AI tools must be designed to accommodate diverse learning needs without reinforcing stereotypes. For example, an AI-driven language tutor in an immersive environment must recognize and support non-native speakers without penalizing dialectal variations. These challenges require not only interdisciplinary design but also ongoing teacher training and iterative feedback loops with students to ensure AI tools remain aligned with pedagogical goals.

5 TOWARD AN INTERDISCIPLINARY RESPONSE: A FRAMEWORK FOR INTEGRATION

The preceding analysis reveals that the challenges posed by AI in education are not siloed; they are woven from cognitive, social, and ethical threads (Tong, 2024). Addressing them requires moving beyond isolated solutions to an integrated, interdisciplinary framework (Chiu, 2024). This section proposes a structure for such collaboration, focusing on dialogue, design principles, and actionable recommendations that collectively steer AI's integration toward humane and effective ends, particularly within innovative learning contexts like immersive simulations.

5.1 Bridging the Silos: Dialogue Between Disciplines

To dismantle disciplinary silos, we must establish structured forums for sustained dialogue. This involves creating shared vocabulary and collaborative spaces where computer scientists, educators, psychologists, sociologists, ethicists, and policymakers can co-construct understanding. Practical mechanisms include interdisciplinary research consortia, "translator" roles for experts who can mediate between fields, and design charrettes that bring diverse stakeholders together at the inception of AIED projects—including those for immersive learning—not merely as evaluators after the fact (Butson & Spronken-Smith, 2024).

The goal of this dialogue is to develop a holistic understanding of the "socio-technical-educational" system. For instance, a psychologist can illuminate how an AI's feedback mechanism in a VR simulation impacts a student's self-efficacy, while a sociologist can examine how that same tool disproportionately affects students from different cultural backgrounds. An ethicist can then frame these insights into guidelines for justice, and a computer scientist can implement technical safeguards (Allen & Kendeou, 2024). It is in this iterative exchange that truly robust and responsive educational AI can emerge.

5.2 Principles for Human-Centric AIED (AI in Education) Design

Moving from dialogue to design, we propose four core principles for Human-Centric AIED. First is Augmentation, Not Automation: AI systems should be designed to enhance and extend the capabilities of educators and learners, not replace them, preserving the irreplaceable human elements of mentorship, inspiration, and care

(Nowrozy & Jam, 2024). Second is Equity and Justice by Design, requiring proactive auditing for bias, inclusive data practices, and designs that actively close—rather than widen—educational disparities, ensuring tools are accessible and fair for all learners in both physical and digital spaces.

The third principle is Transparency and Interpretability, mandating that AI systems provide intelligible explanations for their recommendations and outputs to both teachers and students, fostering trust and enabling informed oversight. Finally, Agency and Data Sovereignty must be central, ensuring that learners and educators retain control over their learning journey and personal data (Bhambri & Khang, 2024a). This means designing for meaningful consent, editable learner models, and options to opt-out of certain automated features, thereby reinforcing human autonomy within the technologically mediated environment (Hu, 2025).

5.3 Policy and Pedagogical Recommendations for the Future

Translating these principles into action requires concrete policy and pedagogical shifts. Policymakers must establish agile regulatory frameworks that set minimum standards for algorithmic fairness, data privacy, and accountability in educational tools—including those used in immersive environments—while also funding independent audits and long-term research on AI's societal impact. Simultaneously, institutions should develop "AI in Education" strategic plans that include infrastructure, professional development, and clear acceptable-use policies that align with their core educational mission (Kamali et al., 2024).

For educators, the recommendations focus on empowerment through continuous professional development. This includes training not just on how to use AI tools, but how to critically evaluate them, interpret their outputs, and integrate them pedagogically to support diverse learning objectives (Bhambri & Khang, 2024b). Furthermore, curriculum designers must embed digital and AI literacy for students, teaching them to be critical consumers of AI-generated content, to understand the ethical implications of these technologies, and to use them as powerful assistants in their own lifelong learning journeys, thus preparing them for a future of human-AI collaboration.

6 CONCLUSION: STEERING THE SYMBIOSIS

The integration of Artificial Intelligence into education is not a fleeting trend but a fundamental shift, demanding we move beyond viewing it as a simple tool. As this chapter has illustrated through interdisciplinary lenses, AI's most significant challenges and opportunities lie in its profound influence on the human dimensions of learning—how students think, what they believe, and how they relate to knowledge and each other. The cognitive, affective, and ethical layers of this integration are deeply intertwined; a change in one precipitates ripple effects across the others (Przegalinska & Triantoro, 2024). Therefore, the central challenge is no longer merely technical but socio-technical, requiring us to consciously steer the evolving relationship between human minds and machine intelligence toward a productive and ethical symbiosis, rather than allowing it to develop haphazardly. This imperative is magnified in the context of immersive and inclusive learning, where AI's influence is both more pervasive and potentially more transformative.

To navigate this symbiosis, a proactive and collaborative framework is essential. This entails moving from isolated disciplinary actions to integrated responses where educators, technologists, psychologists, ethicists, and policymakers co-create the future of learning. Such a framework must be built on three pillars: first, Human-Centric Design, ensuring that AI tools are developed to augment, not replace, educator expertise and student agency, especially in complex simulated environments. Second, Transparent Pedagogical Integration, where the use of AI is explicitly discussed in the classroom, its limitations are taught, and its outputs are critically evaluated as part of the curriculum (Bhambri & Khang, 2025). Third, Continuous Ethical Auditing, establishing ongoing processes to assess AI systems for bias, equity, and data privacy, with mechanisms for adaptation and accountability.

Ultimately, the goal is to forge a future where AI serves to amplify the best of human education: fostering creativity, critical thinking, and compassionate collaboration within diverse and engaging learning ecosystems. By consciously steering this symbiosis, we can harness the power of AI to provide unparalleled personalization and support, freeing educators to focus on the deeply human acts of mentoring, inspiration, and care (Moemeke, 2024). The success of this endeavor will not be measured by the sophistication of the algorithms, but by our ability to cultivate wiser, more empathetic, and more empowered learners, prepared to thrive in a complex world alongside intelligent machines. The responsibility lies with us to ensure that in the classroom of the future—whether physical or immersive—the mind remains firmly in the lead, with the machine as its most capable and carefully guided partner (Rana & Bhambri, 2024b).

The future of AI in education—especially within immersive and inclusive learning ecosystems—depends on our ability to translate interdisciplinary principles into classroom practice. This requires:

- Co-design with educators and students in the development of AI tools for VR/AR environments.
- Pilot programs in real immersive classrooms to test AI's impact on engagement, equity, and learning outcomes.

- Professional development modules that train teachers to critically evaluate and pedagogically integrate AI in immersive settings.

By taking these steps, we can ensure that AI serves as a guided partner in education—enhancing human potential without diminishing human agency.

REFERENCES

Allen, L. K., & Kendeou, P. (2024). ED-AI Lit: An interdisciplinary framework for AI literacy in education. *Policy Insights from the Behavioral and Brain Sciences*, *11*(1), 3–10.

Allison, J., Hwang, G. J., Mayer, R. E., Pellas, N., Karnalim, O., de Freitas, S., & Sanusi, I. (2025). From generative AI to extended reality: Multidisciplinary perspectives on the challenges, opportunities, and future of educational computing. *Journal of Educational Computing Research*, *63*(6), 1327–1363.

Bhambri, P., & Kant, S. (2025a, February 1-2). A taxonomy of bias in machine learning: Classification, sources, and implications for ethical AI [Paper presentation]. Lincoln-SPAST Global Sustainability Programme (SGS-24), 1st International Conference of L-GPR Program, Lincoln University College, Malaysia. SPAST Proceedings, 1(2). https://spast.org/techrep/article/view/5387/724

Bhambri, P., & Kant, S. (2025b, April 26-27). Ethical AI systems: A comprehensive framework for bias mitigation and fairness in machine learning [Paper presentation]. Lincoln-SPAST Global Sustainability Programme (SGS-24), 2nd International Conference of L-GPR Program, Lincoln University College, Malaysia. SPAST Proceedings, 1(2). https://spast.org/techrep/article/view/5385/698

Bhambri, P., & Khang, A. (2024a). The human-machine nexus with art-making generative AIs. In Hai-Jew, S. (Ed.), *Making art with generative AI tools* (pp. 73–85). IGI Global., DOI: 10.4018/979-8-3693-1950-5.ch004

Bhambri, P., & Khang, A. (2024b). Machine learning advancements in E-health: Transforming digital healthcare. In *Medical robotics and AI-assisted diagnostics for a high-tech healthcare industry* (pp. 174–194). IGI Global., DOI: 10.4018/979-8-3693-2105-8.ch012

Bhambri, P., & Khang, A. (2025). Edge computing for enhancing efficiency and sustainability in green transportation systems. In Khang, A. (Ed.), *Driving green transportation system through artificial intelligence and automation* (pp. 43–65). Springer., DOI: 10.1007/978-3-031-72617-0_3

Bhambri, P., & Rani, S. (2025). Advancements in educational technology: Navigating the landscape of user experience in Web 3.0. In Pelet, J.-É. (Ed.), *Architecting the digital future: Platforms, design, and application* (pp. 365–396). IGI Global., DOI: 10.4018/979-8-3693-2973-3.ch014

Butson, R., & Spronken-Smith, R. (2024). AI and its implications for research in higher education: A critical dialogue. *Higher Education Research & Development, 43*(3), 563–577.

Chen, J. J. (2025). From Turing's conception of machine intelligence to the evolution of AI in early childhood education: Conceptual, empirical, and practical insights. AI. *Brain and Child, 1*(1), 1.

Chiu, T. K. (2024). Future research recommendations for transforming higher education with generative AI. *Computers and Education: Artificial Intelligence, 6*, 100197.

Creely, E., & Blannin, J. (2025). Creative partnerships with generative AI. Possibilities for education and beyond. *Thinking Skills and Creativity, 56*, 101727.

Elamin, M. O. I. (2024). AI through the ages: Unlocking key opportunities and navigating challenges in the history and future of artificial intelligence. *International Journal of Religion, 5*(12), 1152–1166.

Hu, Y. (2025). Creating interactive AI learning environments: Integrating interdisciplinary approaches and Taoist art principles. *Interactive Learning Environments*, •••, 1–20.

Huang, X., & Qiao, C. (2024). Enhancing computational thinking skills through artificial intelligence education at a STEAM high school. *Science & Education, 33*(2), 383–403.

Jain, K., & Raghuram, J. N. V. (2024). Unlocking potential: The impact of AI on education technology. *Multidisciplinary Reviews, 7*(3), 2024049–2024049.

Kamali, J., Alpat, M. F., & Bozkurt, A. (2024). AI ethics as a complex and multifaceted challenge: Decoding educators' AI ethics alignment through the lens of activity theory. *International Journal of Educational Technology in Higher Education, 21*(1), 62.

Kayyali, M. (2024). Future possibilities and challenges of AI in education. In *Transforming education with generative AI: Prompt engineering and synthetic content creation* (pp. 118–137). IGI Global Scientific Publishing.

Khogali, H. O., & Mekid, S. (2024). Perception and Ethical Challenges for the Future of AI as Encountered by Surveyed New Engineers. *Societies (Basel, Switzerland), 14*(12).

Lamberti, P. M., Bombaerts, G., & IJsselsteijn, W. (2025). Mind the gap: Bridging the divide between computer scientists and ethicists in shaping moral machines. *Ethics and Information Technology, 27*(1), 2.

Lobanova, A., Hrabovets, I., Prykhodko, O., Karytka, V., Kalashnikova, L., & Chernous, L. (2024). Artificial intelligence in teaching social disciplines: Opportunities and challenges of tools. *Educational Technology Quarterly, 2024*(4), 360–377.

Moemeke, C. D. (2024). Artificial intelligence and machine learning in enhancing science learning experiences: Exploring possibilities and concerns. *NIU Journal of Educational Research, 10*(2), 59–72.

Ng, D. T. K., Su, J., Leung, J. K. L., & Chu, S. K. W. (2024). Artificial intelligence (AI) literacy education in secondary schools: A review. *Interactive Learning Environments, 32*(10), 6204–6224.

Nishat, A. (2025). Rethinking Intelligence: An Interdisciplinary Framework for AI Research. *Pioneer Research Journal of Computing Science, 2*(2), 162–169.

Nowrozy, R., & Jam, D. (2024). Embracing the generative AI revolution: advancing tertiary education in cybersecurity with GPT. arXiv preprint arXiv:2403.11402.

Parker, J. L., Richard, V. M., Acabá, A., Escoffier, S., Flaherty, S., Jablonka, S., & Becker, K. P. (2025). Negotiating meaning with machines: AI's role in doctoral writing pedagogy. *International Journal of Artificial Intelligence in Education, 35*(3), 1218–1238.

Patel, N. S., & Indurkhya, N. (Eds.). (2025). *The Rise of Intelligent Machines: A Multi-disciplinary Perspective from Industry and Impact on Higher Education.* CRC Press.

Peters, M. A., Jackson, L., Papastephanou, M., Jandrić, P., Lazaroiu, G., Evers, C. W., & Fuller, S. (2024). AI and the future of humanity: ChatGPT-4, philosophy and education–Critical responses. *Educational Philosophy and Theory, 56*(9), 828–862.

Przegalinska, A., & Triantoro, T. (2024). *Converging minds: The creative potential of collaborative AI.* CRC Press.

Rana, R., & Bhambri, P. (2024a). Artificial Intelligence and Internet of Things (IoT) facilitated digital twin for Industry 4.0 application domains. In Rani, S., Bhambri, P., Kumar, S., Pareek, P. K., & Elngar, A. A. (Eds.), *AI-driven digital twin and Industry 4.0* (pp. 168–181). CRC Press., DOI: 10.1201/9781003395416-11

Rana, R., & Bhambri, P. (2024b). Generative AI in web application development: Enhancing user experience and performance. In Shah, I. A., & Jhanjhi, N. Z. (Eds.), *Generative AI for web engineering models* (pp. 471–486). IGI Global., DOI: 10.4018/979-8-3693-3703-5.ch021

Rani, S., Kataria, A., Bhambri, P., Pareek, P. K., & Puri, V. (2024). Artificial intelligence in personalized health services for better patient care. In Gupta, S. K., Karras, D. A., & Natarajan, R. (Eds.), *Revolutionizing healthcare: AI integration with IoT for enhanced patient outcomes* (pp. 89–108). Springer., DOI: 10.1007/978-3-031-65022-2_6

Rong, J., Terzidis, K., & Ding, J. (2024). Kids AI Design Thinking Education for Creativity Development. *Archives of Design Research*, *37*(3), 119–133.

Simões, J. M., & Caldeira, W. (2024). Ethics concerns in the use of computer-generated images for human communication. *Journal of Ethics in Higher Education*, (4), 169–192.

Stolpe, K., & Hallström, J. (2024). Artificial intelligence literacy for technology education. *Computers and Education Open*, *6*, 100159.

Storozhyk, M. (2024). Philosophy of future: Analytical overview of interaction between education, science, and artificial intelligence in the context of contemporary challenges. *Futurity Philosophy*, *3*(1), 23–47.

Tong, Y. (2024). Integration of artificial intelligence into the general education curriculum: Importance, approaches, challenges, and a conceptual framework for liberal arts universities. In INTED2024 Proceedings (pp. 7582-7589). IATED.

Vatankhah, S., Bamshad, V., Arici, H. E., & Duan, Y. (2024). Ethical implementation of artificial intelligence in the service industries. *Service Industries Journal*, *44*(9-10), 661–685.

Yıldız, T. (2025). The minds we make: A philosophical inquiry into theory of mind and artificial intelligence. *Integrative Psychological & Behavioral Science*, *59*(1), 10. PMID: 39743649

Zahra, S. T., Bibi, E., & Younus, Z. (2025). Artificial Intelligence (AI) and Human Mind: Struggles and Strengths in the Education Sector. In Artificial Intelligence and Human Agency in Education: Volume One: The Nexus Between AI and Human Agency in Educational Contexts (pp. 265-289). Springer Nature Singapore.

Chapter 8
Practical Inclusive Education Approaches in Immersive Learning Environments

Marubini Christinah Sadiki
https://orcid.org/0009-0001-3655-9610
University of South Africa, South Africa

ABSTRACT

Immersive learning environments, driven by cutting-edge technologies such as virtual reality (VR), augmented reality (AR), and interactive simulations, present substantial opportunities to enhance inclusive education. These technologies empower educators to create engaging and personalized learning experiences that cater to a diverse array of learning styles, abilities, and preferences. Central to this inclusive strategy is the Universal Design for Learning (UDL) framework, which advocates for adaptable methods of content delivery, learning assessment, and student engagement. When combined with immersive technologies, UDL facilitates the development of accessible educational resources that are advantageous for learners with disabilities, as well as those from varied linguistic and cultural backgrounds. An essential aspect of this methodology is the incorporation of multi-sensory learning tools, which are particularly beneficial for students facing cognitive or sensory challenges.

INTRODUCTION

Inclusive education, based on the principles of equity and access, affirms the right of every learner to receive a quality education, irrespective of their ability,

DOI: 10.4018/979-8-3373-5188-9.ch008

background, or circumstances (Makweya & Sepadi, 2025). In the 21st century, this dedication increasingly aligns with advancements in technology, particularly through immersive learning environments (Pramanik, 2024). Instruments such as virtual reality (VR), augmented reality (AR), mixed reality (MR), simulations, and gamified platforms are transforming the delivery and experience of education (AlGerafi et al., 2023; Thangavel, 2025). When purposefully designed, these technologies act as significant tools for inclusion, offering equitable opportunities for all learners to engage actively and achieve success (Yeganeh et al., 2025). Immersive learning emphasizes experiential, interactive, and learner-centered methodologies (Wagner & Liu, 2021; Oyelana, Olson, & Caine, 2022). These tools can simulate real-world contexts, tailor instruction to individual needs, and stimulate multiple senses, making them especially advantageous for students with varied learning requirements (Damaševičius & Sidekerskienė, 2024).

For example, environments enriched with audio can assist learners who have visual impairments, whereas controlled simulations can help students with autism in managing social situations (Gatcho, Manuel, & Sarasua, 2024; Patterson, 2022). Additionally, multilingual or language-support features integrated within augmented reality can help linguistically diverse learners to overcome language obstacles (Nteliou et al., 2021). Consequently, immersive technologies play a crucial role in enhancing inclusive teaching and learning methodologies (Yeganeh et al., 2025; Lazou & Tsinakos, 2023). However, the implementation of immersive tools in inclusive education necessitates more than mere access; it requires a deliberate and pedagogically sound approach. The utilization of technology must be in accordance with the Universal Design for Learning (UDL) framework, which promotes various modes of representation, engagement, and expression (Sewell, Kennett, & Pugh, 2022). Immersive environments informed by UDL enable learners to access information, interact with content, and exhibit understanding in personalized manners through visuals, narration, scaffolding, or interactive feedback (Vasinda & Pilgrim, 2023; Zhang et al., 2022). For instance, virtual laboratories may integrate step-by-step voice instructions, emphasized visual cues, and adaptive feedback mechanisms (Reyes et al., 2024; Matovu et al., 2023). The integration of these technologies must be guided by intentional curriculum design and inclusive pedagogy (Lazou & Tsinakos, 2023; Molloy & Farrell, 2024). Educators should create assignments that are socially equitable, culturally responsive, and rooted in the lived experiences of students (Ladson-Billings, 2023).

Immersive tools can enhance this experience by enabling students to investigate virtual cultural environments, participate in storytelling that validates their identity, or collaborate across various contexts in digital realms (Hashmi, 2025; Moss & McKeeman, 2025). The success of such tools hinges on educators' capacity to align technology with inclusive objectives a challenge that necessitates professional development, collaboration, and critical reflection (Shireesha & Jeevan, 2024; MacDonald et al., 2022). Furthermore, accessibility and digital equity remain vital issues. Despite the potential of immersive learning, access to dependable technology, internet connectivity, and digital infrastructure is still inconsistent (Zallio & Clarkson, 2022; Dudley et al., 2023). If these disparities are not addressed, there is a danger of exacerbating the digital divide (Christanti et al., 2024; Pittman et al., 2021). Proposed solutions encompass investing in inclusive infrastructure, creating content that is relevant to local contexts, and engaging communities in co-creation and feedback mechanisms to guarantee that technologies address genuine needs (Khribi, Othman, & Al-Sinani, 2022; Nikolakopoulou & Koutsabasis, 2025).

Teacher preparation and capacity-building are of equal importance. Educators need to be proficient in utilizing immersive tools and adept at implementing them to foster diversity, inclusion, and learner engagement (Alam & Mohanty, 2023; Weisberg & Dawson, 2023). Techniques such as collaborative virtual teaching, avatar-based simulations, and digital storytelling can enhance engagement, particularly when rooted in inclusive pedagogical practices (Graham, 2022). The intersection of inclusive education and immersive technology offers a unique opportunity to broaden access to learning and ensure success for all students (Muhammad, 2023; Kokkinos, 2024). To achieve this goal, educators must transcend mere novelty and employ these tools in ways that prioritize learner diversity and equity (Bowen et al., 2024; Couture & Murgatroyd, 2024). With careful design, inclusive pedagogy, and equitable access, immersive environments can serve as powerful tools for transforming education (Selvakumar et al., 2025; Alam & Mohanty, 2024). As systems develop, the emphasis must remain on establishing inclusive learning environments, whether virtual or physical, where every learner is recognized, supported, and empowered to succeed (Tiwari & Fahrudin, 2024; Rana et al., 2024).

WHAT ARE IMMERSIVE LEARNING ENVIRONMENTS?

Immersive learning environments are technology-enhanced educational spaces designed to fully engage learners through interactive, realistic, and often multisensory experiences (Baxter & Hainey, 2024). When thoughtfully implemented, these environments can be adapted to meet the needs of students with disabilities, language challenges, or diverse learning preferences, making them powerful tools for promoting equity and inclusion (Molloy & Farrell, 2024; Monica et al., 2025).

OPPORTUNITIES TO PROMOTE INCLUSIVE EDUCATION IN IMMERSIVE LEARNING ENVIRONMENTS

Immersive learning environments possess the transformative potential to enhance inclusive education by offering adaptable, engaging, and learner-centered experiences (Asif et al., 2024; Maulidah & Christyodetaputri, 2025). By utilizing technologies such as virtual reality (VR), augmented reality (AR), and simulation-based platforms, these environments contribute to bridging accessibility gaps and catering to a wide array of learning needs (Thangavel, 2025; Yeganeh et al., 2025). They empower educators to develop flexible and inclusive learning spaces where learners of diverse abilities, backgrounds, and preferences can engage in meaningful ways (Dikilitas & Fructuoso, 2023; Setiawan & Qamariah, 2023). This represents a significant shift from traditional, uniform instruction towards more personalized and equitable educational practices that acknowledge and celebrate learner diversity (Khelifi & Hamzaoui-Elachachi, 2024).

A notable strength of immersive technologies is their alignment with Universal Design for Learning (UDL) principles, which advocate for multiple means of engagement, representation, and expression (Zaugg, 2024; Sanguinetti, 2024). For instance, visual content can be augmented with audio narration and captions, while simulations can facilitate hands-on or experiential learning, allowing students to interact with content in ways that best accommodate their individual needs (Jiang, Phutane, & Azenkot, 2023; von Gillern & Nash, 2023).This adaptability guarantees that students with disabilities, language differences, or diverse learning styles can fully and equitably participate in the learning process

(Khanna & Bhola, 2023). In addition to facilitating access, immersive environments promote core values of inclusive education such as empathy, cultural awareness, and social responsibility (Rambaree, et al 2023; Hoter et al., 2024). By replicating real-world situations and various cultural contexts, learners are able to examine viewpoints that differ from their own, thereby nurturing a more profound comprehension of identity, inclusion, and justice (Hollombe, Yablon, & Iluz, 2024; Ulla et al., 2024). These experiences are especially significant in equipping students to engage with diverse educational and social environments with respect and sensitivity (Guberina, 2023; Markey et al., 2021). Moreover, immersive learning technologies promote collaboration and the development of community. Virtual environments can enable inclusive group activities, peer interactions, and collaborative problem-solving, effectively addressing challenges related to physical location or ability (Rocha et al., 2023; Chalkiadakis et al., 2024). When intentionally designed, these environments foster equitable participation by encouraging diverse contributions and recognizing the importance of each learner's role (Curtin & Sarju, 2021; Farley & Burbules, 2022). Thus, immersive learning not only enhances academic engagement but also contributes to the creation of inclusive, supportive, and empathetic learning communities (Miller, 2024; Davis, Nolen, & Koretsky, 2024).

ADDRESSING MULTIPLE AND DIVERSE EDUCATIONAL NEEDS

In modern educational settings, teachers are increasingly required to address a broad spectrum of diverse learning needs. Students differ in their cognitive skills, language abilities, cultural backgrounds, socio-economic status, and physical or sensory challenges (Kormos & Smith, 2023; Mensa, 2023). These variations necessitate teaching methods that extend beyond traditional instruction to adopt more inclusive and adaptive strategies (Andrin et al., 2024). Inclusive education fosters a transformation in perspective recognizing learner diversity not as a hindrance but as a significant asset to the educational atmosphere (Baglieri, 2022; Akintayo et al., 2024). By recognizing that students contribute distinct viewpoints, experiences, and learning preferences, educators can cultivate environments that are more effectively tailored to accommodate a diverse array of educational requirements (Tomlinson & Jarvis, 2023; Zamiri & Esmaeili, 2024).

To effectively meet these varied needs, it is essential to implement flexible curricula and adaptive teaching strategies (Yesil & Aras, 2024; Alawneh et al., 2024). The Universal Design for Learning (UDL) framework provides a strong basis for inclusive education by encouraging

multiple means of representation, engagement, and expression (Bray et al., 2024; Zhang et al., 2024). UDL enables educators to customize content delivery and assessment methods to suit different learning styles for instance, utilizing infographics or videos for visual learners and promoting hands-on or discussion-based activities for others (Cai et al., 2024; Arsyad, Mujahiddin, & Syakhrani, 2024). These inclusive approaches guarantee equitable learning opportunities for all students, irrespective of their backgrounds or abilities (Villarreal & Scott, 2024).

Technology serves a crucial function in facilitating these initiatives (Strielkowski et al., 2025). Instruments such as assistive technologies, speech-to-text software, captioned multimedia, and interactive digital platforms assist in closing educational disparities (Trivedi & Bindewari, 2025; Omiegbe, 2024). Immersive technologies, including virtual reality and simulations, provide customized, engaging learning experiences that can aid students with disabilities or those who find traditional classroom environments challenging (Fitrianto & Saif, 2024; Riyat, Kakkar, & Kakkar, 2025). When these resources are employed thoughtfully and inclusively, they not only improve accessibility but also cultivate a greater sense of belonging and active engagement among all learners (Mohseni, Silvennoinen, & Correia, 2025; Jenks, Onufer, & Guberman, 2025). Ultimately, effectively tackling educational diversity necessitates a comprehensive approach that integrates inclusive teaching methods, adaptable curricula, and technology-based solutions to empower every student to thrive (Bhattacharya, 2025; Adeshina, 2024).

IMMERSIVE TECHNOLOGIES TO SUPPORT LEARNERS WITH DISABILITIES

Immersive technologies, including virtual reality (VR), augmented reality (AR), and mixed reality (MR), are transforming education by providing inclusive, engaging, and personalized learning experiences, especially for students with disabilities (Boowuo & Dittman, 2025). These technologies facilitate the development of interactive environments that can be customized to meet individual learning requirements, effectively minimizing obstacles and fostering equitable access to high-quality education (Navas-Bonilla et al., 2025). For learners who encounter challenges in traditional classrooms, immersive technologies present alternative pathways to engage with material, cultivate essential skills, and actively participate in the educational experience (Serrano-Ausejo & Mårell-Olsson, 2024). A significant advantage of immersive technologies is their ability to support multisensory learning (Baxter & Hainey, 2024). For example, students with visual impairments can explore virtual environments

through auditory signals and haptic feedback, while those with hearing impairments gain from captioning, visual simulations, and sign-language avatars (Mokhtar et al., 2024). Learners with autism or cognitive processing difficulties often excel in structured, predictable virtual environments that minimize distractions and provide safe spaces for repetition and exploration (Dahlstrom-Hakki et al., 2024). These characteristics contribute to building confidence, improving comprehension, and promoting independence.

Furthermore, immersive technologies enable differentiated instruction and can be aligned with individualized education plans (IEPs), allowing learners to manage the pace, difficulty, and format of their interactions (Estaiteyeh & DeCoito, 2024). For instance, a student with physical limitations can engage in a virtual science lab without the physical restrictions of a conventional classroom (Deriba, Saqr, & Tukiainen, 2024). Virtual simulations also create opportunities to practice social skills, daily routines, and vocational tasks in realistic yet controlled settings, thereby better equipping learners for real-world scenarios (Lawson McLean & Lawson McLean, 2024). The effective integration of immersive technologies relies on careful implementation that emphasizes inclusive design, sufficient teacher training, and collaboration with special education experts (Tafazoli, 2025). When utilized properly, these tools can eliminate obstacles, enhance educational experiences, and promote the full inclusion and success of learners with disabilities (Creed et al., 2024). The immersive learning promotes equity, engagement, and lifelong learning opportunities for all students, ensuring that educational environments are dynamic, accessible, and empowering (Pradhan & Naik, 2024).

INCLUSIVE APPROACHES IN IMMERSIVE LEARNING ENVIRONMENTS

Inclusive strategies within immersive learning environments are transforming the educational landscape by addressing learner diversity and promoting accessible, engaging, and equitable experiences for all students (Papadakis & Kalogiannakis, 2024). Technologies like virtual reality (VR), augmented reality (AR), and mixed reality (MR) offer distinctive opportunities to create educational settings that cater to a diverse array of abilities, backgrounds, and learning styles (Crogman et al., 2025). These innovations help to eliminate conventional barriers, allowing students who might otherwise be marginalized to engage actively and meaningfully in their educational journeys (Ribeiro, Farias, & Mesquita, 2024). At the heart of inclusive immersive learning is the Universal Design for Learning (UDL) framework, which promotes various means of engagement, representation, and expression (Sasanelli, Ranieri, & Campanale 2025).

Immersive environments effectively reflect these principles by enabling access to content through visual, auditory, tactile, or interactive modalities, thus accommodating learners with diverse sensory and cognitive requirements (Bhowmik, 2024). For instance, students with visual impairments may find audio descriptions beneficial, while those with hearing impairments can take advantage of captioning and sign language avatars incorporated into the virtual environment (Shidende et al., 2024). This flexibility guarantees that instruction is inclusive and responsive, fostering full participation and reducing exclusion (El Galad, Betts, & Campbell, 2024). Furthermore, immersive technologies enhance social-emotional learning and promote cultural responsiveness (Lau & Shea, 2024). By simulating a variety of real-world scenarios, these environments motivate learners to cultivate empathy and understand multiple viewpoints (Visscher, 2024). Such experiences are crucial in equipping students to thrive in multicultural societies, rendering education not only more accessible but also more significant and empowering (Maspul, 2024).

Collaborative tools integrated into immersive platforms significantly improve inclusion by fostering peer interaction, teamwork, and the establishment of supportive learning communities (Asrifan & Aini, 2025). Overall, inclusive strategies in immersive education leverage emerging technologies to develop educational settings where every student can succeed (Indumathy & Mujra, 2025). When carefully designed and implemented, these methods not only broaden access and engagement for learners with disabilities but also enhance the educational experience for all, cultivating a culture of respect, inclusion, and lifelong learning (Zaky, 2025).

SUPPORTING INCLUSIVE EDUCATION VIA IMMERSIVE LEARNING PLATFORMS

Immersive learning platforms, including virtual reality (VR), augmented reality (AR), and mixed reality (MR), are increasingly acknowledged as revolutionary instruments for enhancing inclusive education (Quintero et al., 2019; Lalotra & Kumar, 2024). These technologies foster dynamic and interactive environments where learners from various backgrounds and abilities can engage meaningfully with educational materials (Kumi-Yeboah et al., 2020). By incorporating inclusive design principles, immersive learning platforms work to remove barriers to participation and offer customized learning experiences that cater to individual needs, thereby promoting equity and accessibility in education (Samaniego López et al., 2025).

A significant advantage of these platforms is their capacity to deliver information through multiple sensory modalities (Rubio-Tamayo, Gertrudix Barrio, & García García, 2017). This adaptability aligns closely with the Universal Design for Learning (UDL) framework, which supports diverse means of engagement, representation, and expression (Zhang et al., 2022; Chamo & Yarom-Cohen, 2025). For instance, students with hearing impairments can take advantage of captioned audio and visual indicators, while learners with physical disabilities may utilize adaptive tools such as voice commands or specialized controllers (Ekpete, 2024). This level of customization enables students to access and interact with content in ways that accommodate their unique abilities, thereby enhancing comprehension and retention (Sridevi, Ashokkumar, & Sathish, 2024).

In addition to tailored learning experiences, immersive platforms also foster collaboration and social interaction, which are essential components of inclusive education (Toto et al., 2024; Cabrera-Duffaut, Pinto-Llorente, & Iglesias-Rodríguez, 2024). These technologies have the capability to replicate real-world situations that enhance social skills, empathy, and cross-cultural awareness (Hoter et al., 2024). This is especially advantageous for learners who may find traditional educational environments challenging, such as students on the autism spectrum (Jardinez & Natividad, 2024). The immersive quality of these experiences offers a secure and nurturing environment for learners to engage socially and develop confidence (Illi & Elhassouny, 2025). Ultimately, the incorporation of immersive platforms into inclusive education signifies a hopeful transition towards more adaptive and fair teaching methodologies (Ahmad et al., 2024). By utilizing the flexibility and interactivity of these technologies, educators can design engaging, customized, and collaborative learning experiences that cater to the diverse needs of learners (Kokkinos, 2024). This advancement not only improves accessibility but also fosters a sense of belonging, contributing to the development of a more inclusive and equitable educational environment for all students.

COOPERATIVE INCLUSIVE STRATEGIES WITHIN IMMERSIVE LEARNING ENVIRONMENTS

Collaborative inclusive strategies within immersive learning environments present a powerful means to promote equity, engagement, and collaboration among a diverse range of learners (Wang & Huang, 2025). Technologies such as virtual reality (VR), augmented reality (AR), and mixed reality (MR) create interactive digital environments where students can work together, irrespective of their physical capabilities or geographical locations (Crogman et al., 2025). These platforms facilitate cooperative learning by fostering teamwork, communication, and collective problem-solving, while ensuring comprehensive inclusion and support for learners with disabilities or varying educational requirements (D'Elia et al., 2025). A notable benefit of these strategies is their capacity to eliminate conventional barriers to participation (Berrezueta-Guzman & Wagner, 2025). For example, students with physical disabilities can fully participate in virtual activities, and those facing communication challenges can utilize tools such as avatars or speech-to-text features to contribute effectively (Troussas, Krouska, & Sgouropoulou, 2025). When educators create tasks that necessitate collaboration and highlight mutual support, they establish inclusive environments where all learners can leverage their strengths and feel acknowledged and valued (Pradhan & Naik, 2024). Moreover, these collaborative methods enhance social-emotional learning and cultural awareness (Efthymiou et al., 2025).

Activities like group simulations, collaborative storytelling, and role-playing scenarios enable students to investigate diverse perspectives and cultivate empathy (Golubovschi, 2024). These experiences are instrumental in developing crucial interpersonal skills and equipping learners for life in a globalized world (Bilderback & Thompson, 2025). Immersive platforms also facilitate differentiated pacing and scaffolded interactions, allowing each student to engage according to their individual abilities and comfort levels (Procel et al., 2024). Ultimately, the adoption of cooperative inclusive strategies in immersive learning environments is essential for providing meaningful and equitable education (Pattiasina, Lamaloang, & Santoso, 2025). By harmonizing the collaborative capabilities of immersive technologies with inclusive pedagogy, educators can foster learning communities in which every student is acknowledged, listened to, and empowered to succeed (Lazou & Tsinakos, 2025).

APPROPRIATE TRAINING AND SUPPORT TO INTEGRATE TECHNOLOGY IN IMMERSIVE LEARNING ENVIRONMENTS

The successful incorporation of technology into immersive learning environments is significantly reliant on educators receiving adequate training and ongoing support (Fitrianto & Saif, 2024; Buragohain et al., 2024). Immersive technologies, including virtual reality (VR), augmented reality (AR), and mixed reality (MR), possess considerable potential to transform education by providing engaging and interactive learning experiences (Al Balushi et al., 2024). Nevertheless, in the absence of adequate preparation, teacher educators and instructors may encounter difficulties in meaningfully integrating these tools into their teaching, which could restrict their effectiveness and potentially exacerbate existing educational inequalities (Best et al., 2024). Comprehensive training provides educators with the necessary technical skills and pedagogical knowledge to effectively leverage immersive technologies (Khamis et al., 2024). This training encompasses familiarizing teachers with the functionalities of various platforms, troubleshooting common technical challenges, and crafting instructional activities that align with curriculum goals while catering to the diverse needs of learners (Thelma et al., 2024). A focus on Universal Design for Learning (UDL) principles within training guarantees that technology integration fosters accessibility and inclusivity (Bray et al., 2024).

When educators are proficient in adapting content and instructional strategies through immersive tools, they are more capable of engaging students with diverse abilities and learning preferences. Continuous support is equally crucial for maintaining and enhancing the application of immersive technologies in educational contexts (Hutson & Hutson, 2024). Such support may manifest as professional learning communities, mentoring, technical assistance, and access to updated resources, allowing educators to keep up with rapidly evolving technologies and refine their teaching methods based on experience and student feedback (Muzapparovna, 2024).

Furthermore, effective school leadership along with supportive policy frameworks create an atmosphere that prioritizes innovation and inclusivity, encouraging educators to engage in experimentation and collaboration (Lijun & Te, 2024). Proper training and ongoing support are essential for the successful integration of technology within immersive learning environments (Gutierrez-Bucheli et al., 2024). By committing to comprehensive professional development and continuous assistance, educational institutions can enable teachers to leverage immersive technologies in ways that enhance learning, foster inclusivity, and equip students for the demands of a digital future (Sulaimon & Adebayo, 2024).

FUNDAMENTAL STRATEGY FOR INCLUSION IN IMMERSIVE EDUCATIONAL ENVIRONMENTS

In immersive educational settings, the implementation of a fundamental inclusion strategy is essential to guarantee that all learners, irrespective of their abilities or backgrounds, can fully participate in and benefit from these advanced technologies (Bhambri, 2025). Technologies such as virtual reality (VR), augmented reality (AR), and mixed reality (MR) offer unique opportunities to provide engaging, interactive, and accessible learning experiences (Thangavel, 2025). Nevertheless, without a meticulously planned and structured approach to inclusion, these powerful tools may inadvertently exclude learners with diverse needs, thereby perpetuating existing inequalities. A core inclusion strategy in immersive learning emphasizes the creation of experiences that are adaptable, accessible, and responsive to individual learner differences (Johnson, Idaka, & Offiong, 2025). This strategy aligns with the principles of Universal Design for Learning (UDL), which promote multiple means of engagement, representation, and expression to cater to various learning styles and abilities (Melhem & Al-Zoubi, 2025). For example, immersive environments can be customized with adjustable sensory features such as audio descriptions for students with visual impairments or captioning for those with hearing challenges (Patel et al., 2025). These adjustments ensure that immersive experiences are not only engaging but also equitable.

Collaboration among educators, technology developers, and the learners themselves is another vital component of this strategy (Catherin et al., 2025). Involving diverse stakeholders in the design and implementation process allows immersive learning environments to more effectively tackle the real challenges that learners encounter (Villada Castillo et al., 2025). This inclusive collaboration aids in identifying and removing barriers, integrating culturally relevant materials, and creating supportive spaces where every student feels valued and empowered to achieve success (Benabid, El Imadi, & Alqatawneh, 2025). Continuous feedback loops facilitate the continuous enhancement of immersive tools and practices, thereby reinforcing inclusivity over time.

The core inclusion strategy converts immersive educational settings from mere technological novelties into significant spaces that welcome and uphold diversity (Jatto & Aladesusi, 2025). By means of deliberate design and cooperative initiatives, educators can leverage immersive technologies to promote equity, engagement, and academic success for every learner, thereby laying a robust groundwork for a truly inclusive digital education future (Mena-Guacas, 2025).

DESIGNING SPACES THAT SUPPORT SHARED LEARNING AND A SENSE OF COMMUNITY

Creating educational environments that foster collaborative learning and nurture a robust sense of community is vital for establishing inclusive, engaging, and effective learning settings (Pattiasina, Lamaloang & Santoso, 2025). Whether in physical or virtual formats, these environments should transcend the mere transmission of information; they ought to motivate collaboration, mutual respect, and a shared dedication to growth among a diverse group of learners (Vettriselvan, 2025). In the context of today's increasingly digital and diverse classrooms, purposeful design is essential in promoting peer interaction, empathy, and collaborative problem-solving (Ribis, 2025). Shared learning environments thrive on interaction and active involvement (Montague et al., 2025). Features such as adaptable seating arrangements, specific areas for group work, and collaborative digital tools all enhance settings where students can engage meaningfully with each other (Wilson, Vallis, & Yeoman, 2025).

In immersive educational contexts, supported by technologies like virtual reality and simulations, shared experiences can be intentionally designed to promote group exploration, dialogue, and the joint accomplishment of tasks (Youssef, Al Malak, & Bayoumy, 2025). These collaborative experiences not only enhance cognitive development but also cultivate vital interpersonal and communication skills. Equally significant is the cultivation of a sense of community, especially for students who may feel marginalized due to their abilities, backgrounds, or languages (Scoulas & Kim, 2025). Inclusive design must guarantee that every student feels acknowledged, valued, and respected (Lteif et al., 2025). This requires the integration of culturally responsive materials, accessible technological features, and environments where students can share their viewpoints and experiences. Establishing consistent engagement practices such as peer feedback sessions, learning circles, and group reflections is crucial for strengthening relationships and building trust within the classroom community (Gonzalez, Kokozos, & Byrd, 2025).

CONCLUSION

Immersive learning environments have the potential to significantly improve inclusive education by leveraging technologies such as virtual reality (VR), augmented reality (AR), and interactive simulations. When these technologies are applied in alignment with Universal Design for Learning (UDL) principles, they offer flexible, accessible, and engaging experiences that cater to the varied needs of all learners. By utilizing multi-sensory approaches and adaptive features, immersive technologies aim to eliminate barriers to participation and promote deeper learning for students with disabilities, language differences, or diverse learning preferences. The incorporation of immersive tools within inclusive frameworks not only enhances learner engagement but also guarantees equitable access to valuable educational opportunities for every student.

REFERENCES

Adeshina, A. E. (2024). From theory to practice: A framework for inclusive technology integration in education. *International Journal of Instructional Technology and Educational Studies*, *5*(1), 1–6. DOI: 10.21608/ihites.2024.380764

Ahmad, I., Sharma, S., Singh, R., Gehlot, A., Gupta, L. R., Thakur, A. K., & Twala, B. (2024). Inclusive learning using Industry 4.0 technologies: Addressing student diversity in modern education. *Cogent Education*, *11*(1), 2330235. DOI: 10.1080/2331186X.2024.2330235

Akintayo, O. T., Eden, C. A., Ayeni, O. O., & Onyebuchi, N. C. (2024). Inclusive curriculum design: Meeting the diverse needs of students for social improvement. *International Journal of Applied Research in Social Sciences*, *6*(5), 770–784. DOI: 10.51594/ijarss.v6i5.1145

Al Balushi, J. S. G., Al Jabri, M. I. A., Palarimath, S., Maran, P., Thenmozhi, K., & Balakumar, C. (2024). Incorporating artificial intelligence powered immersive realities to improve learning using virtual reality and augmented reality technology. In *Proceedings of the 3rd International Conference on Applied Artificial Intelligence and Computing* (pp. 760–765). IEEE. DOI: 10.1109/ICAAIC60222.2024.10574231

Alam, A., & Mohanty, A. (2023). Educational technology: Exploring the convergence of technology and pedagogy through mobility, interactivity, AI, and learning tools. *Cogent Engineering*, *10*(2), 2283282. DOI: 10.1080/23311916.2023.2283282

Alam, A., & Mohanty, A. (2024). Integrated constructive robotics in education (ICRE) model: A paradigmatic framework for transformative learning. *Cogent Education*, *11*(1), 2324487. DOI: 10.1080/2331186X.2024.2324487

Alawneh, Y. J. J., Sleema, H., Salman, F. N., Alshammat, M. F., & Oteer, R. S., & ALrashidi, N. K. N. (2024, April). Adaptive Learning Systems: Revolutionizing Higher Education through AI-Driven Curricula. In 2024 International Conference on Knowledge Engineering and Communication Systems (ICKECS) (Vol. 1, pp. 1-5). IEEE.

AlGerafi, M. A., Zhou, Y., Oubibi, M., & Wijaya, T. T. (2023). Unlocking the potential: A comprehensive evaluation of augmented reality and virtual reality in education. *Electronics (Basel)*, *12*(18), 3953. DOI: 10.3390/electronics12183953

Andrin, G., Kilag, O. K., Groenewald, E., Benitez, J., Dagala, F., & Ubay, R. (2024). Borderless learning environments: Impacts on educational management strategies. [IMJRISE]. *International Multidisciplinary Journal of Research for Innovation, Sustainability, and Excellence*, *1*(2), 43–49. DOI: 10.5281/zenodo.11138470

Arsyad, M., Mujahiddin, M., & Syakhrani, A. W. (2024). The efficiency of using visual learning media in improving science concept understanding. *Indonesian Journal of Education*, *4*(3), 775–787. DOI: 10.30596/ijoe.v4i3.15341

Asif, M., Mondal, A., Soumil, S., Das, A., & Sahoo, P. (2024). Augmented reality and virtual reality in education: A transformative journey. In *Advances in Computational Solutions* (pp. 185–198). Swami Vivekananda University Press.

Asrifan, A., & Aini, N. (2025). The future of education in the metaverse. In *Harnessing chatbots for effective language teaching* (pp. 75–116). IGI Global., DOI: 10.4018/979-8-3693-2938-2.ch004

Baglieri, S. (2022). *Disability studies and the inclusive classroom: Critical practices for embracing diversity in education* (3rd ed.). Routledge., DOI: 10.4324/9781003138808

Baxter, G., & Hainey, T. (2024). Using immersive technologies to enhance the student learning experience. *Interactive Technology and Smart Education*, *21*(3), 403–425. https://di.org/10.1108/ITSE-01-2024-0012

Benabid, A., El Imadi, I., & Alqatawneh, K. (2025). Encouraging quality: Approaches for increasing student achievement in higher education. In *Emerging technologies transforming higher education* (pp. 145–178). IGI Global., DOI: 10.4018/979-8-3693-1181-4.ch008

Berrezueta-Guzman, S., & Wagner, S. (2025). *Immersive multiplayer VR: Unreal Engine's strengths, limitations, and future prospects*. IEEE., DOI: 10.1109/ACCESS.2025.3457712

Bhambri, P. (2025). Virtual and augmented reality for immersive learning experiences: Practical applications and challenges. In *Architecting the digital future: Platforms, design, and application* (pp. 17–46). IGI Global., DOI: 10.4018/979-8-3693-2973-3.ch002

Bhattacharya, D. (2025). Teachers' competencies in effective technology-enabled assessment for holistic development of students. *Indian Journal of Educational Technology*, *7*(1), 83–104. https://journals.ncert.gov.in/IJET/article/view/843

Bhowmik, A. K. (2024). Virtual and augmented reality: Human sensory–perceptual requirements. *Journal of the Society for Information Display*, *32*(8), 605–646. DOI: 10.1002/jsid.1351

Bilderback, S. L., & Thompson, C. B. (2025). Developing global leadership competence: Redefining higher education for interconnected economies. *Higher Education. Skills and Work-Based Learning*, *15*(4), 724–739. DOI: 10.1108/heswbl-10-2024-0301

Boowuo, H., & Dittman, K. (2025). Immersive technologies for special students in higher education. *Journal of Higher Education Theory and Practice, 25*(2), 43–61. DOI: 10.33423/jhetp.v25i2.7634

Bowen, A. E. J., Palmer, L. R. J., Perry, R. C., Thomas, M. S., Tolmie, A., Borst, G., & Van Herwegen, J. (2024). Evaluating what works in the classroom: Best practice and future opportunities. *Mind, Brain and Education : the Official Journal of the International Mind, Brain, and Education Society, 18*(4), 474–484. DOI: 10.1111/mbe.12430

Bray, A., Devitt, A., Banks, J., Sanchez Fuentes, S., Sandoval, M., Riviou, K., & Terrenzio, S. (2024). What next for universal design for learning? *British Journal of Educational Technology, 55*(1), 113–138. DOI: 10.1111/bjet.13347

Buragohain, D., Deng, C., Sharma, A., & Chaudhary, S. (2024). The impact of immersive learning on teacher effectiveness: A systematic study. *IEEE Access : Practical Innovations, Open Solutions, 12*, 35924–35933. DOI: 10.1109/ACCESS.2024.3373541

Cabrera-Duffaut, A., Pinto-Llorente, A. M., & Iglesias-Rodríguez, A. (2024). Immersive learning platforms: Analyzing virtual reality contribution to competence development in higher education—A systematic literature review. *Frontiers in Education, 9*, 1391560. DOI: 10.3389/feduc.2024.1391560

Cai, J., Wen, Q., Bi, M., & Lombaerts, K. (2024). How universal design for learning (UDL) is related to differentiated instruction (DI): The mediation role of growth mindset and teachers' practices factors. *Social Psychology of Education*. Advance online publication. DOI: 10.1007/s11218-024-09874-1

Catherin, T. C., Vettriselvan, R., Mathur, S., Regins, J. C., & Velmurugan, P. R. R. (2025). Integrating AI and learning analytics in distance learning: Strategies for educators and institutions. In *AI and learning analytics in distance learning* (pp. 207–228). IGI Global Scientific Publishing., DOI: 10.4018/979-8-3693-2461-9.ch010

Chalkiadakis, A., Seremetaki, A., Kanellou, A., Kallishi, M., Morfopoulou, A., & Mastrokoukou, S. (2024). Impact of artificial intelligence and virtual reality on educational inclusion: A systematic review of technologies supporting students with disabilities. *Education Sciences, 14*(11), 1223. DOI: 10.3390/educsci14111223

Chamo, N., & Yarom-Cohen, T. (2025). *Landscapes in the professional identity of special education teachers: Perceptions and practices related to Universal Design for Learning (UDL)*. In *Inclusive Special Education – Research to Practice* [Working Title]. IntechOpen. DOI: 10.5772/intechopen.1010446

Christanti, M. F., Mawangir, M., Arevin, A. T., Ramadhan, I., & Limijadi, E. K. S. (2024). The digital divide in education: Bridging gaps in the era of online learning. *Migration Letters : An International Journal of Migration Studies, 21*(S4), 1070–1079. DOI: 10.59670/ml.v21iS4.5621

Couture, J. C., & Murgatroyd, S. (2024). *Education futures for school leadership: Evidence-informed strategies for managing change*. Taylor & Francis., DOI: 10.4324/9781003449750

Creed, C., Al-Kalbani, M., Theil, A., Sarcar, S., & Williams, I. (2024). Inclusive AR/VR: Accessibility barriers for immersive technologies. *Universal Access in the Information Society, 23*(1), 59–73. DOI: 10.1007/s10209-023-00974-9

Crogman, H. T., Cano, V. D., Pacheco, E., Sonawane, R. B., & Boroon, R. (2025). Virtual reality, augmented reality, and mixed reality in experiential learning: Transforming educational paradigms. *Education Sciences, 15*(3), 303. DOI: 10.3390/educsci15030303

Curtin, A. L., & Sarju, J. P. (2021). Students as partners: Co-creation of online learning to deliver high-quality, personalized content. In *Advances in online chemistry education* (pp. 135–163). American Chemical Society., DOI: 10.1021/bk-2021-1386.ch009

D'Elia, P., Stalmach, A., Di Sano, S., & Casale, G. (2025). Strategies for inclusive digital education: Problem/project-based learning, cooperative learning, and service learning for students with special educational needs. *Frontiers in Education, 9*, 1447489. DOI: 10.3389/feduc.2024.1447489

Dahlstrom-Hakki, I., Alstad, Z., Asbell-Clarke, J., & Edwards, T. (2024). The impact of visual and auditory distractions on the performance of neurodiverse students in virtual reality (VR) environments. *Virtual Reality (Waltham Cross), 28*(1), 29. DOI: 10.1007/s10055-023-00854-6

Damaševičius, R., & Sidekerskienė, T. (2024). Virtual worlds for learning in metaverse: A narrative review. *Sustainability, 16*(5), 2032. DOI: 10.3390/su16052032

Davis, S. C., Nolen, S. B., & Koretsky, M. D. (2024). Inclusive excellence in practice: Integrating equitable, consequential learning and an inclusive climate in higher education classrooms and institutions. *Frontline Learning Research, 12*(4), 22–54. DOI: 10.14786/flr.v12i4.808

Deriba, F. G., Saqr, M., & Tukiainen, M. (2024). Assessment of accessibility in virtual laboratories: A systematic review. *Frontiers in Education, 9*, 1351711. DOI: 10.3389/feduc.2024.1351711

Dikilitas, K., & Fructuoso, I. N. (2023). Conceptual framework for flexible learning design: The context of flipped classroom. *[Journal details unclear]*. DOI: 10.31265/usps.267

Dudley, J., Yin, L., Garaj, V., & Kristensson, P. O. (2023). Inclusive immersion: A review of efforts to improve accessibility in virtual reality, augmented reality and the metaverse. *Virtual Reality (Waltham Cross)*, *27*(4), 2989–3020. DOI: 10.1007/s10055-023-00763-8

Efthymiou, E., Katsarou, D. V., Sofologi, M., Argyriadis, A., Argyriadi, A., & Megari, K. (2025). Neuropsychological interventions in inclusive education: Strategies for supportin cognitive and emotional development in diverse learners. In *Clinical applications of pediatric neuropsychology from infancy to adolescence* (pp. 411–448). IGI Global Scientific Publishing., DOI: 10.4018/979-8-3693-1936-3.ch018

Ekpete, O. H. (2024). *Assistive listening devices for individuals with hearing impairment. Faculty of Natural and Applied Sciences Journal of Mathematics and Science Education, 5*(2), 78–81. Retrieved from https://fnasjournals.com/index.php/FNAS-JMSE/article/view/390

El Galad, A., Betts, D. H., & Campbell, N. (2024). Flexible learning dimensions in higher education: Aligning students' and educators' perspectives for more inclusive practices. *Frontiers in Education*, *9*, 1347432. DOI: 10.3389/feduc.2024.1347432

Estaiteyeh, M., & DeCoito, I. (2024). Differentiated instruction in digital video games: STEM teacher candidates using technology to meet learners' needs. *Interactive Learning Environments*, *32*(7), 3768–3782. DOI: 10.1080/10494820.2023.2246023

Farley, I. A., & Burbules, N. C. (2022). Online education viewed through an equity lens: Promoting engagement and success for all learners. *Review of Education*, *10*(3), e3367. DOI: 10.1002/rev3.3367

Fitrianto, I., & Saif, A. (2024). The role of virtual reality in enhancing experiential learning: A comparative study of traditional and immersive learning environments. *International Journal of Post Axial: Futuristic Teaching and Learning*, *2*(2), 97–110. DOI: 10.59944/postaxial.v2i2.300

Gatcho, A. R. G., Manuel, J. P. G., & Sarasua, R. J. G. (2024). Eye tracking research on readers' interactions with multimodal texts: A mini-review. *Frontiers in Communication*, *9*, 1482105. DOI: 10.3389/fcomm.2024.1482105

Golubovschi, O. (2024). Interactive teaching and learning techniques in the context of multicultural education. In *Educaţia multiculturală, spaţiu formativ pentru educaţia valorilor* (pp. 227–233). Chi inău, Republic of Moldova: Universitatea Pedagogică de Stat „Ion Creangă"

Gonzalez, M., Kokozos, M., & Byrd, C. M. (2025). Trust, community, and connection: Laying the groundwork for authentic storytelling. In *Teaching storytelling in classrooms and communities* (pp. 35–60). Routledge.

Graham, R. (2022). *Crisis and catalyst: The impact of COVID-19 on global practice in engineering education* (Research report). CEEDA & 4TU Centre for Engineering Education. Retrieved from https://www.rhgraham.org/resources/Crisis-and-catalyst .pdf

Graham, R. (2022). *Crisis and catalyst: The impact of COVID-19 on global practice in engineering education.* 4TU Centre for Engineering Education / Consortium of Universities. https://www.rhgraham.org/resources/Crisis-and-catalyst.pdf

Guberina, T. (2023). Cultivating inclusive learning environments: Incorporating diversity through culturally responsive pedagogy. *Social Science Chronicle, 3*(1), 1–14. DOI: 10.56106/ssc.2023.003

Gutierrez-Bucheli, L., Goh, J. T., Rashidi, A., Maxwell, D., Digby, R., Fang, Y., & Arashpour, M. (2024). *Adopting immersive technologies in construction training: Determining educational decision-making criteria through a Delphi technique.* Smart and Sustainable Built Environment., DOI: 10.1108/SASBE-01-2024-0012

Gutierrez-Bucheli, L., Goh, J. T., Rashidi, A., Maxwell, D., Digby, R., Fang, Y., & Arashpour, M. (2024). *Adopting immersive technologies in construction training: Determining educational decision-making criteria through a Delphi technique.* Smart and Sustainable Built Environment., DOI: 10.1108/SASBE-01-2024-0012

Hashmi, S. U. (2025). Digital influence on identity within multilingual educational contexts. In *Global Goals, Global Languages: 2025 Report of the Central States Conference on the Teaching of Foreign Languages* (pp. 63–82). Central States Conference on the Teaching of Foreign Languages.

Hollombe, S., Yablon, Y. B., & Iluz, S. (2024). Navigating conflict in the multicultural classroom: The use of simulation-based learning for peace education in teacher training. *Zeitschrift für Pädagogik und Theologie, 76*(3), 253–264. DOI: 10.1515/zpt-2024-2029

Hoter, E., Yazbak Abu Ahmad, M., & Azulay, H. (2024, August). Enhancing language learning and intergroup empathy through multi-user interactions and simulations in a virtual world. *Virtual Worlds, 3*(3), 333–353. DOI: 10.3390/virtualworlds3030018

Hutson, J., & Hutson, P. (2024). Immersive technologies. In *Inclusive smart museums: Engaging neurodiverse audiences and enhancing cultural heritage* (pp. 153–228). Palgrave Macmillan / Springer Nature Switzerland AG., DOI: 10.1007/978-3-031-43615-4_5

Indumathy, I., & Mujra, P. (2025). Sustainable learning. In *Smart education and sustainable learning environments in smart cities* (pp. 381–402). IGI Global Scientific Publishing., DOI: 10.4018/979-8-3693-7723-9.ch023

Jardinez, M. J., & Natividad, L. R. (2024). The advantages and challenges of inclusive education: Striving for equity in the classroom. *Shanlax International Journal of Education, 12*(2), 57–65. DOI: 10.34293/education.v12i2.7182

Jatto, E. O., & Aladesusi, G. A. (2025). Empowering pre-service teachers for inclusive education through technology: Strategies, tools, and innovations. In *Empowering pre-service teachers to enhance inclusive education through technology* (pp. 301–336). IGI Global Scientific Publishing., DOI: 10.4018/979-8-3693-8759-7

Jenks, A., Onufer, L., & Guberman, D. (2025). Emergent questions of access: Disability and the integration of generative AI in teaching and learning. *Higher Education Research & Development, 44*(4), 932–945. DOI: 10.1080/07294360.2024.2442611

Jiang, L., Phutane, M., & Azenkot, S. (2023, October). Beyond audio description: Exploring 360° video accessibility with blind and low vision users through collaborative creation. In *Proceedings of the 25th International ACM SIGACCESS Conference on Computers and Accessibility (ASSETS 2023)* (pp. 1–17). Association for Computing Machinery. DOI: 10.1145/3597638.3608381

Johnson, I. E., Idaka, E. I., & Offiong, A. E. A. (2025). Understanding and distinguishing immersive realities for effective instructional delivery. *Global Journal of Educational Research, 24*(1), 107–117. DOI: 10.4314/gjedr.v24i1.10

Khamis, H., Khairudin, M., Jantan, A. H., Roslan, N. A., & Abdullah, L. N. (2024). Systematic review of adapting immersive technology in enhancing teaching and learning for students in higher education. *Journal of Advanced Research in Applied Sciences and Engineering Technology, 63*(3), 28–32. DOI: 10.37934/araset.63.3.2832

Khanna, P., & Bhola, S. (2023). Designing integrative and collaborative learning for students with special needs and learning disabilities in an inclusive classroom. In *Sustainable blended learning in STEM education for students with additional needs* (pp. 173–194). Springer Nature Singapore., DOI: 10.1007/978-981-99-3497-3_9

Khelifi, K., & Hamzaoui-Elachachi, H. (2024). Beyond "one-size-fits-all" teaching: Embracing the learner-centered paradigm through differentiated instruction.*(At-Talimia), 14*(2), 708–726. DOI: 10.52127/2240-014-002-054

Khribi, M. K., Othman, A., & Al-Sinani, A. (2022, July). Toward closing the training and knowledge gap in ICT accessibility and inclusive design harnessing open educational resources. In *2022 International Conference on Advanced Learning Technologies (ICALT)* (pp. 289–291). IEEE. DOI: 10.1109/ICALT55036.2022.00065

Kokkinos, L. (2024). Revolutionizing education: The dynamic intersection of technology and learning. [IJMCER]. *Educational Research, 6*(1), 26–32. https://www.ijmcer.com/wp-content/uploads/2024/01/IJMCER_E061026032.pdf

Kormos, J., & Smith, A. M. (2023). *Teaching languages to students with specific learning differences* (2nd ed., Vol. 18). Channel View Publications., DOI: 10.21832/KORMOS8615

Kumi-Yeboah, A., Kim, Y., Sallar, A. M., & Kiramba, L. K. (2020). Exploring the use of digital technologies from the perspective of diverse learners in online learning environments. *Online Learning : the Official Journal of the Online Learning Consortium, 24*(4), 42–63. DOI: 10.24059/olj.v24i4.2281

Ladson-Billings, G. (2023). "Yes, but how do we do it?": Practicing culturally relevant pedagogy. In *White teachers/diverse classrooms* (pp. 33–46). Routledge., DOI: 10.4324/9781003448709-6

Lalotra, G. S., & Kumar, V. (2024). The impact of virtual reality and augmented reality in inclusive education. In *Applied assistive technologies and informatics for students with disabilities* (pp. 71–94). Springer Nature Singapore., DOI: 10.1007/978-981-23-9557-0_5

Lau, W. S., & Shea, M. (2024). Empowering English learners in the classroom through culturally responsive social-emotional teaching practices. *Journal of Multilingual and Multicultural Development, 45*(7), 2880–2897. DOI: 10.1080/01434632.2022.2078337

Lawson McLean, A., & Lawson McLean, A. C. (2024). Immersive simulations in surgical training: Analyzing the interplay between virtual and real-world environments. *Simulation & Gaming, 55*(6), 1103–1123. DOI: 10.1177/10468781241287892

Lazou, C., & Tsinakos, A. (2023). Critical immersive-triggered literacy as a key component for inclusive digital education. *Education Sciences*, *13*(7), 696. DOI: 10.3390/educsci13070696

Lazou, C., & Tsinakos, A. (2025). A framework for participatory creation of digital futures: A longitudinal study on enhancing media literacy and inclusion in K-12 through virtual reality. *Information (Basel)*, *16*(6), 482. DOI: 10.3390/info16060482

Lijun, W., & Te, H. C. (2024). The role of primary school principals and administrators in promoting student achievement, teacher effectiveness, and a positive school culture. *Journal of Roi Kaensarn Academi*, *9*(8), 727–739. https://so02.tci-thaijo.org/index.php/JRKSA/article/view/272236

Lteif, L., van der Sluis, H., Block, L. G., Cian, L., Patrick, V. M., & Scott, M. L. (2025). Creating equity by design: A conceptual framework for marketplace inclusion. *Journal of Public Policy & Marketing*, *44*(2), 214–231. DOI: 10.1177/07439156251315371

MacDonald, L., Thomas, E., Javernick-Will, A., Austin-Breneman, J., Aranda, I., Salvinelli, C., & Linden, K. (2022). Aligning learning objectives and approaches in global engineering graduate programs: Review and recommendations by an interdisciplinary working group. *Development Engineering*, *7*, 100095. DOI: 10.1016/j.deveng.2022.100095

Makweya, P. P., & Sepadi, M. D. (2025). Inclusive education and lifelong learning: Beyond school walls. In *Global practices in inclusive education curriculum and policy* (pp. 261–280). IGI Global., https://www.igi-global.com/book/global-practices-inclusive-education-curriculum/741b5cad-7f6f-4c70-a6f3-e44c3de2652

Markey, K., O'Brien, B., Kouta, C., Okantey, C., & O'Donnell, C. (2021). Embracing classroom cultural diversity: Innovations for nurturing inclusive intercultural learning and culturally responsive teaching. *Teaching and Learning in Nursing*, *16*(3), 258–262. DOI: 10.1016/j.teln.2021.03.006

Maspul, K. A. (2024). Discovering the underlying motivations for empowering education through innovation. *Journal of Information System and Education Development*, *2*(1), 27–32. DOI: 10.62386/jised.v2i1.58

Matovu, H., Ungu, D. A. K., Won, M., Tsai, C. C., Treagust, D. F., Mocerino, M., & Tasker, R. (2023). Immersive virtual reality for science learning: Design, implementation, and evaluation. *Studies in Science Education*, *59*(2), 205–244. DOI: 10.1080/03057267.2022.2082680

Maulidah, G., & Christyodetaputri, J. H. (2025). Beyond engagement: Integrating AR and VR for inclusive learning in K–higher education. *Sinergi International Journal of Education, 3*(1), 26–40. https://journal.sinergi.org/id/article/view/abc

Melhem, D. Z., & Al-Zoubi, A. M. (2025). The effect of Universal Design for Learning (UDL)-based VARK model in students with learning difficulties and various learning preferences. *Educational Process: International Journal, 15*, e2025152. Advance online publication. DOI: 10.22521/edupij.2025.15.152

Mena-Guacas, A. F., López-Catalán, L., Bernal-Bravo, C., & Ballesteros-Regaña, C. (2025). Educational transformation through emerging technologies: Critical review of scientific impact on learning. *Education Sciences, 15*(3), 368. DOI: 10.3390/educsci15030368

Mensa, A. A., Sarpong, C., Kubi, F. N., & Donkor, O. (2023). Akan traditional games: An indispensable tool in Ghanaian language classroom in respect to classroom interaction. *Integrated Journal for Research in Arts and Humanities, 3*(4), 69–75. https://ijrah.org/article/view/226/abstract

Miller, J. (2024). *Exploring the lived experiences of educators implementing a program focusing on inclusivity, empathy, resilience, and collaboration: Perceptions of student learning and behavior* (Doctoral dissertation). Cabrini University. https://repository.cabrini.edu/etd/12345

Mohseni, H., Silvennoinen, J., & Correia, A. (2025). Inclusive interactions for place-belongingness: Lessons from citizen science. In D. Glowacka, C. Santoro, & Z. Xiao (Eds.), *IUI-WS 2025: Workshops at the International Conference on Intelligent User Interfaces (IUI) 2025* (Article 8). CEUR Workshop Proceedings, 3957. https://ceur-ws.org/Vol-3957/SOCIALIZE-paper08.pdf

Mokhtar, E. S., Aziz, N., Hamzah, S. S., Ahmad, S. Z., Supli, A. A., & Omar, A. C. (2024, May). Unveiling the conceptual analysis in the direction of developing a fusion virtual reality model for hearing-impaired visual interaction. In *2024 IEEE 14th Symposium on Computer Applications & Industrial Electronics (ISCAIE)* (pp. 89–94). IEEE. DOI: 10.1109/ISCAIE59752.2024.10303841

Molloy, C., & Farrell, R. (2024). Cultivating positive classroom environments: Exploring the efficacy of immersive technologies in removing barriers to learning among primary school students. *Computers in the Schools, 41*(2), 164–192. DOI: 10.1080/07380569.2024.2325441

Monica, J. A., Malar, J. H., Arun, C., Sharmila, L., & Arif, M. (2025). Leveraging technology and universal design for inclusive and engaging learning in Indian higher education. In *Educational philosophy and sociological foundation of education* (pp. 177–212). IGI Global., DOI: 10.4018/979-8-3693-3587-1.ch008

Montague, J., Tsui, J., Kamstra-Cooper, K., Connell, M., Atack, L., & Haghiri-Vijeh, R. (2025). Adapting to change: Undergraduate nursing students' sense of belonging transitioning from online to in-person learning environments. *Journal of Advanced Nursing*, *81*(1), 513–522. DOI: 10.1111/jan.16389 PMID: 39140749

Moss, G. D., & McKeeman, L. (Eds.). (2025). *Report of the Central States Conference on the Teaching of Foreign Languages* (2025 edition). Central States Conference on the Teaching of Foreign Languages., https://files.eric.ed.gov/fulltext/ED671436.pdf

Moss, G. D., & McKeeman, L. (Eds.). (2025). *Report of the Central States Conference on the Teaching of Foreign Languages: Global goals, global languages* (2025 edition). Central States Conference on the Teaching of Foreign Languages., https://files.eric.ed.gov/fulltext/ED671436.pdf

Muhammad, G. (2023). Trends and innovations in the prospects of distance learning. *Journal of Education and Finance Review*, *2*(1), 41–53. https://journal.example.org/article/view/xyz

Muzapparovna, N. G. (2024). Advancements in continuing education: Exploring innovative approaches to teaching in the modern era. *International Journal of Advances in Scientific Research*, *4*(04), 89–96. http://journal.example.org/ijasr/v4i04/123

Navas-Bonilla, C. D. R., Guerra-Arango, J. A., Oviedo-Guado, D. A., & Murillo-Noriega, D. E. (2025, February). Inclusive education through technology: A systematic review of types, tools and characteristics. *Frontiers in Education*, *10*, 1527851.

Nikolakopoulou, V., & Koutsabasis, P. (2025). The 'making' of participatory and co-design for digital experiences in cultural heritage: A review. *CoDesign*. Advance online publication. DOI: 10.1080/15710882.2025.1135228

Nteliou, E., Koreman, J., Tolskaya, I., & Kehagia, O. (2021, July). Digital technologies assisting migrant populations overcome language barriers: The case of the EasyRights research project. In Antona, M., & Stephanidis, C. (Eds.), *Human-Computer Interaction – INTERACT 2021* (pp. 108–124). Springer International Publishing., DOI: 10.1007/978-3-030-85686-1_8

Omiegbe, O. (2024). Artificial intelligence in higher education: Bridging the gap for students with disabilities. *Brock Journal of Education*, *12*(12), 38–50. DOI: 10.37745/bje.2013/vol12n123850

Oyelana, O. O., Olson, J., & Caine, V. (2022). An evolutionary concept analysis of learner-centered teaching. *Nurse Education Today*, *108*, 105187. DOI: 10.1016/j.nedt.2021.105187 PMID: 34741919

Papadakis, S., & Kalogiannakis, M. (2024). Epilogue: Inclusive education: Fostering equity and diversity in modern schools. *Education, Development and Intervention: Toward Participatory and Integrated Solutions*, *23*, 231.

Patel, P., Pampaniya, S., Ghosh, A., Raj, R., Karuppaih, D., & Kandasamy, S. (2025). Enhancing accessibility through machine learning: A review on visual and hearing impairment technologies. *IEEE Access : Practical Innovations, Open Solutions*, *13*, 33286–33307. DOI: 10.1109/ACCESS.2025.3539081

Patterson, B. A. (2022). *Traditional and electronic data collection methods* (Unpublished doctoral dissertation). The Chicago School of Professional Psychology. https://www.proquest.com/openview/fbbdbac006d2bfe8594c2374e14ba0b3/1?pq-origsite=gscholar&cbl=18750&diss=y

Pattiasina, P. J., Lamaloang, L. K., & Santoso, R. Y. (2025). The role of communication in creating inclusive and collaborative learning environments. *The International Journal of Social Education*, *2*(3), 577–591. https://languar.net/index.php/INJOSEDU/article/view/133

Pittman, J., Severino, L., DeCarlo-Tecce, M. J., & Kiosoglous, C. (2021). An action research case study: Digital equity and educational inclusion during an emergent COVID-19 divide. *Journal for Multicultural Education*, *15*(1), 68–84. DOI: 10.1108/JME-04-2021-0027

Pradhan, K. C., & Naik, M. S. (2024). Inclusive education: A foundation for equality and empowerment at the elementary stage. *International Journal of Multidisciplinary Research in Arts, Science and Technology*, *2*(2), 1–8. https://ijmrast.org/vol2issue2/ijmrast2024v2i2001

Pramanik, S. (2024). Immersive innovations: Exploring the use of virtual and augmented reality in educational institutions. In *Augmented reality and the future of education technology* (pp. 66–85). IGI Global., DOI: 10.4018/979-8-3693-2857-6.ch013

Procel, G. J. O., Medina, M. L. F., Sotomayor, D. J., & Sanchez, M. A. P. T. (2024). Using technology in English teaching. *Journal of Environmental Research and Public Health*, *17*(9), 9. DOI: 10.3390/ijerph17093009

Quintero, J., Baldiris, S., Rubira, R., Cerón, J., & Velez, G. (2019). Augmented reality in educational inclusion: A systematic review on the last decade. *Frontiers in Psychology*, *10*, 1835. DOI: 10.3389/fpsyg.2019.01835 PMID: 31456716

Rambaree, K., Nässén, N., Holmberg, J., & Fransson, G. (2023). Enhancing cultural empathy in international social work education through virtual reality. *Education Sciences*, *13*(5), 507. DOI: 10.3390/educsci13050507

Rana, S., Sheshadri, T., Malhotra, N., & Basha, S. M. (2024). *Transdisciplinary teaching and technological integration for improved learning: Case studies and practical approaches*. IGI Global., DOI: 10.4018/979-8-3693-8217-2.ch001

Reyes, R. L., Isleta, K. P., Regala, J. D., & Bialba, D. M. R. (2024). Enhancing experiential science learning with virtual labs: A narrative account of merits, challenges, and implementation strategies. *Journal of Computer Assisted Learning*, *40*(6), 3167–3186. DOI: 10.1111/jcal.13061

Ribeiro, E., Farias, C., & Mesquita, I. (2024). "The game changers": How equity-driven pedagogical scaffolding reduces participation disparities in physical education. *Education Sciences*, *14*(10), 1077. DOI: 10.3390/educsci14101077

Ribis, E. V. (2025). Fostering creativity, advanced technology, and personal growth: The impact of a magic-themed learning experience in primary education. *Revista Catalana de Pedagogia*, *27*, 4–35. DOI: 10.2436/20.3007.01.215

Riyat, M. K., Kakkar, R. K., & Kakkar, A. (2025). Creating immersive learning experiences in education domain through virtual and augmented reality. In *Enhancing learning experiences with digital tools: AI, ChatGPT, and virtual and augmented reality* (pp. 123–156). IGI Global Scientific Publishing., DOI: 10.4018/979-8-3693-9811-1.ch006

Rocha, F., Correia, F., Neto, I., Pires, A. C., Guerreiro, J., Guerreiro, T., & Nicolau, H. (2023, April). Coding together: On co-located and remote collaboration between children with mixed-visual abilities. In *Proceedings of the 2023 CHI Conference on Human Factors in Computing Systems* (pp. 1–14). DOI: 10.1145/3544548.3580924

Rubio-Tamayo, J. L., Gertrudix Barrio, M., & García García, F. (2017). Immersive environments and virtual reality: Systematic review and advances in communication, interaction and simulation. *Multimodal Technologies and Interaction*, *1*(4), 21. DOI: 10.3390/mti1040021

Samaniego López, M. V., Orrego Riofrío, M. C., Barriga-Fray, S. F., & Paz Viteri, B. S. (2025). Technologies in inclusive education: Solution or challenge? A systematic review. *Education Sciences*, *15*(6), 715. DOI: 10.3390/educsci15060715

Sanguinetti, H. (2024). *Exploring the implications: The impact of universal design for learning on student engagement and motivation in diverse classroom environments* (Doctoral dissertation, George Fox University). George Fox University. https://digitalcommons.georgefox.edu/edd/235

Sasanelli, L. D., Ranieri, G., & Campanale, R. (2025). Embodied education in the framework of Universal Design for Learning: Connections and synergies. *Journal of Inclusive Methodology and Technology in Learning and Teaching*, *5*(2). https://www.inclusiveteaching.it/index.php/inclusiveteaching/article/view/350

Scoulas, J. M., & Kim, J. C. (2025). Reevaluating assessment practices for marginalized groups. *Journal of Library Administration*, *65*(2), 244–254. DOI: 10.1080/01930826.2025.2021315

Selvakumar, P., Hemalatha, C., Indumathy, I., Gandhimathi, S., & Mujra, P. (2025). Smart education and sustainable learning environments. In *Smart education and sustainable learning environments in smart cities* (pp. 381–402). IGI Global Scientific Publishing., DOI: 10.4018/979-8-3693-7723-9.ch023

Serrano-Ausejo, E., & Mårell-Olsson, E. (2024). Opportunities and challenges of using immersive technologies to support students' spatial ability and 21st-century skills in K-12 education. *Education and Information Technologies*, *29*(5), 5571–5597. DOI: 10.1007/s10639-023-12528-9

Setiawan, M. A., & Qamariah, Z. (2023). A practical guide in designing curriculum for diverse learners. *PUSTAKA: Jurnal Bahasa dan Pendidikan, 3*(3), 260–275. https://journal.example.org/pustaka/v3i3/260-275

Sewell, A., Kennett, A., & Pugh, V. (2022). Universal Design for Learning as a theory of inclusive practice for use by educational psychologists. *Educational Psychology in Practice*, *38*(4), 364–378. DOI: 10.1080/02667363.2022.2127807

Shidende, D., Kessel, T., Treydte, A., & Moebs, S. (2024, September). A personalized captioning strategy for the deaf and hard-of-hearing users in an augmented reality environment. In De Paolis, L. T., Arpaia, P., & Sacco, M. (Eds.), Lecture Notes in Computer Science: Vol. 15028. *Extended Reality: XR Salento 2024* (pp. 3–21). Springer Nature Switzerland., DOI: 10.1007/978-3-031-71704-8_1

Shireesha, M., & Jeevan, J. (2024). The role of artificial intelligence in personalized learning: A pathway to inclusive education. *Library Progress – Library Science, Information Technology & Computer, 44*(3), 21746–21752. https://bpasjournals.com/library-science/index.php/journal/article/view/2813

Shireesha, M., & Jeevan, J. (2024). The role of artificial intelligence in personalized learning: A pathway to inclusive education. *Library Progress – Library Science, Information Technology & Computer, 44*(3), 21746–21752. https://bpasjournals.com/library-science/index.php/journal/article/view/2813

Sridevi, R., Ashokkumar, P., & Sathish, V. (2024). Empowering minds: Cognitive learning strategies for higher education success. In *Implementing interactive learning strategies in higher education* (pp. 123–150). IGI Global Scientific Publishing., DOI: 10.4018/979-8-3693-3559-8.ch005

Strielkowski, W., Grebennikova, V., Lisovskiy, A., Rakhimova, G., & Vasileva, T. (2025). AI-driven adaptive learning for sustainable educational transformation. *Sustainable Development, 33*(2), 1921–1947. DOI: 10.1002/sd.2365

Sulaimon, J. T., & Adebayo, A. A. (Eds.). (2024). *Empowering educators: Enhancing teacher professional development for sustainable education*. Routledge.

Tafazoli, D., McCallum, L., Fatemeh, R. M., Kusuma, I. P. I., Nami, F., Roe, J., & Waters, K. (2025). A conceptual model for inclusive computer-assisted language learning: A collaborative ethnography. *Computer-Assisted Language Learning Electronic Journal, 26*(2), 1–28. DOI: 10.11139/callejon.26.02.001

Thangavel, S., Sharmila, K., & Sufina, K. (2025). Revolutionizing education through augmented reality (AR) and virtual reality (VR): Innovations, challenges and future prospects. *Asian Journal of Interdisciplinary Research, 8*(1), 1–28. DOI: 10.54392/ajir2511

Thelma, C. C., Sain, Z. H., Mpolomoka, D. L., Akpan, W. M., & Davy, M. (2024). Curriculum design for the digital age: Strategies for effective technology integration in higher education. *International Journal of Research, 11*(07), 185–201. DOI: 10.5281/zenodo.13123899

Tiwari, S. P., & Fahrudin, A. (2024). *Evolving school dynamics and emerging technologies in education: Critical success factors*. SciFormat Publishing Inc., DOI: 10.69635/978-1-0690482-0-2

Tomlinson, C. A., & Jarvis, J. M. (2023). Differentiation: Making curriculum work for all students through responsive planning & instruction. In *Systems and models for developing programs for the gifted and talented* (pp. 599–628). Routledge.

Toto, G. A., Marinelli, C. V., Cavioni, V., di Furia, M., Traetta, L., Iuso, S., & Petito, A. (2024). What is the role of technologies for inclusive education? A systematic review. In *Higher education learning methodologies and technologies online* (pp. 533–565). Springer Nature Switzerland., DOI: 10.1007/978-3-031-67351-1_36

Trivedi, M., & Bindewari, S. (2025). Artificial intelligence: An educational advancement for students with visual disabilities. In *Impacts of AI on Students and Teachers in Education 5.0* (pp. 155–192). IGI Global Scientific Publishing., DOI: 10.4018/979-8-3693-8191-5.ch006

Troussas, C., Krouska, A., & Sgouropoulou, C. (2025). A novel framework of human–computer interaction and human-centered artificial intelligence in learning technology. In *Human-Computer Interaction and Augmented Intelligence: The Paradigm of Interactive Machine Learning in Educational Software* (pp. 387–431). Springer Nature Switzerland AG., DOI: 10.1007/978-3-031-84453-9_9

Ulla, M. B., Advincula, M. J. C., Mombay, C. D. S., Mercullo, H. M. A., Nacionales, J. P., & Entino-Señorita, A. D. (2024). How can GenAI foster an inclusive language classroom? A critical language pedagogy perspective from Philippine university teachers. *Computers and Education: Artificial Intelligence*, *7*, 100314. DOI: 10.1016/j.caeai.2024.100314

Vasinda, S., & Pilgrim, J. (2023). Technology supports in the UDL framework: Removable scaffolds or permanent new literacies? *Reading Research Quarterly*, *58*(1), 44–58. DOI: 10.1002/rrq.484

Vettriselvan, R. (2025). Empowering digital education: The future of value-based learning in the digital era. In Sousa, B., & Veloso, C. (Eds.), *Empowering value co-creation in the digital era* (pp. 199–228). IGI Global Scientific Publishing., DOI: 10.4018/979-8-3373-1742-7.ch009

Villada Castillo, J. F., Bohorquez Santiago, L., & Martínez García, S. (2025). Optimization of physics learning through immersive virtual reality: A study on the efficacy of serious games. *Applied Sciences (Basel, Switzerland)*, *15*(6), 3405. DOI: 10.3390/app15063405

Villarreal, A. R., & Scott, S. M. (2024). Fostering inclusive and resilient classroom environments in the post-COVID-19 era: Strategies for underserved and underrepresented students. In *Building resilient education models post crisis* (pp. 17–41). IGI Global Scientific Publishing., DOI: 10.4018/979-8-3693-8125-0.ch002

Visscher, K. (2024). Experiencing complex stakeholder dynamics around emerging technologies: A role-play simulation. *European Journal of Engineering Education*, *49*(2), 370–388. DOI: 10.1080/03043797.2023.2196940

von Gillern, S., & Nash, B. (2023). Accessibility in video gaming: An overview and implications for English language arts education. *Journal of Adolescent & Adult Literacy*, *66*(6), 382–390. DOI: 10.1002/jaal.1284

Wagner, C., & Liu, L. (2021). Creating immersive learning experiences: A pedagogical design perspective. In *Creative and collaborative learning through immersion: Interdisciplinary and international perspectives* (pp. 71–87). Springer International Publishing., DOI: 10.1007/978-3-030-72512-8_5

Wang, D., & Huang, X. (2025). Transforming education through artificial intelligence and immersive technologies: Enhancing learning experiences. *Interactive Learning Environments*, •••, 1–20. DOI: 10.1080/10494820.2025.2465451

Weisberg, L., & Dawson, K. (2023). The intersection of equity pedagogy and technology integration in preservice teacher education: A scoping review. *Journal of Teacher Education*, *74*(4), 327–342. DOI: 10.1177/00224871221101234

Wilson, S., Vallis, C., & Yeoman, P. (2025). Walking through the future in the present: Teaching practices in postdigital learning spaces. *Postdigital Science and Education*, *7*, 1–21. DOI: 10.1007/s42438-025-00321-4

Yeganeh, L. N., Fenty, N. S., Chen, Y., Simpson, A., & Hatami, M. (2025). The future of education: A multi-layered metaverse classroom model for immersive and inclusive learning. *Future Internet*, *17*(2), 63. DOI: 10.3390/fi17020063

Yesil, L. B., & Aras, İ. S. (2024). The significance of flexible learning spaces and student-centred pedagogies in school settings: A comparative case study. *International Education Journal: Comparative Perspectives*, *23*(1), 1–24. DOI: 10.1111/iej.2024.23.issue-1

Youssef, E., Al Malak, M., & Bayoumy, M. (2025). Metaverse in education: A survey-based investigation of collaborative learning and immersive experiences. *Emerging Science Journal*, *8*, 379–395. DOI: 10.28991/ESJ-2024-SIED1-022

Zaky, H. (2025). Quality higher education: Accommodate diverse learning needs in classrooms. *SSRN*. DOI: 10.2139/ssrn.5158830

Zallio, M., & Clarkson, P. J. (2022). Designing the metaverse: A study on inclusion, diversity, equity, accessibility and safety for digital immersive environments. *Telematics and Informatics*, *75*, 101909. DOI: 10.1016/j.tele.2022.101909

Zamiri, M., & Esmaeili, A. (2024). Strategies, methods, and supports for developing skills within learning communities: A systematic review of the literature. *Administrative Sciences*, *14*(9), 231. DOI: 10.3390/admsci14090231

Zaugg, T. (2024). Future innovations for assistive technology and universal design for learning. In *Assistive technology and universal design for learning: Toolkits for inclusive instruction* (pp. 275–318). IGI Global., DOI: 10.4018/978-1-7998-9018-4.ch012

Zhang, L., Carter, R. A.Jr, Basham, J. D., & Yang, S. (2022). Integrating instructional designs of personalized learning through the lens of universal design for learning. *Journal of Computer Assisted Learning*, *38*(6), 1639–1656. DOI: 10.1111/jcal.12675

Zhang, L., Carter, R. A.Jr, Greene, J. A., & Bernacki, M. L. (2024). Unraveling challenges with the implementation of universal design for learning: A systematic literature review. *Educational Psychology Review*, *36*(1), 35. DOI: 10.1007/s10648-023-09733-2

Chapter 9
STEAM Camp Impact on Mexican Female Teachers' Technological, Pedagogical, and Disciplinary Knowledge

Ricardo Murillo Alfaro
https://orcid.org/0000-0003-4198-0191
Centro Regional de Formación Docente e Investigación Educativa, Mexico

Alhelí Segovia Sánchez
https://orcid.org/0000-0002-0420-6642
Escuela Normal federal de Educadoras Maestra Estefanía Castañeda, Mexico

Ezra Federico Parra-González
https://orcid.org/0000-0002-1192-6568
Center for Research in Mathematics (CIMAT), Zacatecas, Mexico

ABSTRACT

This chapter per the authors examines the impact of a STEAM camp on the technological, pedagogical, and disciplinary knowledge of female upper secondary school teachers in priority groups within the COBAT system in Tamaulipas, Mexico, utilizing the TPACK model as a theoretical framework. Methodologically, it employs a quantitative, explanatory, longitudinal, non-experimental design with a sample of 20 female teachers, using the validated TPACK-21 questionnaire administered after three STEAM camps. Results reveal solid baseline strengths in CK, PK, and PCK, with significant improvements in TCK ($p = .042$), TPK ($p = .030$), and TPACK (p

DOI: 10.4018/979-8-3373-5188-9.ch009

= .037) dimensions, indicating enhanced integration of technology with pedagogy and content through hands-on activities. The discussion interprets these findings in light of gender equity and regional inequalities, while conclusions underscore the camp's role in empowering teachers, promoting equitable STEAM education, and informing policies for sustainable professional development in vulnerable contexts.

1. INTRODUCTION

Upper Secondary Education (Educación Media Superior, EMS) in Mexico represents the level at which students between 15 and 18 years of age receive an education that fosters reflection, data exploration, and knowledge assimilation across various developmental domains. This level encompasses programs such as general high school, technical professional baccalaureate, and their equivalents, as well as professional education that does not require a high school degree or its equivalents, which may be delivered through seven different types of services (Ley General de Educación [LGE], 2024).

According to data from the Dirección General de Planeación, Programación y Estadística Educativa (DGPPE, 2024), during the 2023–2024 academic year, Mexico registered an enrollment of 5,508,572 students served by 425,826 teachers across 21,249 schools. In the state of Tamaulipas, within the same academic cycle, 144,543 students were enrolled, taught by 7,981 teachers across 511 schools distributed among 16 different federal and state subsystems (Secretaría de Educación de Tamaulipas [SET], 2024). This educational level faces specific challenges in the state, including limited coverage in rural areas, restricted access to technologies, and the need for continuous teacher professional development. These challenges directly affect student learning outcomes, particularly in areas such as mathematics and science.

One of the subsystems offering upper secondary education with both terminal and preparatory functions in the state is the Colegio de Bachilleres del Estado de Tamaulipas (COBAT). Established in June 1988, the first students were admitted in September of that same year across four campuses in different municipalities. Currently, COBAT serves 18,875 students distributed across 522 groups, taught by 657 teachers in 73 schools under four different modalities, plantel, CEMSADET, telebachillerato, and extension, located in urban, semi-urban, and rural areas throughout Tamaulipas (Colegio de Bachilleres del Estado de Tamaulipas [COBAT], 2022; SET, 2024).

This subsystem, like the entire upper secondary level in the state, faces major challenges in enhancing teacher education in key areas that foster scientific and technological competencies among students. These, together with essential and long-lasting skills such as problem-solving, argument construction, decision-making, communication, and participation, are critical for thriving in a dynamic, highly technological, and knowledge-driven society (Organización de las Naciones Unidas para la Educación, la Ciencia y la Cultura [UNESCO], 2021).

At the national level, following the Acuerdo Secretarial 09/08/23, upper secondary education began implementing the Marco Curricular Común de la Educación Media Superior (MCCEMS) starting from the 2023–2024 academic year (SEP, 2024). This curricular framework aims to cultivate a new generation of individuals with free-thinking minds, capable of using their own judgment to evaluate internal and external situations, working collaboratively, and acting according to ethical values. Its sociocognitive foundations contribute to developing communication skills, logical-mathematical reasoning, the capacity to analyze current events based on historical facts, and technological literacy. The included knowledge domains encompass the natural, experimental, and social sciences, technology, and the humanities. The framework emphasizes experiential learning, which connects directly with the principles of engineering education.

To improve teaching in science and mathematics, it is essential to strengthen teacher professional development through innovative strategies such as the STEAM approach (science, technology, engineering, arts, and mathematics). This model promotes the integration of these disciplines through active methodologies that prepare students for the challenges of contemporary society (Camacho-Tamayo et al., 2024). It aims to bridge theory and practice through interdisciplinary projects and the use of innovative technologies (Pazmiño Núñez et al., 2025). Its main goal is to foster creativity, innovation, and problem-solving, while developing key 21st-century skills that enable students to face current global challenges (Sanchez Junior & Alves de Sousa, 2023; Arias Villalba et al., 2024; Prieto Murillo, 2024).

Therefore, teacher education in the STEAM approach is of paramount importance in the current and future educational landscape. This training extends beyond mastering technological tools; it involves a deep understanding of how to interconnect diverse knowledge domains. A primary motivation for training teachers in this approach lies in the difficulty many educators face in demonstrating the application, scope, and potential of the STEAM framework to enrich science and other subject areas in their daily teaching practices (Soto Calderón et al., 2022; Camacho-Tamayo & Bernal-Ballé, 2023).

This challenge often stems from insufficient pre-service or in-service preparation. Therefore, specific training programs can play a crucial role in clarifying the purpose, practice, and supports needed for successful STEAM implementation (Soto Calderón et al., 2022). Furthermore, a positive correlation has been observed between teachers "perceived self-efficacy in implementing STEAM approaches and improvements in students" academic performance. Teacher´s belief in their own capacity (self-efficacy) within the STEAM context is a fundamental factor for effective teaching (Soto Calderón et al., 2022).

Educational policies in various contexts, including Mexico and Colombia, have expressed a convergent interest in promoting training related to STEAM disciplines, recognizing their strategic importance for economic development, innovation, and competitiveness. However, despite these initiatives, significant gaps remain in ensuring equitable access to quality in STEAM education (Silva-Hormazábal & Alsinab, 2023). These gaps may result from the absence of a systemic perspective that coherently integrates curriculum, pedagogy, teacher development, and infrastructure. Not all educators have adequate opportunities to develop STEAM-oriented practices (Silva-Hormazábal & Alsinab, 2023).

Despite these challenges, teachers increasingly acknowledge the intrinsic value of the STEAM approach in fostering meaningful learning opportunities tied to authentic problem-solving and the acquisition of essential 21st-century skills. Professional development can also help mitigate resistance to change that some educators express toward innovative pedagogical methodologies such as STEAM (Soto Calderón et al., 2022; Silva-Hormazábal & Alsinab, 2023).

In this regard, continuous teacher education is imperative, and the STEAM approach poses particular demands that require up-to-date, specialized preparation (Soto Calderón et al., 2022). Thus, the professional development of COBAT female teachers in STEAM represents a key strategy for improving educational outcomes in the state. Beyond training in these disciplines, it is equally important to support teachers in effectively incorporating digital tools into their instructional planning and fostering technological and disciplinary learning among students (Camacho-Tamayo et al., 2024; Moreno Rando, 2024). Digital literacy is essential for educators to design teaching processes that overcome technological barriers and harness the potential of digital tools (Silva & Antunes, 2024; Camacho-Tamayo et al., 2024).

Similarly, the STEAM approach not only empowers teachers in their educational role but also creates valuable opportunities for students' holistic development, better preparing them to face the challenges and seize the opportunities of the present and the future (López García & López García, 2024; Bañuelos Márquez, 2024; Rodríguez Pinzón et al., 2024). STEAM enables students to thrive in a society that demands complex and versatile skills such as critical thinking, creativity, collaboration, and problem-solving.

Gender gap in STEAM education

Although the STEAM framework fosters the development of multiple competencies, girls, adolescents, and women continue to face barriers to participation in STEAM education, skill development, and access to technical-scientific professions.

The main challenges include gender-based prejudice in career choice, limited access to training, especially in rural contexts and sociocultural and economic barriers. These factors contribute to women's underrepresentation in STEAM fields (UNICEF, 2023; Organización Internacional del Trabajo [OIT], 2020).

Reports indicate that in higher education, male enrollment predominates in engineering, manufacturing, construction, and technology programs, while women are more represented in social sciences, humanities, health, and education. This trend occurs in many countries. For instance, in Spain, female participation in STEAM education remains low: in high school, the percentage of girls choosing STEAM-related subjects is significantly smaller than that of boys. At the university level, although women account for half of total enrollment, fewer than 8% pursue STEAM-related fields, and in vocational training, female participation does not exceed 3.6% (Grañeras et al., 2022; Universidad Pontificia Comillas, 2021; OIT, 2020).

According to the Centro de Investigación de Política Pública (2022), in Mexico during the 2021–2022 academic year, women represented 54% of university students; however, in the labor market they face higher rates of informality, lower employment levels, and lower wages compared to men. Although career choice is a personal decision, it is influenced by individual preferences and skills, educational costs, local academic offerings, and gender roles. Gender representation varies across professional fields: for example, in psychology, three out of four students are women, whereas in engineering, nine out of ten students are men.

The gender gap in STEAM education represents a major challenge for achieving Sustainable Development Goals (SDGs) 4 ensuring inclusive, equitable, and quality education and promoting lifelong learning opportunities for all, and 5, achieving gender equality and empowering all women and girls of the 2030 Agenda. The exclusion of women from STEAM fields results in a significant loss of talent and creativity and undermines global efforts to build equitable and inclusive societies. This underscores the urgent need for strategies encompassing curriculum design, social awareness, and transformative public policies (Naciones Unidas [NU], 2015).

Relevance of the study for teacher education in highly marginalized contexts

Mexico is a heterogeneous country characterized by demographic and territorial diversity. Among its defining features is regional inequality, which generates social asymmetry and limits equitable access to development opportunities, leading to poverty, exclusion, and marginalization. Highly marginalized areas (typically rural) are marked by restricted access to political, economic, and basic services

(Consejo Nacional de Población [CONAPO], 1994; Consejo Estatal de Población [COESPO], 2019).

Due to their location and limited accessibility, educational institutions in these contexts often face insufficient infrastructure and lack of instructional resources, resulting in unequal opportunities for students. Teachers, in turn, encounter difficulties in their professional growth due to resource scarcity, institutional organization, and geographic isolation.

It is therefore essential that teachers promote relevant and contemporary topics suited to their educational contexts, ensuring local prosperity and educational sustainability. This highlights the need to prepare teachers capable of guaranteeing quality education for all students, particularly in communities experiencing deep social inequalities. Current educational demands call for an expansion of foundational knowledge through innovative approaches that foster critical thinking, creativity, and problem-solving (Barbero et al., 2020).

Description of the research and structure of the document

The objective of this study is to determine the influence of a STEAM camp on technological, pedagogical, and disciplinary knowledge (based on the TPACK model) among female teachers of upper secondary education working in priority-group schools within the COBAT subsystem. This objective is guided by the research question: What is the influence of a STEAM camp on the technological, pedagogical, and disciplinary knowledge, under the TPACK model, of female teachers from priority-group schools in the COBAT subsystem?

The study aims to test the alternative hypothesis that participation in a STEAM camp significantly enhances female upper secondary teachers' technological, pedagogical, and disciplinary knowledge, according to the TPACK model, in priority-group COBAT schools.

This paper presents the scientific background and theoretical framework supporting the study, followed by a detailed description of the methodological design, and concludes with the presentation of the results and final conclusions derived from the research.

2. BACKGROUND

Implementing the STEAM approach in educational settings requires teachers to be prepared to design, manage, implement, and evaluate learning in an integrated and contextualized manner. In recent years, various educational institutions have launched teacher education initiatives, recognizing that educators give meaning to the teaching–learning process by addressing social, health, and environmental issues that reflect the intersection of multiple disciplines.

In Chile, Silva-Hormazábala and Ángel Alsinab (2023), acknowledging that the STEAM methodology serves as a means to advance toward a fairer and more sustainable society, conducted a study aimed at designing and validating a training program for early childhood educators. Their work followed a design-based research approach, a methodology centered on the design and testing of educational interventions through iterative cycles involving collaboration between researchers and practitioners familiar with the topic (Anderson & Shattuck, 2012).

The results highlighted that during the first phase, fundamental elements of the program's design were identified such as theoretical conceptualization, disciplinary integration, contextualization, sustainability, active methodologies, a focus on practice, and teacher collaboration. In the second phase, co-evaluation was incorporated as a key strategy, and in the third iteration, the program was implemented with a group of 31 teachers. The final version of the training program, called Pro-STEAM, consisted of three modules: Education for the 21st Century, STEAM Education, and STEAM Implementation.

This study underscores the need to design training programs tailored to teachers' contextual realities. It is essential that educational programs consider both the participants' needs and the input of expert reviewers to ensure meaningful feedback and improved outcomes.

Similarly, Camacho-Tamayo and Bernal-Ballén (2024) conducted a study to evaluate the implementation of a teacher education strategy on STEAM for natural science teachers, using Kirkpatrick's evaluation model. This model includes four levels:

1. Reaction: captures participants' perceptions of the training program through feedback and opinions.
2. Learning: assesses the degree to which participants acquire new knowledge and skills during the training.
3. Behavior: focuses on how participants apply what they learned in their professional practice.
4. Results: examines the final outcomes and the overall impact on the organization.

The educational program was delivered in an m-learning modality to twenty natural science teachers from four educational institutions in Bogotá. The effectiveness of this intervention was evaluated using four data collection instruments distributed via Google Forms and WhatsApp.

The results revealed that the STEAM education implemented through m-learning facilitated participation and collaborative work among teachers. The flexible structure of the program allowed participants to access training materials easily and at any time, accommodating their schedules and responsibilities while promoting asynchronous learning. Furthermore, the instructor could update resources and materials in real time, keeping participants engaged with current content. The program also encouraged dynamic learning through diverse evidence-based tasks and artifacts submitted by participants.

In the same vein, Boice et al. (2021) identified that STEAM implementation poses challenges for teachers. Their study evaluated the GoSTEAM@Tech program, designed to analyze the functioning and potential outcomes of this professional development initiative. The researchers used a descriptive case study with a mixed-methods triangulation design that combined quantitative survey data, qualitative focus groups and interviews, and open-ended questions.

The instruments were administered to 17 teachers who participated in the first year of GoSTEAM@Tech: 8 elementary school teachers, 5 middle school teachers, and 4 high school teachers. Findings indicated that the program's content was valuable for helping teachers understand and apply STEAM-based lesson plans. Data from the instruments revealed that teachers demonstrated a high level of arts integration in their lesson planning and achieved a deeper understanding of how to incorporate the arts within the STEAM framework, despite encountering challenges in classroom implementation.

Collectively, these studies highlight the importance of training those responsible for facilitating knowledge acquisition in the classroom, especially as new methodologies emerge that transform teaching and learning. The diversity of formats available for professional development represents an advantage, as it allows participants to balance training with their personal, social, and professional obligations. Finally, the results of these STEAM education initiatives demonstrate a positive transformation in teachers' professional practices, particularly in their instructional planning and classroom interactions.

The pedagogical foundations of the STEAM approach and the theoretical framework of the Technological Pedagogical Content Knowledge (TPACK) model share a common epistemological core centered on the integration of knowledge domains to enhance teaching and learning. Both perspectives emphasize that meaningful learning emerges from the dynamic interaction between disciplinary content, pedagogical strategies, and technological tools. In this sense, STEAM provides the what and why of interdisciplinary teaching promoting creativity, innovation, and problem-solving across science, technology, engineering, arts, and mathematics while TPACK offers the how by articulating the specific intersections among technological, pedagogical, and content knowledge that teachers must master to effectively design and implement STEAM-based instruction. Integrating both frameworks thus supports a more comprehensive understanding of teachers' professional competencies, enabling the development of educational practices that are both contextually relevant and technologically enriched.

Previous studies on the application of the TPACK model in teacher education

In the field of educational technology research, the Technological Pedagogical Content Knowledge (TPACK) model has attained a prominent position as a key theoretical framework for understanding the complex relationship between technology, pedagogy, and disciplinary content in teaching practice. This model, grounded in Shulman's seminal concept of Pedagogical Content Knowledge (PCK), expands its scope by incorporating technological knowledge as an essential pillar for effective and relevant teaching in the digital era (Rivera-Robles et al., 2021; Mishra & Koehler, 2006).

Previous studies have extensively explored the applicability of the TPACK model in teacher education, covering both pre-service teacher preparation and in-service professional development. These investigations have employed diverse methodological approaches, including quantitative studies featuring surveys, statistical data analysis, and instrument validation (Rivera-Robles et al., 2021; Paula-Bonifacio & Marcelo-García, 2023; Shafie et al., 2022; Zhan et al., 2013; Suryani et al., 2021; Başaran, 2020) qualitative studies using case studies, in-depth interviews, detailed classroom observations, and analysis of curricular documents and lesson plans (Salas-Rueda, 2018; Rivera-Robles et al., 2021; Zhubi & Ismajli, 2022) and mixed-methods research that combines both perspectives to provide a more holistic understanding of the phenomenon (Salas-Rueda, 2019; Hayati et al., 2022).

In the context of pre-service teacher education, research has delved into prospective teachers' perceptions of their own TPACK levels (Leal Urueña & Rojas Mesa, 2020; Suryani et al., 2021), the assessment of intervention programs specifically designed and implemented to strengthen their TPACK competencies (Zhan et al., 2013), and the rigorous development and validation of measurement instruments aimed at accurately evaluating TPACK proficiency (Başaran, 2020; Paula-Bonifacio & Marcelo-García, 2023; Suryani et al., 2021; Shafie et al., 2022; Saz-Pérez et al., 2024).

Findings from these studies reveal a recurring trend: while pre-service teachers tend to demonstrate acceptable familiarity with technological tools, they often show lower confidence and proficiency in effectively integrating these technologies with appropriate pedagogical strategies and specific disciplinary content. Teacher education programs that adopt learning by design approaches (Mishra & Koehler, 2006; Zhan et al., 2013) where future educators actively participate in creating technological resources and solutions to address authentic educational challenges, while engaging in critical reflection on their own pedagogical practice have proven particularly effective in promoting TPACK development among teacher candidates (Castillejos-López et al., 2014; Rivera-Robles et al., 2021).

Additionally, a line of research has emphasized the necessity of contextualizing the TPACK model to the specific characteristics and requirements of different disciplines such as mathematics, natural sciences, reading and writing, and social sciences recognizing that effective technological integration varies considerably across knowledge domains (Hayati et al., 2022; Leal Urueña & Rojas Mesa, 2020; Paula-Bonifacio & Marcelo-García, 2023; Rivera-Robles et al., 2021; Salas-Rueda, 2019; Suryani et al., 2021).

Research focusing on in-service teachers, on the other hand, has examined educators' self-perception of their TPACK competencies (Ortiz-Colón et al., 2020), as well as the contextual and individual factors influencing their ongoing TPACK development throughout their careers (Leal Urueña & Rojas Mesa, 2020; Rivera-Robles et al., 2021; Zhubi & Ismajli, 2022). Other studies have evaluated the impact of professional development programs specifically designed to enhance pedagogical practices through the effective integration of technology in the classroom (Rivera-Robles et al., 2021; Salas-Rueda, 2018; Zhan et al., 2013).

Findings indicate that in-service teachers generally exhibit greater confidence and mastery of their pedagogical and disciplinary knowledge compared to their technological competencies, particularly regarding the coherent and meaningful integration of these three components in daily instruction. Furthermore, studies have identified notable differences in teachers' self-perception and TPACK development associated with variables such as gender, age, years and quality of teaching experience, and access to technology, as well as frequency and purpose of technology use in both personal and professional contexts (Leal Urueña & Rojas Mesa, 2020; Ortiz-Colón et al., 2020; Rivera-Robles et al., 2021).

In summary, prior research reveals a sustained and growing interest in applying the TPACK model as a foundational framework for teacher education and professional development across multiple educational levels and disciplines. Studies have explored teachers' perceptions, beliefs, and attitudes toward technology integration, as well as the measurable impact of training interventions designed to cultivate and strengthen their TPACK competencies. The wide range of evaluation instruments and methodological approaches used in these investigations underscores the inherent complexity of the TPACK construct and highlights the ongoing need for further research to achieve a more nuanced and generalizable understanding of technological integration in everyday pedagogical practice. The limitations identified in previous studies such as the heavy reliance on self-reported data, variability in sample sizes, and the specificity of educational contexts suggest future directions for research seeking a more robust and transferable comprehension of the TPACK model within teacher education (Rivera-Robles et al., 2021).

3. THEORICAL FRAMEWORK

STEAM Education and Its Impact on Teaching and Learning

STEAM education, an acronym denoting the integration of Science, Technology, Engineering, Arts, and Mathematics, has emerged as a twenty-first-century educational paradigm that transcends the mere sum of individual disciplines to foster a synergistic convergence of knowledge and skills (Castro-Campos, 2022). This holistic, interdisciplinary approach recognizes the inherent interconnectedness among these fields, promoting a vision of learning that mirrors the complexity of the real world, where problems rarely confine themselves to a single area of study (Arias Villalba et al., 2024; López-Gamboa et al., 2020). STEAM is not simply STEM plus the arts; rather, it reconceptualizes education by valuing creativity and design thinking as foundational pillars on par with scientific rigor and technological innovation. It is a model that seeks to integrate and develop artistic and scientific-technical subjects within an interdisciplinary framework.

This model originates in 2008, when Yakman introduced the initial "A" for "Arts" into the existing STEM acronym. The goal was to promote interdisciplinarity through problem- and project-based learning (Yakman, 2008, as cited in Meza González & Duarte Abarca, 2020). Yakman distinguishes two markedly different approaches: (1) the traditional approach, which treats STEM as four independent "plots" developed separately, and (2) the recent or integrative approach, which conceives the four STEM subjects jointly. To underscore the separation between subjects, the author differentiates the concepts typographically, referring to the former as S-T-E-M and the latter as STEM (Yakman, 2008; Yakman y Lee, 2012, as cited in Meza González & Duarte Abarca, 2020).

Definitions of STEAM are multifaceted. It is conceived as an active teaching methodology, an interdisciplinary pedagogical model, a learning culture that values creativity and collaboration, and an educational approach that seeks to contextualize learning in the real world (Arias Villalba et al., 2024; Arrigui Torres & Andrés Mosquera, 2022; Correa-Delgado, 2024; Pabón-Rúa et al., 2024; Santillán-Aguirre et al., 2021).

At its core, STEAM dissolves artificial barriers between disciplines, encouraging students to draw on knowledge and skills from multiple areas to investigate, design, create, and solve authentic problems. According to Aguilera y Vílchez-González (2024), Castro-Campos (2022), and Silva-Díaz et al. (2023), the approach rests on the premise that learning is more meaningful and enduring when clear connections are established between abstract concepts and their practical applications, and when creativity and innovation are integral to the process.

Interdisciplinarity is a hallmark of STEAM: content from different disciplines is woven around common themes or projects, fostering a holistic, integrated understanding of knowledge. Through this integration, students learn to think systemically, recognizing relationships and dependencies among different fields (Perales & Aróstegui, 2024).

With respect to teaching, the STEAM approach demands a reconceptualization of the teacher's role. As Aguilera y Vílchez-González (2024) and Pineda Caro (2022) indicate, the educator moves from being a mere transmitter of information to serving as a facilitator, guide, and mentor of the learning process. This pedagogical shift requires adopting active, student-centered methodologies in which inquiry, experimentation, and real-world problem-solving become the pillars of classroom practice (Monroy-González et al., 2021).

Within this approach, and following Pineda Caro (2022), teachers are compelled to develop interdisciplinary competencies characteristic of STEAM, including an integrated understanding of the various disciplines and the ability to foster creativity and critical thinking in their students. Implementing STEAM encourages educators to integrate a broad range of active methodologies into their curricula, such as Project-Based Learning (PBL), Problem-Based Learning (PBL), inquiry-based learning, and engineering design, among others (Aguilera & Vílchez-González, 2024; Arias Villalba et al., 2024; López-Gamboa et al., 2020).

Likewise, Monroy González et al. (2021), Urgiles-Rodríguez et al. (2022), and Pineda Caro (2022) note that STEAM promotes the creation of innovative learning environments that transcend the traditional classroom by incorporating activities related to robotics, programming, communications, and maker spaces, requiring the effective exploration and use of diverse technological tools.

A central aspect of STEAM's impact on teaching lies in the explicit promotion of creativity and innovation among students, prompting teachers to stimulate idea generation and to provide space for experimentation and reflection (López-Gamboa et al., 2020). Finally, the dynamic, multidisciplinary nature of the approach underscores the need for ongoing teacher professional development and a sustained commitment to self-directed learning, enabling educators to remain current with advances across the STEAM fields.

Regarding learning, the STEAM approach exerts a profound, multifaceted impact on students' educational trajectories. First, it promotes meaningful, contextualized learning whereby abstract knowledge gains relevance through links to authentic, real-world situations and problems, fostering deeper and more durable understanding (Aguilera & Vílchez-González, 2024; Urgiles-Rodríguez et al., 2022). According to Arrigui Torres y Mosquera (2022), Correa-Delgado (2024), and López-Gamboa y Soto (2020), STEAM functions as a key instrument for developing essential twenty-first-century competencies: critical reasoning and complex problem-solving, creativity and innovation, cooperation and effective communication, digital literacy, and autonomous learning. Students learn to integrate knowledge and skills from multiple disciplines synergistically, transcending traditional boundaries to investigate, design, create, and solve problems from a holistic, integrated perspective (Castro-Campos, 2022; Lam-Byrne, 2023).

Aguilera & Vílchez-González (2024), Monroy-González et al. (2021), and Lam-Byrne (2023) report that STEAM's real-world connections and the inclusion of the arts awaken students' intellectual curiosity and significantly increase their motivation and interest in scientific and technological areas, counteracting the traditional perception of these disciplines as abstract or inaccessible.

Similarly, Arias Villalba et al. (2024) and Pineda Caro (2022) indicate that inquiry and problem-solving (core to STEAM) strengthen critical and reflective thinking, enabling students to analyze information, pose questions, and evaluate evidence rigorously. Through active, participatory methodologies, learners become agents of their own learning, experimenting, manipulating, and constructing knowledge autonomously, while teamwork and collaboration are cultivated as essential tools for tackling complex challenges and developing projects jointly.

Finally, various studies, such as Arias Villalba (2024) and Santillán-Aguirre et al. (2021), document that STEAM implementation can lead to notable gains in academic performance, underscoring the effectiveness of this educational paradigm in consolidating knowledge.

Teacher Education in Technology and Pedagogy

The effective integration of information and communication technologies (ICT) in education has become a crucial undertaking that demands adequate teacher preparation (Blanco Iturralde et al., 2024; Luna-Romero et al., 2019). In today's society, characterized by rapid technological development and constant connectivity, educational institutions have not remained static; they are integrating ICT in both administrative and academic domains. This transformation requires relevant teacher education that enables educators to incorporate these tools deliberately and pedagogically into their practice (Luna-Romero et al., 2019; Valarezo Castro & Santos Jiménez, 2019).

Blanco Iturralde et al. (2024) argue that teacher education in technology is essential to maximizing the potential of technological and digital tools in the teaching–learning process (PEA). However, acquiring technical or instrumental skills is insufficient; it is also necessary to develop pedagogical competencies that allow for meaningful technology integration through continuous professional development, given the constant evolution of technology (CAYACHOA-Amaya & ALVAREZ-Araque, 2020; Guimarães Carvalho et al., 2019; Luna-Romero et al., 2019). Planning teacher education that prioritizes the development of digital competencies is indispensable for professional growth and overall educational progress; crucially, such training must go beyond purely instrumental mastery of technological tools (Guimarães Carvalho et al., 2019; Prendes Espinosa, 2018).

Luna Romero et al. (2019) emphasize that training should help teachers keep the horizon of the teaching–learning process in view amid technological advances, channeling efforts into developing ICT-supported didactics. This entails the capacity to select appropriate technological resources and use them to design technology-enhanced instruction. The fundamental purpose is for teachers to serve as facilitators of the teaching–learning process, capable of transforming their own practice and promoting situations that develop learner´s capacities (Morales Soza, 2020; Valarezo Castro & Santos Jiménez, 2019). Educators are thus expected not only to apply technologies but also to design new educational scenarios that optimize student learning.

A recurrent issue identified in the literature is that training often focuses narrowly on technical aspects, detached from solid pedagogical and methodological underpinnings (Arteaga-Alcívar et al., 2022; Valarezo Castro & Santos Jiménez, 2019). In many cases, emergent training has been reduced to procedure-oriented workshops, fracturing the link between how to teach, how to learn, and the content to be taught. Insufficient or inadequate training, particularly the lack of didactic-pedagogical preparation for using technology, is frequently cited by teachers themselves as a major obstacle to effective ICT inclusion in educational processes (CAYACHOA-Amaya & ALVAREZ-Araque, 2020). As noted by Morán Peña et al. (2017), some teachers report that their initial preparation did not address technology integration, compelling them to self-update using personal resources. This lack of didactic-pedagogical training significantly reduces the possibilities afforded by technology.

For technological integration to be truly effective and transformative, teacher education must be comprehensive and continuous, planned and structured to address needs that are both pedagogical and digital (Arteaga-Alcívar et al., 2022; Luna-Romero et al., 2019; Salinas Esparza et al., 2021). Training should be designed to connect instructional strategies, the role of ICT, and the disciplinary field in which teaching is situated.

According to Pinto-Sudario et al. (2021) and Cedeño Ávila et al. (2024), training should develop technical capacities and, critically, pedagogical and methodological competencies. The aim is that teachers not only acquire skills for personal use of ICT tools but also master educational paradigms that employ them, competently use them as teaching tools, and become adept at assessment paradigms supported by ICT (CAYACHOA-Amaya & ALVAREZ-Araque, 2020; Luna-Romero et al., 2019).

Luna Romero et al. (2019) emphasize that training should help teachers keep the horizon of the teaching–learning process (PEA) in view amid technological advances, channeling efforts into developing ICT-supported didactics. This entails the capacity to select appropriate technological resources and use them to design technology-enhanced instruction. The fundamental purpose is for teachers to serve as facilitators of the PEA, capable of transforming their own practice and promoting situations that develop learners' capacities (Morales Soza, 2020; Valarezo Castro & Santos Jiménez, 2019). Educators are thus expected not only to apply technologies but also to design new educational scenarios that optimize student learning.

In sum, Arteaga-Alcívar et al. (2022) and Pinto-Sudario (2021) contend that teacher education should be grounded in practice and reflection on practice, addressing real problems faced by educators and fostering active participation, specifically, in technology and pedagogy. Strategies such as collaborative and cooperative learning among colleagues are fundamental for sharing experiences, developing instructional materials, and strengthening research capacities (CAYACHOA-Amaya & ALVAREZ-Araque, 2020).

A relevant conceptual model that addresses the complex integration of knowledge required for effective technology-enhanced teaching is the TPACK (Technological, Pedagogical, and Content Knowledge) model proposed by Mishra y Koehler in 2006. This model, elaborated further in subsequent sections, highlights the intricate interplay among three interrelated knowledge bases: content or disciplinary knowledge (CK), pedagogical knowledge (PK), and technological knowledge (TK) (Koehler et al., 2015).

TPACK posits that success in using ICT in education is achieved when teachers combine these forms of knowledge for didactic purposes; its value lies in the centrality of the didactic component and its connection with other curricular variables, beyond merely instrumental training (CAYACHOA-Amaya & ALVAREZ-Araque, 2020; Morales Soza, 2020; Luna-Romero et al., 2019).

Since the early 2000s, programs to introduce ICT into classrooms, as well as diverse initiatives for ongoing teacher professional development, have been designed and implemented by national and state governments and educational institutions, which have established public policies and invested in ICT implementation and relevant human-resource training (Abarca-Reyes, 2020; López de la Madrid et al., 2021; Secretaría de Educación Pública, 2020).

Guimarães Carvalho (2019) and Morales Soza (2020) note that teacher education in technology and pedagogy is an ongoing, fundamental challenge aimed at equipping educators with the competencies required for effective, meaningful ICT integration in pedagogical practice. Overcoming the limitations of purely technical approaches and focusing on the deep articulation of technological, pedagogical, and content knowledge (as proposed by the TPACK model) is essential for transforming education and enhancing student learning in the digital era (CAYACHOA-Amaya & ALVAREZ-Araque, 2020; Morales Soza, 2020; Palominos Bastias & Marcelo García, 2021).

TPACK Model

Teacher´s knowledge constitutes a foundational element that underpins effective pedagogical practice. Teaching is a complex activity that demands the integration of multiple forms of specialized knowledge, continually adapted to the dynamic and demanding contexts of the classroom (Koehler et al., 2015). In this landscape, the Technological, Pedagogical, and Content Knowledge (TPACK) model, conceptualized by Mishra y Koehler (2006), emerges as an essential theoretical framework for understanding how technology can be integrated meaningfully into teaching and learning processes.

TPACK rests on the premise that merely adding technological tools to instruction does not guarantee improved educational outcomes (Samperio Pacheco & Barragán López, 2018). Instead, the model emphasizes the complex interaction and deep understanding of three core domains: content or disciplinary knowledge (CK), pedagogical knowledge (PK), and technological knowledge (TK) (Leal Urueña & Rojas Mesa, 2020; Samperio Pacheco & Barragán López, 2018; Ortiz-Colón et al., 2020; Koehler et al., 2015).

Content knowledge (CK), according to Mishra y Koehler (2006), Rivera-Robles et al. (2021), and Cabero Almenara et al. (2015), refers to the substantive knowledge of the subject taught by the teacher. It includes understanding concepts, theories, ideas, organizational frameworks, evidence, and established practices and approaches for developing content within a specific discipline.

Cabero Almenara et al. (2015), Paula-Bonifacio y Marcelo-García (2023), and Mishra y Koehler (2006) state that pedagogical knowledge (PK) encompasses knowledge of teaching and learning processes and methods. This includes classroom management, effective teaching strategies, learning theories, assessment methods, and the ability to adapt instruction to diverse student needs. It involves understanding how students learn, how to design effective learning activities, and how to create environments conducive to learning.

Finally, Cabero Almenara et al. (2015), Paula-Bonifacio y Marcelo-García (2023), and Koehler et al. (2015) define technological knowledge (TK) as knowledge of various digital technologies, computing tools, and their applications in education. This domain goes beyond the ability to use a given software or device; it entails understanding the capacities and limitations of technologies to support learning, recognizing when a technology may help or hinder an educational objective, and continually adapting to rapid technological advances.

The true power of the TPACK model lies in integrating these three foundational forms of knowledge, giving rise to four interrelated knowledge types (Rivera-Robles et al., 2021). The first is Pedagogical Content Knowledge (PCK), emerging from the intersection of CK and PK. Teachers with strong PCK understand how to teach specific content effectively, considering typical student difficulties and selecting pedagogical strategies best suited to facilitate understanding (Salas-Rueda, 2018; Leal Urueña & Rojas Mesa, 2020). Shulman (1987, as cited in Koehler et al., 2015) argued that this knowledge is more than the sum of CK and PK, representing a teacher-specific category of professional knowledge.

Technological Content Knowledge (TCK) arises from the intersection of TK and CK. This dimension involves understanding how technology can be used to represent or communicate content more effectively. Teachers with strong TCK know how digital tools can transform the ways students interact with and understand subject matter (Cabero Almenara et al., 2015; Samperio Pacheco & Barragán López, 2018; Salas-Rueda, 2018; Castillejos-López et al., 2014).

In the same vein, Technological Pedagogical Knowledge (TPK) is generated by integrating TK and PK. This dimension refers to understanding how technology can support and enhance pedagogical strategies. Teachers with robust TPK can leverage technology to implement diverse teaching and learning methodologies, optimizing student engagement and participation (Alemán-Saravia et al., 2023; Cabero Almenara et al., 2015; Castillejos-López et al., 2014; Salas-Rueda, 2019).

Finally, Technological Pedagogical Content Knowledge (TPACK) represents the core of the model, the dynamic, complex integration of all three knowledge bases. Teachers with well-developed TPACK can teach specific content effectively using appropriate technologies and pedagogical strategies suited to the learning context. This knowledge is contextual and flexible, enabling educators to make informed decisions about how and when to use technology to enhance instruction (Castillejos-López et al., 2014; Paula-Bonifacio & Marcelo-García, 2023; Samperio Pacheco & Barragán López, 2018; Rivera-Robles et al., 2021; Salas-Rueda, 2019; Torres et al., 2021).

Since its introduction, the TPACK model has undergone significant development in educational research. Early efforts focused on clarifying and strengthening the model's theoretical bases. Subsequent work turned to designing and validating instruments to measure teachers' TPACK (Castillejos-López et al., 2014). These instruments (often self-report questionnaires) seek to assess teachers' perceptions of their knowledge and skills across TPACK domains. Nonetheless, scholars have recognized the need to complement self-reports with performance-based evaluations, such as lesson-plan analyses, classroom observations, and reflective accounts of pedagogical practice, to gain a deeper understanding of TPACK competence in action (Balladares-Burgos & Valverde-Berrocoso, 2022; Cabero Almenara et al., 2015; Koehler et al., 2015).

Education in Priority Groups

Education is a fundamental right that must be guaranteed for all. However, some segments of the population, considered vulnerable or priority groups, are at greater risk of educational inequality and discrimination. Despite progress in expanding and making education more inclusive in recent years, girls and women, migrants, and people with disabilities are among those who continue to experience the greatest educational disadvantage (UNESCO, 2022).

The Fifth Global Report on Adult Learning and Education (2022) notes that, although women's participation has increased, adults, Indigenous students, rural populations, migrants, older adults, persons with disabilities, and people in prison remain excluded from learning opportunities. Approximately 60% of member countries reported no improvements in participation among people with disabilities, migrants, and prisoners. Moreover, participation among rural populations and older adults declined in 24% of the 159 countries surveyed.

In Mexico, there is a legal obligation to provide educational services grounded in equity and excellence, ensuring that no one is excluded from the National Education System. To this end, the Secretaría de Educación Pública (SEP) has implemented actions to enable communities facing significant educational disadvantage, geographic dispersion, or risk to attend school regularly, thereby promoting their economic, social, and cultural development and extending educational coverage to all social sectors and regions of the country (Dirección General de Acreditación, Incorporación y Revalidación [DGAIR], s.f.).

These observations underscore that serving priority groups in education is a persistent challenge worldwide and nationally. Although progress has been made in recent decades, it remains an area requiring focused attention.

4. METHODOLOGY

a. Research Design

This study adopts a quantitative, explanatory, longitudinal, and non-experimental design, grounded in the Technological, Pedagogical, and Content Knowledge (TPACK) model (Mishra & Koehler, 2006). Its objective is to evaluate the impact of a STEAM camp–based intervention on the technological, pedagogical, and disciplinary competencies of female upper secondary school teachers working in vulnerable rural schools of the COBAT subsystem in Tamaulipas, Mexico. The longitudinal design incorporates three measurement points conducted after each camp (February 2024, November 2024, and April 2025), allowing for the analysis of changes in TPACK competencies over time without manipulation of variables, thus maintaining a non-experimental approach.

The explanatory nature of this research seeks to demonstrate how participation in STEAM camps influences the seven dimensions of the TPACK model: Content Knowledge (CK), Pedagogical Knowledge (PK), Technological Knowledge (TK), Pedagogical Content Knowledge (PCK), Technological Content Knowledge (TCK), Technological Pedagogical Knowledge (TPK), and the integrative TPACK dimension (Koehler & Mishra, 2009). This longitudinal approach facilitates the identification of trends and sustained effects of the intervention, as reflected in preliminary findings indicating significant improvements in the TPK and TPACK dimensions.

The decision to employ a non-experimental longitudinal design was based on both ethical and contextual considerations intrinsic to the educational environments under study. Random assignment and experimental manipulation were not feasible due to institutional constraints and the voluntary nature of teacher´s participation in professional development programs organized by the COBAT subsystem. Additionally, the intervention "STEAM training camps" was implemented as part of a broader governmental initiative aimed at teacher professionalization, which required inclusive participation rather than selective sampling. Therefore, a non-experimental design was the most appropriate and ethically sound choice, allowing the researchers to observe real-world educational dynamics while maintaining ecological validity. The longitudinal approach, in turn, enabled the identification of sustained changes in TPACK competencies over time, offering a more comprehensive view of the intervention's educational impact in authentic school contexts.

b. Population and Sample

Population: The target population consisted of female upper secondary school teachers employed in COBAT subsystem schools located in rural or vulnerable areas of Tamaulipas, Mexico. These schools, classified as priority groups, face socioeconomic and geographic limitations that restrict access to technological resources and opportunities for continuous professional development (Rivera-Robles et al., 2021).

Inclusion criteria:

- Female upper secondary school teachers employed in COBAT institutions.

- Teachers working in schools situated in rural or socioeconomically vulnerable areas, according to established criteria of social and geographic marginalization.
- Teachers who participated in the STEAM camps conducted in February 2024, November 2024, and April 2025.

Exclusion criteria:

- Female teachers not employed in COBAT upper secondary schools.
- Teachers working in urban or non-vulnerable educational centers.
- Teachers who did not participate in the STEAM camps.

Sample: A **convenience sampling method** was employed, selecting 20 female teachers from COBAT schools located in vulnerable areas who participated in all three STEAM camps. The same 20 participants were evaluated at each of the three post-intervention measurement points to ensure consistency in the longitudinal analysis. Although the sample size is limited, it is appropriate given the study's focus on a hard-to-reach population and the logistical constraints inherent in rural contexts (Creswell & Creswell, 2018). Nonetheless, this limitation will be addressed in the discussion section to reflect on its implications for the generalization of findings.

c. Data Collection Instrument

The data collection instrument used was the **TPACK-21 questionnaire**, validated by Valtonen et al. (2017) and adapted to the Latin American context by Alemán-Saravia, Deroncele-Acosta, and Robles-Mori (2023). This instrument evaluates the seven dimensions of the TPACK model and is structured as follows:

- **5 sociodemographic items:** Gather information about age, teaching experience, and other relevant variables.
- **7 academic training items:** Assess participants' educational qualifications and prior professional development.
- **36 items distributed across seven dimensions:** Measure CK (4 items), PK (7 items), TK (4 items), PCK (6 items), TCK (4 items), TPK (6 items), and TPACK (5 items), using a five-point Likert scale (1 = "I need extensive knowledge about the topic"; 5 = "I have a comprehensive understanding of the topic").

The TPACK-21 was selected for its psychometric validity and cultural adaptability, ensuring its suitability for the target population (Valtonen et al., 2017). Its administration at three post-intervention points allowed for the assessment of cumulative effects of the STEAM camps on teachers' TPACK competencies.

d. Intervention: STEAM Camps

The intervention consisted of three STEAM camps conducted in February 2024, November 2024, and April 2025. These camps were designed to strengthen teachers' technological, pedagogical, and disciplinary competencies through a combination of workshops, lectures, and hands-on activities focused on STEAM-related topics aligned with the upper secondary curriculum. The activities promoted "learning by design" approaches, which have been shown to effectively enhance TPACK competencies in teacher education contexts (Mishra & Koehler, 2006; Castillejos-López et al., 2014).

The intervention specifically targeted female teachers working in vulnerable rural schools, addressing persistent gaps in access to professional training and technological resources (Ortiz-Colón et al., 2020).

e. Data Collection Procedure

Data collection followed three distinct phases, each conducted after the completion of a STEAM camp:

1. **Post-Intervention 1 (February 2024)**:
   - After the first camp, the TPACK-21 questionnaire was administered to the 20 participants to assess the initial effects of the intervention across the seven TPACK dimensions.
   - Sociodemographic and academic training data were collected to contextualize the sample.
2. **Post-Intervention 2 (November 2024)**:
   - Following the second camp, the TPACK-21 was administered again to measure cumulative changes in teachers' competencies.
   - This stage aimed to capture the combined effects of the first two camps.
3. **Post-Intervention 3 (April 2025)**:
   - After the third camp, the TPACK-21 was applied to evaluate the sustained effects of the intervention over time.
   - This final measurement point enabled analysis of the consolidation of TPACK competencies.

Before each administration of the instrument, all participants signed an informed consent form, ensuring voluntary participation and full understanding of the study's objectives and procedures. Data collection was carried out under standardized conditions to ensure reliability.

f. Data Analysis

Data analysis was conducted using R Studio (version 4.3.1), selected for its versatility in advanced statistical analysis and open-source accessibility (R Core Team, 2023).

g. Normality Test

The Shapiro–Wilk test was applied to data from each TPACK dimension to assess distribution normality. Based on the results, the data did not follow a normal distribution, leading to the use of non-parametric statistical tests, which were more appropriate for the data type and sample size.

h. Statistical Tests

- Friedman test:
    - Given the longitudinal design with repeated measures for the same subjects, the Friedman test, a non-parametric alternative to repeated-measures ANOVA, was employed to detect significant differences in TPACK scores across the three measurement points for each dimension (Field, 2018). Partial results indicated statistically significant differences in the TCK dimension, suggesting a notable impact of the STEAM camps on the integration of technology with disciplinary content.
- Post-Hoc analysis:
    - When the Friedman test yielded statistically significant results ($p < .05$), paired comparisons were conducted using the Wilcoxon signed-rank test, with p-values adjusted via Bonferroni correction to control Type I error in multiple comparisons. These analyses identified specific moments in which significant changes occurred (Field, 2018).
        - Effect size (Rosenthal's r): Calculated for significant paired comparisons to evaluate the magnitude of change across measurements, with interpretation based on conventional thresholds: small ($r \approx .10$), medium ($r \approx .30$), and large ($r \geq .50$).
        - Kendall's W coefficient: Used as an additional measure to assess the degree of agreement among the three measurements and the overall intensity of observed change.

i. Descriptive Analyses

Descriptive statistics (means, standard deviations, and medians) were computed for each TPACK dimension at the three measurement points, providing a comprehensive view of trends in teachers' competencies. These analyses complemented the inferential tests by offering broader contextual information to aid interpretation of the results.

j. Ethical Considerations

The study adhered to strict ethical principles aligned with international standards for human subjects research (American Psychological Association, 2017):

- **Informed consent**: Each participant signed an informed consent form before every administration of the instrument, ensuring voluntary participation and understanding of the study´s objectives, procedures, and participant rights.
- **Confidentiality**: Data were anonymized through alphanumeric codes to protect participant´s identities.
- **Voluntary participation**: No incentives were offered that could influence participation, thereby avoiding coercion.

k. Limitations

- **Sample Size**: The sample of 20 participants, while appropriate for the study context, limits statistical power and generalizability to larger populations (Creswell & Creswell, 2018).
- **Convenience sampling**: The non-random selection method may introduce bias, affecting sample representativeness.
- **Self-Reported data**: The use of the TPACK-21 self-report instrument may be subject to social desirability bias or inaccuracies in teachers' self-assessment (Podsakoff et al., 2003).
- **Lack of control group**: The non-experimental design lacks a control group, which limits causal inferences regarding the observed changes.

5. RESULTS

This section presents the findings derived from the application of the TPACK-21 questionnaire to a sample of 20 female upper secondary school teachers from the COBAT subsystem, assigned to vulnerable rural schools in the state of Tamaulipas, Mexico. Data were collected at three post-intervention measurement points corresponding to February 2024 (first administration), November 2024 (second administration), and April 2025 (third administration), as part of a longitudinal design evaluating the impact of STEAM camps on teachers' TPACK competencies. Analyses were conducted using R Studio software (version 4.3.1; R Core Team, 2023), encompassing normality testing, descriptive statistics, nonparametric analysis of variance through the Friedman test, and post hoc Wilcoxon signed-rank tests, complemented by Kendall's W coefficient and Rosenthal's r as measures of effect size. The interpretation followed the methodological guidelines established by Field (2018) and was framed within the context of prior research on the TPACK model (Mishra & Koehler, 2006).

Normality Analysis

To determine the distribution of scores across the seven dimensions of the TPACK model, the Shapiro–Wilk test was applied at each measurement point.

In the first administration (February 2024), the p-values indicated that the distributions for TK ($p = .062$) and TPK ($p = .175$) did not reject the null hypothesis of normality ($p > .05$), whereas PK ($p = .033$), CK ($p = .036$), PCK ($p = .047$), TCK ($p = .009$), and TPACK ($p = .150$) exhibited significant deviations from normality.

In the second administration (November 2024), only TK ($p = .202$) maintained a normal distribution, while PK ($p = .024$), CK ($p = .014$), PCK ($p = .001$), TCK ($p = .014$), TPK ($p = .0004$), and TPACK ($p = 3.72E–05$) displayed clear non-normality.

By the third administration (April 2025), all dimensions showed non-normal distributions: TK ($p = .001$), PK ($p = .031$), CK ($p = .013$), PCK ($p = .010$), TCK ($p = .021$), TPK ($p = .002$), and TPACK ($p = .008$).

This consistent non-normality across measurement points justified the selection of nonparametric methods for inferential analyses, aligning with Field's (2018) recommendations for data characterized by asymmetric distributions or the presence of outliers.

Descriptive analysis

Descriptive statistics, including means and medians, were calculated for each TPACK dimension across the three measurement points to characterize teachers' competencies before and after each STEAM camp.

In the first administration, the mean scores were as follows: PK ($M = 4.43$), PCK ($M = 4.36$), CK ($M = 4.33$), TK ($M = 3.86$), TPK ($M = 3.84$), TCK ($M = 3.72$), and TPACK ($M = 3.71$), reflecting a stronger initial mastery in pedagogical dimensions (PK, PCK, CK) compared with those integrating technology (see Figure 1).

Figure 1. Mean Scores by Dimension after the First STEAM Camp.

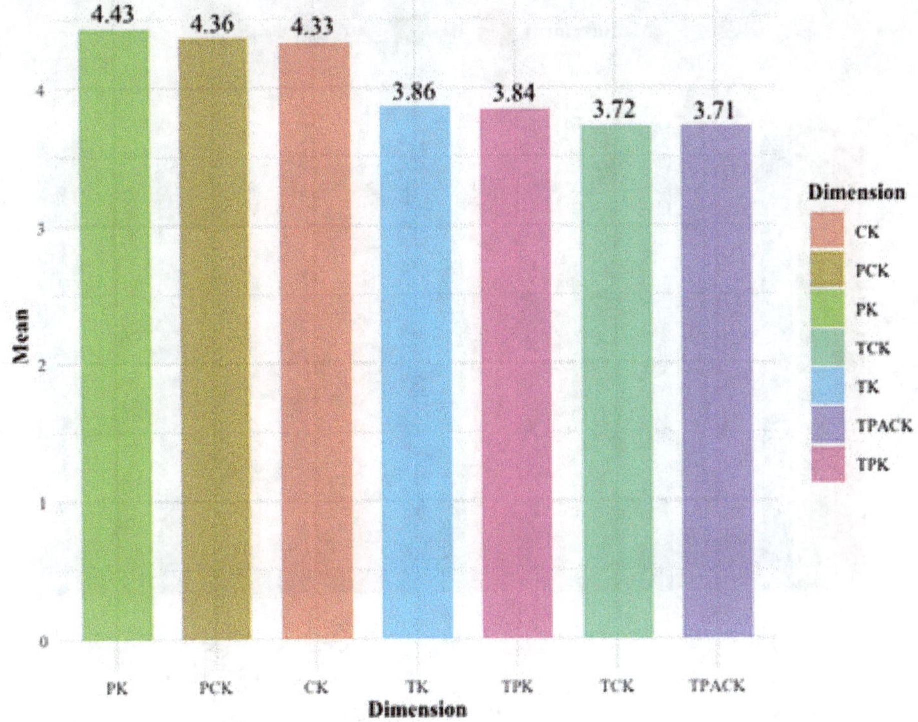

The comparisons of means and medians across the three administrations, illustrated in the bar charts (see Figures 2 and 3), revealed that the pedagogical dimensions maintained consistently high levels (means between 4.0 and 4.5; medians around 4.0–4.2) over time, suggesting stability in these preexisting competencies. In contrast, the technological dimensions (TK, TCK, TPK, and TPACK) started from lower baseline values (initial means ranging from 3.5 to 3.9) and showed gradual increases: TCK reached an approximate median of 3.9 in the third administration, TPK approached 4.0, and TPACK reached 3.9, according to the point plots tracing their evolution throughout the successive camps (see Figure 4).

Figure 2. Comparison of Mean Scores by Dimension across the Three STEAM Camps.

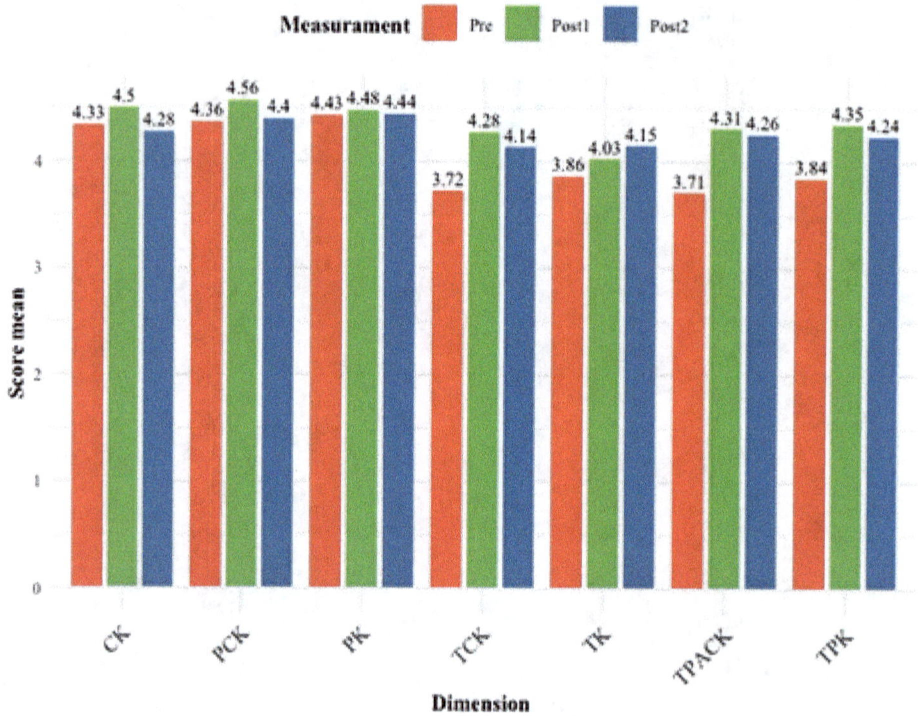

Figure 3. Comparison of Median Scores by Dimension across the Three STEAM Camps.

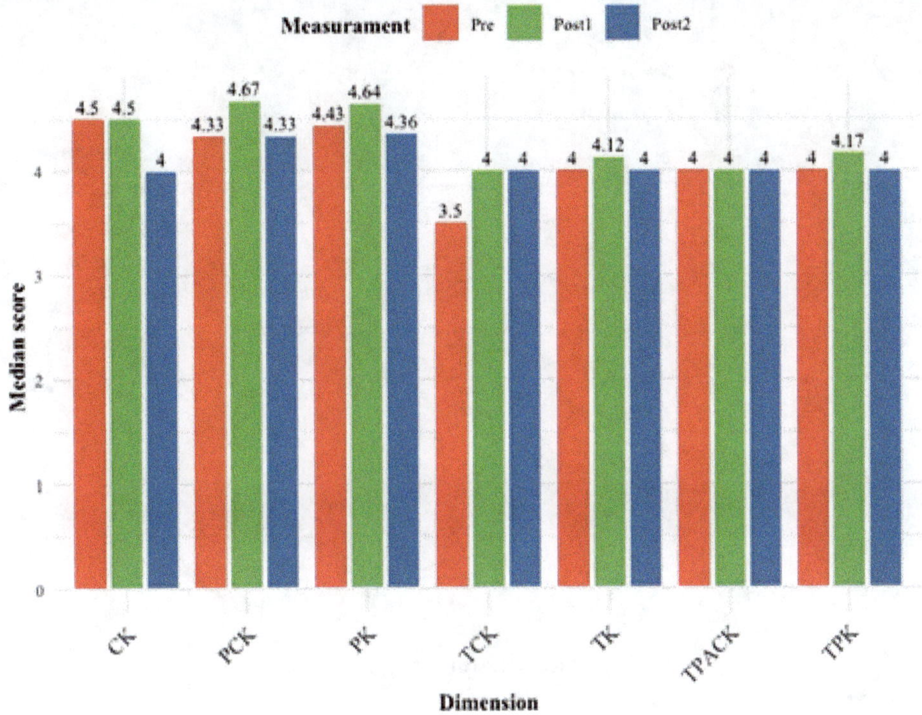

Figure 4. Evolution of Median Scores by Dimension across the Three STEAM Camps

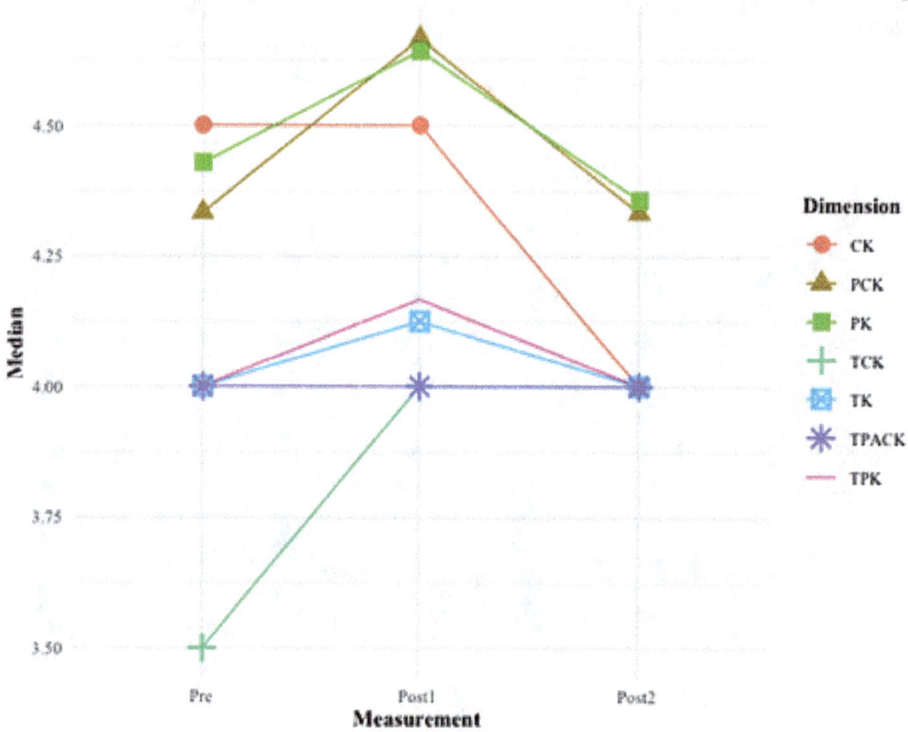

The box plot corresponding to the TCK dimension (see Figure 5) revealed an increase in the median from 3.7 to 3.9 between the first and third measurements, accompanied by a reduction in interquartile dispersion. This pattern indicates greater homogeneity in the scores following the STEAM camps, suggesting a progressive consolidation of technological–content integration among the participating teachers.

Figure 5. Distribution of TCK Scores across the Three STEAM Camps.

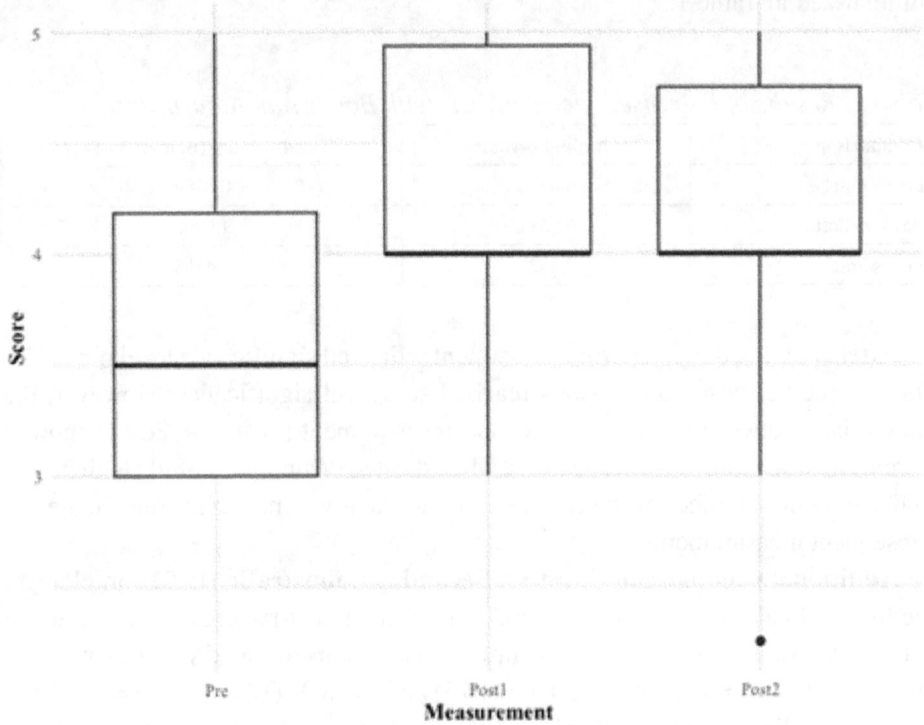

Inferential Analysis

Friedman test: To evaluate differences in TPACK scores across the three measurement points, the Friedman test was applied, a nonparametric method suitable for longitudinal designs with nonnormally distributed data (Field, 2018). The results indicated that only the TCK dimension showed statistically significant differences ($p = .0424$), while the remaining dimensions did not exhibit significant variation: TK ($p = .386$), PK ($p = .410$), CK ($p = .356$), PCK ($p = .488$), TPK ($p = .0863$), and TPACK ($p = .172$). To quantify the effect size for TCK, Kendall's coefficient of concordance ($W = .124$) was calculated, suggesting a small yet detectable effect, consistent with the magnitude typically observed in medium-duration educational interventions (Cohen, 1988).

Post-Hoc Analysis: Since the Friedman test identified significant differences in the TCK dimension, pairwise Wilcoxon signed-rank tests with Bonferroni correction were conducted to explore specific comparisons among the three measurement points (Post1 vs. Post2, Post2 vs. Post3, and Post1 vs. Post3). The results are summarized in Table 1.

Table 1. Results of Pairwise Wilcoxon Tests with Bonferroni Adjustment.

Comparison	Original p-valor	Adjusted p (Bonferroni)
Pre vs Post1	0.0296	0.0889
Post1 vs Post2	0.5511	1.0000
Pre vs Post2	0.1523	0.4568

After applying the Bonferroni adjustment (adjusted significance level $p < .017$), none of the pairwise comparisons reached statistical significance. However, the comparison between the first and second measurement (Post1 vs. Post2) showed a trend approaching significance (p_{adjusted} = .0889), which may indicate an initial effect of the first intervention that was not fully consolidated in subsequent measurements.

Additional Comparison (First vs. Second Administration): To complement the longitudinal analysis, an additional Wilcoxon signed-rank test was conducted between the first and second administrations. The results revealed significant differences in TPK ($W = 21.5$, $p = .030$, $r = .513$) and TPACK ($W = 27.5$, $p = .037$, $r = .491$). According to Rosenthal's r index, these effect sizes are classified as moderate to large ($r > .40$), suggesting a notable impact of the first two STEAM camps on the integration of technological and pedagogical knowledge. The remaining dimensions did not exhibit significant differences, as presented in Table 2. The overall Wilcoxon statistic was highly significant ($p = 5.46 \times 10^{-14}$), indicating a general effect of the intervention across dimensions.

Table 2. Wilcoxon Test Results and Rosenthal's r between the First and Second Measurements.

Dimension	W	p (wilcoxon)	Interpretation	R (Rosenthal)
TK	55	0.517766502872979	non-significant results	0.152450361096792
PK	53.5	0.467621481726538	non-significant results	0.171203395590979
CK	45.5	0.423237261136477	non-significant results	0.188754513331769
PCK	38.5	0.395325896556399	non-significant results	0.200346577806686
TCK	38	0.0710465474323053	non-significant results	0.425484964416331
TPK	21.5	0.0296314303063321	Significant results	0.512648283727024
TPACK	27.5	0.0372813492930711	Significant results	0.490889934911684

6. DISCUSSION

The findings align with the main objective of the study: to understand the influence of a STEAM camp on the development of technological, pedagogical, and disciplinary knowledge under the TPACK framework among female high school teachers working in COBAT institutions located in priority communities in Tamaulipas, Mexico. This objective is reflected in the central research question: How does participation in a STEAM camp impact technological, pedagogical, and disciplinary knowledge from the TPACK perspective among female teachers in this context?

The proposed hypothesis suggested that participation in such formative experiences would positively influence these areas of knowledge. The results partially confirm this assumption, based on a quasi-experimental design with repeated measures and both descriptive and non-parametric inferential analyses (Friedman and Wilcoxon tests). The sample consisted of 20 purposefully selected female teachers, all working in highly marginalized contexts.

From a theoretical standpoint, the TPACK model (Mishra & Koehler, 2006) serves as a key conceptual reference, as it enables a deeper understanding of how disciplinary knowledge (CK), pedagogical knowledge (PK), and technological knowledge (TK) interrelate, along with their combined forms (PCK, TCK, TPK, and TPACK). The descriptive results revealed a solid foundation in content and pedagogical dimensions, with pre-intervention values above 4.0, reflecting the teachers' initial training in traditional models where pedagogical and disciplinary components have historically been emphasized over the technological dimension (UNESCO, 2021). These dimensions remained stable across the three measurements, confirming that TPACK operates as a transformative framework rather than a simple sum of its parts, where CK and PK serve as the foundational bases enabling more complex interactions (Koehler et al., 2015).

In contrast, the technological dimensions started at intermediate levels (between 3.5 and 3.9) and showed progressive improvement, approaching 4.0 by the final measurement. This trend supports the hypothesis that STEAM camps, as practical and experiential learning spaces, foster the development of technological competencies, particularly in contexts with limited digital resources, such as rural areas of Tamaulipas (Silva-Hormazábal & Alsinab, 2023).

The inferential analysis reinforces this interpretation. The Friedman test identified significant changes only in TCK ($\chi^2 = 6.167$, p = .0424, W = .124), indicating a modest but relevant impact on the integration of technology with disciplinary content. Although the post-hoc analyses with Bonferroni adjustment did not reach significance, a marginal trend was observed between the initial and first post-test (p_{adjusted} = .0889), suggesting an initial effect that would require continuity to consolidate. Additionally, Wilcoxon comparisons revealed significant improvements in TPK (Z = -2.165, p = .030, r = .513) and TPACK (Z = -2.091, p = .037, r = .491), with moderate-to-large effect sizes. These results confirm that hands-on, project-based activities promoted during the camps enhance pedagogical–technological integration, helping to bridge both gender and digital divides faced by female teachers in vulnerable educational environments (United Nations Children's Fund [UNICEF], 2023; Grañeras et al., 2022).

Comparison with previous research helps contextualize these findings. For instance, recent studies in Colombia (Pazmiño Núñez et al., 2025) report similar outcomes in STEAM programs for rural teachers, attributing improvements to the contextualization of local problems, a focus also present in this study. In Mexico, other investigations (Bañuelos Márquez, 2024; Rodríguez Pinzón et al., 2024) have highlighted how such initiatives contribute to reducing gender gaps in upper secondary education. However, the absence of significant improvements in TK and other strictly technological dimensions can be explained by structural limitations, such as inadequate digital infrastructure in priority areas (Consejos Estatales de Población [COESPO], 2019), which aligns with criticisms of the TPACK model for not explicitly incorporating socioeconomic factors (Voogt et al., 2013).

It is also important to acknowledge the study's limitations. The quasi-experimental design without a control group restricts the ability to establish absolute causal relationships and leaves room for external influences such as participants' intrinsic motivation (Creswell & Creswell, 2018). The use of a self-report questionnaire may introduce social desirability bias, and the small sample size (n = 20) limits generalizability. Nevertheless, these conditions are justified within a mixed-methods approach, characteristic of research in marginalized contexts, and do not invalidate the findings, though they suggest the need for future studies employing more robust designs.

In terms of implications, the results provide empirical evidence to identify gaps in STEAM teacher education in Tamaulipas and support educational policies aligned with the Marco Curricular Común de la Educación Media Superior (MCCEMS; SEP, 2024), which promote inclusive and equitable education (SDG 4 and 5; UN, 2015). For female teachers from priority groups, the STEAM camps emerge as a transformative strategy that not only strengthens their technological and pedagogical competencies but also empowers them within their professional practice. In the long term, this empowerment may lead to improved learning outcomes for their students (Sanchez Junior & Alves de Sousa, 2023).

7. CONCLUSIONS

The conclusions of this research represent a significant contribution to the field of STEAM education in vulnerable contexts, particularly within the COBAT subsystem in Tamaulipas. The primary objective was to analyze how participation in a STEAM camp influences the technological, pedagogical, and disciplinary knowledge of female high school teachers working in schools serving priority groups, using the TPACK model as a theoretical framework. From this objective, the central research question emerged: What impact does participation in a STEAM camp have on teachers' technological, pedagogical, and disciplinary knowledge, as conceptualized by the TPACK model?

The initial hypothesis posited a positive effect, which was partially confirmed, though the findings proved more nuanced than initially expected. Employing a quasi-experimental design with repeated measurements and non-parametric statistical tests made it possible to observe tangible changes in the teachers' TPACK competencies.

In terms of results, one of the most noteworthy findings concerns the stability of the core TPACK dimensions, disciplinary, pedagogical, and pedagogical content knowledge, which consistently exhibited high averages (above 4.0 across all three measurements). This stability reflects the teachers' strong initial preparation, still largely grounded in content-focused and traditional pedagogical practices, a common feature in many educational settings in Mexico where technological integration has progressed slowly. In contrast, dimensions involving technology (TK, TCK, TPK, and TPACK) demonstrated measurable improvement, starting from intermediate levels (3.5–3.9) and approaching 4.0 following participation in the camp.

The statistical analyses confirmed these improvements. The Friedman test revealed significant differences in TCK ($\chi^2 = 6.167$, $p = .0424$, $W = .124$), while Wilcoxon tests identified significant increases in TPK ($Z = -2.165$, $p = .030$, $r = .513$) and TPACK ($Z = -2.091$, $p = .037$, $r = .491$). These moderate-to-large effect sizes indicate that STEAM camps serve as effective environments for fostering stronger technological–pedagogical integration, an especially valuable outcome in rural communities where limited access to resources often constrains such development.

From a theoretical standpoint, the findings reaffirm the relevance of the TPACK model proposed by Mishra and Koehler (2006), while also demonstrating its adaptability to nontraditional learning experiences such as STEAM camps. The observed growth in TPK and TPACK aligns with previous studies showing that interventions designed to reflect local conditions yield more lasting effects. Moreover, the inclusion of transdisciplinary activities, such as literacy workshops and artistic projects within the STEAM framework, suggests that the model can also extend to broader competencies such as creativity and collaborative problem-solving.

In practice, these results hold several implications. For female teachers in marginalized areas of Tamaulipas, participation in STEAM camps not only enhances their professional profiles but also provides spaces for empowerment in fields where women's participation has traditionally been limited (Grañeras et al., 2022; UNICEF, 2023). Strengthening their TPACK equips them with tools to promote more active and student-centered learning, aligning with the requirements of the Marco Curricular Común de la Educación Media Superior (MCCEMS) and UNESCO's framework of 21st-century competencies. At the institutional level, the COBAT system may view these results as an opportunity to expand rural coverage and improve teacher training, even through low-cost digital resources adapted to local school conditions.

In relation to educational policy, this study underscores the importance of equity-oriented strategies consistent with Sustainable Development Goals 4 and 5 (UN, 2015). A potential pathway forward would be to expand STEAM camps to additional schools across the state, integrating gender mentorship programs and formative assessments to help overcome resistance to pedagogical innovation among educators.

It is also important to acknowledge the study's limitations. The absence of a control group prevents definitive causal inferences, and the use of self-report questionnaires may have introduced social desirability bias. Nevertheless, the results open avenues for future research employing more robust designs, possibly through mixed methods approaches that capture both quantitative data and teachers' perceptions and emotional experiences.

Looking ahead, longitudinal studies could assess whether the observed improvements in TPACK are sustained (or even amplified) over time as teachers apply what they learned in their classrooms. Future research might also explore how emerging technologies, such as artificial intelligence, can be integrated into similar learning experiences. Cross-country comparisons with other Latin American contexts could further illuminate how public policies and institutional support shape the implementation and success of these initiatives.

In closing, this study demonstrates that STEAM camps can serve as a viable and effective strategy to transform teacher professional development in vulnerable educational contexts. Although the initial hypothesis was only partially confirmed, the evidence shows that these experiences strengthen key dimensions of TPACK and, beyond statistical outcomes, pave the way for building a more just, inclusive, and forward-looking educational system.

REFERENCES

Abarca-Reyes, J. F. (2020). Evolución histórica de las tecnologías educativas en México. *Revista Tecnológica-Educativa Docentes 2.0, 9*(2), 254–263. https://doi.org/DOI: 10.37843/rted.v9i2.171

Aguilera, D., & Vílchez-González, J. M. (2024). ¿De qué hablamos cuando hablamos de educación STEAM? Una revisión de experiencias educativas. *Revista Fuentes, 26*(2), 211–224. DOI: 10.12795/revistafuentes.2024.15412

Alemán-Saravia, A. C., Deroncele-Acosta, A., & Robles-Mori, H. (2023). Traducción, adaptación cultural y validación del cuestionario TPACK-21 en docentes en servicio. *Revista de Ciencias Sociales, XXIX*(3), 453–469.

Anderson, T., & Shattuck, J. (2012). Design-based research: A decade of progress in education research? *Educational Researcher, 41*(1), 16–25.

Arias Villalba, W. O., & Mejía Carrillo, M. de J., Carranza Basantes, S. F., & Alvarado Jaya, H. G. (2024). Educación STEAM (ciencia, tecnología, ingeniería, artes y matemáticas) en la educación básica: Integración curricular y efectividad, una revisión desde la literatura. *Polo del Conocimiento, 9*(2), 2026–2045. DOI: 10.23857/pc.v9i2.6651

Arrigui Torres, E., & Andrés Mosquera, J. (2022). Aportes de la educación STEAM a la enseñanza de las ciencias: Una revisión documental entre 2018 y 2021. *Revista Latinoamericana de Educación Científica, Crítica y Emancipadora (LadECiN), 1*(1), 49–61. https://revistaladecin.com/index.php/LadECiN/article/view/40

Arteaga-Alcívar, Y., Guaña-Moya, J., Begnini-Domínguez, L., Cabrera-Córdova, M. F., Sánchez-Cali, F., & Moya-Carrera, Y. (2022). Integración de la tecnología con la educación. *RISTI – Revista Ibérica de Sistemas e Tecnologias de Informação, E54*(11), 182–193. https://www.researchgate.net/publication/378635135_Integracion_de_la_tecnologia_con_la_educacion

Balladares-Burgos, J., & Valverde-Berrocoso, J. (2022). El modelo tecnopedagógico TPACK y su incidencia en la formación docente: Una revisión de la literatura. *Revista Caribeña de Investigación Educativa, 6*(1), 63–72. DOI: 10.32541/recie.2022.v6i1.pp63-72

Bañuelos Márquez, A. M. (2024). Modelos de evaluación de la calidad en programas educativos a distancia. In *CIVINEDU 2024: Conference proceedings* (pp. 48–52). REDINE. https://doi.org/DOI: 10.58909/adc24377766

Başaran, B. (2020). Examining preservice teachers' TPACK-21 efficacies with clustering analysis in terms of certain variables. *Malaysian Online Journal of Educational Technology*, *8*(3), 84–99. DOI: 10.17220/mojet.2020.03.005

Blanco Iturralde, J. A., Rocha Cajas, E. P., Criollo Llumiquinga, L. J., Rocha Cajas, J. A., & Rocha Cajas, M. E. (2024). La necesidad de capacitación docente para una implementación efectiva de la tecnología educativa en el aula. *Ciencia Latina*, *8*(2), 2347–2367. DOI: 10.37811/cl_rcm.v8i2.10676

Cabero Almenara, J., Marín Díaz, V., & Castaño Garrido, C. (2015). Validación de la aplicación del modelo TPACK para la formación del profesorado en TIC. *@tic. Revista d'Innovació Educativa*, (14), 13–22. DOI: 10.7203/attic.14.4001

Camacho-Tamayo, E., & Bernal-Ballé, A. (2023). Elementos teóricos sobre la formación docente en ciencias naturales con enfoque STEAMH: Revisión sistemática. *Ciencia Latina*, *7*(1), 1598–1618. DOI: 10.37811/cl_rcm.v7i1.4508

Camacho-Tamayo, E., Bernal-Ballén, A., & González Fernández, M. O. (2024). Análisis de la autopercepción sobre el uso del enfoque STEAM en las estrategias de aula de docentes de ciencias naturales de México y Colombia. [RECIE]. *Revista Caribeña de Investigación Educativa*, *8*(1), 117–143. DOI: 10.32541/recie.2024.v8i1.pp117-143

Castillejos-López, B., Torres-Gastelú, C. A., & Lagunes-Domínguez, A. (2014). El enfoque del conocimiento tecnológico pedagógico del contenido (TPACK): Revisión del modelo. In Esquivel Gámez, I. (Ed.), *Los modelos tecno-educativos, revolucionando el aprendizaje del siglo XXI* (1st ed., pp. 237–252). Ismael Esquivel Gámez., https://www.researchgate.net/publication/280301257_Los_Modelos_Tecno-Educativos_revolucionando_el_aprendizaje_del_siglo_XXI

Castro-Campos, P. A. (2022). Reflexiones sobre la educación STEAM: Alternativa para el siglo XXI. *Praxis (Bern)*, *18*(1), 158–175. DOI: 10.21676/23897856.3762

CAYACHOA-Amaya. I. D. C., & ALVAREZ-Araque, W. O. (2020). El modelo TPACK como estrategia para integrar las TIC en el aula escolar a partir de la formación docente. *Revista ESPACIOS, 41*(16), 6–16. https://www.revistaespacios.com/a20v41n16/a20v41n16p06.pdf

Cedeño Ávila, J. R., Rivadeneira Barreiro, L., & Piedad Rivadeneira Barreiro, M. P. (2024). Programa de capacitación docente para mejorar las competencias en el uso de las herramientas tecnológicas. *Tesla Revista Científica*, *4*(1), 1–13.

Cohen, J. (1988). Set correlation and contingency tables. *Applied Psychological Measurement*, *12*(4), 425–434. DOI: 10.55204/trc.v4i1.e345

Colegio de Bachilleres del Estado de Tamaulipas. (2022). *Historia*. https://www.cobat.edu.mx/cobat/historia/

Correa-Delgado, J. S. (2024). La investigación como estrategia pedagógica: Una alternativa latinoamericana a la educación STEAM. *Prospectiva. Revista de Trabajo Social e Intervención Social*, (37), 1–20. DOI: 10.25100/prts.v0i37.13065

General de Planeación, D., & Programación y Estadística, E. (2024, September). *Principales cifras del Sistema Educativo Nacional 2023–2024* (1st ed.). https://www.planeacion.sep.gob.mx/Doc/estadistica_e_indicadores/principales_cifras/principales_cifras_2023_2024_bolsillo.pdf

Guimarães Carvalho, I. S., Tejeda, J., & Pozos Pérez, K. V. (2019). Formación docente para la educación a distancia: La construcción de las competencias docentes digitales. *Série-Estudos*, *24*(51), 69–87. DOI: 10.20435/serie-estudos.v24i51.1296

Hayati, N., Kadarohman, A., Sopandi, W., Martoprawiro, M. A., & Rochintaniawati, D. (2022, August). Chemistry teachers' TPACK competence: Teacher perception and lesson plan analysis. *Technium Social Sciences Journal*, *34*, 237–247.

Koehler, M. J., Mishra, P., & Cain, W. (2015). ¿Qué son los saberes tecnológicos y pedagógicos del contenido (TPACK)? *Virtualidad, Educación y Ciencia*, *6*(10), 9–23. https://dialnet.unirioja.es/servlet/articulo?codigo=5115245

Lailatussaadah, L., Hayati, S., Bin Jamil, A. I., & Abdul Kadir, F. A. B. (2023, December). Mapping TPACK components in implementing edupreneur-profiled curriculum at teacher training and education institutions in Aceh. *Tadris: Jurnal Keguruan dan Ilmu Tarbiyah*, *8*(2), 373–387. https://doi.org/DOI: 10.24042/tadris.v8i2.16755

Lam-Byrne, A. G. (2023). El aprendizaje STEAM: Una práctica inclusiva. *Revista Científica Episteme y Tekne*, *2*(1), e466.

Leal Urueña, L. A., & Rojas Mesa, J. E. (2020). Percepciones de autoeficacia y conocimientos TPACK en profesores en formación. *Diversitas: Perspectivas en Psicología*, *16*(2), 283–296. DOI: 10.15332/22563067.6295

López de la Madrid, M. C., Flores Guerrero, K., & Tejeda Mercado, C. (2021). Las TIC en el diseño de las políticas educativas: El caso de México. *Archivos Analíticos de Políticas Educativas*, *29*(32), 1–34. DOI: 10.14507/epaa.29.4408

López-Gamboa, M. V., Córdoda González, C., & Soto Soto, J. F. (2020). Educación STEM/STEAM: Modelos de implementación, estrategias didácticas y ambientes de aprendizaje que potencian las habilidades para el siglo XXI. *Latin American Journal of Science Education*, *7*(1), 1–16. http://www.lajse.org/may20/2020_12002.pdf

López García, M., & López García, C. (2024). Deserción escolar de primer semestre en la carrera de Ingeniería Electromecánica. In *CIVINEDU 2024: Conference proceedings*. REDINE. https://doi.org/DOI: 10.58909/adc24377766

Luna-Romero, Á. E., Vega Jaramillo, F. Y., & Carvajal Romero, H. R. (2019). Formación docente en el uso de las TIC. *Universidad, Ciencia y Tecnología, Volumen Especial*(2), 46–52. https://uctunexpo.autanabooks.com/index.php/uct/article/view/66

Mishra, P., & Koehler, M. J. (2006). Technological pedagogical content knowledge: A framework for teacher knowledge. *Teachers College Record, 108*(6), 1017–1054.

Monroy-González, L. A., Mendoza-Hernández, L. E., & Alarcón-Acosta, H. (2021). Educación STEAM en preparatoria. *UNO Sapiens. Boletín Científico de la Escuela Preparatoria No. 1, 4*(7), 12–15. https://repository.uaeh.edu.mx/revistas/index.php/prepa1/article/download/7285/7893/

Morales Soza, M. G. (2020). TPACK para integrar efectivamente las TIC en educación: Un modelo teórico para la formación docente. *Docente. Revista Electrónica de Conocimientos. Saberes y Prácticas, 3*(1), 133–148. DOI: 10.5377/recsp.v3i1.9796

Moreno Rando, M. (2024). Análisis actual de la actividad formativa TIC en centros de formación de profesorado no universitario. In *CIVINEDU 2024: Conference proceedings* (pp. 76–81). REDINE. https://doi.org/DOI: 10.58909/adc24377766

Ortiz-Colón, A. M., Ágreda Montoro, M., & Rodríguez Moreno, J. (2020). Autopercepción del profesorado de Educación Primaria en servicio desde el modelo TPACK. *Revista Electrónica Interuniversitaria de Formación del Profesorado, 23*(2), 53–65. DOI: 10.6018/reifop.415641

Pabón-Rúa, J. D., López-Ríos, S. Y., & Cardona-Zapata, M. E. (2024). Perspectivas teóricas y metodológicas sobre creatividad en educación STEAM: Una revisión sistemática. *Revista Científica (Maracaibo), 51*(3), 1–21. DOI: 10.14483/23448350.21959

Palominos Bastias, M., & Marcelo García, C. (2021). Uso de tecnologías digitales para atender necesidades educativas especiales en la formación docente del educador diferencial. *Píxel-Bit. Revista de Medios y Educación*, (61), 231–256. DOI: 10.12795/pixelbit.78020

Paula-Bonifacio, E., & Marcelo-García, C. (2023). Validación de un instrumento TPACK: Enseñanza de la lectura para docentes de educación primaria. *Campus Virtuales, 12*(1), 103–120. DOI: 10.54988/cv.2023.1.1092

Pazmiño Núñez, G. A., Sauca Banegas, M. A., Vasquez Garcia, M. N., Ruano Armijos, G. A., Morocho Cabrera, L. N., Bayas Chacha, L. M., & Santillán Sevillano, N. D. C. (2025). El impacto de las metodologías STEAM en el desarrollo de competencias digitales y creativas en estudiantes. *Ciencia Latina, 9*(1), 2690–2709. DOI: 10.37811/cl_rcm.v9i1.16035

Perales, F. J., & Aróstegui, J. L. (2024). The STEAM approach: Implementation and educational, social and economic consequences. *Arts Education Policy Review, 125*(2), 59–67. DOI: 10.1080/10632913.2021.1974997

Pineda Caro, D. Y. (2023). Enfoque STEAM: Retos y oportunidades para los docentes. *Revista Internacional de Pedagogía e Innovación Educativa, 3*(1).

Pinto-Sudario, G. C., & Plaza-Andrade, J. N. (2021). Determinar la necesidad de capacitación en el uso de las tecnologías de la información y las comunicaciones para la formación docente. *593 Digital Publisher CEIT, 6*(1), 169–181. https://doi.org/DOI: 10.33386/593dp.2021.1.426

Podsakoff, P. M., MacKenzie, S. B., Lee, J. Y., & Podsakoff, N. P. (2003). Common method biases in behavioral research: A critical review of the literature and recommended remedies. *The Journal of Applied Psychology, 88*(5), 879. PMID: 14516251

Prendes Espinosa, M. P. (2018). La tecnología educativa en la pedagogía del siglo XXI: Una visión en 3D. [RIITE]. *Revista Interuniversitaria de Investigación en Tecnología Educativa*, (4), 6–16. DOI: 10.6018/riite/2018/335131

Prieto Murillo, M. (2024). Educando con el enfoque STEAM para la solución de problemas. *Umbral Científica, 49*(1), 3–21.

Rivera-Robles, S. B., Salcedo-Lagos, P. A., Valdivia-Guzmán, J. R., & López-Jara, O. A. (2021). Estudios empíricos del modelo sobre conocimiento didáctico tecnológico del contenido (TPACK) en matemáticas, incluidos en bases bibliográficas internacionales. *Información Tecnológica, 32*(4), 109–120. DOI: 10.4067/S0718-07642021000400109

Rodríguez Pinzón, M. D., Alvarez Araque, W. O., Jiménez Orozco, H. L., Romero Forero, A., & Vanessa Bernal, I. (2024). Perspectivas sobre los obstáculos que enfrentan los educadores al adoptar el enfoque STEAM. In *Conference Proceedings CIVINEDU 2024* (pp. 40–47). REDINE. https://doi.org/DOI: 10.58909/adc24377766

Salas-Rueda, R. A. (2018, June). Uso del modelo TPACK como herramienta de innovación para el proceso de enseñanza-aprendizaje en matemáticas. *Perspectiva Educacional. Formación de Profesores, 57*(2), 3–26. DOI: 10.4151/07189729-vol.57-iss.2-art.689

Salas-Rueda, R. A. (2019). Modelo TPACK: ¿Medio para innovar el proceso educativo considerando la ciencia de datos y el aprendizaje automático? *Entreciencias, 7*(19), 51–66. DOI: 10.22201/enesl.20078064e.2018.19.67511

Salinas Esparza, M. de C., Flores Crespo, P. A., & Escudero Nahón, A. (2021). La formación docente en el uso de tecnología: Una necesidad constante. In *Congreso Nacional de Investigación Educativa (CNIE 2021)* (pp. 1–10). https://www.comie.org.mx/congreso/memoriaelectronica/v16/doc/1598.pdf

Samperio Pacheco, V. M., & Barragán López, J. F. (2018). Análisis de la percepción de docentes, usuarios de una plataforma educativa, a través de los modelos TPACK, SAMR y TAM3 en una institución de educación superior. *Apertura (Guadalajara, Jal.), 10*(1), 116–131. DOI: 10.32870/Ap.v10n1.1162

Sanchez, S. L., Junior., & Alves de Sousa, R. R. (2023). The importance of STEAM education in training future professionals. *Diálogo e Interação, 17*(1). https://revista.faccrei.edu.br/revista-dialogo-e-interacao/article/view/166

Santillán-Aguirre, J. P., Santos-Poveda, R. D., & Jaramillo-Moyano, E. M. (2021). STEAM: Educación para el sujeto del siglo XXI. *Revista Dominio de las Ciencias, 7*(4), 1461–1478. DOI: 10.23857/dc.v7i4.2181

Saz-Pérez, F., Pizà-Mir, B., & Lizana Carrió, A. (2024). Validación y estructura factorial de un cuestionario TPACK en el contexto de inteligencia artificial generativa (IAG). *Hachetetepé. Revista Científica de Educación y Comunicación*, (28), 1–14. DOI: 10.25267/Hachetetepe.2024.i28.1101

Secretaría de Educación de Tamaulipas. (2024). *Anuario de la estadística educativa del Estado de Tamaulipas, ciclo escolar 2023–2024* [Informe]. https://www.tamaulipas.gob.mx/educacion/wp-content/uploads/sites/3/2024/04/anuario-educacion-2023-2024_v-e.pdf

Secretaría de Educación Pública. (2020). *Agenda Digital Educativa* [Website]. https://infosen.senado.gob.mx/sgsp/gaceta/64/2/2020-02-05-1/assets/documentos/Agenda_Digital_Educacion.pdf

Shafie, H., Majid, F. A., & Ismail, I. S. (2022). Developing a 21st-century technological pedagogical content knowledge (TPACK) instrument: Content validity and reliability. *International Journal of Education, 14*(3), 100–115. DOI: 10.5296/ije.v14i3.19980

Silva, N., & Antunes, M. C. (2024). Oficinas de escrita e bem-estar entre idosos: A ação das Universidades Séniores. In *CIVINEDU 2024: Conference proceedings* (pp. 113–116). REDINE. https://doi.org/DOI: 10.58909/adc24377766

Silva-Díaz, F., García-Yeguas, A., & Carrillo-Rosúa, J. (2023). Integración de tecnologías emergentes para la educación STEAM: Proyecto TECNOSTEAM. In *Las nuevas realidades educativas: El uso de tecnologías emergentes para el aprendizaje* (pp. 129–136). Dykinson., https://www.researchgate.net/publication/372782412

Silva-Hormazábal, M., & Alsinab, Á. (2023). Promoviendo el desarrollo profesional docente en STEAM: Diseño y validación de un programa de formación. [REXE]. *Revista de Estudios y Experiencias en Educación*, *22*(50), 99–120. DOI: 10.21703/rexe.v22i50.1986

Soto Calderón, A., Oliveros Ruiz, M. A., & Roa Rivera, R. I. (2022). Curso-taller STEAM para docentes: Una evaluación formativa. *Entreciencias*, *10*(24), 1–19. DOI: 10.22201/enesl.20078064e.2022.24.82377

Suryani, T., Rahayu, W., & Saptono, A. (2021, August). Development and validation of a technological pedagogical content knowledge (TPACK) instrument for elementary school mathematics teachers. [IJMMU]. *International Journal of Multicultural and Multireligious Understanding*, *8*(8), 445–457. DOI: 10.18415/ijmmu.v8i8.2951

Torres, C. A., Espinosa, W. A., Romero, D. M., Herrera, R. S., & Herrera, D. A. (2021, February 15). TPACK: Aplicabilidad docente del modelo en Educación General Básica Elemental. *Espacios*, *42*(3), 102–115. DOI: 10.48082/espacios-a21v42v03p08

Urgiles-Rodríguez, B. E., Tixi-Gallegos, K. G., & Allauca-Peñafiel, M. E. (2022). Metodología STEAM en ambientes académicos. *Revista Científica Dominio de las Ciencias*, *8*(1), 113–125. DOI: 10.23857/dc.v8i1.2482

Valarezo Castro, J. W., & Santos Jiménez, O. C. (2019). Las tecnologías del aprendizaje y el conocimiento en la formación docente. *Revista Conrado, 15*(68), 180–186. http://conrado.ucf.edu.cu/index.php/conrado

Valtonen, T., Sointu, E., Kukkonen, J., Kontkanen, S., Lambert, M. C., & Mäkitalo-Siegl, K. (2017). TPACK updated to measure pre-service teachers' twenty-first century skills. *Australasian Journal of Educational Technology*, *33*(3).

Zhan, Y., Quan, J., & Ren, Y. (2013). An empirical study on the technological pedagogical content knowledge development of pre-service mathematics teachers in China. *International Journal of Social Media and Interactive Learning Environments*, *1*(2), 199–212. DOI: 10.1504/IJSMILE.2013.053600

Zhubi, A., & Ismajli, H. (2022). The interconnection between technological, pedagogical and content knowledge in primary school lesson planning. *Journal of Social Studies Education Research*, *13*(2), 125–146. https://files.eric.ed.gov/fulltext/EJ1355509.pdf

Chapter 10
The Short Story as a Teaching Tool for Educating Readers in Primary School

Oscar Ernesto Cabral Mier
https://orcid.org/0009-0006-3632-2927
Escuela Normal Rural "Gral. Matías Ramos Santos", Mexico

Selso Loera-Serrano
https://orcid.org/0000-0001-5579-7764
Benemérita Escuela Normal "Manuel Ávila Camacho", Mexico

Sergio Rodríguez-Ayala
https://orcid.org/0000-0002-6022-4431
Escuela Normal Benemérita "Manuel Ávila Camacho", Mexico

ABSTRACT

This research examines the effectiveness of short stories as a teaching tool for strengthening the development of literary readers and reading comprehension in primary school. A project conducted with fourth-grade elementary school students, based on the strategies of Isabel Solé (1992) and a constructivist approach, was carried out in twelve public schools in the municipality of Loreto, Zacatecas, during the 2023–2024 school year. Using a mixed methodology and an action research process, 286 students and 24 teachers participated, applying teaching sequences centered on short stories. The results showed a 32% increase in reading comprehension and an improvement in motivation for recreational reading. From a qualitative perspective, three categories emerged: reading motivation, teacher mediation, and

DOI: 10.4018/979-8-3373-5188-9.ch010

reading as a social practice. Therefore, it is concluded that short stories, when approached pedagogically, constitute an effective means to promote critical reading, the pleasure of reading, and reading autonomy in rural school settings.

INTRODUCTION

The development of reading skills in Mexican basic education continues to be one of the most complex and persistent structural challenges of the national education system, particularly in rural contexts that have historically faced conditions of social, economic, and cultural inequality. Despite institutional efforts to improve literacy and reading comprehension levels through curricular reforms, compensatory programs, and educational materials, the results in terms of developing competent, critical, and autonomous readers remain limited, especially in communities where material resources are scarce, family support is irregular, and school conditions do not always favor innovative and sustained pedagogical practices.

This study is situated in the municipality of Loreto, Zacatecas, a rural context that representatively reflects the tensions and contradictions that characterize basic education in peripheral regions of the country. In this setting, fully organized schools coexist with multigrade schools, the latter characterized by the simultaneous instruction of various grade levels by a single teacher. This imposes additional challenges in lesson planning, time management, the diversification of teaching strategies, and addressing the individual needs of students. Furthermore, the sociocultural environment, while placing high value on orality as a means of transmitting community knowledge, traditions, and everyday experiences, does not always promote reading as a systematic, pleasurable, and socially significant habit. In this context, the development of competent and independent readers at the primary level emerges as a fundamental pillar of education, not only for its academic relevance but also for its profound impact on children's cognitive, emotional, social, and cultural development. Undoubtedly, reading cannot be conceived solely as the technical skill of decoding. Graphic signs or locating explicit information in a text; on the contrary, it involves a complex process of meaning construction, interpretation, critical reflection and dialogue with the world.

Reading is an essential tool for acquiring knowledge, understanding reality, and actively participating in social and democratic life. However, everyday educational reality shows that in many primary school classrooms, reading practices continue to be reduced to instrumental and reproductive approaches. These approaches prioritize students learning to "read correctly" in terms of fluency and accuracy, and to answer literal questions that demand the extraction of explicit information, relegating to a secondary role the exploration of implicit meanings, personal interpretation, critical evaluation, and the aesthetic enjoyment of texts.

This limited conception of reading tends to strip it of its comprehensive formative potential, relegating its playful, emotional and creative dimension; as a consequence, a growing disinterest and low motivation of students towards reading is observed, particularly in the school context. Reading is often perceived as a curricular obligation disconnected from children's interests, experiences, and life realities. This negative perception is reinforced by traditional pedagogical practices that tend to present texts selected exclusively from the teacher's interests or strictly aligned with the curriculum, without considering the cultural, emotional, and cognitive diversity of the students. Furthermore, assessments centered on multiple-choice tests prioritize the correct answer over the process of comprehension, reflection, and interpretation. In this scenario, reading becomes a passive, mechanical, and insignificant act, where teacher intervention is superficial or limited, and didactic conditions that facilitate students' transition to more complex levels of comprehension, such as inferential and critical reading, are not created. The absence of intentional pedagogical mediation prevents students from developing the cognitive and metacognitive strategies necessary to monitor their understanding, establish relationships between ideas, formulate hypotheses, make value judgments, and engage with texts from a reflective perspective.

Faced with this problem, there is an urgent need to seek, discover, and create methodologies, tools, and teaching activities that allow us to redefine reading in elementary school, reclaiming it as an act of awareness, sensitization, and encounter with knowledge, imagination, and emotion.

Various studies have documented that elementary school students, particularly those in fourth grade, present significant cognitive obstacles in reading comprehension. These difficulties manifest as problems integrating scattered information, making inferences, identifying text structure, and establishing relationships between the content read and their prior knowledge. Such limitations not only affect academic performance in Language Arts but also have cross-cutting repercussions in all areas of knowledge, since reading is the primary means of accessing school knowledge. A student with reading comprehension difficulties faces barriers to learning Science, Mathematics, History, and other subjects, which increases the risk of academic underachievement and school exclusion.

Available empirical evidence indicates that among the main cognitive obstacles hindering reading comprehension in fourth-grade students are metacognitive deficiencies, vocabulary limitations, working memory problems, and difficulties with executive functions. Jaramillo Arana et al. (2025), in a study conducted with 60 fourth-grade children, identified severe metacognitive deficiencies, particularly in the ability to monitor comprehension, detect errors, and make inferences while reading.

Similarly, Tabullo et al. (2022) found that inhibitory control and vocabulary level significantly influence reading comprehension, especially when students encounter expository texts that demand greater cognitive effort. Likewise, Carrillo López et al. (2024) identified multiple causes associated with poor reading comprehension, including limited vocabulary, decoding deficiencies, memory problems, and a lack of prior knowledge.

Ares Ferreirós et al. (2021) documented weaknesses in fundamental cognitive processes such as simultaneous processing, sustained attention, and planning. While this evidence is consistent, it is important to note that most of these studies have been conducted in urban contexts, which limits their generalizability to rural environments with different sociocultural characteristics. However, focusing the analysis solely on cognitive factors is insufficient to understand the complexity of the reading comprehension problem. Reading involves much more than processing information; it entails a strong interconnection of ideas, emotions, experiences, and senses that give meaning to what is read. Reading is an act of encountering creative imagination, the knowledge generated by letters, and the possibility of understanding and reinterpreting reality. From this perspective, reading is also an act of sensitization that contributes to developing a love of reading and to the formation of critical and conscious individuals.

Decisions made regarding reading promotion in schools have profound implications for students' holistic development, as they influence opportunities for encountering science, culture, ethics, and the construction of meaning in life. In this sense, reading not only fulfills an academic function but also constitutes a cultural practice that shapes identity, broadens horizons, and fosters social participation. In addition to cognitive factors, there are didactic, institutional, and sociocultural obstacles. The school environment, students' personal habits, family culture, and the community context decisively influence the relationship children establish with reading. In many cases, families lack established reading practices and printed materials at home, limiting early exposure to written texts. Furthermore, in some rural contexts, reading is not seen as a tool for improving living conditions or expanding development opportunities, which weakens its social value.

This complex web of multidimensional factors has been highlighted by recent research that underscores the need to analyze reading comprehension from a holistic perspective, considering not only the reader's individual abilities but also the didactic, institutional, and cultural conditions in which reading takes place. Hence the importance of creating literacy-rich environments in the classroom, school, family, and community, understood as spaces where reading is promoted systematically, meaningfully, and collaboratively, involving diverse educational and social actors.

A review of ten studies conducted in urban and rural contexts in Latin America identifies three main problem areas that limit reading comprehension in fourth-grade students.

First, obstacles in decoding and reading fluency are identified. Seven studies report difficulties in word recognition, while five point to fluency problems. Nine studies highlight that limitations in extracting propositions and processing text structure directly affect overall text comprehension; For this synthesis, ten studies conducted in urban and rural contexts in Latin America were selected. The inclusion criteria were: 1) research focused on fourth-grade primary school students, 2) studies that addressed cognitive, pedagogical, or assessment obstacles in reading comprehension, and 3) works published in regional scientific databases. Studies that did not present empirical results on literal, inferential, or critical levels in that grade were excluded; likewise, vocabulary restrictions and shortcomings in the use of cognitive and metacognitive strategies are identified.

Second, barriers in pedagogical design are evident. At least four studies point to the use of inadequate teaching methods, and six underscore the lack of explicit instruction in handling different types of texts, such as differentiating between narratives and expositions. This deficiency hinders the development of effective reading strategies and limits students' ability to adapt to diverse textual demands. Other findings include irrelevant assessments, a lack of supplementary teaching resources, and adverse school conditions, such as overcrowded classrooms or insufficient time for reading.

Third, limitations in assessment and diagnostic processes are identified. Four studies primarily rely on standardized tests, while four others employ qualitative methods, which in some cases restricts the depth of the diagnosis and hinders the precise identification of reading difficulties. Overall, these studies agree that deficiencies in teacher training, the application of appropriate pedagogical methods, and diagnostic assessment are associated with significant impediments in students' reading comprehension.

Conversely, there is ample evidence justifying the need to continue exploring the importance of creating reading environments as a strategy to achieve the formative goals of education and promote holistic human development. In particular, several studies highlight the didactic potential of children's literature, and specifically, of stories, as a resource for strengthening reading comprehension in fourth-grade elementary school students.

Galindo Guerra and Martínez Becerra (2022) indicate that the systematic use of stories in the classroom is related to significant improvements in reading comprehension levels. Strategies based on interactive storytelling, story analysis, creative writing, and story mapping have been shown to strengthen literal, inferential, and critical comprehension. Arévalo Suárez et al. (2019) document that 91% of participating students achieved significant progress in literacy over an eight-month period, highlighting the importance of teacher mediation and the cultural relevance of the texts used. These strategies not only favor the development of cognitive skills but also promote emotional engagement and a love of reading. Other studies confirm consistent results across different educational levels. Galindo Guerra et al. (2022) found that fourth-grade students achieved critical comprehension levels, establishing complex inferences and adopting reflective stances toward texts. Estepa et al. (2019) reported significant progress through the change of literary genre, while research at elementary levels documents improvements in inferential comprehension and in analysis and reflection skills (Tambaco Quintero et al., 2024; Núñez-Naranjo et al., 2021; Ávila-Negrinis et al., 2021).

Based on this literature review, the need to document new research experiences that contribute to the state of knowledge on reading comprehension is evident, particularly in understudied rural contexts. In this sense, the present study is justified by the need to analyze the effects, implications, and challenges involved in generating literacy environments oriented towards the formation of a reading culture that transcends the school space and extends to the daily lives of students, recognizing the teacher as a key agent in the transformation of reading practices and in the formation of critical, autonomous readers committed to their reality.

Research Questions

To address the problem posed, this research will be guided by the following questions:

Central Question:

- How does short stories, used as a teaching resource and articulated with reading strategies (before, during, and after), promote the development of literary readers and the development of reading comprehension (literal, inferential, and critical) in elementary school students?

Secondary Questions:

- What are the optimal teaching conditions that should be generated in the classroom so that story reading and spaces for the exchange of opinions among readers promote deep understanding and interest in literature in elementary school students?
- How does the teacher's intervention, as a mediator, influence the construction of interpretations and value judgments by students during story reading situations and subsequent discussions?

- What impact does the diversity of stories (e.g., traditional, contemporary, multimodal, picture books) have on motivation, the development of reading strategies, and the reading comprehension levels of elementary school students?
- How can Solé's specific strategies (updating prior knowledge, predicting, question formulation, summarizing, inferring, and elaborating on the main idea) be effectively integrated into storytelling to enhance autonomy and the ability to learn from texts at the primary level?

THEORETICAL FRAMEWORK

This theoretical framework is based on an interactive, cognitive, and constructivist conception of reading and school learning. From this perspective, it is recognized that understanding a text involves a complex process of meaning construction, mediated by cognitive, metacognitive, affective, and sociocultural strategies. In accordance with the research question, this study assumes that reading comprehension does not develop spontaneously or automatically, but rather requires explicit, systematic, and intentional instruction, as well as didactic conditions that foster the reader's active participation in culturally meaningful reading practices.

The theoretical framework is structured around several interrelated conceptual axes: reading as an interactive and constructive process; the constructivist approach to school learning; the explicit instruction of reading comprehension strategies, particularly based on Isabel Solé's proposal; the short story as a narrative genre and didactic resource; the development of literary readers; and the role of the teacher and the necessary didactic conditions for creating literacy-rich environments.

Reading as an Interactive and Constructive Process

From a contemporary perspective, reading is conceived as an interactive process in which the reader is not limited to decoding graphic signs or extracting information linearly, but actively participates in constructing an interpretation of the text. In this process, the reader formulates hypotheses, anticipates meanings, verifies predictions, establishes inferences, and articulates textual information with prior knowledge, personal experiences, and cultural frameworks. This conception differs from traditional approaches that reduced reading to a mechanical and passive activity, focused exclusively on accuracy and fluency.

Cognitive and constructivist literature has emphasized that reading comprehension is the result of the dynamic interaction between the text, the reader, and the context. This interaction is based on at least three fundamental conditions: the ability to decode, the effective use of reading strategies, and metacognition, understood as the awareness and control that the reader exercises over their own comprehension process. Undoubtedly, a competent reader not only recognizes words and syntactic structures but is also able to regulate their comprehension, identify difficulties, and apply strategies to resolve them.

In this sense, a distinction is made between expert and novice readers. Expert readers typically apply comprehension strategies automatically and unconsciously, allowing them to process information fluently. However, when faced with an obstacle such as unfamiliar vocabulary, a complex text structure, or a semantic inconsistency, they activate a "strategic state" in which they become aware of their reading process, plan actions, evaluate their understanding, and make decisions to overcome it. This strategic behavior is a central feature of advanced reading proficiency.

Conversely, developing readers, such as primary school students, do not always possess these strategies or the metacognitive capacity necessary to use them independently. Hence the importance of explicit instruction that allows them to understand what reading means, why they read, and how comprehension can be improved. From this perspective, reading is conceived as a cognitive and cultural practice learned through interaction with others, particularly in the school context.

The Constructivist Approach to School Learning and Teaching

In this research, learning is based on the constructivist approach, which views the student as an active subject who constructs their knowledge through interaction with learning materials, peers, and the teacher. From this perspective, teaching does not mean directly transmitting information, but rather providing pedagogical support that allows students to progressively construct their learning. As Edwards and Mercer (1988) point out, school learning is a "joint construction" of meaning, in which teachers and students participate actively and collaboratively. In this process, the teacher's role is irreplaceable. Far from being a mere presenter of content, the teacher acts as a mediator of learning, offering cognitive and didactic scaffolding that supports students in the appropriation of new knowledge. Undoubtedly, this scaffolding can take various forms: modeling strategies, guiding questions, timely feedback, selection of relevant materials, and creation of challenging didactic situations. As students acquire greater mastery, this support is gradually withdrawn, favoring autonomy.

The constructivist approach involves recognizing that meaningful learning occurs when students are able to activate their prior knowledge, compare it with new information, and reorganize it to integrate it in a non-arbitrary way. In the context of reading, this means that comprehension occurs when the reader establishes relationships between what they already know and what the text proposes, generating new meanings. Therefore, reading instruction should start from the students' knowledge, interests, and experiences, as well as their sociocultural context. Likewise, this model recognizes that the educational situation is dynamic and requires constant adaptation from the teacher to the characteristics of the group, the learning pace, and individual needs. In rural and multi-grade contexts, this flexibility is especially relevant, since students present heterogeneous reading trajectories and diverse learning conditions. In this sense, constructivism offers a solid theoretical framework for designing didactic interventions that promote reading comprehension from an inclusive and contextualized perspective.

Reading Comprehension Strategies According to Isabel Solé

Isabel Solé's theoretical proposal (1992) is one of the central references for this research, as it offers a clear, systematic, and pedagogically relevant model for teaching reading comprehension.

Solé defines reading comprehension strategies as high-level procedures that involve formulating objectives, planning actions to achieve them, evaluating the results, and potentially modifying the strategies used. From this perspective, strategies are not isolated techniques or infallible recipes, but rather flexible and transferable procedures that allow readers to face diverse reading situations.

A fundamental principle of this proposal is that strategies do not develop spontaneously: they do not mature, emerge, or appear on their own; they are taught or they are not taught, and they are learned or they are not learned. Therefore, their teaching must be explicit, conscious, and systematic, allowing students to understand not only what they are doing when they read, but also why they are doing it and in what situations it is useful to apply certain strategies.

Solé organizes the teaching of reading comprehension strategies into three key moments of the reading process: before, during, and after reading. Each of these moments fulfills a specific function in the construction of meaning and requires the teaching of particular strategies. Before reading, the main objective is to prepare the reader for the encounter with the text. At this stage, motivation and goal setting are promoted, generating a positive disposition toward reading. Students must understand the purpose of the activity: why they are going to read and what they are expected to do with the text. Likewise, prior knowledge is activated through questions that invite reflection on what they already know about the topic, the author, or the type of text. This process fosters meaningful learning and facilitates the integration of new information. Furthermore, the formulation of predictions and hypotheses based on the title, illustrations, or paratext is encouraged, as well as the generation of questions that guide the reading.

During reading, the reader actively constructs comprehension, monitoring their process and resolving difficulties. In this phase, strategies such as verifying predictions are taught, which involves confirming or modifying initial anticipations. The establishment of inferences, which allows going beyond explicit information; the review and control of comprehension, detecting errors or gaps and applying mechanisms such as rereading; and the identification of essential information, distinguishing what is relevant from what is accessory according to the purposes of reading.

After reading, the goal is to consolidate and deepen understanding, promoting reflection and the transfer of what has been learned. Strategies include identifying the main idea, creating summaries, formulating value judgments and opinions, and connecting the text with other readings and personal experiences. This moment is key to developing critical understanding, as it allows the reader to reinterpret the text, discuss it with others, and generate new ideas based on what they have read.

The Short Story as a Narrative Genre and Didactic Resource

The short story belongs to the narrative genre and is characterized by the presentation of a sequence of events organized chronologically, generally structured with an initial state, a complication, a series of actions, a resolution, and a final state. This narrative structure functions as a cognitive framework that facilitates comprehension, as it allows the reader to anticipate the development of the story and organize the information coherently.

The choice of the short story as a didactic resource in this research is based on several reasons. First, the short story has a high motivational potential, as it combines fictional elements with everyday situations, generating an emotional connection that sparks the reader's interest. Second, it fosters the development of creative imagination, empathy, and sensitivity to understand diverse contexts and perspectives. Furthermore, it allows for the transfer of knowledge and practical experience, since stories often present conflicts, values, and dilemmas that invite reflection.

From a pedagogical standpoint, the short story is particularly well-suited for teaching reading comprehension strategies, given that its structure facilitates making predictions, identifying causal relationships, drawing inferences, and constructing overall meaning. However, it is important to emphasize that the short story should not be the only type of text used in the classroom. Developing competent readers requires exposure to diverse genres and text structures so that students can develop the ability to adapt to different reading demands.

The impact of diverse stories (traditional, contemporary, multimodal, and picture books) is a determining factor in the motivation and development of reading strategies. Research shows that exposure to diverse textual superstructures allows fourth-grade students to expand their reading experience beyond the basic narrative paradigm. In particular, stories that blend fictional elements with everyday situations create an emotional connection that helps overcome cognitive obstacles such as metacognitive deficits and memory limitations identified in this age group.

The Development of Literary Readers

The ultimate goal of this research is to contribute to the development of literary readers, understood as individuals who go beyond simply deciphering the written code and who turn to reading out of both necessity and desire. A literary reader reads regularly for pleasure, establishes emotional connections with texts, discusses and shares their reading with others, and uses reading as a tool for understanding the world. Furthermore, the development of this type of reader does not occur immediately or individually, but rather is built gradually through participation in cultural reading practices. In this process, the classroom becomes a privileged space for providing the necessary conditions: access to varied and high-quality texts, time dedicated to reading, teacher guidance, dialogue among readers, and recognition of reading as a social and cultural experience.

Teacher Role and Didactic Conditions

The teacher plays a central role in developing readers, going beyond the function of simply transmitting knowledge. Their role involves diagnosing and contextualizing, understanding students' prior knowledge, interests, and motivations, as well as the socio-educational context in which the school is situated. Likewise, they must select and adapt materials, choosing stories and other texts appropriate to the age, interests, and learning objectives.

Creating a climate conducive to reading is another essential function of the teacher; generating enthusiasm, curiosity, and intrigue fosters a positive attitude toward reading. Strategic interventions such as relevant questions, rereading, and contextualizing the work allow for deeper comprehension and enrich the reading experience. Finally, fostering autonomy involves providing scaffolding that helps students develop self-control strategies and assume an active role as readers.

From this perspective, assessment should be formative, process-centered, and geared toward continuous improvement. Monitoring comprehension, providing feedback, and adjusting instruction to students' needs are fundamental to fostering meaningful learning.

The articulation of these theoretical elements underpins the research proposal, which aims not only to explain the phenomenon of reading comprehension but also to transform educational practice by promoting storytelling as a key tool in building communities of active, competent readers who enjoy reading in primary education.

Teacher mediation must evolve from simply evaluating responses to creating a "strategic framework." The teacher acts as a professional mediator who not only transmits knowledge but also provokes and guides. This intervention is fundamental to activating the reader's "strategic state": when the student encounters an obstacle in the text, the mediator guides the conscious planning and deliberation to resolve it. Furthermore, the transformation observed in the participating schools, where teaching shifted from textbook-centered instruction to dialogue and the exchange of opinions, validates that reading is, above all, a joint co-construction between teacher and student.

METHODOLOGY

This research adopts a rigorous and systematic approach, consistent with the objectives, to explore and describe the effectiveness of short stories in developing readers at the primary level. The research approach is mixed, as this allows for a deep understanding of reading practices, classroom interactions, and the subjective experiences of students and teachers. It should be noted that the qualitative approach is ideal for understanding life experiences through case studies and for investigating the complexity of teaching and learning processes in real-life contexts.

The research was based on action research (AR). This type of research is particularly relevant for addressing problems in the educational context, seeking not only to understand but also to transform practice. AI is characterized by its cyclical and participatory nature, involving the researcher (teacher) in a continuous process of diagnosis, planning, action, observation, reflection, and evaluation. These phases, proposed by Monje (2011) and Latorre (2003), will serve as a guide for structuring this process.

Context and Participants

The study was conducted in the municipality of Loreto, Zacatecas, a region with a predominance of rural communities and fully organized or multi-grade schools. Twelve public elementary schools participated in the research, selected based on accessibility and institutional availability.

The total population was 286 students (132 girls and 154 boys) and 24 teachers, all in fourth grade; the students ranged in age from 9 to 11 years.

Table 1. School Location Students Teachers Type of organization

School	Localition	Students	Teachers	Type of organization
1. Ricardo Flores Magón	Loreto Centro	28	2	Completa
2. Adolfo López Mateos	La Victoria	24	2	Completa
3. Rafael Ramírez	El Naranjal	25	2	Multigrado
4. Club de Leones	Loreto, centro	27	2	Completa
5. Belisario Domínguez	Loreto	21	2	Completa
6. 20 de Noviembre	La Alquería	25	2	Completa
7. José Vasconcelos	Loreto	26	2	Completa
8. Francisco Villa	El Salitre	24	2	Multigrado
9. Ignacio Zaragoza	San Isidro	25	2	Multigrado
10. Jaime Torres Bodet	Loreto Norte	24	2	Completa
11. Amado Nervo	Norias de San Miguel	19	2	Completa
12. Francisco García Salinas	Guadalupe de Trujillo	18	2	Multigrado

Instruments

The following instruments were used:

1. Diagnostic and final reading comprehension test, based on three levels of analysis (literal, inferential, and critical).
2. Reading Motivation Scale (EML-Prim), adapted from the Wigfield and Guthrie (1997) model.
3. Teacher observation guide, focused on mediation strategies, reading climate, and student participation.
4. Semi-structured interviews with teachers and focus groups with students.

Procedure

1. Diagnostic phase (January 2023): administration of initial tests and observation of common reading practices.
2. Intervention phase (February–May 2023): implementation of 8 teaching sequences based on classic and regional stories, taught twice a week.

The intervention consisted of eight teaching sequences based on the 'Live Reading with Stories' model. Each session was structured in five phases: Connection (activation of prior knowledge), Literary Exploration (dramatized reading), Construction of Meaning (debate on literal, inferential and critical levels), Creation (rewriting of endings) and Social Projection (sharing of products).

3. Evaluation phase (June 2023): administration of final instruments and interviews to assess changes in reading comprehension and motivation.

RESULTS

Quantitative Results

The data obtained show a significant improvement in overall reading comprehension, as the overall average went from 58.4% (diagnostic level) to 77.2% (final level), representing an increase of 32%.

Table 1. Reading comprehension averages by school (percentage correct answers)

School	Diagnostic (%)	Final (%)	Increase (%)
1. Ricardo Flores Magón	61	81	+33
2. Adolfo López Mateos	54	73	+35
3. Rafael Ramírez	57	75	+31
4. Crub de Leones	63	82	+30
5. Belisario Domínguez	56	76	+36
6. 20 de noviembre	55	73	+32
7. José Vasconcelos	62	83	+34
8. Francisco Villa	53	70	+32
9. Ignacio Zaragoza	55	74	+34
10. Jaime Torres Bodet	60	80	+33
11. Amado Nervo	54	71	+31
12. Francisco García Salinas	52	69	+33

Overall average: Diagnostic 58.4% → Final 77.2% → Average increase: +32%. The most notable results were observed at José Vasconcelos, Miguel Hidalgo, and Emiliano Zapata schools, where teacher mediation was more consistent and dramatized readings and reading clubs were promoted.

Descriptive Graph (Narrative)

In the overall analysis, nine of the twelve schools achieved a reading comprehension level classified as "satisfactory" (more than 75% correct answers), while three were in the "medium-high" range (70–74%). No school maintained "low" levels at the end of the cycle.

Qualitative Results

Three main categories emerged from the analysis of interviews, observations, and teacher narratives:

a) Reading Motivation

Teachers reported an increase in students' willingness to read. 87% of students said they enjoyed storytelling sessions, and 68% requested to take books home. One teacher commented, "Before, children read because the teacher asked them to; now they read because they want to know what comes next in the story" (Melchor Ocampo School).

b) Teacher Mediation

A transformation in pedagogical practice was identified, with teachers shifting from textbook-centered teaching to active mediation based on questions, dialogue, and role-playing. One teacher comments, "Storytelling allowed me to understand how my students think. I learned to listen to their interpretations, not just evaluate their responses" (José Vasconcelos School).

c) Reading as a Social Practice

In several schools, collective reading spaces were created (corners, fairs, role-playing). This strengthened the sense of community and family participation, something that truly motivated everyone. One principal comments, "Parents came to the storytelling fair; it was the first time some of them heard their children read in public" (Benito Juárez School).

Table 2. Narrative summary of categories

Category	Main Evidence	Perceived Impact
Reading Motivation	Enjoyment, participation, voluntary book lending	Increased reading frequency
Teacher Mediation	Use of active strategies, reading aloud, dramatization,	improvement in oral comprehension and expression
Social Reading	Community events, family collaboration	strengthening of school-community ties

DISCUSSION

The results obtained in the twelve primary schools of the municipality of Loreto, Zacatecas, support the claim that storytelling, when incorporated as a planned, systematic, and pedagogically mediated teaching resource, significantly enhances both reading comprehension and intrinsic motivation for reading. This finding not only validates the relevance of the implemented strategy but also aligns with a solid body of research that highlights the role of children's literature as a privileged mediator in the construction of meaning and the development of symbolic thought in childhood (Colomer, 2005; Mendoza, 2011).

The 32% increase in reading comprehension levels recorded at the end of the intervention is a significant quantitative indicator, especially considering the rural and multi-grade context in which the study was conducted. This progress was primarily evident in literal and inferential comprehension, suggesting that story-based teaching strategies helped strengthen fundamental skills such as identifying explicit information, establishing causal relationships, and drawing inferences from the text. These results align with previous research indicating that narrative texts, due to their sequential and coherent structure, facilitate overall comprehension and access to progressively more complex levels of interpretation.

However, the qualitative analysis of the experience allows us to affirm that the most significant achievements of the intervention were not limited to the cognitive realm. Classroom observations, narrative records, and interviews with teachers and students demonstrate that the most profound gain occurred in the affective and social aspects of reading. The children not only read more frequently, but also began to embrace reading as a form of personal expression, aesthetic enjoyment, and collective interaction. Reading ceased to be perceived solely as a mandatory school activity and became a shared experience, imbued with meaning and symbolic value.

This finding is especially relevant, since the specialized literature has indicated that intrinsic motivation is a key factor in consolidating long-term reading habits. In this sense, the study's results reinforce the idea that a love of reading is not imposed, but rather built upon positive, meaningful, and emotionally rewarding experiences.

The opportunity to discuss the stories, dramatize scenes, reinterpret characters, and connect the narratives to everyday life allowed students to establish a closer and more personal relationship with the texts.

Teacher mediation emerged as a determining factor in the impact of the intervention. Teachers who supported the reading process through active strategies—such as expressive read-alouds, dramatizations, literary circles, and open-ended questions—achieved more significant progress compared to those who limited themselves to a more instrumental application of the materials. This result validates the arguments of Cassany (2006) and Solé (1992), who maintain that teaching reading is a co-constructive process between teacher and student, in which intentional pedagogical intervention is essential for the development of comprehension strategies and for the cultural appropriation of reading.

From this perspective, the teacher acts not only as a facilitator of texts, but also as a cultural mediator who guides, models, and accompanies the reading process. The quality of pedagogical interventions, more than the quantity of texts read, proved to be a key element in deepening comprehension and fostering active student participation. This finding is especially relevant in rural contexts, where material conditions may be limited, but where pedagogical creativity and teacher commitment can generate high-impact reading experiences.

In contexts like Loreto, Zacatecas, characterized by scarce resources and the presence of multigrade schools, the short story acquires even greater pedagogical value. Its brevity, flexibility, and symbolic richness allow it to be adapted to diverse levels of comprehension and ages, facilitating attention to diversity within the classroom. Likewise, its narrative structure favors simultaneous work with students of different grades, making it a particularly relevant resource for multigrade classrooms.

A particularly significant aspect of the intervention was the incorporation of traditional narratives from the Zacatecas region into the lesson plans. This decision allowed for the integration of reading instruction with local culture, strengthening students' sense of identity and giving greater meaning to reading activities. The stories, by reflecting experiences, values, and issues relevant to the community, fostered greater identification among the children and promoted intergenerational dialogue, contributing to the development of a dynamic and contextualized curriculum.

The cultural variable in this study transcends mere geographic location, becoming a "cognitive bridge." By integrating traditional narratives from Zacatecas, the school curriculum is transformed into a practice of identity and a sense of community. This is undoubtedly crucial in environments where family culture values oral communication but has not institutionalized daily reading. By using regional stories, a "situated reading" is achieved, reducing the gap between children's life experiences and academic demands. This allows the story to function as a familiar framework for interpretation, facilitating anticipation and deep understanding.

The overall analysis of the intervention allows us to affirm that reading, when conceived and practiced as a shared experience, transcends the classroom and extends into the community. Story fairs, open reading circles, and dramatizations not only functioned as teaching strategies but also as spaces for cultural interaction that involved families, teachers, and other community members. These experiences strengthened a sense of belonging and reaffirmed education as a social practice, in line with Freire's perspective (1997), who conceives of reading the world as a process inseparable from reading the word.

In short, the discussion of the results demonstrates that the didactic use of storytelling, mediated by conscious and contextualized teacher intervention, not only improves reading comprehension but also contributes to building a reading culture in rural contexts. The findings reinforce the need to promote reading practices that integrate the cognitive, affective, and social dimensions, recognizing children's literature as a powerful tool for the holistic development of students and for transforming the educational experience in primary school.

Derived Pedagogical Proposal: "Live Reading with Stories"

Derived from the experience developed in the schools of Loreto, the pedagogical model "Live Reading with Stories" is proposed, a replicable strategy in rural or semi-urban contexts that seeks to consolidate reading instruction from a comprehensive perspective.

General Objective

To promote reading comprehension and literary appreciation through the use of short stories as a cross-cutting theme in teaching practice, integrating cognitive, emotional, and sociocultural dimensions.

Model Structure

The "Live Reading with Stories" model operationalizes Solé's strategies (before, during, and after) in five highly interactive phases. The "Connection" phase is not only preparatory but also activates prior knowledge and predictions essential for meaningful learning. The "Meaning Construction" phase integrates literal, inferential, and critical levels of analysis, allowing students not only to decode but also to associate and make value judgments based on their situated reality. This model proposes live literature as a cross-cutting axis where assessment is formative and focuses on the process of cultural appropriation of reading.

Table 3. Model Structure

Phase	Description	Suggested Activities	Assessment
1. Connection	Activate prior knowledge and emotions associated with the story's theme.	Brainstorming, discussion of expectations, title prediction	Teacher anecdotal record.
2. Literary Exploration	Guided or dramatized reading of the story, with active group participation	Choral reading, dramatization, shared reading aloud.	Participation checklist.
3.Meaning Construction	Analysis of the text from different levels of comprehension (literal, inferential, critical)	Debate, open-ended questions, character maps, narrative timelines	Reading comprehension rubric.
4. Creation and Recreation	Textual and artistic production derived from the story	. Creative rewriting, illustration, alternative version of the ending	Formative assessment with feedback.
5. Social Outreach	Socialization of products and public reading	Story fair, reading mural, family participation.	. Self- and peer-assessment.

Pedagogical Principles

1. Living Literature: the story as a text that is felt, thought, and transformed.
2. Mediating Teacher: the teacher as a guide who listens, provokes, and accompanies.
3. Situated Reading: the connection between literature and the reality of the rural context.
4. Cooperative Learning: reading as a collective practice.
5. Formative Assessment: focused on the process, not just the outcome.

This model is proposed as an adaptable strategy, useful for reading promotion projects in public schools, rural teacher training colleges, and teacher training programs, where its effectiveness is based on a socioconstructivist approach and an understanding of reading as a living cultural practice; in multigrade school settings, time management and addressing age diversity presented an operational challenge for teachers.

Sociocultural obstacles: The report indicates that the lack of printed materials in homes and a family culture that prioritizes oral communication over systematic reading can limit the long-term impact of the intervention.

CONCLUSIONS

The research conducted in twelve primary schools in the municipality of Loreto, Zacatecas, allows us to assert, with a solid foundation, that storytelling is a highly effective teaching resource for developing competent, critical, and sensitive readers at the primary education level, provided its incorporation into the classroom is mediated by an active, intentional, and reflective pedagogical approach. The results obtained confirm that reading stories should not be conceived as an accessory or recreational activity disconnected from the curriculum, but rather as a central pedagogical strategy capable of articulating students' cognitive, emotional, social, and cultural development.

From a quantitative perspective, the data show significant improvements in the reading comprehension levels of the participating students, particularly at the literal and inferential levels. These advances reflect that systematic work with stories, accompanied by explicit comprehension strategies before, during, and after reading, fosters the construction of meaning, the identification of main ideas, the formulation of inferences, and reflection on the textual content. In rural and multi-grade contexts, where educational challenges are greater due to the scarcity of resources and the heterogeneity of the student body, these results acquire special relevance, since they demonstrate that it is possible to improve reading performance through relevant, contextualized and pedagogically sound teaching proposals.

However, the most profound findings of the research emerge from the qualitative analysis of the experience. Classroom observations, testimonies from teachers and students, as well as records of group activities, reveal substantial transformations in the children's attitudes toward reading. Throughout the intervention, reading ceased to be perceived as a mandatory or evaluative task and became a meaningful, desired, and shared experience. The students showed a greater willingness to participate, express opinions, formulate questions, and connect the texts to their own experiences, demonstrating a progressive appropriation of reading as a cultural practice and a form of personal expression.

In this sense, the research confirms that reading stories not only contributes to strengthening linguistic skills but also directly impacts the students' holistic development. Through the narratives, the children developed empathy by identifying with the characters and their conflicts, strengthened their identity by recognizing elements of their cultural and social context in the stories, and began to exercise critical thinking by making judgments, comparing situations, and proposing alternative interpretations. Children's literature, and in particular the short story, thus became established as a privileged space for ethical reflection, the recognition of the other, and the construction of meaning.

A key finding of this research is the impact the project had on teaching practices. Participating teachers progressively moved from traditional approaches centered on textbooks and rote comprehension activities toward teaching strategies that promoted interpretation, dialogue, and creation. Reading aloud, dramatizations, literary circles, the production of alternative endings, and linking stories to community experiences allowed for a redefinition of the teacher's role as a cultural mediator and reader development facilitator. This process involved the development of new professional skills, such as the critical selection of texts, the formulation of open-ended questions, the management of classroom dialogue, and the formative assessment of reading comprehension. Furthermore, the research demonstrates that teacher mediation not only influences student learning but also transforms the pedagogical culture of schools.

Reading became a central element of school life, creating spaces for encounter, dialogue, and collective creation. Activities such as story fairs, dramatizations open to the community, and intergroup reading circles encouraged the participation of families and other local stakeholders, extending the project's impact beyond the classroom and reaffirming the social nature of education. In this way, the school consolidated itself as a space of culture, where reading functions as a shared practice and as a means to strengthen community ties.

Another relevant aspect of the findings is the appropriateness of using local narratives as part of the reading development process. The integration of traditional tales and stories linked to the culture of Zacatecas allowed students to recognize themselves in the texts, strengthening their sense of belonging and cultural identity. Undoubtedly, this contextualized approach demonstrated that reading acquires greater meaning when it engages with the student's environment and when the cultural richness of rural communities is recognized as a valuable pedagogical resource. In this sense, the research provides evidence in favor of building more flexible and context-sensitive curricula, capable of integrating local knowledge and cultural practices into formal education.

Based on the results obtained, it is recommended that reading promotion programs based on the didactic use of storytelling, similar to the "Living Reading with Stories" proposal, be institutionalized as part of local and regional educational policies. These programs should include ongoing teacher training in reading mediation strategies, the provision of relevant and diverse literary resources, and the creation of school and community spaces for shared reading. Furthermore, it is suggested that basic education curricula and programs place greater emphasis on children's literature as a formative tool, beyond its instrumental function in developing linguistic skills.

Finally, this research reaffirms that reading stories is, in essence, about fostering humanity. In rural contexts like Loreto, Zacatecas, where the school represents a central space for encounter and socialization, reading can become a powerful tool for building reading communities with meaning, sensitivity, and social commitment. From its simplicity, accessibility, and cultural richness, the Mexican rural school has the potential to promote profound reading experiences that contribute not only to academic learning but also to the formation of critical, empathetic individuals who are aware of their reality. In this sense, the story reveals itself not only as a didactic resource but also as a means to humanize education and strengthen the social fabric from the earliest stages of school life.

REFERENCES

Ares Ferreirós, M., Alfonso Gil, S., & Deaño, M. (2021). Effectiveness of the Planning Facilitation program for the prevention of reading comprehension difficulties.

Ávila-Negrinis, L., Daza-Cuello, D. M., & González-Roys, G. A. (2021). *The Magical World of Children's Stories: A Teaching Strategy for Developing Inferential Reading Comprehension*. UNIMAR Journal.

Cassany, D. (2006). *Behind the Lines: On Contemporary Reading*. Anagrama.

Colomer, T. (2005). *Walking among books: literary reading in school*. Fondo de Cultura Económica.

Edwards, D., & Mercer, N. (1988). *El conocimiento compartido: el desarollo de la comprensión en el aula*. Paidós.

Estepa, F. Lida Maritza, A., & Arciniegas, W. E. (2019). Encountering the Story: A Strategy to Improve Reading Comprehension. In Education and Science

Freire, P. (1997). Pedagogy of Autonomy: Necessary Knowledge for Educational Practice. 21st Century.

Guerra, G., Alfonso, D., Becerra, M., & Mercedes, Y. (2022). The Story as a Teaching Strategy to Strengthen Critical Reading in Fourth-Grade Students. In Criterios Magazine

Jaramillo Arana, A., Montaña de la Cadena, G., & Rojas Reina, L. M. (2025). Error detection in the metacognitive process of monitoring children's reading comprehension. Latin American Journal of Social Sciences. *Childhood and Youth*, *4*(2). Advance online publication. DOI: 10.11600/rlcsnj.4.2.396

Latorre, A. (2003). *La investigación-acción. Conocer y cambiar la práctica educativa*. GRAÓ.

López, C., Lucero, P., Medina, J., Gladys, H. P., Carolina, A., Celedón, S., Judith, Y. C. A., & Titzé, M. (2024). Deciphering Horizons: An In-Depth Analysis of Reading Comprehension in Elementary School Students. In Estudios y Perspectivas, Scientific and Academic Journal.

Mendoza, A. (2011). *Children's stories and their teaching: a guide for teachers and mediators*. Paidós.

Núñez-Naranjo, A. F., Guevara, A. W. P., Pérez, V., & Yancha, K. R. Y. (2021). El cuento: estrategia didáctica para la comprensión lectora. ConcienciaDigital, 4(1.2), 119-130.

Quintero, T., Renato, A., Valencia, Q., Paola, K., Santana, G., Junior, W., Valdez, F., Lisbeth, J., Muñoz, S., & Manuel, J. (2024). *Storytelling as a Teaching Strategy to Improve Reading Comprehension in the Elementary Sublevel of Basic General Education.* Ciencia Latina, Multidisciplinary Scientific Journal.

Solé, I. (1992). *Reading strategies*. Graó.

Arévalo Suárez, Diana Liyiny, Quintero Antolínez, Leonardo Alfredo, M. Vásquez (2019). Understanding Stories. Education and Science

Tabullo, Á. J., Wainselboim, A., & París, L. A. (2022). La comprensión de textos expositivos y narrativos y su relación con el vocabulario. °: La eficacia lectora y el control inhibitorio en niños de cuarto grado. Traslaciones. *Revista Latinoamericana de Lectura y Escritura*, *9*(17), 39–59.

Wigfield, A., & Guthrie, J. T. (1997). Relationships of children's motivation for reading to the amount and breadth of their reading. *Journal of Educational Psychology*, *89*(3), 420–432.

Chapter 11
Virtual Reality-Based Intensive Care Unit (VRIcuLAB) Design

Cem Deniz Kumral
https://orcid.org/0000-0002-1326-4537
Isparta University of Apllied Sciences, Turkey

Mevlüt Ersoy
Süleyman Demirel University, Turkey

Sıddıka Ersoy
https://orcid.org/0000-0001-8094-8042
Süleyman Demirel University, Turkey

Hamit Armağan
https://orcid.org/0000-0002-8948-1546
Süleyman Demirel University, Turkey

Tuncay Yiğit
Süleyman Demirel University, Turkey

ABSTRACT

The integration of immersive technologies has transformed nursing education, yet existing solutions often lack holistic ICU workflow experiences. This chapter presents VRicuLAB, a Virtual Reality-Based Intensive Care Unit designed to provide nursing students with a realistic, risk-free, and process-oriented learning environment. VRicuLAB enables users to perform procedures, operate virtual devices, and monitor patients through high-fidelity simulations. Beyond technical architecture, the system integrates data-driven tracking and educator dashboards for objective

DOI: 10.4018/979-8-3373-5188-9.ch011

assessment and personalized feedback. By combining engineering precision with instructional design, VRicuLAB aims to enhance accessibility, inclusivity, and engagement. The chapter discusses theoretical foundations, educational rationales for design decisions, and sustainable immersive learning approaches, bridging the gap between engineering and healthcare disciplines.

INTRODUCTION

Integration of immersive and interactive technologies into healthcare education has reshaped how clinical competencies are taught, practiced, and assessed. In nursing education where precision, empathy, and evidence-based decision-making must intersect technology-enhanced learning environments provide a powerful complement to limited clinical placements and resource-constrained skills labs (Cho & Kim, 2024). Global disruptions to clinical access in recent years further accelerated the shift toward scalable, simulation-based training (Martin et al., 2023). Within this landscape, Virtual Reality (VR) has emerged as a credible medium for high-fidelity, repeatable, and risk-free experiential learning (Chen et al., 2020). VR supports not only cognitive understanding but also affective engagement and psychomotor skill acquisition the triad that underpins clinical performance (Efendi et al., 2023).

In Intensive Care Unit (ICU) contexts, where the density of monitoring data, technology, and time-sensitive decisions is high, VR can safely expose learners to scenario complexity that would be risky or logistically impractical at the bedside (Kim & Yoo, 2025). Recent studies consistently report gains in knowledge, skills, and self-efficacy following VR-based simulation compared with traditional methods, albeit with effect sizes varying by task fidelity and instructional design (Ryan et al., 2022; Obeid et al., 2025; Cho & Kim, 2024). Learners also benefit from deliberate practice: VR enables frequent repetition, graduated difficulty, and immediate feedback without patient risk (Lok et al., 2006). These advantages align with experiential and mastery learning frameworks that emphasize cycles of performance, reflection, and corrective action (Chang et al., 2025). Despite encouraging outcomes, gaps remain. Many implementations target isolated procedures (e.g., injection technique or single-device operation) rather than end-to-end ICU workflows that require integrated reasoning across monitors, ventilators, infusion pumps, and alarms (Adil et al., 2026). Few systems provide multi-user coordination mirroring real ICU teamwork or data-driven analytics that capture the nuance of decision paths and timing (Lee et al., 2025). Moreover, the literature calls for clearer reporting on usability, accessibility, and cost-effectiveness, especially for institutions with heterogeneous hardware capacity (Gentili et al., 2022). Finally, while several reviews highlight positive learning effects, they also note variability in study design and a need for longitudinal follow-up to confirm retention and transfer to clinical practice (Daneshfar & Moonaghi, 2025).

Virtual Reality-Based Intensive Care Unit (VRicuLAB) model was conceived to address these gaps through an architecture that combines technical fidelity with pedagogical structure. To explicitly define the educational context, VRicuLAB is targeted at undergraduate nursing students in their junior or senior years. Regarding curricular integration, the system is designed to be embedded within advanced practicum modules or specific 'Critical Care Nursing' courses. Its pedagogical role is strictly defined as a complementary tool rather than a substitute for physical laboratories; it acts as a preparatory bridge, allowing learners to master complex equipment workflows in a risk-free environment before transitioning to high-stakes clinical practice. Furthermore, acknowledging the variability in digital literacy within this learner profile, the interaction design minimizes technical complexity to ensure that the cognitive load remains focused on clinical reasoning rather than hardware manipulation. VRicuLAB simulates an ICU bay with virtual patients and key technologies bedside monitors, ventilators, infusion devices, and electrocardiogram (ECG) modules each modelled to reflect clinically plausible states and parameter behaviours (Angelucci et al., 2025). Learners interact via joystick and hand-tracking to adjust ventilator settings, titrate infusions, acknowledge alarms, and interpret multi-parameter trends (Khundam et al., 2021). Crucially, every action and state transition is captured as a structured log, enabling reconstruction of the clinical "storyline" for debriefing and assessment (Liao et al., 2023). From an instructional design perspective, VRicuLAB operationalizes core principles of deliberate practice and scaffolded progression. Scenarios are authored in an Extensible Markup Language (XML)-based engine that defines initial conditions, device parameters, triggers, branching logic, and expert-validated success criteria This modularity permits rapid authoring and continuous improvement: educators can calibrate difficulty, insert reflective pauses, or add failure-mode branches to surface common pitfalls. The same infrastructure supports multi-user participation, allowing learners to practice communication, task allocation, and shared situational awareness competencies frequently cited as determinants of ICU safety (Khalili, 2021).

A distinctive innovation of the platform is data-driven performance analytics. Because interactions are logged with timestamps and semantic labels, educators can quantify completion time, error frequency, alarm handling latency, parameter-setting accuracy, and help-seeking behaviour. These metrics move evaluation beyond global checklists to evidence-oriented profiles that reveal how learners arrive at outcomes, not merely whether they finish (Ma et al., 2024). Integrated dashboards support real-time monitoring and formative feedback, transforming instructors from passive observers into active mentors (Pei et al., 2024). In turn, learners can review replays and analytics to build metacognitive insight why an action worked, when it was timed poorly, and how an alternative path might reduce risk (Ki & Ryu, 2024). Accessibility and inclusivity are central to the design. Traditional labs face capacity, scheduling, and maintenance constraints; VR offers time- and place-independent access and reduces dependence on expensive consumables (Somerville et al., 2024). By supporting Oculus Quest 2 and Quest 3 headsets, VRicuLAB scales across budgets while maintaining acceptable framerates and interaction quality. Inclusive design considerations readability, interaction ergonomics, and graded cognitive load were incorporated to accommodate diverse learner needs without diluting clinical authenticity (Brisson, 2024). These features align with current calls to make simulation equitable and sustainable, particularly in regions where clinical exposure is difficult to guarantee (Gavilanes, 2024). Beyond skill acquisition, immersive simulation contributes to emotional preparedness and ethical awareness. High stakes yet psychologically safe scenarios allow learners to practice under pressure, rehearse communication with families and teams, and reflect on priority setting when resources are constrained. Debriefings leverage the log-derived timeline to anchor discussion in concrete events rather than recollection, enhancing validity and uptake of feedback. Collectively, these elements suggest that immersive platforms like VRicuLAB can bridge engineering and nursing education by offering inclusive, interactive, and measurable pathways from theory to practice.

This chapter introduces the conceptual foundations, system design, and educational implications of VRicuLAB. We first position VR in the broader context of nursing and ICU education, emphasizing gaps in comprehensive workflows, teamwork, and analytics. We then describe the architecture Unity/C# implementation, XML-based scenario engine, hand-tracking/joystick interaction, logging scheme, and educator dashboards highlighting design choices that balance fidelity with usability. Finally, we discuss how data-driven evaluation and inclusive access can help institutions scale high-quality ICU training while maintaining pedagogical rigor. By aligning technological precision with instructional intent, VRicuLAB advances a sustainable model of immersive learning attuned to the evolving demands of contemporary nursing education.

OVERVIEW OF VIRTUAL REALITY TECHNOLOGY

Virtual Reality (VR) technology is defined as an interactive computer-generated environment that enables users to experience a realistic sense of presence in a simulated three-dimensional world (Britannica, 2025). Through a combination of hardware components such as head-mounted displays (HMDs), motion trackers, and handheld controllers and sophisticated software architectures, VR systems deliver sensory stimuli that replicate or augment the real world. These environments allow users not only to observe but also to act and react within immersive virtual spaces (Chen et al., 2020). The fundamental pillars of VR systems are immersion, interactivity, and navigation (or agency) (Landwehr, 2024; Petersen et al., 2022). Immersion provides the feeling of being enveloped in a virtual setting, minimizing awareness of the physical surroundings. Interactivity ensures that the system responds in real-time to user input, while navigation grants the user freedom to move within and manipulate the environment. Together, these features establish a dynamic human–computer interaction framework that can significantly enhance experiential learning outcomes (Huang et al., 2021).

VR has become a transformative technology across diverse disciplines, including education, healthcare, engineering and entertainment (Javvaji et al., 2024; Ersoy et al., 2022). In education, VR simulations enable learners to perform complex or hazardous procedures in a controlled, repeatable, and feedback-driven setting. This capability is particularly valuable in medical and nursing training, where hands-on experience is essential yet often constrained by ethical or logistical barriers. However, the widespread adoption of VR still faces challenges related to technical limitations, usability issues, and cost-effectiveness. For instance, display latency, low resolution, and motion–visual incongruence can cause "cybersickness," reducing user comfort and engagement (Porcino et al., 2020). From a technical standpoint, VR systems typically consist of an HMD for visual presentation, motion tracking modules for position and orientation detection, input devices for user interaction, and a high-performance graphical processing unit (GPU) to render real-time environments (Britannica, 2025). The software component defines the physics, logic, and behaviour of virtual objects and manages synchronous communication between hardware and user actions. For example, when a user adjusts a control knob on a virtual ventilator, the system immediately displays the corresponding change in pressure or airflow, mimicking a real clinical interaction (Javvaji et al., 2024).

In recent years, systematic reviews have highlighted the pedagogical benefits of VR-based learning environments, especially in nursing and healthcare education contexts (Ryan et al., 2022). These studies report improvements in knowledge retention, psychomotor skill acquisition, and self-efficacy among students exposed to virtual simulation-based training (Cho & Kim, 2024; Saab et al., 2023). To support this skill acquisition, VRicuLAB utilizes a motion-based interaction architecture. This design replaces abstract controller clicks with realistic manual tasks, allowing learners to practice the precise physical movements required in an intensive care setting. Nevertheless, most current implementations are task-specific and do not yet replicate the complex dynamics of an intensive care unit (ICU) or other real-world healthcare scenarios (Souza et al., 2025). Hence, designing immersive, modular, and pedagogically integrated VR systems remains a critical research priority in educational technology (Berezi, 2025). Moreover, VR's potential extends beyond technical training to support affective and ethical competence. In clinical education, VR can simulate emotionally charged situations that help learners develop empathy, decision-making skills, and situational awareness without risk to patients (Wu, 2025; Elendu et al., 2024). When coupled with advanced analytics such as log recording and performance tracking, these environments can also generate quantitative evidence of learning progress (Liao et al., 2023).

In conclusion, while the reviewed literature establishes VR as a potent tool for psychomotor skill acquisition, it explicitly calls for the next generation of simulators to move beyond isolated task training. VRicuLAB is architecturally designed to directly answer three specific demands identified in recent studies. First, to address the scarcity of 'full-flow' simulations and workflow fragmentation, the system integrates multiple device interactions (ventilator, infusion pump, monitor) to replicate the cognitive load of a holistic ICU bay, unlike systems limited to single procedures. Second, responding to the critical lack of collaborative platforms, it implements a synchronous multi-user engine to facilitate the team-based communication essential for patient safety. Third, to bridge the gap in objective evaluation, VRicuLAB incorporates a granular logging infrastructure (JSON/SQL) that transforms abstract decision-making processes into measurable data points. Consequently, the system's design is not merely technical but is a direct architectural response to these identified pedagogical gaps. To visualize how these architectural decisions translate into the learning process, Figure 1 illustrates the system's techno-pedagogical framework, mapping the flow from student interaction to data-driven assessment.

Figure 1. VRicuLAB Techno-Pedagogical Framework

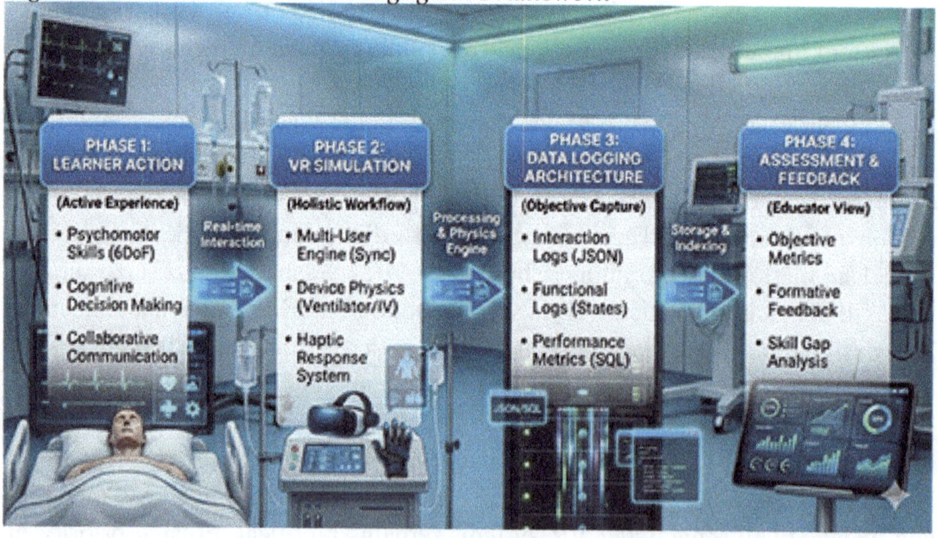

The operational flow depicted in Figure 1 serves as the architectural blueprint for the proposed solution, directly addressing the limitations of isolated task training highlighted in the literature. While the first two phases (Learner Action and VR Simulation) focus on establishing the 'experiential fidelity' required for immersion, the subsequent phases (Data Logging and Assessment) are engineered to solve the 'analytical gap' by transforming subjective performance into objective data. Guided by this four-phase techno-pedagogical framework, the following section details the specific technical implementation of VRicuLAB, demonstrating how each phase is constructed to support high-fidelity intensive care training. The techno-pedagogical framework of VRicuLAB. The diagram illustrates the system's operational flow across four distinct phases: (1) Learner Action, where psychomotor and cognitive inputs are captured via real-time interaction; (2) VR Simulation, which processes these inputs through a multi-user physics engine; (3) Data Logging Architecture, where raw actions are serialized into objective JSON/SQL datasets; and (4) Assessment & Feedback, where data is synthesized into actionable insights for educators.

SYSTEM DESIGN AND ARCHITECTURE OF VRICULAB

VRicuLAB was designed to provide nursing students with an immersive and interactive learning environment replicating real ICU conditions. The system combines visual realism, data-driven interaction, and role-based access to create a multi-layered simulation platform that supports both student learning and instructor monitoring. The overall design of VRicuLAB follows a modular and scalable architecture built using Unity 3D and C#, integrated with a secure SQL Server database and optimized for VR headsets.

General System Architecture

Architecture of VRicuLAB adopts a client–server model that facilitates simultaneous access by multiple users. The client side, developed in Unity, renders the 3D ICU environment and manages real-time user interactions. The server side is responsible for handling authentication, log management, and data storage, ensuring synchronization between users and maintaining the continuity of sessions. Each component within the system (patient monitor, ventilator, infusion pump, or control interface) is represented as a functional object, designed with independent behaviors defined through modular C# scripts. To ensure high performance and compatibility across devices, the VRicuLAB architecture uses asynchronous data transfer for communication between Unity and the SQL database. This allows each user's actions (e.g., adjusting ventilator parameters or connecting infusion lines) to be recorded and analyzed in real time without disrupting system performance. The network structure also supports scalability, enabling additional modules or new ICU rooms to be incorporated without altering the existing codebase. In the basic architecture, the VR application, developed in the Unity environment, communicates with the database server and the educator web application in the web environment. The VR application, in turn, runs on virtual reality glasses. General system architecture diagram is presented in Figure 2.

Figure 2. General system architecture

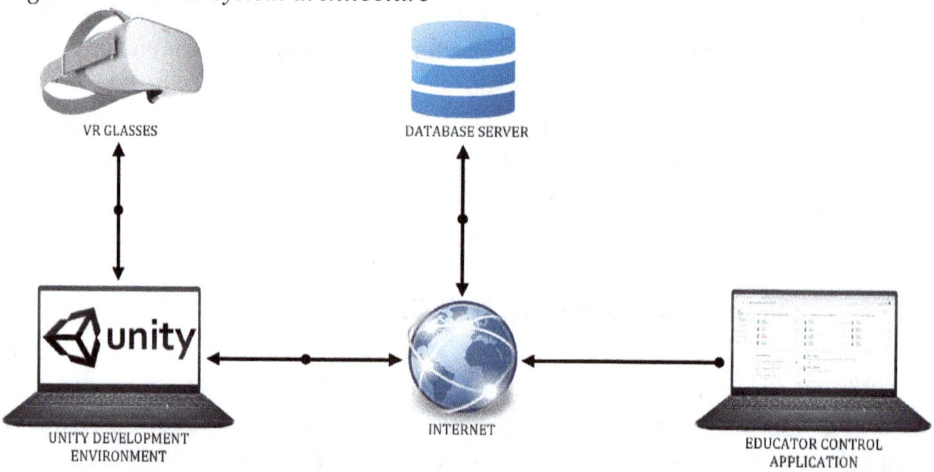

From an educational standpoint, this client–server architecture is not merely a technical necessity but a pedagogical enabler. By offloading complex data processing to the server, the system ensures that the learner's VR experience remains fluid and free of latency-induced distractions, which is critical for maintaining 'cognitive presence' in simulation. Furthermore, the modular design supports curriculum scalability; educators can seamlessly introduce new clinical modulesinto the existing architecture as students advances in their academic progression, ensuring the technology grows alongside the learner's competency.

VRicuLAB Use-Case Diagram

Use-case diagram presented in Figure 3 provides a conceptual overview of the interaction flow between the primary user roles students and educators within the VRicuLAB environment. This diagram outlines the hierarchical and functional relationships among system components, illustrating how users' access, perform, and manage experimental activities in the virtual intensive care unit. Designed in accordance with the Unified Modeling Language (UML) framework, the diagram highlights the dependencies and inclusions between critical actions such as login, verification, experiment execution, data management, and log monitoring.

Figure 3. VRicuLAB use-case diagram

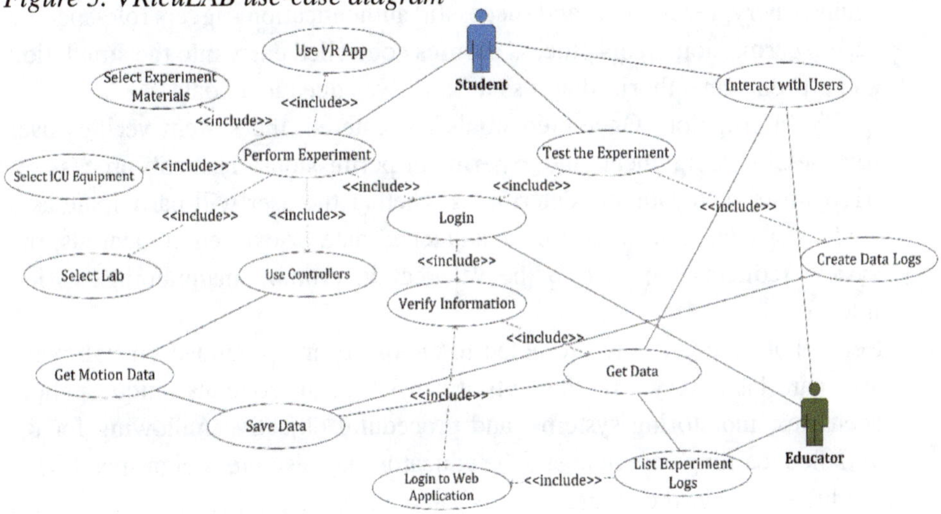

From a pedagogical perspective, this use case structure emphasizes the dual focus of VRicuLAB: enabling students to perform immersive, hands-on experiments, and empowering educators to supervise and evaluate performance through integrated data collection and feedback mechanisms. On the technical side, each interaction represented in the diagram corresponds to a specific module within the system's architecture implemented through modular scripts and database transactions to ensure real-time synchronization between virtual actions and recorded data.

Overall framework reinforces the role-based interaction logic of VRicuLAB. Students are primarily responsible for initiating and performing experimental procedures through VR controllers, while educators function as supervisory entities who verify information, access data, and review experimental outcomes. This division of roles ensures a structured, secure, and trackable workflow that mirrors the collaborative nature of real ICU environments. The individual functions and relationships outlined in the use case diagram are described below to provide a more detailed understanding of the operational logic and educational intent of each component.

- Use VR App: This function represents the initial stage of user engagement, where students launch the VRicuLAB application using the Oculus headset. The system automatically connects to the main server and loads the configured ICU simulation environment. This step also performs preliminary system checks, such as verifying the headset connection, initializing controllers, and synchronizing user position in the virtual space.

- Login: The login process authenticates both student and educator accounts via the secure SQL-based verification system. User credentials are validated against encrypted records, and successful authentication triggers role-specific access permissions. This process ensures controlled entry into the simulation and prevents unauthorized access to sensitive educational data.
- Verify Information: Once credentials are entered, the system verifies user role, session assignment, and experiment permissions. This sub-process retrieves user metadata and determines whether the user will participate as a student or educator. In case of mismatched data or expired credentials, the system redirects the user to the verification prompt, maintaining session integrity.
- Select Lab: Students are prompted to choose from predefined virtual intensive care laboratory environments. Each lab setup contains unique patient scenarios, monitoring systems, and procedural objectives, allowing for diversified learning experiences. The educator may also pre-assign specific lab modules to each student group based on course objectives.
- Select ICU Equipment: Within the chosen lab environment, students interactively select the required ICU devices such as ventilators, syringe pumps, ECG monitors, and defibrillators from the equipment library. This process simulates real-world preparation before a clinical procedure and reinforces knowledge of device functions and placement.
- Select Experiment Materials: This step involves choosing consumables or clinical components required for the training scenario, such as IV lines, electrodes, or syringes. Each selection is logged by the system for later performance evaluation.
- Use Controllers: Students manipulate virtual equipment using Oculus handheld controllers. Each controller's trigger and joystick inputs are mapped to specific interaction functions, including grabbing, rotating, connecting, or activating medical devices. The HoldObject() and DropObject() scripts manage object state transitions, ensuring smooth and realistic control responses.
- Perform Experiment: Students carry out assigned clinical procedures such as patient monitoring, adjusting ventilator parameters, or performing basic resuscitation steps. The system records every input, tool usage, and timing data to generate individual performance logs. This stage represents the core interactive learning process within VRicuLAB.
- Test the Experiment: After performing the experiment, students can simulate patient responses or device feedback based on predefined physiological

models. This allows them to test the outcome of their interventions, such as changes in oxygen saturation or heart rate, promoting applied learning and diagnostic reasoning.

- Get Motion Data: The system continuously tracks user hand and head movements via the Oculus sensors. Motion data are collected to evaluate precision, response speed, and ergonomic posture during procedures. These metrics are essential for assessing the accuracy of manipulative skills in a clinical context.
- Save Data: All recorded actions, timing, and motion parameters are automatically stored in the SQL database in JSON format. This ensures that performance data can be later retrieved for evaluation or replay. The save function operates asynchronously, preventing interruptions in real-time simulation flow.
- Get Data: The educator's dashboard retrieves stored data for review. This includes experiment outcomes, device interactions, and timestamps for all actions taken during a session. The system also supports filtering logs by user, experiment type, or date range.
- Create Data Logs: During each session, the system generates categorized logs interaction logs, functional logs, and performance logs automatically labelled with user ID and session ID. These structured datasets form the basis for performance evaluation and research analytics.
- List Experiment Logs: Educators can view aggregated summaries of experiment activities, displaying completion status, accuracy rates, and response times. The listing interface provides export functionality for further analysis using external statistical tools.
- Login to Web Application: Educators access the web-based control panel, where they can monitor session progress, review logs, and assign new experiments. This interface serves as the bridge between the virtual simulation and administrative oversight.
- Interact with Users: The educator role also includes direct engagement with students during active simulations. Through the shared virtual space, educators can observe user behaviour, provide real-time feedback, and adjust experiment parameters dynamically.

This functional separation mirrors the 'Preceptor Model' common in clinical nursing education. By distinguishing the student role (focused on experiential action) from the Educator role (focused on observation and formative assessment), the system technically enforces a pedagogical boundary that encourages learner autonomy while preserving the safety net of instructor supervision.

Role-Based Access and User Management

To ensure controlled access and structured supervision, the VRicuLAB platform implements a role-based access control (RBAC) mechanism that differentiates permissions between students and educators directly within the VR environment. Each user role is registered in the SQL Server database with distinct access privileges and functionality scopes defined through unique role identifiers. Student accounts grant access to the virtual simulation modules, enabling learners to interact with ICU devices, manipulate parameters, and complete structured practice scenarios. These users operate exclusively within the immersive VR environment, where all actions such as device interaction, parameter adjustment, or scenario progression are managed through real-time event triggers. Each student session is automatically assigned a unique session ID that ensures data traceability and supports subsequent performance analysis.

Educator accounts, on the other hand, are designed to provide enhanced control and flexibility within the same VR environment. In addition to the capabilities available to students, educators can initiate and terminate simulations, switch between different training modules, monitor scenario status, and assist learners directly within the virtual space. This multi-level role hierarchy enables instructors to participate in the simulation as observers, supervisors, or co-participants, depending on the instructional objective. The authentication process for both user types is managed through a secure login interface integrated with the central SQL Server database. Upon entering credentials, the client-side application locally hashes the password using the SHA-256 encryption algorithm before transmitting it via HTTPS to the server. The server then compares the received hash with the stored encrypted value in the database's Users table. Once validated, a session token containing the user's role, device ID, and login timestamp is generated and stored in the ActiveSessions table. This token governs session continuity and enables the system to dynamically load the corresponding VR modules based on user role.

If authentication fails due to incorrect credentials, inactive accounts, or expired sessions the system triggers an exception handler that records the event with an error code (e.g., AUTH_FAIL_401) and a timestamp. Failed attempts are limited to three per account; upon reaching this threshold, the system locks the account temporarily and flags it for verification. All login activities are recorded in a dedicated AuthLogs table that maintains records of username, IP address, device type, and login result for audit purposes.

Unlike the educators' web-based analytics interface, which is used solely for reviewing detailed log and performance data, the VR-based educator account focuses on in-simulation management and supervision. This separation between immersive training and administrative analysis ensures system stability and enhances data security by isolating real-time simulation processes from external monitoring tools. The integration of secure hashing, encrypted communication, and session management protocols ensures confidentiality and role-based integrity within the VR environment. This structure provides the foundation for future integration with institutional authentication systems and allows educators and students to collaborate within a unified but permission-aware simulation space. VRicuLAB login interface is shown in Figure 4.

Figure 4. VRicuLAB login interface

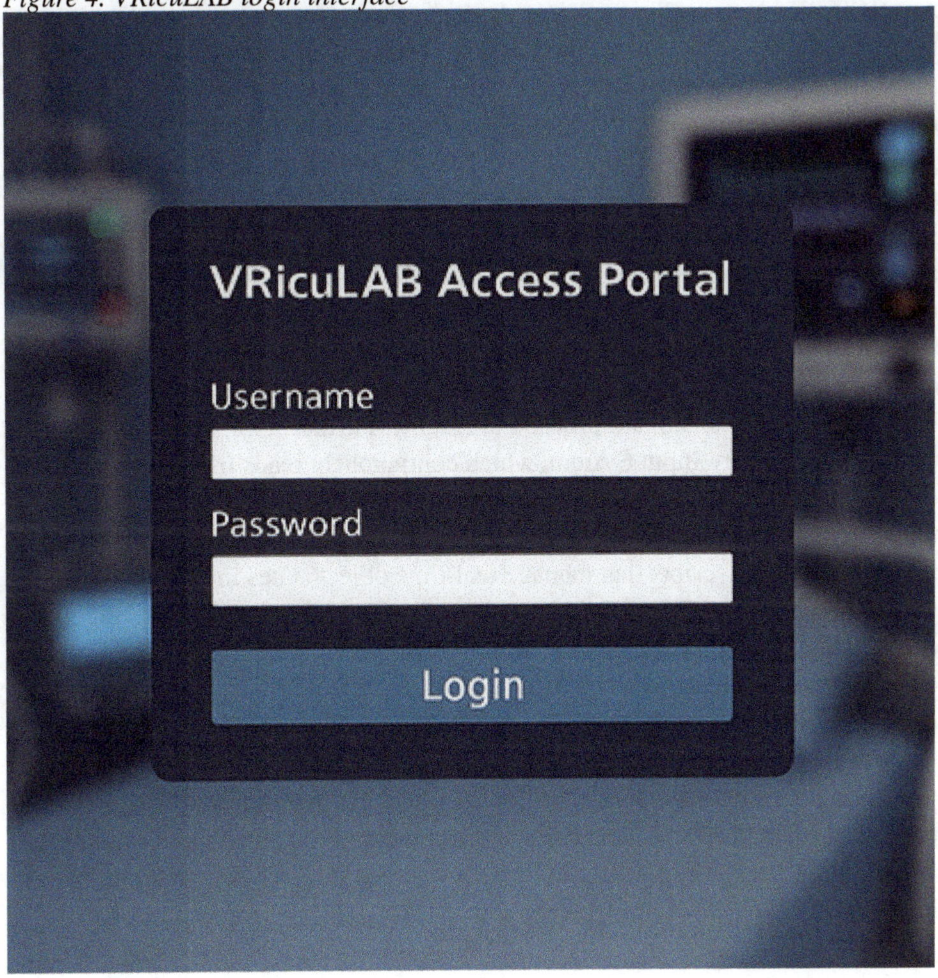

Beyond data security, this rigorous authentication protocol serves a vital academic function: 'Assessment Integrity.' By ensuring that every action is irrefutably linked to a specific user session, the system prevents data contamination between learners.

This guarantees that the performance analytics generated for grading or feedback reflect the student's true individual competency, establishing VRicuLAB as a valid tool for summative assessment within the nursing curriculum.

User Interaction and Control Mechanisms

The interaction between the user and the virtual environment in VRicuLAB is achieved through the Oculus controllers, which serve as the primary input devices for all object manipulation and navigation tasks within the virtual intensive care unit (ICU). Each controller tracks six degrees of freedom (6DoF), enabling precise hand movements such as grabbing, rotating, pushing, and releasing objects in real time. The ergonomic design of these controllers, equipped with analog triggers and thumbsticks, allows for intuitive engagement with virtual medical equipment such as ventilators, monitors, infusion pumps, and patient beds. The right-hand controller is typically assigned to object manipulation functions, whereas the left-hand controller handles navigation and auxiliary actions such as menu selection and interface activation. The trigger button corresponds to the "grab" event, the grip simulates mechanical grasping pressure, and the thumbstick facilitates fine-tuned rotational adjustments of interactive objects. This configuration replicates the tactile experience of interacting with real medical devices, ensuring that the system maintains both educational realism and procedural fidelity. Furthermore, each interaction is tracked by the Unity Input System, which continuously reads trigger pressure and orientation vectors to synchronize the user's hand model with physical gestures. At the core of this interaction logic lies the "grab-and-release" mechanism, implemented via specialized C# scripts that manage real-time object states in Unity.

The functions HoldTheObject() and DropTheObject() control the activation and deactivation of objects within the virtual environment. The logic ensures that an object cannot be simultaneously held and interacted with by multiple users, maintaining data integrity and realistic control behavior. A coroutine (DropTheObjectE()) introduces a short delay (0.2 seconds) to simulate the natural release interval that occurs during hand movement transitions in physical environments. This delay also prevents unwanted double-interactions, thereby improving interaction stability and minimizing simulation errors. Simplified source code used for grab and release interactions is presented in Figure 5.

Figure 5. Grab and release interactions code script

```
public void DropTheObject()
{
    onHand = false;

    StartCoroutine(DropTheObjectE());
}
IEnumerator DropTheObjectE()
{
    stopToInteract = true;
    yield return new WaitForSeconds(0.2f);
    stopToInteract = false;
}

public void HoldTheObject()
{
    onHand = true;

    startToInteract = true;
    stopToInteract = false;
}
```

From a functional perspective, this script defines a binary state system in which onHand acts as the key flag representing user-object attachment. When the trigger is pressed, onHand becomes true, marking the object as actively manipulated. Once released, the coroutine resets interaction variables to ensure the object's collider can respond to other events. This structure mirrors real-world hand–object dynamics and creates an intuitive bridge between the user's physical movement and virtual response.

The overall control architecture ensures seamless synchronization between physics-based object motion, animation systems, and haptic feedback. Each successful grab triggers a short haptic pulse, while a release action produces a subtle vibration cue providing users with tactile feedback that enhances immersion and task precision. In a nursing education context, these features enable trainees to perform detailed clinical actions such as adjusting ventilator knobs, repositioning sensors, or connecting IV lines with procedural accuracy.

VRicuLAB creates a realistic, low-latency interaction framework by combining responsive control algorithms with real-time haptics, ensuring that every movement is naturally transferred to the virtual intensive care unit. This human-centred design not only ensures usability and accessibility but also enhances the transfer of cognitive skills from simulation to real-world medical applications.

These technical specifications are directly grounded in the theory of 'embodied cognition.' By mapping 6DoF movements directly to clinical tasks, the system fosters psychomotor fidelity, ensuring that the muscle memory developed in VR such as the precise rotation of a fine-tune knob or the angle of an IV insertion translates accurately to physical equipment. Furthermore, the programmed haptic feedback acts as a sensory reinforcement mechanism, helping learners distinguish between successful and failed interactions without relying solely on visual cues.

Functional Components of the Virtual ICU

Virtual Reality–Based Intensive Care Unit (VRicuLAB) was designed as a modular and scalable environment, replicating real-world ICU operations with an emphasis on interactive learning, system responsiveness, and data-driven training. The system architecture integrates both software-defined components and hardware-simulated elements, each designed to emulate critical ICU functionalities such as patient monitoring, device interaction, and clinical decision-making support.

At the software layer, the system was developed using the Unity 3D engine with C# scripting, chosen for its real-time rendering capabilities, cross-platform compatibility, and flexible integration with external databases. The Unity physics engine was employed to model the physical behaviour of objects, enabling realistic responses such as cable dynamics, medical equipment collisions, and haptic feedback synchronization. Each interactive component in the virtual ICU including ventilators, infusion pumps, and defibrillators was modelled as an independent GameObject with specific behavioural scripts defining their response to user input. For instance, a ventilator's control panel includes parameter adjustment scripts that simulate changes in respiratory rate or tidal volume, visually reflected in both display values and patient monitor waveforms. The database management layer, hosted on a Microsoft SQL Server, provides persistent storage for user profiles, simulation configurations, and activity records.

Each object in the virtual environment is registered in a relational schema that links user interactions to timestamped database entries. This structure allows real-time retrieval and updating of simulation states, ensuring that any parameter modification made by the user (e.g., adjusting oxygen levels or pump flow rate) is immediately synchronized with both the virtual device and the database record. Additionally, a data caching mechanism using asynchronous calls minimizes latency between user actions and visual feedback, maintaining frame rates above 90 FPS to support an uninterrupted VR experience.

The interaction layer is built upon an event-driven architecture, which continuously monitors user input from VR controllers and translates them into predefined simulation commands. The system recognizes gestures, controller triggers, and object collisions, each corresponding to distinct event codes. These inputs are processed through the InteractionManager class, which determines the context of the action such as whether an object is being grasped, adjusted, or activated and executes the relevant procedural script. This modular approach allows the addition of new medical instruments or training modules without altering the underlying system architecture.

From a visual and sensory standpoint, realism and immersion were prioritized to enhance cognitive engagement and knowledge retention. Lighting, sound design, and spatial audio were dynamically configured to replicate ICU conditions, including alarm notifications, patient monitor beeps, and device startup sounds. The materials and textures were optimized to reduce rendering overhead while maintaining clinical realism. The communication layer ensures synchronization between the client application (VR headset) and the SQL server through a RESTful API that manages real-time requests such as data submission, session updates, and role validation.

Each simulation instance establishes a unique connection token that maintains data consistency throughout the user's active session. This design allows multiple students to perform simulations concurrently while preserving the integrity of individual datasets and preventing cross-session interference. The basic communication and user interaction architecture of the system is given in Figure 6.

Figure 6. Communication and user interaction architecture

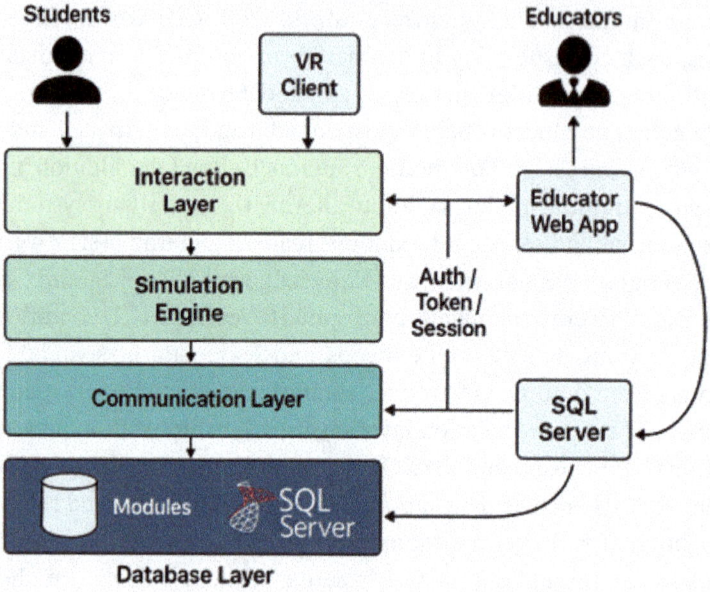

A core element of the VRicuLAB system is its modular simulation framework, which supports dynamic scene loading and progressive complexity levels. Scenarios are categorized into three tiers:

- Fundamental skills modules (e.g., patient observation, device familiarization),
- Procedural simulations (e.g., infusion setup, airway management), and
- Critical decision-making scenarios (e.g., cardiac arrest response, equipment malfunction management).

Each module integrates interactive indicators that provide real-time guidance, such as highlighting incorrect actions or displaying visual cues for next procedural steps. Educators can also configure custom scenarios by modifying XML-based configuration files, which define the set of available devices, patient states, and learning objectives for a given training session. Example images from the VRicuLAB environment containing functional objects are given in Figure 7 and Figure 8.

Figure 7. VRicuLAB environment 1

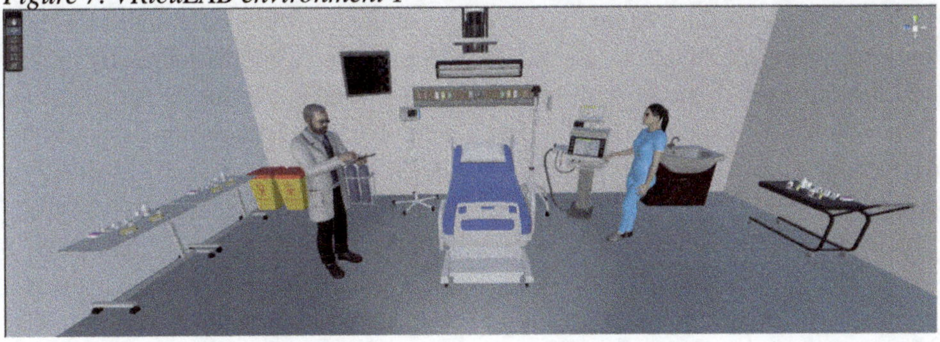

Figure 8. VRicuLAB environment 2

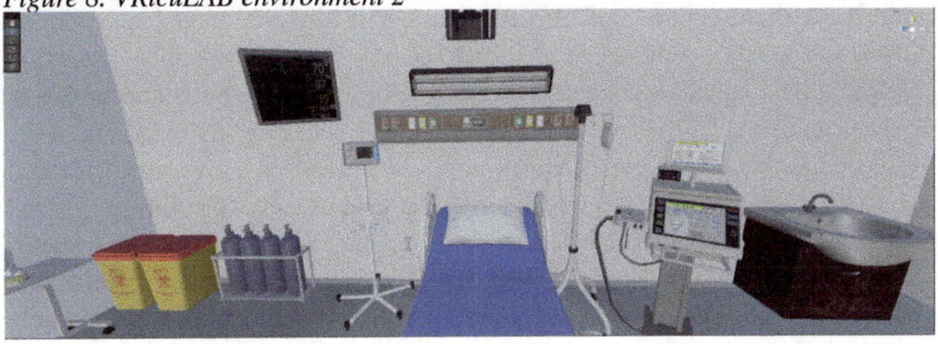

Pedagogically, this rigorous physics and interaction simulation is essential for establishing 'ecological validity.' By ensuring that medical devices obey real-world physical laws (e.g., cable dynamics, gravity-dependent fluid flows) and respond instantly to inputs, the system minimizes the 'gulf of execution.' This allows learners to immerse themselves fully in the clinical scenario without being distracted by unrealistic mechanics, thereby keeping their cognitive load focused purely on clinical reasoning.

Data Management and Log Synchronization

VRicuLAB database infrastructure employs a hybrid storage architecture that combines relational (SQL) and document-oriented (JSON-based) data models to balance consistency, scalability, and flexibility. Static information such as user credentials, roles, and session metadata is maintained in normalized relational tables, whereas dynamic and frequently changing data including user interactions, device parameters, and procedural outcomes are serialized and stored as JSON documents. This design allows the system to efficiently handle the wide variability of events that occur during simulation sessions without imposing a rigid schema structure.

Each log entry in the system is composed of several key-value pairs that define event characteristics such as user ID, session number, object name, interaction type, device state, and timestamp. For example, a student's adjustment of ventilator pressure parameters would trigger a JSON log entry containing attributes like "eventType": "parameterChange", "device": "ventilator", "oldValue": "12 cmH_2O", "newValue": "15 cmH_2O", "timestamp": "2025-09-20T14:35:12Z". This fine-grained approach enables event reconstruction, allowing educators and developers to trace the complete sequence of user interactions for analysis and debugging purposes.

The log management subsystem operates asynchronously, ensuring minimal latency between user actions and data registration. Interaction data are queued in a temporary local buffer within the Unity environment and then periodically synchronized with the central SQL Server through RESTful API endpoints. Each log entry is assigned a unique event identifier (UUID) to prevent duplication during concurrent data uploads or network instability. In the event of a connection loss, the system automatically switches to offline mode, locally caching logs until the server connection is restored at which point the cached data are batch-uploaded and verified against existing entries for integrity consistency. To optimize retrieval performance, an indexing mechanism was implemented for frequently queried fields such as user ID, session date, and event type. This enables rapid aggregation and filtering of logs, which is particularly valuable when analysing trends over multiple sessions or identifying recurring procedural errors. Additionally, the log system incorporates checksum validation to detect and discard corrupted entries during synchronization, thereby enhancing the overall reliability of the dataset. Beyond individual event tracking, the log system generates derived analytics metrics that summarize user performance, such as total interaction count, error frequency, and completion time per scenario. These aggregated data points form the foundation for the educator analytics module, which supports comparative assessments and longitudinal tracking of student learning progression. After each completed session, a session summary file is automatically archived in the system's backup directory, ensuring full data recoverability and long-term research value. All collected logs are stored in structured JSON format within the database under their respective session identifiers, making it possible to retrieve both raw event data and summarized metrics. Educators access and interpret these logs through dedicated web-based dashboards, which visualize performance indicators and behavioural trends. This interface enables instructors to monitor learner engagement in real time, identify recurring issues, and adjust training strategies accordingly thus bridging the gap between virtual simulation data and educational decision-making. The architectural structure of the data flow and log synchronization process is given in Figure 9.

Figure 9. The architectural structure of the data flow and log synchronization process

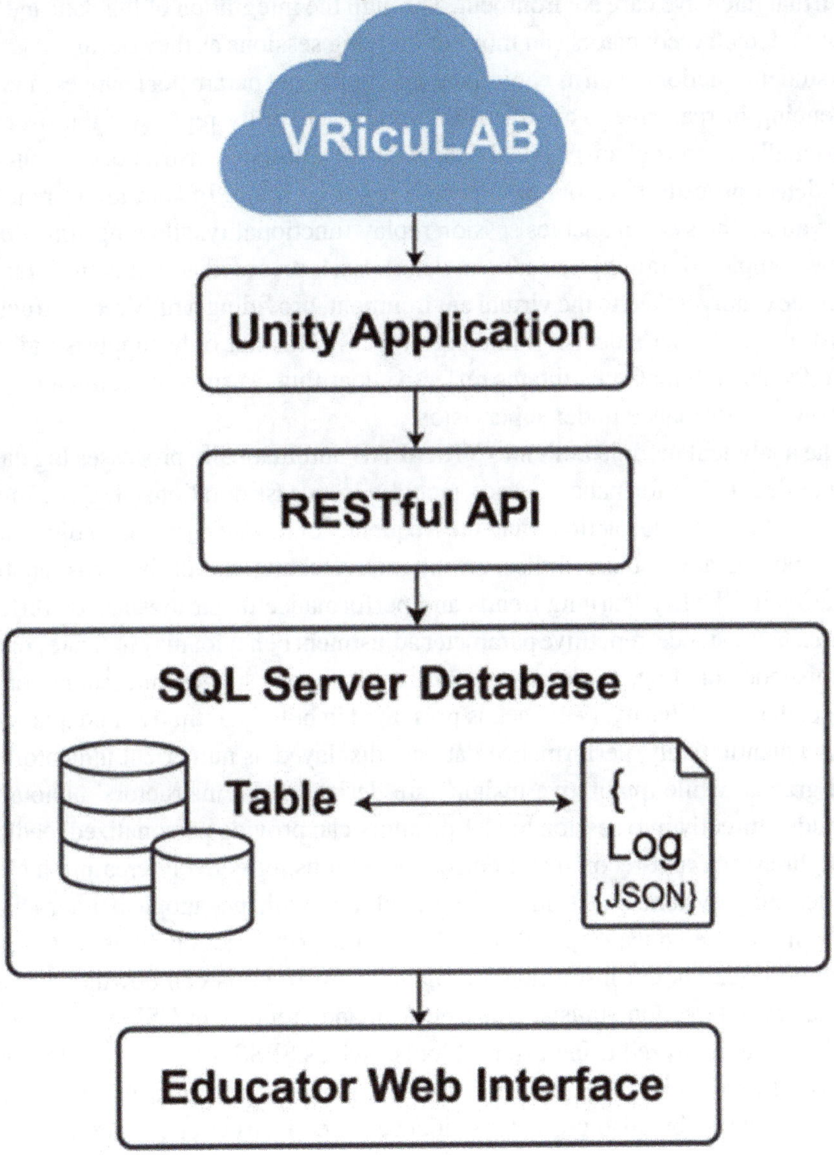

Educator Monitoring and Feedback System

VRicuLAB system is its educator feedback interface, designed to provide instructors with real-time and retrospective oversight of student performance within the virtual intensive care environment. Through the integration of log data and simulation telemetry, educators can monitor ongoing sessions as they occur, observing each student's actions such as equipment manipulation, parameter changes, and task sequencing in real time. This live observation capability replicates the oversight traditionally exercised in physical laboratories, allowing instructors to immediately detect procedural errors or delays in task execution. In addition to real-time observation, the system enables session replay functionality, allowing educators to review completed training sessions in detail. Each recorded action is timestamped and contextually linked to the virtual environment, providing a fully reconstructable record of the learner's decision-making process. This not only supports individualized feedback but also facilitates reflective learning, as students can later review their own performance under supervision.

The analytical module built into VRicuLAB automatically processes log data to produce detailed performance metrics, including total task duration, idle time, number of successful and failed actions, and the frequency of device parameter adjustments. These metrics are visualized through interactive charts and dashboards, enabling educators to identify learning trends and performance disparities across different cohorts. For instance, repetitive parameter adjustment behavior may indicate conceptual misunderstanding, while longer task durations may suggest uncertainty or lack of procedural familiarity. Feedback is presented in both quantitative and qualitative forms. Quantitatively, performance data are displayed as numerical indicators and trend graphs, while qualitative insights are derived from instructors' annotations embedded directly into session logs. Educators can provide personalized feedback, highlight errors, and recommend corrective actions, effectively creating a closed loop learning system that bridges data analytics with pedagogical intervention. Furthermore, the educator panel includes data export functionalities that support academic research and institutional evaluation. Instructors can download session summaries, interaction statistics, and performance reports in CSV format, which can be further analyzed using external tools such as SPSS, Excel, or Python-based analytics frameworks. This feature not only enhances the transparency of the assessment process but also promotes evidence-based instructional design.

Overall, the educator interface transforms the VRicuLAB platform from a passive simulation environment into an active learning analytics ecosystem. By enabling real-time monitoring, post-session review, and comprehensive performance analysis, the system empowers instructors to deliver adaptive feedback, improve learner engagement, and elevate the overall pedagogical value of immersive virtual reality–based nursing education. The educator control panel is depicted in Figure 10.

Figure 10. Educator control panel

VRicuLAB Educator Console serves as the primary interface through which instructors can monitor and manage student activity within the virtual intensive care training environment. The dashboard displays all active users in tabular form, with each row representing an individual learner and their associated experimental session. The "Experiment" column lists the assigned training modules (e.g., ICU Monitoring, Pain Management, Emergency Response Simulation), while the "Status" column visually indicates progress.

Each record includes the start time of the session, enabling educators to track both participation patterns and temporal distribution of activities across different training modules. The "Actions" column provides two primary control options View and Pause. Selecting View opens a detailed session summary displaying real-time logs, interaction history, and recorded telemetry data from the VR environment. Through this feature, educators can review precise student actions such as device adjustments, task sequences, and response times. The Pause option temporarily halts a live session, allowing the instructor to intervene directly either to provide guidance, correct procedural errors, or reassign the student to a different module.

This structure allows instructors to perform both macro and micro-level supervision, integrating pedagogical assessment with system analytics. By offering color-coded visual indicators and interactive action buttons, the console effectively transforms complex datasets into an intuitive, actionable interface. Furthermore, detailed log analyses corresponding to each experiment type are presented in subsequent sections, providing a deeper insight into system functionality and learner behaviour.

Multi-User Interaction Framework

VRicuLAB is its multi-user interaction capability, which enables several participants to access and operate within the same virtual intensive care unit (ICU) environment simultaneously. The purpose of this feature is to reproduce the collaborative dynamics of a real ICU, where healthcare professionals must coordinate procedures, share information, and perform synchronized actions around a patient. The system was designed as a client–server-based multiplayer architecture, ensuring that every user perceives consistent and synchronized updates of the shared simulation environment. The underlying architecture relies on Unity's Mirror networking framework, configured to operate through a dedicated central server. Each VR headset functions as an independent client that connects to the main node, where all simulation states are stored and validated. The server maintains control over the ICU environment, handling object ownership, synchronization, and consistency checks. When a user manipulates a device such as adjusting a ventilator setting or repositioning a patient monitor the change is processed by the server and broadcast to all connected users with minimal latency. This ensures that all participants experience an identical, synchronized environment at any given moment.

Each participant is represented in the system by a customized virtual avatar that mirrors their real-time head and hand movements. These avatars are designed not only to visually identify users but also to support nonverbal communication through gestures, positioning, and gaze direction. For instance, an instructor's avatar standing beside a trainee and pointing toward a device provides a clear contextual cue without requiring verbal instructions. This visual interaction design fosters intuitive teamwork and allows educators to supervise student performance effectively within the virtual ICU. To further enhance situational awareness, the avatars of educators are color-coded differently from those of students, and each carries an on-screen name label for easy identification.

The interaction layer supports simultaneous manipulation of medical equipment by multiple users, using a controlled object ownership model. Each interactive device in the ICU scene such as infusion pumps, ECG monitors, and syringe drivers has a dynamically assigned "owner." The ownership is granted to the user who first interacts with the object and revoked once the action is complete or the object is released. During ownership transfer, the system locks the object state to prevent data conflicts or simultaneous modifications. This model ensures consistent and deterministic system behaviour even when several users operate within the same environment.

Data exchange between clients and the central server is conducted via synchronized state packets, optimized through delta compression to transmit only the changes in object properties rather than full-state updates. Each packet is timestamped and validated to maintain temporal accuracy and prevent overlapping updates. This optimization minimizes network bandwidth usage while maintaining real-time responsiveness in the VR headset, even in high-load multi-user scenarios. The platform also integrates session-level concurrency management and user presence tracking. Each connected user is assigned a unique session ID, allowing the server to monitor entry and exit events, device usage history, and task completion states. Educators can observe all active participants in real time through a monitoring interface that displays user positions, interaction frequencies, and device utilization metrics. This provides an analytical layer for evaluating teamwork patterns, coordination efficiency, and procedural adherence within the ICU training scenario.

Security and integrity remain a core focus of the system's design. All multiplayer sessions are secured through TLS 1.3 encryption, and authentication is managed by the SQL-based login infrastructure that verifies user credentials before allowing access to the shared simulation. To ensure scalability, the VRicuLAB architecture supports multiple concurrent sessions, each running as an isolated "virtual ICU" instance. This allows multiple classes or training groups to operate simultaneously without interference. Beyond real-time collaboration, the system includes a record and replay mechanism that captures all multi-user activities for later review. During playback, instructors can observe avatars' interactions, equipment manipulations, and sequence timing to analyse coordination and identify training gaps. This replay mode transforms the VRicuLAB environment from a static training tool into a dynamic performance analysis platform, capable of evaluating both individual competence and group collaboration effectiveness. By combining multi-user synchronization, avatar-based visual communication, and real-time procedural feedback, VRicuLAB effectively replicates the cooperative and highly organized nature of intensive care practice. The architecture provides a technically robust, scalable, and pedagogically valuable foundation for teaching teamwork and situational awareness in virtual healthcare environments.

This architecture is explicitly designed to support 'Collaborative Constructivism.' In a real ICU, patient safety depends on the synchronized efforts of the care team. By enabling real-time multi-user presence, VRicuLAB transcends individual skill training to address 'Interprofessional Education (IPE)' competencies. The shared environment forces learners to practice closed-loop communication and maintain shared situational awareness, skills that are often lost in isolated desktop simulations.

VRICULAB LOG ANALYSIS

Comprehensive log management and analysis framework was integrated into VRicuLAB to enable objective evaluation of user performance and system behaviour during virtual training sessions. Every user action, device interaction, and procedural sequence is recorded in real time, forming a detailed digital footprint of each simulation. This logging architecture was designed not only for debugging or system optimization but also as a pedagogical tool to assess learning processes and user engagement. By capturing granular data such as object manipulation frequency, sequence of actions, and time spent on individual tasks the system provides both educators and researchers with deep insights into how learners interact with the virtual ICU environment. From a technical standpoint, the log collection process operates asynchronously to ensure uninterrupted simulation performance. Each action is timestamped and tagged with a unique session ID and user ID, preventing data duplication and maintaining temporal accuracy even in multi-user sessions. The logs are stored in structured JSON format within the SQL database, enabling flexible data retrieval and integration with analytics tools such as Python, MATLAB, or SPSS. This hybrid architecture allows efficient handling of large datasets while maintaining relational consistency for user records and scenario metadata.

Pedagogically, the logging system bridges the gap between immersive simulation and measurable learning outcomes. It enables educators to trace decision-making paths, detect recurring procedural errors, and identify patterns of progress across training sessions. Moreover, the collected data can be used to refine scenario design, adapt instructional strategies, and promote evidence-based feedback in nursing education. By analysing these logs, instructors gain a clearer understanding of students' clinical reasoning skills and psychomotor performance in complex critical care tasks.

The following subsections describe and illustrate the three primary log categories recorded within the system interaction logs, functional logs, and performance logs each serving distinct but complementary roles in the educational analytics pipeline.

Interaction Logs

Interaction logs capture every tangible action performed by users within the VRicuLAB simulation, focusing on hand–object interactions, spatial manipulations, and equipment engagement sequences. These logs represent the most fundamental layer of behavioural analytics, documenting how participants engage with the virtual

ICU environment through their VR controllers. Each interaction record includes identifiers such as UserID, ObjectName, ActionType, Timestamp, and SessionID.

From a technical perspective, interaction logs are generated by Unity's event-driven input handlers that track controller triggers and collision events in real time. Each event is serialized in JSON format and asynchronously transmitted to the database through a RESTful API. This design ensures minimal latency during high-frequency interactions, preventing data loss or frame delays that might affect the realism of the simulation. The architecture also employs a queue-based caching system, allowing log entries to be temporarily stored locally if an internet connection is interrupted, thus ensuring consistency in multi-user sessions.

Pedagogically, these logs provide an invaluable record of student behaviour patterns how frequently a participant manipulates instruments, whether they follow procedural order, or how efficiently they transition between actions. For example, frequent re-grabbing of the same object might indicate uncertainty or a lack of motor precision, while smooth sequences of actions suggest increasing familiarity and confidence with the ICU workflow. Educators can replay or visualize these logs to reconstruct a student's procedural pathway, enabling personalized feedback and data-driven performance evaluation. A representative example of the interaction log data is presented Table 1.

Table 1. Example of the interaction log data

UserID	ObjectName	ActionType	Timestamp	SessionID
STU001	SyringePump	Grabbed	2025-10-21 10:23:45	S1023
STU001	SyringePump	Released	2025-10-21 10:23:58	S1023
STU002	VentilatorKnob	Adjusted	2025-10-21 11:07:33	S1024
STU003	ECGLead	Connected	2025-10-21 11:41:22	S1025

From the dataset above, it is evident that the system successfully records every micro-level event associated with user manipulation. Each interaction not only provides data for mechanical accuracy but also contributes to developing psychomotor skill profiles for learners. By aggregating multiple sessions, educators can identify common points of confusion (e.g., incorrect electrode connections or device misplacement) and adapt subsequent training modules accordingly. Furthermore, the data structure supports integration with time-series analytics, enabling researchers to compute metrics such as average interaction latency, action frequency per minute, and error density. This transforms the log data into a quantifiable measure of learning efficiency, bridging the gap between immersive simulation and empirical educational evaluation.

Functional Logs

Functional logs represent the operational backbone of VRicuLAB's data monitoring and control architecture. Unlike interaction logs, which capture user actions, functional logs document how the virtual medical devices and subsystems respond to those actions. Each functional entry records key parameters such as device state changes, threshold triggers, sensor readings, and system feedback loops providing a complete overview of the dynamic interaction between user input and system computation.

Technically, each piece of ICU equipment within VRicuLAB is implemented as an independent object-oriented class in Unity, equipped with a custom DeviceState-Controller script. These scripts continuously monitor parameter changes through event listeners and automatically log variations to the system database. For example, adjusting a ventilator knob updates the OxygenFlowRate or TidalVolume properties in real time, while toggling a defibrillator records the ChargeLevel and DischargeEvent values. Each of these operations triggers a functional log entry that includes fields such as DeviceName, Parameter, OldValue, NewValue, and ResponseTime.

All entries are serialized in structured JSON format, optimized for high-frequency recording using a non-blocking I/O pipeline. This allows the system to handle multiple concurrent device updates especially during complex training sessions involving several participants without performance degradation. The logs are subsequently processed through a normalization function to eliminate redundancy and ensure chronological consistency. A representative example of the functional log data is presented Table 2.

Table 2. Example of the functional log data

DeviceName	Parameter	OldValue	NewValue	Response Time (ms)	UserID
Ventilator	OxygenFlowRate	4.0	5.0	45	STU001
SyringePump	InfusionRate	2.5	3.0	52	STU002
ECGMonitor	HeartRateThreshold	120	110	38	STU001
Defibrillator	ChargeLevel	0	200	61	STU003

This dataset illustrates the system's ability to record fine-grained device interactions with millisecond precision. Each entry in the table correlates a user-triggered change with the corresponding system response, enabling quantitative analysis of control accuracy and responsiveness. Such precision is critical in healthcare education, where timing and parameter control directly affect the validity of simulated procedures.

From an analytical standpoint, functional logs are essential for assessing both system stability and user comprehension of device behaviour. For instance, repetitive or rapid adjustments to the same parameter may indicate trial-and-error learning, while consistent and minimal corrections reflect conceptual understanding and procedural confidence. By aggregating this data, educators can evaluate how accurately and efficiently students adapt to different medical devices. Furthermore, these logs support automated system diagnostics. Any delay exceeding the predefined response time threshold (e.g., >100 ms) triggers an internal alert, allowing developers to detect and resolve performance bottlenecks. Over multiple sessions, these logs help refine the virtual device models, ensuring their behaviour aligns with real-world medical equipment standards.

Pedagogically, functional logs provide a measurable link between student actions and clinical outcomes within the virtual ICU. They reveal how learners translate theoretical knowledge into procedural accuracy, bridging the gap between abstract instruction and real-time decision-making. In doing so, VRicuLAB not only measures what students do but also how effectively they interact with complex medical systems an essential competence in intensive care nursing training.

Performance Logs

Performance logs constitute the evaluative layer of VRicuLAB's analytical architecture. While interaction and functional logs capture the how of user behaviour and system responses, performance logs quantify the effectiveness and efficiency of those behaviours within the context of immersive training. These logs consolidate metrics that directly relate to learning outcomes such as task completion time, sequence adherence, procedural accuracy, and error frequency forming the empirical foundation for performance assessment in virtual clinical simulations. From a technical standpoint, performance logs are generated by a session monitoring module integrated with Unity's coroutine system. During each simulation, the system continuously monitors task states, marking transitions such as "initialized," "in progress," and "completed." Each transition event triggers a timestamped entry containing fields such as UserID, TaskName, StartTime, EndTime, Duration, ErrorCount, and CompletionStatus. The collected data are stored in the SQL database and mirrored in JSON format for analytics processing. This hybrid storage approach enables interoperability with external machine learning frameworks for predictive modeling and performance clustering. A representative example of the performance log data is shown in Table 3.

Table 3. Example of the performance log data

UserID	TaskName	StartTime	EndTime	Duration (sec)	Error Count	Completion Status
STU001	Ventilator Setup	2025-10-22 09:10:05	2025-10-22 09:13:42	217	1	Completed
STU002	ECG Monitoring	2025-10-22 09:15:13	2025-10-22 09:20:51	338	0	Completed
STU003	IV Line Connection	2025-10-22 09:23:01	2025-10-22 09:30:17	436	3	Completed
STU004	Syringe Pump Adjustment	2025-10-22 09:32:00	2025-10-22 09:36:50	290	2	Incomplete

As observed in Table 3, the performance log structure provides a clear timeline of user actions and outcomes. For instance, while all participants successfully initiated their assigned tasks, differences in duration and error count reveal individual variations in procedural fluency. The system's capability to timestamp each phase with sub-second precision allows educators to evaluate both speed and accuracy two critical indicators of clinical competence.

Analytically, performance logs support multidimensional evaluation. The system automatically calculates mean task duration, standard deviation across sessions, and error ratios per task type, which can be visualized through the educator dashboard. By correlating these metrics with interaction and functional data, the system can infer complex behavioural insights for example, identifying whether prolonged task completion is due to motor inefficiency (frequent object grabs) or conceptual misunderstanding (repeated parameter changes). These integrated analytics transform raw performance data into actionable educational intelligence.

Pedagogically, performance logs enable evidence-based assessment in nursing education. Rather than relying solely on subjective instructor observations, educators can use objective data to evaluate student progress. For instance, a reduction in error count or shorter completion times over consecutive sessions indicates improvement in psychomotor coordination and procedural accuracy. Conversely, recurrent errors in specific task phases may highlight areas where additional instruction or practice is required. Furthermore, these logs can contribute to adaptive learning mechanisms in future iterations of VRicuLAB. By feeding historical performance data into AI-driven feedback systems, the platform could dynamically adjust scenario complexity to match a learner's proficiency level. Such adaptive feedback loops would create a more personalized and effective training experience, aligning with modern competency-based education frameworks in healthcare.

Ultimately, performance logs bridge the gap between immersive experience and quantifiable evaluation. They transform experiential learning into measurable outcomes, ensuring that the VR-based simulation not only engages learners but also validates their clinical readiness through objective, data-driven evidence.

Ultimately, this data infrastructure serves a 'Learning Analytics' function. By capturing granular behavioral data rather than just final outcomes, the system supports 'Formative Assessment.' Educators can trace the learner's decision-making pathway identifying not just what mistake was made, but why it occurred based on the sequence of preceding actions allowing for targeted pedagogical intervention.

LIMITATIONS AND DESIGN ASSUMPTIONS

While VRicuLAB presents a robust framework for intensive care training, several limitations and design assumptions must be acknowledged to contextualize its application.

First, regarding sensory fidelity, the system relies on standard consumer VR controllers (Oculus Touch), which provide vibrotactile feedback but lack force-feedback capabilities. Consequently, users cannot feel the physical weight of a ventilator tube or the resistance of tissue during an IV insertion. This "haptic gap" means that while the system excels at training procedural sequence and cognitive decision-making, it cannot fully replicate the fine kinesthetic dexterity required for delicate manual skills. Therefore, the design assumes that VRicuLAB acts as a cognitive and procedural preparatory tool, not a total replacement for physical manikin-based training where tactile resistance is critical.

Second, the system operates on a "generic ICU model" assumption. Intensive care protocols and equipment interfaces often vary significantly between institutions. To maintain generalizability, VRicuLAB simulates standardized equipment behaviors rather than replicating a specific brand of medical device. Institutions adopting this platform may need to supplement the VR training with brief bridging sessions to address local variations in equipment interfaces.

Third, technical and physiological constraints pose potential barriers. Although the Oculus Quest 2 and 3 are relatively affordable, their deployment requires institutional infrastructure for device management and hygiene. Furthermore, a small subset of users may experience "cybersickness" (motion sickness) during prolonged sessions. To mitigate this, the design assumes simulation sessions should be limited to 20–30 minutes, focusing on intensive, short-burst scenarios rather than prolonged shifts.

Finally, the assessment logic assumes that "action logs" are reliable proxies for clinical competence. While the system accurately records what a student did and when, it infers the intent behind the action based on the context. Future iterations incorporating eye-tracking or voice analysis would be required to capture the full nuance of student reasoning during complex critical incidents.

EXPERT OPINION AND PRE-IMPLEMENTATION EVALUATION

While a comprehensive quantitative study involving large-scale student data is detailed as a future work in last section, a structured expert consultation was conducted during the final development phase of the system to ensure the system's pedagogical alignment and ergonomic stability. A senior academic specialist in intensive care nursing education performed a heuristic evaluation of the VRicuLAB environment. The focus of this review was not on specific task completion, but rather on the overall suitability of the system architecture for academic use and the intuitiveness of the user interface.

Qualitative feedback from this expert review confirmed that the system's design effectively bridges theoretical knowledge with practical application. The expert emphasized that the interaction logic was consistent with clinical standards. However, the evaluation highlighted specific areas for improvement regarding environmental fidelity and spatial perception. The expert recommended enhancing the realism of hospital surface textures and calibrating the dimensions of virtual medical devices to match their real-world counterparts more precisely. Based on these recommendations, specific refinements were implemented: texture maps were upgraded to photorealistic quality, device scales were adjusted to true-to-life measurements, and interface text panels were rescaled to minimize cognitive load. This expert-guided validation confirms that the platform is technically robust, user-friendly, and pedagogically ready for the planned longitudinal curriculum integration.

DISCUSSION AND EDUCATIONAL IMPACT

The development of VRicuLAB represents a significant paradigm shift in nursing education, extending beyond the simple visualization of clinical environments to the engineering of measurable, active learning ecosystems. Generally, the integration of VR in healthcare has been lauded for providing safe practice spaces; however, a recurring critique in the literature is the lack of objective performance evidence. VRicuLAB addresses this critical gap by harmonizing high-fidelity simulation with rigorous data analytics, thereby bridging the divide between "experiential learning" and "academic assessment."

The most distinct educational contribution of this system lies in its ability to transform ephemeral simulation experiences into persistent, actionable data. Traditional simulation assessment often relies on subjective observation or self-reporting. In contrast, VRicuLAB's architecture leverages the recording and analysis of interactions to support formative assessment. By serializing user actions into granular logs, the system provides a deterministic record of decision-making pathways, latency periods, and procedural sequencing. This enables educators to move from generic feedback (e.g., "you were too slow") to evidence-based coaching (e.g., "the data shows a 40-second hesitation in selecting the correct catheter size").

Furthermore, this analytical depth empowers instructional decision-making. The aggregation of performance data allows faculty to diagnose not just individual student errors, but systemic curriculum gaps. For instance, if a significant cohort consistently fails a specific branching logic regarding ventilator alarms, educators can empirically identify the need to revise the theoretical component of the course. Thus, the platform functions as a diagnostic instrument for the curriculum itself.

Beyond assessment, the system contributes to the democratization of advanced clinical training. By decoupling the "Educator" role (web-based analytics) from the "Student" role (VR immersion), VRicuLAB offers a scalable solution for institutions with limited resources. It allows a single instructor to asynchronously review the detailed performance metrics of multiple students, achieving a supervision ratio that is often unattainable in physical laboratories due to space and personnel constraints.

To rigorously validate the pedagogical efficacy of VRicuLAB, future research initiatives are planned to employ a comparative effectiveness study using a quasi-experimental design. In this proposed framework, the learner cohort will be stratified into two distinct groups: an experimental group, which will engage with the immersive VRicuLAB scenarios, and a control group, which will undergo traditional laboratory instruction (e.g., low-fidelity manikins or standard video demonstrations). Beyond objective performance metrics, the research design will integrate psychometric survey instruments to evaluate the subjective dimensions of the learning experience. Specifically, these instruments will assess critical educational variables such as intrinsic motivation, simulation satisfaction, and self-efficacy. By juxtaposing the engagement levels of the VR-trained group against those of the traditional group, future studies aim to empirically demonstrate how immersive environments can reduce learner attrition and foster a deeper commitment to mastering complex clinical protocols.

In conclusion, VRicuLAB demonstrates that the efficacy of immersive learning depends not merely on graphical realism, but on the tight coupling of technical fidelity with pedagogical accountability. The system successfully addresses the literature's call for holistic, multi-user, and analytically rigorous training environments. Looking forward, the development roadmap focuses on integrating Artificial Intelligence (AI) to close the feedback loop. Future iterations aim to employ machine learning algorithms to analyze log patterns in real-time, providing students with adaptive, "in-simulation" scaffolding without immediate instructor intervention. Ultimately, by fusing engineering precision with nursing pedagogy, VRicuLAB establishes a sustainable, data-driven blueprint for the future of healthcare education.

REFERENCES

Adil, M., Ali, A., Hakim, S. B., Farouk, A., Abulkasim, H., Khan, M. K., & Song, H. (2026). Security and Privacy Challenges in Healthcare Internet of Things Applications in the Era of Agentic AI. *Authorea Preprints*.

Angelucci, A., Greco, M., Cecconi, M., & Aliverti, A. (2025). Wearable devices for patient monitoring in the intensive care unit. *Intensive Care Medicine Experimental, 13*(1), 26. PMID: 40016479

Berezi, I. U. (2025). Virtual Learning Environment: Redefining Higher Educational Delivery for Efficiency and Accessibility. International Journal of Educational Management, Rivers State University., 1(1), 451-467.

Brisson, C. M. (2024). The ergonomic classroom: Best practices for fostering inclusive learning environments. In *Inclusiveness Beyond the (Non) binary in Romance Languages* (pp. 105–119). Routledge.

Britannica. (2025). Virtual Reality. Encyclopaedia Britannica. https://www.britannica.com/technology/virtual-reality

Chang, W., Lin, C. C., Crilly, J., Lee, H. L., Chen, L. C., & Han, C. Y. (2025). Virtual Reality Simulation for Undergraduate Nursing Students for Care of Patients With Infectious Diseases: Mixed Methods Study. *JMIR Medical Education, 11*, e64780. PMID: 39933166

Chen, F.-Q., Leng, Y.-F., Ge, J.-F., Wang, D.-W., Li, C., Chen, B., & Sun, Z.-L. (2020). Effectiveness of virtual reality in nursing education: Meta-analysis. *Journal of Medical Internet Research, 22*(9), e18290. DOI: 10.2196/18290 PMID: 32930664

Cho, M.-K., & Kim, M. Y. (2024). Enhancing nursing competency through virtual reality simulation among nursing students: A systematic review and meta-analysis. *Frontiers in Medicine, 11*, 1351300. DOI: 10.3389/fmed.2024.1351300 PMID: 38774395

Daneshfar, M., & Moonaghi, H. K. (2025). The impact of clinical simulation on bridging the theory–practice gap in nursing education: A systematic review. *BMC Medical Education, 25*(1), 1216. PMID: 40877870

Efendi, D., Apriliyasari, R. W., Prihartami Massie, J. G. E., Wong, C. L., Natalia, R., Utomo, B., & Chen, K. H. (2023). The effect of virtual reality on cognitive, affective, and psychomotor outcomes in nursing staffs: Systematic review and meta-analysis. *BMC Nursing, 22*(1), 170. PMID: 37202768

Elendu, C., Amaechi, D. C., Okatta, A. U., Amaechi, E. C., Elendu, T. C., Ezeh, C. P., & Elendu, I. D. (2024). The impact of simulation-based training in medical education. *Revista de Medicina (São Paulo), 103*(27), e38813. PMID: 38968472

Ersoy, M., Kumral, C. D., Çolak, R., Armağan, H., & Yiğit, T. (2022). Development of a server-based integrated virtual laboratory for digital electronics. *Computer Applications in Engineering Education, 30*(5), 1307–1320.

Gavilanes, J. S. (2024). Diversity, equity and inclusion in simulation-based education: experiences from multiple academic health centers (Doctoral dissertation, Portland State University).

Gentili, A., Failla, G., Melnyk, A., Puleo, V., Tanna, G. L. D., Ricciardi, W., & Cascini, F. (2022). The cost-effectiveness of digital health interventions: A systematic review of the literature. *Frontiers in Public Health, 10*, 787135. PMID: 36033812

Huang, W., Roscoe, R. D., Johnson-Glenberg, M. C., & Craig, S. D. (2021). Motivation, engagement, and performance across multiple virtual reality sessions and levels of immersion. *Journal of Computer Assisted Learning, 37*(3), 745–758.

Javvaji, C. K., Reddy, H., Vagha, J. D., Taksande, A., Kommareddy, A., & Reddy, N. S. (2024). Immersive innovations: Exploring the diverse applications of virtual reality (VR) in healthcare. *Cureus, 16*(3), e56137. PMID: 38618363

Khalili, A. (2021). An XML-based approach for geo-semantic data exchange from BIM to VR applications. *Automation in Construction, 121*, 103425.

Khundam, C., Vorachart, V., Preeyawongsakul, P., Hosap, W., & Noël, F. (2021). A comparative study of interaction time and usability of using controllers and hand tracking in virtual reality training. In Informatics (Vol. 8, No. 3, p. 60). MDPI.

Ki, S., & Ryu, J. (2024). The Effects of Self-Regulation Strategies on Cognitive Load, Self-Efficacy, and Learning Satisfaction in VR Nursing Practical Training. In Society for Information Technology & Teacher Education International Conference (pp. 493-497). Association for the Advancement of Computing in Education (AACE).

Kim, D. R., & Yoo, J. (2025). The effectiveness of 360-degree virtual reality-based mechanical ventilation nursing education for ICU nurses. In Healthcare (Vol. 13, No. 14, p. 1639). MDPI.

Landwehr, K. (2024). Environmental perception: An ecological perspective. In *Environmental perspectives* (pp. 18–38). Routledge.

Lee, I. J., Liao, P. H., & Hung, H. W. (2025). Utilizing VR technology with remote medical guidance for distant collaborative emergency medical training in advanced cardiac life support. *Interactive Learning Environments*, •••, 1–18.

Liao, K. C., Ajjawi, R., Peng, C. H., Jenq, C. C., & Monrouxe, L. V. (2023). Striving to thrive or striving to survive: Professional identity constructions of medical trainees in clinical assessment activities. *Medical Education*, *57*(11), 1102–1116. PMID: 37394612

Lok, B., Ferdig, R. E., Raij, A., Johnsen, K., Dickerson, R., Coutts, J., & Lind, D. S. (2006). Applying virtual reality in medical communication education: Current findings and potential teaching and learning benefits of immersive virtual patients. *Virtual Reality (Waltham Cross)*, *10*(3), 185–195.

Ma, X., Xie, Y., Yang, X., Wang, H., Li, Z., & Lu, J. (2024). Teacher-student interaction modes in smart classroom based on lag sequential analysis. *Education and Information Technologies*, *29*(12), 15087–15111.

Martin, B., Kaminski-Ozturk, N., Smiley, R., Spector, N., Silvestre, J., Bowles, W., & Alexander, M. (2023). Assessing the impact of the COVID-19 pandemic on nursing education: A national study of prelicensure RN programs. *Journal of Nursing Regulation*, *14*(1), S1–S67. PMID: 37012978

Obeid, M. F., Ewais, A., & Asia, M. R. (2025). NursingXR: Advancing Nursing Education Through Virtual Reality-Based Training. *Applied Sciences (Basel, Switzerland)*, *15*(6), 2949.

Pei, B., Cheng, Y., Ambrose, A., Dziadula, E., Xing, W., & Lu, J. (2024). LearningViz: A dashboard for visualizing, analyzing and closing learning performance gaps—a case study approach. *Smart Learning Environments*, *11*(1), 56.

Petersen, G. B., Petkakis, G., & Makransky, G. (2022). A study of how immersion and interactivity drive VR learning. *Computers & Education*, *179*, 104429.

Porcino, T., Trevisan, D., & Clua, E. (2020). Minimizing cybersickness in head-mounted display systems: causes and strategies review. In 2020 22nd symposium on virtual and augmented reality (SVR) (pp. 154-163). IEEE.

Ryan, G. V., Callaghan, S., Rafferty, A., Higgins, M. F., Mangina, E., & McAuliffe, F. (2022). Learning outcomes of immersive technologies in health care student education: Systematic review of the literature. *Journal of Medical Internet Research*, *24*(2), e30082. PMID: 35103607

Saab, M. M., McCarthy, M., O'Mahony, B., Cooke, E., Hegarty, J., Murphy, D., & Noonan, B. (2023). Virtual reality simulation in nursing and midwifery education: a usability study. CIN: Computers, Informatics. *Nursing*, *41*(10), 815–824. PMID: 36749836

Somerville, S., Howden, S., Ker, J., & Schofield, S. (2024). Exploring accessible, inclusive and sustainable simulation-based education in remote and rural communities: A realist review. *International Journal of Healthcare Simulation : Advances in Theory and Practice*, •••, 1–14.

Souza, L. L. (2025). Virtual reality in critical care nursing education: First experiences in low-cost ICU simulation environments. *Education Sciences*, *15*(9), 1258. DOI: 10.3390/educsci15091258

Wu, Y. (2025). The simulation paradox: Does perfecting virtual anatomy risk imperfecting professional empathy? *Anatomical Sciences Education*, *18*(10), 1147–1154. PMID: 40588781

Compilation of References

Abarca-Reyes, J. F. (2020). Evolución histórica de las tecnologías educativas en México. *Revista Tecnológica-Educativa Docentes 2.0, 9*(2), 254–263. https://doi.org/DOI: 10.37843/rted.v9i2.171

Acharya, M., & Mohbey, K. K. (2024). Virtual environment role in higher education students learning enhancement with intellectual disabilities. In *Applied assistive technologies and informatics for students with disabilities* (pp. 35–57). Springer Nature Singapore.

Adeleye, O. O., Eden, C. A., & Adeniyi, I. S. (2024). Innovative teaching methodologies in the era of artificial intelligence: A review of inclusive educational practices. *World Journal of Advanced Engineering Technology and Sciences, 11*(2), 069-079.

Adera, N. (2025). Innovative learning spaces and blended learning: Quest for 21st century competency teaching and learning approaches. *Creating Dynamic Space in Higher Education: Modern Shifts in Policy, Competencies, and Governance*, 139-174.

Ader, L. G. M., Crowley, K., Kuhn, S., Caraffini, F., Altındağ, T., & Colreavy-Donnelly, S. (2023, September). Extended Reality, Augmented Users, and Design Implications for Virtual Learning Environments. In *2023 IEEE International Symposium on Technology and Society (ISTAS)* (pp. 1-8). IEEE.

Adeshina, A. E. (2024). From theory to practice: A framework for inclusive technology integration in education. *International Journal of Instructional Technology and Educational Studies, 5*(1), 1–6. DOI: 10.21608/ihites.2024.380764

Adetunla, A., Akinlabi, E., Jen, T. C., Okokpujie, I. P., & Ajibade, S. S. (2024, April). A review on the Challenges and Prospects in Harnessing Virtual Reality in Education. In *2024 International Conference on Science, Engineering and Business for Driving Sustainable Development Goals (SEB4SDG)* (pp. 1-5). IEEE.

Adil, M., Ali, A., Hakim, S. B., Farouk, A., Abulkasim, H., Khan, M. K., & Song, H. (2026). Security and Privacy Challenges in Healthcare Internet of Things Applications in the Era of Agentic AI. *Authorea Preprints*.

Adl-Amini, K., Meßner, M. T., & Hardy, I. (2025). A simulation game for placement decision-making: Fostering reflection and belief change about inclusion in teacher education. *International Journal of Inclusive Education*, *29*(7), 1197–1213.

Afonso, A., Morgado, L., Noguera, I., Sepúlveda-Parrini, P., Hernandez-Leo, D., Alkhasawneh, S. N., & Carvalho, I. C. (2025). Flexible learning by design: Enhancing faculty digital competence and engagement through the FLeD Project. *Education Sciences*, *15*(7), 934.

Agbabiaka, H. I., Olatunji, S. A., Saleh, M., Sodangi, A. B., & Muhammad, H. (2024). Students with disabilities (SWDs) and facilities accessibility in a northern Nigerian public university: Dismantling exclusion in achieving SDG4. *Facilities*, *42*(11/12), 928–946.

Aghaziarati, A., Nejatifar, S., & Abedi, A. (2023). Artificial intelligence in education: Investigating teacher attitudes. *AI and Tech in Behavioral and Social Sciences*, *1*(1), 35–42. DOI: 10.61838/kman.aitech.1.1.6

Aguilera, D., & Vílchez-González, J. M. (2024). ¿De qué hablamos cuando hablamos de educación STEAM? Una revisión de experiencias educativas. *Revista Fuentes*, *26*(2), 211–224. DOI: 10.12795/revistafuentes.2024.15412

Ahmad, I., Sharma, S., Singh, R., Gehlot, A., Gupta, L. R., Thakur, A. K., & Twala, B. (2024). Inclusive learning using industry 4.0 technologies: Addressing student diversity in modern education. *Cogent Education*, *11*(1), 2330235.

Ahmad, I., Sharma, S., Singh, R., Gehlot, A., Gupta, L. R., Thakur, A. K., & Twala, B. (2024). Inclusive learning using Industry 4.0 technologies: Addressing student diversity in modern education. *Cogent Education*, *11*(1), 2330235. DOI: 10.1080/2331186X.2024.2330235

Ahuja, N. J., Dutt, S., Choudhary, S. L., & Kumar, M. (2025). Intelligent tutoring system in education for disabled learners using human–computer interaction and augmented reality. *International Journal of Human-Computer Interaction*, *41*(3), 1804–1816.

Ai, Y., Hu, Y., & Zhao, W. (2025). Interactive learning: Harnessing technology to alleviate foreign language anxiety in foreign literature education. *Interactive Learning Environments*, *33*(3), 2440–2459.

Akinrinola, O., Okoye, C. C., Ofodile, O. C., & Ugochukwu, C. E. (2024). Navigating and reviewing ethical dilemmas in AI development: Strategies for transparency, fairness, and accountability. *GSC Advanced Research and Reviews*, *18*(3), 50–58. DOI: 10.30574/gscarr.2024.18.3.0088

Akintayo, O. T., Eden, C. A., Ayeni, O. O., & Onyebuchi, N. C. (2024). Inclusive curriculum design: Meeting the diverse needs of students for social improvement. *International Journal of Applied Research in Social Sciences*, *6*(5), 770–784.

Al Balushi, J. S. G., Al Jabri, M. I. A., Palarimath, S., Maran, P., Thenmozhi, K., & Balakumar, C. (2024). Incorporating artificial intelligence powered immersive realities to improve learning using virtual reality and augmented reality technology. In *Proceedings of the 3rd International Conference on Applied Artificial Intelligence and Computing* (pp. 760–765). IEEE. DOI: 10.1109/ICAAIC60222.2024.10574231

AlAli, R., & Wardat, Y. (2024). Opportunities and challenges of integrating generative artificial intelligence in education. *International Journal of Religion*, *5*(7), 784–793.

Alam, A. (2023a). Media multitasking with M-learning technology in real-time classroom learning: Analysing the dynamics in formal educational settings for the future of E-learning in India. In *2023 2nd International Conference on Smart Technologies and Systems for Next Generation Computing (ICSTSN)* (pp. 1-6). IEEE.

Alam, A. (2023b). The secret sauce of student success: Cracking the code by navigating the path to personalized learning with educational data mining. In *2023 2nd International Conference on Smart Technologies and Systems for Next Generation Computing (ICSTSN)* (pp. 1-8). IEEE.

Alam, A., & Mohanty, A. (2022). Facial analytics or virtual avatars: Competencies and design considerations for student-teacher interaction in AI-powered online education for effective classroom engagement. In International conference on communication, networks and computing (pp. 252–265). Springer. https://doi.org/DOI: 10.1007/978-3-031-43145-6_21

Alam, A., & Mohanty, A. (2022, December). Facial analytics or virtual avatars: competencies and design considerations for student-teacher interaction in AI-powered online education for effective classroom engagement. In *International Conference on Communication, Networks and Computing* (pp. 252-265). Cham: Springer Nature Switzerland.

Alam, A., & Mohanty, A. (2023, January). Learning on the move: a pedagogical framework for state-of-the-art mobile learning. In *International Conference on Data Management, Analytics & Innovation* (pp. 735-748). Singapore: Springer Nature Singapore.

Alam, A. (2022). Impact of university's human resources practices on professors' occupational performance: empirical evidence from India's higher education sector. In *Inclusive businesses in developing economies: Converging people, profit, and corporate citizenship* (pp. 107–131). Springer International Publishing.

Alam, A. (2023c). Intelligence unleashed: An argument for AI-enabled learning ecologies with real world examples of today and a peek into the future. In *International Conference on Innovations in Computer Science, Electronics & Electrical Engineering*-2022 (Vol. 2717, No. 1, p. 030001). AIP Publishing LLC.

Alam, A., & Mohanty, A. (2023). Educational technology: Exploring the convergence of technology and pedagogy through mobility, interactivity, AI, and learning tools. *Cogent Engineering*, *10*(2), 2283282. DOI: 10.1080/23311916.2023.2283282

Alam, A., & Mohanty, A. (2024). Integrated constructive robotics in education (ICRE) model: A paradigmatic framework for transformative learning in educational ecosystem. *Cogent Education*, *11*(1), 2324487.

Alam, A., & Mohanty, A. (2024). Integrated constructive robotics in education (ICRE) model: A paradigmatic framework for transformative learning. *Cogent Education*, *11*(1), 2324487. DOI: 10.1080/2331186X.2024.2324487

AlArabi, K., Alsalhi, N. R., Almarashdi, H. S., Zakarneh, B., & Annamalai, N. (2023). The Role of Computer Simulations (CSs) and artificial intelligence on student learning: Moderating the impact of the learning environment. [Social Space]. *Przestrzeń Społeczna*, *23*(3), 103–122.

Alawneh, Y. J. J., Sleema, H., Salman, F. N., Alshammat, M. F., & Oteer, R. S., & ALrashidi, N. K. N. (2024, April). Adaptive Learning Systems: Revolutionizing Higher Education through AI-Driven Curricula. In 2024 International Conference on Knowledge Engineering and Communication Systems (ICKECS) (Vol. 1, pp. 1-5). IEEE.

Alemán-Saravia, A. C., Deroncele-Acosta, A., & Robles-Mori, H. (2023). Traducción, adaptación cultural y validación del cuestionario TPACK-21 en docentes en servicio. *Revista de Ciencias Sociales*, *XXIX*(3), 453–469.

Alfares, N. (2021). The effect of problem-based learning on students' problem-solving self-efficacy through Blackboard system in higher education. *International Journal of Education and Practice*, *9*(1), 185–200.

AlGerafi, M. A., Zhou, Y., Oubibi, M., & Wijaya, T. T. (2023). Unlocking the potential: A comprehensive evaluation of augmented reality and virtual reality in education. *Electronics (Basel)*, *12*(18), 3953. DOI: 10.3390/electronics12183953

Alhazzaa, K., & Yan, W. (2025). Immersive technologies in education: Exploring user experience and engagement in building energy simulations through AR and VR. *Computers & Education: X Reality*, 6, 100097. https://doi.org/DOI: 10.1016/j.cexr.2025.100097

Al-Kfairy, M., Alzaabi, M., Snoh, B., Almarzooqi, H., & Alnaqbi, W. (2024, May). Metaverse-based classroom: the good and the bad. In *2024 IEEE Global Engineering Education Conference (EDUCON)* (pp. 1-7). IEEE.

Allen, L. K., & Kendeou, P. (2024). ED-AI Lit: An interdisciplinary framework for AI literacy in education. *Policy Insights from the Behavioral and Brain Sciences*, *11*(1), 3–10.

Allison, J., Hwang, G. J., Mayer, R. E., Pellas, N., Karnalim, O., de Freitas, S., & Sanusi, I. (2025). From generative AI to extended reality: Multidisciplinary perspectives on the challenges, opportunities, and future of educational computing. *Journal of Educational Computing Research*, *63*(6), 1327–1363.

Almazroui, K. M. (2023). Project-based learning for 21st-century skills: An overview and case study of moral education in the UAE. *Social Studies*, *114*(3), 125–136.

Almuaqel, I. A. (2023). Virtual reality and inclusive learning of individuals with intellectual and developmental disabilities: A review of findings and the path ahead. *IEEE Transactions on Engineering Management*, *71*, 13049–13065.

Almuaqel, I. A. (2023). Virtual reality and inclusive learning of individuals with intellectual and developmental disabilities: A review of findings and the path ahead. *IEEE Transactions on Learning Technologies*, *16*(3), 365–377.

Almusaed, A., Almssad, A., Yitmen, I., & Homod, R. Z. (2023). Enhancing student engagement: Harnessing 'AIED''s power in hybrid education—A review analysis. *Education Sciences*, *13*(7), 632. Advance online publication. DOI: 10.3390/educsci13070632

Aloizou, V., Linardatou, S., Boloudakis, M., & Retalis, S. (2025). Integrating a movement-based learning platform as core curriculum tool in kindergarten classrooms. *British Journal of Educational Technology*, *56*(1), 339–365.

Alqithami, S., Alzahrani, M., Alzahrani, A., & Mostafa, A. (2019). Modeling an augmented reality game environment to enhance behavior of ADHD patients. In *Brain Informatics: 12th International Conference, BI 2019, Haikou, China, December 13–15, 2019* [Springer International Publishing.]. *Proceedings*, *12*, 179–188.

Alvarado, Y., Guerrero, R., & Serón, F. (2023). Inclusive learning through immersive virtual reality and semantic embodied conversational agent: A case study in children with autism. *Journal of Computer Science and Technology, 23*(2), e09–e09.

Al-Zahrani, A. M., & Alasmari, T. M. (2024). Exploring the impact of artificial intelligence on higher education: The dynamics of ethical, social, and educational implications. *Humanities & Social Sciences Communications, 11*, 03432. Advance online publication. DOI: 10.1057/s41599-024-03432-4

Amaya, A., Woolf, C., Devane, N., Galliers, J., Talbot, R., Wilson, S., & Marshall, J. (2018). Receiving aphasia intervention in a virtual environment: The participants' perspective. *Aphasiology, 32*(5), 538–558.

Anderson, T., & Shattuck, J. (2012). Design-based research: A decade of progress in education research? *Educational Researcher, 41*(1), 16–25.

Andrin, G., Kilag, O. K., Groenewald, E., Benitez, J., Dagala, F., & Ubay, R. (2024). Borderless learning environments: Impacts on educational management strategies. [IMJRISE]. *International Multidisciplinary Journal of Research for Innovation, Sustainability, and Excellence, 1*(2), 43–49. DOI: 10.5281/zenodo.11138470

Andujar, A., & Nadif, F. Z. (2022). Evaluating an inclusive blended learning environment in EFL: A flipped approach. *Computer Assisted Language Learning, 35*(5–6), 1138–1167.

Angelucci, A., Greco, M., Cecconi, M., & Aliverti, A. (2025). Wearable devices for patient monitoring in the intensive care unit. *Intensive Care Medicine Experimental, 13*(1), 26. PMID: 40016479

Anwar, M. S., Yang, J., Frnda, J., Choi, A., Baghaei, N., & Ali, M. (2025). Metaverse and XR for cultural heritage education: Applications, standards, architecture, and technological insights for enhanced immersive experience. *Virtual Reality (Waltham Cross), 29*(2), 51.

Ares Ferreirós, M., Alfonso Gil, S., & Deaño, M. (2021). Effectiveness of the Planning Facilitation program for the prevention of reading comprehension difficulties.

Arévalo Suárez, Diana Liyiny, Quintero Antolínez, Leonardo Alfredo, M. Vásquez (2019). Understanding Stories. Education and Science

Arias Villalba, W. O., & Mejía Carrillo, M. de J., Carranza Basantes, S. F., & Alvarado Jaya, H. G. (2024). Educación STEAM (ciencia, tecnología, ingeniería, artes y matemáticas) en la educación básica: Integración curricular y efectividad, una revisión desde la literatura. *Polo del Conocimiento, 9*(2), 2026–2045. DOI: 10.23857/pc.v9i2.6651

Arrigui Torres, E., & Andrés Mosquera, J. (2022). Aportes de la educación STEAM a la enseñanza de las ciencias: Una revisión documental entre 2018 y 2021. *Revista Latinoamericana de Educación Científica, Crítica y Emancipadora (LadECiN), 1*(1), 49–61. https://revistaladecin.com/index.php/LadECiN/article/view/40

Arslan, F., Haydar, B., & Ullah, F. (2024). *Bridging theory and practice: AI applications in learning and teaching in Pakistan's education system.* ResearchGate., DOI: 10.3847/rg.2024.383206313

Arsyad, M., Mujahiddin, M., & Syakhrani, A. W. (2024). The efficiency of using visual learning media in improving science concept understanding. *Indonesian Journal of Education, 4*(3), 775–787. DOI: 10.30596/ijoe.v4i3.15341

Arteaga-Alcívar, Y., Guaña-Moya, J., Begnini-Domínguez, L., Cabrera-Córdova, M. F., Sánchez-Cali, F., & Moya-Carrera, Y. (2022). Integración de la tecnología con la educación. *RISTI – Revista Ibérica de Sistemas e Tecnologias de Informação, E54*(11), 182–193. https://www.researchgate.net/publication/378635135_Integracion_de_la_tecnologia_con_la_educacion

Asatryan, S., Svajyan, A., & Antonyan, S. (2023). Augmented reality in education for children with special needs. *Armenian Journal of Special Education, 7*(1), 56–62. DOI: 10.24234/se.v6i1.304

Asif, M., Mondal, A., Soumil, S., Das, A., & Sahoo, P. (2024). Augmented reality and virtual reality in education: A transformative journey. In *Advances in Computational Solutions* (pp. 185–198). Swami Vivekananda University Press.

Asitah, N., Murni, A. W., Lestari, W. M., Aini, N., & Kartikasari, H. L. (2024, September). Virtual Reality in Inclusive Basic Education: A Systematic Review of Roles and Application for Future Education Directions. In *2024 International Conference on ICT for Smart Society (ICISS)* (pp. 1-6). IEEE.

Asrifan, A., & Aini, N. (2025). The future of education in the metaverse. In *Harnessing chatbots for effective language teaching* (pp. 75–116). IGI Global., DOI: 10.4018/979-8-3693-2938-2.ch004

Ávila-Negrinis, L., Daza-Cuello, D. M., & González-Roys, G. A. (2021). *The Magical World of Children's Stories: A Teaching Strategy for Developing Inferential Reading Comprehension.* UNIMAR Journal.

Avila-Pesantez, D. F., Vaca-Cardenas, L. A., Delgadillo Avila, R., Padilla Padilla, N., & Rivera, L. A. (2018, August). Design of an augmented reality serious game for children with dyscalculia: a case study. In *International Conference on Technology Trends* (pp. 165-175). Cham: Springer International Publishing.

Ayeni, O. O., Al Hamad, N. M., Chisom, O. N., Osawaru, B., & Adewusi, O. E. (2024). AI in education: A review of personalized learning and educational technology. *GSC Advanced Research and Reviews, 18*(2), 261–271.

Babu, C. V. S., & Vinutha, S. (2024). Impact of AR/VR in the Learning Process of Children with Dyslexia. In V. A. Devi, W. Singh, & Y. Kumar (Eds.), *Augmented reality and virtual reality in special education* (pp. 161–188). Scrivener Publishing LLC.

Baglieri, S. (2022). *Disability studies and the inclusive classroom: Critical practices for embracing diversity in education* (3rd ed.). Routledge., DOI: 10.4324/9781003138808

Bali, C., & Zsido, A. N. (2024). Optimizing Learning Outcomes of Educational Applications Enhanced with Multimedia and Interactive Features: A Review. *Education, Development and Intervention: Toward Participatory and Integrated Solutions*, 167-184.

Balladares-Burgos, J., & Valverde-Berrocoso, J. (2022). El modelo tecnopedagógico TPACK y su incidencia en la formación docente: Una revisión de la literatura. *Revista Caribeña de Investigación Educativa, 6*(1), 63–72. DOI: 10.32541/recie.2022.v6i1.pp63-72

Banik, B. G., & Gullapelly, A. (2025). AI-powered gamification and interactive learning tools for enhancing student engagement. In *Driving quality education through AI and data science* (p. 28). IGI Global., DOI: 10.4018/979-8-3693-8292-9.ch013

Bañuelos Márquez, A. M. (2024). Modelos de evaluación de la calidad en programas educativos a distancia. In *CIVINEDU 2024: Conference proceedings* (pp. 48–52). REDINE. https://doi.org/DOI: 10.58909/adc24377766

Baragash, R., Al-samarrie, H., Azahrai, A., & Alfarraj, O. (2020). Augmented reality in special education: A meta-analysis of single-subject design studies. *European Journal of Special Needs Education, 35*(3), 382–397. DOI: 10.1080/08856257.2019.1703548

Barana, A., Marchisio, M., & Sacchet, M. (2021). Interactive feedback for learning mathematics in a digital learning environment. *Education Sciences, 11*(6), 279.

Barbu, M., Iordache, D. D., Petre, I., Barbu, D. C., & Băjenaru, L. (2025). Framework Design for Reinforcing the Potential of XR Technologies in Transforming Inclusive Education. *Applied Sciences (Basel, Switzerland), 15*(3), 1484.

Barley, N., & Mikhailova, I. (2020). Real-time formative assessment in online language classroom. In *ICERI2020 Proceedings* (pp. 4671–4678). IATED.

Başaran, B. (2020). Examining preservice teachers' TPACK-21 efficacies with clustering analysis in terms of certain variables. *Malaysian Online Journal of Educational Technology*, *8*(3), 84–99. DOI: 10.17220/mojet.2020.03.005

Basri, W. S. (2024). Effectiveness of AI-powered tutoring systems in enhancing learning outcomes. *Eurasian Journal of Educational Research*, *110*, 1–15. DOI: 10.14689/ejer.2024.110.003

Baxter, G., & Hainey, T. (2024). Using immersive technologies to enhance the student learning experience. *Interactive Technology and Smart Education*, *21*(3), 403–425.

Bearman, M., Ryan, J., & Ajjawi, R. (2023). Discourses of artificial intelligence in higher education: A critical literature review. *Higher Education*, *86*, 369–385. DOI: 10.1007/s10734-022-00937-2

Bekteshi, L. (2025). Education in the Era of AI and Immersive Technologies: A Systematic Review. *Journal of Research in Engineering and Computer Sciences*, *3*(1), 01-14.

Belda-Medina, J. (2024). Inclusive education through digital comic creation in higher learning environments. *Social Sciences*, *13*(5), 272.

Belhaj, R., Ait Ali, N., & Browlahrouf, I. (2025). Gamified Hybrid Learning for Neurodiverse Students: Designing Universally Accessible Instructional Models. *Journal Neosantara Hybrid Learning*, *3*(1), 38–46.

Bellini, S., Peters, J. K., Benner, L., & Hopf, A. (2007). A meta-analysis of school-based social skills interventions for children with autism spectrum disorders. *Remedial and Special Education*, *28*(3), 153–162.

Benabid, A., El Imadi, I., & Alqatawneh, K. (2025). Encouraging quality: Approaches for increasing student achievement in higher education. In *Emerging technologies transforming higher education* (pp. 145–178). IGI Global., DOI: 10.4018/979-8-3693-1181-4.ch008

Berezi, I. U. (2025). Virtual Learning Environment: Redefining Higher Educational Delivery for Efficiency and Accessibility. *International Journal of Educational Management, Rivers State University.*, *1*(1), 451-467.

Berrezueta-Guzman, S., & Wagner, S. (2025). *Immersive multiplayer VR: Unreal Engine's strengths, limitations, and future prospects*. IEEE., DOI: 10.1109/ACCESS.2025.3457712

Berson, I. R., & Berson, M. J. (2024). AI in K-12 social studies education: A critical examination of ethical and practical challenges. In Artificial intelligence in education conference proceedings (pp. 101–112). Springer. https://doi.org/DOI: 10.1007/978-3-031-64315-6_8

Bhambri, P., & Kant, S. (2025a, February 1-2). A taxonomy of bias in machine learning: Classification, sources, and implications for ethical AI [Paper presentation]. Lincoln-SPAST Global Sustainability Programme (SGS-24), 1st International Conference of L-GPR Program, Lincoln University College, Malaysia. SPAST Proceedings, 1(2). https://spast.org/techrep/article/view/5387/724

Bhambri, P., & Kant, S. (2025b, April 26-27). Ethical AI systems: A comprehensive framework for bias mitigation and fairness in machine learning [Paper presentation]. Lincoln-SPAST Global Sustainability Programme (SGS-24), 2nd International Conference of L-GPR Program, Lincoln University College, Malaysia. SPAST Proceedings, 1(2). https://spast.org/techrep/article/view/5385/698

Bhambri, P., & Khang, A. (2024a). The human-machine nexus with art-making generative AIs. In Hai-Jew, S. (Ed.), *Making art with generative AI tools* (pp. 73–85). IGI Global., DOI: 10.4018/979-8-3693-1950-5.ch004

Bhambri, P., & Khang, A. (2024b). Machine learning advancements in E-health: Transforming digital healthcare. In *Medical robotics and AI-assisted diagnostics for a high-tech healthcare industry* (pp. 174–194). IGI Global., DOI: 10.4018/979-8-3693-2105-8.ch012

Bhambri, P., & Khang, A. (2025). Edge computing for enhancing efficiency and sustainability in green transportation systems. In Khang, A. (Ed.), *Driving green transportation system through artificial intelligence and automation* (pp. 43–65). Springer., DOI: 10.1007/978-3-031-72617-0_3

Bhambri, P., & Rani, S. (2025). Advancements in educational technology: Navigating the landscape of user experience in Web 3.0. In Pelet, J.-É. (Ed.), *Architecting the digital future: Platforms, design, and application* (pp. 365–396). IGI Global., DOI: 10.4018/979-8-3693-2973-3.ch014

Bhattacharya, D. (2025). Teachers' competencies in effective technology-enabled assessment for holistic development of students. *Indian Journal of Educational Technology*, *7*(1), 83–104. https://journals.ncert.gov.in/IJET/article/view/843

Bhowmik, A. K. (2024). Virtual and augmented reality: Human sensory–perceptual requirements. *Journal of the Society for Information Display*, *32*(8), 605–646. DOI: 10.1002/jsid.1351

Bilderback, S. L., & Thompson, C. B. (2025). Developing global leadership competence: Redefining higher education for interconnected economies. *Higher Education. Skills and Work-Based Learning*, *15*(4), 724–739. DOI: 10.1108/heswbl-10-2024-0301

Binhammad, M. H. Y., Othman, A., Abuljadayel, L., Al Mheiri, H., Alkaabi, M., & Almarri, M. (2024). Investigating how generative AI can create personalized learning materials tailored to individual student needs. *Creative Education*, *15*, 1499–1523. DOI: 10.4236/ce.2024.157091

Binytska, K. M., Bilyakovska, O. O., Yankovych, O. I., Greskova, V. V., & Ocheretna, I. P. (2023). Exploring the potential of immersive technologies in university education worldwide.

Blanco Iturralde, J. A., Rocha Cajas, E. P., Criollo Llumiquinga, L. J., Rocha Cajas, J. A., & Rocha Cajas, M. E. (2024). La necesidad de capacitación docente para una implementación efectiva de la tecnología educativa en el aula. *Ciencia Latina*, *8*(2), 2347–2367. DOI: 10.37811/cl_rcm.v8i2.10676

Blasco-Serrano, A. C., González, I. B., & Coma-Roselló, T. (2022). Incorporation of ICT into preservice teacher training using the flipped classroom to enhance inclusive education. *Edutec, 79*. *Article*, *10*, 21556.

Boowuo, H., & Dittman, K. (2025). Immersive technologies for special students in higher education. *Journal of Higher Education Theory and Practice*, *25*(2), 43–61. DOI: 10.33423/jhetp.v25i2.7634

Borah, A. R., Nischith, T. N., & Gupta, S. (2024, January). Improved learning based on GenAI. In *2024 2nd International Conference on Intelligent Data Communication Technologies and Internet of Things (IDCIoT)* (pp. 1527-1532). IEEE.

Bouck, E. C. (2016). A national snapshot of assistive technology for students with disabilities. *Journal of Special Education Technology*, *31*(1), 4–13. DOI: 10.1177/0162643416633330

Bourguet, M. L., & Omfalos, E. (2024). Work-in-Progress—Student's Co-creation of Collaborative Learning Spaces on the Metaverse. Immersive Learning Research-Academic, 217-233.

Bowen, A. E. J., Palmer, L. R. J., Perry, R. C., Thomas, M. S., Tolmie, A., Borst, G., & Van Herwegen, J. (2024). Evaluating what works in the classroom: Best practice and future opportunities. *Mind, Brain and Education : the Official Journal of the International Mind, Brain, and Education Society*, *18*(4), 474–484. DOI: 10.1111/mbe.12430

Bray, A., Devitt, A., Banks, J., Sanchez Fuentes, S., Sandoval, M., Riviou, K., & Terrenzio, S. (2024). What next for universal design for learning? *British Journal of Educational Technology*, *55*(1), 113–138. DOI: 10.1111/bjet.13347

Bredow, C. A., Roehling, P. V., Knorp, A. J., & Sweet, A. M. (2021). To flip or not to flip? A meta-analysis of the efficacy of flipped learning in higher education. *Review of Educational Research*, *91*(6), 878–918.

Bridges, S. A., Robinson, O. P., Stewart, E. W., Kwon, D., & Mutua, K. (2020). Augmented reality: Teaching daily living skills to adults with intellectual disabilities. *Journal of Special Education Technology*, *35*(1), 3–14. DOI: 10.1177/0162643419836411 PMID: 38911489

Brisson, C. M. (2024). The ergonomic classroom: Best practices for fostering inclusive learning environments. In *Inclusiveness Beyond the (Non) binary in Romance Languages* (pp. 105–119). Routledge.

Britannica. (2025). Virtual Reality. Encyclopaedia Britannica. https://www.britannica.com/technology/virtual-reality

Bryant, L., Bailey, B., & Hemsley, B. (2024). Developing and evaluating an immersive augmented reality application for children with developmental communication disability: InterPlay for language learning. *International Journal of Speech-Language Pathology*, •••, 1–14. DOI: 10.1080/17549507.2024.2361734 PMID: 39135408

Bryant, L., Decates, J., Bailey, B., & Hemsley, B. (2024). Views on augmented reality and neurodevelopmental communication disability: Survey of parents, educators, and health professionals. *Journal of Autism and Developmental Disorders*, •••, 1–9. DOI: 10.1007/s10803-024-06686-8 PMID: 39708077

Bryant, L., & Hemsley, B. (2024). Augmented reality: A view to future visual supports for people with disability. *Disability and Rehabilitation. Assistive Technology*, *19*(3), 800–813. PMID: 36149835

Buragohain, D., Deng, C., Sharma, A., & Chaudhary, S. (2024). The impact of immersive learning on teacher effectiveness: A systematic study. *IEEE Access : Practical Innovations, Open Solutions*, *12*, 35924–35933. DOI: 10.1109/ACCESS.2024.3373541

Bu u, A. F. (2024). AI-Powered Classrooms: A Revolution in Learning Environments. *Analele Universităţii din Craiova, Seria Ştiinţe Filologice. Limbi Străine Aplicate*, (1), 96–103.

Butson, R., & Spronken-Smith, R. (2024). AI and its implications for research in higher education: A critical dialogue. *Higher Education Research & Development, 43*(3), 563–577.

Cabero Almenara, J., Marín Díaz, V., & Castaño Garrido, C. (2015). Validación de la aplicación del modelo TPACK para la formación del profesorado en TIC. *@tic. Revista d'Innovació Educativa,* (14), 13–22. DOI: 10.7203/attic.14.4001

Cabrera-Duffaut, A., Pinto-Llorente, A. M., & Iglesias-Rodríguez, A. (2024). Immersive learning platforms: Analyzing virtual reality contribution to competence development in higher education—A systematic literature review. *Frontiers in Education, 9*, 1391560. DOI: 10.3389/feduc.2024.1391560

Cai, J., Wen, Q., Bi, M., & Lombaerts, K. (2024). How universal design for learning (UDL) is related to differentiated instruction (DI): The mediation role of growth mindset and teachers' practices factors. *Social Psychology of Education.* Advance online publication. DOI: 10.1007/s11218-024-09874-1

Cakir, R., & Korkmaz, O. (2019). The effectiveness of augmented reality environments on individuals with special education needs. *Education and Information Technologies, 24*(2), 1631–1659.

Camacho-Tamayo, E., & Bernal-Ballé, A. (2023). Elementos teóricos sobre la formación docente en ciencias naturales con enfoque STEAMH: Revisión sistemática. *Ciencia Latina, 7*(1), 1598–1618. DOI: 10.37811/cl_rcm.v7i1.4508

Camacho-Tamayo, E., Bernal-Ballén, A., & González Fernández, M. O. (2024). Análisis de la autopercepción sobre el uso del enfoque STEAM en las estrategias de aula de docentes de ciencias naturales de México y Colombia. [RECIE]. *Revista Caribeña de Investigación Educativa, 8*(1), 117–143. DOI: 10.32541/recie.2024.v8i1.pp117-143

Campillo-Ferrer, J. M., & Miralles-Martínez, P. (2021). Effectiveness of the flipped classroom model on students' self-reported motivation and learning during the COVID-19 pandemic. *Humanities & Social Sciences Communications, 8*(1), 1–9. PMID: 38617731

Candel, E. C., de-la-Peña, C., & Yuste, B. C. (2024). Pre-service teachers' perception of active learning methodologies in history: Flipped classroom and gamification in an e-learning environment. *Education and Information Technologies, 29*(3), 3365–3387.

Cano, C. A. G., & Troya, A. L. C. (2023). Artificial Intelligence applied to teaching and learning processes. *LatIA*, (1), 2.

Cano, S. R., Delgado-Benito, V., & Gonçalves, V. (2022). Educational technology based on virtual and augmented reality for students with learning disabilities: Specific projects and applications. In *Emerging advancements for virtual and augmented reality in Healthcare* (pp. 26–44). IGI Global Scientific Publishing.

Cao, Y., Ng, G. W., & Ye, S. S. (2023). Design and evaluation for immersive virtual reality learning environment: A systematic literature review. *Sustainability, 15*(3), 1964.

Cao, Y., & Zhai, J. (2022). A survey of AI in finance. *Journal of Chinese Economic and Business Studies, 20*(2), 125–137. DOI: 10.1080/14765284.2022.2077632

Carmigniani, J., Furht, B., Anisetti, M., Ceravolo, P., Damiani, E., & Ivkovic, M. (2011). Augmented reality technologies, systems and applications. *Multimedia Tools and Applications, 51*(1), 341–377. DOI: 10.1007/s11042-010-0660-6

Carreon, A., Smith, S. J., Mosher, M., Rao, K., & Rowland, A. (2022). A review of virtual reality intervention research for students with disabilities in K–12 settings. *Journal of Special Education Technology, 37*(1), 82–99. DOI: 10.1177/0162643420962011

Cassany, D. (2006). *Behind the Lines: On Contemporary Reading*. Anagrama.

CAST. (2024). Universal Design for Learning Guidelines version 3.0. Retrieved June 3, 2025, from https://udlguidelines.cast.org

Castillejos-López, B., Torres-Gastelú, C. A., & Lagunes-Domínguez, A. (2014). El enfoque del conocimiento tecnológico pedagógico del contenido (TPACK): Revisión del modelo. In Esquivel Gámez, I. (Ed.), *Los modelos tecno-educativos, revolucionando el aprendizaje del siglo XXI* (1st ed., pp. 237–252). Ismael Esquivel Gámez., https://www.researchgate.net/publication/280301257_Los_Modelos_Tecno-Educativos_revolucionando_el_aprendizaje_del_siglo_XXI

Castro-Campos, P. A. (2022). Reflexiones sobre la educación STEAM: Alternativa para el siglo XXI. *Praxis (Bern), 18*(1), 158–175. DOI: 10.21676/23897856.3762

Catherin, T. C., Vettriselvan, R., Mathur, S., Regins, J. C., & Velmurugan, P. R. R. (2025). Integrating AI and learning analytics in distance learning: Strategies for educators and institutions. In *AI and learning analytics in distance learning* (pp. 207–228). IGI Global Scientific Publishing., DOI: 10.4018/979-8-3693-2461-9.ch010

CAYACHOA-Amaya. I. D. C., & ALVAREZ-Araque, W. O. (2020). El modelo TPACK como estrategia para integrar las TIC en el aula escolar a partir de la formación docente. *Revista ESPACIOS, 41*(16), 6–16. https://www.revistaespacios.com/a20v41n16/a20v41n16p06.pdf

Cedeño Ávila, J. R., Rivadeneira Barreiro, L., & Piedad Rivadeneira Barreiro, M. P. (2024). Programa de capacitación docente para mejorar las competencias en el uso de las herramientas tecnológicas. *Tesla Revista Científica*, *4*(1), 1–13.

Cevikbas, M., & Kaiser, G. (2022). Student engagement in a flipped secondary mathematics classroom. *International Journal of Science and Mathematics Education*, *20*(7), 1455–1480.

Chalkiadakis, A., Seremetaki, A., Kanellou, A., Kallishi, M., Morfopoulou, A., Moraitaki, M., & Mastrokoukou, S. (2024). Impact of artificial intelligence and virtual reality on educational inclusion: A systematic review of technologies supporting students with disabilities. *Education Sciences*, *14*(11), 1223. DOI: 10.3390/educsci14111223

Chamo, N., & Yarom-Cohen, T. (2025). *Landscapes in the professional identity of special education teachers: Perceptions and practices related to Universal Design for Learning (UDL).* In *Inclusive Special Education – Research to Practice* [Working Title]. IntechOpen. DOI: 10.5772/intechopen.1010446

Chang, W., Lin, C. C., Crilly, J., Lee, H. L., Chen, L. C., & Han, C. Y. (2025). Virtual Reality Simulation for Undergraduate Nursing Students for Care of Patients With Infectious Diseases: Mixed Methods Study. *JMIR Medical Education*, *11*, e64780. PMID: 39933166

Chang, Y. J., Kang, Y. S., & Huang, P. C. (2013). An augmented reality (AR)-based vocational task prompting system for people with cognitive impairments. *Research in Developmental Disabilities*, *34*(10), 3049–3056. DOI: 10.1016/j.ridd.2013.06.026 PMID: 23880030

Chen, F.-Q., Leng, Y.-F., Ge, J.-F., Wang, D.-W., Li, C., Chen, B., & Sun, Z.-L. (2020). Effectiveness of virtual reality in nursing education: Meta-analysis. *Journal of Medical Internet Research*, *22*(9), e18290. DOI: 10.2196/18290 PMID: 32930664

Cheng, M. (2024). *Immersive Virtual Reality for Motor Rehabilitation in Individuals With Neurodevelopmental Disorders* [Doctoral dissertation, Northeastern University]. ProQuest Dissertations & Theses Global. https://www.proquest.com/dissertations-theses/immersive-virtual-reality-motor-rehabilitation/docview/3130515297/se-2?accountid=25074

Chen, J. J. (2025). From Turing's conception of machine intelligence to the evolution of AI in early childhood education: Conceptual, empirical, and practical insights. AI. *Brain and Child*, *1*(1), 1.

Chernikova, O., Heitzmann, N., Stadler, M., Holzberger, D., Seidel, T., & Fischer, F. (2020). Simulation-based learning in higher education: A meta-analysis. *Review of Educational Research, 90*(4), 499–541.

Chernikova, O., Sommerhoff, D., Stadler, M., Holzberger, D., Nickl, M., Seidel, T., & Heitzmann, N. (2025). Personalization through adaptivity or adaptability? A meta-analysis on simulation-based learning in higher education. *Educational Research Review, 46*, 100662.

Chib, S., Mehta, A. K., Selvakumar, P., Saravanan, A., Mishra, B. R., & Manjunath, T. C. (2025). Mental health challenges and solutions in high-pressure work environments. In Harriott, S. (Ed.), *Innovative approaches to managing conflict and change in diverse work environments* (pp. 247–272). IGI Global Scientific Publishing., DOI: 10.4018/979-8-3693-9556-1.ch011

Chiu, T. K. (2024). Future research recommendations for transforming higher education with generative AI. *Computers and Education: Artificial Intelligence, 6*, 100197.

Cho, H. J., Zhao, K., Lee, C. R., Runshe, D., & Krousgrill, C. (2021). Active learning through flipped classroom in mechanical engineering: Improving students' perception of learning and performance. *International Journal of STEM Education, 8*(1), 46. PMID: 34312588

Cho, M.-K., & Kim, M. Y. (2024). Enhancing nursing competency through virtual reality simulation among nursing students: A systematic review and meta-analysis. *Frontiers in Medicine, 11*, 1351300. DOI: 10.3389/fmed.2024.1351300 PMID: 38774395

Christanti, M. F., Mawangir, M., Arevin, A. T., Ramadhan, I., & Limijadi, E. K. S. (2024). The digital divide in education: Bridging gaps in the era of online learning. *Migration Letters : An International Journal of Migration Studies, 21*(S4), 1070–1079. DOI: 10.59670/ml.v21iS4.5621

Chukwuemeka, E. J., & Garba, M. (2024). Technology as a catalyst for learning and unlearning: A tool for navigating education in a dynamic society. *European Journal of Interactive Multimedia and Education, 5*(2), e02404.

Cohen, J. (1988). Set correlation and contingency tables. *Applied Psychological Measurement, 12*(4), 425–434. DOI: 10.55204/trc.v4i1.e345

Colegio de Bachilleres del Estado de Tamaulipas. (2022). *Historia*. https://www.cobat.edu.mx/cobat/historia/

Collado-Valero, J., Rodríguez-Infante, G., Romero-González, M., Gamboa-Ternero, S., Navarro-Soria, I., & Lavigne-Cerván, R. (2021). Flipped classroom: Active methodology for sustainable learning in higher education during social distancing due to COVID-19. *Sustainability, 13*(10), 5336.

Colomer, T. (2005). *Walking among books: literary reading in school.* Fondo de Cultura Económica.

Cook-Chennault, K. (2025). *Examining Access and Inclusion in STEM Fields in Higher Education: Digital Learning Environments.* Personalized Learning, and Institutional Change to Advance Educational Opportunity.

Correa-Delgado, J. S. (2024). La investigación como estrategia pedagógica: Una alternativa latinoamericana a la educación STEAM. *Prospectiva. Revista de Trabajo Social e Intervención Social*, (37), 1–20. DOI: 10.25100/prts.v0i37.13065

Couture, J. C., & Murgatroyd, S. (2024). *Education futures for school leadership: Evidence-informed strategies for managing change.* Taylor & Francis., DOI: 10.4324/9781003449750

Creed, C., Al-Kalbani, M., Theil, A., Sarcar, S., & Williams, I. (2023). Inclusive augmented and virtual reality: A research agenda. *International Journal of Human-Computer Interaction, 40*(20), 6200–6219. DOI: 10.1080/10447318.2023.2247614

Creed, C., Al-Kalbani, M., Theil, A., Sarcar, S., & Williams, I. (2024). Inclusive AR/VR: Accessibility barriers for immersive technologies. *Universal Access in the Information Society, 23*(1), 59–73. DOI: 10.1007/s10209-023-00969-0

Creely, E., & Blannin, J. (2025). Creative partnerships with generative AI. Possibilities for education and beyond. *Thinking Skills and Creativity, 56*, 101727.

Crogman, H. T., Cano, V. D., Pacheco, E., Sonawane, R. B., & Boroon, R. (2025). Virtual reality, augmented reality, and mixed reality in experiential learning: Transforming educational paradigms. *Education Sciences, 15*(3), 303. DOI: 10.3390/educsci15030303

Cueva, A., & Inga, E. (2022). Information and communication technologies for education considering the flipped learning model. *Education Sciences, 12*(3), 207.

Curtin, A. L., & Sarju, J. P. (2021). Students as partners: Co-creation of online learning to deliver high-quality, personalized content. In *Advances in online chemistry education* (pp. 135–163). American Chemical Society., DOI: 10.1021/bk-2021-1386.ch009

D'Elia, P., Stalmach, A., Di Sano, S., & Casale, G. (2025). Strategies for inclusive digital education: Problem/project-based learning, cooperative learning, and service learning for students with special educational needs. *Frontiers in Education, 9*, 1447489. DOI: 10.3389/feduc.2024.1447489

Dahlstrom-Hakki, I., Alstad, Z., Asbell-Clarke, J., & Edwards, T. (2024). The impact of visual and auditory distractions on the performance of neurodiverse students in virtual reality (VR) environments. *Virtual Reality (Waltham Cross), 28*(1), 29. DOI: 10.1007/s10055-023-00854-6

Dai, C. P. (2024). Applying machine learning to augment the design and assessment of immersive learning experience. In *Machine learning in educational sciences: Approaches, applications and advances* (pp. 245–264). Springer Nature Singapore.

Dai, C. P., Ke, F., Dai, Z., & Pachman, M. (2023). Improving teaching practices via virtual reality-supported simulation-based learning: Scenario design and the duration of implementation. *British Journal of Educational Technology, 54*(4), 836–856.

Dalle, J., Aydin, H., & Wang, C. X. (2024). Cultural dimensions of technology acceptance and adaptation in learning environments. *Journal of Formative Design in Learning*, •••, 1–14.

Damaševičius, R., & Sidekerskienė, T. (2024). Virtual worlds for learning in metaverse: A narrative review. *Sustainability, 16*(5), 2032. DOI: 10.3390/su16052032

Daneshfar, M., & Moonaghi, H. K. (2025). The impact of clinical simulation on bridging the theory–practice gap in nursing education: A systematic review. *BMC Medical Education, 25*(1), 1216. PMID: 40877870

Dascal, J., Reid, M., IsHak, W. W., Spiegel, B., Recacho, J., Rosen, B., & Danovitch, I. (2017). Virtual reality and medical inpatients: A systematic review of randomized, controlled trials. *Innovations in Clinical Neuroscience, 14*(1-2), 14. PMID: 28386517

Davis, S. C., Nolen, S. B., & Koretsky, M. D. (2024). Inclusive excellence in practice: Integrating equitable, consequential learning and an inclusive climate in higher education classrooms and institutions. *Frontline Learning Research, 12*(4), 22–54. DOI: 10.14786/flr.v12i4.808

Deniz, E. U., Ceylan, C., Eren, R., & Memiş, O. B. (2024). Advancing empathy and emotional intelligence among pharmacy students: A comparative mixed-methods study with peer role-play simulation intervention. *Currents in Pharmacy Teaching & Learning, 16*(8), 102112. PMID: 38795610

Deriba, F. G., Saqr, M., & Tukiainen, M. (2024). Assessment of accessibility in virtual laboratories: A systematic review. *Frontiers in Education*, *9*, 1351711. DOI: 10.3389/feduc.2024.1351711

DHSC [Department for Health and Social Care] (2001). *Valuing people: A new strategy for learning disability for the 21st century*. Retrieved June 3, 2025, from https://www.gov.uk/government/publications/valuing-people-a-new-strategy-for-learning-disability-for-the-21st-century

Di Natale, A. F., Bartolotta, S., Gaggioli, A., Riva, G., & Villani, D. (2024). Exploring students' acceptance and continuance intention in using immersive virtual reality and metaverse integrated learning environments: The case of an Italian university course. *Education and Information Technologies*, *29*(12), 14749–14768.

Dick, E. (2021). The promise of immersive learning: Augmented and virtual reality's potential in education. *Information Technology and Innovation Foundation*, *1*, 1–10.

Dikilitas, K., & Fructuoso, I. N. (2023). Conceptual framework for flexible learning design: The context of flipped classroom. *[Journal details unclear]*. DOI: 10.31265/usps.267

Dolapcioglu, S., & Doğanay, A. (2022). Development of critical thinking in mathematics classes via authentic learning: An action research. *International Journal of Mathematical Education in Science and Technology*, *53*(6), 1363–1386.

Dudley, J., Yin, L., Garaj, V., & Kristensson, P. O. (2023). Inclusive immersion: A review of efforts to improve accessibility in virtual reality, augmented reality and the metaverse. *Virtual Reality (Waltham Cross)*, *27*(4), 2989–3020. DOI: 10.1007/s10055-023-00763-8

Dwivedi, A., Dsouza, M., & Aggarwal, A. (2024). AI-driven school management system: A React-based web application enhancing educational administration and student performance analytics. *International Journal of Innovative Science and Research Technology*, *8*(5), 811–816. DOI: 10.38124/ijisrt/ijisrt24apr2465

Eager, B., & Brunton, R. (2023). Prompting higher education towards AI-augmented teaching and learning practice. *Journal of University Teaching & Learning Practice*, *20*(5), 1–20. DOI: 10.53761/1.20.5.02

Eden, C. A., Chisom, O. N., & Adeniyi, I. S. (2024). Harnessing technology integration in education: Strategies for enhancing learning outcomes and equity. *World Journal of Advanced Engineering Technology and Sciences, 11*(2), 001-008.

Eden, C. A., Chisom, O. N., & Adeniyi, I. S. (2024). Integrating AI in education: Opportunities, challenges, and ethical considerations. *Magna Scientia Advanced Research and Reviews, 10*(2), 6–13. DOI: 10.30574/msarr.2024.10.2.0039

Edwards, D., & Mercer, N. (1988). *El conocimiento compartido: el desarollo de la comprensión en el aula*. Paidós.

Efendi, D., Apriliyasari, R. W., Prihartami Massie, J. G. E., Wong, C. L., Natalia, R., Utomo, B., & Chen, K. H. (2023). The effect of virtual reality on cognitive, affective, and psychomotor outcomes in nursing staffs: Systematic review and meta-analysis. *BMC Nursing*, *22*(1), 170. PMID: 37202768

Efthymiou, E. (Ed.). (2024). *Revolutionizing Inclusive Education: Mindfulness, Neurodiversity, and Executive Functioning Skills: Mindfulness, Neurodiversity, and Executive Functioning Skills*. IGI Global.

Efthymiou, E., Katsarou, D. V., Sofologi, M., Argyriadis, A., Argyriadi, A., & Megari, K. (2025). Neuropsychological interventions in inclusive education: Strategies for supportin cognitive and emotional development in diverse learners. In *Clinical applications of pediatric neuropsychology from infancy to adolescence* (pp. 411–448). IGI Global Scientific Publishing., DOI: 10.4018/979-8-3693-1936-3.ch018

Ekpete, O. H. (2024). *Assistive listening devices for individuals with hearing impairment. Faculty of Natural and Applied Sciences Journal of Mathematics and Science Education, 5*(2), 78–81. Retrieved from https://fnasjournals.com/index.php/FNAS-JMSE/article/view/390

El Galad, A., Betts, D. H., & Campbell, N. (2024). Flexible learning dimensions in higher education: Aligning students' and educators' perspectives for more inclusive practices. *Frontiers in Education*, *9*, 1347432. DOI: 10.3389/feduc.2024.1347432

Elamin, M. O. I. (2024). AI through the ages: Unlocking key opportunities and navigating challenges in the history and future of artificial intelligence. *International Journal of Religion*, *5*(12), 1152–1166.

Elendu, C., Amaechi, D. C., Okatta, A. U., Amaechi, E. C., Elendu, T. C., Ezeh, C. P., & Elendu, I. D. (2024). The impact of simulation-based training in medical education. *Revista de Medicina (São Paulo)*, *103*(27), e38813. PMID: 38968472

Ellikkal, A., & Rajamohan, S. (2024). AI-enabled personalized learning: Empowering management students for improving engagement and academic performance. *Vilakshan-XIMB Journal of Management*, *22*(1), 88–102. DOI: 10.1108/xjm-02-2024-0023

Eltahir, M. E., & Babiker, F. M. E. (2024). The influence of artificial intelligence tools on student performance in e-learning environments: Case study. *Electronic Journal of e-Learning*, *22*(9), 91–110.

Ersoy, M., Kumral, C. D., Çolak, R., Armağan, H., & Yiğit, T. (2022). Development of a server-based integrated virtual laboratory for digital electronics. *Computer Applications in Engineering Education*, *30*(5), 1307–1320.

Espada-Chavarria, R., González-Montesino, R. H., López-Bastías, J. L., & Díaz-Vega, M. (2023). Universal design for learning and instruction: Effective strategies for inclusive higher education. *Education Sciences*, *13*(6), 620.

Estaiteyeh, M., & DeCoito, I. (2024). Differentiated instruction in digital video games: STEM teacher candidates using technology to meet learners' needs. *Interactive Learning Environments*, *32*(7), 3768–3782. DOI: 10.1080/10494820.2023.2246023

Estepa, F. Lida Maritza, A., & Arciniegas, W. E. (2019). Encountering the Story: A Strategy to Improve Reading Comprehension. In Education and Science

Fang, J., Vong, J., & Fang, J. (2022). Exploring student engagement in fully flipped classroom pedagogy: Case of an Australian business undergraduate degree. *Journal of Education for Business*, *97*(2), 76–85.

Faresta, R. A. (2024). AI-powered education: Exploring the potential of personalised learning for students' needs in Indonesia education. *Traektoriâ Nauki*, *10*(5), 3012–3022. DOI: 10.22178/pos.104-19

Farley, I. A., & Burbules, N. C. (2022). Online education viewed through an equity lens: Promoting engagement and success for all learners. *Review of Education*, *10*(3), e3367. DOI: 10.1002/rev3.3367

Feng, B., & Ng, L. L. (2024). The spatial influence on vocabulary acquisition in an immersive virtual reality-mediated learning environment. [IJCALLT]. *International Journal of Computer-Assisted Language Learning and Teaching*, *14*(1), 1–17.

Fernandes, F. A., Rodrigues, C. S. C., Teixeira, E. N., & Werner, C. M. (2023). Immersive learning frameworks: A systematic literature review. *IEEE Transactions on Learning Technologies*, *16*(5), 736–747.

Ferreira, B., & Menezes, P. (2020). Gamifying motor rehabilitation therapies: Challenges and opportunities of immersive technologies. *Information (Basel)*, *11*(2), 88. DOI: 10.3390/info11020088

Fisher, R., Perényi, A., & Birdthistle, N. (2021). The positive relationship between flipped and blended learning and student engagement, performance and satisfaction. *Active Learning in Higher Education*, *22*(2), 97–113.

Fitrianto, I., & Saif, A. (2024). The role of virtual reality in enhancing Experiential Learning: a comparative study of traditional and immersive learning environments. *International Journal of Post Axial: Futuristic Teaching and Learning*, 97-110.

Fitrianto, I., & Saif, A. (2024). The role of virtual reality in enhancing experiential learning: A comparative study of traditional and immersive learning environments. *International Journal of Post Axial: Futuristic Teaching and Learning*, *2*(2), 97–110. DOI: 10.59944/postaxial.v2i2.300

Fitzpatrick, V., Reed, T., Gilger, J., Brophy, S., & Imbrie, P. K. (2013, October). First-year engineering students with dyslexia: Comparison of spatial visualization performance and attitudes. In *2013 IEEE Frontiers in Education Conference (FIE)* (pp. 1254–1256). IEEE.

Flores-Gallegos, R., Rodríguez-Leis, P., & Fernández, T. (2022). Effects of a virtual reality training program on visual attention and motor performance in children with reading learning disability. *International Journal of Child-Computer Interaction*, *32*, 100394.

Forde, D., Carstens, C., Haihambo, C. K., Sivunen, U., O'Neill, C., & Galletti, A. (2025). Creating a Framework for an Inclusive Learning Environment.

Franze, A., Loetscher, T., Gallomarino, N. C., Szpak, A., Lee, G., & Michalski, S. C. (2024). Immersive virtual reality is more effective than non-immersive devices for developing real-world skills in people with intellectual disability. *Journal of Intellectual Disability Research*, *68*(12), 1358–1373. DOI: 10.1111/jir.13177 PMID: 39169557

Frei-Landau, R., Orland-Barak, L., & Muchnick-Rozonov, Y. (2022). What's in it for the observer? Mimetic aspects of learning through observation in simulation-based learning in teacher education. *Teaching and Teacher Education*, *113*, 103682.

Freire, P. (1997). Pedagogy of Autonomy: Necessary Knowledge for Educational Practice. 21st Century.

Galliers, J., Wilson, S., Marshall, J., Talbot, R., Devane, N., Booth, T., & Greenwood, H. (2017). Experiencing EVA park, a multi-user virtual world for people with aphasia. [TACCESS]. *ACM Transactions on Accessible Computing*, *10*(4), 1–24.

Garzotto, F., Gelsomini, M., Occhiuto, D., Matarazzo, V., & Messina, N. (2017, June). Wearable immersive virtual reality for children with disability: a case study. In *Proceedings of the 2017 conference on interaction design and children* (pp. 478-483).

Gašević, D., Siemens, G., & Sadiq, S. (2023). Empowering learners for the age of artificial intelligence. *Computers and Education: Artificial Intelligence*, *4*, 100130. Advance online publication. DOI: 10.1016/j.caeai.2023.100130

Gatcho, A. R. G., Manuel, J. P. G., & Sarasua, R. J. G. (2024). Eye tracking research on readers' interactions with multimodal texts: A mini-review. *Frontiers in Communication*, *9*, 1482105. DOI: 10.3389/fcomm.2024.1482105

Gavilanes, J. S. (2024). Diversity, equity and inclusion in simulation-based education: experiences from multiple academic health centers (Doctoral dissertation, Portland State University).

General de Planeación, D., & Programación y Estadística, E. (2024, September). *Principales cifras del Sistema Educativo Nacional 2023–2024* (1st ed.). https://www.planeacion.sep.gob.mx/Doc/estadistica_e_indicadores/principales_cifras/principales_cifras_2023_2024_bolsillo.pdf

Gentili, A., Failla, G., Melnyk, A., Puleo, V., Tanna, G. L. D., Ricciardi, W., & Cascini, F. (2022). The cost-effectiveness of digital health interventions: A systematic review of the literature. *Frontiers in Public Health*, *10*, 787135. PMID: 36033812

Getzel, E. E., & Thoma, C. A. (2008). Experiences of college students with disabilities and the importance of self-determination in higher education settings. *Career Development for Exceptional Individuals*, *31*(2), 77–84.

Ghoulam, K., & Bouikhalene, B. (2024). From classrooms to cyberspace: Understanding pedagogical approaches and outcomes in Metaverse learning environments. *Advances in Mobile Learning Educational Research*, *4*(1), 983–993.

Glaser, N., Li, S., Nuguri, S. S., Calyam, P., & Joshi, A. C. (2025). Piloting a Virtual Reality Cybersecurity Game for Neurodivergent Adults: Findings from a User-Centered Formative Evaluation. *Immersive Learning Research-Academic*, 67-77.

Glaser, N., Parishani, Z., Joshi, A. C., & Calyam, P. (2025). Leveraging Virtual Reality for Neurodivergent Representation in Cybersecurity Education: An Emerging Technology Report. *Technology, Knowledge and Learning*, 1-14.

Golubovschi, O. (2024). Interactive teaching and learning techniques in the context of multicultural education. In *Educaţia multiculturală, spaţiu formativ pentru educaţia valorilor* (pp. 227–233). Chi inău, Republic of Moldova: Universitatea Pedagogică de Stat „Ion Creangă"

Gómez-Puerta, M., Chiner, E., Melero-Pérez, P., & Lorenzo Lledó, G. (2019). Research review on augmented reality as an educational resource for people with intellectual disabilities. *International Journal of Developmental and Educational Psychology*, *1*(2), 473–485. DOI: 10.1177/00224669241258225

Gonzalez, M., Kokozos, M., & Byrd, C. M. (2025). Trust, community, and connection: Laying the groundwork for authentic storytelling. In *Teaching storytelling in classrooms and communities* (pp. 35–60). Routledge.

Graham, R. (2022). *Crisis and catalyst: The impact of COVID-19 on global practice in engineering education* (Research report). CEEDA & 4TU Centre for Engineering Education. Retrieved from https://www.rhgraham.org/resources/Crisis-and-catalyst.pdf

Graham, R. (2022). *Crisis and catalyst: The impact of COVID-19 on global practice in engineering education.* 4TU Centre for Engineering Education / Consortium of Universities. https://www.rhgraham.org/resources/Crisis-and-catalyst.pdf

Grant, K. A. (2025). Experiential learning. In *Practical Applications of Experiential and Community-Engaged Learning Methods in Business* (Vol. 1, pp. 91–109). High-Impact Teaching Practices in Business Education.

Grech, A., Wodehouse, A., & Brisco, R. (2024). Empathic empowerment: An exploration and analysis of a situated interaction through empathic modelling and role-play. *Proceedings of the Design Society*, *4*, 2373–2382.

Grigorenko, E. L., Compton, D. L., Fuchs, L. S., Wagner, R. K., Willcutt, E. G., & Fletcher, J. M. (2020). Understanding, educating, and supporting children with specific learning disabilities: 50 years of science and practice. *The American Psychologist*, *75*(1), 37–51. DOI: 10.1037/amp0000452 PMID: 31081650

Guberina, T. (2023). Cultivating inclusive learning environments: Incorporating diversity through culturally responsive pedagogy. *Social Science Chronicle*, *3*(1), 1–14. DOI: 10.56106/ssc.2023.003

Guerra, G., Alfonso, D., Becerra, M., & Mercedes, Y. (2022). The Story as a Teaching Strategy to Strengthen Critical Reading in Fourth-Grade Students. In Criterios Magazine

Guimarães Carvalho, I. S., Tejeda, J., & Pozos Pérez, K. V. (2019). Formación docente para la educación a distancia: La construcción de las competencias docentes digitales. *Série-Estudos*, *24*(51), 69–87. DOI: 10.20435/serie-estudos.v24i51.1296

Gutierrez-Bucheli, L., Goh, J. T., Rashidi, A., Maxwell, D., Digby, R., Fang, Y., & Arashpour, M. (2024). *Adopting immersive technologies in construction training: Determining educational decision-making criteria through a Delphi technique*. Smart and Sustainable Built Environment., DOI: 10.1108/SASBE-01-2024-0012

Haddad, R. J., & Kalaani, Y. (2014). Gaming against plagiarism (GAP): A game-based approach to illustrate research misconduct to undergraduate engineering students.

Hajahmadi, S., Clementi, L., López, M. D. J., & Marfia, G. (2024, March). Arele-bot: Inclusive learning of spanish as a foreign language through a mobile app integrating augmented reality and chatgpt. In *2024 IEEE Conference on Virtual Reality and 3D User Interfaces Abstracts and Workshops (VRW)* (pp. 335-340). IEEE.

Haj-Bolouri, A., Katende, J., & Rossi, M. (2023, May). A mid-range theory for designing sustainable safe spaces of immersive learning environments: a design-science based gamification approach. In *International Conference on Design Science Research in Information Systems and Technology* (pp. 449-469). Cham: Springer Nature Switzerland.

Hardwick, J., Whittington-Walsh, F., Bezanson, K., Miller, A., & Sawatzky, E. (2022). Designing for inclusion. In *Designing for Care.*

Harrison, M., Rowlings, J., White, E. H., Vallence, M., & Potemkin, N. (2024). Neurodiversity and digital inclusion: creating the conditions for inclusive education through universal learning design.

Hashim, H. U., Yunus, M. M., & Norman, H. (2022). 'AReal-Vocab': An augmented reality English vocabulary mobile application to cater to mild autism children in response towards sustainable education for children with disabilities. *Sustainability, 14*(8), 4831.

Hashmi, S. U. (2025). Digital influence on identity within multilingual educational contexts. In *Global Goals, Global Languages: 2025 Report of the Central States Conference on the Teaching of Foreign Languages* (pp. 63–82). Central States Conference on the Teaching of Foreign Languages.

Hayati, N., Kadarohman, A., Sopandi, W., Martoprawiro, M. A., & Rochintaniawati, D. (2022, August). Chemistry teachers' TPACK competence: Teacher perception and lesson plan analysis. *Technium Social Sciences Journal, 34*, 237–247.

Hollombe, S., Yablon, Y. B., & Iluz, S. (2024). Navigating conflict in the multi-cultural classroom: The use of simulation-based learning for peace education in teacher training. *Zeitschrift für Pädagogik und Theologie, 76*(3), 253–264. DOI: 10.1515/zpt-2024-2029

Horak, A., Daly, K., & King, S. (2024). *Creating equity and access for gifted learners: Implementing a problem-based professional learning experience using the ExCEL model*. Routledge.

Hossain, K. I. (2024). Reviewing the role of culture in English language learning: Challenges and opportunities for educators. *Social Sciences & Humanities Open*, *9*, 100781.

Hoter, E., Yazbak Abu Ahmad, M., & Azulay, H. (2024, August). Enhancing language learning and intergroup empathy through multi-user interactions and simulations in a virtual world. *Virtual Worlds*, *3*(3), 333–353. DOI: 10.3390/virtualworlds3030018

Howell, R. A. (2021). Engaging students in education for sustainable development: The benefits of active learning, reflective practices and flipped classroom pedagogies. *Journal of Cleaner Production*, *325*, 129318.

Hrastinski, I., Bonetti, A., & Hedjever, M. (2023). Relationship between auditory processing skills and academic achievement of elementary school children. *Specijalna Edukacija i Rehabilitacija*, *22*(2), 95–116. DOI: 10.5937/specedreh22-37415

Huang, W., Roscoe, R. D., Johnson-Glenberg, M. C., & Craig, S. D. (2021). Motivation, engagement, and performance across multiple virtual reality sessions and levels of immersion. *Journal of Computer Assisted Learning*, *37*(3), 745–758.

Huang, X., & Qiao, C. (2024). Enhancing computational thinking skills through artificial intelligence education at a STEAM high school. *Science & Education*, *33*(2), 383–403.

Hubballi, R. B., Selvakumar, P., Seenivasan, R., Basava Aradhya, S. G., Dinesh, N., & Seelam, P. K. (2025). Overview of current AI technologies in education. In Kyei-Blankson, L., & Ntuli, E. (Eds.), *Transformative AI practices for personalized learning strategies* (pp. 1–26). IGI Global Scientific Publishing., DOI: 10.4018/979-8-3693-8744-3.ch001

Hutama, B. A. A., Sihwi, S. W., & Salamah, U. (2021, November). Kinect based therapy games to overcome misperception in people with dysgraphia using dynamic difficulty adjustment. In *2021 IEEE International Conference on Computing (ICOCO)* (pp. 230-235). IEEE.

Hutson, J., & Ceballos, J. (2023). Rethinking education in the age of AI: The importance of developing durable skills in the Industry 4.0. *Journal of Information Economics*, *1*(2), 9–26. DOI: 10.58567/jie01020002

Hutson, J., & Hutson, P. (2024). Conclusion: Future Directions for Neuro-inclusivity in Museums and Heritage Sites. In *Inclusive Smart Museums: Engaging Neurodiverse Audiences and Enhancing Cultural Heritage* (pp. 229–240). Springer Nature Switzerland.

Hutson, J., & Hutson, P. (2024). Immersive technologies. In *Inclusive brilliant museums: Engaging neurodiverse audiences and enhancing cultural heritage* (pp. 153–228). Springer Nature Switzerland.

Hutson, J., & Hutson, P. (2024). *Inclusive smart museums: Engaging neurodiverse audiences and enhancing cultural heritage*. Springer Nature.

Hutson, J., & McGinley, C. (2023). Neuroaffirmative approaches to extended reality: Empowering individuals with autism spectrum condition through immersive learning environments. *International Journal of Technology in Education and Science*, *7*(3).

Hu, Y. (2025). Creating interactive AI learning environments: Integrating interdisciplinary approaches and Taoist art principles. *Interactive Learning Environments*, •••, 1–20.

Imrie, R. (2011). Universalism, universal design and equitable access to the built environment. *Disability and Rehabilitation*, *34*(10), 873–882. DOI: 10.3109/09638288.2011.624250 PMID: 22054109

Indumathy, I., & Mujra, P. (2025). Sustainable learning. In *Smart education and sustainable learning environments in smart cities* (pp. 381–402). IGI Global Scientific Publishing., DOI: 10.4018/979-8-3693-7723-9.ch023

Intarapreecha, N., & Sangsawang, T. (2023). Incorporating augmented reality to enhance learning for students with learning disabilities: A focus on spatial orientation in physical. *Journal of Applied Data Sciences, 4*(3), 245-253. dhttps://DOI: <ALIGNMENT.qj></ALIGNMENT>10.47738/jads.v4i3.126

Ip, H. H. S., & Li, C. (2021). Introducing immersive learning into special education settings: A comparative review of two studies. In Hui, A., & Wagner, C. (Eds.), *Creative and Collaborative Learning Through Immersion: Interdisciplinary and International Perspectives* (pp. 135–150). Springer., DOI: 10.1007/978-3-030-72216-6

Ip, H. H., Wong, S. W., Chan, D. F., Li, C., Kon, L. L., Ma, P. K., Lau, K. S. Y., & Byrne, J. (2024). Enhance affective expression and social reciprocity for children with autism spectrum disorder: Using virtual reality headsets at schools. *Interactive Learning Environments*, *32*(3), 1012–1035. DOI: 10.1080/10494820.2022.2107681

Jacob, U. S., Pillay, J., Misitura Oyundoyin, B., & Oyundoyin, J. O. (2022). Barriers to and benefits of online learning among special education undergraduates. *Multicultural Education*, *8*(4), 9–21. DOI: 10.5281/zenodo.6416145

Jadán-Guerrero, J., Tamayo-Narvaez, K., Méndez, E., & Valenzuela, M. (2024, June). Adaptive learning environments: Integrating artificial intelligence for special education advances. In *International Conference on Human-Computer Interaction* (pp. 86-94). Cham: Springer Nature Switzerland.

Jain, K., & Raghuram, J. N. V. (2024). Unlocking potential: The impact of AI on education technology. *Multidisciplinary Reviews*, *7*(3), 2024049–2024049.

Jaramillo Arana, A., Montaña de la Cadena, G., & Rojas Reina, L. M. (2025). Error detection in the metacognitive process of monitoring children's reading comprehension. Latin American Journal of Social Sciences. *Childhood and Youth*, *4*(2). Advance online publication. DOI: 10.11600/rlcsnj.4.2.396

Jardinez, M. J., & Natividad, L. R. (2024). The advantages and challenges of inclusive education: Striving for equity in the classroom. *Shanlax International Journal of Education*, *12*(2), 57–65. DOI: 10.34293/education.v12i2.7182

Jatto, E. O., & Aladesusi, G. A. (2025). Empowering pre-service teachers for inclusive education through technology: Strategies, tools, and innovations. In *Empowering pre-service teachers to enhance inclusive education through technology* (pp. 301–336). IGI Global Scientific Publishing., DOI: 10.4018/979-8-3693-8759-7

Javvaji, C. K., Reddy, H., Vagha, J. D., Taksande, A., Kommareddy, A., & Reddy, N. S. (2024). Immersive innovations: Exploring the diverse applications of virtual reality (VR) in healthcare. *Cureus*, *16*(3), e56137. PMID: 38618363

Jdaitawi, M. T., & Kanan, A. F. (2022). A decade of research on the effectiveness of augmented reality on students with special disability in higher education. *Contemporary Educational Technology*, *14*(1), ep332. DOI: 10.30935/cedtech/11369

Jenks, A., Onufer, L., & Guberman, D. (2025). Emergent questions of access: Disability and the integration of generative AI in teaching and learning. *Higher Education Research & Development*, *44*(4), 932–945. DOI: 10.1080/07294360.2024.2442611

Jiang, L., Phutane, M., & Azenkot, S. (2023, October). Beyond audio description: Exploring 360° video accessibility with blind and low vision users through collaborative creation. In *Proceedings of the 25th International ACM SIGACCESS Conference on Computers and Accessibility (ASSETS 2023)* (pp. 1–17). Association for Computing Machinery. DOI: 10.1145/3597638.3608381

Jiang, M. Y. C., Jong, M. S. Y., Lau, W. W. F., Chai, C. S., & Wu, N. (2021). Using automatic speech recognition technology to enhance EFL learners' oral language complexity in a flipped classroom. *Australasian Journal of Educational Technology*, *37*(2), 110–131.

Jiang, Z. (2024). Research on the advancement of equity in higher education driven by artificial intelligence. *Journal of Higher Education Research*, *5*(2), 88–102. DOI: 10.32629/jher.v5i2.2427

Johnson, I. E., Idaka, E. I., & Offiong, A. E. A. (2025). Understanding and distinguishing immersive realities for effective instructional delivery. *Global Journal of Educational Research*, *24*(1), 107–117. DOI: 10.4314/gjedr.v24i1.10

Jones, A., & Bomash, I. (2018, June). Validating mastery learning: assessing the impact of adaptive learning objective mastery in Knewton Alta. In *International Conference on Artificial Intelligence in Education* (pp. 433-437). Cham: Springer International Publishing.

Kamalı-Arslantaş, T., & Baser, D. (2025). Effects of implementing interactive videos in an online flipped classroom on preservice special education teachers. *European Journal of Education*, *60*(4), e70234.

Kamali, J., Alpat, M. F., & Bozkurt, A. (2024). AI ethics as a complex and multifaceted challenge: Decoding educators' AI ethics alignment through the lens of activity theory. *International Journal of Educational Technology in Higher Education*, *21*(1), 62.

Kapetanaki, A., Krouska, A., Troussas, C., & Sgouropoulou, C. (2022). Exploiting augmented reality technology in special education: A systematic review. *Computers*, *11*(10), 143. DOI: 10.3390/computers11100143

Kapsalis, E., Jaeger, N., & Hale, J. (2022). Disabled-by-design: Effects of inaccessible urban public spaces on users of mobility assistive devices – A systematic review. *Disability and Rehabilitation. Assistive Technology*, *19*(3), 604–622. DOI: 10.1080/17483107.2022.2111723 PMID: 35984675

Kasperski, R., & Crispel, O. (2022). Preservice teachers' perspectives on the contribution of simulation-based learning to the development of communication skills. *Journal of Education for Teaching*, *48*(5), 521–534.

Kaur, D. P., Kumar, A., Dutta, R., & Malhotra, S. (2022). The role of interactive and immersive technologies in higher education: A survey. *Journal of Engineering Education Transformations*, *36*(2), 79–86. DOI: 10.16920/jeet/2022/v36i2/22156

Kawinkoonlasate, P. (2024). Utilizing a digital-flipped classroom approach to enhance writing skills and foster an active learning environment among Thai EFL learners.

Kayyali, M. (2024). Future possibilities and challenges of AI in education. In *Transforming education with generative AI: Prompt engineering and synthetic content creation* (pp. 118–137). IGI Global Scientific Publishing.

Kellems, R. O., Eichelberger, C., Cacciatore, G., Jensen, M., Frazier, B., Simons, K., & Zaru, M. (2020). Using video-based instruction via augmented reality to teach mathematics to middle school students with learning disabilities. *Journal of Learning Disabilities, 53*(4), 277–291. DOI: 10.1177/0022219420906452 PMID: 32065040

Kettler, R. J., Elliott, S. N., Davies, M., & Griffin, P. (2012). Testing a multi-stage screening system: Predicting performance on Australia's national achievement test using teachers' ratings of academic and social behaviors. *School Psychology International, 33*(1), 93–111. DOI: 10.1177/01430343114030

Khalid, I. L., Abdullah, M. N. S., & Fadzil, H. M. (2024). A systematic review: Digital learning in STEM education. *Journal of Advanced Research in Applied Sciences and Engineering Technology, 51*(1), 98–115.

Khalili, A. (2021). An XML-based approach for geo-semantic data exchange from BIM to VR applications. *Automation in Construction, 121*, 103425.

Khamis, H., Khairudin, M., Jantan, A. H., Roslan, N. A., & Abdullah, L. N. (2024). Systematic review of adapting immersive technology in enhancing teaching and learning for students in higher education. *Journal of Advanced Research in Applied Sciences and Engineering Technology, 63*(3), 28–32. DOI: 10.37934/araset.63.3.2832

Khanna, P., & Bhola, S. (2023). Designing integrative and collaborative learning for students with special needs and learning disabilities in an inclusive classroom. In *Sustainable blended learning in STEM education for students with additional needs* (pp. 173–194). Springer Nature Singapore., DOI: 10.1007/978-981-99-3497-3_9

Khasawneh, M. A. S. (2024). The potential for utilizing virtual reality technology in educating students with learning disabilities. *Journal of Infrastructure. Policy and Development, 8*(13), 6802. DOI: 10.24294/jipd6802

Khelifi, K., & Hamzaoui-Elachachi, H. (2024). Beyond "one-size-fits-all" teaching: Embracing the learner-centered paradigm through differentiated instruction.*(At-Talimia), 14*(2), 708–726. DOI: 10.52127/2240-014-002-054

Khine, M. S. (2024). Ethics, and the future of education in an AI-driven world. In *Artificial intelligence in education: A machine learning perspective* (pp. 629–735). Springer., DOI: 10.1007/978-981-97-9350-1_6

Khogali, H. O., & Mekid, S. (2024). Perception and Ethical Challenges for the Future of AI as Encountered by Surveyed New Engineers. *Societies (Basel, Switzerland), 14*(12).

Khribi, M. K., Othman, A., & Al-Sinani, A. (2022, July). Toward closing the training and knowledge gap in ICT accessibility and inclusive design harnessing open educational resources. In *2022 International Conference on Advanced Learning Technologies (ICALT)* (pp. 289–291). IEEE. DOI: 10.1109/ICALT55036.2022.00065

Khundam, C., Vorachart, V., Preeyawongsakul, P., Hosap, W., & Noël, F. (2021). A comparative study of interaction time and usability of using controllers and hand tracking in virtual reality training. In Informatics (Vol. 8, No. 3, p. 60). MDPI.

Ki, S., & Ryu, J. (2024). The Effects of Self-Regulation Strategies on Cognitive Load, Self-Efficacy, and Learning Satisfaction in VR Nursing Practical Training. In Society for Information Technology & Teacher Education International Conference (pp. 493-497). Association for the Advancement of Computing in Education (AACE).

Kim, D. R., & Yoo, J. (2025). The effectiveness of 360-degree virtual reality-based mechanical ventilation nursing education for ICU nurses. In Healthcare (Vol. 13, No. 14, p. 1639). MDPI.

Kirk, V. (2025). A sensory-friendly learning environment through design: user experience and implementation.

Klimova, B., Pikhart, M., & Kacetl, J. (2023). Ethical issues of the use of AI-driven mobile apps for education. *Frontiers in Public Health, 10*, 1118116. Advance online publication. DOI: 10.3389/fpubh.2022.1118116 PMID: 36711343

Klochko, O., Fedorets, V., Tkachenko, S., & Maliar, O. (2021). The use of digital technologies for flipped learning implementation. *IEEE EAEEIE Annual Conference Proceedings,* 1–6.

Kochurina, S. A., Fedorova, O. O., & Zakharov, K. P. (2022, April). Learning Motivation of Students of Adaptive Learning Platforms. In Proceedings of the Conference "Integrating Engineering Education and Humanities for Global Intercultural Perspectives" (pp. 303-310). Cham: Springer International Publishing.

Koehler, M. J., Mishra, P., & Cain, W. (2015). ¿Qué son los saberes tecnológicos y pedagógicos del contenido (TPACK)? *Virtualidad, Educación y Ciencia, 6*(10), 9–23. https://dialnet.unirioja.es/servlet/articulo?codigo=5115245

Kokkinos, L. (2024). Revolutionizing education: The dynamic intersection of technology and learning. [IJMCER]. *Educational Research, 6*(1), 26–32.

Kolenbrander, J., & Michaels, A. J. (2025). Personality emulation utilizing large language models. *Applied Sciences (Basel, Switzerland), 15*(12), 6636. Advance online publication. DOI: 10.3390/app15126636

Kormos, J., & Smith, A. M. (2023). *Teaching languages to students with specific learning differences* (2nd ed., Vol. 18). Channel View Publications., DOI: 10.21832/KORMOS8615

Kotte, K. R., & Attaluri, V. (2025). Revolutionising retail banking with AI and virtual technologies: AI-driven financial training. In Nair, A. J., Manohar, S., Limbu, Y. B., & Huhmann, B. A. (Eds.), *Intersecting natural language processing and FinTech innovations in service marketing* (pp. 421–440). IGI Global Scientific Publishing., DOI: 10.4018/979-8-3693-9944-6.ch020

Kozyar, M. M., Pasichnyk, S. M., Kopchak, M. M., Burmakina, N. S., & Suran, T. (2022). Simulation-based learning as an effective method of practical training of future translators. *Journal of Curriculum and Teaching, 11*(1), 298–308.

Kumar, K. S., Selvan, T., Mahendraprabu, M., Ganesan, K., Ramnath, R., & Kumar, N. S. (2024). Examining the Role of Virtual Reality, Augmented Reality, and Artificial Intelligence in Adapting STEM Education for Next-Generation Inclusion. *International Journal of Emerging Knowledge Studies, 2*(12), 876–883.

Kumi-Yeboah, A., Kim, Y., Sallar, A. M., & Kiramba, L. K. (2020). Exploring the use of digital technologies from the perspective of diverse learners in online learning environments. *Online Learning : the Official Journal of the Online Learning Consortium, 24*(4), 42–63. DOI: 10.24059/olj.v24i4.2281

Kurtts, S. A. (2006). Universal design for learning in inclusive classrooms. *Electronic Journal for Inclusive Education, 1*(10), 7.

Kusmawan, U. (2023). Redefining teacher training: The promise of AI-supported teaching practices. *Journal of Advances in Education and Philosophy, 7*(9), 332–335.

Labadze, L., Grigolia, M., & Machaidze, L. (2023). Role of AI chatbots in education: Systematic literature review. *International Journal of Educational Technology in Higher Education, 20*, 56. Advance online publication. DOI: 10.1186/s41239-023-00426-1

Ladson-Billings, G. (2023). “Yes, but how do we do it?”: Practicing culturally relevant pedagogy. In *White teachers/diverse classrooms* (pp. 33–46). Routledge., DOI: 10.4324/9781003448709-6

Lailatussaadah, L., Hayati, S., Bin Jamil, A. I., & Abdul Kadir, F. A. B. (2023, December). Mapping TPACK components in implementing edupreneur-profiled curriculum at teacher training and education institutions in Aceh. *Tadris: Jurnal Keguruan dan Ilmu Tarbiyah, 8*(2), 373–387. https://doi.org/DOI: 10.24042/tadris.v8i2.16755

Lamberti, P. M., Bombaerts, G., & IJsselsteijn, W. (2025). Mind the gap: Bridging the divide between computer scientists and ethicists in shaping moral machines. *Ethics and Information Technology, 27*(1), 2.

Lam-Byrne, A. G. (2023). El aprendizaje STEAM: Una práctica inclusiva. *Revista Científica Episteme y Tekne, 2*(1), e466.

Lampropoulos, G. (2023). Augmented reality and artificial intelligence in education: Toward immersive intelligent tutoring systems. In *Augmented reality and artificial intelligence: The fusion of advanced technologies* (pp. 137–146). Springer Nature Switzerland.

Landwehr, K. (2024). Environmental perception: An ecological perspective. In *Environmental perspectives* (pp. 18–38). Routledge.

Langan, L., Frazer, K., Darley, A., Goodman, L., Browne, F., Fulfilled, P., & Redmond, C. (2025). Inclusive pedagogy in online simulation-based learning in undergraduate nursing education: A scoping review. *Journal of Advanced Nursing, 81*(2), 591–606. PMID: 38940383

Latorre, A. (2003). *La investigación-acción. Conocer y cambiar la práctica educativa.* GRAÓ.

Lau, W. S., & Shea, M. (2024). Empowering English learners in the classroom through culturally responsive social-emotional teaching practices. *Journal of Multilingual and Multicultural Development, 45*(7), 2880–2897. DOI: 10.1080/01434632.2022.2078337

Lawson McLean, A., & Lawson McLean, A. C. (2024). Immersive simulations in surgical training: Analyzing the interplay between virtual and real-world environments. *Simulation & Gaming, 55*(6), 1103–1123. DOI: 10.1177/10468781241287892

Lazou, C., & Tsinakos, A. (2023). Critical immersive-triggered literacy as a key component for inclusive digital education. *Education Sciences, 13*(7), 696. DOI: 10.3390/educsci13070696

Lazou, C., & Tsinakos, A. (2025). A framework for participatory creation of digital futures: A longitudinal study on enhancing media literacy and inclusion in K-12 through virtual reality. *Information (Basel), 16*(6), 482. DOI: 10.3390/info16060482

Leal Urueña, L. A., & Rojas Mesa, J. E. (2020). Percepciones de autoeficacia y conocimientos TPACK en profesores en formación. *Diversitas: Perspectivas en Psicología, 16*(2), 283–296. DOI: 10.15332/22563067.6295

Lee, I. J., Liao, P. H., & Hung, H. W. (2025). Utilizing VR technology with remote medical guidance for distant collaborative emergency medical training in advanced cardiac life support. *Interactive Learning Environments*, •••, 1–18.

Levesque, E., & Duncan, J. (2024). Inclusive education for deaf students: Pass or fail. *Deafness & Education International, 26*(2), 125–126.

Levterova-Gadjalova, D., Terlemezyan, H., Tagareva, K., & Tsokov, G. (2024). Metaverse of Learning Disabilities in Higher Educational Institutions. In *Applied Assistive Technologies and Informatics for Students with Disabilities* (pp. 209–234). Springer Nature Singapore.

Liao, K. C., Ajjawi, R., Peng, C. H., Jenq, C. C., & Monrouxe, L. V. (2023). Striving to thrive or striving to survive: Professional identity constructions of medical trainees in clinical assessment activities. *Medical Education, 57*(11), 1102–1116. PMID: 37394612

Light, J., McNaughton, D., Beukelman, D., Fager, S. K., Fried-Oken, M., Jakobs, T., & Jakobs, E. (2019). Challenges and opportunities in augmentative and alternative communication: Research and technology development to enhance communication and participation for individuals with complex communication needs. *Augmentative and Alternative Communication, 35*(1), 1–12. DOI: 10.1080/07434618.2018.1556732 PMID: 30648903

Li, H. (2023). AI in education: Bridging the divide or widening the gap? Exploring equity, opportunities, and challenges in the digital age. Advances in Education. *Humanities and Social Sciences, 8*(1), 355–370. DOI: 10.56028/aehssr.8.1.355.2023

Lijun, W., & Te, H. C. (2024). The role of primary school principals and administrators in promoting student achievement, teacher effectiveness, and a positive school culture. *Journal of Roi Kaensarn Academi, 9*(8), 727–739. https://so02.tci-thaijo.org/index.php/JRKSA/article/view/272236

Lin, X. F., Luo, G., Luo, S., Liu, J., Chan, K. K., Chen, H., & Li, Z. (2024). Promoting pre-service teachers' learning performance and perceptions of inclusive education: An augmented reality-based training through learning by design approach. *Teaching and Teacher Education, 148*, 104661.

Li, R., Lund, A., & Nordsteien, A. (2023). The link between flipped and active learning: A scoping review. *Teaching in Higher Education, 28*(8), 1993–2027.

Liu, R., Salisbury, J. P., Vahabzadeh, A., & Sahin, N. T. (2017). Feasibility of an autism-focused augmented reality smartglasses system for social communication and behavioral coaching. *Frontiers in Pediatrics*, *5*, 145. PMID: 28695116

Liu, R., Wang, L., Koszalka, T. A., & Wan, K. (2022). Effects of immersive virtual reality classrooms on students' academic achievement, motivation and cognitive load in science lessons. *Journal of Computer Assisted Learning*, *38*(5), 1422–1433. DOI: 10.1111/jcal.12688

Liu, Y., & Pásztor, A. (2022). Effects of problem-based learning instructional intervention on critical thinking in higher education: A meta-analysis. *Thinking Skills and Creativity*, *45*, 101069.

Liu, Y., Razman, M. R., Zakaria, S. Z. S., Ern, L. K., Hussain, A., & Chamola, V. (2024). Utilizing ubiquitous learning to foster sustainable development in rural areas: Insights from 6G technology. *Computers in Human Behavior*, *161*, 108418.

Lobanova, A., Hrabovets, I., Prykhodko, O., Karytka, V., Kalashnikova, L., & Chernous, L. (2024). Artificial intelligence in teaching social disciplines: Opportunities and challenges of tools. *Educational Technology Quarterly*, *2024*(4), 360–377.

Löfstrand, P., & Zakrisson, I. (2025). Exploring the impact of role-playing exercises on cognitive and emotional processes: A social-and educational psychological perspective. *Frontiers in Psychology*, *16*, 1645213. PMID: 41030334

Lok, B., Ferdig, R. E., Raij, A., Johnsen, K., Dickerson, R., Coutts, J., & Lind, D. S. (2006). Applying virtual reality in medical communication education: Current findings and potential teaching and learning benefits of immersive virtual patients. *Virtual Reality (Waltham Cross)*, *10*(3), 185–195.

López de la Madrid, M. C., Flores Guerrero, K., & Tejeda Mercado, C. (2021). Las TIC en el diseño de las políticas educativas: El caso de México. *Archivos Analíticos de Políticas Educativas*, *29*(32), 1–34. DOI: 10.14507/epaa.29.4408

López, C., Lucero, P., Medina, J., Gladys, H. P., Carolina, A., Celedón, S., Judith, Y. C. A., & Titzé, M. (2024). Deciphering Horizons: An In-Depth Analysis of Reading Comprehension in Elementary School Students. In Estudios y Perspectivas, Scientific and Academic Journal.

López-Gamboa, M. V., Córdoda González, C., & Soto Soto, J. F. (2020). Educación STEM/STEAM: Modelos de implementación, estrategias didácticas y ambientes de aprendizaje que potencian las habilidades para el siglo XXI. *Latin American Journal of Science Education,* *7*(1), 1–16. http://www.lajse.org/may20/2020_12002.pdf

Lteif, L., van der Sluis, H., Block, L. G., Cian, L., Patrick, V. M., & Scott, M. L. (2025). Creating equity by design: A conceptual framework for marketplace inclusion. *Journal of Public Policy & Marketing*, *44*(2), 214–231. DOI: 10.1177/07439156251315371

Lu, A., Chan, S., Cai, Y., Huang, L., Nay, Z. T., & Goei, S. L. (2018). Learning through VR gaming with virtual pink dolphins for children with ASD. *Interactive Learning Environments*, *26*(6), 718–729.

Luca, E. (2023). Transforming education with AI: Cloud-based personalized learning and data protection strategies. *International Journal of AI in Education*, *15*(6), 225–240.

Luna-Romero, Á. E., Vega Jaramillo, F. Y., & Carvajal Romero, H. R. (2019). Formación docente en el uso de las TIC. *Universidad, Ciencia y Tecnología, Volumen Especial*(2), 46–52. https://uctunexpo.autanabooks.com/index.php/uct/article/view/66

Lyon, G. R. (1996). Learning disabilities. *The Future of Children*, *6*(2), 54–75. PMID: 8689262

MacDonald, L., Thomas, E., Javernick-Will, A., Austin-Breneman, J., Aranda, I., Salvinelli, C., & Linden, K. (2022). Aligning learning objectives and approaches in global engineering graduate programs: Review and recommendations by an interdisciplinary working group. *Development Engineering*, *7*, 100095. DOI: 10.1016/j.deveng.2022.100095

Macdonald, S. J., & Clayton, J. (2012). Back to the future, disability and the digital divide. *Disability & Society*, *28*(5), 702–718. DOI: 10.1080/09687599.2012.732538

Maheswaran, K., Selvakumar, P., Shaikh, M., Shashank, G., Gupta, S., & Manjunath, T. C. (2025). The evolution of smart urban mobility with emerging technologies. In Ponnusamy, S., Assaf, M., Youssef, B., Jeon, G., & Kalyanaraman, S. (Eds.), *Leveraging VANETs and blockchain technology for urban mobility* (pp. 1–28). IGI Global Scientific Publishing., DOI: 10.4018/979-8-3373-0265-2.ch001

Makweya, P. P., & Sepadi, M. D. (2025). Inclusive education and lifelong learning: Beyond school walls. In *Global practices in inclusive education curriculum and policy* (pp. 261–280). IGI Global., https://www.igi-global.com/book/global-practices-inclusive-education-curriculum/741b5cad-7f6f-4c70-a6f3-e44c3de2652

Malaquias, O., & Malaquias, R. F. (2016). The role of virtual reality in the learning process of individuals with intellectual disabilities. *Technology and Disability*, *28*(4), 133–138. 10.3233_TAD-160454

Manekar, A., Gade, V., Unhale, R., Manker, H., & Dhole, R. (2024). Exploring an Immersive AR/VR Pedagogical Approach: Experiential Learning for Autism Spectrum Disorder (ASD). *Education*.

Maresca, G., Corallo, F., De Cola, M. C., Formica, C., Giliberto, S., Rao, G., Crupi, M. F., Quartarone, A., & Pidalà, A. (2024). Effectiveness of the use of virtual reality rehabilitation in children with dyslexia: Follow-up after one year. *Brain Sciences*, *14*(7), 655. DOI: 10.3390/brainsci14070655 PMID: 39061396

Marín, V., Sampedro, B. E., & Morales-Diaz, M. (2025). Secondary education teacher's views on mixed reality in inclusive environments. *Journal of New Approaches in Educational Research*, *14*(1), 4.

Markey, K., O'Brien, B., Kouta, C., Okantey, C., & O'Donnell, C. (2021). Embracing classroom cultural diversity: Innovations for nurturing inclusive intercultural learning and culturally responsive teaching. *Teaching and Learning in Nursing*, *16*(3), 258–262. DOI: 10.1016/j.teln.2021.03.006

Marques, B., Santos, B. S., & Dias, P. (2024). Ten years of immersive education: Overview of a virtual and augmented reality course at postgraduate level. *Computers & Graphics*, *124*, 104088.

Martin, B., Kaminski-Ozturk, N., Smiley, R., Spector, N., Silvestre, J., Bowles, W., & Alexander, M. (2023). Assessing the impact of the COVID-19 pandemic on nursing education: A national study of prelicensure RN programs. *Journal of Nursing Regulation*, *14*(1), S1–S67. PMID: 37012978

Maskati, E., Alkeraiem, F., Khalil, N., Baik, R., Aljuhani, R., & Alsobhi, A. (2021). Using virtual reality (VR) in teaching students with dyslexia. [IJET]. *International Journal of Emerging Technologies in Learning*, *16*(9), 291–305. DOI: 10.3991/ijet.v16i09.19653

Maspul, K. A. (2024). Discovering the underlying motivations for empowering education through innovation. *Journal of Information System and Education Development*, *2*(1), 27–32. DOI: 10.62386/jised.v2i1.58

Matovu, H., Ungu, D. A. K., Won, M., Tsai, C. C., Treagust, D. F., Mocerino, M., & Tasker, R. (2023). Immersive virtual reality for science learning: Design, implementation, and evaluation. *Studies in Science Education*, *59*(2), 205–244. DOI: 10.1080/03057267.2022.2082680

Maulidah, G., & Christyodetaputri, J. H. (2025). Beyond engagement: Integrating AR and VR for inclusive learning in K–higher education. *Sinergi International Journal of Education, 3*(1), 26–40. https://journal.sinergi.org/id/article/view/abc

Ma, X., Xie, Y., Yang, X., Wang, H., Li, Z., & Lu, J. (2024). Teacher-student interaction modes in smart classroom based on lag sequential analysis. *Education and Information Technologies*, *29*(12), 15087–15111.

McDermott, G., Byrne, A., McLaughlin, R., O'Connor, N., & Griselain, S. (2023). *Exploring the use of immersive technologies to enhance the student experience.* Ubiquity Proceedings.

McMahon, D., Cihak, D., & Wright, R. (2015). Augmented reality as a navigation tool to employment opportunities for postsecondary education students with intellectual disabilities and autism. *Journal of Research on Technology in Education*, *47*(3), 157–172. DOI: 10.1080/15391523.2015.1047698

Melhem, D. Z., & Al-Zoubi, A. M. (2025). The effect of Universal Design for Learning (UDL)-based VARK model in students with learning difficulties and various learning preferences. *Educational Process: International Journal*, *15*, e2025152. Advance online publication. DOI: 10.22521/edupij.2025.15.152

Mena-Guacas, A. F., López-Catalán, L., Bernal-Bravo, C., & Ballesteros-Regaña, C. (2025). Educational transformation through emerging technologies: Critical review of scientific impact on learning. *Education Sciences*, *15*(3), 368. DOI: 10.3390/educsci15030368

Mendoza, A. (2011). *Children's stories and their teaching: a guide for teachers and mediators.* Paidós.

Mensa, A. A., Sarpong, C., Kubi, F. N., & Donkor, O. (2023). Akan traditional games: An indispensable tool in Ghanaian language classroom in respect to classroom interaction. *Integrated Journal for Research in Arts and Humanities*, *3*(4), 69–75. https://ijrah.org/article/view/226/abstract

Mercier, S. (Ed.). (2025). *Design for All Learners: Create Accessible and Inclusive Learning Experiences.* American Society for Training and Development.

Meyer, A., & Rose, D. H. (2005). The future is in the margins: the role of technology and disability in educational reform. In Rose, D. H., Meyer, A., & Hitchcock, C. (Eds.), *The Universally Designed Classroom: Accessible Curriculum and Digital Technologies* (pp. 18–51). Harvard Education Press.

Mhlongo, S., Mbatha, K., Ramatsetse, B., & Dlamini, R. (2023). Challenges, opportunities, and prospects of adopting and using smart digital technologies in learning environments: An iterative review. *Heliyon*, *9*(6). PMID: 37274691

Microsoft. (2024, March 7). Ability Summit 2024: Advancing accessibility with AI technology and innovation. The Official Microsoft Blog. Retrieved May, 29, 2025 from https://blogs.microsoft.com/blog/2024/03/07/ability-summit-2024-advancing-accessibility-with-ai-technology-and-innovation/

Miles, P., & Boltin, K. (2025). Creation and use of SBS's The Boat; principles for the co-creation of online interactive learning environments for innovative digital pedagogy. *Pedagogies*, *20*(3), 364–380.

Miller, J. (2024). *Exploring the lived experiences of educators implementing a program focusing on inclusivity, empathy, resilience, and collaboration: Perceptions of student learning and behavior* (Doctoral dissertation). Cabrini University. https://repository.cabrini.edu/etd/12345

Minghelli, V., D'anna, C., & Vastola, R. (2023). A biopsychosocial approach to plan inclusive learning environments in physical education. *Journal of Physical Education and Sport*, *23*(9), 2492–2502.

Mintz, J., Connolly, C., O'Brien, E., Daniela, L., & Ceallaigh, T. Ó. (2024). Inclusive digital education: Contexts, practices and perspectives. *Computers in the Schools*, *41*(2), 115–119.

Mirari, K. (2022). The effectiveness of adaptive learning systems in personalized education. *Journal of Education Review Provision*, *2*(3), 70–76. DOI: 10.55885/jerp.v2i3.194

Mishra, P., & Koehler, M. J. (2006). Technological pedagogical content knowledge: A framework for teacher knowledge. *Teachers College Record*, *108*(6), 1017–1054.

Mishra, S., Afaq, A., Mishra, T. K., & Mathur, N. (2025). Integrating generative AI-driven learning programs to enhance marketing skills. In *Generative artificial intelligence and ethics: Standards, guidelines, and best practices* (p. 38). IGI Global., DOI: 10.4018/979-8-3693-3691-5.ch009

Mitsea, E., Drigas, A., & Skianis, C. (2023). VR gaming for meta-skills training in special education: The role of metacognition, motivations, and emotional intelligence. *Education Sciences*, *13*(7), 639.

Moemeke, C. D. (2024). Artificial intelligence and machine learning in enhancing science learning experiences: Exploring possibilities and concerns. *NIU Journal of Educational Research*, *10*(2), 59–72.

Mohseni, H., Silvennoinen, J., & Correia, A. (2025). Inclusive interactions for place-belongingness: Lessons from citizen science. In D. Glowacka, C. Santoro, & Z. Xiao (Eds.), *IUI-WS 2025: Workshops at the International Conference on Intelligent User Interfaces (IUI) 2025* (Article 8). CEUR Workshop Proceedings, 3957. https://ceur-ws.org/Vol-3957/SOCIALIZE-paper08.pdf

Mokhtar, E. S., Aziz, N., Hamzah, S. S., Ahmad, S. Z., Supli, A. A., & Omar, A. C. (2024, May). Unveiling the conceptual analysis in the direction of developing a fusion virtual reality model for hearing-impaired visual interaction. In *2024 IEEE 14th Symposium on Computer Applications & Industrial Electronics (ISCAIE)* (pp. 89–94). IEEE. DOI: 10.1109/ISCAIE59752.2024.10303841

Mokmin, N. A. M., & Rassy, R. P. (2024). Review of the trends in the use of augmented reality technology for students with disabilities when learning physical education. *Education and Information Technologies*, *29*(2), 1251–1277. DOI: 10.1007/s10639-022-11550-2

Mokmin, N. A. M., & Ridzuan, N. N. I. B. (2022). Immersive technologies in physical education in malaysia for students with learning disabilities. *IAFOR Journal of Education*, *10*(2), 91–110.

Molloy, C., & Farrell, R. (2024). Cultivating positive classroom environments: Exploring the efficacy of immersive technologies in removing barriers to learning among primary school students. *Computers in the Schools*, *41*(2), 164–192. DOI: 10.1080/07380569.2024.2325441

Monica, J. A., Malar, J. H., Arun, C., Sharmila, L., & Arif, M. (2025). Leveraging technology and universal design for inclusive and engaging learning in Indian higher education. In *Educational Philosophy and Sociological Foundation of Education* (pp. 177–212). IGI Global.

Monica, J. A., Malar, J. H., Arun, C., Sharmila, L., & Arif, M. (2025). Leveraging technology and universal design for inclusive and engaging learning in Indian higher education. In *Educational philosophy and sociological foundation of education* (pp. 177–212). IGI Global., DOI: 10.4018/979-8-3693-3587-1.ch008

Monroy-González, L. A., Mendoza-Hernández, L. E., & Alarcón-Acosta, H. (2021). Educación STEAM en preparatoria. *UNO Sapiens. Boletín Científico de la Escuela Preparatoria No. 1, 4*(7), 12–15. https://repository.uaeh.edu.mx/revistas/index.php/prepa1/article/download/7285/7893/

Montague, J., Tsui, J., Kamstra-Cooper, K., Connell, M., Atack, L., & Haghiri-Vijeh, R. (2025). Adapting to change: Undergraduate nursing students' sense of belonging transitioning from online to in-person learning environments. *Journal of Advanced Nursing*, *81*(1), 513–522. DOI: 10.1111/jan.16389 PMID: 39140749

Moon, J. (2024). Learning experience design of verbal prompts in virtual reality-based training for autistic children. *Research in Learning Technology*, •••, 32.

Morales Soza, M. G. (2020). TPACK para integrar efectivamente las TIC en educación: Un modelo teórico para la formación docente. *Docente. Revista Electrónica de Conocimientos. Saberes y Prácticas*, *3*(1), 133–148. DOI: 10.5377/recsp.v3i1.9796

Morris, J. R., Hughes, E. M., Stocker, J. D., & Davis, E. S. (2022). Using video modeling, explicit instruction, and augmented reality to teach mathematics to students with disabilities. *Learning Disability Quarterly*, *45*(4), 306–319.

Moss, G. D., & McKeeman, L. (Eds.). (2025). *Report of the Central States Conference on the Teaching of Foreign Languages* (2025 edition). Central States Conference on the Teaching of Foreign Languages., https://files.eric.ed.gov/fulltext/ED671436.pdf

Moss, G. D., & McKeeman, L. (Eds.). (2025). *Report of the Central States Conference on the Teaching of Foreign Languages: Global goals, global languages* (2025 edition). Central States Conference on the Teaching of Foreign Languages., https://files.eric.ed.gov/fulltext/ED671436.pdf

Mouboua, P. D., Atobatele, F. A., & Akintayo, O. T. (2024). Multilingual education and social equity: A comparative study of integration policies in multicultural societies. *GSC Advanced Research and Reviews, 19*(2), 032-042.

Mounkoro, I., & Rafique, T.. (2024). AI-powered tutoring systems: Revolutionizing individualized support for learners. *Library Progress International*, *44*(2), 1–20. DOI: 10.48165/bapas.2024.44.2.1

Muhammad, G. (2023). Trends and innovations in the prospects of distance learning. *Journal of Education and Finance Review*, *2*(1), 41–53. https://journal.example.org/article/view/xyz

Munthe, R. G., Abbas, M., Fernandez, R., & Ulita, N. (2024). The impact of educational information systems on learning accessibility in higher education. [ITEE]. *International Transactions on Education Technology*, *3*(1), 94–103.

Muthusubramanian, M., Jangoan, S., Sharma, K. K., & Krishnamoorthy, G. (2024). Demystifying explainable AI: Understanding, transparency and trust. *International Journal of AI Ethics and Governance*, *6*(2), 88–102. DOI: 10.36948/ijfmr.2024.v06i02.14597

Muzapparovna, N. G. (2024). Advancements in continuing education: Exploring innovative approaches to teaching in the modern era. *International Journal of Advances in Scientific Research*, *4*(04), 89–96. http://journal.example.org/ijasr/v4i04/123

Mystakidis, S., & Lympouridis, V. (2023). Immersive learning. *Encyclopedia*, *3*(2), 396–405.

Nabors, L., Monnin, J., & Jimenez, S. (2020). A scoping review of studies on virtual reality for individuals with intellectual disabilities. *Advances in Neurodevelopmental Disorders*, *4*(4), 344–356. DOI: 10.1007/s41252-020-00177-4

Naruka, V. S., & Upadhyay, S. (2024). Virtual Reality (VR) and Neurodiversity: Therapeutic and Educational Applications. *As the editors of Transforming Learning. Power and Education*, •••, 151.

Navas-Bonilla, C. D. R., Guerra-Arango, J. A., Oviedo-Guado, D. A., & Murillo-Noriega, D. E. (2025, February). Inclusive education through technology: A systematic review of types, tools and characteristics. [). Frontiers Media SA.]. *Frontiers in Education*, *10*, 1527851.

Newman, L., Wagner, M., Knokey, A. M., Marder, C., Nagle, K., Shaver, D., Wei, X., Cameto, R., Contreras, E., Ferguson, K., Greene, S., & Schwarting, M. (2011). The post-high school outcomes of young adults with disabilities up to 8 years after high school: A report from the National Longitudinal Transition Study-2 (NLTS2). National Center for Special Education Research. Retrieved May, 28, 2025 from https://files.eric.ed.gov/fulltext/ED524044.pdf

Ng, D. T. K., Su, J., Leung, J. K. L., & Chu, S. K. W. (2024). Artificial intelligence (AI) literacy education in secondary schools: A review. *Interactive Learning Environments*, *32*(10), 6204–6224.

Ni, A., & Cheung, A. (2023). Understanding secondary students' continuance intention to adopt AI-powered intelligent tutoring system for English learning. *Education and Information Technologies*, *28*, 3191–3216. DOI: 10.1007/s10639-022-11305-z PMID: 36119127

Nikolakopoulou, V., & Koutsabasis, P. (2025). The 'making' of participatory and co-design for digital experiences in cultural heritage: A review. *CoDesign*. Advance online publication. DOI: 10.1080/15710882.2025.1135228

Nishat, A. (2025). Rethinking Intelligence: An Interdisciplinary Framework for AI Research. *Pioneer Research Journal of Computing Science*, *2*(2), 162–169.

Nowrozy, R., & Jam, D. (2024). Embracing the generative AI revolution: advancing tertiary education in cybersecurity with GPT. arXiv preprint arXiv:2403.11402.

Nteliou, E., Koreman, J., Tolskaya, I., & Kehagia, O. (2021, July). Digital technologies assisting migrant populations overcome language barriers: The case of the EasyRights research project. In Antona, M., & Stephanidis, C. (Eds.), *Human-Computer Interaction – INTERACT 2021* (pp. 108–124). Springer International Publishing., DOI: 10.1007/978-3-030-85686-1_8

Nugraha, R. A., Sunardi, S., Asrowi, A., Murwaningsih, T., Yusuf, M., & Supratiwi, M. (2025). Development and validation of augmented reality media for social and emotional learning in children with learning disabilities (SEAKAR). *AL-ISHLAH: Jurnal Pendidikan, 17*(1), 1355–1366.

Nuguri, S. S., Kambhampati, A., Glaser, N., Calyam, P., Li, S., Bates, C., . . . Nuguri, S. (2025, January). Adaptive Virtual Reality Learning Environment with a Reinforcement Learning-Driven Pedagogical Agent. In *2025 IEEE 22nd Consumer Communications & Networking Conference (CCNC)* (pp. 1-4). IEEE.

Núñez-Naranjo, A. F., Guevara, A. W. P., Pérez, V., & Yancha, K. R. Y. (2021). El cuento: estrategia didáctica para la comprensión lectora. ConcienciaDigital, 4(1.2), 119-130.

Nurfadila, M. Y., Hajar, S., & Arsyad, N. F. (2024). Utilizing quizizz for game-based learning in elementary science education. *Journal of Education and Computer Applications, 1*(1), 12–19.

Nurhaswinda, N., Pebriana, P. H., & Nurmalina, N. (2025). The Impact of Technology-Driven Adaptive Learning on Mathematical Conceptual Mastery in Primary Education. G-Couns: Jurnal Bimbingan dan Konseling, 9(3), 2383-2397.

Obaid, M. A. S. (2013). The impact of using multi-sensory approach for teaching students with learning disabilities. *Journal of International Education Research, 9*(1), 75.

Obeid, M. F., Ewais, A., & Asia, M. R. (2025). NursingXR: Advancing Nursing Education Through Virtual Reality-Based Training. *Applied Sciences (Basel, Switzerland), 15*(6), 2949.

Okeke, N. I., Alabi, O. A., Igwe, A. N., & Ofodile, O. C. (2024). AI in customer feedback integration: A data-driven framework for enhancing business strategy. *World Journal of Advanced Research and Reviews, 24*(1), 2036–2052. DOI: 10.30574/wjarr.2024.24.1.3207

Omiegbe, O. (2024). Artificial intelligence in higher education: Bridging the gap for students with disabilities. *Brock Journal of Education, 12*(12), 38–50. DOI: 10.37745/bje.2013/vol12n123850

Ortiz-Colón, A. M., Ágreda Montoro, M., & Rodríguez Moreno, J. (2020). Autopercepción del profesorado de Educación Primaria en servicio desde el modelo TPACK. *Revista Electrónica Interuniversitaria de Formación del Profesorado, 23*(2), 53–65. DOI: 10.6018/reifop.415641

Osypova, N., Kokhanovska, O., Yuzbasheva, G., & Kravtsov, H. (2021). Implementation of Immersive Technologies in Professional Training of Teachers. In Bollin, A. (Eds.), *Information and Communication Technologies in Education, Research, and Industrial Applications. ICTERI 2020. Communications in Computer and Information Science, 1308*. Springer., DOI: 10.1007/978-3-030-77592-6_4

Owan, V. J., Abang, K. B., Idika, D. O., & Etta, E. O. (2023). Exploring the potential of artificial intelligence tools in educational measurement and assessment. *Eurasia Journal of Mathematics, Science and Technology Education, 19*(4), 13428. Advance online publication. DOI: 10.29333/ejmste/13428

Owoade, S. J., Uzoka, A., Akerele, J. I., & Ojukwu, P. U. (2024). Innovative cross-platform health applications to improve accessibility in underserved communities. *International Journal of Applied Research in Social Sciences, 6*(11), 2727–2743. DOI: 10.51594/ijarss.v6i11.1723

Oyelana, O. O., Olson, J., & Caine, V. (2022). An evolutionary concept analysis of learner-centered teaching. *Nurse Education Today, 108*, 105187. DOI: 10.1016/j.nedt.2021.105187 PMID: 34741919

Oyeniran, C. O., Adewusi, A. O., Adeleke, A. G., Akwawa, L. A., & Azubuko, C. F. (2022). Ethical AI: Addressing bias in machine learning models and software applications. *Computer Science & AI Ethics Journal, 9*(3), 88–102.

Pabón-Rúa, J. D., López-Ríos, S. Y., & Cardona-Zapata, M. E. (2024). Perspectivas teóricas y metodológicas sobre creatividad en educación STEAM: Una revisión sistemática. *Revista Científica (Maracaibo), 51*(3), 1–21. DOI: 10.14483/23448350.21959

Palominos Bastias, M., & Marcelo García, C. (2021). Uso de tecnologías digitales para atender necesidades educativas especiales en la formación docente del educador diferencial. *Píxel-Bit. Revista de Medios y Educación*, (61), 231–256. DOI: 10.12795/pixelbit.78020

Pangestu, Y., Wulandari, S., & Handayani, I. (2024). Implementation of augmented reality in animal introduction learning for students with intellectual disabilities. [IJSECS]. *International Journal Software Engineering and Computer Science, 4*(1), 263–272. DOI: 10.35870/ijsecs.v4i1.2214

Papadakis, S., & Kalogiannakis, M. (2024). Epilogue: Inclusive education: Fostering equity and diversity in modern schools. *Education, Development and Intervention: Toward Participatory and Integrated Solutions*, *23*, 231.

Papaioannou, G., Volakaki, M. G., Kokolakis, S., & Vouyioukas, D. (2023). Learning spaces in higher education: A state-of-the-art review. *Trends in Higher Education*, *2*(3), 526–545.

Parker, J. L., Richard, V. M., Acabá, A., Escoffier, S., Flaherty, S., Jablonka, S., & Becker, K. P. (2025). Negotiating meaning with machines: AI's role in doctoral writing pedagogy. *International Journal of Artificial Intelligence in Education*, *35*(3), 1218–1238.

Patel, N. S., & Indurkhya, N. (Eds.). (2025). *The Rise of Intelligent Machines: A Multi-disciplinary Perspective from Industry and Impact on Higher Education*. CRC Press.

Patel, P., Pampaniya, S., Ghosh, A., Raj, R., Karuppaih, D., & Kandasamy, S. (2025). Enhancing accessibility through machine learning: A review on visual and hearing impairment technologies. *IEEE Access : Practical Innovations, Open Solutions*, *13*, 33286–33307. DOI: 10.1109/ACCESS.2025.3539081

Patterson, B. A. (2022). *Traditional and electronic data collection methods* (Unpublished doctoral dissertation). The Chicago School of Professional Psychology. https://www.proquest.com/openview/fbbdbac006d2bfe8594c2374e14ba0b3/1?pq-origsite=gscholar&cbl=18750&diss=y

Pattiasina, P. J., Lamaloang, L. K., & Santoso, R. Y. (2025). The role of communication in creating inclusive and collaborative learning environments. *INJOSEDU: International Journal of Social and Education*, *2*(3), 577–591.

Pattiasina, P. J., Lamaloang, L. K., & Santoso, R. Y. (2025). The role of communication in creating inclusive and collaborative learning environments. *The International Journal of Social Education*, *2*(3), 577–591. https://languar.net/index.php/INJOSEDU/article/view/133

Patty, J. (2024). The use of AI in language learning: What you need to know. Jurnal Review Pendidikan dan Pengajaran (JRPP), 7(1), 642–658.

Paula-Bonifacio, E., & Marcelo-García, C. (2023). Validación de un instrumento TPACK: Enseñanza de la lectura para docentes de educación primaria. *Campus Virtuales*, *12*(1), 103–120. DOI: 10.54988/cv.2023.1.1092

Pazmiño Núñez, G. A., Sauca Banegas, M. A., Vasquez Garcia, M. N., Ruano Armijos, G. A., Morocho Cabrera, L. N., Bayas Chacha, L. M., & Santillán Sevillano, N. D. C. (2025). El impacto de las metodologías STEAM en el desarrollo de competencias digitales y creativas en estudiantes. *Ciencia Latina, 9*(1), 2690–2709. DOI: 10.37811/cl_rcm.v9i1.16035

Pei, B., Cheng, Y., Ambrose, A., Dziadula, E., Xing, W., & Lu, J. (2024). LearningViz: A dashboard for visualizing, analyzing and closing learning performance gaps—a case study approach. *Smart Learning Environments, 11*(1), 56.

Perales, F. J., & Aróstegui, J. L. (2024). The STEAM approach: Implementation and educational, social and economic consequences. *Arts Education Policy Review, 125*(2), 59–67. DOI: 10.1080/10632913.2021.1974997

Perelmutter, B., McGregor, K. K., & Gordon, K. R. (2017). Assistive technology interventions for adolescents and adults with learning disabilities: An evidence-based systematic review and meta-analysis. *Computers & Education, 114*, 139–163. DOI: 10.1016/j.compedu.2017.06.005 PMID: 29276334

Pérez-Muñoz, S., Castaño Calle, R., Morales Campo, P. T., & Rodríguez-Cayetano, A. (2024). A systematic review of the use and effect of virtual reality, augmented reality and mixed reality in physical education. *Information (Basel), 15*(9), 582. DOI: 10.3390/info15090582

Petersen, G. B., Petkakis, G., & Makransky, G. (2022). A study of how immersion and interactivity drive VR learning. *Computers & Education, 179*, 104429.

Peters, M. A., Jackson, L., Papastephanou, M., Jandrić, P., Lazaroiu, G., Evers, C. W., & Fuller, S. (2024). AI and the future of humanity: ChatGPT-4, philosophy and education–Critical responses. *Educational Philosophy and Theory, 56*(9), 828–862.

Pillai, R., Sivathanu, B., Metri, B., & Kaushik, N. (2024). Students' adoption of AI-based teacher-bots (T-Bots) for learning in higher education. *Information Technology & People, 37*(1), 328–355. DOI: 10.1108/ITP-02-2021-0152

Pineda Caro, D. Y. (2023). Enfoque STEAM: Retos y oportunidades para los docentes. *Revista Internacional de Pedagogía e Innovación Educativa, 3*(1).

Pinto-Sudario, G. C., & Plaza-Andrade, J. N. (2021). Determinar la necesidad de capacitación en el uso de las tecnologías de la información y las comunicaciones para la formación docente. *593 Digital Publisher CEIT, 6*(1), 169–181. https://doi .org/DOI: 10.33386/593dp.2021.1.426

Pittman, J., Severino, L., DeCarlo-Tecce, M. J., & Kiosoglous, C. (2021). An action research case study: Digital equity and educational inclusion during an emergent COVID-19 divide. *Journal for Multicultural Education, 15*(1), 68–84. DOI: 10.1108/JME-04-2021-0027

Pitychoutis, K. M., & Al Rawahi, A. (2024). Smart teaching: The synergy of multiple intelligences and artificial intelligence in English as a foreign language instruction. In *Forum for Linguistic Studies* (Vol. 6, No. 6, pp. 249-260).

Pivik, J. R. (2010). The perspective of children and youth: How different stakeholders identify architectural barriers for inclusion in schools. *Journal of Environmental Psychology, 30*(4), 510–517. DOI: 10.1016/j.jenvp.2010.02.005

Podsakoff, P. M., MacKenzie, S. B., Lee, J. Y., & Podsakoff, N. P. (2003). Common method biases in behavioral research: A critical review of the literature and recommended remedies. *The Journal of Applied Psychology, 88*(5), 879. PMID: 14516251

Porcino, T., Trevisan, D., & Clua, E. (2020). Minimizing cybersickness in head-mounted display systems: causes and strategies review. In 2020 22nd symposium on virtual and augmented reality (SVR) (pp. 154-163). IEEE.

Pradeep, K., Sulur Anbalagan, R., Thangavelu, A. P., Aswathy, S., Jisha, V. G., & Vaisakhi, V. S. (2024, December). Neuroeducation: Understanding neural dynamics in learning and teaching. [). Frontiers Media SA.]. *Frontiers in Education, 9*, 1437418.

Pradhan, K. C., & Naik, M. S. (2024). Inclusive education: A foundation for equality and empowerment at the elementary stage. *International Journal of Multidisciplinary Research in Arts, Science and Technology, 2*(2), 1–8. https://ijmrast.org/vol2issue2/ijmrast2024v2i2001

Pramanik, S. (2024). Immersive innovations: Exploring the use of virtual and augmented reality in educational institutions. In *Augmented reality and the future of education technology* (pp. 66–85). IGI Global., DOI: 10.4018/979-8-3693-2857-6.ch013

Prendes Espinosa, M. P. (2018). La tecnología educativa en la pedagogía del siglo XXI: Una visión en 3D. [RIITE]. *Revista Interuniversitaria de Investigación en Tecnología Educativa*, (4), 6–16. DOI: 10.6018/riite/2018/335131

Prieto Murillo, M. (2024). Educando con el enfoque STEAM para la solución de problemas. *Umbral Científica, 49*(1), 3–21.

Procel, G. J. O., Medina, M. L. F., Sotomayor, D. J., & Sanchez, M. A. P. T. (2024). Using technology in English teaching. *Journal of Environmental Research and Public Health, 17*(9), 9. DOI: 10.3390/ijerph17093009

Przegalinska, A., & Triantoro, T. (2024). *Converging minds: The creative potential of collaborative AI*. CRC Press.

Pulivarthy, P., & Whig, P. (2025). Bias and fairness addressing discrimination in AI systems. In *Ethical dimensions of AI development* (pp. 103–126). IGI Global., DOI: 10.4018/979-8-3693-4147-6.ch005

Qian, C., Videla, R., Videla, R., Parada, F. J., Aros, M. B., Ramírez, P., ... & Molina, B. (2025). Breaking barriers in education: leveraging 3E approach and technology to foster inclusion for SEN students.

Quintero, J., Baldiris, S., Rubira, R., Cerón, J., & Velez, G. (2019). Augmented reality in educational inclusion: A systematic review on the last decade. *Frontiers in Psychology*, *10*, 1835. DOI: 10.3389/fpsyg.2019.01835 PMID: 31456716

Quintero, T., Renato, A., Valencia, Q., Paola, K., Santana, G., Junior, W., Valdez, F., Lisbeth, J., Muñoz, S., & Manuel, J. (2024). *Storytelling as a Teaching Strategy to Improve Reading Comprehension in the Elementary Sublevel of Basic General Education*. Ciencia Latina, Multidisciplinary Scientific Journal.

Rahman, N. A., Mailok, R., & Husain, N. M. (2020). Mobile augmented reality learning application for students with learning disabilities. *International Journal of Academic Research in Business & Social Sciences*, *10*(2), 133–141. DOI: 10.6007/IJARBSS/v10-i2/6896 PMID: 40715120

Rajora, R., Rajora, A., Sharma, B., Aggarwal, P., & Thapliyal, S. (2024, February). The integration of IoT in learning environments: Assessing the impact of educational empowerment and addressing its challenges. In *2024 4th International Conference on Innovative Practices in Technology and Management (ICIPTM)* (pp. 1-5). IEEE.

Ralabate, P. K. (2011). Universal design for learning: Meeting the needs of all students. *ASHA Leader*, *16*(10), 14–17. DOI: 10.1044/leader.FTR2.16102011.14

Rambaree, K., Nässén, N., Holmberg, J., & Fransson, G. (2023). Enhancing cultural empathy in international social work education through virtual reality. *Education Sciences*, *13*(5), 507. DOI: 10.3390/educsci13050507

Rana, S., Sheshadri, T., Malhotra, N., & Basha, S. M. (2024). Creating Digital Learning Environments: Tools and Technologies for Success. In *Transdisciplinary Teaching and Technological Integration for Improved Learning: Case Studies and Practical Approaches* (pp. 1-21). IGI Global.

Rana, M., Norbisrath, U., Vainikko, E., & Rossi, B. (2023, September). Transforming affordable virtual reality headsets into effective learning environments. In *2023 International Conference on Intelligent Metaverse Technologies & Applications (iMETA)* (pp. 1-8). IEEE.

Rana, R., & Bhambri, P. (2024a). Artificial Intelligence and Internet of Things (IoT) facilitated digital twin for Industry 4.0 application domains. In Rani, S., Bhambri, P., Kumar, S., Pareek, P. K., & Elngar, A. A. (Eds.), *AI-driven digital twin and Industry 4.0* (pp. 168–181). CRC Press., DOI: 10.1201/9781003395416-11

Rana, R., & Bhambri, P. (2024b). Generative AI in web application development: Enhancing user experience and performance. In Shah, I. A., & Jhanjhi, N. Z. (Eds.), *Generative AI for web engineering models* (pp. 471–486). IGI Global., DOI: 10.4018/979-8-3693-3703-5.ch021

Rana, S., Sheshadri, T., Malhotra, N., & Basha, S. M. (2024). *Transdisciplinary teaching and technological integration for improved learning: Case studies and practical approaches*. IGI Global., DOI: 10.4018/979-8-3693-8217-2.ch001

Rane, N. (2023). Chatbot-enhanced teaching and learning: Implementation strategies, challenges, and the role of ChatGPT in education. *Challenges, and the Role of ChatGPT in Education (July 21, 2023).*

Rane, N. (2023). Roles and challenges of ChatGPT and similar generative artificial intelligence for achieving the sustainable development goals (SDGs) [Preprint]. *SSRN*. https://doi.org/DOI: 10.2139/ssrn.4603244

Rani, S., Kataria, A., Bhambri, P., Pareek, P. K., & Puri, V. (2024). Artificial intelligence in personalized health services for better patient care. In Gupta, S. K., Karras, D. A., & Natarajan, R. (Eds.), *Revolutionizing healthcare: AI integration with IoT for enhanced patient outcomes* (pp. 89–108). Springer., DOI: 10.1007/978-3-031-65022-2_6

Rashidi, H. H., Pantanowitz, J., Hanna, M. G., Tafti, A. P., Sanghani, P., Buchinsky, A., Fennell, B., Deebajah, M., Wheeler, S., Pearce, T., Abukhiran, I., Robertson, S., Palmer, O., Gur, M., & Tran, N. K. (2025). Introduction to artificial intelligence and machine learning in pathology and medicine: Generative and nongenerative artificial intelligence basics. *Modern Pathology*, *38*(4), 100688. Advance online publication. DOI: 10.1016/j.modpat.2024.100688 PMID: 39755237

Rekha, K., Gopal, K., Satheeskumar, D., Anand, U., Doss, D., & Elayaperumal, S. (2024). AI-powered personalized learning system design: Student engagement and performance tracking system. In *Proceedings of the 4th international conference on advanced computing and intelligent technologies* (Vol. 28, pp. 1125–1130). IEEE. https://doi.org/DOI: 10.1109/icacite60783.2024.10617155

Reyes, R. L., Isleta, K. P., Regala, J. D., & Bialba, D. M. R. (2024). Enhancing experiential science learning with virtual labs: A narrative account of merits, challenges, and implementation strategies. *Journal of Computer Assisted Learning*, *40*(6), 3167–3186. DOI: 10.1111/jcal.13061

Ribeiro, E., Farias, C., & Mesquita, I. (2024). "The game changers": How equity-driven pedagogical scaffolding reduces participation disparities in physical education. *Education Sciences*, *14*(10), 1077. DOI: 10.3390/educsci14101077

Ribis, E. V. (2025). Fostering creativity, advanced technology, and personal growth: The impact of a magic-themed learning experience in primary education. *Revista Catalana de Pedagogia*, *27*, 4–35. DOI: 10.2436/20.3007.01.215

Rivera-Robles, S. B., Salcedo-Lagos, P. A., Valdivia-Guzmán, J. R., & López-Jara, O. A. (2021). Estudios empíricos del modelo sobre conocimiento didáctico tecnológico del contenido (TPACK) en matemáticas, incluidos en bases bibliográficas internacionales. *Información Tecnológica*, *32*(4), 109–120. DOI: 10.4067/S0718-07642021000400109

Riyat, M. K., Kakkar, R. K., & Kakkar, A. (2025). Creating immersive learning experiences in education domain through virtual and augmented reality. In *Enhancing learning experiences with digital tools: AI, ChatGPT, and virtual and augmented reality* (pp. 123–156). IGI Global Scientific Publishing., DOI: 10.4018/979-8-3693-9811-1.ch006

Roberts, K. D., Park, H. J., Brown, S., & Cook, B. (2011). Universal design for instruction in postsecondary education: A systematic review of empirically based articles. *Journal of Postsecondary Education and Disability*, *24*(1), 5–15.

Rocha, F., Correia, F., Neto, I., Pires, A. C., Guerreiro, J., Guerreiro, T., & Nicolau, H. (2023, April). Coding together: On co-located and remote collaboration between children with mixed-visual abilities. In *Proceedings of the 2023 CHI Conference on Human Factors in Computing Systems* (pp. 1–14). DOI: 10.1145/3544548.3580924

Rohm, A. J., Stefl, M., & Ward, N. (2021). Future proof and real-world ready: The role of live project-based learning in students' skill development. *Journal of Marketing Education*, *43*(2), 204–215.

Rong, J., Terzidis, K., & Ding, J. (2024). Kids AI Design Thinking Education for Creativity Development. *Archives of Design Research, 37*(3), 119–133.

Rose, D. H., & Strangman, N. (2007). Universal design for learning: Meeting the challenge of individual learning differences through a neurocognitive perspective. *Universal Access in the Information Society, 5*, 381–391. DOI: 10.1007/s10209-006-0062-8

Rosenstrauch, D., Mangla, U., Gupta, A., & Masau, C. T. (2023). Artificial intelligence and ethics. In *Digital health entrepreneurship* (pp. 225–239). Springer., DOI: 10.1007/978-3-031-33902-8_16

Rousi, R., Alanen, H. K., & Wilson, A. S. (2024). Data privacy, ethics and education in the era of AI–A university student perspective. In Proceedings of the 7th conference on technology ethics (TETHICS 2024) (Vol. 3901, pp. 81–95). CEUR-WS.

Rubio-Tamayo, J. L., Gertrudix Barrio, M., & García García, F. (2017). Immersive environments and virtual reality: Systematic review and advances in communication, interaction and simulation. *Multimodal Technologies and Interaction, 1*(4), 21. DOI: 10.3390/mti1040021

Rueda, J., & Lara, F. (2020). Virtual reality and empathy enhancement: Ethical aspects. *Frontiers in Robotics and AI, 7*, 506984. DOI: 10.3389/frobt.2020.506984 PMID: 33501297

Ryan, G. V., Callaghan, S., Rafferty, A., Higgins, M. F., Mangina, E., & McAuliffe, F. (2022). Learning outcomes of immersive technologies in health care student education: Systematic review of the literature. *Journal of Medical Internet Research, 24*(2), e30082. PMID: 35103607

Saab, M. M., McCarthy, M., O'Mahony, B., Cooke, E., Hegarty, J., Murphy, D., & Noonan, B. (2023). Virtual reality simulation in nursing and midwifery education: a usability study. CIN: Computers, Informatics. *Nursing, 41*(10), 815–824. PMID: 36749836

Sabri, S. M., Ismail, I., Annuar, N., Rahman, N. R. A., Abd Hamid, N. Z., & Abd Mutalib, H. (2024). A conceptual analysis of technology integration in classroom instruction towards enhancing student engagement and learning outcomes. *Integration (Amsterdam), 9*(55), 750–769.

Sajja, R., Sermet, Y., Cwiertny, D., & Demir, I. (2023). Integrating AI and learning analytics for data-driven pedagogical decisions and personalized interventions in education [Preprint]. arXiv. https://doi.org//arXiv.2312.09548DOI: 10.48550

Sakthivel, M., Jaganathan, A., & Mohanraj, M. Mohit, & Manjunath, T. (2025). Brand loyalty through AI and personalisation: AI-generated content for financial marketing. In A. J. Nair, S. Manohar, Y. B. Limbu, & B. A. Huhmann (Eds.), Intersecting natural language processing and FinTech innovations in service marketing (pp. 77–96). IGI Global Scientific Publishing. https://doi.org/DOI: 10.4018/979-8-3693-9944-6.ch006

Salas-Rueda, R. A. (2018, June). Uso del modelo TPACK como herramienta de innovación para el proceso de enseñanza-aprendizaje en matemáticas. *Perspectiva Educacional. Formación de Profesores*, *57*(2), 3–26. DOI: 10.4151/07189729-vol.57-iss.2-art.689

Salas-Rueda, R. A. (2019). Modelo TPACK: ¿Medio para innovar el proceso educativo considerando la ciencia de datos y el aprendizaje automático? *Entreciencias*, *7*(19), 51–66. DOI: 10.22201/enesl.20078064e.2018.19.67511

Salinas Esparza, M. de C., Flores Crespo, P. A., & Escudero Nahón, A. (2021). La formación docente en el uso de tecnología: Una necesidad constante. In *Congreso Nacional de Investigación Educativa (CNIE 2021)* (pp. 1–10). https://www.comie.org.mx/congreso/memoriaelectronica/v16/doc/1598.pdf

Salvador, R., Barros, M. V., Barreto, B., Pontes, J., Yoshino, R. T., Piekarski, C. M., & de Francisco, A. C. (2023). Challenges and opportunities for problem-based learning in higher education: Lessons from a cross-program Industry 4.0 case. *Industry and Higher Education*, *37*(1), 3–21.

Sá, M. J., & Serpa, S. (2023). Metaverse as a learning environment: Some considerations. *Sustainability*, *15*(3), 2186.

Samal, A., & Misra, L. I. Mohit, Pougajendy, S., Chandel, P. S., & Manjunath, T. C. (2025). Musealization and tourism practices. In S. Oflazoğlu & M. Dora (Eds.), Preserving cultural heritage in post-disaster urban renewal (pp. 115–142). IGI Global Scientific Publishing. https://doi.org/DOI: 10.4018/979-8-3693-9097-9.ch006

Samaniego López, M. V., Orrego Riofrío, M. C., Barriga-Fray, S. F., & Paz Viteri, B. S. (2025). Technologies in inclusive education: Solution or challenge? A systematic review. *Education Sciences*, *15*(6), 715. DOI: 10.3390/educsci15060715

Samperio Pacheco, V. M., & Barragán López, J. F. (2018). Análisis de la percepción de docentes, usuarios de una plataforma educativa, a través de los modelos TPACK, SAMR y TAM3 en una institución de educación superior. *Apertura (Guadalajara, Jal.)*, *10*(1), 116–131. DOI: 10.32870/Ap.v10n1.1162

Sanchez, S. L., Junior., & Alves de Sousa, R. R. (2023). The importance of STEAM education in training future professionals. *Diálogo e Interação, 17*(1). https://revista.faccrei.edu.br/revista-dialogo-e-interacao/article/view/166

Sanguinetti, H. (2024). *Exploring the implications: The impact of universal design for learning on student engagement and motivation in diverse classroom environments* (Doctoral dissertation, George Fox University). George Fox University. https://digitalcommons.georgefox.edu/edd/235

Santillán-Aguirre, J. P., Santos-Poveda, R. D., & Jaramillo-Moyano, E. M. (2021). STEAM: Educación para el sujeto del siglo XXI. *Revista Dominio de las Ciencias, 7*(4), 1461–1478. DOI: 10.23857/dc.v7i4.2181

Sapkaroski, D., Mundy, M., & Dimmock, M. R. (2022). Immersive virtual reality simulated learning environment versus role-play for empathic clinical communication training. *Journal of Medical Radiation Sciences, 69*(1), 56–65. PMID: 34706398

Sasanelli, L. D., Ranieri, G., & Campanale, R. (2025). Embodied education in the framework of Universal Design for Learning: Connections and synergies. *Journal of Inclusive Methodology and Technology in Learning and Teaching, 5*(2). https://www.inclusiveteaching.it/index.php/inclusiveteaching/article/view/350

Sato, E., Shyyan, V., Chauhan, S., & Christensen, L. (2024). Putting AI in fair: A framework for equity in AI-driven learner models and inclusive assessments. *Journal of Measurement and Evaluation in Education and Psychology, 15*(Special Issue), 263–281. DOI: 10.21031/epod.1526527

Saunders, T. L., Coleman, M. B., Smith, C. C., Carter, A., & Alshehri, A. (2024). The effects of using augmented reality on phoneme and word reading for first grade students with autism and developmental delays. *Journal of Special Education Technology, 0*(0), 1–13. 10.1177_01626434251314007

Savickaite, S., Oyebisi, J., Stockman, T., & Bourguet, M. L. (2024). Instructional Design and Authoring of Accessible and Inclusive Extended Reality Learning Experiences. *The Journal of Applied Instructional Design, 13*(4).

Saz-Pérez, F., Pizà-Mir, B., & Lizana Carrió, A. (2024). Validación y estructura factorial de un cuestionario TPACK en el contexto de inteligencia artificial generativa (IAG). *Hachetetepé. Revista Científica de Educación y Comunicación*, (28), 1–14. DOI: 10.25267/Hachetetepe.2024.i28.1101

Sbeiti, S. A. (2024). Technology Integration in Support of Wellness for Neurodiverse Students. *Journal of Educational Informatics, 5*(1), 58–73.

Schmidt, M., Lu, J., Huang, R., Francois, M. S., Lee, M., Wang, X., & Feijóo-García, P. G. (2024). Participatory, human-centered, equitable, neurodiverse, and inclusive XR. *Journal of Educational Technology & Society*, *27*(4), 283–301.

Schmidt, M., Newbutt, N., Lee, M., Lu, J., Francois, M. S., Antonenko, P. D., & Glaser, N. (2024). Toward a strengths-based model for designing virtual reality learning experiences for autistic users. *Autism*, *28*(7), 1809–1827. PMID: 37937531

Scoulas, J. M., & Kim, J. C. (2025). Reevaluating assessment practices for marginalized groups. *Journal of Library Administration*, *65*(2), 244–254. DOI: 10.1080/01930826.2025.2021315

Secretaría de Educación de Tamaulipas. (2024). *Anuario de la estadística educativa del Estado de Tamaulipas, ciclo escolar 2023–2024* [Informe]. https://www.tamaulipas.gob.mx/educacion/wp-content/uploads/sites/3/2024/04/anuario-educacion-2023-2024_v-e.pdf

Secretaría de Educación Pública. (2020). *Agenda Digital Educativa* [Website]. https://infosen.senado.gob.mx/sgsp/gaceta/64/2/2020-02-05-1/assets/documentos/Agenda_Digital_Educacion.pdf

Seol, H. Y., Kang, S., Lim, J., Hong, S. H., & Moon, I. J. (2021). Feasibility of virtual reality audiological testing: Prospective study. *JMIR Serious Games*, *9*(3), e26976. DOI: 10.2196/26976 PMID: 34463624

Serafin, S., Adjorlu, A., & Percy-Smith, L. M. (2023). A review of virtual reality for individuals with hearing impairments. *Multimodal Technologies and Interaction*, *7*(4), 36. DOI: 10.3390/mti7040036

Serrano-Ausejo, E., & Mårell-Olsson, E. (2024). Opportunities and challenges of using immersive technologies to support students' spatial ability and 21st-century skills in K-12 education. *Education and Information Technologies*, *29*(5), 5571–5597. DOI: 10.1007/s10639-023-12528-9

Sethi, S. S., & Jain, K. (2024). AI technologies for social emotional learning: Recent research and future directions. *Journal of Research in Innovative Teaching & Learning*, *17*(2), 213–225.

Setiawan, M. A., & Qamariah, Z. (2023). A practical guide in designing curriculum for diverse learners. *PUSTAKA: Jurnal Bahasa dan Pendidikan, 3*(3), 260–275. https://journal.example.org/pustaka/v3i3/260-275

Sewell, A., Kennett, A., & Pugh, V. (2022). Universal Design for Learning as a theory of inclusive practice for use by educational psychologists. *Educational Psychology in Practice*, *38*(4), 364–378. DOI: 10.1080/02667363.2022.2127807

Sgambelluri, R., & Placanica, F. (2024). Designing educational-inclusive contexts through artificial intelligence from the perspective of Life Designing.

Shaaban, T. S., & Mohamed, A. M. (2024). Exploring the effectiveness of augmented reality technology on reading comprehension skills among early childhood pupils with learning disabilities. *Journal of Computers in Education, 11*(2), 423–444. DOI: 10.1007/s40692-023-00269-9

Shadmehr, R. (2024). Designing an Individualized Virtual Reality Environment for Training: A Design Case Study with Autistic Learners.

Shafie, H., Majid, F. A., & Ismail, I. S. (2022). Developing a 21st-century technological pedagogical content knowledge (TPACK) instrument: Content validity and reliability. *International Journal of Education, 14*(3), 100–115. DOI: 10.5296/ije.v14i3.19980

Shanthi, B., Ravichandran, C., Manimegalai, V., Parashar, A. K., & BS, H. (2025). Critical Thinking in Higher Education Through Innovative Strategies: Out-of-the-Box Thinking. In *Global Practices in Inclusive Education Curriculum and Policy* (pp. 365-398). IGI Global.

Shidende, D., Kessel, T., Treydte, A., & Moebs, S. (2024, September). A personalized captioning strategy for the deaf and hard-of-hearing users in an augmented reality environment. In De Paolis, L. T., Arpaia, P., & Sacco, M. (Eds.), Lecture Notes in Computer Science: Vol. 15028. *Extended Reality: XR Salento 2024* (pp. 3–21). Springer Nature Switzerland., DOI: 10.1007/978-3-031-71704-8_1

Shireesha, M., & Jeevan, J. (2024). The Role of Artificial Intelligence in Personalized Learning: A Pathway to Inclusive Education. *Library of Progress-Library Science, Information Technology & Computer, 44*(3).

Shireesha, M., & Jeevan, J. (2024). The role of artificial intelligence in personalized learning: A pathway to inclusive education. *Library Progress – Library Science, Information Technology & Computer, 44*(3), 21746–21752. https://bpasjournals.com/library-science/index.php/journal/article/view/2813

Silva-Díaz, F., García-Yeguas, A., & Carrillo-Rosúa, J. (2023). Integración de tecnologías emergentes para la educación STEAM: Proyecto TECNOSTEAM. In *Las nuevas realidades educativas: El uso de tecnologías emergentes para el aprendizaje* (pp. 129–136). Dykinson., https://www.researchgate.net/publication/372782412

Silva-Hormazábal, M., & Alsinab, Á. (2023). Promoviendo el desarrollo profesional docente en STEAM: Diseño y validación de un programa de formación. [REXE]. *Revista de Estudios y Experiencias en Educación*, *22*(50), 99–120. DOI: 10.21703/rexe.v22i50.1986

Simões, J. M., & Caldeira, W. (2024). Ethics concerns in the use of computer-generated images for human communication. *Journal of Ethics in Higher Education*, (4), 169–192.

Singh, B., Kaunert, C., Lal, S., & Arora, M. K. (2025). Enhancing AI-Augmented Classrooms: Teacher-Centric Integration of Intelligent Tutoring Systems and Adaptive Learning Environments. In *Fostering Inclusive Education With AI and Emerging Technologies* (pp. 99-130). IGI Global.

Singh, M., Sun, D., & Zheng, Z. (2024). Enhancing university students' learning performance in a metaverse-enabled immersive learning environment for STEM education: A community of inquiry approach. *Future in Educational Research*, *2*(3), 288–309.

Singh, T. M., Reddy, C. K. K., Murthy, B. V. R., & Nag, A. (2025). AI and education: Bridging the gap to personalized, efficient, and accessible learning. In *Internet of behavior-based computational intelligence for smart education systems* (p. 30). IGI Global., DOI: 10.4018/979-8-3693-8151-9.ch005

Solé, I. (1992). *Reading strategies*. Graó.

Soler Costa, R., Tan, Q., Pivot, F., Zhang, X., & Wang, H. (2021). Personalized and adaptive learning: Educational practice and technological impact. *Texto Livre*, *14*(3), 33445. Advance online publication. DOI: 10.35699/1983-3652.2021.33445

Solmaz, S., Kester, L., & Van Gerven, T. (2024). An immersive virtual reality learning environment with CFD simulations: Unveiling the Virtual Garage concept. *Education and Information Technologies*, *29*(2), 1455–1488. PMID: 37361838

Sombilon, E. V., Rahmanov, S. S., Jachecki, K., Rahmanov, Z., & Peisachovich, E. (2024). Ethical considerations when designing and implementing immersive realities in nursing education. *Cureus*, *16*(7). PMID: 39130836

Somerville, S., Howden, S., Ker, J., & Schofield, S. (2024). Exploring accessible, inclusive and sustainable simulation-based education in remote and rural communities: A realist review. *International Journal of Healthcare Simulation : Advances in Theory and Practice*, •••, 1–14.

Soto Calderón, A., Oliveros Ruiz, M. A., & Roa Rivera, R. I. (2022). Curso-taller STEAM para docentes: Una evaluación formativa. *Entreciencias, 10*(24), 1–19. DOI: 10.22201/enesl.20078064e.2022.24.82377

Soundariya, A., Behera, N. K., Chandel, P. S., Gupta, S., & Manjunath, T. C. (2025). AI and environmental ethics: The role of AI in addressing climate change—Ethical considerations in AI-driven environmental solutions. In Chakraborty, S. (Ed.), *Human values, ethics, and dignity in the age of artificial intelligence* (pp. 321–346). IGI Global Scientific Publishing., DOI: 10.4018/979-8-3693-9035-1.ch013

Sousa, M. J., & Costa, J. M. (2022). Discovering entrepreneurship competencies through problem-based learning in higher education students. *Education Sciences, 12*(3), 185.

Souza, L. L. (2025). Virtual reality in critical care nursing education: First experiences in low-cost ICU simulation environments. *Education Sciences, 15*(9), 1258. DOI: 10.3390/educsci15091258

Sowell, J. (2023). Making Learning Inclusive in Digital Learning Environments. In *English Teaching Forum* (Vol. 61, No. 1, pp. 2-13). US Department of State. Bureau of Educational and Cultural Affairs, Office of English Language Programs, SA-5, 2200 C Street NW 4th Floor, Washington, DC 20037.

Sridevi, R., Ashokkumar, P., & Sathish, V. (2024). Empowering minds: Cognitive learning strategies for higher education success. In *Implementing interactive learning strategies in higher education* (pp. 123–150). IGI Global Scientific Publishing., DOI: 10.4018/979-8-3693-3559-8.ch005

Stalmach, A., D'Elia, P., Di Sano, S., & Casale, G. (2024). Digital methods to promote inclusive and effective learning in schools: A mixed methods research study. *Open Education Studies, 6*(1), 20240023.

Stolpe, K., & Hallström, J. (2024). Artificial intelligence literacy for technology education. *Computers and Education Open, 6*, 100159.

Storozhyk, M. (2024). Philosophy of future: Analytical overview of interaction between education, science, and artificial intelligence in the context of contemporary challenges. *Futurity Philosophy, 3*(1), 23–47.

Strielkowski, W., & Grebennikova, V.. (2025). AI-driven adaptive learning for sustainable educational transformation. *Sustainable Development, 33*(2), 1921–1947. DOI: 10.1002/sd.3221

Suh, A., & Prophet, J. (2018). The state of immersive technology research: A literature analysis. *Computers in Human Behavior, 86*, 77–90. DOI: 10.1016/j.chb.2018.04.019

Sulaimon, J. T., & Adebayo, A. A. (Eds.). (2024). *Empowering educators: Enhancing teacher professional development for sustainable education*. Routledge.

Sundari, M. S., Penthala, H. R., & Nayyar, A. (2024). Transforming education through AI-enhanced content creation and personalized learning experiences. In *Impact of artificial intelligence on society* (p. 21). Chapman and Hall/CRC., DOI: 10.1201/9781032644509-7

Suryani, T., Rahayu, W., & Saptono, A. (2021, August). Development and validation of a technological pedagogical content knowledge (TPACK) instrument for elementary school mathematics teachers. [IJMMU]. *International Journal of Multicultural and Multireligious Understanding*, *8*(8), 445–457. DOI: 10.18415/ijmmu.v8i8.2951

Sviridova, E., Yastrebova, E., Bakirova, G., & Rebrina, F. (2023). Immersive technologies as an innovative tool to increase academic success and motivation in higher education. *Frontiers in Education*, *8*, 1192760. DOI: 10.3389/feduc.2023.1192760

Tabullo, Á. J., Wainselboim, A., & París, L. A. (2022). La comprensión de textos expositivos y narrativos y su relación con el vocabulario. °: La eficacia lectora y el control inhibitorio en niños de cuarto grado. Traslaciones. *Revista Latinoamericana de Lectura y Escritura*, *9*(17), 39–59.

Tafazoli, D., McCallum, L., Fatemeh, R. M., Kusuma, I. P. I., Nami, F., Roe, J., & Waters, K. (2025). A conceptual model for inclusive computer-assisted language learning: A collaborative ethnography. *Computer-Assisted Language Learning Electronic Journal*, *26*(2), 1–28. DOI: 10.11139/callejon.26.02.001

Tan, S. Z. K., Shendyapina, M., & Tay, L. N. S. (2024). Evaluating the use of immersive interactive mixed reality (i2MR) technology in special needs education in Singapore. *Technology. Knowledge and Learning*, *29*(2), 781–802. DOI: 10.1007/s10758-023-09648-8

Tariq, M. U. (2025). AI in the Classroom: Revolutionizing Instruction and Student Engagement. In M. Kessinger, G. Nelson, L. Lennex, & K. Nettleton (Eds.), *Enhancing Classroom Instruction and Student Skills With AI* (pp. 35-62). IGI Global Scientific Publishing. https://doi.org/DOI: 10.4018/979-8-3373-4576-5.ch002

Tariq, M. U. (2026). AI-Powered Assessment Platforms: Transforming Higher Education Evaluation. In *Innovating Assessment and Evaluation in Higher Education: Inclusive Practices and Technological Advancements* (pp. 117-146). IGI Global Scientific Publishing.

Tariq, M. U. (2025). Integrating Advanced Technologies for Multi-Stakeholder Collaboration: Driving Sustainability in Supply Chains Through Industry 4.0. In Frichi, Y., & Jawab, F. (Eds.), *Multi-Stakeholder Collaboration for Sustainable Supply Chain* (pp. 313–334). IGI Global Scientific Publishing., DOI: 10.4018/979-8-3693-8925-6.ch014

Taylor, D. L., Yeung, M., & Bashet, A. Z. (2021). Personalized and adaptive learning. In *Innovative learning environments in STEM higher education* (pp. 17–34). Springer., DOI: 10.1007/978-3-030-58948-6_2

Tene, T., Marcatoma Tixi, J. A., Palacios Robalino, M. D. L., Mendoza Salazar, M. J., Vacacela Gomez, C., & Bellucci, S. (2024). Integrating immersive technologies with STEM education: A systematic review. *Frontiers in Education*, *9*, 1410163. DOI: 10.3389/feduc.2024.1410163

Thangavel, S., Sharmila, K., & Sufina, K. (2025). Revolutionizing education through augmented reality (AR) and virtual reality (VR): Innovations, challenges and future prospects. *Asian Journal of Interdisciplinary Research*, *8*(1), 1–28. DOI: 10.54392/ajir2511

Thelma, C. C., Sain, Z. H., Mpolomoka, D. L., Akpan, W. M., & Davy, M. (2024). Curriculum design for the digital age: Strategies for effective technology integration in higher education. *International Journal of Research*, *11*(07), 185–201. DOI: 10.5281/zenodo.13123899

Thirunagalingam, A., & Selvakumar, P. (2025). Application of automation and robotics in the oil and gas industry. In Abdullayev, V., & Khang, A. (Eds.), *Revolutionizing AI and robotics in the oil and gas industry* (pp. 229–244). IGI Global Scientific Publishing., DOI: 10.4018/979-8-3693-8156-4.ch011

Tiwari, S. P., & Fahrudin, A. (2024). *Evolving school dynamics and emerging technologies in education: Critical success factors*. SciFormat Publishing Inc., DOI: 10.69635/978-1-0690482-0-2

Tomlinson, C. A., & Jarvis, J. M. (2023). Differentiation: Making curriculum work for all students through responsive planning & instruction. In *Systems and models for developing programs for the gifted and talented* (pp. 599–628). Routledge.

Tong, Y. (2024). Integration of artificial intelligence into the general education curriculum: Importance, approaches, challenges, and a conceptual framework for liberal arts universities. In INTED2024 Proceedings (pp. 7582-7589). IATED.

Torres, C. A., Espinosa, W. A., Romero, D. M., Herrera, R. S., & Herrera, D. A. (2021, February 15). TPACK: Aplicabilidad docente del modelo en Educación General Básica Elemental. *Espacios*, *42*(3), 102–115. DOI: 10.48082/espacios-a21v42v03p08

Tosto, C., Hasegawa, T., Mangina, E., Chifari, A., Treacy, R., Merlo, G., & Chiazzese, G. (2021). Exploring the effect of an augmented reality literacy programme for reading and spelling difficulties for children diagnosed with ADHD. *Virtual Reality (Waltham Cross)*, *25*, 879–894.

Toto, G. A., Marinelli, C. V., Cavioni, V., di Furia, M., Traetta, L., Iuso, S., & Petito, A. (2024). What is the role of technologies for inclusive education? A systematic review. In *Higher education learning methodologies and technologies online* (pp. 533–565). Springer Nature Switzerland., DOI: 10.1007/978-3-031-67351-1_36

Toto, G. A., Marinelli, C. V., Cavioni, V., di Furia, M., Traetta, L., Iuso, S., & Petito, A. (2024). What is the role of technologies for inclusive education? A systematic review. In *International Conference on Higher Education Learning Methodologies and Technologies Online* (pp. 533–565). Springer, Cham.

Trivedi, P. (2024). Immersive Learning's Promise: The educational potential of augmented and virtual reality. *Augmented Reality and Virtual Reality in Special Education*, 91–102.

Trivedi, M., & Bindewari, S. (2025). Artificial intelligence: An educational advancement for students with visual disabilities. In *Impacts of AI on Students and Teachers in Education 5.0* (pp. 155–192). IGI Global Scientific Publishing., DOI: 10.4018/979-8-3693-8191-5.ch006

Troussas, C., Krouska, A., & Sgouropoulou, C. (2025). A novel framework of human–computer interaction and human-centered artificial intelligence in learning technology. In *Human-Computer Interaction and Augmented Intelligence: The Paradigm of Interactive Machine Learning in Educational Software* (pp. 387–431). Springer Nature Switzerland AG., DOI: 10.1007/978-3-031-84453-9_9

Ulla, M. B., Advincula, M. J. C., Mombay, C. D. S., Mercullo, H. M. A., Nacionales, J. P., & Entino-Señorita, A. D. (2024). How can GenAI foster an inclusive language classroom? A critical language pedagogy perspective from Philippine university teachers. *Computers and Education: Artificial Intelligence*, *7*, 100314. DOI: 10.1016/j.caeai.2024.100314

United Nations. (2015). Transforming our world: The 2030 agenda for sustainable development Retrieved May, 28, 2025 from https://sdgs.un.org/2030agenda

Upadhyay, M., & Malik, F. A. (2024). Societal and economic impact of Atmanirbhar Bharat: A long-term vision through education. Empowering India's Future: NEP. Skill Development and Cultural Expression, 17.

Upadhyaya, A. N., Debnath, P., Rani, P., Manjunath, T. C., & Bhattacharya, S. (2025). AI-based disaster prediction and early warning systems. In Mobo, F. (Ed.), *AI and emerging technologies for emergency response and smart cities* (pp. 55–74). IGI Global Scientific Publishing., DOI: 10.4018/979-8-3693-9770-1.ch003

Urbaite, G. (2024). The role of technology in modern language education. *Euro-Global Journal of Linguistics and Language Education*, *1*(1), 3–10.

Urgiles-Rodríguez, B. E., Tixi-Gallegos, K. G., & Allauca-Peñafiel, M. E. (2022). Metodología STEAM en ambientes académicos. *Revista Científica Dominio de las Ciencias*, *8*(1), 113–125. DOI: 10.23857/dc.v8i1.2482

Valarezo Castro, J. W., & Santos Jiménez, O. C. (2019). Las tecnologías del aprendizaje y el conocimiento en la formación docente. *Revista Conrado, 15*(68), 180–186. http://conrado.ucf.edu.cu/index.php/conrado

Valiente-Riedl, E., Anderson, L., & Banki, S. (2022). Practicing what we teach: Experiential learning in higher education that cuts both ways. *Review of Education, Pedagogy & Cultural Studies*, *44*(3), 231–252.

Valtonen, T., Sointu, E., Kukkonen, J., Kontkanen, S., Lambert, M. C., & Mäkitalo-Siegl, K. (2017). TPACK updated to measure pre-service teachers' twenty-first century skills. *Australasian Journal of Educational Technology*, *33*(3).

Vasinda, S., & Pilgrim, J. (2023). Technology supports in the UDL framework: Removable scaffolds or permanent new literacies? *Reading Research Quarterly*, *58*(1), 44–58. DOI: 10.1002/rrq.484

Vasquez, E., Nagendran, A., Welch, G. F., Marino, M. T., Hughes, D. E., Koch, A., & Delisio, L. (2015). Virtual learning environments for students with disabilities: A review and analysis of the empirical literature and two case studies. *Rural Special Education Quarterly*. Advance online publication. DOI: 10.1177/875687051503400306

Vatankhah, S., Bamshad, V., Arici, H. E., & Duan, Y. (2024). Ethical implementation of artificial intelligence in the service industries. *Service Industries Journal*, *44*(9-10), 661–685.

Velazquez-Solis, P. E., Correa, M. E. G., Martinez, M. A., Arroyo, J. G., & Marquez, M. Y. (2025). Designing Teaching Strategies Using Artificial Intelligence for Neurodivergent Students in Higher Education. In *Exploring Psychology, Social Innovation and Advanced Applications of Machine Learning* (pp. 191-208). IGI Global Scientific Publishing.

Vermunt, J. D. (2023). Understanding, measuring and improving simulation-based learning in higher education: Student and teacher learning perspectives. *Learning and Instruction, 86*, 101773.

Vettriselvan, R. (2025). Empowering digital education: The future of value-based learning in the digital era. In Sousa, B., & Veloso, C. (Eds.), *Empowering value co-creation in the digital era* (pp. 199–228). IGI Global Scientific Publishing., DOI: 10.4018/979-8-3373-1742-7.ch009

Vibhuti, Kumar, N., Kataria, C., & Aroura, S. (2025). Assessing the efficacity of immersive computing and electroencephalogram in the rehabilitation of upper extremity neuro-motor dysfunctions: A systematic review. *International Journal of Human-Computer Interaction*, •••, 1–27. DOI: 10.1080/10447318.2025.2470284

Videla, R., Aros, M. B., Parada, F., Kausel, L., Sandoval-Obando, E., Jorquera, D., & Ramírez, P. (2025). Neurodiversity: Post-cognitivist foundations of the 3E approach for educational inclusion of autistic students with technology. *Frontiers in Human Neuroscience, 18*, 1493863. PMID: 39963287

Videla, R., Parada, F. J., Aros, M. B., Ramírez, P., Sarzosa, A., Jorquera, D., & Kausel, L. (2025, June). Breaking barriers in education: Leveraging 3E approach and technology to foster inclusion for SEN students. [). Frontiers Media SA.]. *Frontiers in Education, 10*, 1554314.

Villada Castillo, J. F., Bohorquez Santiago, L., & Martínez García, S. (2025). Optimization of physics learning through immersive virtual reality: A study on the efficacy of serious games. *Applied Sciences (Basel, Switzerland), 15*(6), 3405. DOI: 10.3390/app15063405

Villarreal, A. R., & Scott, S. M. (2024). Fostering inclusive and resilient classroom environments in the post-COVID-19 era: Strategies for underserved and underrepresented students. In *Building resilient education models post crisis* (pp. 17–41). IGI Global Scientific Publishing., DOI: 10.4018/979-8-3693-8125-0.ch002

Vinumol, K. P., Chowdhury, A., Kambam, R., & Muralidharan, V. (2013, May). Augmented reality based interactive text book: An assistive technology for students with learning disability. In *2013 XV symposium on virtual and augmented reality* (pp. 232–235). IEEE. https://doi.org/DOI: 10.1109/SVR.2013.26

Visscher, K. (2024). Experiencing complex stakeholder dynamics around emerging technologies: A role-play simulation. *European Journal of Engineering Education, 49*(2), 370–388. DOI: 10.1080/03043797.2023.2196940

von Gillern, S., & Nash, B. (2023). Accessibility in video gaming: An overview and implications for English language arts education. *Journal of Adolescent & Adult Literacy, 66*(6), 382–390. DOI: 10.1002/jaal.1284

Voultsiou, E., & Moussiades, L. (2025). A systematic review of AI, VR, and LLM applications in special education: Opportunities, challenges, and future directions. *Education and Information Technologies*, •••, 1–41. DOI: 10.1007/s10639-025-13550-4

Vullamparthi, A. J., Nelaturu, S. C. B., Mallaya, D. D., & Chandrasekhar, S. (2013). Assistive learning for children with autism using augmented reality. Speaking albums and visual auditory schedulers. In *2013 IEEE Fifth International Conference on Technology for Education* (pp. 43-46). doi: DOI: 10.1109/T4E.2013.18

Wagner, C., & Liu, L. (2021). Creating immersive learning experiences: A pedagogical design perspective. In *Creative and collaborative learning through immersion: Interdisciplinary and international perspectives* (pp. 71–87). Springer International Publishing., DOI: 10.1007/978-3-030-72512-8_5

Wang, D., & Huang, X. (2025). Transforming education through artificial intelligence and immersive technologies: Enhancing learning experiences. *Interactive Learning Environments*, •••, 1–20.

Wang, Q., & Yu, Z. (2024). Deep Learning-Based Scene Processing and Optimization for Virtual Reality Classroom Environments: A Study. *TS. Traitement du Signal, 41*(1).

Wang, Y., Liang, J., Yu, J., Shan, Y., Huang, X., Lin, W., Pan, Q., Zhang, T., Zhang, Z., Gao, Y., Yu, X., Wei, L., & Yang, Z. (2024). Multiscale haptic interfaces for metaverse. *Device, 2*(6), 100326. Advance online publication. DOI: 10.1016/j.device.2024.100326

Weisberg, L., & Dawson, K. (2023). The intersection of equity pedagogy and technology integration in preservice teacher education: A scoping review. *Journal of Teacher Education, 74*(4), 327–342. DOI: 10.1177/00224871221101234

Weiss, P. L., Bialik, P., & Kizony, R. (2003). Virtual reality provides leisure time opportunities for young adults with physical and intellectual disabilities. *Cyberpsychology & Behavior, 6*(3), 335–342. PMID: 12855092

Weng, X., Chiu, T. K., & Tsang, C. C. (2022). Promoting student creativity and entrepreneurship through real-world problem-based maker education. *Thinking Skills and Creativity*, *45*, 101046.

Wigfield, A., & Guthrie, J. T. (1997). Relationships of children's motivation for reading to the amount and breadth of their reading. *Journal of Educational Psychology*, *89*(3), 420–432.

Williams, L., & Sembiante, S. F. (2022). Experiential learning in US undergraduate teacher preparation programs: A review of the literature. *Teaching and Teacher Education*, *112*, 103630.

Williams, R., Cloete, R., Cobbe, J., Cottrill, C., Edwards, P., Markovic, M., Naja, I., Ryan, F., Singh, J., & Pang, W. (2022). From transparency to accountability of intelligent systems: Moving beyond aspirations. *Data & Policy*, *4*, e7. Advance online publication. DOI: 10.1017/dap.2021.37

Wilson, S., Vallis, C., & Yeoman, P. (2025). Walking through the future in the present: Teaching practices in postdigital learning spaces. *Postdigital Science and Education*, *7*, 1–21. DOI: 10.1007/s42438-025-00321-4

Wongvorachan, T., Lai, K. W., Bulut, O., & Tsai, Y. S. (2022). Artificial intelligence: Transforming the future of feedback in education. Journal of Applied Testing Technology, 23(Special Issue 1), 95–116. https://doi.org/DOI: 10.1386/jpm_00003_1

Wu, C.-L., & Tsai, Y.-H. (2023). Effects of video prompting with augmented reality on functional living skills of students with intellectual and developmental disabilities. *Journal of Special Education Technology*, *39*(1), 3–14. DOI: 10.1177/01626434231170594

Wu, J. G., Zhang, D., & Lee, S. M. (2023). Into the brave new metaverse: Envisaging future language teaching and learning. *IEEE Transactions on Learning Technologies*, *17*, 44–53.

Wu, Y. (2025). The simulation paradox: Does perfecting virtual anatomy risk imperfecting professional empathy? *Anatomical Sciences Education*, *18*(10), 1147–1154. PMID: 40588781

Xiao, Y., & Zhi, Y. (2023). An exploratory study of EFL learners' use of ChatGPT for language learning tasks: Experience and perceptions. *Languages (Basel, Switzerland)*, *8*(3), 212. Advance online publication. DOI: 10.3390/languages8030212

Xu, Z. (2024). AI in education: Enhancing learning experiences and student outcomes. *Applied and Computational Engineering*, *51*(1), 104–111.

Yazici, M. S., & Uzuner, F. G. (2024). School-based inclusive mentoring within the scope of an experiential learning model (IEM) for teacher education. *Teaching and Teacher Education, 152*, 104799.

Yeganeh, L. N., Fenty, N. S., Chen, Y., Simpson, A., & Hatami, M. (2025). The future of education: A multi-layered metaverse classroom model for immersive and inclusive learning. *Future Internet, 17*(2), 63.

Yeh, H. C. (2025). The synergy of generative AI and inquiry-based learning: Transforming the landscape of English teaching and learning. *Interactive Learning Environments, 33*(1), 88–102.

Yekollu, R. K., Bhimraj Ghuge, T., Sunil Biradar, S., Haldikar, S. V., & Mohideen Abdul Kader, O. F. (2024). AI-driven personalized learning paths: Enhancing education through adaptive systems. In International conference on smart data intelligence (pp. 507–517). Springer. https://doi.org/DOI: 10.1007/978-981-97-3191-6_38

Yenioglu, B. Y., Yenioglu, S., Sayar, K., & Ergulec, F. (2023). Using augmented reality based intervention to teach science to students with learning disabilities. *Journal of Special Education Technology, 39*(1), 108–119. DOI: 10.1177/01626434231184829

Yesil, L. B., & Aras, İ. S. (2024). The significance of flexible learning spaces and student-centred pedagogies in school settings: A comparative case study. *International Education Journal: Comparative Perspectives, 23*(1), 1–24. DOI: 10.1111/iej.2024.23.issue-1

Yıldız, T. (2025). The minds we make: A philosophical inquiry into theory of mind and artificial intelligence. *Integrative Psychological & Behavioral Science, 59*(1), 10. PMID: 39743649

Yilmaz, O., & Hebebci, M. T. (2022). The use of virtual environments and simulation in teacher training. *International Journal on Social and Education Sciences, 4*, 446–457.

Youngerman, E., & Culver, K. C. (2024). Increasing equity through project-based learning in graduate and professional schools: Problems of practice, cases, and clinics. In *Promoting Meaningful Student-Faculty Experiences in Graduate Education* (pp. 62–84). Routledge.

Youssef, E., Al Malak, M., & Bayoumy, M. (2025). Metaverse in education: A survey-based investigation of collaborative learning and immersive experiences. *Emerging Science Journal, 8*, 379–395. DOI: 10.28991/ESJ-2024-SIED1-022

Zahra, S. T., Bibi, E., & Younus, Z. (2025). Artificial Intelligence (AI) and Human Mind: Struggles and Strengths in the Education Sector. In Artificial Intelligence and Human Agency in Education: Volume One: The Nexus Between AI and Human Agency in Educational Contexts (pp. 265-289). Springer Nature Singapore.

Zaky, H. (2025). Quality higher education: Accommodate diverse learning needs in classrooms. *SSRN*. DOI: 10.2139/ssrn.5158830

Zallio, M., & Clarkson, P. J. (2022). Designing the metaverse: A study on inclusion, diversity, equity, accessibility and safety for digital immersive environments. *Telematics and Informatics*, *75*, 101909. DOI: 10.1016/j.tele.2022.101909

Zamiri, M., & Esmaeili, A. (2024). Strategies, methods, and supports for developing skills within learning communities: A systematic review of the literature. *Administrative Sciences*, *14*(9), 231. DOI: 10.3390/admsci14090231

Zaugg, T. (2024). Future innovations for assistive technology and universal design for learning. *Assistive technology and universal design for learning: Toolkits for inclusive instruction*, 275-318.

Zaugg, T. (2024). Future innovations for assistive technology and universal design for learning. In *Assistive technology and universal design for learning: Toolkits for inclusive instruction* (pp. 275–318). IGI Global., DOI: 10.4018/978-1-7998-9018-4.ch012

Zentall, S. S. (2007). Math performance of students with ADHD: Cognitive and behavioral contributors and interventions. In Berch, D. B., & Mazzocco, M. M. M. (Eds.), *Why is math so hard for some children? The nature and origins of mathematical learning difficulties and disabilities* (pp. 219–243). Paul H. Brookes Publishing Co.

Zhang, H., Wang, Z., Zong, S., Wu, H., Jiang, R., Cui, Y., & Luo, H. (2024). Impact of intelligent learning environments on perception and presence of hearing-impaired college students. *Journal of Educational Technology & Society*, *27*(4), 352–374.

Zhang, L., Carter, R. A.Jr, Basham, J. D., & Yang, S. (2022). Integrating instructional designs of personalized learning through the lens of universal design for learning. *Journal of Computer Assisted Learning*, *38*(6), 1639–1656. DOI: 10.1111/jcal.12675

Zhang, L., Carter, R. A.Jr, Greene, J. A., & Bernacki, M. L. (2024). Unraveling challenges with the implementation of universal design for learning: A systematic literature review. *Educational Psychology Review*, *36*(1), 35. DOI: 10.1007/s10648-023-09733-2

Zhang, M., Ding, H., Naumceska, M., & Zhang, Y. (2022). Virtual reality technology as an educational and intervention tool for children with autism spectrum disorder: Current perspectives and future directions. *Behavioral Sciences (Basel, Switzerland)*, *12*(5), 138. PMID: 35621435

Zhang, Y., & Miao, Z. (2025). Enhancing EFL learners' engagement and motivation through immersive technologies: The role of artificial intelligence, augmented reality, virtual Reality, and mobile applications. *European Journal of Education*, *60*(2), e70128. DOI: 10.1111/ejed.70128

Zhan, Y., Quan, J., & Ren, Y. (2013). An empirical study on the technological pedagogical content knowledge development of pre-service mathematics teachers in China. *International Journal of Social Media and Interactive Learning Environments*, *1*(2), 199–212. DOI: 10.1504/IJSMILE.2013.053600

Zhan, Z., Zhou, X., Cai, S., & Lan, X. (2025). Exploring the effect of competing mechanism in an immersive learning game based on augmented reality. *Journal of Computers in Education*, *12*(2), 449–475.

Zhubi, A., & Ismajli, H. (2022). The interconnection between technological, pedagogical and content knowledge in primary school lesson planning. *Journal of Social Studies Education Research*, *13*(2), 125–146. https://files.eric.ed.gov/fulltext/EJ1355509.pdf

Zhu, Q., & Xie, X. (2023). Users' needs and expectations of immersive learning spaces in an academic library: A survey. *Journal of Librarianship and Information Science*, *55*(2), 371–382.

Zuhair, V., Babar, A., Ali, R., & Oduoye, M. O.. (2024). Exploring the impact of artificial intelligence on global health and enhancing healthcare in developing nations. *Journal of Primary Care & Community Health*, *15*, 1–10. DOI: 10.1177/21501319241245847 PMID: 38605668

About the Contributors

Héctor Cardona-Reyes, Ph.D., earned his Doctorate in Computer Science from the Juárez Autonomous University of Tabasco (Mexico), where he developed computational methods for the production of interactive environments focused on rehabilitation. He also holds a Master's and a Bachelor's degree in Computer Science from the Autonomous University of Aguascalientes. He is currently a Research Professor at the Center for Research in Mathematics (CIMAT), Zacatecas Unit, assigned by SECIHTI Mexico. He teaches in the Master's Program in Software Engineering and the Master's Program in Science with a specialization in Robotics. His main research areas include human-computer interaction, immersive environments applied to health and education, virtual reality, and software engineering. Dr. Cardona-Reyes has published extensively in indexed scientific journals such as IEEE RITA, Universal Access in the Information Society, and Computers, Informatics, Nursing, as well as in book chapters published by Springer and IGI Global. He has served as proceedings editor for international conferences (CEUR-WS volumes) and has supervised multiple master's and doctoral theses on topics related to educational technologies and virtual environments. His recent work focuses on the development of immersive and inclusive learning ecosystems and the assessment of their impact in formal and informal educational contexts.

Klinge Orlando Villalba-Condori holds a Ph.D. in Educational Sciences from the Universidad Nacional de San Agustín de Arequipa, Peru. He also earned a Master's degree in Educational Management and a specialization in Systems Engineering from the same institution. Dr. Villalba-Condori is currently a university professor and researcher affiliated with various national and international institutions, contributing to both undergraduate and postgraduate education. His academic work focuses on the integration of STEAM (Science, Technology, Engineering, Arts, and Mathematics) into education, the development of computational thinking, and the use of emerging technologies to improve learning processes. He has participated in advanced research stays and training programs at globally recognized institutions including Harvard University, the University of Helsinki, Nanyang Technological University, and the University of Salamanca. Dr. Villalba-Condori has authored over 50 peer-reviewed articles indexed in Scopus and Web of Science, covering topics such as educational technology, machine learning in health, learning analytics, and inclusive STEM education. In addition to serving as a guest editor for special issues in indexed journals, he has contributed to several book chapters and authored textbooks addressing digital literacy and didactic strategies in science and mathematics education.

Alexis Edmundo Gallegos Acosta holds a Ph.D. in Applied Sciences and Technology with a specialization in Artificial Intelligence and Statistical Modeling from the Autonomous University of Aguascalientes, Mexico. He currently serves as a postdoctoral researcher at the Center for Research in Mathematics (CIMAT), Zacatecas Unit. His work focuses on the measurement of cognitive load using virtual reality environments and electroencephalographic (EEG) signals to personalize educational interventions for students with learning disorders in basic education. Dr. Gallegos Acosta has held teaching positions at both the Autonomous University of Aguascalientes and Tecnológico de Monterrey, delivering courses in artificial intelligence, machine learning, and quantitative methods. His academic contributions include multiple peer-reviewed publications in areas such as feature selection in EEG signals, educational technology, and evolutionary metaheuristics applied to medical data. He has been recognized with awards such as the Best Paper Award at the XIV Workshop on Hybrid Intelligent Systems and received honorable mention in national thesis competitions. Dr. Gallegos has also served as a thesis advisor at undergraduate, master's, and doctoral levels and continues to contribute to research in artificial intelligence for education and healthcare applications.

Miguel Ángel Ortiz Esparza holds dual Ph.D. degrees—one in Computer Science from the Inter-institutional Doctorate in Computer Science (PNPC) and another in Education Management from the Tecnológico de Estudios Superiores de Naucalpan, Mexico. He also holds a postdoctoral degree in Software Engineering from the Center for Research in Mathematics (CIMAT), Zacatecas Unit, supported by SECIHTI, Mexico. His research has focused on inclusive digital ecosystems, human-computer interaction, and the design of virtual reality environments for improving mathematical competencies in primary education. Dr. Ortiz Esparza currently serves as a research professor at the Autonomous University of Aguascalientes and teaches across multiple institutions, including the Instituto Tecnológico de Estudios Superiores de Monterrey (ITESM), Universidad Panamericana, and Tecnológico Universitario de Aguascalientes. His teaching spans courses in web and mobile development, artificial intelligence, databases, and software engineering. Dr. Ortiz Esparza has authored numerous publications on inclusive technologies, augmented and virtual reality for education, and the development of software tools to support learners with cognitive challenges. His work bridges the gap between engineering and pedagogy, contributing significantly to the design of accessible learning environments in Latin America.

***

Ashraf Alam currently holds the position of Research Faculty at the Centre of Excellence in Public Policy, Sustainability and ESG Research, housed within the Faculty of Law and Policy Studies at Alliance University, Bangalore. Renowned for his transdisciplinary acumen spanning education, technology, and policy studies, Dr. Ashraf has been distinguished as one of the World's Top 2% Scientists by Stanford University and Elsevier, an accolade that highlights the breadth and depth of his scholarly impact. His prolific academic output includes over fifty SCOPUS-indexed publications and more than one hundred conference presentations at esteemed national and international academic forums. His educational trajectory reflects both depth and versatility: a Ph.D. in Education from the Indian Institute of Technology (IIT) Kharagpur, an M.Ed. with a concentration in Mathematics Education, and a B.S. in Computer Science from the University of Delhi. He also holds postgraduate degrees in Public Administration (M.A.) and Mathematics (M.Sc.), supplemented by a suite of postgraduate diplomas in Higher Education, Guidance and Counselling, Educational Technology, Criminology and Police Administration, and Value Education. Dr. Ashraf is an active participant in global scholarly discourse. As Associate Editor of Frontiers in Education, he plays a pivotal role in curating and guiding intellectual contributions across the Educational, Pedagogical, and Learning Sciences. Concurrently, he serves as Founder and Director of Academic Chronicles Private Limited, where he orchestrates editorial board formation and develops strategic frameworks for peer-reviewed publishing in the Social, Behavioural, and Humanistic Sciences. His research has been disseminated through elite academic platforms, including Elsevier, Springer, Taylor & Francis, Wiley, Routledge, Sage, Emerald, and IEEE, and addresses a remarkably diverse array of topics such as pedagogical theories, educational administration, educational psychology, educational sociology, educational policy, technology-integrated learning, mathematics education, educational philosophy, educational technology, teacher education, and AI/ML in learning environments. Dr. Ashraf's scholarly rigor is further demonstrated by his success in qualifying multiple prestigious examinations including UGC-NET-JRF in both Education and Adult and Continuing Education, UGC- NET in Public Administration, and GATE in Humanities and

Social Sciences. At the heart of Dr. Ashraf's intellectual ethos lies a steadfast belief in education as a catalytic and emancipatory force capable of engendering social justice, human flourishing, societal progress, and sustainable transformation. His recent explorations into 'Happiness Engineering' and holistic well- being in school ecosystems articulate a vision of education that transcends instrumentalist paradigms, prioritizing emotional intelligence, global consciousness, empathy, and psychosocial resilience among learners. His research agenda seeks to conceive educational praxis through the affordances of inclusive digital learning, gamified instructional design, and artificial intelligence (AIEd), thereby constructing robust, ethically grounded frameworks for 21st century education. At Alliance University, Dr. Ashraf remains committed to architecting pedagogical models that not only cultivate intellectual dexterity and cognitive excellence but also prepare learners for morally responsive leadership, intellectual nimbleness, and responsible global citizenship in an increasingly volatile, uncertain, complex, and ambiguous (VUCA) world.

Hamit Armağan was born in 1979 in Isparta, Turkey. He received his BS degree from the Department of Mathematics, Süleyman Demirel University, in 2001 and M.Sc. and Ph.D. degrees from the Graduate School of Natural and Applied Sciences, Süleyman Demirel University, in 2008 and 2018, respectively. He is currently an instructor in the Department of Informatics, Süleyman Demirel University, Isparta, Turkey. His research interests include fuzzy logic, genetic algorithm, artificial intelligent, and engineering technology education.

Muralidhar L B is a professionally qualified dental surgeon. He holds a Ph.D. from Canara Bank School of Management Studies, Bangalore University, after his MBA from Christ University. He is qualified in management at UGC - NET and KSET. He has 18 years of total teaching experience spanning across dental education, healthcare management and general management and 4 years of corporate experience. He has worked as a research associate in the Institute for Social and Economic Change, Bangalore in a project entitled as "Management By and For Common Man: An Exploration of the Concept and Direction for Future"post Ph.D. He had secured 28th rank in the S.S.L.C. examination for Karnataka State in 1993. His 25 patents have been published, and 2 design patents have been granted. He has 41 research publications to his credit, of which 23 are Scopus-indexed, 5 are ABDC indexed and 1 is indexed in Web of Science. He has co-authored 11 books and 9 book chapters.. He is supervising Ph.D. research of 3 research scholars at JAIN (Deemed to be University). He works as an assistant professor in the Department of Business Management Studies, School of Commerce, Jain Deemed to be a University in Bangalore.

Pankaj Bhambri is an accomplished Associate Professor in the Department of Information Technology at Guru Nanak Dev Engineering College, Ludhiana, with over 21 years of teaching and research experience. Recognized as a Top 2% Scientist by Stanford University and Elsevier, his expertise spans Artificial Intelligence, Machine Learning, the Internet of Things, and Cloud Computing. A prolific researcher, he has authored numerous patents, published extensively in Scopus and SCIE-indexed journals, and edited several influential books with international publishers like CRC Press and Springer. Dr. Bhambri is also an active academic leader, guiding Ph.D. candidates, serving on technical committees for international conferences, and currently pursuing a Post Doctorate Research at Lincoln University College, Malaysia.

Deepak D is an Assistant Professor at the School of Commerce, Jain (Deemed-to-be) University, Bengaluru.He holds an M.Com degree from Bangalore Central University and is a UGC-NET qualified individual.His academic interests span business finance, financial technology, and sustainable business practices.Deepak has published over 20 research papers in reputed national and international journals. His work explores emerging themes such as AI in marketing, the circular economy, emotional intelligence, and green finance.He has co-invented patents related to leadership strategy and the management of the bullwhip effect.He is actively involved in academic conferences on digital transformation and future-ready business models. Deepak collaborates with multidisciplinary scholars to bridge theory with practical innovation. He is listed on the Vidwan database and holds an ORCID ID: 0009-0004-8493-1474.Outside academics, he has represented his university in national-level wrestling competitions.

Mevlut Ersoy was born in 1985 in Ankara, Turkey. He obtained his B.S. degree in Computer Education from Gazi University Ankara, Turkey in 2007. He completed his Master's degree in Computer Engineering from Suleyman Demirel University, Turkey in 2012. He completed his Ph.D. degree in Suleyman Demirel University Department of Computer Engineering in 2016. He works as an Assistant Professor in Suleyman Demirel University Computer Engineering Department since 2016. His research interests include Artificial Intelligence, FPGA, Embedded Systems, Computer Networks.

Sıddıka Ersoy was born in Isparta, Turkey in 1980. She completed her undergraduate studies at Istanbul University Florence Nightingale School of Nursing in 2000; her master's degree from Marmara University in 2008; and her doctorate from Ege University in 2017. During the first ten years of her professional career, she gained clinical experience in intensive care and emergency nursing. Since 2010, she has held an academic position in the Department of Internal Medicine Nursing at the Faculty of Health Sciences, Süleyman Demirel University, and has continued her work as a faculty member since 2019. She received the title of Associate Professor in 2024. Her academic research areas include internal medicine nursing, chronic disease management, chronic wound and diabetic foot care, spiritual care and holistic nursing approach, quality of care and patient safety, and scale development and psychometric assessment studies.

Purushotham H. C is an Assistant Professor at the School of Commerce, JAIN (Deemed-to-be University), with over 6 years of teaching experience. He is currently pursuing a Ph.D. at REVA University and holds an MBA in Management. His expertise spans consumer behaviour, strategic management, HRM, and marketing. He has published several research papers and book chapters and received multiple Best Paper Awards. He has coordinated academic, cultural, and NSS activities and actively contributes to faculty development and student mentoring. He is also a certified Behaviour and Mentoring Analyst and holds certifications in marketing analytics and digital marketing.

Cem Deniz Kumral was born in 1995 in Erzincan, Turkey. He received his bachelor's degree in Computer Engineering from Süleyman Demirel University in 2018. He received his Master's degree in Computer Engineering from Süleyman Demirel University in 2020. He received his Ph.D degree in Computer Engineering from Süleyman Demirel University in 2025. He continues to work in the fields of virtual reality, virtual laboratories, FPGA and embedded systems,

Rampelli Manojkumar received his Ph.D. in Power Engineering from the Indian Institute of Technology Guwahati in 2023. He obtained his Master of Technology in Power and Energy Systems from the National Institute of Technology Karnataka, Surathkal, India, in 2015. He is currently an Assistant Professor in the Department of Electrical and Electronics Engineering at BVRIT Hyderabad College of Engineering for Women. He is currently the Editorial Board Member of Scientific Reports, Early Career Editor for the International Journal of Ambient Energy and the Guest Editor for PLOS ONE. He has been a speaker at the IEEE Smart Grid webinar series and has contributed to multiple funded research projects on smart transformer-based microgrid systems and distributed generation management. He has published 9 SCI journal papers, including articles in IEEE Transactions on Power Systems, IEEE Transactions on Industrial Informatics, and Sustainable Cities and Society. His research expertise spans energy management, hybrid AC/DC distribution systems, energy storage, and power electronics applications in modern distribution systems. Additionally, he is an active reviewer for around 20 SCI journals, including IEEE

Transactions on Industrial Informatics, IEEE Systems Journal, Journal of Energy Storage, Applied Energy, etc. He has also been actively involved in faculty training programs focused on teaching and learning enhancement, including instructional design, formative assessment, and teaching analytics, thereby strengthening his interdisciplinary expertise in education and technology integration.

Venkanna Mekala Associate Professor of Physics, Department of Basic Sciences and Humanities, BVRIT Hyderabad College of Engineering for Women having 20 years of Teaching experience. Published 3 Text books, 5 Patents, 23 papers and presented in18 national & International Conferences. Life member of OSI and ISCA

Ricardo Murillo Alfaro is a Mechatronic Engineer graduated from the UP of Victoria, a master in educational research and a doctorate in educational policies from CRETAM with a line of research in Educational Technology, Educational Robotics and Educational Statistics. Since 2015, he has worked as upper secondary, high school, and postgraduate teacher in public and private educational institutions in the State of Tamaulipas, focusing on areas of science and technology. He has various investigations, publications and participation in national and international magazines and conferences. He has served as a technical and methodological advisor in various scientific and technological creativity and innovation projects, as well as robotics. Among them, the participation and 4 gold medals obtained in international events such as the London International Youth Science Forum in 2022 held in London, England, Afrika Science Buskers Festival 2021 held in Zimbabwe, 6th stand out. World Invention Competition and Exhibition 2024 held in Selangor, Malaysia and at the 1st Global Sustainabilty Innovation Competition held in Indonesia, as well as at ExpoSiences ASIA 2024 held in Kuwait

Özgür Örün obtained his Ph.D. degree with an interdisciplinary thesis from the Department of Computer Education and Instructional Technology at Anadolu University in 2019. As of 2024, he has started a second graduate program in Neuroscience at the Graduate School of Health Sciences, Ege University, Türkiye. In 2013, he was an Erasmus visiting academic staff for a short term at Adam Mickiewicz University in Poznan, Poland. In 2018, as a researcher focusing on the physiological measurement of learning processes with Electroencephalogram (EEG), he attended the EEGLAB at the Swartz Center for Computational Neuroscience, University of California, San Diego, USA. Since 2021, Dr. Özgür ÖRÜN has been working at the Izmir Institute of Technology, contributing as a researcher and consultant to various projects supported by different institutions, including the Development Agency and the Scientific and Technological Research Council of Türkiye. His interdisciplinary research interests include educational neuroscience, cognitive science, (multimedia) learning, working memory, multitasking, instructional design and technology. He publishes and continues his academic production within this scope.

P. Selvakumar is currently an Associate Professor in the Department of Science and Humanities at Nehru Institute of Technology, Coimbatore, Tamil Nadu, India. Prior to joining Nehru Institute of Technology, he held positions as an Assistant Professor in the Department of Science and Humanities various engineering colleges in Coimbatore, Tamil Nadu, India, spanning from 2011 to 2023. Dr.P. Selvakumar's academic and research interests lie primarily in the field of phytochemistry. He has made significant contributions to his field, with an impressive record that includes 30 journal publications, 12 patents, and 20 conference papers. Additionally, he has organized 5 seminars and conferences, further demonstrating his commitment to academic and scientific exchange. Throughout his career, Dr. P.Selvakumar has been recognized for his dedication and excellence in teaching, having been honored with several awards, including the Best Teacher Awards. He holds a prominent position in the academic community, contributing actively to research.

Ezra Federico Parra González is an academic researcher with experience in the fields of technology and education. He earned his Ph.D. in Computer Science from the Center for Research and Advanced Studies of the National Polytechnic Institute (CINVESTAV) between 2009 and 2013, where he also completed his M.Sc. in Computer Science. He holds a B.Sc. in Informatics from the Interdisciplinary Professional Unit of Engineering and Social and Administrative Sciences (UPIICSA-IPN). From 2013 to 2021, Dr. Parra worked at the Regional Center for Teacher Training and Educational Research (CRETAM), focusing on educational technology, particularly Educational Robotics and Educational Data Mining. Since 2022, he has been an Academic Technician at the Center for Research in Mathematics (CIMAT), Zacatecas Unit, where he conducts research on mobile robotics, virtual reality, and artificial intelligence applied to education. He currently serves as Coordinator of the Master's Program in Robotics and as Head of Outreach at CIMAT.

T. Aditya Sai Srinivas is an accomplished academician currently serving as an Associate Professor in the Department of Computer Science and Engineering at Ravindra College of Engineering for Women, Kurnool. He holds a Ph.D. in Internet of Things (IoT) from the prestigious VIT University, Vellore, where he specialized in cutting-edge IoT frameworks and intelligent systems. With a strong research orientation, he has published over 45 research papers in reputed international journals. His academic contributions extend beyond research, having authored multiple textbooks in computer science and engineering. Dr. Srinivas is actively involved in mentoring students and guiding innovative projects in emerging technologies like ML, IoT, and FL. He is also a regular contributor to academic conferences and technical symposiums. His work reflects a commitment to both scholarly excellence and practical application in the evolving tech landscape.

N Sathyanarayana has over 15 years of teaching experience at both undergraduate and postgraduate levels. He holds a Master of Business Administration degree from VTU and a Master of Commerce degree from Periyar University. He has completed his Ph.D. in Banking and Finance from Dayananda Sagar University. Currently, he serves as an Assistant Professor in the School of Commerce at Jain (Deemed-to-be University), Bangalore. He has published 24 research papers in international journals, including three indexed in Scopus, and seven papers in national journals. Additionally, he has presented 14 research papers at international conferences and 11 at national conferences. He has co-authored two books at the national level and contributed 17 Scopus-indexed book chapters.

Alhelí Segovia Sánchez Full-time professor at the Maestra Estefanía Castañeda Federal Normal School for Preschool Teachers and academic assistant at the Regional Center for Teacher Training and Educational Research. She is also a collaborator in the Emerging Academic Body "ICT in Education." She holds a Bachelor's Degree in Preschool Education from the Maestra Estefanía Castañeda Federal Normal School for Preschool Teachers, a Master's Degree in Teaching Methodology from the Mexican Institute of Pedagogy, and a Doctorate in Educational Policy from the Regional Center for Teacher Training and Educational Research. She teaches at both the undergraduate and graduate levels, offering courses related to the teaching practice training pathway, pedagogical knowledge, and research methodology. Her main research areas include educational policy, teaching practice, and artificial intelligence applied to education.

Muhammad Usman Tariq has more than 17+ year's experience in industry and academia. He is a prolific author of research articles, case studies, book chapters, and academic books, with work spanning a wide range of disciplines. His contributions also include several patents. He is founder and CEO of The Case HQ, a unique repository for courses, narrative and video case studies. Additionally, he is President of Gulf Higher Education (Gulf HE) focused on advancing academic practice. He has been working as a consultant and trainer for industries representing six sigma, quality, health and safety, environmental systems, project management, and information security standards. His work has encompassed sectors in aviation, manufacturing, food, hospitality, education, finance, research, software and transportation. He has diverse and significant experience working with accreditation agencies of ABET, ACBSP, AACSB, WASC, CAA, EFQM and NCEAC. He is a Principal Fellow of Advance HE UK, Senior Fellow of SEDA UK, and Chartered Fellow of CIPD UK other than Senior Member IEEE.

Chetan T.R, PhD in Marketing, serves as Assistant Professor at JAIN (Deemed-to-be University), specializing in Marketing, International Business, and Entrepreneurship. Honored with the Best Faculty Award, he blends academic rigor with real-world relevance through case studies and interdisciplinary insights. His research focuses on ethics, mindset, and time mastery, empowering students through holistic mentoring. With expertise in faculty development, structured academic modules, and impactful communication, he actively contributes to scholarly initiatives. Passionate about innovation and sustainability, Dr. Chetan integrates AI tools to enhance pedagogy and professional growth, fostering a dynamic learning ecosystem that bridges theory with practice.

Mesut Türk received his PhD in Computer Education and Instructional Technology from Anadolu University. He currently works as an Assistant Professor in the Department of Computer Technologies at Amasya University, Türkiye. His research interests focus on educational technologies, instructional design, blended learning, student engagement, digital literacy, and the integration of digital technologies into teaching and learning processes. He has published articles in national and international peer-reviewed journals, particularly on technology integration in education and learners' digital competencies.

Tuncay Yiğit was born in 1972 in Isparta, Turkey. He obtained his B.S. degree in Electrical Education Department from Gazi University, Turkey in 1997. He completed his Master's degree in Electrical Education from Gazi University 2000. He obtained his Ph.D. degree in Gazi University Electrical Education in 2005. He is currently working as a Professor in Suleyman Demirel University Department of Computer Engineering. His research interests include Software Engineering, IT Systems and Electronic Systems.

Index

A

Accessibility 3, 4, 5, 14, 24, 27, 29, 30, 31, 32, 33, 43, 45, 47, 49, 53, 62, 63, 68, 79, 81, 82, 87, 88, 91, 92, 93, 94, 95, 96, 102, 104, 105, 107, 108, 112, 116, 156, 162, 166, 168, 203, 204, 205, 208, 209, 210, 217, 218, 220, 221, 225, 229, 230, 238, 254, 286, 295, 300, 302, 314, 332
Action Research 170, 175, 225, 275, 286
Active Learning 147, 148, 150, 151, 152, 157, 158, 159, 160, 162, 173, 175, 176, 177, 320, 330
AI in Education 2, 21, 23, 112, 119, 121, 122, 123, 124, 125, 129, 140, 141, 142, 143, 144, 182, 183, 184, 186, 190, 191, 192, 193, 194, 197
Algorithmic Fairness 15, 181, 193
Approaches 22, 29, 30, 31, 37, 66, 78, 110, 113, 114, 115, 117, 132, 133, 134, 136, 137, 139, 147, 148, 149, 150, 151, 152, 156, 158, 160, 163, 165, 167, 168, 170, 173, 197, 199, 201, 205, 207, 212, 215, 222, 224, 226, 235, 238, 241, 242, 243, 248, 253, 266, 276, 281, 294, 300
Artificial Intelligence and Adaptive Learning for Equity 1

B

Business Education 176

C

COBAT 233, 234, 236, 238, 251, 252, 255, 263, 265, 266, 269
Constructivism 91, 283, 323

D

Data Governance 11, 15, 45, 91, 104
Data Privacy 15, 81, 128, 129, 146, 162, 181, 184, 190, 193, 194
Digital Inclusion 83, 133, 167
Digital Literacy 15, 17, 107, 122, 124, 125, 128, 132, 133, 136, 149, 161, 236, 245, 301
Digital Pedagogies 97, 147, 148, 149, 150, 151, 152, 153, 156, 167, 173

E

Educational Technology 28, 48, 51, 59, 75, 84, 86, 112, 119, 144, 175, 176, 183, 196, 197, 198, 214, 215, 216, 241, 268, 273, 303
Equity in Education 3, 4, 5, 148
Ethical AI 11, 17, 127, 129, 145, 196
Ethical and Social Considerations In the Deployment of AI in Education 121
Explainable AI 145

F

Flipped Learning 148, 149, 150, 152, 155, 157, 158, 159, 160, 161, 162, 163, 174, 175, 177

G

Generative AI 17, 22, 23, 119, 196, 197, 198, 220

H

Healthcare Education 300, 303, 326, 331

I

Immersive 4, 7, 9, 13, 16, 27, 28, 29, 30, 31, 32, 33, 35, 36, 37, 38, 39, 40, 41, 42, 43, 45, 46, 47, 48, 49, 50, 51, 52, 54, 56, 57, 58, 59, 60, 61, 62, 63, 64, 65, 66, 67, 68, 72, 73, 74, 75, 76, 77, 78, 79, 80, 81, 82, 83, 84, 86, 112, 113, 114, 115, 116, 118, 119, 132, 137, 141, 151, 163, 165, 166, 167, 174, 178, 179, 181, 182, 183, 184,

185, 187, 188, 189, 190, 191, 192, 193, 194, 195, 201, 202, 203, 204, 205, 206, 207, 208, 209, 210, 211, 212, 213, 214, 215, 216, 217, 218, 219, 220, 221, 222, 223, 225, 226, 227, 229, 230, 299, 300, 302, 303, 305, 307, 310, 321, 324, 325, 327, 328, 331, 333, 334
Immersive Learning 9, 29, 32, 33, 49, 51, 56, 59, 61, 63, 66, 67, 68, 74, 75, 79, 81, 83, 113, 114, 116, 118, 119, 151, 184, 187, 191, 192, 201, 202, 203, 204, 207, 208, 209, 210, 211, 212, 215, 216, 218, 226, 230, 300, 302, 331
Immersive Learning Environments 9, 29, 114, 187, 201, 202, 203, 204, 207, 209, 210, 211, 212, 218
Immersive Technology 40, 56, 63, 74, 80, 81, 82, 203, 220
Inclusive Design 17, 66, 67, 68, 125, 126, 127, 137, 152, 206, 208, 212, 221, 302
Inclusive Education 14, 43, 83, 87, 88, 92, 108, 112, 115, 116, 117, 118, 149, 156, 157, 164, 165, 166, 174, 177, 178, 201, 202, 203, 204, 205, 208, 212, 218, 220, 221, 222, 224, 225, 226, 227, 228
Inclusive Instructional Design 33, 147, 148, 150, 151, 152, 173
Instructional Design 29, 33, 39, 41, 42, 45, 84, 87, 89, 92, 93, 95, 147, 148, 149, 150, 151, 152, 155, 172, 173, 300, 301, 320
ITS 1, 2, 4, 5, 7, 8, 9, 14, 36, 63, 73, 75, 100, 117, 122, 128, 134, 136, 138, 141, 148, 158, 161, 162, 169, 172, 181, 182, 183, 184, 193, 194, 197, 234, 235, 237, 241, 243, 247, 249, 250, 252, 254, 263, 265, 276, 277, 278, 284, 286, 291, 293, 294, 295, 301, 314, 316, 320, 322, 329, 330

L

Learning Analytics 7, 13, 24, 87, 89, 100, 155, 162, 185, 216, 320, 329
Learning Disability 33, 34, 35, 40, 49, 50, 54, 57
Learning Environment 2, 32, 76, 83, 84, 111, 112, 113, 117, 118, 160, 174, 175, 177, 178, 299, 305, 332
Learning Gap 12, 13
Literary Readers 275, 280, 281, 285

M

Multilingual Education 116

N

Neurodiversity 61, 64, 65, 66, 70, 83, 84, 85

P

Pedagogy 16, 87, 88, 89, 90, 91, 92, 95, 96, 97, 98, 99, 104, 108, 116, 136, 139, 142, 148, 149, 151, 153, 155, 159, 162, 163, 165, 166, 167, 169, 176, 177, 178, 198, 202, 203, 209, 214, 219, 221, 229, 230, 234, 236, 241, 245, 247, 297, 331
Personalized Learning 2, 3, 4, 5, 6, 7, 14, 19, 20, 22, 23, 24, 25, 28, 31, 32, 35, 83, 111, 112, 118, 128, 141, 143, 144, 155, 157, 186, 190, 201, 206, 227, 228, 231
Practical 31, 42, 59, 62, 63, 81, 98, 117, 131, 140, 141, 143, 149, 152, 153, 169, 170, 172, 176, 177, 182, 191, 192, 197, 201, 215, 216, 225, 226, 227, 244, 263, 284, 330, 333
Problem-Based Learning 147, 150, 151, 169, 171, 172, 173, 174, 177, 178, 244

R

Reading Comprehension 35, 56, 275, 276, 277, 278, 279, 280, 281, 283, 284, 285, 287, 288, 289, 290, 292, 293, 294, 295, 297, 298
Reading Strategies 279, 280, 281, 282, 284, 298

S

Short Stories 275, 276, 280, 286, 292
Simulation-Based Learning 148, 149, 150, 164, 165, 173, 175, 176, 177, 179, 219
STEAM Approach 235, 236, 238, 240, 244, 271
STEAM Camp 233, 238, 250, 253, 256, 263, 265
STEAM Education 234, 236, 237, 239, 240, 243, 265, 272

T

Teacher Education 115, 140, 160, 164, 165, 166, 174, 176, 179, 230, 234, 235, 236, 237, 238, 239, 241, 242, 243, 245, 246, 247, 253, 264, 333
Teaching Resources 279
Technology 1, 13, 15, 20, 21, 22, 23, 25, 27, 28, 30, 33, 35, 36, 40, 41, 43, 45, 46, 47, 48, 49, 51, 52, 53, 54, 55, 56, 57, 58, 59, 60, 63, 66, 67, 68, 70, 71, 72, 73, 74, 75, 80, 81, 82, 83, 84, 85, 86, 88, 89, 97, 98, 110, 111, 112, 113, 114, 115, 116, 117, 118, 119, 121, 125, 128, 129, 131, 132, 133, 134, 135, 139, 140, 141, 142, 144, 145, 146, 148, 149, 154, 157, 159, 162, 168, 170, 172, 174, 175, 176, 178, 183, 187, 188, 196, 197, 198, 199, 202, 203, 205, 206, 210, 211, 214, 215, 216, 218, 220, 221, 224, 225, 226, 227, 228, 229, 230, 234, 235, 237, 240, 241, 242, 243, 245, 246, 247, 248, 249, 254, 256, 263, 265, 268, 273, 300, 302, 303, 306, 332, 333, 334
TPACK 98, 233, 238, 240, 241, 242, 243, 247, 248, 249, 250, 251, 252, 253, 254, 255, 256, 257, 261, 262, 263, 264, 265, 266, 267, 268, 269, 270, 271, 272, 273

V

Virtual Reality 27, 28, 37, 38, 41, 47, 49, 50, 51, 52, 53, 54, 55, 56, 57, 58, 67, 75, 83, 84, 85, 110, 111, 112, 113, 114, 115, 117, 118, 141, 165, 166, 168, 175, 178, 201, 202, 204, 205, 206, 207, 208, 209, 210, 211, 212, 214, 215, 216, 217, 218, 221, 222, 223, 226, 228, 229, 299, 300, 301, 302, 306, 314, 321, 332, 333, 334, 335

www.ingramcontent.com/pod-product-compliance
Lightning Source LLC
LaVergne TN
LVHW062323300926
849161LV00007B/1547
* 9 7 9 8 3 3 7 3 5 1 8 8 9 *